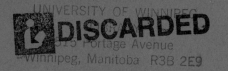

The making of Manchester Jewry
1740–1875

For Joyce and Marc

Bill Williams

The making of
Manchester Jewry

1740–1875

MANCHESTER
UNIVERSITY PRESS

HOLMES & MEIER
PUBLISHERS, NEW YORK

© Manchester University Press 1976

Published by
Manchester University Press
Oxford Road
Manchester M13 9PL

ISBN 0 7190 0631 7

USA

Holmes and Meier Publishers, Inc
101 Fifth Avenue
New York, New York   10003

Library of Congress Cataloging in Publication Data
Williams, Bill, 1931–
    The making of Manchester Jewry.
    Bibliography: p. 434
    Includes index.
    1. Jews in Manchester, Eng.—History.   2. Manchester,
Eng.—History.   I. Title.
DS135.E55M368   942.7'33'004924   75–43635

US ISBN 0–8419–0252–6

Printed in Great Britain by
R. & R. Clark Ltd
Edinburgh

Contents

Illustrations

The author and publishers are indebted to the following for permission to reproduce illustrations: figures 1 and 10: Mr Geoffrey Kershaw of Didsbury; figures 2, 4, 8, 9 and maps 1, 2 and 3: Manchester Central Reference Library; figure 3: Mocatta Library, University College, London; figures 5 and 6: Salford City Library; figure 7 and plate III: Manchester Great and New Synagogue; plate I: Mrs Eileen Kay of Liverpool; plate II: Mrs Leonard Stein of London.

Preface

In this book I have tried to trace the origins of what has become the largest, and perhaps the most influential, Jewish community in provincial England. There are now at least thirty synagogues in the Greater Manchester area, over 120 Jewish societies and charities, forty-five Zionist organisations, two local Jewish newspapers, and a Jewish population conservatively estimated at forty thousand persons spread between Whitefield and Prestwich in the north and Cheadle and Gatley to the south. It is an important community, both for the depth and versatility of its inner life and for the influence it has exercised, and continues to exercise, both within the Jewish sphere and on the social and economic development of Manchester. The planning of this work was itself a local communal enterprise, initiated by correspondence between Walter Wolfson and Hymie Gouldman soon after the Six Day War and subsequently guided with great charm by the late Leonard Cohen. It was at their invitation that in 1970 I became a member of the Committee for the Publication of a History of Manchester Jewry, of which Mr Wolfson was the chairman, and Mr Gouldman the vice-chairman.

No earlier attempt has been made to write a coherent history of the community. There were monographs on particular aspects of communal life—most notably, perhaps, Israel Slotki's studies of the Shechita Board and the Talmud Torah and Hymie Gouldman's sensitive centenary history of the Great Synagogue—but the threads had not been drawn together, except in a most tentative manner by Neville Laski in two articles for the *Manchester Review*. A great wealth of sources lay virtually untapped in the offices, attics and cellars of synagogues and societies throughout the city. Part of the preparatory work for this book was the location of these documents and the safe preservation of as many of them as possible in the archives of the Manchester Central Reference Library, which now has one of the finest collections of modern Anglo-Jewish records in the country. I have used some of this material in seeking out the origins of the characteristic pattern of life, work and worship of Manchester Jewry.

It is this frame of reference which has fixed the period I have covered in this volume, for the foundations of communal life lie not, as has often been supposed, in the 'mass immigration' of 1881–1914 but in a much earlier period. Manchester Jewry grew with Manchester. It originated, like the modern industrial city, at the end of the eighteenth century and assumed its distinctive social, economic and religious character during the first three quarters of the nineteenth.

A significant movement of Eastern European immigration is itself older than has been supposed—dating back, perhaps, to the mid-1840s, or even earlier. By 1875 over half of Manchester's Jewish population was of Russian or Polish origin. The balance of communal life has undergone many subsequent shifts of emphasis. It has become subject to a greater degree of co-ordination and has developed a wider range of political commitments. But its basic structure has remained that of the mid-1870s. The time-scale itself is significant, for it emphasises that in no sense can the Jewish community be regarded as 'alien' to Manchester. It was not a late addition to an established pattern of urban life, but an integral part of the pattern itself. Its role, like that of other minorities—the Germans, the Italians, the Greeks, and, particularly, the Irish—was not peripheral and derivative, but central and creative, in a city which has always been cosmopolitan in character.

In considering this interplay between the town and one of its many cultural components, I have sought to shed some light upon the role of the minority group in the life of the Victorian city. If the place of 'class' is well known, comparatively little attention has been devoted to the more autonomous groupings which centre upon nationality and religion. The degree of their individuality and independence, the process of their integration, their interaction both with each other and with the city as a whole, the attitudes and feelings they evoked, and the influence they exerted are all matters of concern for the urban historian. While not attempting a comparative study on any scale, I have been aware that, apart from its intrinsic importance, the development of Manchester Jewry provides the case history of a nineteenth-century urban minority.

There was a further interplay between the Manchester community and Anglo-Jewry. The local community to some extent shared the changes experienced by Anglo-Jewry as a whole. Throughout its early history it was deeply affected by Jewish developments in other urban centres, London in particular, but also Liverpool and Birmingham. But it also evolved a distinctive personality of its own, derived in part from its unique human composition, in part from its central place on a major route of transmigration between Eastern Europe and the United States, in part from the influence of Manchester's dynamic rise in economic and political importance during the nineteenth century. In the early 1850s, in particular, Manchester mounted a challenge to the Chief Rabbinate which arose at least in part from the prominence of Manchester's role in the life of the nation. More adventurous in outlook, and less restrained by precedent than the metropolitan community, Manchester's initiative has helped to determine the pattern of Anglo-Jewish life.

Manchester
February 1976

Acknowledgements

My special thanks are due to Mr Daniel Cohen and his fellow-trustees of the Leonard Cohen Trust for their generous and sustained help towards the expenses involved in the preparation and publication of this book; to the executor of the late Mrs Rosina Asser of Manchester for assistance towards the establishment of a Jewish History Unit in Manchester Polytechnic; to the Council of the Jewish Historical Society of England and to the Council of Manchester and Salford Jews for their sponsorship of this project; to Mr Walter Wolfson and Mr Hyman Gouldman, chairman and vice-chairman of the Committee for the Publication of the History of Manchester Jewry, and to the other members of that committee for their constant help and advice; to the Executive of the Manchester Great and New Synagogue for permission to make use of the congregation's archives, now deposited in the Manchester Central Library; to Mr Jacob Schwalbe, the former Secretary of the Great and New Synagogue, for his care in preserving those records for posterity and for his friendly tolerance of my many interruptions of his work; to the Executives of the Spanish and Portuguese Synagogue, Cheetham Hill Road, and of the South Manchester Synagogue, Wilbraham Road, for access to the records of those congregations; to Mr Abraham Berman and to the Council of the Manchester Jewish Social Services, for permission to make use of the early records of the Manchester Jewish Board of Guardians, now deposited in the Manchester Central Library; to Mr Sampson Goldstone for information related to the Salford origins of his family; to the late Mr Alex Jacob of Manchester for his help in the preservation of Jewish records in private hands; to Mrs Joan Behrens, for permission to use the earliest minute book of the Jewish Ladies Clothing Society, in her possession; to Mrs Dorothy Goldstone of Cheadle for access to her collection of Franks family records and for her kind hospitality on numerous occasions; to Mrs Eileen Kay of Liverpool for permission to reproduce the portrait of Jacob Franks; to Mrs Leonard Stein of London for access to her family records and for permission to reproduce the portrait of Louis Beaver; to Mr Geoffrey Kershaw of Didsbury for access to family records relating to Jacob Nathan; to the Reverend Gabriel Brodie of the Great and New Synagogue for his frequent and invaluable help in introducing an outsider to the religious life and customs of Judaism; to Mr Marcel Glaskie of Sale for permission to make use of data from his study of the Census of 1871, which is incorporated in Appendix B; to the editors of the local communal newspapers, the *Jewish Telegraph* and the *Jewish Gazette*, particularly for their help in the location of source materials; to the Executive of the Princes Road Synagogue, Liverpool, for permission to make use of their archive collection; to Mr Karl Abrahams of Liverpool for his help in the location of these and other records in the Liverpool area; to Dr W. H. Chaloner of Manchester University for reading my original manuscript and for his helpful criticism and encouragement; to Mr John Shaftesley, O.B.E., the Editor of Publications of the Jewish Historical Society; Dr Aubrey Newman of Leicester University, and Dr Richard Barnett, C.B.E., for their constructive comments upon the final typescript; to the many librarians and archivists who have assisted in my long search for records, in particular Miss Jean Ayton and Miss Dora Rayson of the Archives Department of the Manchester Central Reference Library, Mr Christopher Makepeace and Mr David Taylor, successive Local History Librarians in Manchester, and Mr C. R. Fincken of the Mocatta Library, University College, London; to the Director and Board of Governors of Manchester Polytechnic for a period of sabbatical leave which made the completion of this book possible and for other help in promoting research in the field of Anglo-Jewish History; to Mr Ray Howorth, Dean of the Institute of Advanced Studies, Manchester Polytechnic, for his kindness and encouragement; to the student helpers who gave assistance to the committee and to myself; and, particularly, to Mrs Miriam Steiner, my Research Assistant during the past year, whose help has proved invaluable in bringing this work to fruition.

Finally, I wish to thank the Manchester Jewish community as a whole, and the many individuals within it whom I have had occasion to approach, for their invariable courtesy and immense warmth. The findings recorded in this book, including any errors they may contain, are, of course, mine alone.

1   The foundations, 1740–1815

The foundation and early development of provincial Anglo-Jewry was a remote and at first a relatively insignificant consequence of the westward flow of Ashkenazi Jews which followed the renewal of persecution in Central and Eastern Europe in the middle of the seventeenth century.[1] The atrocities associated with the Cossack rebellion of 1648–51 had the effect of reversing the eastward drift of Jewish migration into the kingdom of Poland, and of driving a flood of penniless refugees across Western Europe into the new urban centres of Holland and Germany, where their arrival nearly coincided with Cromwell's reopening of England to Jewish settlement in 1657. Within twenty years, at most, a few had reached London, where wealthy Sephardi traders and financers had re-established the basis of communal life, and before the end of the century the first pioneers had moved on into the provinces, as often as not with the encouragement of those who might otherwise have borne the cost of their relief. They came to the notice, too, of London's Court of Aldermen, which in July 1677 ordered 'that no Jew without good estate be admitted to reside or lodge in London or the liberties thereof'.[2]

I

Most of those who left London made for the flourishing seaports of the south and east coasts, but the more adventurous were to be found as far north as Edinburgh, far from the security of royal patronage and beyond the protective influence of their wealthier and more indispensable co-religionists. They were without political rights. They were barred by law from owning land. They were the butt of a firmly entrenched religious prejudice which laid them open to frequent insult and occasional violence. Their lack of experience, capital and local connections combined with their religious scruples to drive them into economic functions which, however necessary, lacked the esteem of traditional trades and crafts. They travelled the country selling whatever portable and easily saleable commodities lay within their means, either on their own account or, on a commission basis, as the agents of established provincial shopkeepers or London dealers. They made, sold, exchanged or repaired articles in common use in the country household—umbrellas, brushes, cast-off clothing, quill pens, trinkets, smallware—which made no demand on specialised expertise. A few of the less scrupulous or more enterprising lived on their wits, as travelling entertainers, street artists, 'itinerant pawnbrokers', quacks, and, occasionally, as criminals. A mid-eighteenth-century critic believed the great mass of Anglo-Jewry (some seven thousand persons, he calculated) to consist of

a train of *hawkers*, and *pedlars*, and *traffickers* in every imaginable commodity, in every *imaginable* way, but very few in that which is deemed *regular*, *honourable*, and according to the ordinary rules of civil polity. In this general line, we must include those who buy, and sell, stolen goods.[3]

There was little inducement for any Jew to settle in a town or village where popular feeling was likely to be hostile, economic opportunities were few, land ownership impossible, and social advancement unlikely. Initially, at least, the tendency was to return to London, where, however hostile the local authorities, communal life was relatively secure; or, at all events, to remain within easy reach of the religious facilities and charitable agencies of metropolitan Jewry.

Although itinerant Jews were probably familiar enough in the English countryside during the first four decades of the eighteenth century, and a few had accumulated sufficient capital and courage to open small shops in seaports and market towns, nowhere in the provinces did Jewish settlement exist on a scale sufficient for a separate communal life. Observant Jews who were too far from London to return weekly for the celebration of the Sabbath organised temporary *minyanim* in lodging houses where they were well known or in shops or warehouses from which they obtained their supplies. Although it was many years in the making, it is probable that in 1740 there already existed the first links in a chain of lodging houses in which Jewish travellers were familiar and which could be used as stepping stones in long provincial journeys.[4] In its mature form,

the landlord . . . especially to gain their custom, kept a cupboard or closet containing cooking utensils for their use, so that they might eat Kosher . . . [and] kept the cupboard locked and guarded the key on his own person . . .[5]

In cleaning the pots and pans after use, each successive Jewish guest inscribed on them in chalk his name, the date, and the portion of the Law read on the Sabbath of that week. Groups of pedlars who surrounded more populated areas congregated in such inns on a Friday evening, stayed over Saturday, and set out again on Sunday morning.

They generally formed a club, and one of their number, who was licensed by the rabbi to slaughter animals, was paid by the club for one day's loss of profit from his

business to get to the hotel early enough on Friday to kill animals or poultry, purchase fish, etc, and either cook or superintend it that it should be quite Kosher by
the time the brotherhood came there.[6]

Such brotherhoods were in effect small embryonic communities, lacking only
a climate of opinion conducive to permanent settlement, or the resources for
its establishment. They worshipped wherever circumstances allowed and
buried their dead in the cemeteries of whichever churches would accept them.

Although the greater part of the early Jewish itinerant trade outside London
was centred on the ports of the south and east coasts, as far north as King's
Lynn, and as far west as Falmouth, there is some evidence of hawkers in the
vicinity of Birmingham, Hull, Liverpool, and the growing textile towns of Lancashire and the West Riding of Yorkshire. A Jewish chapman named Samuel
Emanuel had reached Morpeth in Northumberland by 1744, when he sought
the benefit of an Act for the Relief of Insolvent Debtors.[7] The appearance of
the name 'Synagogue Alley' on a town plan of Manchester and Salford first
published in 1741[8] (see Map 1) suggests the headquarters of a group of hawkers
who met occasionally to replenish their stocks, exchange communal gossip,
and make up a quorum for public worship, a supposition strengthened by the
robbery of one such hawker, Isaac Soloman, at Thornham Lane End, on the
road between Manchester and Rochdale, on 26 February 1740.[9] Soloman was
waylaid by

two Men on Foot . . . the one a Low Broad-set Man, wearing a whitish caped Close
Coat, and a brown Bob Wig; the other a tall thin Man, of pale complexion, wearing a
Drab-colour'd Coat, white Metal Buttons, Blue Waistcoat, Check'd Shirt, and dark
colour'd Hair

who relieved him (according to his own account) of

Nine Guineas, one Portugese Piece Value Three Pounds Twelve Shillings, Three Moi-
dores Value Four Pounds One Shilling, One Half Guinea, and Ten Shillings in Silver;
and the Goods hereafter mentioned, being of the value of Ten Pounds and upwards,
viz two Pair of carved Silver Shoe Buckles, two Pairs of Silver Tea Tongs, one Pinchbeck Watch Chain, four Gold Rings, one Pinchbeck Head for a Cane, ten Pair of
Chrystal Buttons, a Silver Watch Chain, three Silver Stock Buckles, one large Silver
Clasp, a silver carved snuff-box, several pair of white Metal Buckles, several Japan
Snuff-Boxes and Silver Thimbles.

Soloman was perhaps typical of an upper echelon of itinerant traders—a
travelling jeweller, the agent of a shopkeeper in London or Liverpool,[10] who
supplied the rising middle classes with their minor luxuries. Manchester in 1740
was already 'a spacious, rich and populous' town and a growing centre for
the domestic manufacture of woollen, linen and cotton goods 'whereby its
immensely enriched and many 100 poor families employed from several

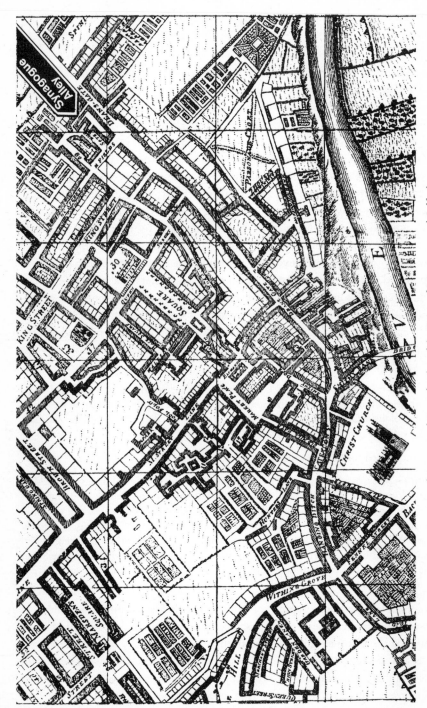

MAP I Section of Casson and Berry's *Plan of the Town of Manchester and Salford*, 1741.

Counties'.[11] St Ann's Square, laid out in 1712, served as the nucleus of new streets 'several of them . . . large, open and well-paved' which contained the 'elegant and magnificent' mansions of merchants and manufacturers.[12] The population had probably doubled over the preceding thirty years to a total of around fifteen thousand.[13]

During the 1740s the kaleidoscope of isolated pedlars and shifting brotherhoods began to shape itself into a pattern of permanent settlement. Itinerant dealers who acquired a little capital and goodwill rented small shops in the towns which had served as the bases of their operations and began to create around themselves the essentials of a corporate religious life. The oldest community of certain date outside London was at Portsmouth, where public worship began during 1746–47 and a burial ground was leased by four of the founders in 1749.[14] Communities were in existence at Birmingham, Falmouth, Ipswich, King's Lynn, Norwich and Penzance before 1750, in Bristol by 1753, and at Liverpool by 1755–56, when John Wesley spoke of the tolerance of the townspeople towards the Jews 'who live among them', and an eccentric 'yeoman of Martinscroft' (near Warrington) addressed himself to their conversion in three letters, one addressed 'to the learned Rabbi of the Jews Synagogue at Liverpool', the others 'to the poor, miserable, Christless, but innocent Jews' in and about the town.[15] While lending a measure of stability to provincial Jewish life, such communities retained something of their earlier character, in that a core of settled shopkeepers was in each case surrounded by hawkers, some of whom plied goods on their behalf. In Liverpool, when a *minyan* could not be made up within the town,

a messenger was sent out . . . to the neighbouring places—as Chester, Newton, Parkgate, etc, where there existed Jewish lodging houses—to invite the struggling Hebrew in his capacity of hawker, to attend divine worship . . .[16]

In Falmouth during the 1750s Alexander Moses (better known as Zender Falmouth) kept a stock of buckles and cutlery, jewellery and watches, which he supplied on credit to young pedlars, often with an advance of £4, sufficient to cover the cost of a hawker's licence, on condition that they returned every Friday early enough to make up the Sabbath *minyan*. After squaring their accounts on Sunday morning, they were given fresh stock and sent out on another circuit. Zender Falmouth exercised a patriarchal authority over his economic dependants, insisting on their retention of a Jewish name, arranging their marriages, and keeping a watchful eye over their lives and characters.[17] Similar functions were performed by Benjamin Yates, a Liverpool seal engraver, in the 1760s, by Moses Aaron, a Birmingham pencil maker, in the 1770s, and probably by scores of other settled shopkeepers up and down the country, who served to strengthen the religious framework of itinerant Jewish life.

In the middle years of the eighteenth century, Liverpool rather than Manchester served as the focus of Jewish settlement in the north-west. During the 1750s Liverpool was an established port, Manchester an expanding village. In 1756 Manchester was already moving out of its cocoon of relative self-sufficiency into a 'wicked and debauched Age' of increasing commercial wealth and private luxury, but a period was well within living memory when there was only one inn, when 'Wine and Spiritous Liquors' were to be found in 'not above 3 or 4 Private Houses', and when 'not six Families in Town drank Tea'.[18] The retail trades in milk, butter and coal were still 'new methods of gaining a livelihood unknown in the Town till very lately'.[19] In 1758 a private coach was acquired for the first time by a family which owed its wealth to trade rather than patrimony.[20] Manchester's population at that time was little over seventeen thousand, Liverpool's over thirty thousand.[21] While the Liverpool congregation moved from its original premises in Cumberland Street to a larger room in Turton Court, in or about 1775,[22] the brotherhood which had centred on Manchester's Synagogue Alley had broken up within a decade of 1741.[23] At the time of the acrimonious public debate on the issue of Jewish naturalisation during 1753–54 the Manchester press reprinted the anti-Semitism of the metropolitan newspapers, but the only local allusion was to the escape from Salford Gaol at the end of 1753 of a man suspected of robbing and murdering a Jewish pedlar in Wales.[24] The editorial view of the *Mercury* was the popular one that the naturalisation of Jews was 'repugnant both to Scripture and sound Policy'.[25] During the formative years of provincial Anglo-Jewry Manchester provided no more than a market for the Jewish hawker and a haven for the Jewish outlaw.

Although there were perhaps twenty settled communities in England and Scotland before the outbreak of the revolutionary wars with France, their total population was probably exceeded in size by the floating body of rootless immigrants who used the facilities in one or more of them, sometimes as 'strangers' at the cost of an offering, sometimes as the lessees of seats for the Holy Days, often as permanent seat holders at reduced 'country' rates which assured them of burial rights and the services of congregational officials. A retrospective register of births, marriages and deaths, drawn up in Liverpool during the years 1808–09, reveals isolated families in Wakefield (1756), Barnstaple (1780), Totnes (1780), Hull (1784) and Market Harborough (1790).[26] A Jewish clockmaker and silversmith lived in Leeds from at least 1758 until his conversion to Christianity in 1772;[27] another worked in Hull in 1770.[28] The 'country' members of the Great Synagogue in London included Jews trading in Nottingham (1763–64) and Brighton (1766–67).[29] Isolated families who depended on the services of Reb Leib Aleph, the Portsmouth *mohel*, between 1762 and 1793 lived at Winchester (1763), Bath (1771), Cowes in the Isle of Wight (1778), Gosport (1783), Arundel (1786) and Poole (1788).[30] At the time of Zender Falmouth's death, in 1791, families dependent on the Falmouth community lived in Redruth, Truro, Penrhyn, Camborne and St Austell.[31] A variety of other sources reveal Jews at Lincoln (1766),[32] York (1771),[33] Wendover in Buckinghamshire (1778),[34] Witney in Oxfordshire (1770),[35] Whitehaven (1776)[36] and Saffron Walden (1785).[37] Provincial Jewry was swelled throughout the eighteenth century as a result of intermittent persecution in Bohemia, Poland and the Ukraine, and restrictions on the freedom of Jews in many of the smaller German states.[38]

The slender economic basis of their survival in England precipitated a drift into crime, fanned by rumour into the proportions of a crisis. When, on 8 November 1771, a Jew in Aldgate confessed to his part in a brutal murder in Chelsea, Sir John Fielding, the London magistrate, led a witch hunt which reached far out into the provinces. Two Jews were arrested for 'a most violent Robbery' committed at Wormley in Hertfordshire.[39] Three 'notorious Villains' were arrested for the Chelsea murder and other 'extraordinary Burglaries', by Fielding's agents in Birmingham;[40] a fourth was apprehended at Henley a few days later.[41] Rumours spread that

fresh Miscreants had been sent for from abroad, and arrived . . . and had formed some very daring and mischievous plans:[42]

one report put the figure at fifty, a second at 150, adding

they are supposed to be invited here for the worst purposes by the worst of their Brethren.[43]

Of four other Jews—'following an idle gambling Course of Life'—who were arrested at Liverpool in November for passing forged notes and bills at Fairs in Lincolnshire, Nottinghamshire and Yorkshire, one at least had spent some time at the Old Boar's Head in Manchester.[44] A wave of ill-feeling led to raids on Jewish pedlars all over the country, to abortive plans for a second expulsion, and to an offer from Fielding of a free passage to a seaport to any Jew who desired to return to his native land.[45] When four Jews were hanged at Tyburn in December for the Chelsea murder, orders were read out in every synagogue that the community should keep off the streets until the panic subsided.[46]

The occupations into which Jews were forced by circumstance tempted some to crime and laid others open to suspicion. Traditional skills in seal cutting and calligraphy which made some eighteenth-century Jewish immigrants into expert engravers, watchmakers, or miniature painters, turned others towards the arts of forgery, lock picking and private coining. The involvement

of others in pawnbroking and the secondhand trade opened a convenient avenue to theft and receiving. In June 1775 'a Jew who buys and sells old cloathes'
was in court on suspicion of having stolen five guineas from 'an old pair of
breeches' for which he was bargaining with the servant of a Liverpool
householder.[47] The real or assumed international connections of English Jews
invited the kind of fraud practised by 'a noted Jew', who, in 1776, sold a
quantity of glass to a gullible Birmingham merchant at an exorbitant price (8s
a pound, as against the real value of less than a penny) on the pretence of
acting as the agent of a Jewish merchant 'of immense property and strict
honesty' in Amsterdam.[48]

Five years after the Chelsea murder, in the autumn of 1776, Manchester—
still without a settled community—was visited by five robbers and highway-
men, including three Jews, who were responsible for a series of extensive burglaries in Birmingham, Liverpool and Chester.[49] The gang was made up of the
two young Londoners, Christopher Lawless, a baker, and Isaac Hutchinson,
once 'a jockey in the service of the Duke of Ancaster', who had recruited three
Jewish accomplices to act in specialist capacities: Joseph Isaacs and Michael
Lyon, two London seal engravers, to manufacture 'instruments for forcing
locks, bolts, etc', and Alexander Solomon, a Liverpool pawnbroker, who, before he turned to crime, had 'lived in the strictest rectitude . . . as an honest
tradesman, in the cities of London, Dublin and Bristol'.[50] It was in Manchester, in September 1776, that the five planned a series of robberies of shops and
private houses in Chester for which they were subsequently arrested and committed to the House of Correction at Hunt's Bank.[51] In a trial at Chester As-
sizes in December which lasted eleven hours, four were sentenced to death
—'to the satisfaction of a very crowded court'—after Lyon had turned King's
evidence. The affair attracted considerable attention, and the 'cavalcade'
from Northgate Goal in Chester to the place of execution was followed by

many thousands of People . . . Hutchinson and Lawless, attended by the Romish
Priest, in one Cart, and Isaac and Soloman, attended by the Jew Rabbi, in another
Cart, bellowing forth Hebrew all the Way.

From the gallows, where Solomon died protesting his innocence, Isaacs as 'a
penitent', their bodies were taken for burial 'at the Synagogue in Liverpool'.[52]

The chief effect of such incidents was to reinforce existing ill-feeling and
suspicion. A German visitor of 1782 was surprised to find 'anti-pathy and
prejudice' towards the Jews 'far more common [in England] than it is
even with us, who certainly are not partial to them'.[53] Another foreigner, writing nine years later, believed that 'few burglaries, robberies and false coinages'
were committed in which Jews were not in some way involved, and described
the furnaces which supposedly burned throughout the night in Duke's Place

to melt down stolen silver and gold.[54] In London, in the 1790s, a Jewish theatre-goer was an invitation to abuse:

I no sooner put my head into an obscure corner of the gallery, than some fellow or other roars out to his comrades—Smoke the Jew!—Smoke the cunning little Isaac!—Throw him over, says another, hand over the smoutch!—Out with Shylock, cries a third, out with the pound of man's flesh—Buckles and Buttons! Spectacles! bawles out a fourth—and so on through the whole gallery, till I am forced to retire . . . amongst hootings and hissings, with a shower of rotten apples and chewed oranges vollied at my head . . .'[55]

In this atmosphere, Jewish settlement in the provinces in the two decades which preceded the outbreak of war with France in 1793 was cautious and circumspect. Jewish traders tended to concentrate in and around those towns in which the basis for economic and religious survival had already been staked out in the mid eighteenth century, rather than to strike out into unknown territory, however attractive the apparent commercial inducements. Isolated families, in the north-west and elsewhere, sought the safety of established communal life. Simon Joseph, a German silversmith, who had lived in Wakefield from 1756 to 1766, was one of several country shopkeepers who moved with their families into Liverpool during the 1770s and 1780s.[56] When the Liverpool congregation moved from the synagogue in Turton Court, where Isaac and Soloman were buried in 1776, into a house in Frederick Street purchased in 1789,[57] it was composed of some twenty-five jewellers, pawnbrokers, drapers and slop dealers, and an unknown number of dependent pedlars.

Although Manchester's population had risen to over twenty-four thousand in 1773–74 and nearly forty-two thousand by the end of 1788[58] in the wake of the industrial and commercial boom associated with the mechanisation of cotton spinning, it could not compete for security with Liverpool, where tolerance towards the Jews was of long standing. To the generally prevalent currents of anti-Semitism which cast all Jews as 'avaricious out-casts (who make gain their God)',[59] Manchester added its own peculiar fear of 'travelling plagiarists' who threatened to reveal the profitable secrets of the cotton industry to foreign rivals.[60] In the spring of 1774 Prescott's *Manchester Journal* warned its readers that

several JEWS and OTHER FOREIGNERS have for some months past frequented the Town and Neighbourhood, under various Pretences, assuming different Names, the better to effectuate their purposes, and some of them have procured Spinning Machines, Looms, Dressing Machines, Cutting Knives, and other Tools and Utensils used in the manufactures of Fustians, Cotton Velvets, Velverets, and other Manchester goods . . . and have taken opportunities of secreting themselves in several Workshops . . . in order to make themselves acquainted with the process thereof. And . . . frequent Attempts have been made to entice, persuade, and seduce many of our Manufacturers and Artificers to go into foreign Parts out of His Majesty's Dominions . . . the Consequences of which must be the Destruction of the trade of this Country, unless timely prevented.[61]

A Committee of Trade, which was appointed to meet weekly—'or oftener, as occasion shall require'—to deal with suspected persons, offered a reward of twenty guineas for information leading to an arrest.

But after this public Notice it is hoped that no one will be so regardless of his own interest, and so great an enemy to the Community, as to give the least encouragement to such Invaders, whose only Design is to take the Bread out of the Mouths of our Workmen, and deprive us of a Trade which has been the Labour and Experience of so many Years to bring to the present State of Perfection.[62]

Although no Jew is known to have been convicted for the export of machinery or the 'seduction' of cotton operatives, the attitude of the Manchester middle class towards them was coloured for over half a century by fear of their possible implication in industrial espionage.[63]

Although direct evidence of Jewish commercial and professional activity in Manchester during the boom years of the 1770s and 1780s is lacking, the town was occasionally visited by anonymous itinerant dealers in articles in which Jewish hawkers specialised. In January 1771, 'a Person' from London offered for sale bankrupt stock of 'linen drapery, millinery, jewellery, and hosiery goods' at the Rose and Crown in Deansgate.[64] In the spring of 1779, travelling slop sellers spent a fortnight at the King's Arms, Smithy Door, with

a very large Assortment of second hand and some New Cloaths consisting of Wearing Apparil in very great Variety, especially in the Men's Way . . . a variety of which, though they may be called second-hand, are very little worse than New, yet will be sold at half Price or Less.[65]

Amongst the numerous travelling quacks who visited Manchester during the 1770s was one with the equivocal title Dr Jerusalem, who arrived from Leeds in January 1774 and disappeared into obscurity, after effecting a number of miraculous cures, six months later.[66] Manchester was within range of the slop dealers, drapers and silversmiths of the Liverpool community of the 1780s, and of Lazarus Levi, a 'travelling Jew' of Leeds who died there in 1799 at the age of 105.[67] The appearance of Jews in the conjectural role of industrial spies suggests their greater familiarity to the Manchester public in more conventional occupations.

II

The exact sequence of events which converted these occasional contacts into settled communal life must remain to some extent a matter for conjecture. Fragments of evidence suggest that from the late 1780s Jews were beginning to experiment in the retail trades in and around Manchester. Hamilton Levi, who appears in a local trade directory for 1788 as a flower dealer in Long Mill-gate, may have been Jewish. The brothers Simon and Henry Solomon of Liverpool traded as jewellers and watchmakers in Rochdale, where they were declared bankrupt in 1788.[68] Simon Solomon then moved to Shudehill in Manchester, where in 1792–93 his shop was twice burgled.[69] It was the Liverpool connection which proved decisive. Subsequent events would suggest that in the late 1780s and early 1790s a group of ten to twelve hawkers and small shopkeepers based in Liverpool, and dealing chiefly in cheap jewellery, lenses, quills, umbrellas and old clothes, had begun to concentrate their attentions on the Manchester market and to explore the possibilities of a Manchester settlement. It may be, as tradition suggests, that they were held back only by the difficulty of finding a person sufficiently tolerant to lease them land for use as a burial ground.

The leading members of the group were two brothers, Lemon and Jacob Nathan, dealers in slop and watch materials, whose origins lay in Bavaria, where Lemon was born in 1742 and Jacob in 1761. Although their names do not appear in any Liverpool trade directory, they were certainly living in the town before 1786, when Lemon Nathan was a Freemason of some standing in Liverpool's Ancient Lodge No. 53. Indeed, family tradition has it that the elder brother was already an 'active worker' in Liverpool's communal affairs during the early 1770s.[70] At all events, the Nathan brothers provided leadership to a body of tradesmen whose final decision to settle in Manchester has all the appearances of a carefully planned operation.[71] Other prominent members of the group were Aaron Jacob, a slop-seller of Prussian origin, and Isaac Franks, a hawker of lenses, probably born in Holland, whose English career had begun during the 1760s in Norfolk.[72] There he met a Miss Nash, a Quaker girl, with whom he eloped to Dublin, where in 1781 she was converted to Judaism and became his wife. The couple then settled in Liverpool, where their eldest son, Jacob, was born in the following year. The eldest member of the group was Abraham Isaac Cohen, a Hebrew teacher, then in his seventies, whose son, Philip, was an umbrella maker and dealer in ostrich feathers. Others, of whose antecedents little is known, included Henry Isaacs, a dealer in quill pens and his son, Samuel, who was born in Liverpool in 1780; Nathan Samuel, a pencil maker born in Poland in 1775; Benjamin Joel, a brushmaker;

Gershon Israel, a dealer in watch parts; Abraham Levi, an optician; Wolf Polack, a pawnbroker; and the slop-sellers, Simon Nathan, Israel Simon and Myer Lemon, who was born in Tulsberg in south Germany in 1749 and married in Hull in 1784.[73] It seems likely that these men had been (and perhaps still were) linked in the manner of an itinerant 'brotherhood'.

For a period of perhaps six or seven years Manchester was an increasingly important focus of their commercial dealings without becoming their place of permanent residence. The outbreak of war with France in January 1793 was perhaps the most decisive stimulus to settlement. Anti-foreign feeling became more acute, and within a few months it was legally embodied in an Aliens Act which gave the government wide powers over the movement of all foreigner in England, and compelled those already in the country to obtain, and to produce on demand, licences of residence and trade. Although not directed specifically against the Jews, it placed their activities under close official surveillance. At the very least, those Liverpool Jews who traded regularly with Manchester were impressed with the advantage of consolidating these links by establishing a legal right of residence and an organised basis of communal life. A few—including Myer Lemon, Nathan Samuel and Israel Simon—elected to remain in Liverpool. The majority prepared the way for a Manchester settlement by deputing three of their younger members—Isaac Isaacs (another son of Henry Isaacs, the quill dealer), Philip Isaac Cohen and Jacob Franks—to obtain possession of a small parcel of land at the corner of the cemetery at St Thomas' Chapel in Pendleton for the sum of £43 8s 9d and an annual peppercorn rent from Samuel Brierly, a Methodist silk dyer, in a lease sealed on 10 March 1794.[74] Soon afterwards (and certainly before 1796) the new community had begun to worship in the 'small upper chamber' of a warehouse in Garden Street, Withy Grove[75]—'a mean-looking street, the buildings chiefly ancient . . . unclean and disagreeable'[76]—in the heart of Manchester's Old Town, where Aaron Jacob—'affectionately known as "Rabbi Ahron" '—acted as Reader and *shochet* for an honorarium of £10 a year.[77]

This was also the first area of Jewish settlement (see Map 2). A complex of congested streets, narrow, tortuous lanes, and cramped courts radiating from Miller Street, Shudehill and Long Millgate, in the area of the Collegiate Church, the Old Town was the market centre of Manchester and a district of low-lying, decaying seventeenth-century property, engulfed and overshadowed by the smoke and clamour of new factories and warehouses. The trade directory for 1794 locates eleven Jewish settlers—an optician, a book-keeper, two slop-dealers, two dealers in watch materials, a brush maker, a working jeweller, a quill dresser, an umbrella maker, and a 'dealer in cotton goods'—in the area between Oldham Street and the Collegiate Church, all but one within

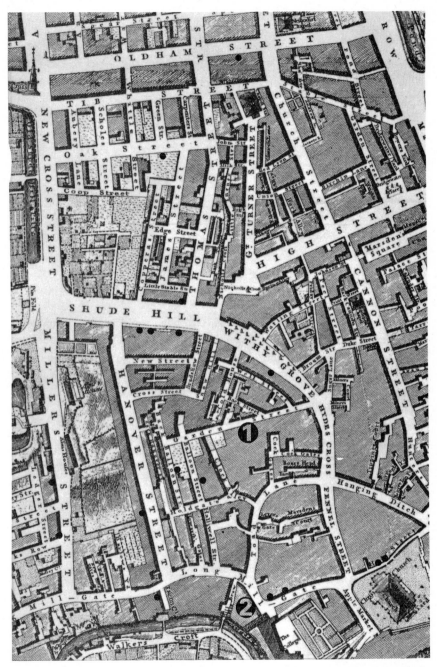

MAP 2   Section of C. Laurent's *Topographical Plan of Manchester and Salford*, 1793. Jewish households (1794–1815) are marked. (1) The warehouse where the community first worshipped; (2) the synagogue in Ainsworth's Court.

a few hundred yards of the synagogue. Although poor, they avoided the 'offensive dark, damp and incommodious cellars' on the river side and the fever-ridden 'nests' of lodging-houses which shocked the sensitivities of John Aiken in 1795.[78] They chose instead a district of cheap but spacious houses in an area already known to them as hawkers, in which they might pass relatively unnoticed and where they could maintain contact with itinerant dealers who continued to use Manchester as a base. Apart from regular daily services, the first official ceremony in the synagogue took place in 1796, when Nathan Samuel came over from Liverpool to marry the daughter of one of his former colleagues.[79]

Fragments of evidence link the new settlers to two quack doctors who had arrived in Liverpool from Dublin, probably together, in or about 1789: Dr Isaac Solomon, a brother of Abraham Solomon, a merchant and the authorised *shochet* of the Cork community in the mid eighteenth century, and his more notorious nephew (Abraham's son) Samuel Solomon, who in 1789 married Elizabeth, the third daughter of the Birmingham pencil maker, Moses Aaron.[80] In 1794 Isaac Solomon practised as a 'surgeon and chemist' in Cleveland Street, Samuel Solomon in the Old Strand. A will proved on 5 December 1796[81] indicates that Dr Isaac Solomon took up residence in Manchester during 1795 and died there in the following year. His two executors—Aaron Jacob and Gershon Israel—were made responsible for the payment of £50, in weekly instalments of 7s 6d, to his brother Abraham, the former Cork *shochet*, then in retirement in Liverpool—'if my said Brother shall so long live'—£125 to the first, and £150 to the second of his daughters, and their families, also in Liverpool, and ten guineas to his servant, Ann Ambrose. To his son, Solomon Solomon, a working jeweller, then living in Falcon Court, Manchester, he bequeathed

the sum of One Shilling, and I will and direct that he shall not be intitled [*sic*] to have or receive any other Benefit of this my will;

and finally £10

unto the Trustees of a certain plot of land in Pendleton . . . intended to be appropriated for the use of the Jews as a Burial Place . . . [to be] applied towards erecting a Wall round the same.

It seems reasonable to assume an estrangement of the two doctors from the Liverpool synagogue, perhaps on some issue of observance, which persuaded both to stake a claim in a new Manchester community in which they were well known.

Only a deduction such as this would explain the terms of a document drawn up on 7 February 1797:

We the undersigned, being the Jewish congregation of Manchester, in consideration of the sum of ten pounds, ten shillings, paid to our manager and overseer [by] Mr Samuel Solomon of Liverpool (Doctor of Medicine) grant and acknowledge the said Samuel Solomon to be equal to either or any of us to have a sufficient place in our burial ground lying in Pendleton near Manchester that will contain the corpse of the said Samuel Solomon when he may depart this life, and also sufficient space and ground in the said burial ground to contain Elizabeth the wife of the said Samuel Solomon and the children of the said Samuel or Elizabeth Solomon either or any of their issue lawfully begotten in wedlock according to the Jewish rites and ceremony, being such as are acceptable to the Jewish Synagogue, not having been converted to any other religion, when it shall please God to take away the life of him or any of his or her children.[82]

The names of the signatories have not survived, but it may be assumed that the congregation's 'overseer' was Jacob Nathan, who by that time had entered into partnership with his brother at 144 Long Millgate, opposite the gates of Chetham's College (see Figure 1), where on 1 August 1798 he was granted an Aliens Licence to live and trade as a jeweller and silversmith.[83]

Although Samuel Solomon took advantage of the agreement to arrange for the burial at Pendleton of his son, Henry, who died on 9 May 1798 at the age of nine months,[84] the progress of his career freed him from dependence on either community.[85] The spectacular success of his miracle cure, the 'Balm of Gilead', in England and America at the turn of the century enabled him in 1804 to build a mansion at Kensington, on the outskirts of Liverpool, which he called Gilead House, and which became, in succeeding years, a centre of politi-

FIGURE 1   Jacob Nathan's house in Long Millgate, indicated by the 'x' of his son, Elias, on a photograph of *c*. 1890.

cal jobbing and high society, and to purchase an estate on Mossley Hill, on which he constructed a private family mausoleum. He severed his connections with Judaism in all but distant sympathy, and his subsequent association with Manchester was confined to the publicity of his remedies. His Balm was widely advertised in the Manchester press, and drew favourable comment from at least one credulous editor, who attributed its wide renown to 'respectably attested cases' of genuine cures.[86] To the many other lotions, tinctures and elixirs available to the vain and fearful Manchester public, he added his 'Anti-Impetigines or Solomon's Drops' for the cure of 'all disorders originating in an impure state of the blood' (at 11s a bottle, or 35s for a four-in-one family pack), and an 'Astergent Lotion' for removing 'all kinds of Pimples, Ringworm, Carbuncles, etc, from the Face and Skin'.[87] In a *Guide to Health*, first published in 1796 and offered for sale at 3s, he played particularly on the effects of the 'divine vengeance' brought down on those 'who . . . unfortunately pursued a dangerous practice in their youth', under the emblem of a spurious coat of arms and the copy of a medical diploma purchased from Marischal College, Aberdeen.[88]

III

During its ten years in the Garden Street warehouse (1796–1806), the Manchester Hebrew Congregation underwent little permanent change in its size or general character. As a body of small shopkeepers, it responded more to the pressures upon Anglo-Jewry than to the fluctuations of the cotton trade, which, in spite of periods of depression and a sharp crisis during 1799–1800, underwent a general, and at times very rapid, expansion. The population of Manchester, Salford and their suburbs rose during these years to a total of around 110,000,[89] probably the largest urban concentration outside London, while the Jewish community did not exceed fifteen families, or perhaps seventy-five persons, in 1806. With immigration from Europe impeded by war and hampered by regulation, internal movement restricted by the Aliens Act (reinforced by fresh legislation in 1798 and 1803) and patriotism intense, there was little cause for any movement of Jews into a town in which feeling towards foreigners was particularly volatile. The reasons for caution were increased by the well-publicised deportation of Wolf Polack, the pawnbroker, then in Shudehill, in February 1800, for undisclosed breaches of the Aliens Act;[90] to ensure his departure, he was escorted to Hull by Joseph Madder, one of the Manchester constables. The resumption of war in May 1803 after the Peace of Amiens, was the signal for a further prolonged outburst of virulent xenophobia. *Wheeler's Manchester Chronicle* told its readers:

At this period of alarm, it appears to be a matter of importance with Government, that Aliens should conform to the law enacted for their regulation. The object of it, when national prejudices have induced many foreigners to deem that political conduct *right*, which Reason and Justice most loudly confirm to be *wrong*, becomes truly serious; and it requires vigilant exertion to counteract principles of such a dangerous tendency.[91]

A separate notice inserted by the Manchester constables reminded local inn-keepers that their failure to check the credentials of any alien lodger made them liable to a £10 fine, half of which might be earned by an alert informer. Aliens who failed to obtain licences of residence or to give 'a true account' of any weapons in their possession to a local magistrate were liable to imprisonment. Licences were subject to forfeit 'if the persons who obtained them be found out of their districts'.[92]

These circumstances did not encourage expansion. The community remained huddled around the synagogue, where its leaders did what they could to emphasise the honesty of their intentions. In 1798 the Nathan brothers contributed 5s to a local fund for national defence.[93] On a 'day of public humiliation' observed in Christian Manchester on 15 March 1800 by 'a very animated sermon' in the Collegiate Church to troops assembled 'in military order',

the solemnity was devoutly observed by the Jews in this town. In a prayer composed for the occasion, is the following pleasing and grateful tribute—After praying for the Royal Family, the Counsellors, the Nobility, the Representatives of the People, and the whole nation, it proceeds, 'Shield them from all evils, and bless them with all kinds of blessing, for it is well unto us with them—the people are peaceable towards us; and their laws are a protection to us and our property.'[94]

With one exception, the changes in the composition of the community were understandably few and relatively insignificant. Abraham Isaac Cohen, who had accompanied the colonists of 1794, perhaps as their spiritual mentor, died in Miller Street at the age of eighty. When Henry Isaacs, the quill dresser, died in 1804, at the age of fifty-nine, his business in Milner's Court, Sugar Lane, was continued by his widow, Esther, and subsequently by his eldest son, Samuel. Jacob and Isaac Cohen, hat makers, arrived from London in 1799; Mordecai Slazenger Moss, a German umbrella maker, in 1800; Asher Cohen, a slop dealer from Firth in Hesse, in 1801; Joseph Braham, a dealer in slop and umbrellas, from Danzig in 1806.[95]

The exception was the young Nathan Meyer Rothschild of Frankfurt[96] —'perhaps the most talented and least polished, even of that astonishing family'[97]—who arrived in Manchester with his father's chief book-keeper, Siegmund Geisenheimer, in the August of 1800 and acquired an office in Brown Street in the central commercial district. Nathan Meyer's father, Meyer Amschel Rothschild, was at that time still in the process of converting a provincial discounting business in Frankfurt into a major banking concern and had only recently gained access to substantial investment funds as the Court Agent to the Elector of Hesse Cassel. It seems likely that it was for this reason that he entered into an elaborate partnership with his sons and began to deploy them in the capitals of Europe as his financial and commercial agents. It was as part of these arrangements that Nathan Meyer travelled to London with Geisenheimer in May 1800,[98] with ready capital of some £20,000, of which a fifth was his own and the rest belonged to the family business.[99] After remaining for three months in London, apparently to acquire direct experience of English commercial practice in the firm of the financier, Levi Barent Cohen,[100] he proceeded to Manchester in August. He knew little or no English,[101] and his acquaintance with the Manchester cotton trade was limited to experience of English agents on the continent, where he had been unfavourably impressed by their high prices and arrogant manners.[102] It was to circumvent these agents and to acquire English textiles at source at the lowest possible price for the German market that the Manchester office was now established.

Although lack of evidence conceals the exact nature of Rothschild's operations, it seems likely that they centred upon the manufacture and finishing of cotton goods in Manchester on behalf of his father in Frankfurt. According to an account attributed to him,

I soon found out that there were three profits—the raw material, the dyeing and the manufacturing. I said to the manufacturers, 'I will supply you with material and dye, and you supply me with manufactured goods.' So I got three profits instead of one, and I could sell goods cheaper than anybody.[103]

At the same time, a series of letters written to Frankfurt during 1800–01 suggest that he was also purchasing textiles in Scotland, in the West Riding of Yorkshire, and perhaps in the Midlands.[104] The possibility of making immediate payment in the form of bills drawn upon his father's bankers in London gave him access to goods at the lowest prices and 'in a short time' he is said to have tripled his outlay.[105] Through shipping firms in Hull, Leith and London goods made their way through forwarding agents in Hamburg to his father's warehouse in Frankfurt, whence they were distributed to the continental market through the great German Fairs. Conditions favoured the enterprise. Following a brief recession during the winter of 1799–1800, Manchester's export trade expanded rapidly, particularly after the signing of the peace with France in October 1801. The pause in hostilities opened up the starved European market to English textiles and stimulated a burst of factory building in Manchester and its vicinity during 1801–03.[106] Rothschild was only one, although probably the most successful, of at least eight German merchants who came to

Manchester during 1800–03 to tap the rich supply of cotton goods at source.[107] Rothschild began only as his father's agent, but before the end of 1801 he was also shipping goods on his own account direct to other customers in Germany, France and Italy.

Little else is known of Rothschild's life and enterprise in Manchester.[108] The records of a Manchester Benefit Society reveal that one at least of his clerks—Joseph Barber—was recruited locally.[109] In 1804, when, with four other Germans, he was granted letters of denization, he appeared in a local trade directory as a 'merchant and manufacturer', with a house in Downing Street, Ardwick—a suburb 'chiefly occupied by the merchants of the town . . . particularly distinguished by the neatness and elegance of its buildings',[110] and likened by a contemporary to London's West End.[111] A vast social gulf separated Rothschild, with his great family wealth and international connections, from the struggling shopkeepers of the Old Town, in whose company he is said to have worshipped. He occupied a seat in the synagogue and 'conformed strictly to all the rites and ceremonies of our faith, his dinner being cooked by a Jewess and taken to him at his warehouse every day'.[112] The *shamash* is said to have 'brought him the palm branch and citron daily during the Tabernacle Festival'.[113] Another story, less reliable in its source, describes him as having taken his meals at a 'public dining room', where his companions included 'Mr Herman . . . an Israelite, a dealer in fine pictures and paintings'.[114] Of the fifteen German merchants in Manchester in 1806, eight were of Jewish descent, but of these only Rothschild maintained his religious affiliations.

Rothschild may perhaps be credited with some, at least, of the communal developments which accompanied the early years of his residence. Soon after his arrival, the congregation secured the services of 'Rabbi' Joseph Crool,[115] an eccentric travelling scholar of Hungarian origin, who in 1802 set up a 'Hebrew Academy' at his home in Oak Street. His stay in Manchester was uneventful, and apparently brief, for by 1805 he was acting as spiritual guide to the small Jewish congregation in Nottingham.[116] Subsequently he moved on to Cambridge, where he earned a comfortable livelihood for over twenty years as a freelance teacher at a time when the Royal Professors of Hebrew were absentees. Nothing is known of his life in Manchester, but those who had attended his lessons in Cambridge later remembered him as a man of great pretensions and little learning, 'abounding in prejudices', and given to the custom 'of wearing a parchment girdle in which were inscribed passages from the Law and the Talmud'.[117] In Manchester, perhaps at Rothschild's prompting, he sounded the patriotic note. Part of his own translation of a rhetorical sermon delivered on 19 October 1803 reads:

We in this country have reason to rejoice . . . We are protected by . . . King George,.

and . . . by his servants . . . they are our guardians against all those who rise up to hurt us.

Of the English, in whose midst Manchester Jews lived 'quietly and peaceably', he wrote:

they are an industrious nation, they eat the labour of their own hands. It hath pleased Thee to exalt them in prosperity above all nations.[118]

Other communal achievements of a lesser order, although traditionally attributed to the Nathan brothers, may have been partially financed by Rothschild. The wall around the burial ground, pending through lack of funds since the death of Dr Isaac Solomon, was completed at the cost of £43 in 1806.[119] In the March of the same year Jacob Nathan made the first quarterly payment of £2 10s to Miss Mary Ainsworth for a warehouse in Ainsworth's Court, Long Millgate, once used as a school, to serve as a new and larger place of worship.[120]

The resumption of war in 1803 had meantime placed a considerable strain upon the trade with Germany in which Rothschild was involved. In the face of blockade and counter-blockade, markets became more inaccessible, freight charges and insurance premiums increased proportionately, long-term planning became difficult. Attempts to evade the French led to costly, dangerous and circuitous routes to Germany via the ports on the Baltic or the Adriatic, while attempts to run the British blockade of the Elbe during 1804–06 ran the risk of interception.[121] At the end of May 1806, a few months before the Elbe was reopened, the agents of the Admiralty in Hull took possession of five ships—the *Jupiter*, the *Pilgrim*, the *Leipzig*, the *Brunswick* and the *Boyton*—and seized from each cargoes of contraband purchased by three Jews—'Leo, Wolfe, and Mayring'—in Manchester for around £20,000. Leo was arrested at Harwich; the other two made their escape to the continent.[122] The uncertainty was increased by the Berlin Decree (November 1806) and the French seizure of Hamburg and Bremen, and reached a point of crisis during 1808, when exports to Europe were shipped chiefly to Heligoland and Gothenberg, and thence smuggled into France and Germany. A brief recovery during 1809–10, as the routes via Baltic and Adriatic became better known, was followed by an acute depression which lasted into the autumn of 1812. Many who had no alternative to the cotton trade survived by exercising extreme care in the study of the market, courage in the selection of routes, and flexibility in their choice of products.[123]

Rothschild was in a different position. In 1805 he acquired a new London office—in St Helen's Place—and although he continued to spend a good deal of time in Manchester, he became increasingly involved in his father's financial transactions with the great London bankers and, from 1808–09, as loan contractor to the British government. His marriage in 1806 to the daughter of his former patron, Levi Barent Cohen (and the sister-in-law of Moses Montefiore) gave him a personal link with the leaders of the Sephardi community, then dominant in London finance by virtue of their connections with Amsterdam. In 1808, using funds supplied by his father, he purchased substantial quantities of gold from the East India Company which he used subsequently to subsidise Britain's continental allies and to finance Wellington's Peninsular Campaign. The profits from these transactions and the commanding position they gave him in the City of London ensured the fortunes of the English House, and the death of Sir Francis Baring and Abraham Goldsmid in 1810 'left him without any very formidable competitor in the London money market'.[124]

According to a story relayed by Moses Margoliouth, Rothschild would not have left Manchester had it not been for

a private pique against one of his co-religionists, which originated by the dishonouring of a Bill which was made payable to him, which disgusted him with the then Manchester community,[125]

but it seems more likely that his movements reflected the changing emphasis of the family business in England from mercantile to financial dealings, against a background of uncertainty in the cotton trade. During 1808–09 Rothschild occupied a 'large and commodious' warehouse in Back Mosley Street adjoining a 'spacious, modern, and well built' town house at 25 Mosley Street,[126] then 'without exception the most elegant street in Manchester'.[127] In 1809 he subscribed £3 3s (for the first time) to the Royal Infirmary in Piccadilly.[128] But during the winter of 1809–10 he began to wind up his affairs in Manchester. His house and business in Mosley Street were sold early in 1810 and vacated the following December, when Rothschild himself moved permanently to London.[129] The closure of a temporary branch maintained for eighteen months at 5 Back Lloyd Street was announced in a notice in the *Manchester Exchange Herald* of 4 July 1811:

that the business heretofore carried on by the undersigned Nathan Meyer Rothschild, at Manchester, under the firm of 'Rothschild Brothers', will cease to be carried on by him from this day, and any persons having dealings with that firm are required to send their demands or pay their accounts to N. M. Rothschild, at his Counting-House, in No. 2 New Court, St Swithins-lane, London.

N. M. Rothschild[130]

A golden handshake perhaps accounts for Joseph Barber's purchase (for nine guineas) of Life Membership of the Commercial Clerks' Association in 1812[131] and his subsequent emergence as a merchant on his own account. Whatever his feelings about the local Jewish community, Rothschild's connections with the town were completely severed. The link with his family was not revived until 1841, when his widow visited Manchester, donated £50 to local charities, and expressed her pleasure 'in thus testifying her remembrance of a town in which she was many years since a resident'.[132]

IV

A revival of trade in Manchester followed the collapse of the continental blockade, Napoleon's retreat from Moscow, and a reopening of the Baltic ports in the autumn of 1812. During 1813 direct trade with the channel·ports was resumed, and by the December of that year Manchester was again 'full of foreign merchants seeking consignments of cloth and yarn'.[133] Of the five German merchants who settled in Manchester during 1812–14, at least three were of Jewish descent, and, of these, two were practising Jews. Solomon Levi Behrens,[134] who succeeded to Rothschild's role as the financial patron of the community, was born in Pyrmont in the independent German principality of Waldeck in 1788, the son of Levy Behrens, one of three brothers who were partners in a business importing English textiles to the markets and fairs of north Germany. In 1806, when their partnership was dissolved, Levy Behrens moved to the free city of Hamburg, where he set up the business in which his sons, Solomon Levi and Wilhelm, served their commercial apprenticeships. The family had social and commercial links with Nathan Meyer Rothschild, who is said to have once sought the hand of Levy's daughter, Lorette,[135] and it was probably Rothschild's example which took the young Solomon Levi Behrens to Manchester, at the beginning of 1814. Like Rothschild, he acquired a house in Mosley Street, and a warehouse in Back George Street from which he exported Manchester goods through his sister, Lorette, who took over the family business in Hamburg and guided its fortunes with an iron efficiency.

While Behrens, like Rothschild before him, maintained communal links with his Manchester co-religionists across a wide social chasm, and took a paternal interest in their affairs, Gustavus Gumpel, who arrived in Manchester during 1814, also from Hamburg, was more aloof. Although apparently observant, Gumpel chose to occupy a seat only at the impressive new synagogue in Seel Street, Liverpool, where the births of his children were subsequently registered during the period 1819–23.[136] His was a half-way position between those German settlers, like Solomon Reinholdt (1798), Louis Magnus (1805), Morris Schlesinger (1812) and M. S. Meyer (1815), whose assimilation was complete before their arrival in Manchester, and those, like Behrens and Rothschild, whose orthodoxy and communal allegiance were unshaken by the assimilatory pressures within German society. He was prepared to accept membership only of a synagogue which gave adequate expression to his social ambitions.[137]

The closing years of the Napoleonic War were an important turning point in the social evolution of the community as a whole, and in the prevailing attitude towards it. Some of the earliest settlers were beginning to improve their economic and social status. Aaron Jacob, the former slop seller, entered the cotton industry in 1808 as a manufacturer of fustians in Hunter's Lane, and acquired a house near Windsor Bridge. By 1811 he owned a factory in Cannon Street, in the commercial centre of Manchester, and a house in Bank Parade,

FIGURE 2   Handbill of Jacob Franks, *c.* 1812.

a fashionable suburban crescent, above the Irwell, on the rural outskirts of Salford. Asher Cohen, also a former slop dealer, became a 'merchant and manufacturer' in Market Street Lane before overstretching his resources in 1810, when his 'last examination' as a bankrupt was conducted in the Dog Tavern in Deansgate.[138] Benjamin Joel, the brushmaker, who moved from Long Millgate to 20 Market Street in 1814, then employed six or eight men in the manufacture of hair, tooth, clothes and nail brushes, which he sold retail at an annual profit of around £500.[139] When his premises were demolished nine years later, under the Manchester Streets Improvement Act, his son-in-law and successor received £711 in compensation.[140] A handbill engraved in about 1810 (see Figure 2) announced the growing enterprise of another of the original brotherhood:

J[acob] Franks, Optician, No. 4 Miller's Lane . . . Makes and Repairs all sorts of optic Glasses, telliscopes, microscopes, Reading glasses, etc, etc. With a variety of spectacles for all Ages, Whether Concave or Convex. Old Ones taken in Exchange in any of the above Articles. Likewise, Excelent tooth powder will make the Blackest Teeth the finest White. Also Excelent eye-water has Cured many almost blind. Excellent Ruburb. Infallible worm Powder for destroying worms in human Bodeys. N.B. Umbrellas made and Neatly Mended.[141]

The local directories added slop dealing to what may be imagined as a retail undertaking with a substantial body of dependent pedlars. On the death of his first wife, Polly Isaacs, in 1810, Jacob Franks embarked on a second marriage with Amelia Cohen, the daughter of a London box maker, who in 1815 gave birth to the fifth of his twenty-four children. When the Liverpool community began to collect funds for the building of a synagogue in Seel Street (1806–08), Lemon Nathan and Joseph Braham were prospering well enough in Manchester to each contribute five guineas.[142] In a letter of thanks to Braham, Elias Joseph expressed the hope that he would long retain the power to 'circulate' his money 'in the like charitable way'.[143] Several of the former hawkers and travellers who settled in Manchester in the period 1806–14 established small but flourishing enterprises: Joseph Marks (1811) as a clothes dealer in Timber Street; Israel Simmons (1813) as a 'dentist and corn-extractor' in Hart Street; Joseph Levy (1813), who arrived in England from Prussia in 1787, at the age of fourteen, as a pawnbroker, jeweller and slop dealer in Shudehill. The general success of Jewish retail trade was marked by its extension into the more fashionable shopping districts. Although still concentrated in the Old Town, there were Jewish shops in Church Street by 1800, Exchange Street by 1802, Tib Street and Deansgate by 1808, and Market Street by 1814.

Although lacking the size and resources to build and maintain a synagogue such as Liverpool's, which in the final reckoning cost £2,224,[144] by 1815 there were two merchants, a textile manufacturer, a broker, and a core of some fifteen well-established shopkeepers in a total community of twenty-five families, or perhaps one hundred and fifty persons. Many were locally born. Others had resided in Manchester for over twenty years, and in England longer still. After a period of enforced separation from Europe and involvement in the high patriotism of war-time England they had ceased to think of themselves as foreign. They were English. English was the mother tongue of some of the older and all of the younger generation. Those who could afford it had contributed to local appeals since 1798, when the Nathan brothers gave their 5s to the National Defence Fund.[145] When, in July 1803, England appeared to be in imminent danger from Napoleon, six Jews contributed to a 'Fund for National Defence'.[146] Ten subscribed to a 'Nelson Fund', opened in November 1805, to support wounded veterans of Trafalgar and the widows of the fallen.[147]

In other ways, Jewish families identified themselves with local society. Jacob Nathan sent two of his sons to Manchester Grammar School, Lewis Henry in 1808, Joseph in 1811.[148] In 1804 Rothschild was one of the subscribers to a Commercial Coffee Room and Tavern for the members of the Manchester Exchange.[149] Jews began to enter Freemasonry, one of the few social institutions which welcomed them on equal terms. Lemon Nathan had joined in Liverpool. Aaron Jacob and Asher Cohen were admitted to the Manchester Lodge of Fortitude No. 64 on 6 May 1801.[150] In 1810 Jacob Franks was inducted into the Lodge of Unity No. 443, which met at the Old Falstaff Tavern in Market Place.[151] Freemasonry was perhaps the only organised body of public opinion in Manchester which favoured the integration of foreigners (including Jews) into local society and sought to influence public attitudes towards them. It was at the request of 'the Provincial Grand Officers and United Lodge of Manchester Freemasons' that Richard Cumberland's comedy The Jew, one of the first English plays to portray Jewry in a favourable light, was performed at the Theatre Royal in January 1795, only a few months after its London run.[152] In 1799 the young Italian looking-glass manufacturer and barometer maker, Baptist Ronchetti, was treasurer of Manchester's Lodge of St John.[153] The Lodge of Unity No. 442 included three German merchants, and there were other Germans in the Lodges of Trinity and Tranquillity from the turn of the eighteenth century.[154]

In London it was possible for ambitious Jewish families like the Rothschilds, the Montefiores and the Goldsmids to achieve social prominence by patronage and to wield political influence through wealth. In the provinces the only avenue to local eminence was assimilation, and it is remarkable, perhaps, that most Manchester Jews confined themselves to levels of integration and indications of loyalty which could be reconciled with religious conformity. The only known exception amongst the earliest settlers was the Abraham Levy who in 1794, at the age of twenty-six, settled as a book-keeper in Oldham Street, on the edge of the Old Town. His rise on the social scale appears to date from 1796, when he accepted a commission in the Manchester and Salford Volunteers after receiving the statutory 'Sacrament of the Lord's Supper' in the Collegiate Church.[155] In the local directory of 1797 he figures as a 'gentleman'. In 1798—described by his Commanding Officer as 'a very respectable officer'—he was sent to London with a letter to the War Office requesting improved pay, better weapons, and more effective training to enable the battalion to be 'more fit for actual service in Case of Invasion'.[156] As Captain and Paymaster, he became entitled to a horse and an allowance of 2s 6d a day to maintain it. In civic affairs, he became successively chairman of a local Watch Committee (1800), a juror on the Court leet (1801), a House Visitor and Inspector of the Infirmary (1801), and 'conductor' of the special constables in St Paul's district (1802). When England again faced what seemed to be an imminent threat of invasion in the summer of 1803, and something like panic swept through Manchester, Levy became a Captain in the Royal Lancashire Militia.[157] In or about 1806 he left Manchester for Temple Sowerby in Westmorland, where in 1811, shortly after the death of his first wife, he married the daughter of Mathew Atkinson, the Comptroller General of Westmorland and Cumberland, and moved into the social circle of the northern gentry.[158] He ended his life as the tenant of Hutton Hall, a fine sandstone mansion in Penrith.[159]

The Aliens Act was still being strictly enforced in Manchester in January 1812, when all aliens in the neighbourhood of Manchester and Salford were called before the magistrates at the New Bailey Court House to produce their licences of residence.[160] 'Householders and others' with whom aliens resided were to attend at the same time to provide the names of their lodgers 'on pain of forfeiting £10'. In May 1812 it was still possible to believe, with a correspondent to the *Manchester Exchange Herald*, that the recent food riots in Manchester had been the work of 'hosts of foreigners, temporary inmates of the nation', and particularly of 'Itinerant Foreign Pedlars' who, as the 'emissaries' of Bonaparte, supposedly possessed 'the power of tinkering with the poorer classes of society'.[161] The remedy proposed was the 'immediate rejection of every Foreigner who is not fully and fairly known to be really and *bona fide* what he seems' and the more careful surveillance of 'all those who are suffered to remain'.[162] Another alarmist believed that Jews were exporting gold and silver to France to undermine the British economy.[163] Towards the end of the year, however, as fear of defeat gave way to anticipation of victory, and Manchester began to rise out of the severe commercial depression of 1810–

1812, the realities of Jewish communal life—its improving economic status, the process of its cultural integration, the demonstrations of its loyalty—began to work their effect upon public opinion. At the same time, religious preju- dice was blunted by the extension to Manchester of the Anglican conversionist organisation, the Society for Promoting Christianity Amongst the Jews, founded in London in 1795, which, however ambivalent and condescending in its attitudes, improved feelings towards the Jews by deploring ridicule and persecution, and promoting (in admittedly insidious charities) their 'temporal and spiritual welfare'.

The earliest known experiment in conversion in Manchester was the free- lance effort of the Rev. John Johnson, an eccentric preacher of the Countess of Huntingdon's Connection, who during 1798 devoted three sermons to the pur- pose from the pulpit of St George's Church, including one entitled 'The Per- fect Beauty out of Zion; or the Appointed Time of the Messiah upon the Earth . . . written in Hebrew . . . with Chosen Testimonies from the Ancient Tal- mudhs and Targums of the Rabbins, translated into English, first preached to God's ancient People, on 25th day of December, 1798'.[164] Johnson died in 1804, and his work was not followed up until 11 November 1812, when a crowded and 'most respectable' meeting convened in the Dining Room of the Exchange by Manchester's ministers and merchants, including Robert Peel (the elder) and James Hibbert, founded a 'Corresponding Committee' of the London Society, which in the following year converted itself into an 'Auxili- ary Branch' for the collection of funds and the dissemination of propaganda.[165] Genteel Penny Societies were organised

under the patronage and superintendance of Ladies for the purpose of affording an op- portunity to the lower classes, and particularly to servants, of contributing to this im- portant institution.[166]

For the first time, Jews figured in local Christian literature as persons worthy of favourable attention. It was still regarded as a matter of regret that (accord- ing to the rector of Burton Latimer) the Jews held up the Saviour 'to scorn and derision', but this was now excusable as an honest 'act of conscience' which might be remedied by conversion.[167]

A movement in the direction of tolerance was slowed down chiefly by the persistent fear of Manchester merchants and manufacturers of losing the me- chanical secrets upon which they believed their prosperity to depend. When an agent of the London Society alluded in the Manchester press to the possi- bility of providing potential converts with industrial training on 'cotton machines',[168] a correspondent to the *Manchester Exchange Herald* asked (in Oc- tober 1812):

Have not foreigners, who are of nations who are at war with England, a right to leave the country when they like? Is it good policy to teach our manufactures to foreigners, who may transplant English ingenuity to the continent, and whilst they enrich our inveterate foes, do us a material injury? Then can it be good policy to instruct Jews, who are foreigners to all intents and purposes, in the use and nature of cotton machinery?[169]

Legh Richmond, a Bedfordshire rector, and a moving force in conversionism, took the letter seriously enough to reply that

it was far from the wish of the Society to instruct persons so intinerant as the Jews in any of the valuable manufactures of this country,

and to apologise for the ignorance of his colleagues in describing 'the simple apparatus for the manufacturing of Candle-wicks' as 'cotton machines'.[170] The editor of the *British Volunteer and Manchester Weekly Express* summed up the Manchester position in January 1815, when he drew to a close a lively correspondence on the danger from travelling spies:

It is commendable for us to receive strangers with all due hospitality . . . but let us vigilantly guard the mysteries of our national inventions, or we shall find the vital prosperity of our trade dangerously assailed.[171]

V

Such reservations were perhaps one reason for the relatively slow growth of Manchester Jewry. Another was the pattern of Jewish economic life in the provinces, which tended to insulate the community from the strong gravitational pull of the manufacturing towns. Jewish expertise lay not in manufacturing, but in the distributive trades, which still appeared to have their most natural centres in market towns or ports, some of which had risen in importance as naval bases in the wars with France. Birmingham alone amongst the manufacturing towns attracted a sizeable Jewish population, not because Jews were drawn into its industries but because the area produced goods more easily adapted to the pedlar's tray than Manchester cottons.[172] In 1815, when there were perhaps ten thousand Jews in provincial England (as against fifteen thousand in London), concentrated in some twenty-five communities,[173] or dependent upon them, Manchester was still exceeded in size by Plymouth, Portsmouth, Falmouth, Birmingham, and in the north-west by Liverpool, where in 1811, when a Hebrew Philanthropic Society was founded, the Jewish population was over four hundred,[174] perhaps three times that of Manchester. When, in March 1813, the congregation of Ainsworth's Court contributed £3 towards

'Soup Shops' for the local poor, the *Exchange Herald* commented that the donation was

particularly worthy of notice and of praise; the congregation consists of only ten persons of different ages and not one with anything like truth could be alluded to if we say, in comparison, 'Rich as a Jew'. Their three pounds we look upon as the largest benevolence the day afforded.[175]

Later in the same year, the congregation appointed its first full-time Reader—Israel Lewis (or 'Lewis Lorino', as he was better known)[176]—but it was still very small. Joseph Aston wrote, in 1816:

The number of persons who composed the congregation being very small, there is little to recommend the synagogue to notice. It exhibits a striking contrast in its embellishments, to the grandeur, described in the sacred writings, with which the children of Israel celebrated their religious rites.[177]

This was in spite of the fact that Aston's Manchester was itself expanding more rapidly than any other town in England. As the working population increased, and warehouses and factories, in search of cheaper land, encroached upon the central residential districts, a town 'engrossed in the spirit of Commerce'[178] was extending its boundaries on every side. The former villages of Ardwick, Hulme, Chorlton Row, Cheetham and Pendleton, had become, in Aston's phrase, 'suburbs', linked by a 'chain of buildings' to their 'mother towns'.[179] For the convenience of merchants and manufacturers who, like Aaron Jacob, had moved away from the smoke of eighty-two spinning factories to semi-rural districts where 'the pure breath of Heaven may more freely blow upon them',[180] new streets were laid out which in 1816 extended 'upwards of two miles from the centre of town'.[181] At the other end of the social scale, pauper dead from the labyrinth of slums and cellars became so numerous that a new 'expeditious and economical' method was devised for disposing of their bodies in a common pit, covered up with planks when not in use, in the cemetery of St Michael's Church in Angel Street.[182] The end of the French Wars brought back 'many thousands' of veterans, and

also by renovating trade [had] given a new spring to the prosperity of Manchester which has brought talent, capital and industry from every part of the kingdom.[183]

The population had increased, on Aston's calculation, by at least twenty thousand between 1811 and 1816,[184] when about one hundred and thirty thousand people lived in Manchester, Salford and their suburban dormitories. The fifty-three watchmen who patrolled the streets at night from the Police Office in King Street, under the antiquated manorial regime of a borough reeve and Court leet, were insufficient to keep order in the community, and in the winter months the town was 'infested by gangs of freebooters',[185] including 'a

man named Davies, stating himself to be a Prussian Jew' who passed counter-
feit notes with the aid of female accomplices in Manchester and Macclesfield
before his arrest and committal to Chester Castle in January 1815.[186] But the absence of a strong municipal corporation was regarded as 'a subject for congratulation amongst the judicious part of the inhabitants', since it made possible an
unrestricted freedom of development, 'facilitated' the settlement of strangers,
and steered the town clear of political in-fighting.[187] Although (in Aston's
estimate) 'not more than half of the adult population (perhaps not more than a
third)'[188] were local-born, very few were foreigners, and even fewer were
Jews.

2   Consolidation, 1815–26

The first post-war decade was an important watershed in the development of the community. By 1825 the original settlement had been transformed by immigration, education and enterprise into a large and respected body of well-to-do shopkeepers, export merchants, and professional men, an integral part of the Manchester bourgeoisie, the third largest Jewish community in the provinces, and probably the most rapidly expanding. Over the same period, public attitudes more favourable to the Jews made substantial headway, in part, perhaps, because the economic status of the community continued to improve, but still more because Manchester's own economic development began to undermine the social and ideological bases of anti-Semitism and xenophobia. Finally, as the community became more secure and self-assured, its cautious struggle for survival gave way to a confident assertion of permanence which culminated in the building of a new synagogue in Halliwell Street during 1824–25. If the acquisition of a burial ground may be taken, as Cecil Roth suggests, as the beginning of an organised communal life, the building of a synagogue marks an important stage in its development, not only to a size and degree of wealth sufficient for the creation and maintenance of a place of worship, but also to a point of self-confidence at which it no longer seems necessary to conceal from non-Jewish society the existence of an active and healthy communal life. It also presupposes a leadership sufficiently coherent and dynamic to give precise and effective institutional shape to the vague aspirations of the community as a whole—a form of leadership which emerged in Manchester during the early 1820s as a tightly-knit oligarchy of some five or six family groups.

I

With the ending of the French War, and the reopening of regular cross-channel communications, provincial Anglo-Jewry began to expand fairly rapidly in and beyond the communities of the war years. Of the immigrants who began to arrive in England from Germany and Poland at a rate of at least three hundred a year,[1] a majority perhaps remained in London, but a steady stream flowed on into the provinces, a few on their way to the United States, but most to join the existing communities, or to swell the floating population of itinerant traders, repair men and petty criminals. Immigrants were still required to obtain official 'certificates' at the ports of entry, and the government retained its powers of deportation, but once in the country (after an amendment to the Aliens Act in 1814) aliens were no longer required to possess licences of residence, and they were free to move about at will and to settle wherever they pleased. Only nine aliens were 'ordered away' from England between 1814 and March 1818, when the government estimated the resident alien population at around twenty-three thousand.[2] Although the twenty-five existing congregations continued to serve as the focal points of Jewish religious and social life, fragments of evidence suggest that provincial Anglo-Jewry entered upon a new era of turbulence as immigrants moved from place to place in search of the community most suited to their tastes and talents, or begged their way across country to Liverpool, the port of embarkation for America; itinerant tradesmen carried Jewish life into new regions; travelling quacks, opticians, dentists and chiropodists served clients in widely separated towns; London gangs made criminal sorties into provincial cities; and settled families of an earlier generation adjusted to the changing economic contours of the nation. Jewish hawkers were to be found in every part of the kingdom. Isolated Jewish shopkeepers, in no instance in sufficient numbers to lay the basis of an organised congregation, had established themselves in North Shields (by 1818), Sheffield (1818), York (1820), Chester (1820), Preston (1821), Leeds (1822), Hull (1822), Doncaster (1825), Hanley (1825) and Newcastle under Lyme (1825).[3] The earliest account books of the Manchester synagogue reveal other Jewish retailers, by the mid-1820s, at Warrington, Wigan, Bolton and Bury in south Lancashire, at Stalybridge in Cheshire, and at Bradford and Huddersfield in the West Riding, and include payments from Simon Lazarus, a Jewish cheese factor, of Whitchurch in Shropshire, where Jews had been trading since 1818. Michael and Joseph Hyman, the one a member of the Manchester congregation, the other of Liverpool, were by 1819 engaged in itinerant trade in and around Holywell and Caernarvon in North Wales.

Most of all, perhaps, Jewish commercial activity intensified in and around the new industrial centres where rapidly growing town populations had outpaced the development of urban shopkeeping. A recent arrival from Poland who in 1818 obtained a hawker's licence and a stock of goods on credit from Trytle Joel, a jeweller in North Shields, and made his way across country to 'the neighbourhood of Manchester, Birmingham and Liverpool',[4] was perhaps typical of many penniless immigrants disembarking in the north-east. Manchester, in particular, was a market for hawkers, a staging point for transmigrants, a source of commodities for export, a target for criminals, and, finally, a place of permanent settlement and trade. Two Polish Jews who were arrested in June 1823 for hawking pencil cases, spectacles, 'and other Jewish merchandise' in the villages of Didsbury and Withington, on the outskirts of the town, had been in the country for only a few months and were both on their way from London to the port of Liverpool 'to embark for America', a journey delayed by two months in the New Bailey Prison.[5] A brief report of their interrogation by a sympathetic magistrate provides the earliest evidence of Jews passing through the town on their way to the United States. 'Foreign strangers' with criminal intent included Noah Lodolski (1817)—'come from the continent to try the accepted character for credulity which John Bull bears in that meridian'—who drew two local Jewish shopkeepers into a conspiracy to defraud Manchester textile firms. For attempting to obtain goods to the value of £25,000 on the security of two trunks said to contain 'Birmingham goods', but found on examination to be filled with bricks, all three were sentenced to terms of imprisonment with hard labour in Lancaster Castle.[6] A gang of swindlers based in London, and including several Jews, operated briefly in Manchester in the winter of 1821–22, when they obtained goods on credit and then 'decamped, leaving an empty warehouse for the consolation of a numerous band of sufferers'.[7] Two Jewish confidence men who had already achieved a measure of success in North Shields, moved into Manchester in 1821 and relieved a grocer in Long Millgate of £7 'for a bundle of clothes not worth 20/-'; one posed as a liveried footman with clothes to sell, the other as a pedlar, to force up the price in bargaining with an unsuspecting third party.[8] The publicity given to the illegal activities of Jewish travellers suggests their presence in more lawful roles on an even greater scale. Jewish professional men— Abraham Abrahams, a Liverpool optician, Dr Lamert, a notorious quack of Bristol and Spitalfields, and many others—visited Manchester regularly and established temporary surgeries, usually in Piccadilly, for their middle-class clients.[9] For the convenience of these and other observant strangers, Mrs Sarah Levy, a widow, established Manchester's first Jewish lodging house and kosher restaurant—in Long Millgate—in 1819.

All this activity reflected the growing size and economic importance of Manchester in the post-war years, particularly between 1821 and the commercial depression of 1824–26, when the town was extended by the addition of over four hundred new streets, lanes and courts, and the population of Manchester, Salford, and their immediate suburbs rose to over two hundred thousand.[10] Within Anglo-Jewry, the growing opportunities in Manchester were emphasised by the achievements of its earliest settlers. There had, indeed, been failures—during the uncertain years of war and again during the brief recession of 1816[11]—but these were more than offset by the success of those who had begun their working lives as pedlars. To their thriving jewellery business in Long Millgate the Nathan brothers added the import and distribution of miscellaneous manufactured goods (including 'Dutch hats of superior qualities'), the discounting of English and Spanish dollars, and the buying and selling of gold bullion. Their advertisements to this effect in *Wheeler's Manchester Chronicle* of 1817 were the first to be inserted by Manchester Jewish tradesmen in the local press.[12] Jacob Franks gave up his many side-lines and settled down as an optician at 283 Oldham Street, a shop 'designated by the sign of gilt skeleton spectacles' near New Cross, where Butterworth described him, in 1822, as 'a person who has knowledge of optics and is also fond of paintings'.[13] Samuel Isaacs of Withy Grove appears in Butterworth's guide as 'one of the most extensive dealers in quills and sealing wax in the town': he employed tied pedlars, some of whom he assisted with the purchase of a licence.[14] When Israel Simmons, the travelling chiropodist, died in 1822, his widow, Rachel, and young son Isaac (born in Liverpool in 1806) opened a jeweller's shop in Long Millgate which rapidly established itself amongst the most fashionable in the town. In 1824 Aaron Jacob turned from the manufacture of fustians to the overseas trade in textiles, in which he was joined by his two sons, Alexander and Morris, while a third son, Henry, set up on his own account as an importer of French and German cigars, toys and fancy goods, and an exporter of textiles to the South American market through Buenos Aires. S. L. Behrens, whose European trade through Hull flourished in the post-war boom, was one of the promoters of a scheme for a railway between Manchester and Leeds which was first put before the public in January 1825.[15]

As Manchester established its reputation as a town in which money and skill might profitably be invested either on a substantial scale, in the textile trade, or, more modestly, in retail enterprises directed towards a growing middle-class clientele, immigration reinforced the middle ranks of the local community. The post-war influx included former hawkers, and penniless adventurers, like John Peiser, a coachlace weaver of Posen in Prussian Poland, who arrived in England in 1823 and, 'after travelling through a great part of the country', took low-paid work as a journeyman weaver in a Manchester mill.[16] But far more characteristic were those who arrived, either direct from Europe or from other towns in provincial England, with varying amounts of capital and commercial or professional experience to sink into shops, surgeries, warehouses or factories in or near the city centre. At least twelve merchants of German-Jewish origin arrived in Manchester between 1815 and 1825, although only two, Isaac Benjamin (1822) and Moritz Heine (1824), retained their Jewish identity. Phineas and Peter Henry came from Mogilev in White Russia to establish a successful silk factory in Fountain Street in 1820.[17] During 1823 shops were acquired in the Old Town by Joseph Gumpelson, a pawnbroker and jeweller from Berlin,[18] and Abraham Lipman, a clothes dealer from Shokken in East Prussia;[19] and typical of other German immigrants were Levy Sampson (1818), a dealer in fents, Henry Mendleson (1821), a jeweller, and the partners Ansell Spier and Samuel Leon (1823), furriers and manufacturers of cloth caps in Crown Square, Salford. Arrivals from London included Simeon Cohen (1820), a trunk maker and furniture broker in London Road (and father-in-law of Jacob Franks), and John Lyons, who in 1823 established a factory in Blackfriars to manufacture straw hats 'at a much lower price than any other house in England'.[20] Most significant of all, perhaps, of Manchester's advancing status in Anglo-Jewry were the handful of shopkeepers and professional men who came from Liverpool, where they had already created successful businesses: the rope maker and draper, Emmanuel Mendel (1817); the jeweller, John Joel Cohen (1820); the dentist, Pascoe Aranson (1822); and, above all, Abraham Franklin (1823), the moving spirit of the Manchester community for over a quarter of a century.

Abraham Franklin was the son and sixth child of Benjamin Wolf Franklin, a religious teacher, and a member of a family originating in Prague, who came to London from Breslau in or about 1763.[21] When Benjamin and his wife died in an epidemic in London during 1785, their five surviving children were dis-

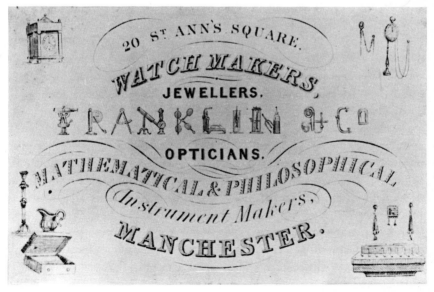

FIGURE 3   Trade card of Abraham Franklin, c. 1830.

tributed amongst friends and relatives, and Abraham (born in England in 1784) was adopted by his aunt Zipporah Marks, the wife of a London silversmith and old clothes dealer, in whose service he began by selling watch-glasses in the parish of St Giles. After his barmitzvah he spent some time as an apprentice to a wholesale watchmaker, John Brogan, before joining his brother Lewis in business in Portsmouth at the turn of the century. There he met and married Miriam Aaron of Portsea, the granddaughter of the Birmingham pencil maker, Moses Aaron, through whose family he acquired a jeweller's shop of his own in 1807. His business prospered, and he played a prominent part in the growth of the local congregation, acting as the trustee of the land upon which the synagogue was built. In 1815 or 1816 he moved to Liverpool, where Lewis was already established as a money changer and foreign banker, and there he carried on business with equal success as a navy agent and silversmith in Pool Lane before moving in 1823 to Manchester, where he opened a jewellery and money-changing enterprise in St Ann's Place and a 'toy warehouse' near the house in Bridge Street in which he lived with his wife and (at that time) nine children. His eldest son, Jacob (born in Portsmouth in 1809), acted as shop-boy in St Ann's Place and attended mathematics classes at the Mechanics' Institute in Cooper Street soon after its foundation in 1825;[22] his second son, Benjamin (born in Portsmouth in 1811), served an apprenticeship as a commercial clerk with Lewis Franklin in Liverpool; his third son, Isaac (born in Portsmouth in 1812), was admitted to Manchester Grammar School in February 1827.[23]

In outlook, Abraham Franklin was perhaps typical of the new Anglo-Jewish bourgeoisie which was taking shape in London and in the provinces. Brought up amongst the hawkers and former hawkers of London, Portsmouth and Liverpool, for whom strictness of observance had provided the only form of social stability and self-respect in a world in which they otherwise lacked security and esteem, his orthodoxy was uncompromising; educated in England, and reaching manhood during the French wars, in which he had served as a volunteer at the time of the invasion crisis of 1803, his loyalties and hopes were centred upon the country of his birth. He belonged to a generation prior to the spread of Reform, which saw no inconsistency between a total commitment to traditional Judaism and full participation as an equal in English social and cultural life. On the contrary, the social and political future of Judaism in England seemed to him to rest with the creation of just such a balance in Jewish life. He was at the same time acutely aware of those disreputable elements in Jewish society and trade which, because they fell short of English moral and commercial standards, seemed to threaten the community's parity of esteem. In the light of the uncertain dealings of the immigrant Jewish hawker, with his 'patriarchal appearance' and 'uncouth dialect, interlarded with a few words of broken English',[24] and the notoriety of the Jewish sharper, he believed it necessary to emphasise the English ideals, social sophistication, stability, and honesty of the settled Jewish tradesman. Hence, perhaps, the remarkable regularity of his appearance in the local press as a guardian of law and order, a paragon of upright trading, and an advocate of social justice. In July 1823 he and his son, Jacob, were instrumental in arranging the arrest in St Ann's Place of two men subsequently found guilty of receiving.[25] In November 1824 he detained in his shop two men (one of them Jewish) attempting to dispose of stolen silver plate.[26] When, in 1826, he received a watch he believed to have been stolen, he advertised a description and later returned it, without charge, to a pawnbroker in Dublin.[27] In the same year, when three men were tried for robbing his house in Bridge Street, he went personally to court to recommend them for mercy 'on the grounds that they had offered no violence when they were discovered, though they had an axe in their hands'. He had made personal enquiries, he told the magistrates, which showed that the family of one of the men was 'in very great distress', and could not afford the loss of its breadwinner.[28]

The community's central problem, as Franklin saw it in the 1820s, was that of adapting its institutions to English conditions without altering, in any significant way, the structure of the religious life which went on in and around them. He did not go along with the handful of German theologians who were beginning to question the Talmudic basis of Jewish custom and to favour assimilatory changes in the ritual of the synagogue, such as those introduced into the services of the first Reform 'Temples' at Berlin and Hamburg during the period 1815–17. The improvements which Franklin believed necessary to the future prestige of the community related to the social quality of congregational life, not to its ritual or ethical content. They could be achieved by what, in religious terms, were peripheral changes which left the liturgy untouched and the Talmud unchallenged: the building of larger and more respectable synagogal accommodation, the creation of a more rational and efficient administration of congregational funds, the introduction of sermons in English, the institution of a choir, improvements in the decorum of services, and the development, as finances allowed, of educational and philanthropic agencies designed to complete the social and occupational integration of the community. It was a programme in which most of Manchester's middle-class Anglo-Jewish families came to believe, to a greater or lesser degree, but Franklin, with his high social standing and long experience of congregational leadership in Portsmouth and Liverpool, was in a strong position to provide a decisive lead. His vision was more comprehensive than that of most of his Manchester contemporaries, whilst his autocratic disposition (not least within his own household) and fierce family pride fitted him for leadership of an anglicised elite.[29] Personal and communal ambitions were inseparably interwoven, since, given the volatility of public opinion towards the Jews, the one was to a very great extent dependent upon the other.

The task of regeneration was not that of starting from scratch but of building upon the strong economic base established during and after the war. By 1825 Manchester Jewry had already acquired the character of a community of shopkeepers with a small élite of merchants and manufacturers; if the 'country' traders are excluded, its working population consisted of fourteen clothes dealers, nine jewellers, five retailers of quills and pencils, five merchants, three hawkers, two hatters, two furriers, two dentists, two silk manufacturers, two fent dealers, an optician, a pawnbroker, a rope maker, and a furniture dealer. Although Jewish residence and trade still centred on the Old Town, Behrens and Gumpel lived near one another in Mosley Street, the most elegant of the diminishing residential districts of central Manchester, Phineas Henry in Clarendon Street, Chorlton Row (the first Jewish resident in the southern suburbs), Aaron Jacob in Bank Parade, and his eldest son, Alexander, in Salford's Crescent, 'a very beautiful suburb . . . recently ornamented with iron palisades'.[30] There were Jewish shops in St Ann's Place (Franklin) and King Street (Mendelson); Pascoe Aranson's surgery was in Princess Street; Jacob Freeman, a painter of miniatures, lived for a time in a studio in Brazennose Street. Although most Jews were in occupations and professions dictated by common experience, there were occasional, although usually short-lived exceptions; during the period 1825–26 Israel Moses, a confectioner and fruiterer, opened an employment exchange at 8 Oldham Street which offered to supply 'servants of respectable character' to the householders of Manchester and Salford.[31] Non-resident Jewish shopkeepers and travellers who depended on the services of the Manchester Synagogue included Casper Eisenburgh, a jeweller in Warrington, Samuel Levy of Bradford, Barnett Cohen of Huddersfield, Simon Lazarus of Whitchurch, Michael Hyman, a hawker of jewellery based in Bangor, Isaac Joel of Preston, Abraham Franks (Jacob's brother) in Newcastle-under-Lyme, and George Mayer, a jeweller who arrived in England from Warsaw in 1820 and in 1825 settled with his two sons, Saul and Nathan, at Shelton, a suburb of Hanley in the Potteries.[32] When Mordecai Slazenger Moss, the Manchester umbrella maker, died soon after the war, his sons entered the trade in old clothes in the smaller towns of the Lancashire cotton belt, Joseph (born in Manchester in 1807) in Warrington, Lewis (born 1796) and Ralph in Bury. With a settled Jewish population of around two hundred and fifty to three hundred (perhaps fifty families), Manchester had become the fourth largest community in England, the third largest in the provinces. The 'opulent and rather numerous body'[33] of Jews in Liverpool was probably in excess of one thousand;[34] there were perhaps five hundred Jewish residents of Birmingham,[35] five times as many as in any other community out of London.

II

Parallel to the numerical and economic growth of the community, and only in part arising out of it, was the continuing development of a spirit of greater tolerance towards the Jews. Although fear of industrial espionage persisted so doggedly that in 1822 James Butterworth decided to omit from his description of Manchester such details of cotton manufacturing

as might prove injurious to the trade of the Kingdom at large, as opening the eyes of those Foreigners who have settled here . . . in order to transport our different improvements and inventions to distant countries,[36]

it was neither attributed specifically to the Jews, nor suspected of every stranger of foreign birth. Butterworth added:

all foreigners are not to be classed with the above, nor to be generally considered as spies, who are come here merely for the sake of plunder:—No! I am sure there are amongst the great Body mercantile very many strangers and Foreigners of excellent dispositions who (I have no doubt) are well-wishers to the land they live in.[37]

Although a substantial body of enlightened men, including the proprietor of the *Manchester Guardian* (founded in May 1821), still feared the ill-effects of the export of machinery, xenophobia in its more virulent forms survived only in the narrow circles of the Manchester Pitt Club, a High Tory society dedicated to the 'Protestant Ascendancy' and the containment of both 'Foreign Enemies' and 'domestic foes',[38] or the small and ineffective Manchester Literary Society, whose members decided in 1827 that it was 'not politic' to allow foreigners to have 'manufacturing and commercial establishments in this country'.[39] In the period 1815–1826 Jews gained from almost every shift of local opinion, and all immigrants, the Irish excepted, from most.

In the five immediate post-war years, the attention of the influential, propertied sections of Manchester society was diverted from 'Jews and other foreigners' towards the 'pestilential doctrines and opinions' of the radical demagogues, besides whose supposedly 'unlawful and nefarious designs' on England's 'well regulated liberty'[40]—culminating at Peterloo in August 1819—the activities of the most unscrupulous Jewish sharper appeared relatively innocuous. Jewish shopkeepers were also seen during these years of crisis to be identified not with the doctrines and methods of Cobbett and Hunt but with the defence of property, order and the political *status quo*. Bernard Cohen was amongst the many signatories of a declaration published in January 1817 which applauded the authorities for the drastic measures they had taken to restrain 'those who are seeking to involve us in riot and confusion';[41] and in July 1819, on the eve of Peterloo, Jacob Nathan was one of three prominent Jews who pledged themselves, with hundreds of other Manchester citizens, to uphold the constitution and to co-operate with the borough reeve and his constables in the preservation of public peace.[42] Faced with the apparent alternative of social disorder, Manchester Jews chose to support a 'Protestant' constitution which, *inter alia*, denied them any office under the crown, and excluded them from civic government, Parliament, and the older universities; they acted according to their interests, not as Jews, but as merchants and shopkeepers concerned about the orderly conduct of business and trade. Under these circumstances it became possible even for the conservative press to distinguish between the 'speculating lower orders of Jews' implicated in crime or in the shadier underworld of commerce, and 'respected' Jewish tradesmen of proven integrity with a substantial stake in local society. When, in May 1817, two local Jewish shopkeepers were implicated in the frauds of Noah Lodolski, 'a considerable feeling' was at first excited in their favour, since their

character and conduct were presumed to have been prior to this transaction irreproachable. Many respectable persons, indeed, gave evidence to this effect on the trial, and it was conjectured that they had become the innocent dupes of the foreigner.[43]

So great was this shift of emphasis from assumed guilt to presumed innocence, that only when their part in the conspiracy was proved beyond doubt did public sympathy dissolve and the press concur in their imprisonment at Lancaster for the 'protection of the commercial community'.[44] In reporting another trial, in 1823, the *Guardian* was able to distinguish sharply between an 'unintelligible' Polish immigrant caught hawking without a licence, and 'a very respectable Jew of this town' (Joseph Levy, of Shudehill) who acted as the court's interpreter.[45] The new settlers of the 1820s, particularly Franklin, served to consolidate this new concept of 'Jewish respectability', at a time when social order was intermittently threatened by the violence of the unemployed.

As the political panic subsided after Peterloo, the Jewish community made even more solid gains from the liberal climate of opinion created by the cotton manufacturers, brokers and textile merchants who emerged during the early 1820s as the dominant force in Manchester society and politics. Through the

Manchester Guardian, whose founder and owner, J. E. Taylor, was himself drawn from the entrepreneurial class, the new captains of industry began for the first time to convert the rationalism, individualism and inventiveness upon which their economic success was based into a distinctive pattern of ideas and attitudes. As the founders of industrial dynasties, their belief in the rights of property was no less insistent than that of the magistrates at Peterloo; but to men who owed their good fortune to personal initiative and the novelty and rationality of their business methods, every other inherited tradition (including traditional prejudice) was open to suspicion and subject to criticism. Men and institutions alike were to be judged not by their pedigree but according to their effects on the promotion of commerce within an orderly society. At the same time, the leaders of what was to become a new ruling class felt the need for a corporate image which would in some way offset the conspicuous evidence of their profits and counterbalance the less salubrious side-effects of their enterprise. Those who in 1823 founded the Royal Manchester Institution for the Promotion of Literature, Science and the Arts (in effect a museum, art gallery, lecture theatre, and social club) did so in part to suggest that 'liberal and rational tastes' were

perfectly compatible with that steady and ardent devotion to commercial pursuits, which is so honourable and becoming in the character of a British merchant.[46]

Many of the *grande bourgeoisie* were no doubt actually liberal in their opinions, cultured in their tastes, and humanitarian in their sympathies; all felt the need to appear so. Civic pride underwent a parallel extension, since the local image of the new middle class appeared to depend to some extent upon the national repute of the town; new bridges were thrown across the Irwell, roads in the town centre were widened and macadamised, learned and specialist societies blossomed, a Mechanics' Institute was founded in Cooper Street, a new Town Hall built in King Street.

An important thread running through all these developments was the gradual extension of religious tolerance, at least within the influential and articulate middle-class leadership of Manchester society. Religious prejudice offended the rational tastes of the new generation of merchants and industrialists, threatened their progressive image, and seemed to belong to a less confident phase of Manchester's economic expansion: it was associated, the *Guardian* believed, with 'a state of circumstances that can no more be recalled than the age during which it existed'.[47] It was unbecoming to 'one of the most opulent towns of the British Empire'.[48] The new urban élite—'the enlightened and liberal parts of this widely scattered and in some respects unconnected population'[49]—saw itself, quite consciously, and with more than a little self-idealisation, as the spearhead of an attack upon 'the gross and sordid spirit which is too often the result of an undivided attention to mercenary pursuits',[50] and 'particularly upon effete prejudice and petty animosities. The Royal Manchester Institution, for example, which within a month of its promotion had attracted over £5,000 in subscriptions, was to have, amongst other results, 'the pleasing effect of removing prejudice, and of softening the asperity of party feeling', and was to become a focal point of liberal opinion.[51] The Manchester Anti-Slavery Society and public meetings in favour of the liberal rebels in Spain or Greece, issued from the same desire to educate public opinion; 'to heighten and ameliorate the general character of our society'.[52] L. D.', who wrote to the *Guardian* in September 1823, expressed a view of religious discrimination which was shared by a majority of the *nouveaux riches*:

every year will see it yield still more to the increasing force of rational and liberal opinions, till it shall be trampled, finally and forever, in the dust, and the people of Manchester shall be freed from the thraldom of ignorance and bigotry . . . The progress of enlightened views cannot now be stayed by petty obstacles.[53]

When, in April 1825, a local pressure group petitioned parliament against 'further concessions' to Roman Catholics, the *Guardian* correctly insisted that the memorial expressed only a minority opinion:

Manchester is not wanting in men who, prepared to defend their own civil and religious rights, would not seek to withhold those of others, from a groundless apprehension of their intentions, or a childish want of confidence in themselves.[54]

A counter-petition favouring Catholic Emancipation was sponsored by Taylor in May and supported by most other leading radical entrepreneurs—Robert Hyde Greg, Mark Philips, Archibald Prentice, Richard and Thomas Potter, G. W. Wood, and the rest[55]—whose names were associated with almost every other liberal and civic cause. The strength of the middle-class support for Benjamin Sandford's new Manchester branch of the British Catholic Association during 1824–25 suggested that at a later stage, once Christian dissent had found full political satisfaction, Jews might count upon the backing of the Manchester plutocracy in their own struggle for civil rights; in the meantime, they were assured of an intellectual climate favourable to the full and free expression of their religious identity. In particular, the *Guardian* remained consistently firm and unequivocal in its support for the rights of religious minorities.

Anti-foreign feeling also subsided during the early 1820s, in part because, like religious prejudice, it was offensive to the new middle-class ethic, in part because, as war fever and fear of industrial espionage faded into distant memory, foreign immigrants gradually acquired a more favourable local image.

The typical immigrants of the post-war years were merchants (sixty by 1825), shopkeepers, private teachers of languages, music or dancing, artists, musicians, actors, commercial clerks and foreign correspondents, most of whom adapted quickly to middle-class English standards and performed services of evident commercial or cultural value. Language teachers, whose proliferation was itself an indication of widening cultural horizons, included Signor Agnelli of Rome (1821), Señor don Jose Garcia Y Villalta of Seville (1825), and the Parisians Emil Vembergue (1821) and Alexandre Mordacque (1825). Most of the German merchants (of whom there were at least forty-six in Manchester by 1825) played as conspicuous a part as their English counterparts in civic, philanthropic and cultural ventures, the names of Leo Schuster, H. D. Dressler, Martin Schunck, P. F. Willert and Emil Liebert appearing in almost every list of subscribers to worthy causes. Foreign street hawkers, particularly young Italian barrel-organists, with their monkeys, racoons and white mice, were tolerable, at least until their numbers became inconvenient to pedestrians and offensive to civic taste in the mid-1830s. When two poor Savoyards 'who could not speak a word of English' were brought before the New Bailey Court in May 1821, on a charge of vagrancy (for 'traversing the streets with a barrel organ') the presiding magistrate ordered their immediate release 'and directed that in future, travelling musicians should not be molested, so long as they conduct themselves with propriety'.[56] A young Italian baker, John Bianchi, served as a Special Constable during the early 1820s, and in 1827 became a permanent police officer, in which role he was better known to the Manchester public as 'Beau Canky'.[57] Joshua Ronchetti, an Italian optician and barometer maker, wrote the *Guardian*'s meteorological reports.

Foreigners also gained from the waves of middle-class sympathy which went out to the European revolutionaries of the 1820s. In June 1823, Manchester committees were set up to assist those who were fighting for the 'great principle of public liberty and national independence' in Greece and Spain,[58] and in the following September, in the face of the apathy of the borough reeve, a meeting in Greg's house in King Street asserted the right of Manchester to voice its opposition to the French invasion of Spain, notwithstanding the 'strict neutrality' of the British government;[59] during 1825 funds went out from Manchester to assist Spanish and Italian political refugees in London.[60] Other foreign causes also attracted Manchester money. During 1822 the Manchester Quakers organised a fund for the victims of the Turkish atrocities on the Greek island of Chios,[61] and in November 1824, at the request of a local German committee led by Leo Schuster, Martin Schunck and J. C. Harter, subscriptions were raised for the victims of floods in South Germany.[62] The prevailing attitude towards foreigners, apart from the declared proponents of

political reaction, was one of sympathy; and although an occasional visitor
—like the 'Russian mechanic of celebrity named Andel' in November 1823—
might be expected to possess subversive or even criminal intentions (in Andel's
case, industrial espionage for Russian cotton mills),[63] the emphasis of public
opinion was on the 'excellent disposition' of the majority. A leader in the
Guardian of 24 April 1824, disposed of another skeleton in the civic cupboard
when it advocated a repeal of the law against the export of machinery, on the
grounds that the security and primacy of Manchester's trade was no longer at
stake. It was better to supply British machines at a profit than to encourage
foreigners, who already knew most of the principles involved, to build their
own, and the fact of foreign competition, if it arose, would in any case serve
only as a further stimulus to British inventive skills.[64] Although it took some
time for the Chamber of Commerce to come round to the same view, the over-
sensitive patriotism of the war years had all but disappeared. The Pitt Club,
the last reservoir of ultra-loyalist feeling, suffered a drastic decline in membership which (by 1823) had left 'little more than a residuum of more weight than
members . . . undisturbed at the bottom'.[65]

Confidence was perhaps the key. The Manchester of 1825, even if its fortunes were liable to fluctuations, was no longer a town of uncertain experiment which required protection from its foreign enemies and competitors; it
had become the established centre of a well-organised international trade and
the metropolis of a vast manufacturing region. The *Guardian* spoke with satisfaction of 'the rapid pace at which a taste for elegant and refined pursuits are
advancing amongst us',[66] and the promoters of the Royal Manchester Institution saw Manchester industrialists in the same role as the merchant-patrons of
Renaissance Italy.[67] The threat to Manchester's prosperity and prestige came
not from foreigners or Jews (many of whom, like Behrens, were members of
the urban élite) but from those who challenged property and public order:
radical demagogues and their followers, 'turn-outs' and their 'piquets', the rootless poor: not the 'bulk' of the working classes, according to the *Guardian*, but
'that rabble without conduct or fixed principles which is always to be found
amongst the population of an immense town'.[68] For all its liberalism, the *Guardian* stopped short of support for those who seemed to undermine public mor-
ale or the rights of property: all those, that is, whose riotous conduct, lack of
enterprise, subversive politics or culpable poverty suggested that they possessed an inadequate 'stake' in the existing social and economic order. The
Irish, in particular, began to emerge in the 1820s as the scapegoats of industrial
civilisation: the Protestants in their 'secret Orange confederacies', but more
especially the Irish Catholics of the cellar-dwellings and illicit stills of Newtown and Little Ireland: desperately poor, squalid, prone to drunkenness and

crime, violent, and, as often as not, associated with some extreme form of radical dissent. An Irish row in Angel Meadow in May 1825, which began as a quarrel between an Irish labourer and his local girl,

gave rise to the most extravagant and alarming rumours one of which was that the Irish Catholics had risen in a body, and were murdering indiscriminately all the Protestants who came their way.[69]

No such rumours surrounded the Jews. Apparently peaceable, law-abiding, propertied, enterprising, and politically cautious, the victims of ancient prejudice and still without full political rights, the Jews attracted the sympathy and the support of middle-class Manchester.

Explicit anti-Jewish feeling survived only within the extreme Evangelical wing of the Church of England. Most of Manchester's new middle-class leaders were religious nonconformists, many Unitarian, like their spokesman, J. E. Taylor, who had no reservations about promoting the interests of groups outside the Protestant Establishment and who did not feel called upon to defend a 'Protestant' constitution against the inroads of Catholics and Jews. On the contrary, religious equality was an integral part of their political programme. Amongst local Anglicans, however, many, particularly in the ministry, were acutely aware of the vulnerability of the Church of England, particularly in an urban environment, where it appeared to be threatened not only by many variants of Christianity, including the Catholicism of the Irish poor, but also by many kinds of apathy and atheism. At one level, this led to the creation of Anglican missions to the poor which attempted to reproduce within the town something of the coherence and warmth supposedly present in the rural parish; at another, it led to a theoretical defence of the Anglican position and an opposition to the claims (including the political claims) of other groups, which bordered on bigotry. Ironically, although the local branch of the Anglican Society for Promoting Christianity Amongst the Jews had at the time of its foundation (in 1812) contributed to the growth of respect for the Jews, in the post-war years it gradually fell under the influence of Evangelical extremists, whose genuine essays in persuasion and marks of tolerance were interspersed with anti-Catholic asides and accompanied by intransigent opposition to the political rights both of Catholics and of unconverted Jews. In consequence, from the early 1820s, the meetings of the society were periodically interrupted by militant Catholics,[70] and on at least two occasions (1821 and 1826) by an out-spoken Jew. On 3 September 1821, after 'several reverend gentlemen' had addressed the society's annual meeting in the Exchange Dining Room,

Mr A[lexander] Jacob, a Jew, rose and at some length combated their arguments and statements. The Jewish religion, he observed, was upwards of 4,000 years old: it had stood the test of time, and was not likely to be now overturned by a religion of so much shorter standing. The society might, it is true, buy over a few reprobate and abandoned Jews . . . but these would be no acquisition to the Christians, and they would, assuredly, be no loss to the Hebrews.[71]

The report adds no more than that the son of Aaron Jacob was given an 'attentive hearing'.

The local defence of the Anglican Establishment reached its most paranoic form in the writings, speeches and sermons of Hugh Stowell (1799–1865),[72] born in Douglas, Isle of Man, the son of a local vicar, and a divinity graduate of St Edmund Hall, Oxford, who in 1825 became rector of St Stephen's Church in Salford:

He could see no infirmities [in the Church of England], he could allow no faults . . . except such as arose from the want of fidelity in those to whom her interests were entrusted . . . nor in the Prayer Book, except that a few of its terms were obsolete.[73]

A master of rhetorical invective, Stowell's main attacks were levelled at Catholic causes—emancipation, the re-establishment of the hierarchy, the Maynooth grant—or at the deserters in the Oxford Movement, but he was prepared to wage war on almost any dissenting group. In a vicious pamphlet, he questioned the right of Unitarians to describe themselves as Christians;[74] he chaired a committee which opposed the attempt of the Owenites to spread socialism from their Hall of Science;[75] and although he did not regard Jews as formidable enemies, he detected 'the curse of God . . . on the wicked and miserable Jewish nation', identified modern Jewry with the crucifixion, and denied to unconverted Jews the right to participate in the making of laws for a Christian country.[76] He was an active member of the Society for Promoting Christianity Amongst the Jews, and professed to believe that their conversion had been delayed only by the Papist caricature of Christianity:

He regarded the Prayer Book as the second book in the world; the Bible being the sun of the system, the Prayer Book the morning star of promise and hope to the Jews.[77]

Stowell occasionally came under attack in the Manchester and London press both for his bigotry and as 'a clap-trap declaimer' of commonplaces,[78] but in Manchester his passionate oratory and championship of every Anglican cause earned him a large following. On the platform, according to his admirers, he was 'fervid, vehement, flowing, and energetic'; in the pulpit, 'quiet, argumentative, persuasive, and deeply interesting'.[79] He became incumbent of Christ Church, Salford, built for him by his supporters at a cost of £15,000 and opened in 1831; for twenty-five years he was President of the Manchester and Salford Protestant Association; his own church honoured him with a canonry of Chester, a chaplaincy of the Cathedral Church, and a rural deanship of Salford, from which positions of prestige he continued to inject a stream of prejudice into an otherwise increasingly tolerant milieu.

The views of Stowell and his supporters were given wider currency by the *Manchester Courier*, founded by Thomas Fowler early in 1825 specifically to counteract the programme of reform advocated by the *Guardian* and its backers, and most immediately to oppose the movement towards Catholic emancipation. The *Courier* represented the declining Tory and Anglican interest, which still dominated the obsolescent institution of local government, against the whole liberal trend of opinion and events, but in particular it set out to defend the privileged position of the established church against the ideal of religious equality to which the *Guardian* had given priority. Its most virulent attacks, like those of Stowell, were reserved for the Catholics, but when the occasion arose it showed itself equally opposed to Jewish claims. If the *Guardian* provided the Jewish community with the support of the largest and most influential sector of local middle-class opinion, and the one which in the course of time determined the social and political future of the town, Stowell and the *Courier* were constant, and sometimes frightening, reminders of more reactionary tendencies.

It was an address by Stowell to a conversionist meeting in the Manor Court Room in October 1826 which drew another public retort from Alexander Jacob, who 'read to the meeting the thirteen fundamental articles of the Jewish faith', and went on:

In your opinions of the Jews you do them a great injustice. There may be men amongst us, as there are amongst every people, who are disposed to barter their God for gold; but, generally speaking, we are possessed of as much honour and humanity as yourselves . . .

We receive no proselytes from interested motives. I am sorry to have to remark, that children are enticed away from their parents by the agents of your society. This is a proceeding which is utterly devoid of humanity. The present is the commencement of our new year. Tomorrow evening the festival will be concluded; and if any gentleman or lady will attend the synagogue, they will be welcome to hear and see our mode of worship. We are possessed of as much compassion and humanity as you are. I consider all mankind as my brethren. In Liverpool, a few weeks ago, when there was a fire in the yard of the Saracen's Head Inn, I was going home from a party; I could not persuade any of your sect to rescue a man who was in the most imminent danger of his life, so I pulled off my coat, and rushed in, and rescued him. I do not state this for the purpose of praising myself, but merely to show that we are possessed of feeling as well as you. The times are at present very bad. You should clothe the poor; go to the town hall tomorrow, and spend your money at the [charity] bazaar; but do not meddle with our nation, for it is quite useless. If you have any arguments to advance, or doctrines to discuss, our rabbis are ready to meet you.[80]

After a further exchange, in which Christianity was referred to, supposedly on biblical evidence, as the 'perfection of Judaism', Jacob replied

I have read all the chapter to which you refer, and I am ready to meet you and discuss the subject not in private but in public, whenever you choose to appoint a time.

He was received with 'good-humoured' applause, which was more than could be said for a Catholic who attempted a parallel interjection three years later: he was immediately 'overpowered by the disapprobation of the assembly, and expelled from the room'.[81]

There is no evidence that the conversionists met with any success in Manchester either by bribery or persuasion. The only known case of apostasy was that of a sister of Joel Hart, a pencil maker of Fennel Street, who in 1821, 'to the great mortification of her friends', eloped with a Christian neighbour and subsequently married him. When Joel Hart and his friends attempted to reach her in her new home, they were driven back by her mother-in-law, a Mrs Day, 'who, with a besom in her hand, successfully resisted the attack and made good her position at the kitchen door'. Hart was taken to court and there ordered to find bail to keep the peace for six months after the prosecution had claimed that the real motive of the *coup de main* was the recovery of gold and silver jewellery which his sister had taken with her.[82]

III

In their different ways, Jacob's intervention in conversionist proceedings, and Hart's unsuccessful *coup*, were minor symptoms of the increasingly confident and assertive mood of the community as a whole—a reflection both of its expanding size and wealth and of the new and generally more favourable trend of public opinion. An advertisement in the *Guardian* of 24 April 1824 addressed to 'You who are not prejudiced against my brethren', and announcing the intended publication of *The Cedar of Lebanon; or, The Jewish Defender*, included the words: 'Cease to despise the Jews: because, as men, they are your brethren, and as Jews, your fathers.'[83] There no longer seemed any good reason why the community should camouflage its religious existence or react to criticism with silence and forbearance. Moreover, the middle class within the Jewish community felt as keenly as their social peers outside it the need for institutions of conspicuous repute to confirm their elevated status. It seems probable that the community was carried along, as much by this general impulse for improvement and display as by its inner momentum, towards the creation of a more solid and respectable institutional structure. Soon after 1820, the Reader at Ainsworth's Court (who had himself replaced the deranged Lewis Lorino in 1817) was superseded by Abraham Abrahams, who, whatever his actual

MAP 3   The centre of the Old Town on Joseph Adshead's *Map of the Township of Manchester*, 1850.

qualifications, was known to his congregation by the title 'Rabbi'. The earliest evidence of his appointment dates from June 1822, when he acted as the medium for a congregational contribution of £5 towards a local fund for the relief of distress in Ireland.[84] Although he served the congregation until his death in 1839, little is known of his life or work; for acting as minister and religious teacher, he received £75 a year and rent-free accommodation in Ainsworth's Court (and later Holdgate Street); an unconfirmed tradition suggests that he was also associated with the wine trade from the West Indies, where at least one of his sons is said to have settled.[85] At all events, his appointment marks the beginning of a concerted effort to raise the level of congregational life, issuing chiefly from the initiative of the Jacob family, but immensely strengthened by the arrival of Franklin in 1823.

On 11 August 1824, the congregation assembled at its 'temporary place of worship' in Ainsworth's Court, 'and after usual daily prayers . . . walked in procession . . . to lay the first stone of an intended new synagogue' on a site in the Old Town between Halliwell Street and the courtyard of the Lamb Inn in Toad Lane (see Map 3); in the evening thirty congregants sat down to an 'excellent' celebratory dinner at the Wilton Arms.[86] When Edward Baines completed his *History, Directory, and Gazetteer of the County Palatine of Lancaster* during the winter of 1824, the building of the 'neat' new synagogue was in progress.[87] It was completed in the following summer and consecrated on 2 September 1825 by M. S. Oppenheim, the Reader of the Seel Street Congregation in Liverpool, accompanied by a 'well-trained choir' (another innovation) of 'juvenile choristers', and a 'co-religionist of the name of Jackson (from Liverpool) who was famous . . . as one of the best violoncello performers in the country'.[88] Jewish businesses in the town suspended their operations during the ceremony, which was fully reported, with all its pomp and circumstance, in every Manchester paper. 'Plain, built of red brick, and possessed [of] no conspicuous front elevation or design' (according to one eyewitness), 'externally much resembling other places of worship at that time existing' (according to another),[89] it cost about £1,700 to build, a sum 'raised with some difficulty from amongst the members'.[90] Within a year (in May 1826) the roof of the building collapsed with a noise like thunder, shattering a 'beautiful glass gas chandelier' and destroying the gallery rail and other furnishings only half an hour after a committee meeting had broken up, but the building was repaired to serve the community for a further thirty-two years. It expressed, if not ostentation, at least the permanence and security of communal life. For the time being at least, the old meeting place in Ainsworth's Court was taken over as a Sunday School by Rev. Samuel Bradley of the Cannon Street Chapel.

It seems reasonable to suppose that Abraham Franklin was closely associated both with this development and with the subsequent foundation of the Manchester Hebrew Philanthropic Society in the autumn of 1826. He had been a leading member of the synagogue in Portsmouth: he came to Manchester direct from Liverpool, where the community already possessed a fine synagogue (1808) and a small but (for the time) efficient and adequate agency of relief (1811). After moving to Manchester he retained an expensive seat at Seel Street and kept up an annual subscription to the Liverpool Hebrew Philanthropic Society, of which he had been a member since 1818, and treasurer during the period 1818–19.[91] In 1824, at the request of the Society's secretary (who wrote: 'I have reason to fear we shall continue troublesome, as long as you are charitable')[92] he arranged the sale of tickets for its anniversary dinner to his new Manchester friends Samuel Isaacs, Simon Jacob, Joseph Marks, Isaac Benjamin, Moritz Heine, Simon Feistel (a clothes dealer of Sugar Lane), and Aaron Jacob, and to Isaac Joel of Preston. S. L. Behrens and Jacob Nathan had been independent subscribers to the society's funds since 1821. The initiative in creating a Philanthropic Society in Manchester, however, was taken by Alexander Jacob, who perhaps saw it in part as a defence against conversionist bribery, and who was also (as his anecdote suggests) in close touch with Jewish families in Liverpool, the source of his imported goods. He was named as the society's 'founder' when, in 1828, he was presented by his fellow workers with a silver snuff box at a special dinner held at the kosher restaurant of Mrs Sarah Levy, then in Deansgate.[93] At that time the vice-chairman was Ansell Spier, the furrier, and Samuel Isaacs was secretary. None of the society's records have survived, but it seems likely that, as in Liverpool, it was at first intended simply 'to afford relief to poor inhabitants . . . of the Jewish persuasion during the inclement season of winter'[94] by providing small weekly allowances of between 2s and 5s to widows, orphans, the aged and the infirm, between New Year and Passover. 'Casual' payments to non-residents, or to the temporary victims of illness or misfortune as well as regular pensions to the permanently incapacitated, were made by the synagogue from its own funds: the Philanthropic Society supplemented the income of the most deserving at the time of year when the effects of their destitution were at their most severe.

The special problem of Jewish poverty had long since exercised the authorities of the Great Synagogue in London:

Parochial relief being principally given in work-houses, our indigent brethren are in consequence [of their dietary laws and Sabbath observance] deprived of such assistance,

and since the law did not permit

a compulsory tax to be raised by any separate community, without a special act of parliament, the only resource and hope of the Congregation rests on the voluntary contributions of its members.[95]

The nature of the English Poor Law threw the Jewish community back upon
its own resources, and since neither charity nor expediency permitted the poor
to be ignored, each synagogue devised its own form of relief which became a
charge upon the total congregational income. In Manchester in the mid-1820s
the incidence of Jewish poverty was relatively small: during the year
1827–28, when records of relief payments are first available, the congregation
paid out casual relief to a total of £15 6s 9d in 102 payments of between 1s 6d
and 2s 6d, and a further £2 11s 11d on Passover Relief, out of a total expenditure of £337. The foundation of the Philanthropic Society marked not the
emergence of poverty as a serious problem but the community's recognition of
its special obligation towards its permanent dependants, particularly the old,
and of the need for sources of revenue over and above the income of the synagogue to meet unforeseen emergencies, such, in the event, as the cholera epidemic of 1832:

as soon as the cholera made its appearance in this town, the subscribers unanimously
agreed to set aside a certain part of their funds for the purpose of supplying the resident
indigent Jews with flannels, meat, rice, and bread, during the period the disease might
exist in the town.[96]

The foundation of the Society at this stage provided further evidence of the
community's increased awareness of its importance and local standing. The
first communal organisation to lie beyond the orbit of the synagogue, it
marked the first stage of the community's emergence from its congregational
chrysalis.

The synagogue, however, was to remain the central pillar of communal
life, not only as the focus of religious worship, and the source of assistance in
times of trouble, but also as the community's chief medium of communication
with the Gentile world, and as the touchstone of Jewish identity at a period before the emergence of secular forms of group expression. Those who did not
rent seats at Halliwell Street, at least for the Holy Days, or take advantage of
the free-sittings available to the poor, ceased to be part of the community in
any meaningful sense, and could be expected to lose their Jewish identity in
every sense, if they had not already done so. The synagogue was the local cus-
todian of Jewish observance, providing services and facilities which made it
possible for Manchester's Jewish residents to live and die within the Mosaic
dispensation. The congregational *shochet* killed for the community according
to the traditional rules of *Kashruth*, and supervised the sale of kosher meat at
the shops of licensed butchers, who paid a tax to the synagogue for his ser-

vices; when no suitable abattoir was available, the congregation rented a slaughtering yard of its own. The synagogue authorities ordered (usually from London) the *matzoth* required by the community at Passover, and arranged for their sale, and free distribution to the poor; provided a *mikvah*, which was contracted out for a small rent to a lady of the congregation, who collected fees; arranged for the elementary religious education of the young by the rabbi in the synagogue chambers (a service exaggeratedly described by Baines as a 'Hebrew Academy'); and provided facilities for circumcision, marriage and burial according to Jewish rites. Jacob Franks, the optician, served as honorary *mohel* of the community until Abraham Franklin's son, Isaac, qualified as a surgeon (and was subsequently licensed to circumcise by the Chief Rabbi) in the late 1830s.[97] The services in the synagogue conformed to the orthodox Jewish tradition as this was interpreted by the Chief Rabbi in London. In the eighteenth century, when no provincial synagogue could have afforded a rabbi of its own, even if suitably qualified persons had been available in England, the rabbi of the Great Synagogue in London had become generally acknowledged as 'Chief Rabbi' of the Ashkenazim and spiritual head of Anglo-Jewry. With the assistance of a *Beth Din*, usually of two *Dayyanim*, he arbitrated in religious disputes, gave *ex cathedra* answers to religious questions referred to him, licensed *shochetim*, authorised marriages, and ordained what liturgical practices lay within (or beyond) the bounds of orthodoxy. Manchester, no less than other provincial communities, accepted his moral authority as a matter of course, and organised its religious life on the basis of his guidance and advice. Even if (as seems unlikely) Abraham Abrahams was qualified as a rabbi, he was expected to exercise no independent jurisdiction. The synagogue was also the public face of Judaism, so that the reputation of the community seemed to depend, in some degree, upon the efficiency with which it managed its affairs, and the order and decorum of its services. When Alexander Jacob sought to counter the prejudice of Stowell and his colleagues, he did so in part by inviting them to attend the service at Halliwell Street; more generally, in organising its congregational life, the community always had one eye on the effect that its structure and ritual might have upon the Gentile mind.

For the financing of its organisation and services, the synagogue relied chiefly upon the income from seat rents which varied, according to the wealth of the occupant, from one guinea to five: in 1827–28 there were sixty-one seat holders at Halliwell Street, twenty-five paying £1 1s a year, fourteen £2 2s, fourteen £3 3s, seven £4 4s and one (S. L. Behrens) £5 5s, a low maximum compared with the rentals in Birmingham and Liverpool. Other income derived from fines for non-attendance at committee meetings or at synagogue on Sabbaths and Holy Days, fines for the refusal of elected office (£6 6s in the case of the Warden, £5 5s by the Treasurer, £2 2s by the Secretary), offerings from members and strangers called to the reading of the Law, the sale of *mitzvaoth*, marriage and burial fees, taxes paid by the butchers for the services of the congregational *shochet*, and profit from the sale of Passover cakes. The congregation did no more than pay its way. When the burial ground at Pendleton was 're-covered' with soil in 1827–28, the congregation met the expense by raising loans from fourteen members, to be repaid 'as soon as the Congregational Funds will allow'.[98] Since the synagogue was a voluntary body, it could use no means of compulsion greater than the loss of privilege or (more rarely) membership. As later events were to suggest, secession on any scale was regarded as much in terms of financial loss as of religious danger.

The social and governmental structure of the synagogue in Halliwell Street was oligarchic in flavour.[99] Those who rented seats were divided into Free or Privileged Members, who were entitled to attend general meetings, to take part in the making or alteration of congregational laws, and to vote in the election of honorary and salaried officials; and seat-holders, who, although they paid as heavily for their seats, were allowed no part in the government of the synagogue, had no vote on any matter, and were ineligible for honorary office. The original Free Members at Halliwell Street (perhaps two-thirds of the total membership in 1825) were those who had contributed financially to the building of the synagogue. Others could be admitted to Free Membership after five years' residence in Manchester, with the approval of a General Meeting, and on the payment of a fee of up to five guineas, but given the reluctance of the early Free Members to add to their numbers, the Free Membership tended to become increasingly exclusive in character as the community expanded around it. Admittance to Free Membership was made to depend upon the 'character' as well as the wealth of the applicant. This system, which prevailed throughout England, varying only in detail, is said to have derived from the practice of Central European congregations, in which a distinction was made between heads of settled families or households (*Ba'ale Batim*), and unattached persons, or persons who travelled in business and returned home only for the festivals,[100] but, if so, it also corresponded to the realities of Jewish life in England. An élite of founder families saw themselves as the creators of congregational life, and custodians of its prestige: the social image of the community, the husbanding of its resources, the order and decorum of its services, all seemed to depend upon the guidance of an anglicised few who knew best how the community could sink strong roots in English soil. Although it was possible to deprive of his privileges anyone who endangered the reputation of the congregation or the quality of its life, it seemed preferable to reserve Free Membership in the first place for those of solid means and proven character. In some respects, the situation within the synagogue resembled that outside it, where a middle-class élite feared the ill effects of those who lacked an adequate 'stake in society': men like Behrens and Franklin, indeed, adopted a similar role in both spheres. It was to some extent appropriate to the stage which Anglo-Jewry had reached in the 1820s, when its leaders were conscious of throwing off the disrepute of the past but not yet convinced that, with the changing climate of public opinion, the future could look after itself; but within it were the seeds of a conflict between established families and new immigrants which was to provide communal history with much of its nineteenth century dialectic.

The synagogue was very much a political body, and although its most prosperous members preferred mostly to buy exemption rather than to serve as honorary officers, the underlying struggle for power and prestige, often reflecting personal and social conflicts within the community at large, was often bitter and prolonged. Tension between the families of Aaron Jacob and Abraham Franklin, arising perhaps from the challenge of a comparative newcomer to the pride of place of a founder family, led to deep synagogal intrigue early in 1832 as a result of which Aaron's eldest son, Henry, then President of the congregation, was able to impose a fine on the young Isaac Franklin for a minor and unwitting breach of congregational rules,[101] an episode which estranged the two families for almost a decade.[102] Until the early 1840s, while the community remained uncertain of its future, personal rifts were not allowed to affect the unity of the congregation as a whole, but in the times of greater confidence and more rapid expansion during the 1840s and 50s social tensions within the community not infrequently erupted as party dispute within the synagogue.

The oligarchy governed the synagogue through a Select Committee of ten persons: the two wardens and two treasurers who were elected annually by secret ballot (each to serve for six months), the four retiring officers, and two others elected by the Free Members from amongst themselves. The Select Committee administered the affairs of the synagogue at its own discretion between Quarterly General Meetings of Free Members, whose confirmation was required only for the alteration of laws, the appointment or dismissal of paid servants (the 'Rabbi', *shochet*, clerk and doorkeeper), and the levy of new taxes. No distinction was made between the religious and the secular life of the congregation: the Select Committee determined applications for Free Membership, allocated seats in the synagogue, distributed poor relief (acting in rotation as relieving officers), supervised the honorary and salaried officials, arbitrated in disputes, investigated complaints, and organised the religious routine of the synagogue, including the timing and form of services, the distribution of honours, and the administration of *Shechita*, without reference to the minister or the *shochet*, who were expected to do as they were told, to be strict in their observance, and punctual in the fulfilment of their duties. In dealing with such matters as alterations in the ritual, the examination of *shochetim*, or the licensing of marriages, the Select Committee dealt directly with the Chief Rabbi in London.

There was nothing exceptional about an exclusive oligarchy in the England of the 1820s, when the whole political system was based upon privilege and patronage. It was not until 'Jewish Emancipation' emerged as a live political issue in the early 1830s, after the English franchise had itself been widened and the Catholics emancipated, that the political structure of the congregation came to be regarded by some of its members as bad publicity for the Jewish cause. Until that time, the concentration of synagogal power in the hands of the few served useful purposes, since it was to some extent true that only an anglicised élite knew where the best interests of the community lay.

3 The two communities, 1826–34

There were, in effect, two communities in Manchester during the later 1820s and early 1830s, the one increasingly anxious to live down the reputation of the other. On one side, there was a settled community of shopkeepers, overseas merchants, share brokers, and professional men, anglicised in speech and custom, comfortably off (or reasonably so), generous to local causes, the providers of essential goods and services to the middle classes; on the other, a flotsam of pedlars and petty criminals, some the unsuccessful residuum of eighteenth-century Jewry, others pauper immigrants of the post-war years, illiterate in English, incoherent in speech, uncouth in appearance, often associated with the criminal underworld, most frequently as the receivers of stolen jewellery and plate. The fact that Manchester's settled community was itself shaped out of the itinerant population of an earlier age if anything served to emphasise the social divide. The further the early members moved from their itinerant origins, the more they were plagued by the memory of them.[1] To many, it seemed that they had purchased acceptance by a success upon which the reputation of the community now depended; evidence of Jews in crime, or in occupations such as hawking and slop selling, which were no longer economically viable or socially reputable, seemed to endanger the communal image, and, with it, the prestige of its resident members. The hawker and the petty criminal occupied within the Jewish milieu a role similar to that of the 'rootless' poor, the subversive radicals and the riotous Irish in the wider society, but added to the fear of their internal corrosive effect was the belief, however inaccurate, that any signs of social degeneration, any association of the community with low standards of public morality would be followed, almost inevitably, by a fresh outburst of anti-Jewish feeling. Jewry as a whole, it was feared, would be implicated in the crime of social disruption: only the paternal guidance of experienced leaders, drawn exclusively from the most anglicised group, could maintain the community's new standards and status, and the security which these appeared to ensure.

I

Although Jewish fears were exaggerated, there were, in fact, constant reminders that prejudice lay just below the surface, even of enlightened middle-
class society. The *Guardian*, for all its general tolerance, was given to occasional
relish over anti-Semitic titbits such as the apprehension of a Jewish pedlar in
Barnsley, in October 1829, in the act of stealing a ham.[2] Reports of crimes involving Jews never failed to include the racial ascription: it was 'a jew pedlar'
who in February 1831 obtained a pair of gold ear-rings by false pretences,[3]
'an Israelite named Reiss' who, in 1829, defrauded a Manchester lodging-house
keeper of £3.[4] When 'a very respectable Manchester gentleman' came before
the local magistrate for stealing a seal from a Jewish pedlar in a pub in Rochdale 'as a lark', the *Guardian* respected the anonymity of the thief and the court
let him off with a caution.[5] The speech of the Jewish hawker lent itself to ridicule. Isaac Jacob, a pickpocket arrested in Hanover Street for stealing a watch,
is reported to have told the police, 'Me hungry belly; no moneysh; so me
took tic-tac.'[6] When Isaac Cohen, who in February 1831 induced a 'simple
girl' to trade her gold ear-rings for 3s each and two pairs in brass, was ordered
by the magistrate to return the money, he replied that he had only 1s 6d, but,
when threatened with committal, he is reported to have 'exclaimed, "Shtop a
beet!" ' and to have drawn from his watch fob the remaining eighteen pence.[7]
Another report of court proceedings (in December 1827) told how a Jewish
housewife (Mrs Jacob Casper) saw a loiterer near her husband's shop and
judged from his looks, correctly, as it turned out, 'dat he vanted to shteal'.[8]

   Stowellite oratory and the local conservative press provided evidence of
more explicit anti-Jewish feeling. In its earliest editorial on Jewish emancipation, on 22 May 1830, the *Manchester Courier* applauded the defeat of Grant's
Bill and rejected without reservation the idea of Jews administering the laws of
a Christian country. The Jews, it was true, were 'less dangerous' than the
Catholics who had become eligible for entry to the House of Commons in the
previous year, but parliament deserved some praise for not compounding its
earlier 'error'. In a leader of the same date, *Wheeler's Manchester Chronicle* conceded that 'much may be said on both sides' but emphasised its serious objections to emancipation. In particular, Wheeler argued, the Jews 'kept up the
form of a distinct *nation* . . . scarcely recognising, except as a matter of compulsion', the authority of a Christian government. 'Under these circumstances
it is impossible to expect the full allegiance of a Jew.' A letter to the *Chronicle*
a week later pressed the attack. Jews were in no way committed to the welfare
of the nation in which they resided. They were also economically 'unproduc-

tive'. They would 'not affect to emulate those who invent or those who execute' but simply waited for goods to come on to the market: 'then they buy and sell, and truck and barter, and pocket the difference in cash'.

There is also a good deal of circumstantial evidence to suggest that, however the readers of the middle-class press felt, ancient prejudice was still more deeply ingrained in the working-class consciousness. The Christian followers of Johanna Southcote, who believed in the unlikely emergence of a New Jerusalem in Ashton-under-Lyne, and whose sectarian faith compelled them to wear beards, complained (in 1827) that they were frequently mistaken for Jews, and subjected, for that reason, 'to all sorts of insulting and opprobrious epithets'.[9] In April 1828 a drunken woman burst into the shops of Ansell Spier and Samuel Isaac (both furriers) in the Old Town, and, calling each a 'Jew-looking thief, and some other such names, swore by Moses and the Prophets that she would carve his bacon with a razor'.[10] If the community overreacted to these and other suggestions of malice, it was because they were regarded as the tip of an anti-Semitic iceberg upon which the communal ship might well founder without the aid of respectable middle-class pilots.

The communal leaders were also sensitive to the frequent and well-reported examples of itinerant criminality, the more notorious because Jewish expertise was concentrated in particular areas of illegality, chiefly receiving and false pretences, which lent themselves to caricature. The Jewish pedlar, with his portable stock, easy mobility, and numerous commercial outlets, was well placed to serve as a receiver. The goods he obtained could be concealed without difficulty in his hawker's box, taken to a convenient centre (particularly Birmingham) for melting down, or absorbed into his pedlar's tray like the goods found on Joseph Masper, an Italian Jewish pedlar, arrested in a house in Tib Street in July 1829, with the proceeds of a robbery in Ducie Place—'tortoiseshell combs, coral necklaces, silver thimbles, pencil cases, tooth picks, pen knives, and razors'.[11] Receiving involved a web of intrigue only rarely visible to the naked eye of the press. 'The Jew' Abraham Samuels, a London hawker, arrived in Manchester by coach on 19 November 1826—in 'a plaid cloak . . . and a hawker's box under his arm'—and took lodgings in the Sawyer's Arms in the Old Town, informing a waiter that he had come to town to purchase stock. Next day at the White Lion in Spear Street, he met by appointment a gang of three men who wished to dispose of the proceeds of a robbery committed in Appleby in Westmorland. A price was agreed, and a day later the goods were carried from the thieves' hideout in a basket on the head of a servant girl (paid 10s for her trouble) to a hut on Kersal Moor where Samuels with his hawker's box waited with £45. In spite of six character witnesses (five of them Jewish), Samuels was sentenced at Salford Sessions in January

1827 to fourteen years' transportation—'the utmost . . . allowed by the law'.[12] When Aaron Gainsborg and Abraham Jacob were caught in June 1831 trying to pawn a silver butter-boat stolen from the bar of the Palace Inn, they were found to have pawned stolen plate to the value of £60 for £11 17s 6d; amongst the goods found in their possession were pieces of silver from the churchwarden's staves of St Stephen's Church in Salford, the incumbency of Hugh Stowell.[13] In September 1831, Moses Benjamin of Birmingham was on trial in Manchester for receiving plate stolen from houses in Ardwick Green and Chorlton Row and sent to him by post in exchange for cash.[14]

Jews involved more directly in theft in and around Manchester included Joseph Jacobs, a 'well-known thief', who served three months on the treadmill during 1826,[15] Edward Samuels of Hamburg who stole an umbrella from the Portico Library in November 1831,[16] and the diminutive thirteen-year-old Joseph Mayer, sentenced a month later to a whipping and three months' imprisonment (one in solitary confinement) for services to a gang of thieves, for whom he squeezed through the grid-holes of shops.[17] In September 1834, Raphael and Bernard Magnus, pill-box manufacturers and purchasers of old clothes, who had already travelled by gig from Frying Pan Alley in London to Exeter, Bristol, Bath, Hull and Liverpool, were in court in Manchester for the theft of silver plate from the Crown and Shuttle in Miller Street.[18]

Common theft was less prevalent than confidence trickery in its various forms. In December 1829 three Jews—John Jacobs, Moses Jacobs and John Ramus—posed as French traders when they attempted (in bad French and worse Spanish) to obtain £7 10s from a druggist in Pendleton on the (false) security of 18 lb of opium and some Cashmere shawls, said to be part of a cargo of silks, leghorns, tobacco, cigars and drugs lying under excise on board the flat *Louisa* in Old Quay Docks. The druggist followed the three men for long enough to hear one of them say, in English, 'what a pity it was that they had not been able to do the doctor'. In court, Moses Jacobs claimed that at no time in his life had he dealt in anything but quills and pens, Ramus complained only of the aspersions cast by the prosecution on his Spanish, and all three were sentenced to a month on the treadmill as vagrants.[19] In May 1830 Samuel Isaacs was a victim of the new and zealous Manchester Guardian Society for the Protection of Traders (against 'swindlers and sharpers') which, for a subscription of 7s a year, alerted its members to possible cases of fraud; on the initiative of the Society, Isaacs was prosecuted successfully for obtaining thread from local manufacturers under false names and with forged bills while lodging in the house of a hairdresser in Bridge Street.[20] Although, as in Isaacs' case, most swindlers were non-residents, the most notorious case involved Sergei Tournoff, a resident in Manchester since the early 1820s, a Free Member since 1825, and son-in-

law of Sarah Levy, the keeper of the restaurant and lodging-house in Deansgate at which Alexander Jacob had been fêted in 1828. In partnership with a recent German immigrant, Charles Rosenberg, Tournoff obtained substantial
goods on credit on the basis of a non-existent account in the Manchester and
Liverpool District Bank. The main offence was against a Birmingham hardware dealer, who was fraudulently dispossessed of copper kettles, frying pans,
candlesticks, bellows, carbines, pistols and swords (said to be for an overseas
order) to the value of £1,500, but a more prominent local victim was Mark
Philips (of the cotton firm J. & N. Philips), a leading merchant and manufacturer, an outstanding protagonist of middle-class enlightenment, and a favourite to serve as one of the two Members of Parliament acquired by Manchester
under the Reform Act of 1832. On receiving dyed goods at Philips' warehouse
(in 1832), Tournoff is reported to have said, 'This is bad cotton, what a difference there is in it, but all Manchester people are cheats.'[21] The impact of the
scandal was the greater because at the time the people of Manchester were already suffering from the combined effects of cholera and industrial depression.

   In many ways, the episode seemed to confirm the worst fears of communal
leaders, since it brought into sharp relief the contrast between the most disreputable elements of Jewry and the most respected segments of Manchester society, and cast Jews in the role of the enemies of legitimate commerce, and all
this at a time of severe social stress. For his part in the affair Tournoff was deprived of all his privileges in the synagogue, and 'ceased to be a Free
Member',[22] and his example seemed to emphasise the need for extreme care
in the election of future members. Viewed against the total background of
crime in Manchester, Jewish illegality was relatively insignificant, most Jewish lawbreakers were petty in their misdemeanours, and few were members
of the resident community, but in each instance, however insignificant, the criminal was publicly linked with the religious group to which he belonged, and
those who represented the group in Manchester felt the need to defend themselves, however cautiously. In a much less cautious and sophisticated way, the
itinerant community watched over its own. When George Simon, a licensed
hawker of jewellery, was before the magistrates for receiving, in July 1829,

The court was excessively crowded with Simon's friends, and immediately on the ver-
dict [an acquittal] being announced, several persons clapped their hands, but were
immediately silenced by the chairman ordering that any who were found clapping
their hands, be taken into custody.[23]

However great the fear, Jewry was in fact as well protected by the law as by
dominant middle-class opinion. Before his trial, Simon, who spoke English
very badly, read a paper to the court

to the effect, that he was a foreigner, and understood, by the laws of England, he was entitled to be tried by a jury composed of half foreigners; but he had not availed himself of that privilege, confident that he should meet with as much, perhaps more, justice from a jury composed entirely of Englishmen.[24]

But the brighter facts of the immediate situation tended to be overshadowed by the remnants of political discrimination, the novelty (and apparent uncertainty) of social acceptance, and an underlying sensitivity to the pinpricks of petty prejudice derived from centuries of persecution. In this distorted context, the receiver of goods stolen from Chorlton Row offset the reputation of Jews who lived there; the Jewish snatch-thief of an umbrella from the Portico Library loomed larger than its Jewish subscribers; Sergei Tournoff seemed more likely to influence public opinion than S. L. Behrens.

II

The contrasts within Jewish society were sharpened by the declining economic importance of hawking and the increasing part played by retailers in meeting the needs of the town's population. Statistical evidence of trading from fixed shops in Manchester suggests a very rapid expansion (probably the most rapid in the first half of the century) in the period 1822–34;[25] the number of boot and shoe makers, for example, increased from forty-one to 226, of tailors and drapers from thirty-nine to 208, of pawnbrokers from sixty-two to 146; and, although expansion was rather less spectacular in other lines, the overall picture is one of retail trading establishing a strong hold on the urban market, almost certainly at the expense of the pedlar. Other evidence suggests that shopkeepers were aware of the ground they were gaining, and were anxious to consolidate it, by improving streets in the town centre, for example, by easing communications within the town (particularly between the centre and the suburbs), and by attempting to limit the 'undue competition of hawkers and pedlars with tradesmen liable to heavy national and local rates'.[26] Little could be done to 'suppress' properly licensed itinerant traders, except by applying pressure on the government to restrict their activities, but the unlicensed hawker was vulnerable to attack since he added a breach of the law to his low overheads and freedom from taxes and rates. Early in 1823 the retailers of Manchester formed a Trade Society to initiate prosecutions against those found (by its paid informers) to be hawking without a licence or engaging in 'mock auctions'.[27] The society's activities were marked, particularly in its early stages, by a notorious excess of zeal: a Manchester tea retailer, arrested with part of his stock, sued for false arrest;[28] two informers who demanded bribes from an unlicensed hawker were themselves taken to court and told by the magistrate that their evidence was no longer admissible;[29] two others were ordered to pay the court's expenses and the cost of a warrant after the trial of a supposed unlicensed hawker of clay pipes who turned out to be the apprentice of a pipe maker.[30] Magistrates were often sympathetic to unlicensed hawkers, particularly to immigrants ignorant of the law; in passing sentence on, a Jewish hawker (in 1823) the magistrate commented, 'Others have brought [the case] here; and if it is pressed, I must convict';[31] in at least one other case involving Jews, the society was persuaded by the court to drop its charges.[32]

However benevolent the law, the prosecution of hawkers was symptomatic of economic changes over which it had no control: itinerant country traders were losing their economic value, many (perhaps for that reason) were drifting into crime, and few remained high in public esteem. Legitimate country hawking flourished in the period 1790–1830, when the growth of large towns opened new markets not yet adequately supplied by the retail trade. During the 1820s, as shopkeeping developed within the new industrial centres, the hawker's market contracted, and he found himself under attack from retailers anxious to remove the remaining annoyance of itinerant competition. The Trade Society's net caught not only Jews, but Italian hawkers of pictures, looking-glasses, barometers, and plaster figures, some at least the agents of Manchester-Italian shopkeepers like Vincent Zanetti and Antonio Peduzzi,[33] Irish women hawking linen in the expanding suburbs, and English pedlars of Staffordshire china, Birmingham hardware and libellous pamphlets. A whole network of itinerant trade was on the brink of collapse, and those who remained within it (according to the Trade Society) were as often as not involved in theft, shoplifting, and (most often) in the distribution of stolen goods or of articles manufactured for the purpose of fraud, particularly brass trinkets offered as gold. Again, Jewish 'duffers' figured amongst the itinerant criminals of the mid-1830s. In December 1835 a young German-Jewish pedlar 'calling himself Julius Rosenheim' was before the New Bailey charged with obtaining money 'by the very common trick of selling as gold ear rings and other trinkets made of common yellow metal'. In court, Rosenheim

protested that it was all a mistake to suppose that he could offer gold ear rings at such a price [3s to 5s]—a thief might sell them for that price, but no honest man could. One of the women . . . had only paid him a shilling and he had worn out a shilling's worth of shoes in looking after the rest of the money, but she always deceives him.[34]

In November 1836 Charles Hart of London, an unlicensed hawker, was found in Manchester

haranging a large multitude of people, flourishing in his hand a number of cards containing brass rings, which he was representing as gold, at the same time saying that he had made a bet with a gentlemen, who had dared him to sell gold rings for a penny each, and he was not going to lose his wager, which was a large one.[35]

Rosenheim (who pleaded innocence) received one month's hard labour; Hart (who offered no defence) was treated more sympathetically:

The Magistrate: Prisoner, if you are forgiven, will you promise to leave town?
Prisoner: I'll not only promise, but I will leave it.

Within the Jewish milieu, the moral as well as the economic basis of itinerant life was giving way. Although a Jewish hawker still knew his fellow travellers well enough to provide trustworthy evidence of their whereabouts, the coherent brotherhoods of the late eighteenth century based on kosher lodging houses and temporary *minyanim*, and often protected by settled shopkeepers who supplied stock on credit, had all but disappeared by 1830. Moses Davies, an itinerant dependant of the Manchester quill dresser, Samuel Isaacs of Withy Grove, by 1832 could no longer afford the down payment required for a licence and stock on credit, and, like many others, fell back on the charity of the synagogue.[36] Michael Hyman, and his younger brother, Joseph, pedlars of jewellery in North Wales in the 1820s, were receiving hand-outs from the Liverpool congregation in the following decade.[37] Michael's son, Louis, began hawking at the age of ten (in 1833) to keep the family above subsistence level;[38] in 1836, Joseph sought help to put him 'in some small way of Business in Liverpool'.[39] Another Liverpool hawker, having pawned all his stock, asked for a congregational subsidy towards making a fresh start in America.[40] As the capital outlay required for viable trade increased beyond his reach, the hawker was replaced by the 'traveller', paid on a wage or commission basis, and by the shopkeeper who occasionally offered part of his stock for sale in a town other than his own. When a Liverpool Jewish hawker had his box stolen from a bar in Oldham in November 1834, he claimed that it contained gold to the value of £75, and gold and silver watches, rings and other trinkets worth over £100, stock which perhaps represented the minimum amount required for profitable itinerant trade on an independent basis.[41] By way of contrast, John Joel Cohen, with a permanent jeweller's shop in Young Street, Manchester, made periodic visits to the smaller towns of the textile belt, carrying 'gold and silver watches, diamond brooches, rings and pins, gold and silver pencil cases, pearl ornaments, silver snuff boxes, silver spoons' and other miscellaneous items of jewellery and plate in two carpet bags packed with cotton; a bag stolen from his gig outside an inn at Haslingden in January 1833 contained stock valued at over £1,000.[42] The old-time country hawker, operating independently or on a credit basis, became a traveller or a shopkeeper, entered crime, became an urban pedlar (extending the facilities of central shops to the growing outer suburbs), or, like the Hyman brothers, fell upon hard times.

III

The lowly position of the Jewish hawker was emphasised by the continued expansion and increasing prosperity of a middle stratum of Jewish shopkeepers, for whom the prototype was Abraham Franklin. Franklin's eldest son, Jacob, was an outstanding student at the Mechanics' Institute. At the prize-giving ceremony of January 1829, the teacher of mathematics paid tribute to two members of his class 'John Stansfield and Jacob Abraham Franklin . . . without whose assistance he could not carry on the business of his class'; the two men had declined to compete for prizes 'in consequence of the students objecting to being competitors, as they expressed it, with their teachers', but were presented with special awards for outstanding merit.[43] In September 1830 Jacob Franklin entered business on his own account in a shop next door to his father's in St Ann's Place as an 'optician and manufacturer of philosophical and mathematical instruments'. He advertised in the *Guardian* at frequent intervals, usually to publicise one of his own novelties—'Eye Preservers' which 'deprive artificial light of its mischievous glare, and at the same time render minute objects more distinctly visible'[44]—'a Portable Hot Air Bath', 'a desirable little apparatus for the general purposes of a family', simple in design, cheap in price.[45] He also supplied apparatus for industrial chemists, engineers, architects, and surveyors, and between times he wrote (but did not publish) a short treatise on the human eye.[46] Jacob Franks, the optician, took into partnership his eldest son, Abraham, who acquired some local repute as a public lecturer on 'the anatomy of the human eye' and the author of a tract on the 'Anatomical Delineations of the Eye-ball'. The fortunes of other jewellers, opticians and dealers in miscellaneous 'fancy goods' were founded upon a growing middle-class market for domestic luxuries and (to a lesser extent) on a steady rise in the real income of artisans, for whom the old aristocratic bias of trade, 'disdaining to display its wares', was quite inappropriate. At 77 King Street Henry Mendleson announced a typical 'depot' for

English and foreign jewellery and Bijouterie, fancy toys, Beads, Berlin and Dresden China, Chimney Ornaments, Musical, Work and Snuff Boxes, Musical Clocks and Watches . . . Satin and Morocco Shoes and slippers with and without fur, Eau de Cologne, playing cards, games, and puzzles in great variety.[47]

In March 1832 Isaac Simmons (son of the itinerant chiropodist) took over a shop in St Ann's Square (see Figure 4), where he offered jewellery, watches, curiosities, and Tunbridge ware at 'unprecedentally [sic] low prices'.[48] Soon after Aaron Jacob's death, in January 1832, his eldest son Alexander (founder of the Philanthropic Society) left the cotton trade and opened a shop at 58 King Street for the sale of foreign shawls, merinos, cigars, snuff, toys, clocks

I. SIMMONS,

SILVERSMITH, JEWELLER, WATCH MAKER,

ELECTRO-PLATE MANUFACTURER,

AND

AGENT FOR BRAHAM'S PATENT PANTOSCOPIC SPECTACLES,

WHICH ARE ADAPTED TO ALL DEFECTS OF SIGHT,

7, ST. ANN'S SQUARE, MANCHESTER.

FIGURE 4   Isaac Simmons' shop in St Ann's Square.

and fancy goods, of which his brothers, Morris and Henry, were the importers. Jacob Nathan's younger son, Elias, set up shop as a jeweller, watchmaker and optician in Chapel Street, Salford—the first Jewish tradesman to explore this busy centre—in 1829.

Under the stimulus of similar economic opportunities, tailoring underwent a major revolution which passed through its most crucial stages between 1829 and 1834. Before the 1820s the clothing trade in Manchester had little to offer the public between the expensive bespoke work of independent master-craftsmen and their apprentices, and the rough-and-ready slop of down-town retailers. Jews were involved exclusively in the lower and more precarious sector of the trade: they stood outside their slop shops soliciting custom, most of it working-class; hovered between clothes dealing and pawnbroking; exchanged waistcoats for watches; occasionally bought and sold fents; dealt roughly with awkward clients (once to the point of manslaughter);[49] sometimes handled stolen goods, often innocently; and felt the full brunt of every spell of industrial unemployment. In 1827 Abraham Hart, a slop seller of Shudehill, applied for the benefit of the Act for the Relief of Insolvent Debtors.[50] Shortly before 1830 there were some indications that the clothing trade as a whole was beginning to respond to the growth of a large lower-middle-class market, for which slop was too disreputable and clothing made by craftsmen too expensive.[51] The move was not so much towards ready-made wear, although some items of ready-made clothing were on sale in Manchester by May 1830, as towards cheapening and accelerating the manufacture of clothing to order, and improving the techniques of advertisement and distribution. The general move was in the direction of mass sales at a low profit margin based upon a sub-structure of domestic out-work and 'sweat shops'. Apart from the initial cutting, which remained the province of the skilled craftsman, the tasks involved in tailoring were therefore separated, simplified, and given out to unskilled labourers, women as well as men, working either at home, or in cramped workshops at low, piece-work rates, for retailers who were not necessarily craftsmen themselves. The old craft basis of the trade, with masters and apprentices working together on a similar range of tasks, and selling finished products direct to the customer, began to give way to a structure of retail middle-men whose main roles (whatever their experience as tailors) were to provide capital and accommodation, to order cloth, to organise unskilled labour and to distribute the completed garments. Although the absence of tailors' records makes it difficult to locate the precise stages of transition, or to identify their prime movers, the change would seem to be associated not so much with local initiative as with the arrival of tailors from the south of England: Francis Grace (from London to King Street in 1829), John Armstrong (from Taunton to Market Street in 1829), Benjamin Hyam (from Ipswich to 22 St Mary's Gate, in August 1832), and, no doubt, others. In each case an immigrant entrepreneur appears either to be applying in Manchester methods which he had evolved elsewhere or to be arriving with a clear understanding that a mass urban market required a radical adaptation of manufacturing and business techniques. Although Hyam was the only Jew amongst them, he was the most significant both in the scale of his enterprise and in the extent of his influence outside as well as inside the community.

Although little is known of his early life, Hyam's family was of pedlar origin and had been established in the retail trade in Ipswich since the end of the eighteenth century, when Simon Hyam (of Hamburg) and his son Hyam Hyam (Benjamin's father) played an important role in laying the basis of communal life.[52] His movement to Manchester at the age of twenty-two was almost certainly an early part of that drift towards the economic opportunities of the growing industrial towns which was finally to eliminate some of the older market-town communities, including Ipswich. His background, however, in common with that of many other British-born Jews of his generation, gave him a close insight into the popular market and helped him both to follow the vagaries of public taste and to meet (and create) demand. Out of this family expertise, considerable energy and organisational skill, a flare for invention and advertisement, and a modicum of capital, Hyam created modern mass-tailoring in Manchester. He relied not upon high prices for each article sold but upon bulk sales at a low margin of profit, fixed but competitive prices, cash on delivery, economy in manufacture, and speed in production, probably in workshops attached to his retail premises. His first advertisements offered to make a complete suit at six hours' notice.[53] For cash payments in advance, clients could contract for two or three suits a year, each to be returned on the arrival of its successor. His advertising, chiefly on the front page of the *Guardian*, was extensive, flamboyant, full of practical detail, frequently accompanied by doggerel verse which occasionally occupied a full column of newsprint, topical in its allusions, and carefully designed to appeal to the social aspirations (and the pocket) of the petite bourgeoisie. His elegant suits, so he had the public believe, were a necessary part of the struggle for social survival; they were cut 'in a first rate London style', but offered at prices which represented a saving of 30–40 per cent on those of his traditional rivals; they were made by 'only first-rate cutters . . . under the superintendance of a cutter of the first eminence, from one of the most fashionable houses in the West of England'. To overcome the 'prejudice' (as he put it) of those who feared that low prices meant poor quality, he offered to refund the cost of any suit 'not fully approved of'. The size of his work-force is not known. John Stubbs, with a rather smaller rival establishment in St Ann's Square, employed seventy to one hundred people (depending on the season) in his workshop in Back Square.[54] His cloth he bought in bulk direct from the manufacturers in the west of England, while most of his competitors were compelled by the smaller scale of their operations to buy at higher prices from local drapers. Hyam's stature may perhaps be judged from a Poor Law circular issued in 1836 which sought to persuade labourers from the south of England to move to Manchester by quoting (amongst other statistics) his low prices for 'wearing apparel'.[55]

Hyam's influence within the Jewish milieu was increased by the degree of his orthodoxy and the strictness of his observance; his advertisements emphasised (to the point of provoking anti-Semitic retorts)[56] the closure of his shop at sunset on Fridays; he was admitted to Free Membership without waiting the statutory five years and was soon paying heavily for the non-acceptance of honorary office. With Franklin and Behrens he formed a kind of communal triumvirate which represented also the three major directions of Jewish enterprise: clothing, jewellery and cotton. Within four years of his arrival, a number of his co-religionists, all former slop sellers, had followed him into tailoring—Marcus Rosenthal, Joseph Levy (also a pawnbroker), Joseph Marks and Jacob Casper, all of Shudehill; Marcus Abraham of Hanging Ditch; Joseph Braham and his son, Isaac, at Hyde's Cross; Abraham Lipman in Deansgate; and, beyond Manchester, Joseph Slazenger Moss in Warrington, Mark Jacobs in Stockport, and Isaac Joel in Preston. The 1832 Trade Directory lists no Jews amongst the 124 Manchester and Salford tailors and drapers, and fifteen amongst thirty-seven clothes dealers (that is, slop sellers); by 1836 seven of the clothes dealers had become tailors. All operated on a very much smaller scale than Hyam, some with only a handful of assistants, Rosenthal with fourteen,[57] almost certainly non-Jewish.

The internal effects of these new methods upon the traditional structure of tailoring began to make themselves felt throughout the industry during 1833–34. In particular, journeymen tailors in traditional workshops began to face the competition of 'women and other inferior outdoor workers', and of unskilled labourers prepared to accept a lowering of wages and a deterioration of workshop conditions. An early indication of mounting anger was an assault upon Abraham Lipman by two journeymen, John and Michael Smith, in March 1833;[58] a three-gill bottle of vitriol they hurled through a shop-window was intended for Lipman, but broke on a cross-board and destroyed or damaged clothes to a value of £40. Early in June, one hundred tailors came out on a strike which was apparently provoked by the conditions of work imposed by 'six Jews and six Gentile masters';[59] the demands included a limitation of the number of 'apprentices' (presumably being used as a euphemism for cheap labour), a reduction of the working day from twelve to eleven hours, and the total elimination of out-work. Jewish masters under attack included Jacob Casper and Marcus Rosenthal, at whose shop on Shudehill crowds of 'turnouts' gathered daily, and behaved in so disorderly a manner that on several occasions he had been obliged to shut up his shop and send for Booth of the Shudehill lock-ups;

Rosenthal was abused and threatened by the leaders of the men as he stood at the roadside 'inviting customers into his shop', and his work-force was cut from fourteen to three.[60] Discontent was tinged with anti-Semitism: crowds of journeymen who went to see *The Tailor*, a burlesque tragi-comedy, at the Queens Theatre, 'hissed, hooted and howled' whenever the hero, Abrahamides, appeared, and showered the theatre manager with apples, pears, eggs, potatoes, turnips and stones.[61] Unable to form a united front, the masters gave way to the demands of their men, who went on to form a local union, probably at the beginning of 1834. Not, however, as a radical gesture: far from seeking reform, they were attempting to bolster up an economic structure upon which they believed their livelihood to depend; their union was a purely local body and existed chiefly (according to its leaders) 'for the regulation of our labour, the diffusion of sound morals and industrious habits, the Support of our Sick, the Burial of our Dead'.[62]

The first strike proved inconclusive. The failure of the masters to implement the terms of their agreement led the unions to make fresh demands, 'some of which', according to the *Guardian*, 'were in the highest degree unreasonable and tyrannical',[63] and which included a closed shop, a ban on women workers and out-work, and the provision by masters of 'good lights and wholesome workshops'.[64] This time, however, the masters were prepared: a meeting of sixty-two of them convened by John Stubbs in June 1834, announced its refusal of the men's demands, decided against the employment of union members, and called on 'friends and customers' of the trade to withhold their orders until the union had been broken up.[65] A bitter twenty-three-week strike began in June. Picketing was often tough and sometimes violent; backed by the *Chronicle* and the *Guardian*, which described the union as the 'bane of the working-classes', the masters imported blacklegs from Liverpool; the union set up a co-operative in Nicholas Croft, offering clothes at prices lower even than Hyam's, or the services of its members in private houses at 4s 6d a day; the masters sent orders to be made up in Knutsford, Stockport (where they were refused), Liverpool, and even London, where Stubbs' son spent several weeks supervising their completion. Finally, in November, shortage of funds and loss of members (two hundred of whom returned to work, while others left town) caused the union to capitulate. Complaining bitterly, and with some cause, at 'the malignant conduct of the master tailors, and the press they employ to gain their avaricious and demoralising ends', the leaders gave way on all counts. The journeymen tailors did not strike again until 1845, and with no greater success; a new order of mass tailoring was gradually consolidated; ready-made clothing, an almost inevitable refinement of the new system, was being sold by Hyam in 1836 and had become common by the end of the decade, ten years before the invention of the lock-stitch sewing machine. Although not named in the second strike, and not amongst the sixty-two masters mobilised by Stubbs, Jewish tailors were deeply implicated in its effects: the outcome of the crisis furthered the movement from slop selling to tailoring which gradually left the old clothes trade of Manchester to the immigrant Irish.[66] The effect of the economic tran-sition of which the strike was a symptom was, in this way, to move a whole category of retailers from a barely reputable fringe occupation to the centre of respectable (and profitable) trade, and so, once again, to reinforce the new Jewish bourgeoisie, and to emphasise its separation from an older Jewish econ-omy rooted in the eighteenth century. Although the activities of Jewish tailors may have kindled some latent popular anti-Semitism, middle-class opinion was on their side: the *Guardian*, in particular, kept up a one-sided running com-mentary upon the alleged brutality of the union's methods.

IV

The Jewish middle class was again reinforced by the nature of the immigration which increased the size of the community from 250–300 in 1825 to around 350–400 in 1834. If an expansion of pauper immigration from Central and East-ern Europe is suggested by an increase in the total congregational payments to the casual poor from about £15 in 1827–28 to nearly £29 in 1833–34, it was probably the case that most recipients of relief were moved on before they be-came a permanent burden on congregational funds or a threat to the commun-al reputation; one evocative entry (in 1834) reads: 'Given him the Polack for leaving Town 8/6.'[67] At all events, it seems probable that most of those who found their way to Manchester were on their way to the Unites States, and re-quired little from the local community but the price of a bed and a meal. The annual number of destitute arrivals was relatively small (between one hundred and fifty and two hundred), and, of these, very few remained. The new resi-dents of the period 1825–34 were on the whole those who had set their sights on Manchester as a place where they might invest a little capital and obtain a good return for their enterprise, either in middle-class retailing, in the profes-sions, or in the manufacture and export of textiles. They included the furriers, Simon Joseph, who was born in Manchester in 1806 (probably the son of an itinerant umbrella maker) and who in 1827 returned from London to establish a branch of 'Reuben Joseph & Son', hat manufacturers and hatters' furriers of Houndsditch, and the brothers Lewis and Samuel Isaac, probably from Liverpool, whose New Fur Establishment in Old Millgate opened in October 1827, with

a perfectly new, elegant, extensive, and fashionable assortment of FURS, consisting of Chinchilla, Russia Fitch, Ermine, Lynx, Minx, Squirrel, and Sable, which they have manufactured into Muffs, Tippets, Mantillas, Pelerences, Cloak linings, Flouncings, Collars, Cuffs, and every other article used in Fur . . . [and] an extensive assortment of fur, cloth and leather caps.[68]

Henry Leveaux, a resident of Preston until 1834, and a former member of the Liverpool synagogue, arrived in Manchester soon afterwards and set up a 'French Bazaar and Temple of Fancy' in the Town Hall Buildings at the corner of Cross Street and King Street in the city centre; 'this Elegant Lounge' (as Leveaux called it in his advertisement) sold a wide range of imported fancy goods from clocks and watches to perfumery and glassware.[69] In the late 1820s Lewis Lyon (of London) established a quill warehouse in Withy Grove; soon afterwards he became a Special Constable of the town, in which capacity, in January 1833, he arrested the receiver of one thousand stolen quills.[70] Other settlers were Philip Solomon and Israel Jacobs (1828), partners in a slop shop on Shudehill, and John Michael Isaac, member of a long-established Liverpool family, who settled in Chapel Street, Salford, in 1834, as a pawnbroker. Joel Benjamin, of Schneidemuhl in Prussia, settled in Bolton, as a rag dealer, in 1830.[71] This was not a period of rapid immigration, the number of seat-holders rising only from fifty-two in 1825 to sixty in 1833 (an increase which included children coming of age); what made it significant for the community was the consolidation of the Jewish middle class.

Social division within the community was increased by the departure of some of its more affluent members to the northern and southern suburbs. The 'smoke and exhalations of a large manufacturing city',[72] the increasing influx of 'barbarous' Irish labourers, 'debased alike by ignorance and pauperism',[73] the outbreak of cholera, and the threat of political disorder all served to persuade anyone in Manchester who could afford it to abandon the centre of the town to shops, warehouses, factories, and 'the narrow, unpaved and almost pestilential streets' of working-class cottages and cellar-dwellings,[74] and to move out into the surrounding countryside. The conversion of the townships of Ardwick, Chorlton Row, Broughton and Cheetham Hill into middle-class suburbs, a process of which Aston had observed the small beginnings in 1815, gathered pace after 1825, and by 1832 Mosley Street had become one of the few streets near the town centre still occupied 'by the dwellings of some of the more wealthy inhabitants'.[75] By that time, the richest of Manchester's citizens

chiefly reside in the countryside, and even the superior servants of their establishments inhabit the suburban townships.[76]

Merchants with business which occasionally kept them in town overnight used the 'elegantly furnished' apartments of the Union Club in Mosley Street, which offered all the 'comforts of an establishment in town' for an entrance fee of forty guineas and an annual subscription of five.[77]

The building of new trunk roads both followed and facilitated the movement into the suburbs. In 1816 work began on a new bridge across the Irk to connect

a line of road from the foot of Millers' Lane . . . into what was formerly Strangeways Park; by which the dangerous turn of the old road over Scotland Bridge and the sharp ascent of Red Bank are avoided,[78]

and which made possible the opening of a new road—York Street (or Cheetham Hill Road)—running out towards Cheetwood Village, Cheetham Cottage Town, and Smedley Lane. In 1830 *Wheeler's Manchester Chronicle* forecast that with the completion of 'a good avenue' from the centre of the town to Miller Street

Cheetham Hill would become a favourite one for gentlemen's residences. It has always been considered the most healthy of all the environs of Manchester.[79]

On the west side of Strangeways Park, the building of Bury New Road, striking out across Stoney Knolls into Higher Broughton, between 1826 and 1830, improved access to the growing suburbs in Strangeways, Mount Pleasant and Broughton; the population of the chapelry of Cheetham increased from 2,027 in 1821 to 4,025 in 1831, of Broughton from 900 to 1,589. On the south side of the town, where in Grosvenor Square there was only one mansion fit for gentlemen in 1816,[80] the rich pushed southwards along the line of Oxford Road and Upper Brook Street into Chorlton-on-Medlock (once Chorlton Row), Ardwick, Rusholme and Greenheys: new 'groves' of villas radiating from Upper Brook Street by 1830 were believed to bear 'a strong resemblance to the neighbourhood of London, on the Surrey Road'.[81] The pretentiousness of these 'tradesmen's dormitories'—'groves' without trees, vast 'cottages', 'green banks' without grass, lawns and grottoes 'pil'd high with pebbles sent from afar, Stalactites, sea-shells, Peak or Matlock spar' were already, in 1833, a subject for biting satire.[82]

Jewish businessmen began to move into the suburbs at the same time and for the same reasons. Aaron Jacob and his sons had lived out in suburban Salford since the first decade of the century; Phineas Henry had lived in Chorlton Row since 1827; but a more steady and continuous drift began in 1832 (accelerated, perhaps, by cholera) when Behrens left Mosley Street for a house in Nelson Street, Chorlton-on-Medlock. Two years later he moved to Plymouth

Grove, which was to remain for over a quarter of a century the main pivot of Jewish settlement in the south. Equidistant from the synagogue, but in a northerly direction, was Gesunde Cottage, built for Abraham Franklin, at the junction of Broughton Lane and Bury New Road, in 1834. During the later 1830s and early 40s further Jewish settlement in the suburbs tended to concentrate around the houses of Behrens and Franklin, who, in each case, provided a social focus for an orthodox élite. Before 1834, however, the movement into the suburbs had achieved little momentum, since the community consisted largely of shopkeepers who were reluctant to leave their premises at night: when Franklin moved to Gesunde Cottage his two elder sons continued to live above the shop in St Ann's Place, where in 1835 they foiled an intruder who claimed that his only object had been an apple pie found half-eaten in his pocket.[83]

V

The Manchester of the early 1830s was, in fact, a society suffering from all the social and political malaise of a rapidly expanding industrial centre with a constant influx of immigrants from rural England and Ireland. The population of the township alone exceeded 142,000 by 1831, when it was 'the capital of discontent',[84] in which nascent class antagonism was sharpened by the endemic fluctuations of an industrial economy:

The Police formed . . . so weak a screen against the power of the mob [according to Dr Kay] that popular violence is now in almost every instance, controlled by the pressure of a military force.[85]

Dr Kay feared that the town might be given over to 'turbulent riots', machine-breakers, arsonists, and 'political desperadoes', unless something was done to counteract the 'contagious example' of Irish depravity and improve the physical condition and moral fibre of the working classes.[86] The *Guardian* led the 'enlightened' middle-class attack upon political sedition, Trade Union tyranny, Irish violence, and the immorality of life amongst the lowest orders:

notwithstanding the various countervailing efforts of many benevolent societies and individuals, the most gross habits of intoxication still prevail to an enormous extent in this town.[87]

The Catholic Irish had now assumed, beyond question, the putative role of social saboteurs. Manchester police who attempted to break up some of the hundred or so illegal whiskey stills in Ancoats and Little Ireland were subject to 'the almost murderous spirit of violence that exists in the breasts of some of the lower orders of Irish',[88] according to the *Guardian*, which reported that one constable had broken his staff on the operators of the Brannigan still in Old-ham Road;[89] when, on St Patrick's Day, 1830, the Irish Fusiliers marched from Salford Barracks to St Augustine's Catholic Chapel in Granby Row, they were followed by crowds of Irish working folk with shamrocks in their hats who, when refused free passage through the toll bar on Regent's Bridge, set up 'a cry peculiar to the Irish' and assaulted three policemen, including Beau Canky.[90] The Catholic Irish were associated with the wrecking of Orange Lodges and the disruption of Stowellite meetings; they were conspicuously im-plicated in Trade Unionism and Chartism; it was they who seemed, most of all, to inhabit the cellars and courts which were just beginning to attract ad-verse public comment. They lacked both the incentive to protect their reputa-tion and the strong middle-class leadership which might have achieved it in the face of pauper immigration on an expanding scale. Their arrival (Dr Kay believed) was a

colonisation of savage tribes . . . attended with effects on civilisation as those which have marked the progress of the sand flood over the fertile plains of Egypt.[91]

Other immigrant groups were in every case more affluent, less numerous and less vulnerable than the Irish. German immigrants of the period 1825–34 were for the most part merchants, professional men and exiled revolutionaries, who were rarely in trouble with the law. The only exceptions on record were three 'gentlemanly' but penniless adventurers—Felix Bernhard Meyer, Carl Kemper and Frederick William Bagdansky—who in May 1833 were caught in the act of robbing the house of the respected German merchant, Martin Schunck, after another compatriot had tipped off the police.[92] Bagdansky (from Prussian Poland), who was caught with a knife in his possession, is re-ported to have boasted that he would murder anyone for £5. Kemper (from Westphalia) was a student who had fled to Belgium after wounding a fellow student in a duel, served for a time in the foreign legion, and enlisted to serve in the army of Don Pedro at Oporto, only to be diverted to Eng-land by Meyer, a fellow Westphalian, the 'chief contriver' of the robbery, and supposedly the son of a university professor. The trio caused a brief stir,[93] but the greater impact upon public opinion was made by the 'great many for-eign gentlemen' who attended the court, and the six in particular who com-posed half the jury—all German merchants, at least one, Ernest Reuss, of Jewish extraction—which sentenced Kemper and Meyer to two years' hard labour, and Bagdansky to one.[94]

The progress of European liberalism also promoted good feeling towards foreigners whose presence in Manchester seemed to link them (however incorrectly) with rebellion and exile rather than with the regimes which were being overthrown. The July Revolution in France was seen as a 'sublime act of retributive justice', particularly since its leaders displayed 'a regard for private property . . . no less striking than their devoted vindication of public rights'.[95] At a fund-raising meeting, Greg spoke of the need for Manchester, as the foremost manufacturing town in the world, to combine the 'pursuit of gain' with continued 'attachment to the principles of just and liberal government'.[96] The proceeds of the fund were taken to Paris by Alexander Kay, Mark Philips and J. C. Dyer, who were entertained by Lafayette at the Hotel de Ville.[97] The heroism of the Polish rebels of 1830–31 also caught the public eye and led to local meetings of protest against Russia's contravention of the Treaty of Vienna.[98] A subscription raised in June 1834 assisted four Polish exiles, who had recently arrived in Liverpool from Trieste, to reach London;[99] another Polish refugee addressed public meetings in Manchester which exposed the cruelties of the Czar, not least towards his Jewish subjects.[100]

In the mid-1830s Italian street musicians and their 'tortured' animals became offensive to an increasingly refined middle-class taste. Complaints of obstruction resulted in ten Italian boys appearing in the New Bailey in June 1834, some with monkeys clinging around their necks, one with a racoon, one with white mice, all arrested at a lodging house kept by another Italian, who was also taken into custody. All were discharged on promising to leave town.[101] In the following December, the local beadles cautioned more than sixteen other boys, and arrested three, at lodging houses in Tib Street, Ancoats Street and Carpenter's Lane, where the house keepers (also Italian) hired out organ boxes at exorbitant rates and demanded rent in proportion to earnings.[102] John Jacko, a young organ grinder, was found guilty, also in 1834, of stealing a monkey from a local street exhibition which included also a brown bear and a camel.[103] Again, however, the relatively innocuous misdemeanours of Italian 'strollers' were more than offset by the repute achieved by a small group of Italian merchants, instrument makers, opticians and print dealers, particularly Joshua Ronchetti, hydrometer and thermometer maker to H.M. Board of Customs, and by the middle-class association of Italians with the cause of liberty. When, in 1830, a beggar with forged credentials claimed to be an Italian 'refugee' the *Guardian* commented:

. . . he may be so—but certainly not from having engaged in the cause of liberty. The true sufferers from this noble cause, the Italians particularly, know how to maintain their dignity in their exile; and by exerting their talents or their industry, do not suffer themselves to be a burthen on foreign generosity.[104]

Local Italians and Germans participated at the meeting at the York Hotel in King Street in February 1830 which prepared plans for a Foreign Library in Manchester;[105] the proceeds of three guinea shares and one guinea subscriptions were to go towards the purchase of books in Italian, German and French, and the library was to be controlled by a committee on which there was only a slight preponderance of Englishmen. Within five years the library, then in a 'flourishing state' with over 1,600 volumes, was being written of by the *Guardian* as the symbol of Manchester's cosmopolitan outlook:

If the present age values itself on the extinction of some national prejudices, to what can this be attributed, but to the extension of our intercourse with foreigners.[106]

No observant Jews were associated with the foundation or early development of the Foreign Library, in part, perhaps, because they did not like to think of themselves as foreigners. When the community presented its first petition to Parliament in favour of Jewish emancipation, in March 1834, S. L. Behrens (born in Pyrmont) classed himself amongst the '*British-born* Jews' whose 'known loyalty' entitled them to complete political freedom.[107] If not all were as British-born as they would like to have been, their loyalty was beyond doubt. When the first Bill for the removal of Jewish 'disabilities' was defeated in the House of Commons by 228 votes to 165 in May 1830 the *Guardian* launched a forthright attack upon the Tory ministers (and those 'degenerate professors of whiggism') who had opposed it. Peel's main speech was described as 'flimsy, and sophistical':

The feebleness of the arguments by which it was sought to justify their [the disabilities] retention, contrasted strongly with the powerful and perspicuous reasoning of those who took the broad ground of universal tolerance; and exposed in forcible terms the inconsistency of parties who, having supported the claims of the Catholics, now oppose those of the Jews.[108]

The growth of 'universal tolerance' was only one of the new foundations of Jewish communal life in Manchester. Equally important was the social and economic standing of the community's settled members and their unequivocal association with the values of the dominant class. Whether as foreigners, as Jews, as citizens, or as tradesmen, members of the local community had achieved acceptance by all but a small, fanatical minority. This was not, however, the way in which the community saw itself. In their construction of the local situation the communal leaders believed the prestige of local Jewry still to be in sufficient peril from its least reputable members to require determined leadership, constant vigilance, and an emphasis upon those virtues—including British birth—which were thought to represent the hallmarks of social quality.

4   The plutocracy, 1834–44

For almost a quarter of a century after 1834, until a Jewish member was admitted to the House of Commons in 1858, the development of Anglo-Jewry was dominated, directly or indirectly, by the issue of Jewish emancipation. Once Protestant Dissenters had attained full political rights in 1828, and the Roman Catholics in 1829, and particularly after the Reform Bill of 1832 had broadened the social base of the House of Commons, Jewish emancipation emerged as a realistic cause with considerable support in non-Jewish quarters. After the emancipation of Negro slaves in the British West Indies in 1833, Jews could claim to be 'the only class of His Majesty's subjects now labouring under civil disqualification'.[1] Already, at the time of Grant's Bill in 1830, the *Guardian* had indicated the support of middle-class Manchester for Jewish rights,[2] and this support was repeated as successive Bills passed through the House of Commons in 1834, 1835 and 1836, only to be defeated by the predominantly Tory House of Lords. Such a stand was consistent with the general tolerance of the new bourgeoisie, and in particular with the open support for Catholic emancipation during 1824–25 and again in 1828–29,[3] against those who believed, with Hugh Stowell and the editor of the *Manchester Courier*, that political concessions to Catholics were 'pregnant with danger to the Protestant constitution'.[4] Public petitions in their favour in Liverpool and other provincial centres in 1830 encouraged Jews to believe that emancipation was at hand, and the subsequent intransigence of the House of Lords only increased their determination to force the issue by effective propaganda on a national scale. The well-publicised formation of the Jewish Association for Obtaining Civil Rights and Privileges by I. L. Goldsmid and Barnard Van Oven in London at the end of 1833[5] was followed by public meetings throughout the country which broadcast the eligibility of Jews for membership of Parliament. The meeting in Manchester on 25 February 1834, chaired by S. L. Behrens and held at the synagogue chambers in Halliwell Street, emphasised the 'known loyalty' of the community and stressed that the Jews of the town

whilst deprived of every opportunity of earning honourable distinction . . . have discharged their social and political duties as good citizens,[6]

a claim which the Select Committee of the congregation was anxious to substantiate in full.

Jewish propaganda was in this one respect significantly different in emphasis from the Catholic agitation which had preceded it. Whilst Jews felt the
need to earn the privilege of emancipation by good civic and social behaviour,
the Catholics had sought only to recover what supposedly had once been
theirs of right—according to a declaration of intent by the Manchester Catholic Association in 1824,

the restoration of our constitutional rights on such terms only as guarantee the integrity of our holy religion, and the independence of our pious and zealous pastors.[7]

In 1824–25 Catholics had spoken, in Manchester and elsewhere, of their 'birth
rights as Britons',[8] and although Jews mirrored this approach in describing
themselves, not always accurately, as 'British-born', the greater emphasis was
placed on the virtues of the community, and particularly its civic virtues.
Neither the tolerance of the surrounding milieu, nor the narrow basis of national and local opposition to Jewish emancipation, was sufficiently reassuring
to stop the community from trying, again and again, to prove itself worthy of
respect. Similar fears seemed to dictate the need for cautious tactics rather than
for any show of militance which might itself have alienated public opinion.
Until 1847, when in the City of London Lionel de Rothschild (Nathan
Meyer's son) began a frontal assault on legislation excluding Jews from Parliament, the community pinned its faith on deferential petitions each of which
stressed the worthiness of Jewish citizens for the exercise of full political rights.
In Manchester, and no doubt in other provincial communities, the prospect of
political equality, instead of allaying the fears of the settled community or persuading it to democratise its own institutions, only served to accentuate the
apparent dangers implicit in the social contrasts thrown into relief by events of
the 1820s and early 1830s, and so to underline the need for an anglicised élite to
continue, through a 'select' system, to maintain the high tone of congregational life. The greater the emphasis which non-Jewish sympathisers placed on the
'credit and respectability' of Jewish life in Manchester—one spoke, for example, of the 'mutual excellences' of local Christian and Jewish society[9]—the
more conscious communal leaders became of the need to eradicate its most
disreputable elements. It was increasingly important that the reality should
correspond more nearly to the ideal, for there was no escaping the fact that as
Behrens spoke of his co-religionists as good enough citizens to enter Parliament, one was arrested by the Manchester police for stealing a watch, two
others—both travelling slop sellers—for the theft of silver plate, and a fourth
was in Lancaster Castle serving out his sentence for fraud.[10]

I

The drive towards greater respectability was immeasurably strengthened in the mid-1830s by the appearance within the community of a rich, sophisticated and coherent mercantile élite of immigrant entrepreneurs. If the 1820s and early 1830s were characterised by the consolidation of the retailing middle-class ranks of the community, the later 1830s were distinguished by the creation of this commercial upper crust into which only the most successful shopkeepers of the preceding years—Hyam, Simon Joseph, Abraham Franklin, the Jacob brothers—were rich enough to be absorbed. The result was a closely knit suburban plutocracy which, within the wider compass of the Free Member-ship, governed the congregation without challenge for almost a decade. In some ways, it resembled the 'cousinhood'[11] which ruled metropolitan Jewry, although its links were as much a matter of commerce as of kin.

The years 1834–36 saw a boom in the cotton industry: trade was exception-ally brisk and there was work enough for all, not only in Manchester but in the smaller towns of the textile belt. A foreign observer (of 1836) believed the annual clear profits of Manchester business to exceed £12 million:

nowhere out of the metropolis is solid capital supposed to be so large as in Manchester. She is wont to say of her rival sister upon the Mersey, that she is able to buy up the whole town of Liverpool, and keep it on hand.[12]

Full employment reduced the incidence of strikes, and for the time being at least Manchester belied her 'unenviable notoriety' as a town with 'rioting propensities'. So preoccupied were merchants and manufacturers in meeting the demand of the market (according to one of their admirers) that few al-lowed themselves more annual relaxation than a fortnight in Southport or a quick trip to Wales,[13] and most could be seen daily 'posting from their country villas to their counting houses between 8 and 9 each morning',[14] their clerks and foremen following in omnibuses which ran at half-hourly intervals from Cheetham Hill and less frequently from Greenheys, Higher Broughton and Upper Brook Street. Prosperity served to harden the lines of class distinc-tion by providing the rich with means enough to place a distance between themselves and the workers upon whom their wealth depended. Houses in Mos-ley Street and other central residential districts were 'converted almost entirely into warehouses'[15] as their occupiers took to the suburbs. The speculators who planned Victoria Park during 1834–35 had in mind those who could afford be-tween £100 and £250 a year to 'combine with the advantages of a close proxi-mity to town, the privacy of a country residence'[16] free from the noise and squalor of 'smoky, dirty, sweltering and toiling Manchester'. On a site of

140 acres in south Manchester the developers laid out houses in crescents and terraces, surrounded by 'ornamental plantations' and served by a new church seating 1,200.[17] As the rich moved into 'miles of pleasant villas peeping out through shrubberied gardens'[18] either in Chorlton-on-Medlock in the south or in Cheetham Hill and Broughton to the north, the centre was left in two layers: 'a grand district of warehouses and counting rooms'[19] in an inner ring around the Exchange, and the suffocating slums and cellars of the operatives in Newtown, Ancoats and Little Ireland.

It was the buoyancy of the market for 'Manchester goods' which induced an increasing number of merchants from London and the Continent to set up agencies in Manchester, and so stake a direct claim, at the most advantageous prices, to commodities for which the world demand seemed far to exceed the local supply. Foreign firms which earlier had relied upon direct purchases from Manchester manufacturers, now found it necessary to keep an agent on the spot to ensure a steady flow of consignments at the most economic rate: the shipping merchants S. A. and J. J. Liebert, whose two senior partners were situated in Hamburg and Berlin, now despatched a third to Manchester, where they had earlier relied on local commission agents.[20] The number of foreign export firms in Manchester rose from seventy-eight in 1834 to 101 (seventy-five of them German) in 1837—a greater increase than in any previous four-year period—and it seems reasonable to assume, on circumstantial grounds, that the number of firms from London increased by an even greater proportion. What made the trend significant for the Jewish community was that thirteen of the newcomers, five from London, eight from Germany, were practising Jews: from London, Philip Lucas and Henry Micholls (of Lucas & Micholls), Henry Moses Salomon and his young Italian-Jewish partner, Giuseppe Rabino di Moro (of Solomon & Moro), and Eleazer Moses (of Moses, Levy & Co.); from Hanover, Henry Hiller (of Furst & Hiller); from Silesia, the partners Edward Nathan and Adolphus Sington; from Hamburg, Augustus Silvester Sichel (of Sichel Brothers), Abraham Bauer and Henry Moritz Lazarus; and Henry Sigismund Straus, and his younger brother, Ralph, from Frankfurt-am-Main, where their family had been the first to live beyond the Judenstrasse after the city had been opened to Jewish residence by Bonaparte.[21] Some, like Lucas, Micholls and Moses, set out to control the whole series of operations in the textile industry, from the manufacturing and finishing of cottons and calicos to their distribution in the overseas market; most confined themselves to the export trade, either on their own account, or, like Hiller and Lazarus, as commission agents who sought out markets for Manchester manufacturers on a percentage basis; Abraham Bauer was a merchant banker. For the most part they were young men in their twenties and early thirties, some prospecting in what had become the world's major centre for the merchanting of cotton goods, most the owners or representatives of firms of established repute, who brought to Manchester some of the 'solid capital' for which the town was becoming famous, to invest in what they regarded as safe and permanent ventures.

The first to arrive, and in many ways the most important, were the partners Philip Lucas and Henry Micholls, who in 1834 set up as merchants and cotton spinners in Brown Street. Micholls, the son of Edward Emmanuel Micholls, originally a watchmaker of Yarmouth, belonged to the third English genera-tion of a family which, like the Jacobs in Manchester, had passed into overseas commerce through the classic stages of country hawking and provincial shop-keeping.[22] Lucas, the senior partner, who was born in 1797 in Kingston, Jamaica, was the son of Sampson Lucas, a cotton trader who had made his for-tune in the West Indies before settling in London, where he died in 1820.[23] Through his elder brother, Louis, Philip Lucas was closely connected with the London plutocracy; through his sister, Anne, who was the wife of S. L. Beh-rens, to the merchant leaders of the Manchester community. In Manchester, he rapidly assumed a high place in middle-class society. In 1834 he was admitted, as its first Jewish member, to the Union Club in Mosley Street,[24] where the to-tal membership was limited to four hundred and which operated a system of exclusion by one black ball in five. In 1836 he helped to promote a Bazaar Fund for the Manchester School for the Deaf and Dumb,[25] and he joined other merchants in opposing the siting of a new Exchange at the lower end of Market Street on the grounds that many 'important houses', including his own, lay to the south-east of Brown Street.[26] In 1839 he was one of the stewards at Manchester's winter Assembly to which no stranger was admitted 'without a personal introduction from a subscriber'.[27] From the later 1830s his name was prominently associated with every important charity and civic cause. It was Lucas and Micholls, themselves uncle and nephew, who, with S. L. Behrens, served as the centre of a mercantile plutocracy the solidarity of which was reinforced by intermarriage. Micholls himself married his cousin, Frederica, Behrens' daughter, in 1838. Although integrated with Manchester's Gentile élite at its highest levels, Lucas and Micholls did not lose touch with the synagogue, to which they were both admitted as Free Members.

It was in this that the new generation of German-Jewish merchants differed most obviously from their predecessors. Of the many immigrant traders of Jewish extraction who had arrived in Manchester since the 1790s, only four had retained their Jewish identity, and by 1834 two of these had left for Liverpool and Gustavus Gumpel had thrown off his allegiance to the synagogue, leaving only S. L. Behrens to represent the community in the Exchange. At least one

German merchant of Jewish origin had become an annual subscriber to the Society for Promoting Christianity Amongst the Jews, and others were active in Unitarian circles.[28] Of the newcomers of 1834–36, on the other hand, only Hiller subsequently lapsed from the Jewish faith.

This was perhaps partly a measure of the social progress which had been made by the Jewish communities of England and Germany since the end of the eighteenth century. Much of the stigma attached to Judaism had disappeared, the movement towards emancipation was gathering pace, and it was becoming possible for culturally sophisticated families to reconcile their social and political ambitions with full religious conformity. Equally important was the influence exerted upon the newcomers by an established Jewish middle class of observant shopkeepers, who served as the community's conscience. Before coming to Manchester, Adolphus Sington had 'neglected for years his religious duties and ceremonial Judaism'. Soon after his arrival, however, he was invited to the house of Abraham Franklin to assist at the ceremony of the First Night of Passover. The atmosphere created such an impression upon him that he returned to a strict observance of Jewish tradition.[29] These trends were of more than passing importance in Manchester, for the existence, from 1836, of a core of rich, westernised, but orthodox and observant Jewish merchants served as a social nucleus which attracted later immigrants who might otherwise have become totally absorbed in Manchester's Christian, or secular, society. Instead, they remained within the community, to play a major role in the struggle for emancipation, and to carry forward the social and institutional improvement of the community on the momentum of their own ambition.

Although Manchester's trade plummeted in 1837 into a depression which continued until 1843, the example which had been set, and the prospect of a dramatic recovery, were sufficient to draw to the town a steady flow of Jewish merchants, particularly from the towns of Holland and northern Germany which lay at the receiving end of Manchester's European trade. Altogether twenty-eight cotton merchants joined the community during the period 1836–43, twenty-four from Germany, chiefly from Hamburg and Frankfurt-am-Main, and two from Holland—Samuel David Bles from The Hague in 1839, and Edward Salomonson from Almelo. The exceptions were Manchester's first two Sephardi merchants, Samuel Hadida of Gibraltar and Abraham Nissim Levy of Constantinople, who arrived, probably together, in 1843 and acquired a joint warehouse in Mosley Street. By the time of the Census of 1841, at least seventy-six Jewish persons were engaged in the Manchester cotton trade—forty-six as merchants, or perhaps commission agents, and twenty as commercial clerks—totals which accounted for rather more than 34 per cent of all employed adult males within the community. Most concentrated exclusively on the export of cotton, but a few—Julius Dyhrrenfurth (of Dyhrren-furth Brothers), Leopold Amschel (of Amschel, Tobler), A. S. Sichel (of Si-chel Brothers) and M. K. Wagner (representing Gustavus Gumpel)—also had warehouses for woollen goods in Bradford, which by the later 1830s had out-stripped the other textile towns of the West Riding to become the major centre of the woollen industry.

The outstanding German-Jewish merchant of Bradford, and one of the first, was Jacob Behrens,[30] a nephew of S. L. Behrens of Manchester, and the eldest son of Nathan Behrens, whose old-established firm in Hamburg imported woollen and cotton goods and distributed them through a network of trav-ellers to the growing urban centres of the Prussian Zollverein, in Mecklen-burg, Brandenburg and Pomerania. According to his own account, it was on a series of visits to Leeds as a buyer for the firm during the period 1832–34, on each of which he failed to persuade local manufacturers to make up goods to his exact specifications, that Jacob Behrens recognised the advantages of a per-manent agency in England.[31] Leaving the Hamburg end of the business to his brother, Edward, he rented a small factory and warehouse in Leeds, where in March 1834, with a single rolling machine and two second-hand wooden presses, he began to manufacture and pack woollen textiles, first on behalf of his father's firm and subsequently as a merchant–manufacturer on his own ac-count.[32] Louis Behrens joined his brother in England as a traveller in 1837, a year before the firm's removal to Bradford, and it was at his suggestion, and apparently against the better judgement of Jacob, that a branch was opened in Tib Lane, Manchester, in August 1840 for the export of cotton cloth.[33] Al-though Jacob Behrens resided occasionally in both towns, the Manchester (and less profitable) end of the business was left substantially to Louis, and the youngest brother, Rudolph. The contrasting religious fortunes of the two branches of the family underline the significance of the situation created in Manchester by the fusion of German-Jewish immigrants of the 1830s with the synagogue built up by shopkeepers during the preceding decade. Although their parents in Hamburg were already, to use Jacob Behrens' phrase, 'emanci-pated from the ceremonial and narrowness of strict Judaism',[34] Louis and Ru-dolph aligned themselves socially with the observant mercantile group in Manchester and joined the synagogue in Halliwell Street, where, as a Free Member, Louis in particular played a key role in the congregation's develop-ment. In Bradford, where no body of Jewish shopkeepers existed, Jacob, and his compatriots, like Martin Schlesinger of Hamburg, failed to create even the loosest framework of Jewish life.[35] On a visit to a synagogue in later life, Jacob found the proceedings

neither impressive nor inspiring. Was it my estrangement . . . or was it the incompetence of the rabbi? . . . There was, at least, not a spark of enthusiasm nor a rag of intelligence in his address . . . All forms of service conducted on lines strictly laid down and according to dogma find no response in me.[36]

It was not until after the arrival of Charles Semon (of Danzig) in the mid-nineteenth century that the German Jews of Bradford even considered the possibility of a religious organisation.[37]

The social status of the new plutocracy, and its coherence, found expression in a pattern of settlement which centred upon two suburban concentrations, each lying roughly two miles from Halliwell Street, on a north–south axis running through the synagogue. One was a northward extension into Higher Broughton and Cheetham Hill of the movement commenced by Franklin in 1834. From Summer Place, Ardwick, Lucas moved to Temple House, on the upper reaches of Cheetham Hill Road, near Temple Bar; Edward Nathan settled in Cheetwood Lane; Sington and Moses in Tivoli Place, Higher Broughton; Bauer in Kew Place in Broughton Lane, near his old friend, Abraham Franklin, whose house served as a focus for the northern élite. Franklin's eldest daughter, Esther, wrote to her Dutch fiancé, Jacob Prins of Arnhem, in 1835:

our family and friends meet alternatively [sic] at each other's houses every week. Last week we were at Mrs Hyam's (where I believe you once had an invitation) and next we are to be at my cousin's Mrs Alexander Jacob where you have an invitation.[38]

Alexander Jacob and his brother Morris lived in the houses inherited from their father in the Crescent, Salford, where Ralph Straus also had rooms, in the lodging house of Ann Jennings. Their brother Henry's house was in Arthur Terrace on Bury New Road. Benjamin Hyam lived over his shop in St Mary's Gate until 1841, when a dramatic expansion of his retail trade in and beyond Manchester provided the means to buy a villa at Cliff Point, Higher Broughton, where his friends, including Franklin and Bauer, joined him on 21 April for a short ceremony of consecration.[39] In the early 1840s a new wave of immigrants reinforced this northern settlement: the Behrens brothers both settled in Higher Broughton, Louis in Camp Street, Rudolph in Tudor Place; S. D. Bles and Gabriel Willing both took houses in Hanbury Terrace, also in Broughton; Wagner in Woodland Terrace nearby. In the southern suburbs Jewish residents were fewer and probably less closely linked. Henry Moses Salomon joined S. L. Behrens in Plymouth Grove; Henry Straus occupied Apsley House on the Hyde Road; Henry Micholls lived in Willow Bank, Moss Side, before also settling in Plymouth Grove, in a house subsequently occupied by Elizabeth Gaskell.[40] A marked disinclination to settle in Greenheys—by 1843 'a German colony . . . the favourite resort of a greater portion of the German residents in Manchester'[41]—again suggests that Jews saw themselves (and acted) not primarily as foreigners but either as Englishmen or as Jews, and in this respect it was significant that the outmarkers of the community in topographic terms were also its richest and most assimilated members—Philip Lucas in the north, and his partner, Henry Micholls, to the south—each representing the height of English social ambition within a Jewish milieu. The Jewish rich were drawn together as much by this ambition as by a common interest in the improvement of communal life.

Their lives consisted, in fact, of striking a balance between a total commitment to Judaism and a full participation in the life of the urban bourgeoisie. There was something of a Jewish social life, in the sense that a group of wealthy, orthodox friends, on regular visiting terms, occasionally made up parties for excursions 'down town' to a recital, a lecture or a play.[42] They took their daily meals together at the establishment of the widow Sophia Leon, who in 1841 opened a lodging house and restaurant in Blackfriars for 'commercial gentlemen of the Jewish persuasion' and offered 'an Ordinary every day at half past one within five minutes walk of the Exchange'.[43] They worshipped together at Halliwell Street and shared an inner world of communal politics and gossip. But they did not regard themselves for this reason as outsiders, nor were they so regarded. They were an integral part of the business community, sharing its fortunes and its fears. S. L. Behrens was one of the twenty-four Manchester merchants who in July 1842, in the lowest depths of the commercial depression, convened a meeting of traders and manufacturers in the borough reeve's room in the Town Hall 'to take into consideration the present appalling state of trade and of the country', while the unemployed operatives waited in a quiet and orderly manner in King Street for a result which offered them little comfort.[44] Sichel and Bauer were founder members of the Anti-Corn Law League, the great new vehicle of Manchester's middle-class ideals, Bauer acting as one of the vice-presidents at the first Great League Banquet held in the Peter Street Pavilion (later to become the Free Trade Hall) on 1 February 1843.[45] Outside the synagogue and the home, the Jewish rich had no distinctive outlook unless it was to shade even more completely into the cultural background. They lived and had their places of business in the same districts as their Gentile peers. Jacob Franklin was a director of the Mechanics' Institute,[46] and an articulate member of the Athenaeum; Lucas was on the executive of the District Provident Society;[47] Micholls was on the committee of the Manchester School of Design.[48] Benjamin Abraham Franklin's fragmentary diary of his visit to Manchester during 1840–41, when he stayed at Gesunde Cottage, reveals a life revolving as much around the commerce and society of the town as the life of the synagogue: he attended plays at the Minor Theatre and the Theatre Royal, visited Knott Mill Fair and Batty's Circus, listened to visiting lecturers at the Royal Manchester Institution, went to a Fancy Dress Ball at the Owenite Hall of Science, where he was impressed by the 'moral demeanour' of the working men and women of the 'dress-making and mechanical class',[49] and became bored at a dance in the 'Chartist Temple', the Carpenter's Hall, where the company was disreputable, the women tipsy, and the entertainment dull.[50]

One immediate effect of the successful assimilation of the Jewish élite was the reproduction within the Jewish community of the class distinctions which existed outside it, above and beyond the political division which already separated the privileged Free Members from the rest of the congregation. A wide social gulf separated Lucas, Bauer, Hyam and Behrens not only from the occasional stranger from Warsaw, the dependent pauper, or the hawker who might still be found in the shabby lodging houses of the Old Town, but also from shopkeepers of modest means from Long Millgate and Shudehill. In their suburban homes S. L. Behrens employed seven servants, including a butler and a seamstress, Salomon and Lucas five each, Moses and Sichel four, Bauer three. When the blockade of Buenos Aires ruined the business of Henry Jacob during 1839–40, the bankruptcy proceedings revealed that his domestic expenses during the 1830s had amounted to over £1,000 a year. To a suggestion from the commissioner that this was somewhat extravagant, he replied:

It requires little explanation . . . It is very well known that I had a large house, and that I kept a good deal of company and that the money has been spent . . . I don't think it is very extravagant £1,000 a year; keeping a gig and horse, and a large establishment, £20 a week is soon gone.[51]

The scale of Bauer's financial operations, which by 1842 had extended beyond Manchester to London and Sierra Leone, and the extent of his connections, may perhaps be deduced from the subsequent careers of his clerks: Isidor Gerstenberg (of Breslau) became the firm's representative in London in 1842, was in business on his own account by 1845, and went on to become an exchange broker, founder of the Council of Foreign Bondholders and one of several Jewish creditors of Karl Marx.[52] Ellis Abraham Franklin (another of Abraham's sons), a junior clerk in 1842, became one of the original partners of Samuel Montagu.[53] In 1841 S. L. Behrens, also in merchant banking in Bradford, Leeds and Glasgow, bought a seventy-horse-power spinning and weaving mill at Catteral near Garstang, with an estate of 50 acres, seventy workers' cottages,[54] and a country house sufficiently well appointed and well protected to attract a 'daring and resolute' gang of burglars armed with bayonets.[55] After Abraham Franklin had given up his jewellery business in 1837 to concentrate on share jobbing, his credit was considered good enough by the joint-stock Northern and Central Bank for it to accept his endorsement, without security, to a bill of exchange for £1,500.[56] The consecration of the community's new burial ground at Prestwich on 4 April 1841 attracted a large crowd of congregants and eleven private coaches.[57]

It was a striking comment upon the hierarchical structure of congregational life that when the new cemetery was planned during 1840—when the Pendleton Burial Ground was declared 'quite full'[58]—it was decided by the Select Committee, at the express wish of Abraham Franklin, that the left side should be reserved for Free Members, the right for seat-holders and strangers.[59] If the plutocracy lived a life of its own outside the synagogue, within the congregation it fought to preserve intact the oligarchic system which seemed to provide a minimal insurance at least against any social dilution of the community's leadership.

II

This was not simply a matter of self-interest, or, if it was, the self-interest was complicated by good intentions. They saw it as their mission to raise the level of the community's social and religious life to meet the increasingly high standards being set by Manchester's middle-class leaders. This was only in part because they believed their own future, social as well as political, to depend upon that of the community. They were also moved by the contagious 'spirit of improvement' amongst the middle classes, which culminated in the incorporation of Manchester in 1838. Market Street was converted by degrees 'from a dirty narrow lane . . . into one of the handsomest streets in England'.[60] The town was punctuated by imposing public institutions, not least the Athenaeum, opened towards the end of 1835. Toad Lane, at the rear exit of the synagogue in Halliwell Street, and once 'so confined that the winds of heaven could scarcely penetrate it',[61] was widened in the early 1830s and then renamed Todd Street as a token gesture to a more squeamish generation.[62] There was a good deal of talk about raising the tone of town life. At the first Annual General Meeting of the Athenaeum in January 1836, James Heywood, the president, spoke of the need for a younger generation of merchants to acquire

more elevated tastes, and improved habits, instead of passing their leisure hours in idleness and dissipation . . . [and so raise themselves] in the estimate of all around them, by their increased intelligence, zeal, and usefulness.[63]

As the Manchester rich became richer, particularly during the boom of 1834–36, their level of expectation for the town increased correspondingly.

The Jewish rich saw themselves as the Cobdens, Gregs, Potters, and Heywoods of the community, who would improve the life of the congregation as their Gentile counterparts had improved that of the town. There was also the particular incentive of Jewish emancipation, for it still seemed that the quality of Jewish communal life would, in the end, decide the issue.

In transmitting the values of the wider society to the Jewish community, however, it was also necessary to translate them into specific communal objectives, and it was towards this end that the plutocracy moved during the period 1837–38. In effect, the trend towards improvement set in motion by Abraham Franklin and Alexander Jacob during the period 1825–26 was revitalised, but in a more ambitious form, to meet more sophisticated tastes. The developments of 1825–26 were perhaps in the main a show of confidence. What was now required was a coherent programme of fundamental change which would raise the level of Jewish social and economic life, and improve the effectiveness and image of its institutions. The creation of a Jewish élite threw the rudimentary character of congregational facilities into sharp relief and highlighted the disreputable vestiges of the community's economic origins.

One remedy at least lay close at hand. In a number of papers and pamphlets Dr Kay and his fellow members of the Manchester Statistical Society (founded in 1833) had emphasised the need for the elementary education of the poorer classes as a means of raising the moral tone of town life. A meeting of the 'Friends of National Education' called together by Mark Philips, James Heywood and others at the Theatre Royal in October 1837 was attended by over two thousand persons, and was believed to have had 'no parallel in England'.[64] It led to the formation, in November, of the Manchester Society for Promoting National Education, which aimed to provide cheap, efficient, and non-sectarian schools, particularly 'for the poorest and most neglected parts' of the town.[65] The movement became bogged down in angry confrontation between those, like Robert Greg, William Nield and Richard Cobden, who believed in a national secular system of schools, in which the entire volume of Scriptures would be read 'without note or comment', and Evangelicals like Stowell who felt that the State would be better advised to support religious voluntary schools.[66] What made it significant for the Jewish community, however, was the stress placed on education as an instrument of social change. English education might be used, as Lucas observed, to

qualify the succeeding generation to remove that odium which, though daily decreasing, still attached to us,[67]

and he and Franklin in particular now saw education as a means by which the Jewish lower orders would be eliminated, or, at the very least, persuaded to accept their lot gracefully and legally. The *Guardian* believed that Jews should have 'as much right as any other class' to share in the benefits of a national, State-aided system, 'in as much as they will be called upon to contribute their full proportion to its expense',[68] but from the Jewish point of view, the problem was too urgent to await a national solution. The need for educational provision was made the more important both by the gradual collapse of hawking as a means of livelihood for the Jewish poor and by the arrival in increasing numbers of pauper immigrants from Eastern Europe. From the mid-1830s Manchester began to feel, for the first time, the full effects of her position on the route across the north of England by road and rail from Hull to Liverpool, and, although most transmigrants could be passed on with a minimal subsidy, a few opted to remain and had somehow to be absorbed into the fabric of the community. Education, so Isaac Franklin believed, 'anticipated' the evil of poverty by assisting immigrants 'to acquire the means of self-dependence'.[69] By the end of 1837, elementary English education for the Jewish poor had become a communal priority.

So had education in Hebrew and religion, chiefly, perhaps, because the Jewish poor were felt to be vulnerable to Christian propaganda. Conversionism was in fact dogged by the same sectarian disputes which undermined so many other Christian projects in the mid nineteenth century. A minister of the Established Church told a meeting of the Society for Promoting Christianity Amongst the Jews (in 1837) that Jews were

a loyal people, and favourable to the Church of England; and if they became Christians at all, they would become so in connection with the Church of England.[70]

Stowell—'spluttering, hissing and sparkling' as usual, according to *Fraser's Magazine*[71]—spent a good deal of time at conversionist meetings attacking papists and Puseyites. The most active local missioner of the society, the convert Rev. H. S. Joseph of Liverpool, believed dissenters 'had lost sight of the Jewish subject', and pinned his own faith on 'affectionate' invitations to his former co-religionists to attend Anglican services.[72] The Christian assault was relatively weak, but its minimal success demanded a measure of inner defence. The provision of Hebrew education had, in fact, fallen well behind the needs of a Jewish population which approached six hundred during the later 1830s. At the synagogue Abraham Abrahams could provide no more than the most elementary instruction to a handful of children, and, at all events, the 'rabbi' declined into a long and incapacitating illness which culminated in his death in 1839. In October 1831, through the columns of the *Guardian*, B. E. Lewis of Hodson Street, Salford, offered private lessons in Hebrew to a limited number of pupils 'who will also be instructed in the Rabbinical Reading [*sic*] if sufficient progress be made in the lessons',[73] but his services—in any case, short-lived—lay beyond the means of those who were believed to be most in need of them. At a meeting of the conversionists in October 1835, Rev. Mr Frost, curate at St Stephen's, Salford, and a protégé of Stowell,

stated that the society having been informed that many of the Jews in this town did not understand Hebrew sufficient to read it, they had distributed a copy of the old and new testaments in the English tongue to every Jewish family in the town, which had been thankfully received.[74]

Although the warm reception given to the New Testament may be doubted, the estimate of the community's background in Hebrew was probably accurate enough, at least in so far as it related to the poorer classes. In the mid-1830s Isaac and Jacob Franklin, and their sister Sarah, ran free Hebrew classes at Gesunde Cottage,[75] but they had no means of devising on their own a systematic solution to the overall problem.

The third element of communal life which appeared to require attention was the quality of synagogal provision. Although Halliwell Street had possessed a choir since its foundation, and its earliest rule book laid great stress on the need for decorum, its organisation was cumbersome and archaic, and its services were thought to compare badly with those of Christian churches, most particularly in the absence of 'pulpit instruction' in the vernacular. Already in 1817, a metropolitan synagogue had begun to experiment with regular English sermons;[76] Bristol followed suit in 1832;[77] Sir Moses Montefiore replaced Spanish with English sermons at Bevis Marks in 1829.[78] The authorities at the Seel Street Synagogue in Liverpool were persuaded in 1827 to erect a pulpit, although it was eight years before anyone could be found to fill it.[79] The person finally selected, in 1835, was David Meyer Isaacs,[80] a young man who now emerged as Anglo-Jewry's leading English rhetorician. Born at Leewarden in Holland in 1810, Isaacs was the third son of a Dutch merchant banker who, on losing all his property during the French Wars, in 1818 migrated to London and opened a private school in Heneage Street, Spitalfields. At the age of fourteen, when his father was Sabbath Lecturer at the New Synagogue in Great St Helens, David Isaacs became companion to the blind wife of Solomon Hirschel, the Chief Rabbi, and read to her in the evenings from the scriptures. Subsequently, while supporting himself as a private tutor to some of London's leading families, he attended the Talmudic classes of Dayan Israel Levy, and, on the strength of this background, in 1832 he obtained the post of lecturer at the synagogue in Bristol. There (in his own estimate) he gave

the most unqualified satisfaction to its respective members . . . I gladly embraced the opportunity of turning the culture of my youth to account by disseminating those salutary doctrines and ennobling lessons of our sacred institutions which I flatter myself have not been altogether ineffectual although insuperable difficulties presented themselves arising from the defective system of Hebraic tuition and local causes,[81]

particularly, it seems, 'unfortunate dissension'[82] within the congregation. In an unsolicited letter of application to the Liverpool synagogue, in October 1834, he wrote:

My mode of lecturing is chiefly extemporaneous, the effusions of a mind deeply imbued with religious zeal remote from sophistry and superstition. My reading in Hebrew is in accordance with the best authorities and the most approved method.[83]

In the following year Isaacs was engaged to deliver English sermons and to serve as Second Reader to the secretary of the Liverpool synagogue, David Woolf Marks. His presence so close to Manchester was an opportunity not to be missed, particularly in the absence of any other English preacher in the provinces. During the years 1837–38 he delivered the occasional invitation sermon at Halliwell Street, and Hyam, then presiding warden, hinted at the possibility of a more regular appointment.[84] Whatever his defects, Isaacs had more to recommend him to the new Manchester élite than a factotum who combined business interests with his congregational duties. On 16 September 1837 Abraham Franklin, Abraham Bauer, Benjamin Hyam and Eleazer Moses invited donations from their co-religionists towards a fund for the establishment of 'periodic lectures in the English language',[85] and towards the end of the following year Isaacs began to deliver fortnightly sermons in Manchester for an annual retainer of £84.[86]

   All these considerations seemed to point to the need for a Jewish communal organisation which would promote Jewish interests in the way that the Manchester Catholic Association had promoted those of the Roman Catholics during the 1820s. Such a body might serve not only to finance Isaacs' sermons and organise suitable facilities for the English and Hebrew education of the poor but also to promote Jewish emancipation and other national and international causes of Jewish interest, and to create the kind of 'concord and confidence' within local Jewry that the Catholic Association had sought to achieve for its community in 1824. By 1838 there existed in Manchester a substantial body of fully assimilated Jews, chiefly in overseas commerce, whose allegiance might conceivably be recovered by providing a focus of Jewish identity outside the synagogue. They included John Peiser, who, after humble beginnings in Manchester, in 1828 entered into partnership with a Gentile patron as a manufacturer of 'coach and livery lace, girth and web and fancy fringes, and whips' in Chancery Lane; although describing himself to the Manchester Unity of Oddfellows, of which he became Provincial Grand Master, as an 'alien' by race and religion,[87] Peiser had abandoned Judaism by

1830. So had Phineas Henry, the Russian silk manufacturer, who occupied a seat at Halliwell Street during the period 1825–27, and Emmanuel Mendel, who only occasionally rented a seat for the Holy days. Mendel had advanced from rope making to the cotton trade, and had also bought a hotel in Bridge Street, where in December 1835 four lectures on Schiller were delivered by a visiting lecturer from Hamburg.[88] Those who broke away from Jewry tended to retain their links, perhaps even to strengthen them, with the local German minority. More recent immigrants of Jewish extraction who held aloof from the synagogue included Salis Schwabe of Oldenburg in Westphalia,[89] who arrived in 1832, took over a factory in Rhodes, Middleton, which had been gutted by Luddites, and converted it into a calico-printing works. Highly successful in business, Schwabe moved easily into local middle-class circles, joined the Anti-Corn Law League, became a close friend of Cobden (and later Mrs Gaskell), played host to Chopin, and was one of Manchester's most perceptive mid-nineteenth-century philanthropists. Amongst other locally prominent assimilated Jews were the merchants Ernest Reuss (of Reuss and King), E. H. Levyssohn, Israel Reiss (of Reiss Brothers), Myer Frank, and Henry Leppoc of Brunswick, subsequently a Poor Law Guardian and City Councillor, Louis Schwabe, a silk manufacturer in Portland Street whose Jacquard looms made Queen Victoria's wedding dress,[90] and Dr Ludwig Bernstein, of Berlin, one of many immigrant linguists, who in July 1837 offered evening classes and private tuition at an address in Faulkner Street.[91] Some observers, at least, believed the process of alienation was due in part to remediable causes and might be arrested:

the synagogue having long been without a preacher, they did not care much to attend it. They took seats in the Socinian [i.e. Unitarian] Chapels and some even in Christian Churches.[92]

They already served local Jewry in one sense, since their virtues were attributed by the Gentile world to the Jewish community, however far they had attempted to move away from it. Was it not at any rate possible that by providing more sophisticated services, with sermons in English, and by creating a non-religious focus, the community might recover their full allegiance?

In this context, it seems likely that those who were beginning to think in terms of an extra-synagogal organisation were influenced by the first rumblings of the Reform Movement in England. As early as July 1837 Sir Moses Montefiore was aware of the possible radical implications of the demands made at Bevis Marks for more decorous services and for the provision of facilities for Divine Worship in the West End: he wrote in his diary

I am most firmly resolved not to give up the smallest part of our religious forms and privileges to obtain civil rights.[93]

At first, this may well have provided the motive of those who sought to modify traditional Jewish liturgy, but under the influence of Geiger's preaching on the Continent during 1838 a few moved into a more extreme position from which they denounced 'Rabbinism' and questioned the divine inspiration of the Oral Law. The matter remained undecided in the later 1830s, but at least it had alerted the more orthodox to a subversive threat against which they needed to arm themselves. In one sense, the community in Manchester during the period 1837–38 was seeking ways of improving Jewish life which would add to its attraction and prestige, without disturbing the traditional framework of orthodoxy, and in devising the means to do so they laid stress throughout on 'the inculcation of religious duties'.

It was for all these reasons that, early in 1838, Franklin, Bauer, Hyam and Moses converted the idea of a Lecture Fund into the wider object of a Hebrew Association which would, in the first instance, sponsor sermons in English and make provision for the free education of the Jewish poor. This second impulse was, if anything, the stronger. At an early meeting, Jacob Franklin

dwelt . . . on the strong temptation which the poor of our nation had to employ their children in business at too early a period, in total disregard of their education, and to the neglect of this, the most favourable time for instilling religious and moral principles . . . he urged how the character of our nation in the estimation of others, was to be best maintained by the early and judicious education of our humbler classes.[94]

The character of our nation in the estimation of others: it was this underlying ideal which held together the Association's diverse objects and which subsequently informed its work. Typically, the first permanent president was Philip Lucas, who placed his 'purse' at the disposal of the Association,[95] and whose 'extensive influence and well-known munificence' were considered by Jacob Franklin, the first Treasurer, to be of decisive importance.[96] Isaac Franklin, the first Secretary, saw the Association as the means by which the Manchester community might help 'to raise the intellectual character of Jews generally' by supporting action on its behalf in England and overseas.[97] The first committee of four consisted of H. M. Salomon, Eleazer Moses, Simon Joseph and Adolphus Sington. The suburban rich had taken the future of the community in hand.

III

For all its good intentions and powerful backing, the Association got off to a shaky start. Isaacs was said to be 'gifted with a forcible, somewhat impulsive and eloquent style of oratory tinged with a peculiarly caustic humour',[98] but his sermons dealt too much with 'undisputed and well-known truths' for the erudite tastes of Abraham Franklin,[99] while his son, Benjamin, during his brief visit from Jamaica in 1841, found the new minister arrogant and 'ungentlemanly' in his conduct, his sermons long-winded, 'unconnected and egotistical', his audiences sparse and apathetic.[100] Alexander Jacob believed that 'it would be well if other congregations emulated the example set by Liverpool and Manchester',[101] but he was speaking in the abstract, as were so many other admirers of 'pulpit oratory' in nineteenth-century Jewry, and no doubt Isaacs made up for his deficiencies as a preacher by his importance as a symbol of the community's aspirations. At all events, his stay was short-lived. Throughout 1841 he was at odds with the authorities at Seel Street over the size of his salary;[102] underlining his discontent, in July he offered himself as a candidate, unsuccessfully as it turned out, for the Lectureship of the Great Synagogue in London.[103] In the autumn, the Select Committee at Liverpool went some way towards meeting his request by appointing him to the additional post of Secretary (recently vacated by David Marks) with an appropriate increase in pay.[104] The new post demanded his full attention, however, and his resignation from his Manchester lectureship resulted in 'the discontinuance for the present of religious discourses in the vernacular'.[105] With the exception of a few months during 1846 they were not resumed at Halliwell Street until the end of 1851.

The earliest stages of the educational experiment were equally unsatisfactory. Lacking the funds, and at first perhaps the inclination, to establish a communal school, in September 1839 the Association appointed a sub-committee

to provide that the children of the Jewish poor have admission into well-ordered and efficient schools, for the ordinary departments of education, to superintend their progress . . . and further, to engage, as soon as the funds will permit, a competent teacher of the rudimentary branches of Hebrew literature.[106]

A rapid survey by Eleazer Moses and the Franklin brothers revealed that there were about twenty-five poor Jewish children in Manchester between the ages of three and a half and five,[107] and in April 1840 arrangements were made for the admission of the youngest into the Ashley Road Infants School, which took pupils under the age of four of every denomination at a fee of 2d a week, and the rest into the Gould Street School,[108] one of the non-sectarian foundations of the Manchester Society for the Promotion of National Education, where 3d a day was charged for a system of tuition described as 'a modification of that of Poussin':

the assembly of all the pupils in the gallery, at stated times, for examination; recreation in the playground, under the eye of the master, who is thereby enabled to observe, and to cherish or restrain the developments of character amongst his charge; and the training of both sexes together, for the sake of the beneficial influence which, under proper regulation, they exercise upon each other.[109]

But even the careful choice of secular and progressive schools could not overcome the problems inherent in sending Jewish children to Gentile institutions. As Jacob Franklin wrote,

> no other religious community has wants so peculiar, both as regards the course of study, and the discipline of conduct; and in no other do youth encounter so many obstacles and disadvantages, when left to ordinary educational establishments.[110]

The movement of all the children to a small private school in July 1840[111] failed to overcome the difficulties presented by Jewish dietary laws and Sabbath observance on the one hand and the implicit Christian content of even the most secular education on the other. Jewish children were no better equipped to enter local schools than Jewish paupers were to enter the local workhouse. In both cases, separate communal provision was required.

This lesson had in fact already been learnt in Liverpool by July 1841, when a 'Hebrew Educational Institution' was opened for ten Jewish boys,[112] and in Birmingham by the following month, when the community founded a 'Jewish National School' in which seventy children of both sexes were 'sheltered and protected against the obstacles of superstition and infidelity'.[113] In the light of these precedents, of its own failure, and of the funds which became available with the resignation of David Isaacs, the Association decided, in January 1842

> to take suitable premises for the use of the association exclusively, and to appoint a competent Hebrew and English master to reside therein, with an assistant if necessary: they do not however, intend to confine their system to the children of the humbler classes, to whom instruction will be afforded gratuitously, but after the manner of the Birmingham School, lately established, they hope the abler classes of the community will be induced to send their children . . . whereby they may secure for them efficient instruction at an economical rate, whilst they will be substantially contributing to the prosperity as well as the respectability of the institution itself.[114]

Necessity became the mother of virtue; since the subscriptions of members seemed unlikely to cover the running costs of an independent school, and State aid was not available, the children of the rich—the 'abler classes' as they were tellingly described—were to be drawn from their suburban homes and private tutors to subsidise the education of the poor. It was a gesture symbolic, perhaps, of the way in which the élite were prepared, at any rate in theory, to commit all their resources to the social elevation of the community. In practice, however, it became more difficult. On 13 November 1842 'a complete Hebrew and English Seminary'[115] opened in rented rooms in Halliwell Street with David Asher, a former assistant at Birmingham, as Headmaster with a salary of £75 a year.[116] A Gentile assistant was paid 5s a week to organise an

'English Department',[117] the girls were 'supervised' and taught needlework by Mrs Sophia Solomons,[118] and Joachim Levy provided instruction in Hebrew for £20 a year.[119] But the weekly total collected from twenty-five boys and thirteen girls amounted to no more than 7s a week.[120] The suburban children held aloof, and the school became dependent for its existence on the benevolence of the Association's subscribers. The committee collected a nominal fee from all the children (in 1843) to remove 'the objectionable name of Free School',[121] moved the children into more spacious and better appointed rooms in St Mary's Street (in 1844),[122] and told its subscribers (in 1845) that 'it should not be objected by the liberal-minded that the communion of the rich and poor is injurious',[123] without making any significant impression on class prejudice. It was still being noted as a 'subject for regret' at the end of 1845 'that a larger number of the children of the more prosperous class are not found in the list of attendants'.[124]

None the less, the school was a conspicuous success, and served as the major agency for the social and economic integration of immigrant children. It was the Hebrew Association's most substantial, and in the end its only tangible achievement. By the beginning of 1845, when Asher left Manchester after an obscure dispute with the committee,[125] there were forty-four pupils, twenty-three boys and twenty-one girls, of whom twenty-four were 'not only taught gratuitously, but provided with books free of expense'.[126] Those 'who else had been unfit to attend the School' were occasionally provided with free clothing by 'Mesdames [S. L.] Behrens and [Philip] Lucas', who visited them in their homes.[127] Corporal punishment was 'altogether interdicted', and in general the committee adopted 'the system of Rewards rather than of Punishments'.[128] The children were taught the Three Rs and Hebrew, and were examined publicly in each at an annual ceremony in the York Hotel in King Street.[129] By 1845 several former pupils were

usefully and profitably employed in the establishments chiefly of members of this Institution, who in their visits to the school room found these youths possessed of the required attainments.[130]

The committee of the Association noted, apparently with some relief, that its original object of

connecting with the ordinary services of the synagogue, the occasional delivery of Lectures for the expounding of the Sacred Writings, and the inculcation of religious duties

had apparently been absorbed into the collateral aim of providing educational facilities for the poor.[131] The Hebrew Association, as such, ceased to exist, and its organisation became the executive and the support of the Manchester Jews School.[132]

The wider objects of the Association had only been achieved in part. It was the agency which in 1840 sponsored a fund to help finance Montefiore's intervention on behalf of the persecuted Jews of Damascus and Rhodes,[133] and which organised a public entertainment in Manchester to celebrate his return;[134] in 1841 it collected £200 from Manchester's 'very small but public spirited' community for the Jewish victims of the Smyrna Fire;[135] but thereafter its efforts became focused exclusively on education. The future initiative in defining the response of Manchester Jewry to wider communal needs passed either back to the synagogue or to individuals prepared to whip up interest and accumulate funds as the need arose. As a cohesive force, it recovered the lost communal allegiance of the German merchant, Leopold Amschel, who subsequently joined the school committee, although without returning to the synagogue. The contribution of many other non-practising Jews—including Bernard Hahn, Nathan Hess, Emmanuel Mendel and Julius Dyrrhenfurth—marked their last surviving link with Judaism.

The school, on the other hand, was seen as part of an Anglo-Jewish renaissance which was moving the community in the direction of social and political equality.[136] The mood of the time was perhaps best expressed in the prospectus of the Liverpool school:

The voice of humanity, the spirit of the age, the love of nationality, and the commands of Heaven, alike demand an immediate provision for the Education of the Poor . . . Knowledge will take the place of Ignorance, Religion of Infidelity, Industry and Handicraft of Idleness and Peddling, and the Blessing of God will rest upon all who labour for its accomplishment.[137]

More was required, however, than divine benediction. Informing all the Hebrew Association's work in the field of education was the undercurrent created by the struggle for political emancipation. While the grand strategy was left to London, each large provincial community felt called upon to create an acceptable social and cultural base for the exercise of political rights.

IV

Apart from the emancipation issue, no external event exercised a greater influence upon the development of the community during these years than the Damascus Affair of 1840.[138] The mysterious disappearance of a Capuchin friar in Damascus shortly before Passover was followed by a revival of the long-discredited accusation of ritual murder, which in turn led first to the imprisonment and torture of prominent Jews and then to anti-Semitic atrocities of medieval barbarism. The sense of shock experienced throughout the Jewish

world by the charge and its consequences was deepened by the credence given
to it, in part for political reasons, by the French Consul, who, under some
pressure from his home government, passed sentences of death on all the accused.
Within weeks the 'blood libel' found an echo on the island of Rhodes, where
it was accompanied by comparable brutalities, and elsewhere there were brief
but telling indications of latent anti-Jewish feeling.

In the spring and early summer of 1840 news of the tragedy awakened the
sympathies of Jewish communities throughout the world. In London, on 21
April, representatives of the metropolitan synagogues met at the house of Sir
Moses Montefiore in Park Lane and appointed a deputation to wait upon
Palmerston and solicit the intervention of the British government. In June the
Board of Deputies decided that Montefiore should lead a mission of interces-
sion to the court of Mehemet Ali, the Ottoman Viceroy of Egypt, and then effective ruler of Syria. In Manchester the Hebrew Association took up the cause
in a meeting held at the York Hotel on 30 June under the chairmanship of
Philip Lucas, and attended by '80 of the principal members of the Jewish persuasion of the town'.[139] In a series of speeches from Lucas, S. L. Behrens,
Bauer, Moses, Sington, Alexander Jacob and the Franklins, the emphasis was
yet again on the respectability of Judaism; in this instance, on the incredibility
of the community's association with the kind of crimes with which the Jews of
Damascus had been accused. The Manchester plutocrats associated themselves
with the measures taken by their counterparts on the Board of Deputies, and a
fund was inaugurated, with Lucas and Jacob Franklin as its trustees, to support
Montefiore's mission to the East. Jews (Lucas said) 'were as enlightened as any
other nation in the world, though they had not the same power as other
nations', and for this reason required the backing of friendly governments.
The recently-established English sermons at Halliwell Street were held out as
an example of Jewish religious life which should dispel the superstitious calum-
nies of Damascus. Alexander Jacob

said that they were all affected individually by the persecution. The question was,
whether they, as Jews were to be taunted with a crime of which neither they nor their
forefathers were ever guilty. He was convinced that, if the public knew more of their
mode of worship, they would be convinced that they were incapable of the crimes
alleged against them; and he trusted, that, as they now had their services in English,
the Christians would go and see how it was conducted.

Those English services were, of course, short-lived, but in more general terms
the effect of Damascus was again to confirm the plutocracy in its belief in the
need for communal improvement, and so to add to the impetus of the
Hebrew Association's educational experiments during the years 1840–44. When
more than enough was contributed to the local Damascus Fund, the trustees

handed a surplus of over £130 to local Jewish charities, the bulk of it to the Association's school.[140]

An important side-effect of the episode was the return to the community, at least in an active, religious sense, of a young intellectual whose estrangement from it was of long standing. Tobias Theodores[141] was born in Berlin in 1808, and had come to Manchester in 1826 to work as an accountant in the counting house of Gustavus Gumpel, who by that time was himself nearing total alienation from the synagogue. At some time, probably in the early 1830s, Theodores resigned from business to become an itinerant teacher of languages in towns throughout Lancashire and Yorkshire, including Halifax, where he met a Miss Sarah Horsfall, a Christian girl, whom he married, apparently in a civil ceremony, in 1839. He returned to Manchester soon afterwards, and at the time of the Census of 1841 he was living with his wife, their five-month-old son Julius, and a single female servant, in Maskell Street, Chorlton-on-Medlock, near the lodging houses in which many German clerks and commission agents, including Jacob Behrens, had their rooms. He is first mentioned in the Manchester press in November 1841, when he twice acted as interpreter for a French lecturer on mesmerism.[142] The first hint of his communal allegiance had been in November 1840, when he wrote a long and famous letter to *The Times* defending the Jews of Damascus,[143] and in March 1841, he attended the dinner given by the Hebrew Association at Hayward's Hotel, Manchester, to celebrate Montefiore's return from his triumphant mission to Egypt. After Lucas had 'left the chair' at one in the morning, Theodores was one of a 'little coterie of 8'—including also the three Franklin and two Jacob brothers (whose inter-family feud was temporarily suspended), Gabriel Willing and David Meyer Isaacs—who remained behind to chat for a further hour.[144] At some time during 1841–42, when he became a regular contributor to the Jewish press, Theodores' wife was received into the Jewish faith in Amsterdam, and on 17 November 1842 their marriage was regularised by a ceremony in the house of Joseph Mirls, the new Second Reader, in Strangeways, and duly recorded in the synagogue's register. His official membership of the synagogue dated only from 1842, but two years later he was present with Montefiore in Birmingham at the opening there of a new building for the Hebrew National School.[145] Much of Theodores' early career remains to be reconstructed, but if, as seems likely, he returned to active Judaism after a period of substantial, perhaps total, assimilation, his earlier cultural experience may in part account for the radical view of Judaism which he was subsequently to adopt, although its intellectual basis was derived from the literature of German Reform. In a review written for the Jewish press in October 1842, in which he gave excessive praise to 'pulpit instruction' as '*the* institution calculated to in-fuse a regenerating spirit into our venerable church', he commented that American and English preachers had 'not yet . . . reached the grade occupied by their German brethren'.[146]

The Damascus episode also provided a suitable climax to the gradual improvement of local middle-class feeling towards the Jews. In a series of public and private meetings which began early in June, declarations of sympathy incorporated and reinforced every element which had gone towards the making of Manchester's tolerance in the preceding thirty years. There was the general enlightenment of the urban middle class (from W. R. Greg):

I am not sorry to take every opportunity of expressing the disgust and detestation which I, in common with all of you, feel at persecution, in whatever country, upon whatever pretext, and under whatever form it is perpetrated;[147]

the first-hand experience of honest and enterprising Jewish traders (from John Brooks, the borough reeve):

We had many Jews resident here, merchants, whom he had known and done business with for the last twenty-five years; and he must confess, that, though he had at first that prejudice against them which is implied in the common expression, 'he has Jew'd you', he found by experience of them, that they were quite as good to deal with as Gentiles. They were a very steady, industrious, persevering people . . . sober and steady[148]

(and from Rev. Daniel Hearne, Catholic pastor of St Patrick's Chapel):

We Christians say they are fond of money, but they sacrifice their money, when put in competition with the observance of their religious rites. Go to their shops in Manchester on the Saturday, which is their Sabbath; and these men, who we say are so fond of money, we find closing their shops and warehouses with a punctiliousness that ought to raise a blush on the face of any Christian;[149]

the conspicuous contributions of Jewish merchants and shopkeepers to local causes (from John Macvicar):

There have been many occasions since I came to live in this town when I have had to apply to the Jewish community here for charitable purposes, and I have ever met with a response from them quite as great as I ever did from the Christian population of this town;[150]

their civic loyalty and commitment to social order (from Absalom Watkin):

discharging faithfully all the duties of citizens, and living amongst us in a manner which, from their credit and respectability, might put to shame many of ourselves;[151]

their associations with Manchester's overseas markets (from 'A Member of the Manchester Chamber of Commerce'):

I need not remind those who know anything of these markets [in the Levant] that a large portion of the trade is in the hands of Jews;[152]

and their identification with the influential body of 'German residents . . . of the Christian faith', many of whom were present at the meeting held in the Town Hall on 22 July, which called upon the government to prevent the recurrence of anti-Semitic outrages in the East.[153] Mercantile Manchester believed, with Alderman Shuttleworth, that Jews were the last persons to deserve exposure to such 'obnoxious odium and obloquy' as had harassed them in Damascus and Rhodes.[154]

Only the die-hard Evangelicals of the Church of England refrained from this euphoric Judaeophilia. The speakers at the July meeting had included a Roman Catholic priest and several dissenting ministers, but the Anglican clergy were conspicuously absent, according to the *Guardian*'s report:

though not so numerously attended as those public meetings where a party struggle is anticipated, or where a formal muster of their relative numbers is made, there was a very respectable attendance, including clergy and ministers of various denominations, and gentlemen of all grades of political opinion. We did not see any church clergymen present . . .[155]

Stowell used the agitation for his own peculiar purposes:

if private and public statements were to be believed, that persecution did not originate in Mohammedan superstition, but had been goaded on by representations of papists.[156]

At conversionist meetings, his ill-feeling towards the Jews was scarcely disguised. When in 1844 a 'gentleman from Halifax', fired by messianic zeal, began to collect subscriptions towards the purchase of Palestine for the Jews, Stowell commented:

there was no railway speculation in the world more wild and enthusiastic than this . . . Convert them to Christianity and leave the rest to God,

and he added,

Many Jews, he was sorry to say, now come over to England, when they heard they could get a begging livelihood, and in that way the Christian had been imposed upon.[157]

His view was coloured also by his defence of the 'Protestant Constitution':

It was no longer the simple British Constitution, once the envy and admiration of the world, but had become a mere composite; and we were still in a transition state; and Jew, Turk, Infidel, jesuit, papist, protestant churchmen, and men of no religion at all, might sit side by side in every court and legislate for this once Christian and protestant land.[158]

Damascus both emphasised the need for a Jewish voice in English politics and increased the public demand for legislation which would put it there. At the July meeting the younger Greg asserted that England owed political equality to the Jews before it could properly assume a 'commanding' attitude of indignation towards the authorities in Syria: the Englishman must remove 'a mote in his own eye as disfiguring as the unsightly beam which obscures the vision of his Turkish brethren'.[159] The *Guardian* increased the tempo of its attack upon the 'particularly harsh and unjustifiable' laws which excluded Jews from Parliament: 'a remnant of the cruelty with which this industrious but ill-fated race were formerly treated in every Christian country'.[160] When in 1845 the Bishop of London argued in the House of Lords that the admission of Jews to Parliament could only destroy the 'Christian fabric' of the nation, the *Guardian* commented:

We trust that the Bishop's fear will be speedily realised, and that we shall soon obtain the practical recognition of the intelligible principle, that, let a man's religious opinions be what they may, they should not affect his rights as a citizen.[161]

The public vote of confidence in the Jewish community, and the growing support for its political struggle, only served to impress upon its members the need to live up to the image of themselves which had been projected, for it was an image which still did not quite match up to the reality. During 1841, when pro-Jewish sentiment was at its most fulsome, a man 'with dark hair and a Jewish cast of countenance' robbed the landlord of the New Inn;[162] 'a box of trinkets of various descriptions' offered for sale by Jacob Isaacs was found to include rings of gilded brass described as gold;[163] a Jewish clothes dealer on Shudehill received plate stolen from a Manchester jeweller;[164] Solomon Benzaquen embezzled money from Benjamin Hyam, by whom he was employed as a salesman and debt collector;[165] and another Isaacs, brother to the crooked pedlar, was involved in a serious robbery in Ashton-under-Lyne.[166] The growing need to eradicate these elements, and to provide pedlars with the means of earning a livelihood within the law, served to add further impetus to the Hebrew Association's work, and seemed to confirm the need for a small and coherent leadership of unimpeachable respectability and undoubted wealth.

V

In emphasising on a wider scale the need for Jewry to project a more 'modern' image, the Damascus Affair probably played some part in persuading those in London who had already sought improvements in the decorum of the synagogue to press for the immediate creation of a Reform congregation on the continental model. The group at Bevis Marks which had pressed without success for a synagogue in the West End and which had already expressed its sympathy for 'the changes introduced in the Reform synagogue in Hamburg and other places',[167] was joined by like-minded men from the Ashkenazi community, and on 15 April 1840, only a few days after news of the Damascus outrage reached London, a total of twenty-four London Jews determined to found a new synagogue in Burton Street, 'under the denomination British Jews', with a revised order of service.[168] Searching about for a minister of sufficient talent, learning and open-mindedness, the dissidents settled on David Woolf Marks, the young secretary and Second Reader at Seel Street in Liverpool, a former pupil of the Jews Free School in London, and a colleague of David Meyer Isaacs, who in 1841 occupied the position which Marks now vacated. Already dissatisfied with the small income from his 'multifarious' duties at Seel Street, Marks accepted the invitation of the Reformers

which whilst it will greatly extend the sphere of my usefulness, and place me in a more comfortable worldly position, will also, with God's blessing, enable me to cast off the abuses which have too long veiled our Holy Religion, and to render its practices and observances more in accordance with its pristine purity.[169]

With no sign of irritation at his departure to more radical territory, the Select Committee at Seel Street released him from part of his contract to enable him to commence his appointment at Burton Street in March 1841.[170] There he formed part of a committee of five, which in August 1841, issued a Sabbath prayer book, *Forms of Prayer*, which defined the liturgy of the new congregation, and which for the next twenty years formed the subject of bitter dispute throughout Anglo-Jewry.

By means of relatively minor changes, chiefly of omission, the Reform Prayer Book sought to erase from the Jewish liturgy those historical elements which were considered offensive to English taste or which appeared, in Marks' phrase, to pervert 'the pure principles of Judaism'.[171] The liturgy, he believed, was derived from a developing tradition, and those parts which owed their origins to an age of persecution 'now fast disappearing' had no place in the tolerant society of nineteenth-century England.[172] This in turn led him to a more fundamental attack upon Rabbinical jurisdiction and the Oral Law, since both seemed to restrict the power of a congregation to modify the ritual in keeping with the particular needs of its time and circumstances. The Oral Law—as enshrined in the *Mishna* and the Jerusalem and Babylonian Talmuds—had to be treated with respect, but it was not to be placed alongside the Bible as an infallible guide to Jewish practice. Marks wrote,

We know that these books are human compositions; and though we are content to accept with reverence from our post-biblical ancestors advice and instruction, we cannot *unconditionally* accept their laws.[173]

It was on this basis that the Reformers attacked the Second Days of Festivals which, for this reason, tended to become a central issue of dispute. The jurisdiction of the Chief Rabbi was unacceptable because it appeared to perpetuate the 'rabbinism' of Talmudic tradition, and to sustain upon it a stultifying uniformity of ritual practice. To the orthodox, the Chief Rabbi seemed to protect an unchanging body of tradition which provided the only bulwark against insidious assimilatory pressures; to Reformers the future of Judaism, particularly its social and political future, appeared to depend upon greater flexibility and a degree of accommodation to the values of the surrounding milieu. Although there remained a wide area for compromise, there was no one, in 1841–42, in a position to exploit it: Solomon Hirschel was old and infirm, the Sephardi Hahamate was vacant, and an appeal to continental rabbis was rendered impossible by their own division on similar issues. After a show of persuasion, Hirschel met what he regarded as a force subversive to Judaism, first with the threat, and then, on 22 January 1842, with the reality, of anathema. His denunciation of the new congregation was endorsed by the Sephardi *Av Beth Din*, and amounted to the imposition of a *cherem*, or ban of excommunication, upon the members of the West London Synagogue.

In Manchester, as in other provincial centres, the *cherem*, and the changes which had given rise to it, posed issues of fundamental importance. Although most congregations accepted the Chief Rabbi's ruling without demur, London's Western Synagogue refused to proclaim the *cherem* from the pulpit,[174] and Liverpool 'tore it up',[175] not because they sympathised with the changes made by the West London Synagogue, but because they did not believe that those changes warranted the action which had been taken or the schism which had resulted.[176] The wardens of the Western Synagogue wrote to Montefiore that many of their members

were entirely opposed to displaying any feeling of intolerance towards their brethren in the faith; deeming it advisable to conciliate rather than by hostile measures to irritate them and thus prevent the possibility of restoring union, peace and brotherly love in Israel.[177]

There is no evidence of Manchester's immediate reaction. Tradition holds that they too rejected the *cherem*,[178] and members were later to claim, correctly enough, that no record of the excommunication existed in the congregation's minutes, but in the absence of letter books covering the period, the question must remain an open one. What the evidence does reveal is the impact made by the emergence of Reform upon Manchester's attitude towards religious change.

There is nothing to suggest that prior to Reform the Manchester congregation did anything but accept the full authority of the Chief Rabbi. The only surviving letter of this period (from August 1836) calls upon Hirschel to examine the fitness for office of Samuel Heilbron of Rotterdam, a candidate for the positions of *shochet* and Reader at Halliwell Street.[179] When the Chief Rabbi confirmed the 'good account of his character' given in Heilbron's testimonials from Holland, he entered the office of Reader, but his appointment as *shochet* was delayed until he reached standards acceptable to Hirschel in 1840.[180] Although the congregation had given expression to 'progressive' tendencies during the period 1838–41 in modernising Jewish education and introducing regular sermons, there is no hint of any changes of which the Chief rabbi might have disapproved. The effect of Reform was probably to hasten changes which were already being considered by the Select Committee to improve the decorum and administrative efficiency of the synagogue. On 6 February 1842 the Free Members accepted changes in the synagogue's financial structure suggested by an 'assessment sub-committee' which had been asked to devise

such plans as will not only increase the income but conduce to the prosperity of the society and provide for the more just division of the expenses and outlay of the congregation.[181]

In a sweeping measure of rationalisation, compulsory offerings, fines for non-attendance, arbitrary seat rents, and the auctioning of honours were replaced by a revised scale of personal assessments closely related to the income of the seat-holders.[182] The changes involved rather more than simplified accounting and a 'fair and equitable' distribution of financial burdens. They also seemed 'likely to add to the proper and decorous observance of the service in the synagogue' by removing the occasion for noisy interruptions of the even and reverential flow of the liturgy.[183] The innovation was highly praised in the Jewish press[184] and was adopted soon afterwards by the Western Synagogue in London.[185] Later in the month, further steps which were taken specifically to tighten up decorum included the imposition of penalties on latecomers, a reduction in the number of *misheberachs* allowed to members 'called up' to the reading of the Law, and the vesting of the distribution of *mitzvaoth* in the wardens alone.[186] There change ended, and there is no hint in the synagogue minutes that any Free Member required anything more. The élite in Manchester was content to raise the quality of synagogal life with improvements which fell far short of Reform, and within the framework of a centralised rabbinical jurisdiction.

The Manchester programme of moderate improvement was more widely promulgated by Jacob Franklin, who in 1841 retired from business and left for

London, where he inaugurated the first successful Anglo-Jewish newspaper, the
Voice of Jacob,

a publication . . . for the promotion of the spiritual and general welfare of the Jews, by
the dissemination of intelligence on subjects affecting their interests, and by the advocacy and defence of their religious institutions.[187]

Impressed by the need for a 'rallying voice' at a time of crisis following the Damascus incident, the Reform schism and the repeated failure of Bills for the
Removal of Jewish Disabilities, Franklin offered a form of enlightened
orthodoxy as a basis of reunion and a point of convergence from which the
community might press its political demands. As a counterpoise to Reform, he
offered the changes which Manchester had already accomplished: greater
efficiency in the administration of congregational affairs, greater decorum,
English sermons, and the removal of such 'unseemly interpolations' as the public sale of honours. Unlike the Reformers, Franklin believed that Judaism
could earn the respect of the Gentile world without abandoning its traditional
orthodoxy. He possessed what an unkind obituarist described as 'a rigidity of
orthodox principles more apt to break than bend',[188] but his views were probably representative of a broad upper-middle stratum of Anglo-Jewish families
which had risen to modest wealth from the rock base of peddling and petty retailing in a less tolerant age.

A much more radical but less representative position was adopted by a
regular contributor to the *Voice of Jacob*, Franklin's new friend, Tobias Theodores, whose social and intellectual roots lay in the Jewish mercantile community of Berlin. Taking up a controversy which began in the correspondence
columns of the paper, in 1842 Theodores published a pamphlet in which he set
out

to consider calmly . . . the force of proofs, positive and negative, adduced in substantia-
tion of the divine origin of the Talmudic traditions.[189]

While doubting the accuracy of the charge that the 'British Jews' of Burton
Street had in fact rejected the divine inspiration of the Oral Law, he set out
to suggest that an acceptance of Judaism did not require 'the ponderous support of the Talmud'.[190] There were, he believed, many valid varieties of
Jewish orthodoxy, and what he called 'rabbinical Judaism', with its emphasis
on oral tradition, was neither more nor less acceptable than the religion of the
Karaites, who rejected the Talmud as a matter of principle.[191] His sharpest
criticism was reserved for rabbis who used the Talmud to bolster up a religious
authority, the historicity of which he doubted.[192] He concluded

We are far from believing that the careful preservation, the study of, or a respect for
the Talmud, can be productive of anything but good to Israel; but we feel convinced,

that the canonisation, and the use made of the Talmud by the rabbis has entailed injury on the best interests of our religion. We see, that wherever the Jewish character rises, the importance of the Talmud is proportionately lowered; and we know that where the Talmud reigns paramount, the moral, intellectual, and social emancipation of the Jews is deplorably retarded.[193]

The passage underlined the dichotomy of the Reform case. On the one hand, Theodores argued, from a conviction shared by the German Reformers, that the Talmud was not divinely inspired, and for that reason was dispensable; on the other, from expediency, that it was a barrier to the cultural, and, implicitly, to the political progress of the Jews. The duality of the argument lent some substance to the fear of the orthodox that Reformers were, in reality, subordinating religion to social and political objectives. But whatever its weaknesses, the pamphlet marked the emergence of Theodores as a key figure in the world of Reform, and a major English representative of the German *Wissenschaft*: in two years he had moved from outside the Jewish pale to the centre of religious controversy. He did not regard himself, however, as a heretic, for it was also in 1842 that he became a member at Halliwell Street. At that time it was still possible to believe that the views which he represented would be absorbed into a 'renovated' orthodox framework, and he perhaps felt that he could best play his part within the synagogue, by converting a desire for modest improvements into more radical inclinations.

It does not seem likely that Theodores found much support in Manchester in the early 1840s. There was perhaps as little sympathy for the opinions of an intellectual nonenity, Michael Hart Simonson, a former teacher at the Birmingham Jews School, who in 1845 was appointed secretary at Halliwell Street. In the previous year Simonson had produced a pamphlet[194] which, while supposedly setting out to defend Second Days of Festivals 'upon strictly Pentateuchal grounds',[195] was in fact a mindless defence of rabbinic tradition and established custom. Of the critics of Second Days, he wrote:

And among the many dissenting parties in matters of religion, there is none so injurious to its cause as that party, which openly sets at defiance a rite, which is as old as the particular state of existence of that sect, tribe, or nation itself, to which *they* belong;[196]

of the Oral Law,

We have no right . . . to have the slightest doubt of the veracity of our pious ancestors and wise Rabbins . . . On the contrary, we should be convinced that it was founded upon philosophical reasoning, critical research, and upon true, divine principles, in accordance with scripture . . . our Rabbins, those acute biblical critics, must have had weighty reasons and substantial arguments [for Second Days] . . . On the varied expressions of Moses, our critical rabbis built and erected lasting monuments.[197]

It was probably the case that in 1844–45 the community as a whole occupied the orthodox middle ground between the radicalism of Theodores and the safe obscurantism of Simonson. At all events, the controversy between 'Talmudist and Anti-Talmudist', to use Simonson's phrase,[198] was temporarily stilled by the death of Hirschel in October 1842. Strife was suspended during the long interregnum, as each side hoped that a new Chief Rabbi would provide peace on its terms, a hope realised for the orthodox by the election of Nathan Marcus Adler of Hanover, who had received the Manchester vote,[199] in 1844, and his arrival in England in July 1845.

VI

Manchester's early response to Reform reflected the balance of social forces within the community of the early 1840s. The communal leadership was in effect a close alliance between the shopkeepers who had founded the synagogue at Halliwell Street and guided its fortunes through the 1820s and early 1830s, and the merchant immigrants of the period after 1834. The shopkeepers had created the oligarchic structure, and the merchants had superimposed upon it their more dynamic influence. The Hebrew Association was the major achievement of this fusion of interests, based as it was upon the drive of Franklin and the 'purse' of Lucas. What held the Association together and determined its policies was the common belief of its leaders that the community would best be served by a sustained attempt to raise the cultural and social quality of life, as a prelude to emancipation. The aspirations of the merchant élite and the anxieties set in motion by the Damascus Affair seemed to confirm this analysis. Beyond this, Reform was a luxury they could not afford, for it seemed calculated, on the London evidence, to create dissension when the occasion demanded concerted action. It was probably also the case that the radical ideas of Theodores, the cultural aspirations of German merchants from the milieu of Reform, and the social and political ambitions of men like Lucas and Micholls—ingredients which in other circumstances might well have created Manchester Reform during 1842—were held in check by a strong shopkeeping middle class, chiefly of pedlar origin, for whom rigid orthodoxy of observance had once provided the only form of social security, and who could not have created communal life in the first place without rabbinical guidance which was available, on terms they could afford, only from the Chief Rabbi. In the early 1840s it was this group—rising high on the flood-tide of urban retailing—which provided the community with its sheet anchor of orthodoxy, which muffled the heresies of Theodores and retained the sophistication of merchant princes within an observant structure not available, for example, in Bradford or Leeds.

The community appeared to them, and to their more plutocratic friends, to demand patriarchal guidance and the unceasing protection of the high social and moral quality of the synagogue's membership. This the 'select' system seemed to provide, and prior to 1844 there was no move to supplant it. The modifications of communal life which seemed necessary in the interests of political equality and social prestige did not include a democratisation of the synagogue: in London, an analogous situation existed, in which the over-whelming need to preserve the community's reputation appeared to require the cautious guidance of Montefiore and an inner cabal of Anglo-Jewish aristo-crats. Only at the Western Synagogue was the Reform crisis followed by the abolition of privileged membership and the opening of Honorary Office to every seat-holder,[200] perhaps because it seemed unlikely that so sophisticated a congregation would attract disreputable applicants. Congregational élitism was also a reflection of the sharpening of class divisions in English society, for middle-class Jews tended to expect within the synagogue the same social status to which they aspired outside it. At the Mechanics' Institute Jacob Franklin was one of those who in November 1840 opposed the creation of a 'general newsroom' on the grounds that it was the beginning of a move to provide the 'working-class' members with dangerous 'instruction in politics': if this continued, he believed, the Institute might well 'become a theatre for dis-cussion of political subjects, and controversial theology'.[201] The Franklins wanted no more political subjects and controversial theology in the synagogue than in the Institute: the role of the rank and file in both was to hold their deferential silence and accept the leadership of their cultural betters.

5 The retail trades, 1840–45

The effectiveness of the shopkeeping bourgeoisie as religious ballast was increased by their growing economic importance in the early 1840s, and particularly after Manchester emerged from prolonged slump during 1843. The depression which had commenced with the collapse of the country's overseas trade in 1837 reached the point of its greatest severity during 1841–42. The number of local bankruptcies rose to unique heights, many factories closed down, and the current of townward migration was temporarily checked. When William Cooke Taylor visited the Lancashire cotton districts during 1842 he found them labouring 'under severe and unprecedented distress',[1] and he was surprised to find that so little working-class violence had arisen out of the 'insanity of despair'.[2] The reason, he supposed, was an underlying confidence in the factory system, the benefits of which were recognised even by those to whom it now denied employment, since once in the town they preferred to

submit to the pressure of hunger, and all its attendant sufferings, with an iron endurance which nothing can bend, rather than be carried back to an agricultural district.[3]

The strength of Cooke Taylor's faith in the 'efficacy' of modern industry led him to believe that Manchester's undeniable social ills were the product not of a settled population of factory operatives but of a 'fluctuating'. pool of 'immigrants and strangers' not yet adequately subjected to the influences of a factory economy.[4] It was these 'strangers'—particularly the Irish—who filled the workhouse and the Night Asylum during the bad years; it was they who were responsible for the increase of crime, the large number of disorderly beer houses, 'the high rate of mortality and the low condition of morals'.[5] Other local commentators—like the 'member of the Athenaeum' who edited Leon Faucher's description of Manchester—shared this myopic but comforting assessment of Manchester's Irish immigrants:

They congregate together, and form in the town a number of distinct communities, each of which is a nucleus for the generation and diffusion of human miasma.[6]

They were said to lack civic pride, to be stupid and lazy, passive towards authority, 'torpid' in their judgements, thriftless, improvident, disorderly, dirty, and excessively radical in their political allegiance,[7] a diagnosis which glossed over the disreputable element in Jewish as well as English society, and which threw into relief the exactly contrary virtues of settled Jewish traders.

During 1843 the trade of the town began to show signs of a recovery which was complete by the summer of 1845. The sepulchral gloom of the Manchester Exchange, described in graphic terms by Cooke Taylor in 1842, gave way to 'feverish speculation'[8] as Manchester became, in Faucher's phrase, the 'diligent spider'[9] at the centre of a growing web of prosperous industrial satellites, efficiently linked by road and rail. By 1844 the population of Manchester and Salford was around 350,000 (perhaps 15 per cent of Irish origin)[10] and a total of over a million persons was believed to inhabit the industrial districts which lay within twelve miles of the Manchester Exchange.[11] S. L. Behrens, Amschel, Micholls and Lucas were amongst the merchants and manufacturers who in March 1845 unsuccessfully requested Manchester bankers not to restrict their hours of business, in the light of 'the great increase now going on in the trade and commerce of this large town';[12] according to their petition, improved road and rail communications with London had made Friday afternoons 'as available in a commercial and banking sense as any other in the week'.[13] Manchester's Jewish merchants also threw their weight behind the struggle for Free Trade which would ultimately, so it was believed, open the world's markets without restriction to Manchester manufacturers. In February 1843 Bauer was one of the platform party for a mass-meeting of the Anti-Corn Law League which pledged its faith in Cobden.[14] In the following November, S. L. Behrens was one of the conveners of a meeting at the Town Hall which launched an appeal on behalf of the League for £100,000.[15] In July 1846, following the Repeal of the Corn Laws and the first national victory of the 'Manchester School', Lucas joined the canvassing committee of the Cobden National Tribute Fund, to which Behrens gave £50 and Sichel £30.[16]

I

A less obvious, but if anything a more substantial, result of economic recovery was a dramatic expansion of the local retail market. According to Cooke Taylor, shopkeepers dependent 'on the supply of commodities to the operative population' were amongst those hardest hit by the depression,[17] and the shopkeepers themselves, meeting in Manchester in June 1842, had no doubt

that existing distress amongst our body is greater than was ever before experienced; that trade has fallen off to an extent without parallel; that the profits on such restricted trade have also been greatly reduced.[18]

They sought 'legislative interposition' to remedy what they saw as an 'alarming' situation. In particular, Cooke Taylor wrote, 'no class of men in business complain more loudly of the pressures of time' than pawnbrokers, for, while there was no shortage of pledges, there was also no market for those which were not redeemed.[19] The shortage of liquid assets had taken some pawnbrokers to the verge of bankruptcy. The distress of the shopkeeper was perhaps as exaggerated as the contentment of the working classes, but it was at least true that the relatively slow pace of retail expansion in the late 1830s and early 1840s underwent a marked acceleration during the period 1843–45, when competition by advertisement between Manchester's retail tradesmen reached new peaks of bombast and invective. These were 'puffing times', according to Hyam,[20] whose own 'puff' was more successful than most, and considerable gains were available to those who were prepared to study, to meet, and to manipulate the tastes not only of middle-class consumers, but of the artisans of the cotton industry, whose real incomes continued to rise with the level of the trade.[21]

This was particularly true of tailoring, the retail industry in which Jews were most conspicuously involved. The enumerators' books for the census of 1841 suggest that eighty-eight Jewish persons, or a little over a third of all Jews then engaged in remunerative employment, were shopkeepers, and that of these forty-four were in the clothing trade (thirty-two as tailors or dressmakers, six as furriers, three as boot and shoe dealers, two as hatters, one as a 'clothes cleaner'), twenty-six in jewellery and hardware (seventeen as jewellers and watchmakers, two as dealers in Birmingham and Sheffield goods, three as opticians and four as pawnbrokers), and nine in stationery (four as general stationers, three as quill dressers, one as a dealer in steel pens, and one as a book-binder). There were also nine general dealers.

In tailoring, the pace was set by Benjamin Hyam, who on 21 April 1841 moved from St Mary's Gate to 'spacious and airy' premises at 26 Market Street, then one of the major retail centres of Western Europe, and renamed it the *Pantechnethica*, in mock deference to the erudition of his clients. His removal at the same time from rooms above his shop to a new house in Higher Broughton marked perhaps the earliest stage in the transfer of mass tailoring from retailer–craftsmen living above their premises and keeping in contact with their workmen through speaking-tubes, to capitalist entrepreneurs exercising a remote control over distribution through a network of travellers and branch enterprises. Hyam then had four branches—in Birmingham, Bristol, Colchester and Bury St Edmunds—and a stock in Manchester alone worth over £25,000. A minor law suit of October 1841 revealed that the clients of his Manchester shop included a cotton broker from Stockport, a surgeon from

Bury, and a cotton manufacturer from Rochdale.[22] Although he offered ready-made suits from 11s and caps for 2d each, his main appeal was to social ambition in a class-conscious society: 'A small income no barrier to a respectable

FIGURE 5 Hyam's *Pantechnethica* in Market Street.

appearance'; clothing as 'the criterion of gentility . . . the surest ladder to fame and fortune'; coats at 15s 'peculiarly adapted . . . to the higher classes of society'.[23] It became increasingly easy to believe his claim to be 'the cheapest and most extensive tailor in the world', to hold 'the largest stock of Ready-made Clothing . . . in the kingdom', and to control an 'Export business to all parts of the world'.[24] In 1847 he moved his 'bespoke department' to special premises in King Street. The number of his branches had risen to six by 1843, ten by 1849 and thirteen by 1851, three of them in the West End of London, their operations co-ordinated by regular April meetings at his warehouse in Pall Mall, Manchester, of managers, salesmen, travellers, collectors and cashiers, who occasionally rented seats for the Passover festival at the synagogue in Halliwell Street.

In the course of the 1840s, Hyam's example was followed by several of his Manchester co-religionists, although never on quite so grand a scale. By 1848 four other Jewish outfitters had shops in Market Street: Lewis Levy, a newcomer to the community, who in 1843 had entered the trade in the premises of the Golden Canister, a former beer parlour in Oldham Street, Jacob Casper, formerly of Hanging Ditch, and Elias and Reuben Levy, the sons of Joseph Levy, who had been established in Manchester as a slop seller, jeweller, and pawnbroker since the war years. Joseph Levy himself ran the successful Bee Hive Outfitting Establishment at 31 and 33 Shudehill. Joel and Adam Casper also remained on Shudehill, where they offered 'unassuming talent' in place of the empty 'puff' of larger concerns. Abraham Lipman's Emporium of Fashion, once in the Old Town, moved in 1847 to Stevenson Square. Another Reuben Levy opened a large shop at 17 Piccadilly, opposite the Royal Infirmary, in 1846. Joseph Braham's shop at Hyde's Cross earned the price of Gorton Hall, a large mansion on the Hyde Road, where in 1851 he and his son, Isaac, were enumerated as 'landed proprietors'. Outside Manchester, Joseph Slazenger Moss of Warrington, son of the one-time umbrella dealer, ran a chain of shops in Bury, Bolton, Preston, Wigan and Heywood, which he inherited from his brother, Ralph, who was killed by a fall from a horse in 1839 while riding home—'in a state of intoxication'—from the Manchester Races.[25] All these men were former dealers in old clothes, and the effect of their enterprise was not simply a conquest of a substantial part of the clothing market, but also the virtual elimination of the Jewish slop seller, whose mantle fell upon the Irish. The clauses of the Police Act of 1844 which required dealers in second-hand goods to have licensed premises were held in abeyance for six years to allow new Irish immigrants 'without a local habitation' to survive on the brickfields of the town by purchasing and bartering a few articles of clothing.[26]

Although there were Gentile tailoring enterprises in Manchester equal to all but Hyam's, the inroads made by Jewish entrepreneurs into their actual or potential market added the occasional anti-Semitic note to what one tailor described as 'the almost terrific *breakers* of a Manchester competition'.[27] In its most usual form, the supposed quality-wear of craftsmen was contrasted with the 'vile old rag shoddy' and 'slop' of Jewish mass-producers. In 1845 Hyam's claim to have rescued the common man from the exorbitant prices of the traditional master-tailor drew from Joseph Mitchell, whose Fair Cloth Trade Hall was also on Market Street, a vitriolic reply which linked 'Jew tailoring' with the topical evils of the Corn Law.[28] Far from alleviating the lot of the common man, the Jews had thrived upon the poverty of industrial civilisation:

Then ragged became man,
The tailor from his work-board was driven;
And 'Old Clo' then came in,
With his 'unshaven chin',
To 'clout what was tattered and riven.

And Newland of old,
With Goldsmid so bold,
Stuck their fingers in every man's 'till';
The Monmouth-street peg shops,
And Jews with their 'rag shops',
Sang 'tol lol' to the starving corn bill.

O! then you soon found,
How much you'd lost ground
By corn-laws and clothing 'Jew-made';
Now upset the one,
And the other's undone,
When you turn fully to free and fair trade.

Hyam's coats—'now so blazoned before us at 15s and boasted of as the dress of the most elite'—were, Mitchell thought, 'worse than Workhouse Greys'. Henry Hewitt, another Market Street tailor, boasted that every garment he sold was made 'on his premises, or at his manufactory in the country', and not mass-produced by 'slop sellers'.[29] There was, of course, every reason for Hyam's competitors to feel apprehensive: within a decade his expansion had embraced Hewitt's shop and driven Mitchell out of business.

Throughout the 1840s Jewish tailors kept up a fierce competition for the lucrative middle-class market, not only with their Gentile rivals, but, perhaps even more bitterly, between themselves. Manchester's various Levy and Casper families publicly disassociated themselves from one another in the columns of the *Guardian* so that the advertisement of one should not add to the trade of a rival. A propaganda war embraced not only prices, styles and quality, but also inventions such as (in 1847) Lewis Levy's 'surprising piece of mechanism' for measuring 'even the most disproportionate'.[30] An act of 1844 which extended copyright law to the patterns of articles manufactured solely 'for the purpose of utility' added a new dimension to advertisements, with crests and patent numbers, and also a new bone of contention. A waterproof coat of 'fairy lightness' registered by Hyam in 1846 sold 3,600 in three months at two guineas each. However, in March 1849 his attempt to register a 'scarf-wrapper vest'—a waistcoat, without buttons, hooks or eyes, supposedly 'worn by the Prince Consort'—was successfully challenged in court by Elias and Reuben Levy as an act of piracy upon their own 'Commercial Vest and Bosom Friend'.[31] After a hearing at the Borough Court in which both waistcoats were solemnly produced and compared, the Levy brothers used the *Guardian* to advertise 'A TRIUMPHANT SUCCESS'.[32]

Although a handful of tailors stressed in their advertisements that they employed only first-class workers on their premises, and did not send work 'to a distance, to be slurred over by women and children in factories and associated poorhouses',[33] the age of mass-tailoring was based in the main upon an underworld of sweated workshops and 'homework'. The three hundred tailors who came out on strike in October 1845 were seeking only the right to work in their masters' shops

instead of in their own badly ventilated dwellings, which were rendered still more uncomfortable by the system of home-working.[34]

In particular, they objected to a system by which master-tailors gave out work in large quantities to 'a sort of middlemen, called "sweaters", who get it done by men and women at starvation prices'.[35] The strike was every bit as militant as that of 1833–34: several employers and their 'knobsticks' were the victims of assaults which resulted in court action; a petition which the Union sent to Parliament called for a committee of enquiry into the 'sanitary condition' of journeymen tailors;[36] workers' co-operatives were seriously considered. Again, however, the courts and the press supported the masters in their refusal to negotiate or to submit the matter to arbitration, and after eight months the men had little choice but to withdraw their demands and go back to work, many to find (as they deserved, according to the *Guardian*) that their jobs had already been taken up.[37] Although Hyam's name was not mentioned in connection with these events, it was coupled with that of 'Moses of London'[38] in February 1850, when Manchester operatives met at the Comet Inn in Lower King Street to drum up support for a local branch of the Journeyman Tailors Society through which they hoped to end the 'system of slop-work' by checking 'the rapid and giant strides of the hydra-headed monster, competition'.[39] Most tailors employed cutters at relatively high wages and then gave out their pieces to be made up by sweated labour for a pittance. Joseph Levy's cutter was employed in 1842 at £2 15s a week, which was raised to £3 when he agreed to move his lodgings from Collyhurst into Manchester.[40] In September 1849 Hyam's foreman cutter, Matthew Kean, had built up sufficient capital to open up as a clothier on his own account in King Street. It was Hyam's custom to employ co-religionists in managerial functions, and for the rest to rely upon Gentile artisans and labourers.

Following the hard times reported by Cooke Taylor in 1842, prosperity returned to the pawnbroker in the mid-1840s. Although possessed of none of the dynamic or competitive qualities of the clothing trades, pawnbroking played a major part in the life of the working man, particularly as a source of short-term loans, and for this reason alone it was a profitable line of trade at a time of regular employment. According to Engels, who was in Manchester as a commercial clerk in the early 1840s, it was common for a working man to pledge 'vast quantities of furniture, Sunday clothes (if they had any) and crockery' in mid-week, only to redeem them again, every Saturday evening, after receiving his wages.[41] The discovery that one of Hyam's porters had pledged stolen goods worth £200 with twenty-one pawnbrokers for a total of only £25 provides some indication of the profit to be made from the sale of unredeemed pledges.[42] Other reported crimes suggest that one of Hyam's suits might be pledged for as much as 24s with an honest pawnbroker, a good quality cap for 1s, a watch worth £7 10s for around £2.[43] Pawn tickets themselves became a form of currency and a medium of exchange in working-class life, as liable to forgery as bank-notes.[44] The pawnshop also played a part in the life of the country pedlar, perhaps an increasing part, as an occasional source of cheap stock and as the means of tiding over a bad spell.[45] There are examples of pedlars pawning watches from their own trays.[46] Joseph Golding, a Jewish hawker living in Salford during 1842–43, was 'accustomed to getting a tolerably good livelihood by buying unredeemed pledges, in articles of gold, silver, etc. and reselling them'.[47] The police used pawnbrokers as informants and expected them to arrest suspects and to report stolen goods.[48] When in April 1846 they retained a solicitor to answer the charge that 'as a body they encouraged felonies', Manchester pawnbrokers were able to instance many occasions on which they had taken the initiative in the detection of crime, including the arrangement of conferences with the Chief Superintendent of police, Richard Beswick.[49] In return they expected the law to enforce their rates of interest.[50]

Although occasionally at odds with the police, always open to abuse, and rarely as wealthy as the successful ready-made tailor, the Jewish pawnbroker was a man of solid substance who commanded respect within and beyond the community. John Michael Isaac of Chapel Street, Salford, married Abraham Franklin's sister-in-law, Sarah Ayrane, in 1842, at Halliwell Street, a ceremony for which Jacob Franklin, then in London, wrote a 'nuptial song'.[51] In March 1849 he was elected an assessor for the Blackfriars Ward in Salford, a post he declined at first under the erroneous impression that it required him to swear an oath 'on the true faith of a Christian'.[52] In March 1850 he was nominated, although not elected, to the Board of Guardians of Salford Union.[53] Philip Solomon and Israel Jacobs, barely literate Polish immigrants when they settled in Manchester as slop sellers in 1828, passed through tailoring into pawnbroking during the succeeding decade, when they employed two orphan apprentices farmed out by the Manchester Poor Law Union at their two branches, in Shudehill and Oldham Street.[54] In October 1842 robbers who entered the shop in Shudehill through the ceiling of an adjacent cellar made away with £35 in cash and £1,000 in gold and silver watches, jewellery and plate.[55] Solomon and Jacobs later insured these premises for £1,500 (£150 for household goods, £800 for pledges, £200 on sale stock, £350 on fixtures) and after a subsequent fire their claim on the Phoenix Fire Office for £1,041 was upheld by the Queen's Bench.[56] The only time they are known to have received stolen goods was when they were confronted by two men armed 'with pistols, powder, balls, and percussion caps' who demanded a loan on the strength of plate stolen from a house in Leeds.[57] They used their contacts within the congregation and their standing with the police to shield Mark Jacobs, the son of one, the son-in-law of the other, when in 1844 he faked the robbery of his clothes shop in Ashton-under-Lyne to salvage a little cash from his impending bankruptcy, and, when he escaped arrest by a hair's-breadth, they packed him off to Baltimore, from which town he later made his way to the goldfields of California.[58]

A negative indication of the expansion of shopkeeping was the continuing decline in fortune of the old-established, independent country hawker, whose lot had been gradually worsening since the early 1830s. The more resilient moved into retailing, often very successfully; others took to urban peddling, probably more extensive in Lancashire than in any other county in England;[59] but most appear to have sunk into obscurity amongst the rotting timbers of the Old Town, for so long the centre of their activity. Of the forty-six hawkers and pedlars in Manchester on Census Night 1841, only six subsequently became settled shopkeepers in the town. All but nine were living in a network of ten streets—'one of the filthiest suburbs of the town', according to Wheeler[60]—centred on the shabby pubs and lodging houses of Hanover Street, Balloon Street and Beswick's Row; eight at the lodging house of Ann Moore in Leadenall Street, two more in the Old Boar's Head at Hyde's Cross, and five at the Nagg's Head in Hanover Street, including an 'artist', Wolf Missel of Ipswich, and a 'comedian', Moses Soloman. Esther Smith's lodging house in Hanover Street included a Jewish pedlar and eighteen other guests, all of them Irish, and other Jewish hawkers figured amongst the guests of the Irish lodging-house keepers, Alice Brogan and Patrick Burke. It was here that the supposed threats to English and to Jewish society co-existed; here were the disreputable elements awaiting conversion to honourable professions through the medium of the Jews School. The local press was punctuated by the petty crimes of ped-lars like Tobias Franklin, caught selling 'spurious gold dust'—to a Jewish shop-keeper in Shudehill—in 1843.[61] Joseph Golding, the salesman of unredeemed pledges, took to drink and violence which in January 1843, drove his wife Amelia to cut her throat with a carving knife, leaving her children on the parish and the synagogue.[62] The communal leaders acted predictably. Sichel appeared in court to recommend Golding for three months' hard labour for neglect;[63] the children, after being supported in turn by the Manchester Union and private subscription, were in 1847 boarded out with a member of the community at a fixed cost.[64] The episode is symbolic not only of the breakdown of hawking, but of the need for the community to tidy away the pieces.

Otherwise, evidence of Jewish activity in shopkeeping is largely subjective and impressionistic. There are indications of a competition between furriers quite as fierce as that which divided tailors. Samuel Leon, of the Old Fur Estab-lishment in Deansgate, fought a running battle with his brother-in-law, Samuel Isaac, of the New, to the point of having him arrested for alleged

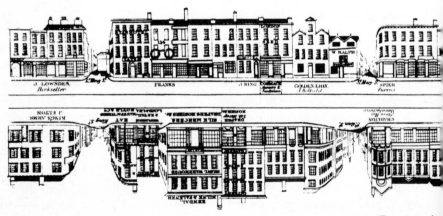

FIGURE 6   Deansgate in

theft.[65] In the jewellery trade the emphasis was upon the search for new commodities to meet the growing demand for domestic luxuries—American glassware, 'philosophical toys', daguerrotypes, electro-plated tableware, 'Irish bog ornaments' (from Isaac Simmons), and so on. Samuel Phillips of London, a dealer in carpets, wall coverings and household ornaments, arrived in Manchester in 1842 and set up a warehouse in Oldham Street, where he also kept a gang of workmen for house decoration and upholstery.[66] David Goodman was the first Jew in Manchester to import and retail tobacco, cigars and snuff, from 1840. At least two Jewish retailers speculated in land and shops other than their own in the city centre. In June 1845 Ansell Spier, the furrier, built four shops for letting on a site in Cateaton Street.[67] Joseph Braham built four more at the junction of St Mary's Gate and Deansgate, which was re-developed during 1845 to remove an 'awkward projecting corner'.[68] In March 1847 Braham was one of seventeen property owners and lessees of the town centre who contributed £1,614—Braham himself gave £107—towards the purchase of the toll-bar on Blackfriar's Bridge, to provide easy access from Salford to the shops in Market Street and Deansgate,[69] while John Michael Isaac contributed to the same cause to ease the flow in the other direction.[70]

For all its enterprise and inventiveness, Jewish retailing expanded almost exclusively on the narrow base established by itinerant traders of the eighteenth century. This was partly, perhaps, because family tradition was not yet adequately counterbalanced by the pull of educational influences and wider experience of an open society. The family of Jacob Franks may be taken as an example, although perhaps an extreme one, for of the eleven boys amongst his twenty-four children, all but three became opticians in their turn, in Manches-

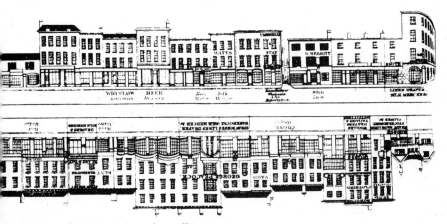

ng the shops of Jacob Franks and Ansell Spier.

ter and elsewhere, usually after serving a family apprenticeship in their father's business, from 1839 located at 114 Deansgate. Louis Franks (born 1818) travelled in the eastern counties, where in 1839 he invented a 'Mechanical Horse'—a proto-bicycle 'of stout wood, tough iron and bold brass'—on which he covered circuits of up to forty miles a day at a maximum speed of ten miles per hour.[71] In 1843 he opened a shop in Leeds.[72] The case-book of Henry Franks (born 1824) shows that he commenced travelling in 1840 in Cambridge-shire before opening a shop in Whitefriars, Hull, in 1842.[73] When Jacob Franks died on a trip to Dublin in 1846, his Manchester business was taken over by his wife, Amelia, and his two eldest sons, Abraham,[74] who remained in Deansgate, and his half-brother, Joseph, who opened a branch in Market Street. Other families had comparable experiences. Of Jacob Nathan's sons, all but one became opticians, jewellers and silversmiths, Elias, the eldest, as con-sulting optician to the Manchester Eye Hospital; the sons of Joseph Levy, of the Bee Hive, were all tailors; Simon Joseph's sons, Morris and Israel, became furriers in their turn; Ansell Spier's son, Joseph, received the royal appoint-ment as a furrier in 1849. The 'Jewish trades' were also sufficiently flexible to absorb immigrants at any level of capital and experience, since each rep-resented, in effect, a continuum from the pedlar's tray to the substantial shop or warehouse.

II

The development of the professions in the Manchester Jewish milieu ran paral-lel to that of shopkeeping, with which they had much in common. Like the re-tail trades, the professions developed with a market which could afford them. They were competitive in the way of shopkeeping, particularly in their least skilled branches, where dentists compared the merits of their artificial teeth, and chiropodists publicised their references. As in retailing, the unskilled or semi-skilled itinerant was giving way under the pressure of urban growth to the settled, experienced and sometimes qualified practitioner. The professions grew more slowly than the shops, because the market for them was more nar-rowly based, and because few provincial Jews of the mid-1840s possessed the educational background which professional status demanded. None the less, by 1844 Manchester possessed the core of a Jewish professional class, particu-larly in medicine and dentistry.

By the early 1840s most of the travelling opticians, dentists, and chiropo-dists of an earlier age had either proved their worth and settled down as shop-keepers and surgeons or else had sunk, with their hawker companions, into an underworld of petty crime, itinerant quackery and dingy lodging houses. Abraham Abrahams, the son of a Bath optician, who moved to Liverpool during the war years, and paid regular visits to Manchester in the 1820s, in the following decade was the president of the Liverpool congregation responsible for the introduction of sermons in English. In 1841 he established a branch of his Liverpool business in Cross Street, Manchester, in partnership with the well-known instrument maker, John Dancer.[75] The typical relic of an older order was the Jewish 'lurcher' whose case-book was quoted by Felix Folio in 1858:

No. 76, Sakery Moses, one of our tribe. Sickness, bad ies, age 57. Fisik, a bottle of my red drops; ped me I shillin, for he wouldn't pay any more; for which reson I med it strong enough to blind him.[76]

In the dingiest lodging-house district of the Old Town, the Census of 1841 revealed Myer Polack, a self-styled 'doctor of medicine' in Timber Street, and a Jewish 'druggist' in Hanover Street, surrounded by their counterparts in commerce. Only a handful of the most resilient, like the optician Samuel Solomons—'Licensed Hawker 1242A'—kept their heads above water by extensive advertising, in Solomon's case, in the *Guardian*, and by a rapid distribution of their services by gig or 'whitechapel'. It was Solomons' custom to hire a temporary surgery in Princess Street, Manchester, and to offer more occasional consultations at pubs in Altrincham, Stockport, Bury and other towns of the cotton belt.[77]

In Manchester, the movement of Jews into the professions had begun when Jacob Nathan sent his son, Lewis Henry, to Manchester Grammar School during the war years, and on to London to train as a surgeon.[78] He was back in Manchester by 1828, when he was living with his father in St George's Street. Isaac Abraham Franklin returned from Edinburgh, also as a surgeon, in 1835, and had entered private practice by 1838, when he was called to attend the victim of an accident in Great Ducie Street.[79] The least ambitious, the most tolerant and the most gentle of the Franklins, Isaac was the outstanding Jewish professional man of the 1840s, earning equal distinction within the profession, the town and the community. In 1835 he replaced Jacob Franks as official *mohel* of the community when Solomon Hirschel, the Chief Rabbi, admitted him to the 'brotherhood of circumcisors'.[80] Later he was to write:

It has ever been my principle to regard the office of Moel as a sacred and religious one, in the discharge of which I have been activated by no motives of pecuniary profit,[81]

and when called upon to help out the Liverpool congregation he charged only two guineas a case to cover his expenses.[82] He offered his free services to the Hebrew Philanthropic Society, of which he was Secretary, and in 1841 received the public thanks of its committee for his 'valuable services . . . to the indigent sick of the town'.[83] He was secretary of the Jews School from its foundation until his death (at a school prize-giving) in 1880.[84] In 1842 he appeared on the local medical scene as the chairman of a meeting at the Athenaeum called specifically to refute the spurious 'neurohypnology' of a fellow surgeon, James Braid of St Peter's Square.[85] In 1844 he became one of the joint secretaries of the Manchester Medical Society.[86] In August 1849, on the recommendation of the Manchester Board of Guardians, he was appointed temporary medical officer at the Canal Street Hospital during the epidemic of Asiatic cholera which swept through the town during the summer and autumn of that year.[87] From the late 1840s until his retirement he worked from a surgery in Long Millgate, in the poorest part of the Old Town. In religion, he held to the strict orthodox tradition of his family, but at times of controversy he was to be found most often building, or trying to build, a bridge between opposing groups in the interests of moderation.

In dentistry, Barnett Moss (or Moses Barnett, as he was known to the synagogue), who had been practising in Manchester since the late 1820s, was overshadowed by two immigrants, both of whom arrived in 1835. Louis Berend, who had migrated to Liverpool from Hanover, with his brother Samuel, in 1823, advertised the opening of his surgery in St George's Street, Manchester, on the front page of the *Guardian*;[88] within a decade he had a country residence at River Lodge, Barton, on the road to Eccles. Frederick Eskell arrived with a similar flourish, probably from London, and established himself at 18 Cooper Street, opposite the Mechanics' Institute, where he claimed that his 'mineral terro-metallic fillings . . . of incorrodible stone . . . without wire or springs' did away 'with the barbarous method of extraction', and guaranteed his artificial teeth 'to bite through the hardest substance without pain or inconvenience'.[89] His prices ranged from a minimum of five guineas to £25 for the finest and most natural quality, on gold plate. Whether or not because of the competition of his co-religionists and other rivals, Barnett Moss fell into debt, tried to recoup his losses on the stock market, and in 1845 cut his throat when the bottom dropped out of his shares in the Manchester, Birmingham and Welsh Continuation Railway.[90] There was the element of the quack in Berend and Eskell, particularly the latter, but there was no gainsaying their solid wealth, which placed them, with Nathan, Franklin and Tobias Theodores, on a par with the solid middle ranks of the shopkeeping bourgeoisie.

III

One of the more striking consequences of the expansion of retail trading was the gradual creation of Jewish 'inner suburbs' in north Manchester between the town centre and the mansions of the rich in Higher Broughton and Cheetham Hill. In south Manchester, the close proximity of the Little Ireland slum in the valley of the Medlock to the expensive villas which began in Grosvenor Square inhibited the settlement there of men in search of comfortable, spacious and reasonably cheap houses within easy travelling range of their shops in the city centre. Along the line of Oxford Road and Upper Brook Street there was simply no space for extensive middle-class settlement between the very rich and the very poor. In the north, however, the merchants who in the 1830s had struck out along York Street and the Bury New Road had leap-frogged over areas of decent, but relatively inexpensive housing in Strange-ways and on the lower reaches of Cheetham Hill, above the sandstone ridge running up from the Irk known as Red Bank. The whole area in fact fell into two separate locations, still divided in 1841 by the toll bar on New Bridge Street: solidly-built, bay-windowed terraced and semi-detached houses in a compact network on either side of Great Ducie Street, and a similar nucleus at the lower end of York Street. It was into both these districts that Jewish shopkeepers and professional men began to move from the early 1840s, hard on the heels of young foreign clerks, some of them also Jewish, who had found board and lodgings in clean and convenient Gentile homes in the later 1830s.

At the time of the Census of 1841 eight Jewish merchants and commission agents were still in lodgings in and around the central warehouse district —chiefly in Mosley Street, Cooper Street, and Portland Street—and fifteen more, including Jacob Behrens, Harry Lazarus and Isidor Gerstenberg, between Grosvenor Square and Dover Street in Chorlton-on-Medlock, but seven had already sought out lodgings in Strangeways and Cheetham Hill, where the encroachment of factories and warehouses was bringing down the rents. Henry Kayser lived in Great Ducie Street, Philip Bauer in New Bridge Street, Benny Simonson in Higher Temple Street, to the south of Philip Lucas in Temple House. The conversion of this spasmodic movement into the beginning of a more continuous and extensive Jewish settlement was the result, in part, of the northwards advance of industry, which drove Gentile families as far up Bury New Road as their means would allow, in part, of the development of the lock-up shop, as significant of a new and more impersonal relationship between the shopkeeper and his enterprise as of his greater social ambition and rising wealth. In the mid-1840s a boy could be persuaded to live above a shop in the town centre for as little as 3s 6d a week and board to free its owner for suburban life.[91] The pioneer was perhaps Joseph Braham, who in 1841 settled in York Street, where, with admirable foresight, he purchased a number of houses subsequently occupied by his co-religionists. There were twelve other Jewish retailers in the area—including Joel Casper, Joseph Levy and Henry Mendleson in Cheetham Hill, Elias Nathan and Jacob Casper in Strangeways—by 1845.

This northward shift in the centre of communal gravity was scarcely visible in 1841, when 228 persons out of a total of around 625 lived in the Old Town, 210 more in shops and lodging houses in the central commercial districts of Manchester and Salford, and there were twenty-seven Jewish households— some eighty-three persons in all—to the south of St Peter's Square.[92] The pattern of Jewish settlement in 1844 is best described as two pyramids, each with its base in Hanover Street, one with its apex in Higher Broughton and embracing Strangeways and Cheetham Hill, the other with its apex in Plymouth Grove and encompassing the petty villadom of commercial and professional men in Chorlton-on-Medlock. It was only after 1844–45 that the northern emphasis became pronounced, and only after 1848–51 that it proved decisive.

IV

Of the thirty-five Free Members of the synagogue in February 1842, eleven were overseas merchants, the rest tailors, furriers, pawnbrokers, jewellers, dentists and surgeons whose arrival in Manchester predated 1836 and whose fortunes had risen with the standard of living. It was an élitist composition which had arisen naturally enough out of the foundation of the synagogue in 1825 and the need to protect the communal reputation in the critical years of the early 1830s. The creation of a mercantile plutocracy with even higher social and political ambitions, the emergence of the emancipation issue, the hopes and anxieties of the middle class of the wider society, and the eddies of feeling flowing from Damascus and Reform, all seemed to confirm that the community's religious integrity and social quality demanded the continued protection of an oligarchic structure. The small group of shopkeepers, merchants and professional men who ruled the synagogue also controlled, as if by right, the ancillary agencies of the community, the Philanthropic Society and the Jews School. To some extent the structure suited the social balance of the community prior to 1840, and reflected the alliance between the merchants and the prosperous shopkeepers who shared the major portion of its wealth.

Their guidance and funds had steered the community through difficult formative years, kept it clear of the whirlpool of Reform, and successfully laid the
basis of a full communal life respected by all, or almost all, of those outside it.
In the late 1830s and early 1840s, however, the situation was complicated by
the emergence of a new group of retail tradesmen—not old-established settlers
like Franks or Spier but either former hawkers making their way up a difficult
economic ladder, new immigrants from the radical milieu of northern and western Germany, or former retailers of the smaller cotton towns, and other provincial centres, drawn into Manchester by the gravitational pull of an expanding urban market. In the early 1840s those same forces which consolidated one
stratum of Jewish shopkeepers made for the emergence of another, if anything
more enterprising and resilient, but blocked from preferment within the
congregation by those who had entered it before them.

Although most of the twenty country hawkers of English birth who lodged
in the Old Town on Census night 1841, declined into poverty and obscurity,
at least six became shopkeepers in Manchester within the succeeding five years.
They included David, Wolf and Moses Misell of Ipswich (and later Liverpool)
who emerged from crowded lodging houses to become retailers, respectively
of tobacco, stationery and pictures, when a small 'half-shop' in a poorer part of
the Old Town might be obtained for as little as £15 a year. Perhaps the most
remarkable career of all was that of Michael Goldstone of Warsaw,[93] who had
survived precariously since his arrival in England in the early 1820s as a
hawker of quills, based first in Liverpool, where for a time he depended upon
the charity of the synagogue,[94] then in Birmingham, and finally, from 1838, in
Manchester. In 1841 he began to manufacture steel pens in Springfield Lane,
Salford; five years later he was a jeweller and watchmaker on Fountain Street
with a house in King Street, Salford.

Much more numerous were the German immigrants of the late 1830s and
early 1840s, many of them exiles from political repression, all from areas deeply affected by the radical feelings, particularly strong within the Jewish milieu,
which finally erupted in 1848. Although most arrived penniless, or nearly so,
they were drawn for the most part from cultured, and sometimes well-to-do
families, and rose rapidly on the economic scale, usually after a brief exploratory
period in urban peddling. Louis Bibergeil,[95] of Bromberg in Prussian Poland,
who arrived in 1840 without funds, was the son of a doctor and nephew of the
German scientist, Aaron Bernstein. With his kinsman, David Falk, also from
Bromberg, he took lodgings in the Old Town, Falk in Timber Street, Bibergeil in Beswick's Row, and became, like Falk, a pedlar of jewellery, steel pens
and smallware. Within four years, both possessed shops, Bibergeil (his name
now anglicised to Beaver) in Cross Street, in partnership with a third immi-

grant, Abraham Wertheim, and Falk in Shudehill. Thieves who entered Beaver's premises in October 1843 by boring a hole through the wall of an adjacent shop escaped with goods worth £500,[96] but notwithstanding the 'ruinous nature' of the robbery, the shop was open for business again within three weeks, although only after the inner walls had been cased with iron.[97] Some arrived, like two silversmiths in Liverpool in August 1846, with

a stock of jewellery and precious stones with which they intended to commence business . . . took a house and shop, obtained a silver licence [and] paid a considerable sum as earnest money.[98]

Other immigrants with a modest amount of capital to invest were the tobacconist and general importer Joel Aaron Kohn of Brodie in Galicia, who arrived in the early 1840s, and David Hesse of Cologne,[99] the son of a rabbi, who shortly before 1840 opened a small draper's shop in London Road, where he was found by the enumerators of the 1841 Census. Within the next few years, Hesse embarked upon the manufacture of shirts, first with Gentile partners and then (from 1845) in his own factory and warehouse in Back Piccadilly. In 1840 Edward Marks, of East Prussian origin, became the first Jewish entrepreneur to specialise in the manufacture of cloth caps, an industry even more easily adapted than general tailoring to mass production for a popular market, and for an even smaller capital outlay. Later experience was to suggest that an energetic immigrant, with capital enough to pay 8s a week for an attic on Shudehill, could earn sufficient profit in a year by making up the cloth of a large retail firm to set up, as Marks did, as a manufacturer on his own account.[100]

Manchester also continued to draw in established shopkeepers from London and from provincial centres, particularly those who already had longstanding links with the Manchester synagogue. Shortly before 1840, Saul and Nathan Mayer, the sons of the Staffordshire shopkeeper, George Mayer, settled in Manchester as pawnbrokers and jewellers, in Shudehill and Swan Street, and other newcomers of the period 1840–44 were Joel Benjamin, the rag dealer from Bolton; Casper Eisenburgh, a jeweller from Warrington; and Morris Harris and Nathan Singer, both tailors from Wigan. Julius Selig, a tobacconist, came from Liverpool; John William Gore, of Lissau in Prussian Poland, from London.

Although these men had little in common beyond their exclusion from congregational privilege, their emergence in the early 1840s was sufficient to upset the social balance and political equipoise of the community of the later 1830s. Some arrived as radicals, others had radicalism forced upon them by the position in which they found themselves. Those who came from Germany in the belief that they were entering a less repressive society found that this was largely true except within their own religious community which, in spite of its struggle for political freedom, was itself content with the domination of an exclusive and self-perpetuating élite. They were unable to cash their economic success in terms of congregational prestige and power. The position was aggravated for former country shopkeepers like Morris Harris and the Mayer brothers, since they had traded and worshipped in Manchester for many years and were well known to those whose privilege they could not share. The new system of assessment of 1842, rational as it was in actuarial as well as religious terms, was a constant source of irritation, since each year those seat-holders who appealed against their financial rating had their cases heard only by the Free Members. A death threw the worst elements of the structure into high relief, since a decision had then to be made as to which side of the burial ground the corpse belonged. Finally, the expansion of retailing added economic to political tension, since those who increasingly found themselves divided between two camps on constitutional issues were also, as often as not, business rivals in tailoring or jewellery.

All this appeared to have no direct religious significance, since there is no evidence that any of the newcomers, at least at this stage, were Reformers or, indeed, had any more radical religious inclinations than the Free Members. None the less, any disturbance of the *status quo* was almost certain to have religious implications. If the shopkeepers of pedlar origin had up to 1840 provided the main ballast of orthodoxy, the question arose as to what would happen to the congregational balloon if that ballast were to be weakened by the admission of foreign immigrants to the Free Membership. At the very least it might be expected that Theodores and a few of the more assimilated merchants like Lucas and the Straus brothers would have greater scope for the propagation of radical views on matters of ritual and ecclesiastical jurisdiction. The question of the Chief Rabbi's power was equally certain to arise in the case of an internal rift, even on political issues. Dr Nathan Marcus Adler, who was elected to office during 1844 and arrived in England in July 1845, was known as an opponent of Reform, and might be expected to intervene in any congregational strife in which Reform might emerge as an issue, even when it had not been the causative factor. A 'well-regulated' decentralised rabbinical structure had been possible in Germany, he believed, because it had evolved over centuries, but in England a rabbinical tradition was lacking, except at the centre, and this central conrol had become necessary to the survival of an orthodox framework of Jewish life.[101] One of his earliest acts was to draw up a code of ritual regulations for use in synagogues throughout the Empire.[102] It was not only a case of whether or not he chose to interpose his authority in a local dispute but also a question of the extent to which German immigrants accustomed to a greater devolution of power in Europe could be made to accept a centralised system in England. In this, as in the political issue, David Hesse, radical by instinct and the son of a rabbi, was potentially a key figure.

The question of congregational autonomy, like that of synagogal democracy, was one upon which communal considerations seemed likely to be complicated by influences stemming from the surrounding town. Middle-class Manchester had no doubts about political rights, at least as they affected shopkeepers, and the immigrants of the early 1840s were moving, therefore, in a society which at many points would reinforce their conviction that privilege belonged to them as of economic right. This was also a militant time in Manchester, when the middle classes launched a sustained campaign against laws believed to be based on class interests other than their own. A 'torrent' of propaganda issued from the Anti-Corn Law League's headquarters in Newall's Buildings during the early 1840s,[103] and Cobden and Bright fought Manchester's battles in London. In these circumstances, the caution of the communal élite in the struggle for Jewish emancipation seemed inappropriate, particularly to those schooled in German liberalism. The idea of earning political rights by good behaviour did not appeal to Hesse or Beaver, who preferred a more direct and positive challenge, and who at a later stage were prepared to serve as the Cobden and Bright of the community in bringing the Manchester approach to bear upon the deliberations of the leaders of Anglo-Jewry. They came to believe that the Manchester community might seek a place in Anglo-Jewry equivalent to that which Manchester was attaining in the affairs of the nation, and in this again lay the basis of strong local loyalty upon which congregational autonomy might subsequently be built. In the events which followed, the questions of equality within the synagogue, religious Reform, and local autonomy, were raised many times, separately and together, and in the course of the following decade and a half each member of the community had ultimately to make up his mind on each.

Manchester itself had reached a point of reappraisal. As the German traveller J. G. Kohl observed in 1844, 'Never since the world began was there a town like it.'[104] Squalor and wealth, progress and decay, coexisted on an unprecedented scale and a new social order had generated tensions unique in kind and in intensity. Each year new urban developments were superimposed, almost piecemeal, upon the old to create a pattern so subtle that only the rationalisations of Cooke Taylor, Engels or Disraeli could reduce it to order. Engels was impressed by the darkness, Disraeli by the light of industrial civilisation. At a Grand Athenaeum Soirée in October 1843, chaired by Charles Dickens, and attended by Richard Cobden and Dr Lyon Playfair, Disraeli spoke of the 'liberalising tendencies of commerce and manufactures'.[105] Answering the charge that the materialism of Manchester men had led them to neglect the arts, he told his audience:

On the contrary, there seems to me something in the pursuits of commerce, something in the very arts of manufacturers, which immediately sympathises with all that human intellect, in its most refined character, can conceive and can produce.

Of all the liberal tendencies the middle classes believed themselves to possess, religious and racial tolerance was probably the most substantial. Manchester had come to terms with its Jewish community, and it was perhaps the major achievement of the oligarchy to help to make this possible. Now it was the turn of the community to resolve its own differences, and in these circumstances the immediate question was: could the oligarchy survive?

6 Communal division, 1844–48

By the beginning of 1844 the social and economic changes of the preceding decade had taken Manchester Jewry to the political crossroads which was approached by one urban community after another during the nineteenth century, as a large body of immigrant shopkeepers, petty manufacturers and professional men developed around the hard core of founder families. The new middle classes, enterprising and resilient in business and socially ambitious, resented a 'select' congregational system which entrusted the making of laws, the allocation of seats and *mitzvaoth*, the levying of taxes, the election of officers, and the future national role and status of the community, to those whose only claim to superiority lay in their earlier arrival. Five years was a long time for a successful foreign immigrant like Louis Beaver, an ambitious professional man like Frederick Eskell, or a former country trader like Morris Harris, to await equality, particularly when its bestowal (and price) depended, even then, upon the whim and fancy of the Select Committee. Their sense of grievance was no doubt aggravated by the way in which a relatively new mercantile élite had given the traditional division within the synagogue the sharper edge of class distinction. Moreover, a movement in a democratic direction was suggested by the prevailing political climate in England, which threw the aristocratic structure of Anglo-Jewry into sharp and unflattering relief, and highlighted the incongruity with which Jewish leaders pressed for a degree of political representation within the nation which they were reluctant to grant to their co-religionists within the synagogue. These same frustrations and fears, which reached a critical point in Manchester during 1844, had made themselves felt six years before in Liverpool, where parallel, but earlier, developments provoked a democratic explosion during the years 1838–42.

I

In Liverpool, where the synagogue in Seel Street had been built in 1808, some seventeen years before Halliwell Street, the founder-contributors, few and wealthy, had raised the barriers of entry against each successive wave of post-war immigration. At the beginning of the century it had been possible to gain admission to Free Membership for a relatively modest fee of between £5 and £7,[1] but once the early members 'got a little richer', then, according to their critics, they came to regard themselves as a 'petty aristocracy' entitled to control the synagogue, 'and they found it necessary, in order to keep up a select circle, to raise the price of admission', until by 1838 it had reached the prohibitive figure of £27 5s,

a larger sum than was ever paid before for a like purpose in the kingdom. But this is not the worst feature in the case for they can, without cause or reason, except that it is their will, prevent a person from taking up their [sic] freedom at any price.[2]

As a result, '30 nominal and 20 real Free Members'[3] (that is, an élite within an élite, as in Manchester) exercised exclusive sway over a prosperous and growing community of some fifteen hundred persons, and in a manner regarded by many seat-holders as arbitrary, partial, and 'irresponsible'. Some of the petty taxes levied by the oligarchy, such as payments exacted for circumcision and the naming of a child, were described by those who paid them, without the compensating benefit of representation, as 'irreligious', 'indecent' and tolerable 'in no other Congregation in the Known World'.[4] High fees extracted from butchers resulted in seat-holders having to pay 'the largest price for the coarsest meat'.[5] As in Manchester, the burial ground itself was subject to class distinction.[6] Abraham Franklin, to whom the division of the Manchester cemetery owed its origin, served as a personal link between the leaders of the two communities. When he moved to Manchester he had retained the privileges which he had purchased in Liverpool in 1820 for what he regarded as the bargain price of £10.[7]

The standard of revolt against the Liverpool aristocracy was raised by a well-to-do jeweller, and a recent arrival in the town from Bristol, Barnett Lyon Joseph, who in October 1838 called a meeting of disaffected seat-holders at the Clarendon Rooms in South John Street,[8] where he succeeded in converting their vague sense of grievance into a sharp attack upon the existing structure and a coherent programme of reform. In a long and eloquent speech, subsequently published for private circulation, he attacked each injustice in turn, and went on to argue that the constitution at Seel Street was fundamentally obsolete:

The day we live in—the things that have passed around us for the last ten years—the constitution of the country—the municipal government of this town—the nature of every public and private society, show that the power of the few over the many is passing away, and that every man in possession of a stake in society is entitled by himself or his representatives to a stake in its management.[9]

The result of the meeting was the presentation to the Free Members, in April 1839, of a 'memorial', 'setting forth the grievances generally felt by the seat holders',[10] and calling, if not for the destruction of the old system, at least for its substantial modification in a liberal direction. The distinction between Free Members and seat-holders was to remain, but the latter were to be given additional powers, including the right to participate in the enactment of laws and the regulation of taxes. The constitution was to be amended to facilitate the acquisition of Free Membership at a 'moderate fixed sum' by men of 'good character' who had resided in Liverpool for three years or more: those, that is, who, on the analogy of the Reform Act of 1832, were regarded as possessing an adequate 'stake in society'. The memorial went on to question the justice of a number of petty impositions and restrictions, and ended with the declaration

That in the eyes of the Supreme Being We are all alike whether rich or poor. That when Death reduces us to a level, distinctions should cease, and the rich and poor be laid side by side.

In life, however, some were to remain more alike than others.

Although Joseph publicly disclaimed any intention of 'forcing a separation', the memorial included the implicit threat of secession in the event of no acceptable answer being received from Seel Street.[11] From London, Solomon Hirschel pleaded for harmony within the community and concessions from the authorities,[12] but in spite of his offer of personal mediation and negotiations stretching over thirteen months, no compromise could be effected. At the end of 1839 fifty-three seat-holders broke away to form the 'Liverpool New Hebrew Congregation', which met first in Hanover Street and acquired land at West Derby for use as a burial ground.[13] Three years later, Elias Mozeley, a Liverpool banker and the leading figure in the ruling clique at Seel Street, tried to persuade the Board of Deputies to abort the new congregation by refusing its secretary permission to register marriages,[14] but neither his attack on the '2 or 3 troublesome and evil-minded persons' behind the revolt and their 'loose principles of government', nor the further intervention of the Chief Rabbi and Sir Moses Montefiore,[15] could effect a reunion.

Although Mozeley professed to believe that the removal of part of the Liverpool community from the 'wholesome control' of its elder statesmen was 'most injurious to our Co-religionists in the provinces',[16] Manchester was not so much moved by Liverpool's example as propelled towards a similar crisis by similar internal changes at a slightly later date. In some respects, the situation in 1844 in Manchester was less oppressive than that of Liverpool in 1838. Since the Manchester synagogue was founded later, the base of its privileged membership was far broader; the proportion of Free Members was greater (thirty-eight out of eighty-two) while the community as a whole was less than half the size; the maximum price of admission had been kept down to five guineas (paid by Samuel Hadida in 1844) and many (Lewis Levy, for example) paid two guineas or less. The disadvantages under which the seat-holders suffered, although considerable, were neither as great nor as numerous as those in Liverpool. They were excluded from power and divided in death, their applications for membership were liable to arbitrary rejection, but they suffered from none of the minor impositions listed in Joseph's memorial. None the less, there existed amongst the Manchester seat-holders a smouldering discontent. Early in 1842 Abraham Lipman, a Free Member of long standing, was persuaded by his seat-holder friends, including his son, Michael, to press for their participation in the passing of a new law. He went so far as to give notice of a motion to that effect to the Select Committee,[17] but was persuaded not to proceed with it, perhaps by his weightier mercantile colleagues, the 'real' Free Members. In March 1842 Joel Benjamin, the rag dealer, and Julius Selig, the tobacconist, threatened to resign their seats unless the Select Committee agreed to a reduction of their annual assessments.[18] The financial issue was an explosive one. Even those able to stomach the absence of a vote found their lack of influence in matters of finance intolerable, particularly when their own assessments were at stake. Possibly the deciding factor was a revised list of assessments issued by the Select Committee on 17 March 1844: the rents of eight seat-holders were raised by a guinea, while those of four Free Members were reduced by a similar amount.

In the following month the seat-holders summarised their grievances in a petition[19] which, like the Liverpool memorial, sought not so much to overturn the old order as to modify the mechanics of class distinction. A privileged membership was to remain, but it was to be open, without partiality or delay, to 'any person who has been a seat-holder for five succeeding years' on the payment of two guineas, provided only that no 'reasonable objection' was raised to his eligibility. The petitioners did not question the right of Free Members to control the general affairs of the synagogue, but they requested that five elected representatives of the seat-holders might attend (with power to vote) those General Meetings which dealt with 'business of importance, such as for dismissals or concluding engagements', and that two of the five might be present (although without a vote) at all meetings of the Select Committee. It was further proposed that, on application to the President, the five representatives might occasionally be 'granted' a committee of Free Members 'for the purpose of redressing any real grievances that may from time to time occur'. The petition ended:

It is your duty, and you are duty bound to sympathise with us, when our feelings are hurt or tampered with, and it becomes your bounden duty, in justice to God and man, to remove all prejudices which have hitherto existed; we are all one flesh and blood, of the same Maker, and the same Redeemer we all look upon.

It was signed by five 'deputies of the Manchester seat holders': Julius Selig, Morris Harris, Joseph Gumpelson, Saul Mayer and John William Gore.

No alterations were sought in the ritual of the synagogue. On the contrary, the dissident seat-holders declared their intention, if pushed to the point of secession,

not to deviate in the smallest particular from [the form of service] established in the Manchester and other orthodox Hebrew congregations . . . [and] to make no alterations whatever in the laws, rites, or liturgy hitherto observed.[20]

A subsequent tradition that one object of the rebels was to install an organ in the synagogue[21] has as little substance as Margoliouth's view that the revolt turned on the price of *misheberachs*.[22] In spite of orthodox fears to the contrary, there was no causal relationship between the movement towards congregational democracy on the one hand and agitation for Reform on the other. Both were attempts to 'modernise' Anglo-Jewish life, and in this sense they both owed their origin in part to an impression, almost certainly incorrect, that an 'anglicisation' of Jewish institutions was a necessary prerequisite for the total acceptance of Jewry into the social and political fabric of the country. But this is as far as the connection went. The objections of the London Reformers concerned matters of theology and ritual; the 'democrats' had no concrete aims beyond a modest extension of the synagogal franchise. There was no logical reason why a Reformer should also be a political radical and, in fact, many were not. Although Tobias Theodores was committed to freedom of religious thought and the elimination of clerical pretensions, later events suggest that he had no objection to the benevolent patriarchy of the laity. He was not amongst the rebels of 1844. There was this further distinction, that whereas English Reform began in London and grew out of currents of thought and ritual fashionable throughout Western Europe, the rebellions of 1838 in Liverpool and 1844 in Manchester were insular and provincial, symptoms of local economic and social change, although strengthened by the prevailing winds of political thought. When, in October 1844, the *Voice of Jacob* reported a 'partial separation' of a number of seat-holders at Halliwell Street, the editor concluded that the break was not based on any 'principle of secession, religiously', and that it was neither 'organic' nor 'permanent' in character.[23]

But although the *Voice of Jacob* believed that the 'liberal policy' at Halliwell Street would 'render unnecessary any separation',[24] the presentation of the petition was followed by a prolonged deadlock from which no compromise seemed likely to emerge. The Select Committee, through its President, Benjamin Hyam, insisted on a fresh petition 'signed by everyone who approves of it' for consideration at a later meeting 'which the delegates will be invited to attend if requisite';[25] the seat-holders, through their secretary, Louis Beaver, demanded 'nothing less than personal representation'.[26] A more or less neutral observer felt that the Select Committee was being unnecessarily punctilious in observing 'the cold forms of etiquette' and the seat-holders too impatient for an immediate solution:[27] he regretted the absence of any intermediary to arrange an 'amicable settlement'.[28] Proposals for a compromise were reportedly put before the seat-holders by a Free Member,

but unfortunately by a VERY insignificant person—a young man notorious only for his meddling propensities and for playing antics and talking nonsense at public meetings,[29]

and who, at all events, was not authorised by the Select Committee to act on its behalf. The intransigence of Hyam and his colleagues precipitated a secession which a more conciliatory attitude might well have avoided. In August 'about 12 or 15 members, mostly young unmarried men',[30] broke away from Halliwell Street, returned to the room in Ainsworth's Court vacated almost twenty years before, purchased land in Miles Platting for use as a burial ground,[31] and wrote to the Chief Rabbi's Office (still vacant at that stage) for permission to appoint their own *shochet*.[32] Although the parent congregation decided that it did 'not intend at present to prevent the new-styled congregation from being provided with meat from our butchers', Joseph Mirls, the Reader, resigned in sympathy with the rebels and set up shop as a Kosher butcher in Quay Street. A decision by the Select Committee in September to allow the seat-holders a voice in the selection of the Chief Rabbi[33] was not regarded by the rebels as sufficient an earnest of its good intentions to warrant their return.

Lacking a leader of the fire and intellectual calibre of B. L. Joseph, the secessionists chose as their first public spokesman

D. E. De Lara Ll.D., Member of the Literary and Philanthropic Society, and of the Institute of Natural and Experimental Science, Professor of Continental Literature in the Royal, the Literary and Scientific, and the Mechanics' Institution,[34]

a very recent arrival, a man of grandiose pretensions and inconsiderable talent, who on 5 September 1844 opened the 'New Synagogue' in Ainsworth's Court with a long, sickly and equivocal oration, 'written [he told the public] on the spur of the moment during a few hours snatched from sleep', and subsequently offered for sale, at 6*d* a copy, 'the proceeds to be given to the poor'.[35] The speech interspersed admiration for the seat-holders with deferential asides on the 'courtesy', 'kindness', and liberality of the Select Committee,[36] and ended:

'whether your [the secessionists'] views were correct or erroneous it does not become me to decide'.[37] De Lara was not himself a member of the New Congregation, and of his subsequent career in Manchester (too short to find him a place in Slater's Directory) we know only that in December 1845 he delivered a lecture to members of the Athenaeum on 'continental literature'.[38]

The young seat-holders who acted as the spearhead of dissent were for the most part men of humble origin and foreign birth who had arrived in Manchester within five years of 1844, three (Louis Beaver, Edward Marks and David Goldman) direct from East Prussia, two (J. W. Gore and Lewis Harris, a quill dresser) from London, the rest from other provincial centres, chiefly in the north-west of England—Julius Selig, David Missel and Frederick Eskell from Liverpool, Morris Harris and Nathan Singer from Wigan, the brothers Mayer from Hanley, Joel Benjamin from Bolton, and Michael Goldstone from Birmingham. They included three capmakers, three retail jewellers, two dealers in rags and cotton waste, two pawnbrokers, two stationers, two tailors, a trimming manufacturer, a confectioner, a tobacconist and a dentist: Eskell apart, a fair occupational cross-section of the new *petite bourgeoisie*. Sharp, ambitious, competitive, self-made men of the city centre and the Old Town, they resented a system which tied the community to the cautious policies of a mercantile and suburban élite. According to its own rather exaggerated circular, the New Congregation was 'commenced under the most unfavourable circumstances, having no wealthy members'.[39]

The revolt might well have proved abortive had it not been for the accession of David Hesse, the German shirt manufacturer, early in 1845. According to his own account, Hesse was not one of the 'original founders' of the New Congregation

nor did I give the founders any direct, or indirect, assistance, until it was formed, although I was invited by them to take a share in their early deliberations. I sent a substitute, in order to hear correctly what was going on at those meetings and I must do honour to the parties who met, that they evinced great moral courage, good sense and aptitude, but still I was not satisfied, I thought it might be, that in a day or two the ardour of all these men will be chilled . . .[40]

When the rebels sustained their enthusiasm through the first difficult months, however, Hesse rented a seat at Ainsworth's Court:

And why? Not because I had any ambitious desires, not because I had any ill-feeling towards any one member of the Old Congregation, not because I had any friends among you (you were then all strangers to me) . . . it was the *principles* upon which your Congregation was founded, those principles which aimed at the destruction of class distinction, and only acknowledged moral and intellectual worth . . . I saw in this little Congregation, and little it was . . . the nucleus of a party that would do much to liberalise our institutions ∴ .[41]

His arrival altered the whole orientation of the movement. Already under the influence of radical thought before his arrival in Manchester, he pushed the more insular members of the New Congregation towards egalitarian ideals which lay far beyond their original intentions, and so moved the revolt into the mainstream of European and English liberalism. A subsequent appeal from the new synagogue, which listed the disabilities under which the seat-holders had laboured at Halliwell Street, ended:

In consequence of a certain degree of British liberality, and improvements in legislative administrations, the persons labouring under the above disabilities could not be governed by those exclusive laws.[42]

Hesse also linked the 'oligarchic' character of Jewish institutions with their lack of practical utility, and he came to regard the New Congregation as a catalyst not only for a process of democratisation but for a more general process of renovation which would render Anglo-Jewish secular organisations 'dynamic' in their pursuit of social welfare, educational improvement and political emancipation. What had begun largely as an insignificant and local upheaval based on the political frustrations of the *nouveaux riches* became, under his influence, an important stage in the adaptation of Jewish institutions to English conditions:

I hope the day is not far distant [he wrote in 1848] when there will be a perfect re-modelling of all the Old Congregations in this kingdom, that they may harmonise with liberal and enlightened opinions.[43]

In business Hesse typified the ambitions and ingenuity of those who had given the revolt its initial momentum. In March 1845, about the time he joined the New Congregation, he and his partner, John Flusheim, registered their first copyright designs—for 'Imperial Patent Shirt Collars' and

improved elastic shirt fronts . . . easy and comfortable without being subject to any of the annoyances which are caused by the old styles,[44]

both of which were distributed by large non-Jewish wholesalers, including J. & N. Philips of Church Street. At the beginning of the following year Flusheim and Hesse were taken to court by a London shirt-maker for pirating his design, but after a two-hour hearing, the Borough Court decided that their manufactures were 'essentially different'.[45] At about this time, Hesse moved out into the southern suburbs, where he acquired a house in Paddock Street, Ardwick, although without losing close contact with his friends in the city centre.

On the basis of Hesse's programme and financial patronage, the New Congregation gradually assumed a permanent form during the year

1845–46. The first marriage to be performed at Ainsworth's Court was registered at the Chief Rabbi's office in London on 20 July 1845. Shortly afterwards, the salaried secretary received official recognition from the Board of Deputies as legal registrar.[46] In September, in spite of charges levelled against him in an anonymous letter to the Chief Rabbi, a 'Mr Brahadi' was elected Reader and recognised as such by Dr Adler.[47] By November, in spite of bitter opposition from Halliwell Street, the Chief Rabbi had given recognition also to the congregational *shochet*.[48] In August 1846 the 'new-styled congregation', as the Select Committee preferred to call it, achieved an important *coup* by obtaining the services of Israel Levy, son of Rev. Aaron Levy of the London Beth Din, as its secretary and 'religious teacher', a resounding answer to those who suspected the congregation of heretical designs:

His discourses in the pulpit [according to a letter in the *Jewish Chronicle*] and his example in practical piety (which are all strictly orthodox) have already stimulated several of our members to pay more attention to religious matters than they did before.[49]

In the estimation of the *Chronicle* his 'learning' was

far above that which we are accustomed to find in this country amongst men of his age; and he would be considered an accomplished Hebrew scholar in any country.[50]

The New Congregation was at pains to stress its good ritual intentions and its subordination to the new Chief Rabbi, who in turn, in spite of his rigid standards, had no hesitation in underwriting its religious respectability. Elated by this early success, in December 1846 a subscription list was opened for

a new synagogue, with school room attached [since] there was no building dedicated to the important purpose of education for the Hebrew Community of this town and . . . synagogue room could only be found for one fourth of the female sex . . .[51]

£673 had been raised within a fortnight, and in December the congregation purchased 2,012 square yards of land on Cheetham Hill Road 'for the purpose of building thereon a synagogue, School Rooms and the congregational institutions'.[52] A circular sent to other provincial congregations in February 1847 sought contributions towards a total of £2,300 required for building operations to begin.[53]

The confident expectations of the New Congregation contrasted sharply with the abject failures of the Old. Since the resignation of David Isaacs in 1841, no suitable candidate had been found to provide sermons at Halliwell Street. The difficulty, as the *Voice of Jacob* noted in 1844, was 'the scarcity of men trained and qualified for the sacred office';[54] most metropolitan synagogues, like Manchester, were 'without anyone publicly to expound the word of God'.[55] Although it would be going too far to accept Margoliouth's view that the absence of 'pulpit instruction' had caused 'a sort of anarchy and manifold striving for mastery' out of which the schism of 1844 had supposedly arisen,[56] both congregations in Manchester were aware of the possible magnetic and cohesive qualities of a highly-regarded and attractive sermoniser. With this thought in mind, following the secession of the New Congregation and the resignation of David Asher from the headmastership of the Jews School early in 1845, the Old Congregation and the Hebrew Association (each controlled by a branch of the same élite) opened negotiations in February 1845, for the appointment of a joint 'lecturer' and headmaster.[57] The result of a series of meetings and some hard bargaining was an advertisement in the *Jewish Chronicle* on 18 April 1845 for

a competent Lecturer and Teacher . . . to deliver Religious Discourses in English at the synagogue, and to conduct the Hebrew and English School connected with the Association:[58]

the salary offered was £180, of which £80 was to be paid by the congregation. For nearly eight months no suitable candidate appeared. Then in March 1846 a Dr Kruger of Berlin was invited to Manchester, where he delivered two sermons characterised, according to the *Voice of Jacob*, by 'erudition and good taste' and 'a much greater mastery of the English language than could have been anticipated'.[59] After a short trial, during which he received 30s a week for six weeks for delivering discourses 'on such days and such topics as the congregation may agree upon', he was elected at a General Meeting of the Old Congregation in May by eighteen votes to eight.[60] In the event, however, Dr Kruger could stomach neither the English language nor the parochial outlook of provincial Anglo-Jewry. After a nostalgic 'address' early in November, 'dwelling much upon the intellectuality of our German brethren', he resigned his post and returned to Berlin.[61] The pulpit at Halliwell Street fell vacant at exactly the time of Israel Levy's arrival to fill that at Ainsworth's Court.

II

During the early winter of 1846–47 it might have appeared that the Manchester community was irreparably divided. The Select Committee at Halliwell Street, where the wealth of the community was still concentrated, showed no signs of compromise on the constitutional issue, while at Ainsworth's Court the growth of the New Congregation was expressly attributed to 'the great principles of our constitution—PERFECT EQUALITY'.[62] As the New Congregation came under the leadership of Hesse and acquired the respectability of Israel Levy's lectures, it began to attract new immigrants of financial standing who were not prepared to await the statutory five years or take the attendant risks involved in an application for Free Membership at Halliwell Street. These included Heinemann Hertz Rosenberg of Westphalia, who arrived during 1846 to open a large-scale business as a retailer of cigars and snuff, and his commercial rivals, Joseph and Louis Goodman of Prussian Silesia, importers of 'fine old Cabana' tobacco, 'choice Old Emperor Cigars' and Meerschaum pipes. Founder-members of the New Congregation continued to rise on the economic scale. Michael Goldstone graduated from hardware to jewellery. Eskell began to send out 'members of his firm' to hold consultations in Manchester's satellite towns. In July 1846 David Misell, then a tobacconist (and a former hawker of stationery), with Julius Seelig, a confectioner from Heilbrunn in Wurttemberg, obtained a copyright for their 'London and Cumberland Prepared Black Lead Pencils', which they sold through seventeen local agents from their warehouse at the corner of Chapel Street and Tib Street, noting, with significant disregard for their own beginnings, that no hawkers were 'under any pretence' to sell goods or solicit orders on their behalf.[63] As the likelihood of the New Synagogue's continuance was increased by these developments, the Old Congregation's opposition to it became the more bitter, particularly since high seat rents were at stake, and the possibility of co-operation correspondingly diminished. Both had plans in mind for new school buildings, similar to those in Liverpool and Birmingham, to replace the rented rooms in St Mary's Street (and so, in theory, attract the children of the rich), but neither possessed the ready cash to accomplish them. More seriously, both were concerned over the dramatic increase of itinerant poverty but neither possessed either the organisation or the funds to create an adequate system of relief.

This was a crucial matter. The number of payments made to casual paupers by the authorities at Halliwell Street, relatively static at between 300 and 350 in the decade preceding 1844, rose during 1844–45 to 689, and in 1845–46 to 956, an annual level below which it fell only once during the remainder of the decade. The attendant cost of the relief rose from £108 in 1843–44 to £139 in 1844–45, £186 in 1845–46 and a record £202 in 1846–47, or nearly 27 per cent of the synagogue's total expenditure. Some of the recipients were no doubt English hawkers and pedlars, the basis of whose livelihood was being gradually undermined; the majority, however, appear to have come from Central and Eastern Europe, and chiefly from the Prussian and Russian segments of the old Kingdom of Poland.[64] In Liverpool, where an increase in casual poverty was experienced at the same time, it was attributed in part to the 'almost indiscriminate' congregational relief, which

induced the application of sturdy mendicants, many of whom visited the town twice or thrice yearly, solely for the purpose of begging,[65]

but chiefly to the 'peculiar circumstances' of

the persecution to which our brethren have been subjected in Northern Europe, and the facility of transit from distant countries by means of steam vessels and railroads.[66]

What Manchester and Liverpool began to experience in the mid-1840s were the effects of a heavy traffic of Jewish transmigration destined for the United States.

From 1840 the Jews of Russian Poland, shielded earlier by a degree of residual autonomy from the full force of Czarist legislation, were subjected to the sudden shock of being placed on an equal footing with their co-religionists in the rest of Russia. A special *ukase* of 1843 extended to the Polish borderlands a mitigated version of the barbarous Conscription Statute in force in the rest of Russia since 1827. Other novel impositions, such as the tax on the wearing of traditional Jewish attire, represented 'a real calamity for the hasidic masses'[67] (and, incidentally, depressed the sale of English textiles at the Leipzig Fair).[68] The pressures from St Petersburg on the whole area of the Pale of Settlement changed in form during the early 1840s without diminishing in intensity. Coercive measures were supplemented by a programme of legislation designed to undermine the political autonomy and cultural integrity of Jewish life. 'Compulsory enlightenment' in Crown Schools, propagated as a preparation for political emancipation, was regarded more realistically as a thinly veiled prelude to forcible conversion, particularly since it was accompanied by a threat to limit still further the area open to Jewish residence. In December 1843 the *Manchester Guardian* reported that the execution of an Imperial *ukase* removing all Jews within fifty *versts* of the western frontier into the interior had caused 'nameless desolation' among the Jewish inhabitants of thirty-three border towns.[69] Further plans projected by the government included increased disabilities for Jews regarded as 'not engaged in productive labour'—the mass of persons, that is, doomed to poverty by the narrow basis of their area of settlement. A visit by Sir Moses Montefiore to the Czar in 1846 took with it the hopes of all Anglo-Jewry (including the Manchester community, which sent him a congratulatory address on his return)[70] but made no significant impression upon Russian policy. A westward movement of fugitives which began within Russia during 1843–44 carried with it impoverished individuals and families from the Polish provinces of East Prussia, where the limited occupational structure of Jewish life had failed to expand with the population, and gathered malcontents, adventurers and the genuine victims of persecution and discrimination from the rest of Central and Western Europe.

The movement of persons was facilitated, as the Liverpool analysis suggested, and later Manchester investigations confirmed, by a substantial improvement of internal rail communications in Central and Eastern Europe and by the creation of regular, reliable and inexpensive facilities for crossing the Atlantic. In the eastern provinces of Prussia, Stettin was linked with Berlin by rail in 1843,[71] and the Lower Silesia–Mark Railway was opened between Breslau and Berlin (a journey occupying thirteen hours) in 1846.[72] By that time it was possible to travel from western Russia to Poznan, and from Poznan to Berlin, if only by way of a lengthy detour through Stettin, and then on the Berlin–Hamburg line to the coast.[73] The completion of a rail route across the north of England with the opening of the Manchester and Leeds Railway on 1 March 1841 gave Liverpool the advantage over Hamburg, Bremen and Le Havre as a port of embarkation for the United States, particularly since a chain of small congregations was known to exist along the way to serve, if necessary, as financial stepping-stones. By 1845 Liverpool was, according to the *Guardian*, 'the great outlet for emigrants'.[74] The linking of the Leeds Extension Line with the Manchester and Liverpool Railway at the new Victoria Station on 1 January 1844 created a direct chain between the largest towns of northern England—Liverpool, Manchester, Leeds and Hull—and was said to have 'brought the German Ocean and the Irish Sea within a few hours' distance of each other'.[75] Letters sent back down the line of transmigration served to disseminate the details of these advantages. Finally, at Liverpool, competition between passenger brokers had reduced the price of a steerage passage to New York from £12 in 1816 to £3 in 1846.[76] By the July of 1846, as a result of all these pressures and changes, the harassed and divided Jewish community in Liverpool was being 'daily applied to by persons who are emigrating to America'.[77]

As the port of embarkation Liverpool bore the brunt of the problem, since those alone stopped off in Manchester, or towns further east, who lacked the immediate means to carry them further. So great was the 'baneful system of itinerant mendicancy'[78] in Liverpool in the spring of 1846 that representatives of the two warring congregations came together in an attempt to clamp down on private almsgiving (which might have encouraged 'able-bodied mendicants to continue their idle mode of life') and to establish in its place 'a Board of Relief, empowered to apportion to each such aid as may be commensurate to its [*sic*] particular merits'.[79] The Liverpool Hebrew Mendicity Society, officially founded in March 1846, was the first serious attempt within Anglo-Jewry to deal in a systematic manner with itinerant poverty and its attendant problems.[80]

From the outset, the problem was construed in Liverpool as more than one of material relief; what was at stake equally was the reputation of the community at a critical moment in the struggle for political emancipation. It was not enough that beggars should be relieved and moved on. The situation required that those who remained should somehow be 'absorbed' discreetly into the social fabric and that others should be discouraged from following. Mendicancy must be 'suppressed'. The society had the declared objects of affording 'reasonable aid in all cases having a shadow of a claim' and of encouraging paupers by their own efforts to 'raise themselves above mendicity'. The 'idle' were to be refused help, or, at most, to be given 'so small a modicum of relief as to prevent application to the institutions of the town for aid'.[81] At all costs, the community must be spared the shame of a flood of Jewish applicants to the local Board of Guardians, which would undermine the cherished claim of the community to 'look after its own'. Small sums were to be distributed to the deserving until such time as they recovered their independence, with the addition, on selected occasions, of small loans and 'judicious advice' 'to enable them to obtain their own livelihood by honourable industrial pursuits'.[82] Subscribers to the society were asked not to give private alms, but to provide applicants with 'tickets of recommendation' to a Board of Relief which met daily at the society's offices to investigate claims. Aid was to be refused on more than two occasions to those who had resided in Liverpool for less than twelve months and, after some hesitation, intending emigrants were declared ineligible for support. There were, in fact, only two reasonable ways of dealing with transmigrants: either by helping them on their way, or by refusing all help in the hope of stemming the flow, and in view of the heavy cost of the former (and the shortage of funds), the latter course was adopted in July 1846, when the relieving officers were instructed to make strict enquiries 'to prevent any imposition or advantage being taken of the funds by persons visiting the Town for this purpose'.[83] The founders declared their ultimate object to be the encouragement of a network of similar organisations throughout the country, which by common action would serve as 'an effectual check . . . to the immigration of idle mendicants',[84] ensure that charity previously misapplied went only to 'the deserving and the industrious'[85] and so produce 'a gradual improvement in the social position of the poor' throughout Anglo-Jewry.[86]

In retrospect, the Mendicity Society was doomed to early failure. Local measures of deterrence, however stringent, were not calculated to stem a flow of 'pauper immigrants' which had its origins in deep economic and political unrest. The problem of the mid-1840s was that modern communications had facilitated the rapid movement of persons from areas of distress to havens of refuge, and the movement was not to be prevented by a single stumbling-block.

No other Anglo-Jewish community followed Liverpool's lead. In December 1846, a 'Mr Barnett' of Birmingham asked for a copy of the constitution of the society 'with a view to instituting a similar one in that town',[87] but did not proceed with his intention. In the absence of any guidance from London, each congregation saw the problem in its own parochial terms, and only in Liverpool was it sufficiently acute to demand an organisational solution. Communities further east, faced at all events with fewer applicants, helped many on towards their port of embarkation. At Liverpool, there was nowhere to 'forward' the poor except the United States, a price too high to pay for their removal. From July 1846 the society contrived the inner contradiction of excluding from its purview the very persons—the transmigrant poor—who constituted the core of the problem. Ineffective though it was, the society struggled on into the autumn of 1847, when the falling off of financial support and the revival of party bickerings combined to destroy it,[88] throwing the poor back on the 'indiscriminate' charity of the two synagogues, supplemented by private alms.

In so far as the Liverpool community found an immediate model, it was, perhaps, in the District Provident Societies, founded in Liverpool in 1829, and in other northern towns, including Manchester, during the early 1830s, for 'the suppression of mendicity and imposture', the occasional relief of 'unavoidable misfortune', and the encouragement of habits of 'frugality and forethought' amongst the poor.[89] The 'pernicious custom' of private almsgiving, supposedly arising from the 'morbid compassion of the thoughtlessly charitable',[90] was discouraged in favour of strict investigation and discriminatory relief based on 'tickets of recommendation' to a Board of Relief. While 'no one need starve . . . who could produce even a feasible claim for relief',[91] the idle were to be refused an assistance which could only perpetuate 'hopeless poverty . . . vagrant and dissipated habits' and the existence of 'a lawless race [of beggars] in the heart of the town'.[92] The deserving were helped to recover their independence by self-help and savings deposits organised by district visitors and so 'uphold the cause of morality generally'.[93] It might be argued that the Liverpool Hebrew Mendicity Society was calculated to achieve for the Jewish bourgeoisie what the Provident societies were intended to accomplish for the middle class as a whole—to suppress the 'annoyance' and scandal of street mendicity, to tide the respectable poor over periods of misfortune or ill luck, and to integrate into the social fabric those who could be salvaged from pauperism, and who might otherwise tarnish the reputation and trouble the conscience of the well-to-do. For the system of voluntary savings devised by the Provident Societies the Mendicity Society substituted a system of loans and advice which bespoke its greater confidence in the capacity of the Jewish poor to achieve economic independence.

In Manchester, where the division of the community was still too recent to allow for co-operative action, the Old Congregation continued to distribute relief on a piecemeal basis from congregational funds, without altering either its machinery or its policies, and scarcely recognising that a special problem existed, except in the spiral of its expenditure. The extent of casual poverty was blamed in part upon the New Congregation, which was accused of serving as an additional incentive to pauper immigrants without playing an adequate part in their relief.[94] Dead paupers were buried, the sick were provided with money for treatment (or 'tickets' for the Royal Infirmary), the able-bodied were given sufficient for a room, a meal, or a pair of shoes (usually between 1s 6d and 2s 6d) and then moved on towards Liverpool, occasionally to Birmingham and London, or, on very rare occasions, when a family without a breadwinner appeared likely to become permanently burdensome, provided with all or part of a transatlantic passage. The New Congregation, more comprehensive in its vision, placed the blame for the whole situation squarely on the shoulders of the Board of Deputies, which was accused of not tackling the problem on a national level.[95]

If the payment of Passover Relief may be used as the approximate index to the growth of the resident poor, the figures suggest an increase from about fifteen families (perhaps sixty to seventy-five persons) in 1843, to about thirty families (about 120–130 persons) in 1845, represented by a growth of expenditure from £15 6s 7½d (about £1 per family) to £30 2s 7d, a sum at which it remained almost static for the rest of the decade, rising to a new level only in 1851–52. In September 1845 the Select Committee at Halliwell Street spoke for the first time of 'the poor of Manchester which belong to the synagogue'[96] and informed Sir Moses Montefiore that it was in no position to contribute to the relief of victims of the 'Smyrna Conflagration', 'when we have so many poor to support both inhabitants and sojourners',[97] but in fact resident poverty was not acute. During 1847 the Hebrew Philanthropic Society voted a total of £49 10s to only ten applicants, each receiving a weekly pension of between 2s and 5s from the Feast of Dedication to the Thursday after Passover,[98] although a loan of £70 to the Old Congregation in November 1846 suggests a substantial reserve of surplus funds.[99] The problem in Manchester was not at first with those who remained, for most of whom there were ready openings in cap making and tailoring, but with the increasing number of 'passengers', who alighted from the train only long enough to beg a bed or a meal, or with itinerant traders and vagrants who came in from time to time to seek alms at the synagogue or in the streets.

III

This threat to the communal reputation was exacerbated by the beginnings of a new style of Christian mission to the Jews, in part stimulated by an increasing number of poor and supposedly vulnerable Jewish immigrants. While the Anglican mission—the Society for Promoting Christianity Amongst the Jews—concentrated upon the abstract mission of universal conversion, and confined its local activities to pious sermons, annual collections and unduly hopeful prayers, it remained relatively innocuous, but towards the end of 1844 a group of dissenters drawn from the Presbyterian, Wesleyan and Baptist congregations of Manchester met together and

finding, on subsequent enquiry, that this town presents an appropriate field of labour, on account of the many Jews who either reside in it or frequently visit it, they determine, in connection with efforts more strictly auxiliary, to support an agent who should be chiefly employed amongst the Jews in Manchester.[100]

On the recommendation of the parent body, the London Society for the Propagation of the Gospel amongst the Jews, they secured the services of Israel Napthali—'for a considerable time a steady and approved convert to the Christian faith'[101]—and, disclaiming any predictions as to the collective future of Jewry, concentrated upon the conversion of individual Jews. Armed with tracts and copies of the New Testament in Hebrew, German and English, Napthali was sent into the community to win converts and to arrange for their baptism at the most convenient chapel. According to his own account (in February 1846) he obtained 'free and frequent access' to Jewish homes:

they generally receive him kindly and listen with attention to his conversation . . . and many accept from him tracts and Bibles. Eight or nine individuals have put themselves under his continued instruction, and are regularly attending places of Christian worship. One has been admitted to a Christian church, having given very satisfactory evidence of a decided change of heart; another has publicly received the rite of baptism preparatory to admission to church fellowship, and others have expressed their desire to partake of the same privilege . . .'[102]

During 1845–46 the periodical of the society published its first 'autobiographies' of Jewish converts whose zigzag path towards Christianity had led them through various shades of secularism and miscellaneous forms of immorality and misadventure into the home of Napthali. Typical was the story of 'Mr Simon, a Jew in middle-life',[103] a native of Mecklenburg Strelitz, whose crooked way began at the age of fifteen when he was apprenticed in Berlin to 'an eminent merchant of infidel opinions' who

led him to read Paine, Voltaire, and other like authors, and rewarded him for his diligence in business by introducing him to places of worldly amusement and dissipation.

On the death of his master, he went to assist in his father's business, but

he could not bear the restraints of the parental roof; and on receiving some property left him by a deceased relative, he went into partnership with a cousin, with whom he went to Hamburg to purchase goods.

Soon even this object was neglected:

Satan now took a complete hold on him, and having returned to Paris he was guilty of deeds which he could not afterwards recollect without shuddering: his property was wasted, and at length he was thrown into prison.

After his release on bail provided by his father, 'he continued to pursue the path of sin and death' and 'to avoid a second imprisonment' he enlisted in a French regiment and was posted to Algiers, where he narrowly escaped death during an outbreak of plague. His parents intervened to buy his discharge, and from Algiers he went to England, where he was first received by relatives at Norwich and Leeds, and finally settled in Manchester. There he married a 'professing Christian', who soon afterwards saved him from suicide during a spell of desperate illness and dire poverty. The saga ended with his introduction to Napthali, who introduced him in turn to the New Testament, provided him with tracts, and subsequently arranged for his baptism at Rusholme Road Chapel on 6 July 1845.

Mr Simon's case is not untypical in that his conversion was preceded by a long period of detachment from the Jewish community in any social or religious sense, by marriage to a Christian and by descent into poverty. So closely associated was poverty with conversion that the witness to another Manchester baptism (of 1845) stressed that the victim was 'in respectable circumstances, not needing pecuniary assistance'.[104] Trouble with the law was also a fairly common feature in the prehistory of a convert. A London Jew baptised in Manchester on 4 January 1846 misspent his youth with 'immoral' associates from whom he 'contracted evil habits, bad expressions, and the utterance of oaths' and in later life was transported for seven years to New South Wales for receiving stolen goods.[105] After settling in Manchester, first as a confectioner, then as a glass and china rivetter, he too married a Christian lady, through whom he met first 'Mr Simon' and then Napthali. Other conversions were the ephemeral product of misfortune or illness, and were often followed in better times by a return to Judaism. Solomon Harris, a Manchester cabinet maker, claimed as a convert in 1846, two years later received 10s 6d from the funds of the Old Congregation 'in case he leaves this town to return to his native country'.[106] Another convert, Reuben Robinson, wrote to the *Jewish Chronicle* from Miller Street, Manchester, in 1848 to confess his error in allowing himself to be baptised.[107] The acid test was a Christian death. In 1849 the Society for the Propagation of the Gospel claimed five converts in Manchester in as many years, adding:

One of these not only lived by faith in the Son of God, but has died happily in the same faith.[108]

Conversions were rare; they were almost always peripheral, affecting most commonly those already estranged from the Jewish faith by marriage, apathy or crime; but they did happen, and the scandal which accompanied them was sufficient to persuade the community to take them seriously. Early editions of the *Voice of Jacob* and the *Jewish Chronicle* are full of warnings of conversionism and its insidious ways, including letters on the subject from Tobias Theodores. From the sensitive vantage point of the Chief Rabbi's office in London, conversionist inroads seemed to add to the dangers and irrationality of a division in which even Gentile butchers were asked to declare their loyalties. The reputation of Anglo-Jewry was at stake; the poor were at risk, spiritually as well as materially, when a pooling of resources and effort might be expected to produce, at the very least, a new school and an effective system of relief.

In Manchester other changes were opening the way towards a rapprochement and providing moderates on both sides with some room for manœuvre. One was the political eclipse of the Franklin family, for over twenty years the mainstay of the Manchester oligarchy. Abraham Franklin's stockbroking enterprise was undermined by the railway crisis of 1845[109] which had precipitated the suicide of Barnett Moss. The failure of his bankers soon afterwards completed the process;[110] he quit Gesunde Cottage, and after a brief residence with his sister-in-law, Esther Segré, in her boarding house (later her private school) in Great Ducie Street, in 1846 he went to stay with his son-in-law, Jacob Prins, in Arnhem, where he spent the remainder of his life.[111] After 1840 Jacob Franklin was fully committed to business and communal politics in London. Of his brothers, Abraham Gabay and Morris struggled on in Manchester with a declining optical and jewellery business until the later 1840s, Ellis had joined Abraham Bauer's London bank in 1842 with two former Manchester clerks, Isidor Gerstenberg and Philip Gowa, and Lewis went out to the West Indies to join Benjamin Franklin, before moving on to the United States.[112] The only influential member of the family left in Manchester was Isaac Franklin, the surgeon, who possessed neither the extreme religious views nor the autocratic disposition of his father and elder brothers. The family of Aaron Jacob suffered a parallel decline. In May 1846 Aaron's eldest son, Alexander, of the Crescent, Salford, brought out issue number one of *The Star of Jacob*, 'a work particularly addressed to the Sons of Israel and the Daughters of Judah',[113] but this enterprise, along with his import business, were ended abruptly in the same year by bankruptcy, and Alexander followed his brother Henry into a painful obscurity. The Free Membership was further weakened by the absence of Abraham Bauer, who had returned to London in 1844, and the isolation of S. L. Behrens, who held aloof from the synagogue and its offices, and, like many of his colleagues in the boom years 1845–46, concentrated on his business affairs. So great was the 'confusion' and delay encountered at election time at Halliwell Street during 1846, as one candidate after another paid the heavy fines for non-acceptance, that the right to purchase freedom from office was finally withdrawn.[114]

IV

The opportunity for the Chief Rabbi to intervene in Manchester's affairs presented itself in November 1846, when he was asked by the secretary at Ainsworth's Court 'to lend his name and influence so as to aid them in the proposed building of a New Synagogue and school'.[115] When he sought the views of the Old Congregation on the need for such developments, Ansell Spier, then presiding warden, replied with a long and circumstantial attack upon the irresponsibility of the rebels.[116] In particular, they had

shown no disposition either in assisting the resident or casual poor, who have increased greatly since that time [1844]; and there can exist no doubt that the influx of the poor has partially been increased in consequence of there being two Congregations.

The New Congregation had no relief agency of its own, and only one of its members subscribed to the Philanthropic Society. The Old Congregation had borne the full burden of the increased cost of poverty, while its income from seat rents and *shechita* had been reduced by secession. There was no need for extra synagogal accommodation, nor was there any lack of places in the Hebrew Association's school, although it was the intention to acquire more permanent premises for it. The burden of the letter was to the effect that, in the circumstances of 1846, there was no place for a duplication of institutions in Manchester, particularly when competition between them undermined the capacity of either to cope with urgent communal problems.

The forceful language of the response decided Dr Adler to act not by showing favour to either side but by inviting representatives from both to a meeting in London. A flurry of correspondence followed[117] for almost two months, as first the Old, and then the New Congregation prevaricated, but delegates were finally elected, David Hesse at Ainsworth's Court and Eleazer Moses at Halliwell Street, and on 31 January 1847 they were persuaded to meet in London under the chairmanship of the Chief Rabbi and in the presence of the *Beth Din* and there to agree to a 'treaty' of nine articles 'for the Benefit of the Poor'. In effect, both congregations agreed to share the profits arising from *shechita* and the burden of relieving the casual poor in a ratio of two to one, which perhaps roughly equated to their relative size. A 'United Board of Relief' was established, consisting of three representatives from each congregation, to supervise the examination of casual applicants and the distribution of relief, the Old Congregation bearing two-thirds, the New Congregation a third, of the total cost. The President of the Board, drawn from each congregation in turn, was to have the casting vote. In the case of resident poverty, each congregation undertook 'to support such of its own poor, as shall have been contributing members to the synagogue from this day's date'. The particularly heavy cost of maintaining 'the orphans of the late [Joseph] Golding' and the children of a young widow, Amelia Bebro, 'during their infancy', and the onerous obligation to bury 'strangers' was shared between the congregations in the same ratio of two to one, the taxes paid by the three butchers (1s 6d for every bullock killed, 6d each for sheep and lambs) and 'any money or moneys received for the burying of strangers' being shared in the same way. In what looks like an attempt to extract some of the bitterness from the dispute between the rival congregations, or, at all events, to stabilise their income, it was agreed

that neither Congregation shall under any circumstance whatever, admit as members or seat holders, any member or seat holder (having held his seat for at least six months) of the other Congregation, unless he or she continues to pay his or her usual contribution towards the Synagogue to which he shall till then have belonged.

The Agreement was to last for three years from 1 February, at the expiry of which period either party was at liberty to annul the treaty 'upon giving six months previous notice of such intention to the other Congregation'. It was a measure of the severity of the problem of itinerant poverty that the two Manchester congregations were able to sink their political differences, however temporarily.

The Select Committee at Halliwell Street wrote to London in February:

we much admire the great ability of the Chief Rabbi in causing the two Hebrew Congregations of Manchester to be on better and more amicable terms . . . which we trust will be of lasting continuance;[118]

but in truth the foundations of the agreement were laid on quicksand. Nothing had been done to heal the social distinctions within the Manchester community or the political differences which had arisen out of them. The rough and ready code of procedure devised by the Board of Relief during its early meetings left it open to partisan manipulation and ill-equipped to cope with the kind of emergency which was the common outcome of transmigration. When the need for relief was often urgent, the machinery for dispensing it was slow and cumbersome. Although Jewish 'distress' increased during the early months of the Board's existence, the influence exerted by the New Congregation's representatives, with fewer resources at their disposal, was towards greater economies than those practised at Halliwell Street. The six members of the Board served in rotation as Relieving Officers, at least one attending each evening at his appropriate synagogue from Sunday to Thursday, but if a pauper arrived after the Thursday evening sitting, however great his need, he was allowed only 9d from synagogal funds to provide him with three nights' lodgings and maintain him over Friday and the Sabbath until the Relieving Officer arrived for his Sunday sitting.[119] A Relieving Officer was empowered to dispense sums of no more than 5s (or 7s 6d if a second member of the Board was present), and, in the ordinary course of events, a pauper was entitled to only one more payment (of not more than 1s) if he returned within three months. No discretionary power was granted to Relieving Officers to make larger payments or to deviate from the agreed procedure even to the extent of reviewing payments in the event of a long illness. 'Special cases' of severe misfortune could be dealt with only by a full meeting of the Board, which was frugal in its charity, particularly when the President came from Ainsworth's Court. If a Relieving Officer acted on his own initiative, he ran the risk of censure by the congregation to which he did not belong, while a system which gave a casting vote to a President drawn alternately from each congregation did little more than provide each in turn with the opportunity of exercising its extravagance or parsimony at the expense of the other. In the last resort, the treaty depended on an amount of good will on both sides which in fact existed on neither.

Within a month of its signing, the treaty itself had become a bone of contention. At the end of February an acrimonious exchange over the charges relating to the upkeep of *shochetim* ended only when the Old Congregation swallowed its pride and paid out what it regarded as an excessive proportion of the total.[120] In June the Old Congregation again backed down when the New Congregation insisted that all six elected delegates were expected to attend every meeting of the Board.[121] In mid-July, however, a more serious rift opened up when the representatives of the New Congregation, temporarily in a voting majority, refused to pass the accounts rendered by Adolphus Sington, a member at Halliwell Street, or to refund money which he had paid out on his own discretion in a case of special need.[122] On 13 August, in a long and angry letter to the Chief Rabbi[123] (delivered by hand by Jacob Franklin), Ansell Spier accused the New Congregation of undermining the whole purpose of the Board by 'so niggardly and parsimonious a disposition as to frustrate the more generous intentions of the old synagogue': its representatives were responsible for the Board's inflexible and restrictive mechanism; they had refused (as in the case of Sington's payment) to sanction discretionary relief in cases of genuine need; they had declined to contribute to the support of three 'old and infirm' paupers, Ralph Rua, Jacob Lyons and Sarah Hyams, who, although long resident in Manchester, had never contributed to the funds at Halliwell Street. It was the case of Sarah Hyams, a widow with four children, which had caused the present difficulty; two of her daughters were grown up and contributed to the family income by taking in lodgers, but this was not enough. Mrs Hyams was supported during the winter months by the Philanthropic Society and private alms, and for the rest of the time was dependent upon the synagogue. After granting her an initial 3s as a 'casual' pauper, however, the Board had first delayed a decision on a second appeal and then, on 13 July, had rejected it, after Sington had already laid out a further 3s. Spier sought Dr Adler's ruling that the cases of Rua, Lyons and Hyams were entitled to joint assistance from the Board on the analogy of the Bebro and Golding children. The Chief Rabbi was also called upon to review the constitution of the Board, to provide 'greater scope' for the 'generous yet discriminating policy of the Old Congregation'. It was suggested that he might consider re-apportioning representation on the Board to give the Old Congregation a two to one majority equivalent to its greater contribution; alternatively, that the Old Congregation might be entrusted with the whole distribution of relief in return for a fixed annual contribution from the New. At all events, Dr Adler was urged by Spier 'to take such measures as may insure a speedy redress to the Poor'.

The degree of truth in Spier's allegations is difficult to determine. The immediate response of the New Congregation was a unilateral withdrawal of its representatives from the Board in early August and counter-complaints to the Chief Rabbi of 'insults' offered to its representatives by those of the Old Congregation.[124] As to the three ageing paupers, it was pointed out that they attended the Old Congregation's services, even if they contributed nothing to its funds.[125] Direct evidence of the New Congregation's attitudes is not available, but it seems likely that the real difficulty was that of justly apportioning the expenses of relief at a time when the tide of vagrancy was running high. A third of a large bill was more than Ainsworth's Court could afford to pay, and its representatives were mandated to press for economies which Halliwell Street represented to the Chief Rabbi as 'niggardly and parsimonious'. It is probable, too, that Hesse, later associated with rigid synagogal economies in matters of charity, was pressing for a greater degree of deterrence and circumspection in the treatment of casual poverty, at least until Anglo-Jewry could agree on some form of concerted action. During 1847 he was pressing through other channels for action at a national level by the Board of Deputies. Certainly it would be rash to consider the New Congregation as illiberal in its attitudes: on 4 April 1847 Israel Levy initiated a collection 'for the relief of the great distress which now prevails' in a charity sermon which, according to the *Manchester Guardian*, 'would have done honour to a minister of the Gentile Christian Church', and which realised a total of over £10.[126] In the early summer the lady members of the congregation, under the lead of the wife of Joel Benjamin, had founded Manchester's first female Jewish charity, the United Sisters Charitable and Benevolent Society, the object of which, according to the *Jewish Chronicle*, was 'to relieve poor Jewish females (legally married) during their confinement in childbed and sickness'.[127] However, the Old Congregation's suggestion to the Chief Rabbi in September that 'puerile complaints' could be avoided if the New Congregation agreed if not to return to the Board at least to bear its proportion of the cost of relief, did nothing to allay the fear at Ainsworth's Court of an extravagant generosity towards vagrants.[128] At all events, Dr Adler had no desire to be caught in the trivial cross-fire of a party dispute in which his intervention could only be misconstrued. Both congregations had accepted the regulations relating to ritual and decorum which he had presented to Anglo-Jewry in February 1847, and with orthodoxy at least secure, other matters were better left to local bargaining.

The real victims were the casual poor. At first, the representatives of the Old Congregation continued to meet as a United Board of Relief 'at the usual time in Halliwell Street' to distribute funds 'on the principles laid down', charging the New Congregation, in its absence, with a third of the cost,[129] but when it became clear that no such bills would be paid at Ainsworth's Court, even for 'the large number of mendicants' who came into Manchester for the Holy days of 1847, the Old Congregation was thrown back on its own resources. In October, it declared the whole treaty 'null and void',[130] and in November the editor of the *Jewish Chronicle*, while refusing, like the Chief Rabbi, to be drawn into the dispute, told one of its correspondents from Manchester: 'We exceedingly regret that the Treaty on behalf of the poor was of so short a duration.'[131] Late in the autumn, as the situation worsened, consideration was given at Halliwell Street to limiting relief to casual applicants to a total of £2 a week,[132] and, when this proved impracticable, the Select Committee turned in December to the novel expedient of 'farming out' its immigrant paupers to a new charity organisation, the Society for the Relief of Really Deserving Distressed Foreigners, at a cost of £40 a year.[133] The Golding orphans were boarded with Paris Cohen, a stationery traveller in Johnson Street, at the joint cost of the Old Congregation and the Manchester Poor Law Union.

Manchester's Society for the Relief of Distressed Foreigners was founded on 4 December 1847[134] by a group of German merchants, most of them non-Jewish, as a 'regular system of dispensing relief' to itinerant foreigners whose presence amongst the 'street mendicants of all ages' who 'hourly infested' the central shopping and warehouse districts, 'forcing pence from the pockets of passers-by', picking pockets, and interrupting 'polite conversation', was as much of an embarrassment to the foreign business community as Jewish mendicants were to the synagogue. The first society of the name was founded at Hull, and, as panic spread along the line of transmigration, others followed in Leeds, Bradford, Huddersfield, and finally Manchester. As an alternative to private almsgiving, which tended, it was believed, to perpetuate 'the continued annoyance of office applicants' and 'the trade of "Any pens or pencils wanted?" ',[135] and to encourage 'a system of fraud',[136] subscribers to the society were requested to distribute tickets which directed applicants to the society's office in Princess Street, where their claims could be properly investigated. With the assistance of information from the sister-societies in other towns, impostors could be weeded out and refused help, while the deserving were furnished with food and lodgings until they could be sent on to another English town, given money or provisions (but not tickets) to assist their emigration to America, or, most commonly, provided with free return passages to their places of origin. In the case of any applicant who could be persuaded to go back to his home, the Manchester society paid the train fare to Hull, where the local society arranged for a steerage passage to Hamburg, Rotterdam or Antwerp. During the first year of the society's operation in Manchester, 140 persons were assisted to return to the Continent, fifty-two were helped across the Atlantic, eighty-eight 'sent forward' to London, Birmingham or Liverpool, and 186 undeserving cases, including 'numerous instances of imposition', were 'detected and exposed'.[137] Foreign beggars were kept away from warehouses, cleared off the streets and eased out of town, either because they were deserving of being assisted by the society or because its strict surveillance cut off their local means of support; for many hopeful travellers, the process of transmigration was either eased, diverted or reversed.

The society was not specifically Jewish in either its membership or its orientation, but it was assured of substantial support from the Jews, both in their role as foreign merchants and because the Old Congregation's initial quarterly subscription of £10 related it directly to communal needs. On the first committee of twelve, chaired by the non-Jewish trader, Martin Schunck, there were four Jews—H. S. Straus (in his new capacity as vice-consul for Holland), David Falk (as the official representative from Halliwell Street), A. S. Sichel and Louis Behrens—and the society received subscriptions of five guineas from S. L. Behrens, three guineas from Benjamin Hyam (who otherwise rarely appeared on non-Jewish subscription lists), two guineas from Adolphus Sington, his partner Edward Nathan and Leopold Amschel, and one from each of Ralph Straus, Ansell Spier, S. D. Bles, Marcus Bauer, Eleazer Moses and Sam Mendel. In the event, however, although the society continued for the rest of the century, it failed to provide even a limited solution to Jewish poverty. Under the terms of its agreement with the Old Congregation, a handful of Jewish immigrants were provided with return fares,[138] but it was found that most could not be kept away from the synagogue, where, in turn, they could scarcely be refused the kind of temporary financial assistance which the society 'avoided as much as possible'. Nor did the society provide for Anglo-Jewish paupers, either resident or itinerant, who applied to the synagogue for 'casual' relief. Early in April 1848 the Old Congregation wrote that its funds necessitated the discontinuance of its subscription.[139] Although many Jews continued to subscribe as individuals and to serve on the society's executive (in particular, Sichel, Louis Behrens and the Straus brothers), Jewish applicants were passed on to one or other of the synagogues, with a single reservation, that if the synagogue was prepared to pay the rail fare of a Jewish pauper as far as Hull, the society undertook to see him across the North Sea.

In December 1841, when he was fêted for his contribution to the work of the Philanthropic Society amongst the resident poor, Isaac Franklin had advocated the formation in Manchester of a 'Strangers' Aid Society'

as a substitute for the present mischievous practise of indiscriminate relief, and as a means of more liberally assisting the truly deserving,[140]

but no one at the time had taken the problem seriously enough to tamper with the piecemeal methods of the synagogue. The marked acceleration of transmigration from 1844–45, with its accompanying threat to the pocket and reputation of the Jewish and foreign communities, gave rise to the first crude alternatives to the 'indiscriminate' distribution of alms. The Hebrew Mendicity Society in Liverpool and the Board of Relief in Manchester may be seen as the earliest provincial attempts to attempt to apply more or less systematic procedures to the relief of the casual poor of the community. The attempts did not succeed, in part because in neither case was there a firm base in communal unity, in part, at least in Manchester, because the community was not agreed in its assessment of the problem. The Old Congregation tended to see it as a temporary local emergency, in which stringent discrimination might be softened by humanity and individual discretion. At the New, attitudes were less paternal and more uncompromising. David Hesse, in particular, appreciated the need for the consistent and economic application of fixed principles, and it was for this reason, perhaps, that Sington's 'liberality' was unacceptable. He also saw the transmigrant poor as part of a national and continuing problem, which included the decay of the itinerant trades, and which, like other issues affecting the future of all Anglo-Jewry, demanded concerted action at a national level from a reinvigorated Board of Deputies.

V

Hesse saw it as part of the crusading role of the New Congregation to bring Jewish institutions back to life after a long period of somnolence, and, in particular, to instill a new dynamism into a Board of Deputies 'apparently instituted for the express purpose of doing nothing'.[141] It was the susbstance of his case that under the benevolent despotism of Sir Moses Montefiore the Board had come to concentrate overmuch on its admittedly important role of watching Parliamentary proceedings for enactments potentially injurious to Jewish interests. Although Montefiore personally was exceptionally active in international causes, in domestic affairs the Board had failed to provide a strong lead in furthering the political, social and educational progress of Anglo-Jewry. Hesse believed that it was the duty of the Deputies

to assist, by their advice, recommendations, influence, and other means at their command, in all matters relating to the political equalisation with our Christian brethren, education of the rising generation, improvement of the character of the adult population, the formation of one great harmonious union of all the metropolitan and provincial congregations, encouragement of industrial pursuits among the lower classes, or any other of the great political and social questions that may be found useful or expeditious.[142]

In the opinion of Hesse, the development of systematic policies along these lines involved the collection by the Board of full and up-to-date statistical information on every aspect of Anglo-Jewish life, the replacement of brief, unconnected meetings of a London clique by regular annual sessions, representative of the whole of Anglo-Jewry, to plan united action in common causes, and the opening of the Board's proceedings, hitherto secret, to the critical scrutiny of the Anglo-Jewish press. A closed oligarchy, and its associated attitude of political caution, was no more acceptable in London than in Manchester, particularly at a time when so many critical problems demanded attention.

His opportunity to act on these beliefs came in the summer of 1847, when both congregations, temporarily tied by treaty, decided that the time was ripe for the community 'to assume its position amongst the large Congregations in

the Empire' by electing its own representatives to the Board.[143] David Hesse
was elected at Ainsworth's Court on 13 June; a fortnight later, Jacob Franklin
and A. S. Sichel were chosen to represent Halliwell Street. In London Franklin
professed views not unlike those of Hesse, and it seems not improbable that it
was his prompting which drew the Old Congregation from its lethargy;
having severed his connection with the *Voice of Jacob* a few months earlier, he
felt inclined to challenge the oligarchy from within. At the first meeting
which they attended together, on 30 August 1847, the two men defended a
common programme.[144]

Franklin began by introducing a resolution which would have made it
necessary for the Board to obtain 'authentic statistical returns' on all matters
connected with the 'social improvement and civil relations' of Anglo-Jewry as
a basis from which the Board might discharge its 'multifarious duties'. Opposed by Louis Lucas on the grounds that a 'numbering of the people' was contrary to biblical precept, the resolution was defeated only by the casting vote
of Montefiore, after a ballot had produced a deadlock of six votes to six. This
was as near as Franklin came to success. His further proposal that the Board
should hold annual sessions at 'a convenient period of the year' to improve the
continuity of its policies and 'better facilitate' the attendance of provincial and
colonial delegates was defeated by seven votes to three, and a subsequent attempt by Hesse to have the meeting adjourned was likewise lost. The only resolution backed by the three provincial delegates (two from Manchester and one
from Liverpool) to receive a majority required that the Board provide its
members with fourteen days' notice of a meeting. Disappointment was acute
in progressive circles in London and Manchester. A member of the New
Congregation wrote:

while the Board of Deputies . . . is very active in all matters relating to foreign countries, they show no symptoms of being desirous to promote the general interests of the
Jewish inhabitants of the Empire,[145]

and a supporting editorial in the *Jewish Chronicle* accused the deputies of
'apathy, listlessness, indolence', pointing with particular scorn to the Board's
failure to support the political struggle of Baron Rothschild in the City of
London.[146] When in January 1848 the Board drew up a petition in support of
Lord John Russell's new bill for the removal of Jewish disabilities, the *Chronicle*
commented: 'Better late than never.'[147]

Hesse carried Franklin's campaign into the spring of 1848. He challenged
the legality of the half-yearly meeting of the Board on 27 March on the
grounds that inadequate notice had been given, and compelled Montefiore to
adjourn until the following month,[148] by which time the New Congregation
had drawn up a 'memorial' of its suggestions and complaints. In this docu-

ment,[149] presented to the Board by Hesse on 27 April, the members of the
New Congregation stated their conviction

that more than an average amount of the following evils prevail amongst us, compared with our Christian brethren, or with the Jews of Germany, France, Holland and
Belgium, viz. A want of Union on nearly all subjects of importance amongst all
classes—A deplorable amount of ignorance—a great want of Employment, and in
consequence an increase of poverty and misery amongst the lower classes.

Since the Board was, in their view, the 'only constituted authority that can
alter this state of things', it should take decisive action, especially when the
movement for emancipation provided 'an additional and powerful motive' for
the improvement of the social condition and moral character of working-class
Jewry. The Board ought to become 'a popular institution', in the limited sense
that it should admit to its meetings members of the Jewish press; it was the
duty of the Board to collect accurate statistical information concerning the community at large; and the successful implementation of its policies demanded
annual plenary sessions, and a permanent executive committee of London
deputies. All of which the Board rejected as lying beyond its traditional
jurisdiction; the collection of information was vetoed by nine votes
to six, the admission of the press by twelve votes to three.[150] Hesse made one
final effort, in June 1848, to rally support for his views by calling on provincial
congregations not represented on the Board to elect 'men of a liberal turn of
mind, men of energy and foresight',[151] but when this appeal met with no
response, he retired from the scene of battle, leaving Franklin to fight on alone.
With Hesse's brief appearance in London, the Manchester community had
made its first independent impression on Anglo-Jewry, and, however ineffective
the immediate impact, the Chief Rabbi and Sir Moses Montefiore were alerted
to the possibility of Manchester becoming a force in national communal
politics with which they would have to come to terms.

VI

Co-operation between Franklin and Hesse in London did nothing to smooth
over the differences between their congregations in Manchester. On 7 January
1848 the *Jewish Chronicle* refused to publish a letter from a Manchester correspondent 'since every communication from the town is unfortunately sure to
give offence to one of the two parties',[152] and the editor went on to ask, in the
light of conversionism and the enemies of Jewish political rights, 'Why do you
not unite to combat a common opposition, rather than waste your strength in
petty contentions?'[153] The difficulty was that, however trivial the arguments

over relief payments and butchers' fees, the major 'contentions' were not petty: they were the symptoms of important changes both in the community and outside it. Manchester Jewry had grown far beyond the point at which it was amenable to government by benevolent patriarchy. Not only was it too big—perhaps ten times as large by 1847 as the community for which the constitution had been intended—it also included a large body of immigrant shopkeepers and manufacturers—an ambitious and sensitive *petite bourgeoisie*—who were anxious to convert the currency of their economic success into the realities of congregational privilege. They could argue, with substantial truth, that the time had arrived for the community to reach political maturity in the shape of a liberal constitution which shared political favours more evenly within the middle classes. An explosion had occurred because the Free Members had lacked the flexibility to accommodate these opinions. They could not quite surrender to the view that the community no longer depended upon the quality of their foresight or upon the extent of their benevolence. They could not quite accept that the lowering of the barriers of privilege to admit the brash young businessmen of Ainsworth's Court, with their noisy advocacy of 'modernity' and practical reform, could do anything but draw unwelcome attention to the growth of the community, and perhaps endanger its religious integrity. Many at Halliwell Street saw as clearly as Hesse the need for a more active prosecution of Jewish political interests, the need for more efficient schools and for a more effective system of poor relief, but they were not convinced that such objectives required a democratic base.

The major issue of the later 1840s, not only in Manchester but throughout Anglo-Jewry, was the extent to which a revision was called for in the institutions of the community and its ways of thought. There was probably general agreement on the need for schools, such as the embryonic institutions in Liverpool, Birmingham and Manchester, in which Hebrew education was combined with 'such a curriculum as is adopted by the respectable academies of Great Britain'. In at least one analysis, such 'national academies' were the *sine qua non* of Jewish progress:

Not until then [according to 'Quizinus' in 1845] will a grand and decisive change be perceived in their moral state; the possession of knowledge will command respect, and dispel illiberality of feeling. Then, those who till now have never dreamt that the Hebrew could rise from the degraded position [in which] he has been placed . . . will . . . be startled by a neglected nation's rising phoenix-like from the ashes of its former grandeur.[154]

The Chief Rabbi himself had given priority to the creation, maintenance and improvement of schools which, although based squarely on religious foundations, included 'efficient instruction in the various branches of a general education'.[155] There was probably also a measure of Anglo-Jewish agreement on the need for a greater political activism than had been encouraged by the Board of Deputies. The man of the moment, in 1847–48, was not Montefiore, aloof within the community, deferential outside it, but Rothschild, the successful Parliamentary candidate for the City of London.[156] This bespoke a general conviction that the Jewish community was sufficiently secure to press for its rights rather than move conspicuously, like a well-behaved child, and under the tutelage of the Deputies, towards the possible rewards of equality and emancipation. There was a sense, too, in which the community as a whole accepted, with the New Congregation, that Jewish social problems required urgent attention. Although kindly outsiders held, with singular obstinacy, to the new Victorian stereotype of the Jew as a respectable merchant, honourable in his dealings, who looked after his own and contributed heavily and conspicuously to public charities, from the inside it was clear (to Jacob Franklin, for example) that the future depended on the eradication of what the New Congregation's memorial had called the 'evils' of ignorance, unemployment and poverty. Differences arose chiefly at those points at which a desire for 'modernisation' appeared to endanger either (as in London in 1840) the religious structure, liturgy or doctrines of the community , or (as in Manchester in 1844) the established hierarchy of privilege, patronage and power.

The most radical Manchester analysis of the national situation was that provided by Theodores in the prospectus of a new monthly periodical, *The Anglo-Jewish Archives*,[157] which he intended to edit but which never appeared. By their 'moral bearing' as individuals and 'their zealous regard for the character of the Jewish name', the founders of the Anglo-Jewish community had succeeded, according to Theodores, 'in battering down one lingering prejudice after the other' and so achieved a remarkable equality of social esteem. In so doing, however, they had not found it necessary to attempt a comparable improvement in Jewish institutional life:

To claim an equality, in this respect, with our (politically enchained) German brethren, were indeed Quixotic. We could hardly bear, with honor, comparison with some of the least numerous sects at home, whose origin, by the side of our religious existence, is but of yesterday. Our public schools are in embryo; our seminaries await the fiat of creation; our theologians speak in foreign tongues; the representatives of Jewish genius in the various arts which embellish life, or in the sciences which render it secure, are not adequately fostered by Jewish care and munificence; even our Charities, though sustained by a quality which flows richly in the Jewish heart, fail in their sacred purpose, and are devoid of becoming grandeur.

The answer, Theodores believed, lay in 'German profundity'; from German writers, 'facts and arguments' could be borrowed to back the case for the removal of Jewish disabilities; from the discourses of Frankfurter, Holdheimer and Mannheimer, could be taken material for Anglo-Jewish sermons and 'family devotion'; in German literature would be found the model for emulation by 'the studious Hebrew youth of Britain'. On other matters, of course, Theodores had already committed himself: he accepted, too, the German attack on the standing of the Talmud; he accepted German standards of religious Reform; he believed in the right of each Jewish congregation to determine its own liturgical future.

Hesse did not share these views. His dealings with the Board of Deputies, and the breakdown of the Chief Rabbi's 'treaty', had no doubt made him cynical about the practical value of the central institutions of Anglo-Jewry, but he had shown no inclination towards either local autonomy or religious heresy. At the opening of the new synagogue in 1844, De Lara expressed the belief that

every congregation has the right, not only to appoint its own slaughterer, but even to select its own Raab or Haham, who is absolutely independent of any other Raab or Haham as one congregation is of any other,

and that 'communication' with London was

a mere matter of courtesy. The London congregation has assumed an authority over every congregation in the kingdom to which it has no right.[158]

But De Lara was speaking out of turn, perhaps anticipating that the New Congregation would experience some difficulty in gaining official recognition, and no evidence exists to suggest any uneasiness in relationships between Ainsworth's Court and the Chief Rabbi's office. Hesse believed in a strong local initiative in secular matters; he believed in a democratic synagogue; but he was not a Reformer, and he had allowed the standing of the New Synagogue to depend upon the Chief Rabbi's blessing. He was, more than anything else, the sharpest of the sharp young businessmen whose grievances had sparked off the revolt. He had no sympathy for the views of Theodores, who had remained throughout at Halliwell Street, amongst the established families whose children came to him for their lessons in German and Hebrew.

But the fluidity of opinion within the community raised the schism of 1844 above the level of a storm in the synagogal teacup. The issues which had been raised in and around it—the constitution of the congregation, the status of the local community, the ritual of the synagogue, the welfare of the poor—remained the burning communal issues for more than a decade. The reappraisal begun in 1844 continued at least until 1858.[159]

It is a measure of the sharpness of the social distinctions created by immigration and social change that they were sufficient to prolong a division which endangered the community's reputation, held up its institutional development, and had no basis in doctrinal or liturgical differences. When Joseph Mitchell of the *Jewish Chronicle* attended services at both the Manchester synagogues towards the end of 1848,[1] the only differences he noted were the absence of 'pulpit instruction' at the Old, and of a well-trained 'voluntary choir' at the New. Otherwise there was little to choose between them. Both were 'thinly attended'. In both, the Readers—Jacob Kantrowitz of Warsaw at the Old, Philip Dessau of Hamburg at the New—were melodious and 'correct'. Both showed striking evidence of 'an improved mode of worship' based upon the rules for decorum contained within the Chief Rabbi's code of 1847. Both were strictly orthodox; the New, if anything, more orthodox than the Old. The attendance by members of one synagogue at the services of the other seemed to emphasise the perversity of their separation. Expediency had in itself proved insufficient to bring them together. The experiment in the joint relief of the immigrant poor had only emphasised the real and apparently irreconcilable social and political differences which kept them apart.

The increasing tempo of the struggle for political emancipation following the election of Baron de Rothschild as M.P. for the City of London in 1847, although it received the unanimous endorsement of the Manchester community,[2] did nothing to strengthen the logic of reunion. So great was the middle-class support for tolerance as an abstract and general ideal that the justice of the Jewish case did not depend upon the internal structure of the congregation, of which most Manchester people were probably totally unaware. Synagogal dispute was reported in the national Jewish, not in the local Gentile press. The *Guardian* described Jewish disabilities, in 1847, as the 'very last remnant of religious persecution', and commented

We trust that the liberal and intelligent spirit of this district will be earnestly and vigorously manifested in favour of the removal of the shackles now oppressing this portion of our fellow-countrymen.[3]

One Manchester citizen saw the achievement of political rights for the Jews as the natural outcome of 'Christian charity and liberal principles' and ascribed

Manchester's failure to promote them more actively to its preoccupation with free trade.[4] Another, in supporting the candidacy of a Roman Catholic for the South Lancashire division, wrote that

it would be a happy incident if the present parliament should open its sittings with a Jew representing the City of London, and a Catholic the still more important constituency of South Lancashire. It would denote a great advance in the public mind in religious liberality.[5]

A form of open petition in favour of Russell's Bill for the Removal of Jewish Disabilities was drawn up by Henry Lyons, a Jew from York who had served in a minor capacity on the administrative staff of the Anti-Corn Law League in Manchester, and in January 1848 it was laid out for signature in Newall's Buildings.[6] The defeat of the Bill in the House of Lords by 163 votes to 128 was characterised by the *Guardian* as 'an obstinate resistance to public opinion . . . fairly and decidedly manifested',[7] and the paper was equally critical of Parliament's failure 'to retrieve the error of the last session' during the period 1849–50.[8] In a series of unequivocal editorials the *Guardian* disposed one by one of the arguments adduced by the opponents of Jewish emancipation.[9]

The realities of Jewish communal life did not enter into the matter. Middle-class Manchester clung to the stereotype of the Jewish citizen which best suited its tolerant inclinations, and only approximated to the facts of the case; the few opponents of Jewish claims took their stand on religious principle. The *Guardian* believed that the 'private worth' and 'active benevolence' of the Jews was 'perhaps better known in Manchester than in any other part of the United Kingdom'.[10] They were the 'distinguished ornaments' of local society.[11] In opening a debate in the Town Council on 19 January 1848, on the expediency of sending an official memorial in favour of Russell's Bill, William Evans emphasised that Jews 'deserved well of this country' as 'respectable . . . merchants, honourable in their dealings, and prominent in their support of objects of benevolence and utility', a view endorsed by the Council by twenty-nine votes to five.[12] Joseph Lamb, one of the five, believed (with Stowell) that

it was inconsistent to give power to persons to make laws in a Christian country, who reject the Saviour whom the Christians worshipped . . . such conduct would bring a judgement upon us.[13]

Canon Stowell, as he had now become, told an audience in the Corn Exchange in November 1847, that he was not prepared to 'violate' the constitution by giving 'the legislative character to an unconverted Jew'.[14] Neither the turmoil within the Jewish community nor the illiberality of the parent synagogue affected the dialogue one way or the other.

The community was also unmoved by an increase of conversionist propaganda and missionary effort. The advent of Reform in England was regarded by Christian missioners as a favourable omen since it supposedly arose from a 'general movement of the mind amongst all classes' which would undermine the 'bigotry and superstition' of Judaism.[15]

Infidelity was fast filling up the gap caused in the minds of the Jews, in consequence of their throwing off their superstitions and old ideas; this offered a fitting opportunity for presenting to the Jews the sacred truth of Christianity.[16]

Stowell spoke of his 'satisfaction' on hearing 'that the Jews were beginning to relinquish their rabbinical traditions'.[17] Napthali believed that most success was to be expected amongst Jews who set a low value on oral tradition.[18] The Rev. A. E. Pearce, also of the local branch of the Society for the Propagation of the Gospel Amongst the Jews, thought that many Jews were

lapsing into open and undisguised Deism . . . some of them are throwing off the Talmud, and endeavouring, perhaps vainly, to find a resting place in the Old Testament.[19]

The Anglicans were encouraged to appoint their own local missionary, J. G. Lazarus—'late superintendent of the Liverpool Institute for Inquiring and Converted Jews'—whose arrival, in November 1849, was advertised on the front page of the *Guardian*.[20] Within two years, Lazarus was 'speaking to many in the streets, . . . visiting others at their dwellings', and 'addressing a considerable number' in the lodging houses of the Old Town, where he was attended, like Napthali, with 'much kindness' and minimal success.[21] In 1849 Pearce believed the 'predicted conversion' of the Jews to be

on the eve of fulfilment, inasmuch as most of the events which are to precede it have been accomplished and there are few intervening prophecies to interfere with that which predicts the conversion of this ancient people,[22]

but, after the initial drama of missionary activity in the mid-1840s, Manchester Jewry no longer took conversionism too seriously. M. H. Simonson, the new secretary at Halliwell Street, believed there was not one in a thousand converts 'who really mean it'.[23] In July 1848 he referred to Dr Adler the case of a shoemaker who had been 'seduced' by a missionary in London and who, although he never accepted 'their Dogma of Salvation', had stayed on with the conversionists to learn a trade. Since his arrival in Manchester a few weeks previously he had begun to attend synagogue and he now sought readmission to the faith in order to be able to say *kaddish* for his mother.[24]

What all this amounted to was that the common political and religious concerns of the community were insufficient to overcome its social differences. The division, after all, was based upon class, and the only forces likely to remove it were those which tended to minimise the class distinctions between

Halliwell Street and Ainsworth's Court. One of these forces was time since, in the Jewish context, length of residence and degree of anglicisation played a major part in determining social and congregational status. Another was the improving prosperity of new immigrants, very marked throughout the 1840s, since this tended to narrow the economic gap between the two congregations. Since orthodoxy was not at stake, it seems likely that, in time, these forces alone would have brought reunion. What hastened the process during the years 1840–51 were two dramatic developments—pauper immigration on an expanding scale and the European revolutions of 1848—each of which emphasised the social interests which the two congregations had in common over the relatively minor constitutional issues on which they were divided. Both developments emphasised the solidarity of the two elements of the Jewish middle class: the first in a negative sense, by creating a Jewish proletariat from which both wished to emphasise their separation; the second, more positively, by dramatising the national interests which German Jews in both synagogues had in common, and which, at the same time, seemed, by highlighting the glory of liberal revolution, to point the community as a whole in a more liberal direction.

I

During the spring of 1848 the democratic secession within the community was overshadowed by liberal insurrection in Europe. The collapse of the French monarchy in February was followed by the fall of Metternich in Vienna, revolution in Berlin, and, in May, the assembly of the national convention at Frankfurt to determine the future of Germany.

In Manchester the immediate effect of these events was to raise the tired spectre of working-class violence, and to unite the middle classes under the Mayor—and cotton manufacturer—Elkanah Armitage, as protectors of public safety and private property. A faint flickering of Chartism, the discovery of pikes in cellars, and a few isolated outbursts of mob violence, chiefly directed against factories and warehouses, were sufficient to bring into being an army of special constables.[25] A force of over six hundred volunteers, chiefly young clerks and warehouse porters, was organised by Armitage as a 'Town Hall Guard', a mobile force, drilled by the police, with white armlets and staves, which could be moved quickly to any trouble spot in the town.[26] It included 'several young foreigners', some of whom had already seen service in anti-revolutionary warfare on the Continent, one in three revolutionary 'contests' in Switzerland.[27] Many smaller shopkeepers came out in quiet, public sympathy for the objects of Chartism,[28] but the general trend of middle-class opinion favoured a massive defence of the *status quo*. A situation which had never been as explosive as the authorities feared was fairly easily brought under control. In his annual crime report the Chief Constable concluded that in spite of the 'great privation and distress' caused by deficient harvests in England and Ireland, and the 'unprecedented excitement and alarm' conjured up by the 'general commotion' in Europe, Manchester had been, throughout 1848, 'less criminal and more orderly than formerly'.[29]

Within the Jewish community, the revolution in Europe had the effect of drawing together the German members of both congregations, with their non-Jewish fellow countrymen, in distant sympathy with the rebels in Berlin and Vienna and the representatives of the German people assembled at Frankfurt. Meeting at the Athenaeum on 30 March 1848, under the chairmanship of Salis Schwabe, two hundred German residents of Manchester voted an address of sympathy to the Frankfurt Assembly—itself a tribute to the 'orderly' methods of the German rebels, as Schwabe was careful to point out—and inaugurated a subscription for the 'martyrs of the holy German cause' who had laid down their lives in Berlin or Vienna 'for the enfranchisement of Germany from arbitrary rule and degrading subjection'.[30] The committee which convened the meeting included Joseph Eller, a German–Jewish commission agent and son-in-law of H. M. Salomon, and amongst the Manchester Germans who assembled before a vast flag bearing the black, crimson and gold emblem of the German Empire, many with tricolour rosettes and ribbons, were many other Jews, including M. K. Wagner and H. S. Straus from the Old Congregation, and David Hesse from the New. In one of the principal speeches Eller denounced the 'evil star' who had ruled at Vienna and welcomed the 'sun of liberty' which was breaking through the clouds of despotism, although he spoke also of those German national virtues—'rectitude', 'industry' and 'practical usefulness'—which he believed had already assured the Germans in Manchester of the respect of their fellow citizens. Other German Jews—Louis Berend, A. S. Sichel, Leopold Amschel, Edward Nathan, David Israel—contributed to a fund which finally totalled £505.[31] The address to the president of the Frankfurt Assembly was drawn up and read to the meeting, in German, by Tobias Theodores. It expressed sympathy for the fallen and prayed for the success of a unity without which liberty could not survive. 'The men who have dictated to the world the laws of thought' were now free, and at Frankfurt their 'sublime spirit' was reshaping the nation as the 'never-fading ornament' of liberty. As Theodores ended, 'The German fatherland for ever! liberty for ever! order for ever!', the whole audience was led by members of the local *Liedertafel* into 'Deutsche Vaterland'.[32]

Although the hope for German unity faded, there was nothing ephemeral about the solidarity of Manchester's German colony, which had been growing more gradually since the early 1840s in keeping with the growth of national feeling in Germany and with the arrival in Manchester of voluntary exiles like David Hesse and Louis Beaver. During 1841 'German gentlemen resident in Manchester' began to hold regular meetings of a *Liedertafel*, 'for the purpose of the practice of their national songs'.[33] Once a year the society held open concerts—usually in the Music Saloon of the Albion Hotel in Piccadilly— at which invited guests were treated, according to the *Guardian*, to 'a fine burst of patriotic spirit and sentiment, in good harmonious blending'.[34] In April 1847, members of the society paid their respects to Dr Felix Mendelssohn—'their distinguished countryman'—who made a short visit to Manchester as the guest of Martin Schunck's partner, Charles Souchay.[35] A Manchester Kegel Club was founded at some time before April 1845, when Emil von Hees, its honorary secretary, advertised for suitable premises in the Broughton area.[36] In the mid-1840s a German tailor from Aix-la-Chapelle set up shop in Princess Street particularly to meet the needs of 'Die Deutschen Herren, ansässig in Manchester',[37] German publications were being advertised, in German, in the *Guardian*; and a new restaurant—the *Eureka*, in Market Street—supplied the *Allgemeine Zeitung* in its public coffee rooms.[38] The exist- ence in Manchester of a German *Verein* which in 1851 welcomed Kossuth on his visit to the town suggests that German feeling found political as well as cultural expression.[39] There were over a hundred German export firms in Manchester by 1851, and the Census of that year suggests the presence of one thousand persons of German birth, of whom at least 292 belonged to observant Jewish families. Apart from those in commerce, there were the German waiters at Manchester hotels who contributed as a body to the Frankfurt Fund, German music teachers and musicians, particularly in the orchestra of Charles Hallé, himself an exile of 1848, and German language teachers in every suburban district and public institution. The house of Elizabeth Gaskell in Plymouth Grove was one social centre for German families, Jewish as well as non-Jewish, although particularly those, like Salis Schwabe, linked with the Cross Street Unitarian Chapel, of which her husband, William, was junior minister.[40] Manchester Jewry was not encased, as were several American communities of this period, within a German enclave which might have slowed down its cul- tural assimilation,[41] but its German members were linked with a wider German colony by ties sufficiently strong, particularly after 1848, to minimise their com- munal differences.

An important feature of those ties was that they were political as well as national. This did not mean simply that liberalism as much as nationalism strengthened the bonds between German Jews of both congregations, but still more that the growth of liberal feeling at Halliwell Street amongt those who welcomed it in Germany inclined them to look with greater favour upon the democratic rebels at Ainsworth's Court. The New Congregation was, after all, as the *Jewish Chronicle* pointed out, 'the advocate of enlightened progression, and of civil and religious liberty',[42] and it was inherently inconsistent for members of the Old Congregation to support freedom in Germany while refusing to countenance the demands of David Hesse. Philip Lucas, perhaps the most influential figure at Halliwell Street after the eclipse of Franklin, had contributed ten guineas to the Frankfurt Fund; Theodores had linked the 'eternal unity' of Germany with her 'eternal freedom'; H. S. Straus was amongst those who had spoken of 'reconciliation and the perfect oblivion of all animosity' as being 'the first and fairest fruit of the people's victory' in Germany.[43] At the very least, the impact of 1848 was to create links of friendship between the most liberal-minded men in both congregations, particularly, perhaps, between Lucas and Hesse, and to strengthen the logic of communal reunion on a wider middle-class franchise. Furthermore, the sympathetic response which the romance of European revolution evoked in middle-class Manchester—coexistent, as in the 1820s, with its fear of mob violence and popular radicalism—created an atmosphere which favoured any modest movement in a democratic direction. Such considerations, however, only made reunion more likely. What made it certain was the creation of a social threat from below within the Jewish milieu which persuaded the middle classes to rationalise their common interests in terms of a political compromise. In English society the threat was posed to the political and economic power of the middle classes by working-class movements; in Jewish, to the reputation of the middle-classes by pauper immigration on a scale far in excess of the influx of 1844–45.

II

When Joseph Mitchell of the *Jewish Chronicle* visited Manchester in November 1848, he was particularly impressed by

an increase in the influx of foreigners, who arrive at Hull and from thence to Manchester, as being the nearest congregation where they may expect relief, the number of Jews at Hull and Leeds being very small.[44]

Communal records endorse this impression, and Mitchell's conclusion that immigration had created in Manchester a poverty 'proportionately still larger than . . . in London'.[45] Early in 1848 the metropolitan synagogues were sufficiently alarmed by the rising tide of pauper immigration to send a circular to the Jewish congregations at Hamburg, Altona, Amsterdam, Rotterdam and Berlin, urging them to use their influence to dissuade Jews passing through their towns from coming to England, where the pressing claims of the resident poor seemed in danger of being 'drowned by the more clamorous and obtrusive demands of their foreign co-religionists'.[46] But the transmigration from Central and Eastern Europe to the United States which had gathered pace in the mid-1840s, when fast English steamships from Liverpool competed successfully with the previously dominant German shipping lines,[47] moved along a route which inevitably made more impact in northern towns, particularly Manchester and Liverpool, than in London. Its increasing scale from 1848 no doubt owed something to the 'disorganised state of politics in Germany and other parts of the continent',[48] but may be accounted for chiefly by a worsening of the political and economic conditions of Jews in those areas of East Prussia and Western Russia in which the movement had its source.[49] The economic basis of petty trades and crafts failed to meet the needs of a rapidly expanding population throughout these regions, but particularly in the narrowing area of Jewish settlement in Russia, where the Imperial campaign against the inner life of Jews through their 'compulsory enlightenment' in State schools reverted to the more direct methods of discriminatory legislation and enforced conscription as part of the government's intense anti-revolutionary activity.

The payments recorded in the account books of the Old Congregation suggest that at least two thousand paupers—more than twice the resident Jewish population of Manchester—were supplied with relief in money and kind between September 1848 and March 1851,[50] a total which takes no account either of those who passed through without requiring relief or of those who may have obtained it at Ainsworth's Court. Of those whose place of origin can be traced, four per cent came from other Jewish communities of the English provinces, seven per cent from London, six per cent from Holland and Belgium, fifty-three per cent from the Russian and Prussian provinces of Poland, fifteen per cent from the rest of Germany, six per cent from the rest of Russia, and nine per cent, in insignificant proportions, from Austria–Hungary, France, Rumania and Sweden. The largest single concentration of immigrants came from the towns and townlets around Warsaw and Posen, the main districts of Jewish settlement in Eastern Europe. Since only sixty-five of the 742 persons named in the account books remained in Manchester long enough to be enumerated in the Census taken at the beginning of April 1851, it may perhaps be assumed that most of the remainder found their way, by steerage-passage, to the United States. Manchester was only one of a chain of European congregations from which a transmigrant expected to obtain temporary support, medical attention or a small subsidy towards a continuance of his journey.

Most of those on the move were probably young and able-bodied men, but there were also 'old men with long beards', boys travelling alone and barefoot, the seriously ill, the partially blind, the lame and the deformed. At least twenty-three women travelled unaccompanied, and there were also more than sixty-two family groups of between two persons and eight, in thirteen of which the father was absent. One lone woman—Hinda Chime—was described as travelling 'in search of her Husband Abraham', and it seems safe to assume that other families without their breadwinners were following menfolk who had gone on ahead, often to uncertain destinations. The occupations of most recipients of relief are not known, but they included capmakers, book-binders, tailors, cabinet makers, glaziers, shoe and slipper makers, a lithographer, a coppersmith, a working jeweller, a watch maker, an umbrella maker, a 'fighter', two 'painters', three soldiers from the Russian Imperial army, a sailor, an officer in the French army, and fourteen persons who described themselves as 'rabbis', one of whom accompanied, and perhaps led, a group of poor men who received a joint subsidy of 2s 6d. Many, perhaps most, were petty traders and casual labourers who in Russia were particularly vulnerable to legal disabilities and whose occupations in Prussia were being gradually attenuated by newer economic developments. They included also adventurers, professional beggars and petty criminals like Joseph Jacobs and Braman Eneyenberg who arrived in Manchester on 11 May 1848 and left for Liverpool a few days later with silver plate, spectacles and foreign coins stolen from the co-religionist with whom they had lodged.[51] In October 1848 two German Jews—'one called Blumenbach'—stole a piece of canvas from the warehouse of Lomnitz and Co. under the pretence of begging.[52] Henry Bendorf was fined for the theft of silver plate in May 1849 before falling back on the relief of the synagogue.[53] A member at Halliwell Street described 'the usual numbers of itinerant paupers' who arrived in Manchester during the winter of 1849–50 as

mostly idle dissolute young men encouraged in some instances by lodging-house keepers to play cards with the alms bestowed upon them by the charitably disposed.[54]

This was too harsh a judgement. What it represented more accurately than the facts of the case were the fears and irritations of the settled community, for pauper immigration meant not only a constant drain on congregational resources but also a renewed and ill-timed threat to the communal reputation. From the late 1840s penniless immigrants from Central and Eastern Europe came to occupy the place vacated by the pedlars of an earlier period, sometimes literally, more often in the sense of becoming the new Achilles' heel of the community, a new social element which threatened to distort the accepted image of local Jewry. They were, in the words of Ansell Spier, a 'growing evil upon society'.[55] It was probably this aspect of the problem which seemed most acute, and which accounts for the parsimony of the synagogue and for the cold, sometimes almost inhuman phraseology of the account books—'a quantity of poor people', or the even more evocative 'job lot of lads' who received 2s 6d to divide between them at the beginning of 1851. The problem as it presented itself at Halliwell Street, and probably also at Ainsworth's Court, was not how to assist in the best way possible the fugitives from poverty and persecution but how to provide only such relief as would guarantee their survival without persuading them to remain. Measures of integration were carefully avoided in favour of keeping up the momentum, at all events considerable, of transmigration. This was the brief of the three members of the Select Committee who attended at Halliwell Street as Relieving Officers twice a week—'not once a month only, as in the metropolis'[56]—to dispense sums of up to 5s at their own discretion and larger amounts with the authorisation of the Select Committee, on precedents set by the Joint Board of Relief during 1847–48. Once it became clear that the problem of transmigrant poverty was more than a temporary inconvenience, the authorities of the Old Congregation developed something of the 'parsimony' of which they had once accused the New, particularly since they now faced the problem alone.

This austere outlook was reflected in the relief provided. Of the 1,222 disbursements made to unattached men in which the amounts are specified, nineteen were of 3d, 102 between 6d and 9d, 227 of 1s, 373 of 1s 6d, 233 of 2s and 219 of 2s 6d. Only forty-nine persons were relieved on the highest scale (3s to 5s) reserved for 'rabbis', 'decent' or 'respectable' men, and for those 'recommended', or in two instances 'highly recommended' by a Free Member or a congregational official. Those, that is, received most who were most acceptable as members of the settled community, or whose stated intention to move on was above suspicion. Relief was always accompanied by pressure upon the applicant to 'leave town', preferably under his own steam, but if necessary with the aid of a ticket, occasionally for London, Hull or Birmingham, but, most frequently, for Liverpool. As far as they were able, the Relieving Officers continued the practice of making only two payments of relief within a three-month period, the second of not more than 1s. Of the 742 recipients who are named in the account books of 1848–51, only 153 were relieved more than once, and only thirty-one more than twice. The policy towards family groups, particularly those in which there was no breadwinner, was to relieve them according to size on a gradually descending scale, and if this did not persuade them to depart, or to find some means of self-support, then to move them

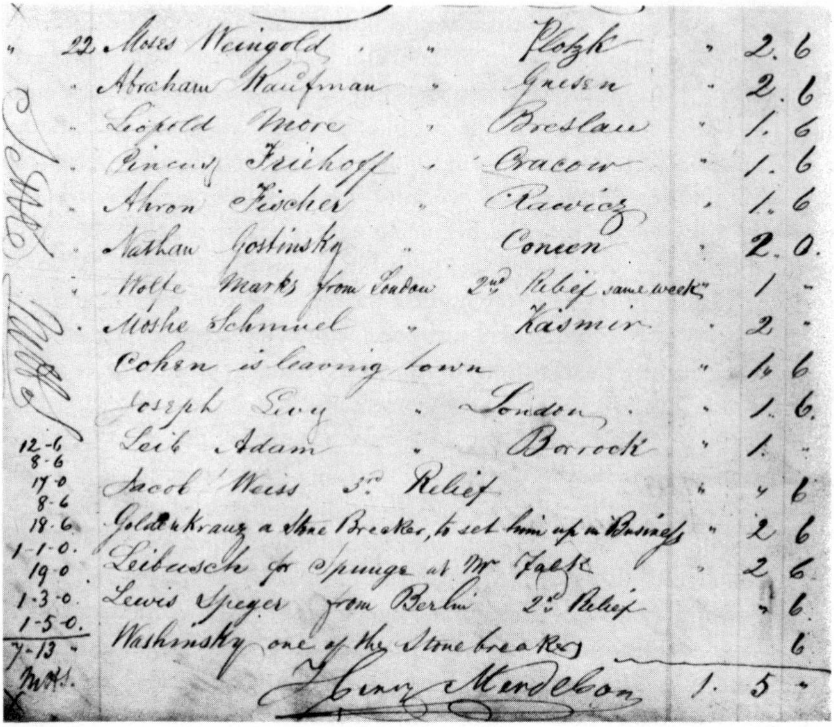
22 Moses Weingold . " Plotzk . 2. 6
Abraham Kaufman . Gnesen . 2. 6
Leopold Moore , Breslau . 1. 6
Pincus Freihoff . Cracow . 1. 6
Ahron Fischer . Rawicz . 1. 6
Nathan Gostinsky " Coneen : 2. 0.
Wolfe Marks from London 2nd Relief same week 1 -
Moshe Schmuel . Kasmir . 2 -
Cohen is leaving town 1. 6
Joseph Levy . London . 1. 6.
12-6 Leib Adam . Borrock 1. -
8-6
17-0 Jacob Weiss 3rd Relief 4 6
8-6
18-6 Goldenkranz a Stone Breaker, to set him up in Business 2 6
1-1-0 Leibusch for Sponge at Mr Falk 2 6
19-0
1-3-0 Lewis Speyer from Berlin 2nd Relief 6
1-5-0
7-13 Washinsky one of the Stonebreakers 6
MHS Henry Mendelson 1. 5 -

FIGURE 7 Extract from the Account Book of the Old Congregation's Board of Relief, March 1849.

on towards America, even at a relatively high cost, before they became a permanent burden. Gittel Pick, who arrived with her only child from Oborniki in November 1848, was given 2*s* 6*d*, then 1*s* 6*d*, and finally three successive weekly payments of 1*s* before receiving a 'special grant' of 6*s* 6*d*

> towards the pound which Mrs Behrens desired her to bring as a portion of the expenses to bring her to America,[57]

and a further 7*s* 6*d* to get her safely to the docks in Liverpool. David Adler, his wife and three children, who were delayed by illness in Manchester in April 1849, were given a special 'Committee Grant' of a guinea towards their tickets for America.[58] Other dependent families, most of them fatherless, were sent, at varying cost, to Hull, London, Birmingham and, in one case, to Dublin. The aged were treated in much the same way. Samuel Solomon, an 'old man', was given two payments of 2*s* at the beginning of December 1848, and a third of 2*s* 6*d* on the 28th of the month after he had 'promised to leave town'. Although never handing out full transatlantic fares, the synagogue occasionally paid out sums as subsistence for the voyage. Those few who could be persuaded to reverse their direction of travel— Samuel Melzak of Warsaw and his wife, in December 1848, Solomon Jacobs in November 1850—were assisted to Hull, where the Society for the Relief of Really Distressed Foreigners provided tickets for Hamburg.

A few who could not be persuaded to move in either direction were provided with small stocks of cheap goods to keep them going as pedlars until they were more amenable to reason. 1s 6d was sufficient to provide a basket of sponges, or the 2 lb of rhubarb that was given to Joseph Shimelman of Poland, with 6d as relief, in August 1850. The aim was to economise on payments to persistent applicants, not to absorb them into the local economy; a hawker's licence was provided very rarely, and then only to those under threat of prosecution for trading without one. In a unique experiment conducted during the hard winter of 1848–49, six disreputable but incorrigible applicants—Abraham Lowenstein of Cracow, Moses Everbach of Vilna, Lewin Hirsch Cohen of Riga, Jeremiah Brust of Hungary, David Goldencranz, Isaac Daniel, and Reuben Washinsky—were set to 'work at stones' in a 'stoneyard', possibly provided by the congregation, to earn first 2s and then 1s a week by hard labour until one by one they were either set up in business or persuaded to leave the town. Daniel 'left England' in February 1849, Brust on 12 March, and the experiment was wound up ten days later with the exclamatory entry in the account book, 'Cohen is leaving town 1s 6d' (see Figure 7). Even the opportunity of survival by stone-breaking was then abandoned as providing too great an inducement to the destitute to outstay their welcome.

Within its own narrow frame of reference, the system of relief achieved a large measure of success. The overall cost of poverty, which had reached £202 during 1846–47, was kept down to £285 at a time of greater immigration in 1850–51, when it represented a rather smaller percentage of the total expenditure of the synagogue. Between 1848 and 1851 the Old Congregation ended each year with a small credit balance of between £40 and £70. Potential dependants upon synagogal relief were for the most part successfully passed on, and in the spring of 1851 the congregation was left with only four permanent pensioners, one of whom was the deranged ex-Reader, Lewis Lorino. What the Relieving Officers did not, and could not, do was prevent the settlement in Manchester of those who had the wish to remain and the means to do so without turning to the synagogue for help or advice.

III

The evidence of the Census of 1851 suggests that by that time the settled Jewish population of Manchester had reached 1,100, a figure which is consistent with contemporary conversionist estimates. Israel Napthali, whose interests were perhaps best served by an exaggeration of his mission, wrote of Manchester and Salford in 1846

that there are about 300 Jewish families resident in those towns, besides a large number of travelling Jews who occasionally visit the place on business, and at their great religious fasts and festivals,[59]

and three years later, Rev. A. E. Pearce made an estimate of between ten and fifteen hundred 'resident' Jews, 'besides hundreds of occasional visitants to this mart of commerce'.[60] Of the 1,092 Jews enumerated in the Census, only 293 were born in Manchester or Salford; since many of these were the children of immigrants, it is probably safe to assume that around 80 per cent of the total is to be accounted for by immigration, chiefly of the preceding fifteen years. The 298 who were born in other parts of England suggest the extent to which Manchester was establishing its primacy amongst provincial congregations, but it was still the case that the largest proportion—comprising 591 persons—of the Jewish population was foreign-born. Although the European places of origin provided in the enumerators' books are difficult to interpret—particularly those in Prussia, Poland, and Russia—it seems certain that at least 9 per cent of the Jewish population, and probably many more, were born in Prussian or Russian Poland, and that most of the 104 persons represented by this 9 per cent arrived in Manchester at the time of extensive transmigration, between 1844 and 1851. If the period before 1836 saw the creation of Manchester's anglicised élite, and the succeeding ten years were distinguished by the creation of a new *petite bourgeoisie*, the later 1840s were characterised by the settlement of a nucleus of poor families of Eastern European origin, the local residue of a movement destined chiefly for the United States. Similar pockets of Eastern European settlement, although in each case smaller than that in Manchester, had built up in other towns along the way, in Hull, Sunderland, Newcastle-upon-Tyne, North Shields, Sheffield and Leeds.[61]

It was not a matter simply of place of origin. The immigrants from Eastern Europe created a new pattern of Jewish settlement, evolved a new occupational structure, and brought with them a religious outlook markedly more orthodox than that of the most conservative member at Halliwell Street. Although a few entered the lodging houses of Charter Street and Hanover Street in the Old Town, in one instance as landlord, the place of settlement of the majority was on Red Bank, a high sandstone ridge which fell away from the area of middle-class settlement on Cheetham Hill down to the railway in the valley of the Irk. Here the houses were arranged in cramped rows along excavated shelves separated and supported by flimsy retaining walls, which on at least one occasion collapsed and killed a recent refugee from Russian persecution.[62] Two parallel roads—Verdon Street and Fernie Street—attracted the bulk of Jewish settlement, and became the heart of what, in succeeding years, acquired the character of a voluntary ghetto. Most of the streets were unlit. Seventy to eighty yards of Verdon Street were illuminated by a single lamp not bright enough for the victim of a garotte robbery in December 1851 to identify his assailants.[63] The drains were choked by the lie of the land, the wells tainted, the air polluted by the 'pestilential effluvia' of the Irk—that 'turbid river, loaded with the refuse of every kind of manufacture and decomposing matter' which played even greater havoc with the health of the Irish on its southern bank, in the 'abominable' courts of Gibraltar.[64] Verdon Street was one of the areas in which Isaac Franklin, as a medical officer of health, treated cases of cholera in 1849. Red Bank once had been a middle-class district, but the construction of a railway at the bottom of the ridge, the steady deterioration of the Old Town and the industrialisation of the Irk Valley had driven most early residents to more salubrious suburbs. The displacement of population from the Old Town by the construction of the Leeds Extension Line and New Victoria Station during 1843–44, and the subsequent demolition to prepare the way for Corporation Street, contributed to the steep social decline of Red Bank in the later 1840s. What then attracted Jewish immigrants was the existence of spacious, but cheap and easily subdivided houses, as suitable for workshops as for homes, within easy reach of the two synagogues, and adjacent to districts in which Jews had already settled. Although Jewish families had occasionally lived in the district at an earlier period, continuous and extensive settlement began only with the arrival of Pincus Nathan, a cap maker, in Verdon Street in 1845. By 1851 twenty-one Jewish households, totalling 130 persons, resided in a network of streets effectively cut off from the town centre to the south by railway viaducts and divided from the middle-class suburb to the north by the steep incline from York Street.

A typical immigrant household amongst those enumerated in the Census of 1851 was 27 Verdon Street, where Raphael Libernich, a Polish hawker, lived with his wife, and daughter, Eliza, also a hawker, and four lodgers: Harris Cohen, a glazier from Posen, Adolphus Frankenstein, a tailor from Breslau, Joseph Weiss, a pedlar from Prussian Poland, and David Goldenkranz, a Silesian glazier and former 'stone-breaker' for the synagogue. At 34 Verdon Street there lived fifteen persons: Abraham Levi, a tailor, his wife, five children—one a glazier, another a cap maker—an Irish servant, and seven Jewish lodgers. In crowded homes such as these, penniless immigrants found *landsleit* with similar backgrounds of experience who might occasionally testify to their characters when the need arose, facilities for worship in *minyanim* which preserved something of the warmth and informality of the European ghetto, and work amongst co-religionists at tasks which demanded little initial skill and which, none the less, offered good prospects to the more enterprising piece-worker. It was in the later 1840s, and particularly between 1848 and 1851 in Red Bank, that Manchester Jewry's 'immigrant trades'[65]—cap making, tailoring, slipper making, cabinet making, waterproofing and glaziery—first took shape.

In tailoring, Jewish enterprise had hitherto been confined to the retailing of clothing for the mass market, prepared by Gentile cutters and made up, in most instances, by Gentile outworkers on piece rates. The effect of Eastern European immigration was to create a Jewish work-force of piece-work tailors, some of whom arrived in Manchester with a little experience, while others were introduced to the rudimentary skills of making-up and finishing by co-religionists who had arrived before them. Given the growing demand for cheap clothing, and the existence of many Jewish shops to meet it, the setting up of a tailoring workshop on a team basis, with the tasks involved broken down into a series of elementary skills and sub-skills, from seaming to button-holing and felling, was an immediate means of earning a livelihood in which every member of an immigrant family might profitably participate. The same was true of slipper making, and particularly cap making, in which the demands upon skill were at their smallest. In the most usual form of the economic structure which resulted, a team of between six and twelve persons, of whom only one or two needed to be experienced artisans, made up clothing, caps or slippers on a contract basis, often through a middleman who provided the capital and equipment, either for a wholesale warehouse or for local retailers, some of them Jewish. Although it preceded mechanisation, the workshop system was given a decided boost by the introduction of the lockstitch sewing machine, patented in America by Isaac Singer in 1851. The line between domestic outwork and workshop labour was not sharply drawn. Houses in Verdon Street and Fernie Street in which the head of the household was enumerated in 1851 as a master tailor, cap maker, or slipper maker, and in which there lived six or seven 'lodgers' of the same trade, seem likely to have been workshops in which groups of workers—often *landsleit*—lived-in with the controlling family. At 29 Verdon Street, for example, where the head of the house was Levy Jacobs, a slipper maker from Russian Poland, the six lodgers were all slipper makers, all Polish, all but one from Warsaw. The distinction between master and men was also difficult to define, and then easy to cross in both directions. The Census of 1851 suggests that there were then at least thirty-two Jewish piece-work tailors in Manchester, forty-seven cap makers, seven of them women, seven slipper makers, and seven cabinet makers, all of Eastern European origin.

Cap making was the boom industry of the late 1840s and 1850s. The first in the field as entrepreneurs—Edward Marks and David Goldman in the mid-1840s, Saul Oppenheim, a Prussian immigrant, in 1848—rose rapidly on the economic scale, Marks to the point of establishing an important agency for the tobacco trade in the early 1850s. Successful retailers in other lines—Joseph Mirls, the former Reader and marine store dealer, Marcus Brandt, a tobacconist, Isaac Kessing in stationery—switched direction to cap making on the basis of immigrant labour. More resilient paupers—Amelia Bebro, the widow, whose children were a subject in the Treaty of 1847; Joseph Shimelman, set up by the Relieving Officers as a hawker of rhubarb—found in cap making the means to substantial independence. In the early 1850s there were Jewish workshops in Red Bank, in the Old Town, and in Lower Bridge Street, in which the lower floors were used as work-rooms, the middle for residence, the upper as storerooms in which caps were aired by open fires or movable gas-lights.[66]

Of the other immigrant trades, glaziery and waterproofing were both introduced into the Manchester Jewish economy by immigrants of 1848–51. Glaziery, which required only a cutting diamond, a few panes of glass carried easily on the back and a rapid turn-over of urban windows, is perhaps best regarded as the most profitable form of urban peddling. The first recorded Jewish glazier in Manchester appears in the synagogue account book of December 1848 as a recipient of relief, and in a form which suggests that his trade was then regarded as unusual, if not unique, in the community.[67] Of the fourteen Jewish glaziers in the Census, all had arrived in Manchester in the preceding three years. One effect of pauper immigration was to revive the itinerant trades, particularly within an urban compass, as an easily capitalised means of immediate survival; the Census enumerates twenty-seven Jewish hawkers, chiefly of trinkets and stationery, but also of the rhubarb and sponges occasionally supplied by the synagogue. The first Jewish 'india rubber waterproofer' in Manchester, and the only one enumerated in the Census, was Morris Friedlander, who arrived from Russian Poland in 1849 and settled in Johnson Street, Red Bank. Within the succeeding two or three years he was followed by other entrepreneurs—Hyman Hart in Verdon Street, Elias Jacobs in Fernie Street—who set up workshops in which immigrant workers smeared cloth with the vulcanised indiarubber developed earlier, in Manchester, by the firm of Charles Mackintosh.[68]

The effect of Eastern European immigration, and of the social and economic tendencies which accompanied it, was to create, for the first time, a Jewish working class in a modern sense: not a body of hawkers working alone towards the day when they might open up shops, but an industrial work-force in domestic workshops, sharing common conditions and rates of pay, and living together in an area of low-cost housing which possessed both a physical and a cultural coherence. It was the sharp social outlines and distinctive standards of the new immigrants which served to emphasise the common characteristics and interests of an anglicised middle class which stretched from the shops of the city centre to the outer suburbs, particularly since the social differences within the Jewish bourgeoisie were being eroded by time and economic change. According to the *Jewish Chronicle*, 'the pecuniary losses caused by the political convulsions in Europe' had 'diminished the property of the wealthy classes in Manchester'.[69] What is more certain is the growing prosperity of the men at Ainsworth's Court. Saul Mayer moved out of the Old Town in December 1847 into a 'half-shop', in Market Street, 'at the sign of the Golden Clock', a few doors from Benjamin Hyam. In 1848 David Hesse patented 'the imperial shirt without buttons or button holes', acquired a factory in St Mary's, and moved into a new suburban house in Islington, Salford. In 1851 Heinemann Hertz Rosenberg had five branches of his tobacco business in central Manchester, and was using the columns of the *Guardian* to find a sixth. Henry Brower was part-owner of a factory in Bridge Street making wood-tips and fancy boxes. John William Gore moved into cap making shortly before his death in October 1849, when the business was continued successfully by his wife, Ann. A few of the more intransigent democrats of the New Synagogue moved on, Joseph Gumpelson to Birmingham in 1850, others to the United States, particularly after the discovery of gold in California in 1849. The three strangers—'Tanchum, Marks and Dantziger'—who made offerings at Halliwell Street in August 1850, before 'going to California',[70] were followed by Selig Davies, a waste dealer, Julius Bywood, a cap maker, and Halkin Harris, a tailor, all from Ainsworth's Court, and John Levy, a quill dresser, who left the Old Congregation with irrecoverable bad debts. The last remnant of Franklin commercial enterprise in Manchester ended abruptly in 1850 with the departure of Morris Franklin for San Francisco.[71] A further unifying factor was the arrival in Halliwell Street of Joseph Slazenger Moss, who in January 1850 moved from Warrington to Manchester, where he succeeded to the tailoring business of William Hulme at 23 Market Street.[72] Although superior in wealth to all but Hyam in the retail trades, and bound by social, economic and marital ties to members of the Old Congregation, he shared the background, and friendship, of the country traders in the New. Some of the edge was also taken off the dispute by the arrival from further afield of new merchants and shopkeepers who took up membership of both congregations and who knew nothing of the bitterness of 1844.

There was still a higher élite which ruled at Halliwell Street—Benjamin Hyam of Park Hill, with his eight servants, Philip Lucas of Temple House, with his seven, and other suburban plutocrats in north and south Manchester—but their best social interests now seemed to lie in an alliance with the *nouveaux riches*. Faced with a new flood of pauper applicants, the paternal leaders of the Old Congregation had been forced to adopt tougher measures than they had been prepared to accept in 1847, and by 1851 their view of poverty probably differed little from that of David Hesse. At the same time, expediency suggested to the radicals at Ainsworth's Court that some modification of their ideal of 'Perfect Equality' might be in their interests as a class. Again, as in the early 1830s, there were, in effect, two Manchester communities, in this new context an anglicised middle class and an immigrant poor, and it seemed to be in the best interests of the one to mitigate the ill effects of the other, by strengthening the agencies of assimilation and relief and by emphasising, in institutional terms, the highest and most English cultural standards of the community.

One explicit effect of these considerations during the period 1849–51 was the planning of a new school building, not only in the interests of the 'welfare' of Jewish youth but, as the Hebrew Educational Association told its members, to further 'the intelligence and respectability of the whole House of Israel'.[73] It was not simply that larger premises were needed to accommodate the seventy children who attended the school in Hanover Street in 1849. What was required was 'an edifice' 'worthy of the noble purposes of education', '*creditable to its benevolent promoters*',[74] and attractive to the children of the rich, whose fees were expected to subsidise the assimilation of the poor. It seemed inappropriate that 'a large, respectable, and intelligent' community such as Manchester had supposedly become should not possess school buildings of its own, 'in an eligible situation', such as those which existed in Birmingham and Liverpool. The increasing local pride of the Jewish middle classes—itself a factor making for reunion—could find satisfaction only in a school which would reflect their own dignity and wealth, while providing a 'cheap and useful' means of raising the social level of the poor. In time, as one of the school's founders remarked, the children of the poor would 'imitate the superiority of the rich'.[75]

An appeal was launched by Philip Lucas at Hayward's Hotel on 18 March 1849,[76] and within eight months donations to the Association—assisted by London Jewish and local Christian sources, and by contributions from members of both Manchester synagogues—totalled £1,200.[77] Early in November 1850, after negotiations with the Earl of Derby had proved abortive, a small piece of land on Cheetham Hill Road was purchased from Louis Beaver,[78] and building began to a plan devised by the prominent local architect and leading Classical revivalist, J. E. Gregan.[79] The corner-stone was laid by Philip Lucas in December,[80] and by the spring of 1851 the building—'a pleasing though modest specimen of skilful architecture'[81]—was nearing completion. It is a measure of the underlying fear of immigrant poverty, and the desire to deter immigrant settlement, that in the 'Fundamental Laws' adopted in the previous May, 'necessitous parents' were not allowed to send their children to the school 'without they shall have resided at least twelve months in the town or its immediate vicinity'.[82] The school was the community's second line of defence.

IV

It might have appeared to an outsider that by 1851 the bonds of union and cooperation between the two congregations were more than sufficient to bring them together. Since the autumn of 1848 observers had noticed a 'more amicable feeling' between them,[83] members of one congregation had been seen at the services of the other,[84] and each had referred to its rival in polite, even affectionate terms. Israel Levy, lecturer at the New until his departure to the London *Beth Din* in 1849, spoke of the 'cordial feeling' which had bound members of both congregations in support for David Hesse's policies at the Board of Deputies[85] and Abraham Franks, a leading member at Halliwell Street, declared publicly that 'he entertained the purest and best feelings' towards Ainsworth's Court.[86] There remained, however, the matter of honours. It was the peculiar genius of the Jewish community that its constituent parts might remain close enough together to suggest the outlines of an integrated whole, and yet far enough apart to remain institutionally discrete, and one reason for this was the need for a reasonable distribution of synagogal honours. It may be inferred that the lack of honours and offices available to the seatholders at Halliwell Street had been one of the mainsprings of their revolt; what still held the community apart during 1850–51 was the loss of prestige which might be involved in bringing them together. What was perhaps required was a focal point so attractive in itself that the two congregations could coalesce around it without either losing face.

This was unexpectedly provided during the summer of 1850 by the arrival in Manchester of Rabbi Dr Solomon Marcus Schiller-Szinessy,[87] a political refugee from the Hungarian Revolution of 1848–49. The late 1840s and early 1850s were a golden age of intinerant 'rabbis', during which the foundations were laid of a local rabbinate both in England and in the United States, where in 1845 there is said to have been only one 'licentiate rabbi'—Abraham Rice of Baltimore—in the whole country.[88] In England Dr Adler possessed a virtual monopoly of rabbinic authority, a strength which served both to consolidate his central control of religious affairs and to weaken the claims of Reform, which, unlike equivalent movements in Germany, and later in the United States, lacked the moral support of men of rabbinical status. Of the self-designated 'rabbis' moving westwards in the later 1840s—at least fifteen of whom passed through Manchester during the years 1848–52—it seems likely that few were in possession of genuine *semikhah*, and that many were lesser dignitaries from the synagogal hierarchies of Central and Eastern Europe, some with a modicum of Talmudic training and a little ministerial experience, others total upstarts whose pretensions were shielded by the confusion of the times. Some were adventurers; others genuine refugees, whether from persecution or poverty; yet others in search of suitable appointments in a western world of fabled wealth and easy accessibility. In September 1846 one travelling rabbi, 'Professor' Hirsch Dannemark, gave an exhibition of his 'marvellous powers' before a mixed audience at the Jews School, then in St Mary's Street, where he undertook to read the first words of the first line of any page selected from five volumes of the Talmud loaned for the occasion by Tobias Theodores.[89] A reporter from the *Manchester Guardian*, who complained of the high entrance fee (5s and 2s 6d), was sceptical of the rabbi's claim to occult or supernatural powers but impressed by the speed of his sight and the power of his memory. At Halliwell Street the Board of Relief gave all but two of its 'rabbinical' applicants a standard 5s gratuity (or 10s if like Gerson Landsberg in September 1848 they were accompanied by their families) to speed them on their transatlantic journeys, or to provide suitably respectable accommodation in the city. Most originated in Central and Eastern Europe—Hyam Bach of Hungary, for example, Rabbi Katzenellenbogen of Posen, or Meyer Frankel—but they included Rabbi Nissim Schlomo of Persia, a 'Rabbi Moshe' of Jerusalem, and Rabbi Meyer Hertz of Dusseldorf.

Of the fifteen, only one remained in Manchester. Forty-nine-year-old 'Rabbi' Hirsch Longhaar from Russian Poland, who arrived in June 1850, became a lodger in the house of Harris (or Hirsch) Portuguese, a Polish cap maker of 29 Verdon Street in Red Bank, and earned a precarious livelihood as a Hebrew teacher in a tenement packed with hawkers and petty artisans of recent Polish or Prussian origin. Harris Portuguese was later to come under official attack for harbouring a private place of worship outside the orbit of synagogal control, and it may well be that as early as 1850 'Rabbi' Longhaar (or Lanker) was leading services in a style, language and setting better suited to the tastes of pauper immigrants, many of whom settled in or near Verdon Street, than the cold and sophisticated ceremonies at Halliwell Street and Ainsworth's Court. This was perhaps the *minyan* which emerged in 1854 as the *Chevra Tehillim* under more reputable guidance.[90]

Dr Schiller-Szinessy was set apart from other fugitives by the credibility of his claims, the quality and breadth of his scholarship, the strength of his ambitions, and his ability, by the time he reached Manchester, to deliver sermons in both English and German. Unlike most of his contemporaries he combined a strong background of western academic training with the possession of Rabbinical *semikhah* endorsed by European rabbis of unquestioned repute. Dr Schiller was born in Budapest in 1820 to an orthodox Jewish family which combined strong mercantile and rabbinic traditions. After an early private education in religion and Hebrew, he studied philosophy and mathematics at the Lutheran College at Eperies in Upper Hungary, proceeding to a. doctorate in these subjects at the University of Jena in 1845. At Jena he accompanied his western education with religious studies which culminated in his ordination as a rabbi in 1843. The quiet pastoral and academic life which he then commenced as spiritual guide to the small Jewish congregation at Eperies and Lecturer in Hebrew and Jewish History at the Lutheran College, was interrupted in 1848 by the outbreak of revolution. With many other young Jews, he threw in his lot with Kossuth's nationalists, first stumping the country on a vigorous recruiting campaign and then, early in 1849, joining the revolutionary army in its desperate combat with Imperial troops. In March he was wounded by an Austrian detail, captured, imprisoned in the fortress of Tamesvar, and sentenced to death. On the eve of his execution, however, he engineered an escape with the help of his Galician warders and made his way to Trieste, where he boarded a Scots boat bound for Cork. From Ireland he moved on to England, first to Stoke Poges, where two elderly retired governesses taught him the elements of English, and then on to London in the early summer of 1850.

The arrival of so erudite, dynamic and eloquent a personality in the dull and introverted world of Anglo-Jewry created something like a sensation. At the end of June the *Jewish Chronicle* published as leaders two articles he had written on anti-Semitism in the Austrian Empire, in which he had emphasised the role of Jews as the protagonists of liberty and Hungarian nationality.[91]

The Jews, from their birth, are friends and devotees of liberty; their whole faith, all their sacred books, breathe liberty, and inspiration for the same, in the highest degree.[92]

A former 'inspector' of the Lutheran College in Eperies, then in exile in London, was moved to writing a letter of congratulation, in which he acquainted the public with Dr Schiller's career and virtues.[93] At Eperies, where he had been known for his 'amiable character' and 'deep learning', Dr Schiller had become the first Jew to hold a public professorship in Hungary, while his 'eloquent lectures' in the local synagogue had 'excited public attention'. The letter ended: 'I am convinced that in England he will be able, in a short time, to acquire the same respect he enjoyed in Hungary.' His first sermon, delivered in German,[94] on Sabbath *Nahamu*, apparently to a metropolitan congregation, breathed a fiery revivalism which caught the public imagination when a full translation appeared in the *Chronicle*.[95] On 'God's Love of Israel', it dwelt in resounding rhetoric upon the duties implied in divine support for the House of Israel, and upon the need for a revitalisation of religious life:

And indeed I already see it in my mind, how Israel again renders herself worthy of the love manifested by God; I already see, it is again awake—the great spirit, which is the true characteristic of the God-believing, God-inspired Israelite . . .

Within weeks, his sermons were being published in translation at 1d each, 'in order to bring them within reach of the humbler classes'.[96]

He made his first official excursion into the provinces on the Second Day of the New Year Festival—8 September 1850—when he preached an invitation sermon, again in German, at the synagogue in Birmingham, where he was greeted with equal enthusiasm.[97] Printed in translation at the expense of the Birmingham authorities,[98] the sermon again touched upon the theme of liberty—

What other religion taught earlier than the Jewish, Liberty, Equality, and Fraternity for whose sake the present age is in full excitement . . .

but its central message was a return to religious enthusiasm and a strict observance of Jewish law, even if, on this account 'one has been despised and scoffed at by others who think differently'. He also stressed for the first time his deep concern for the education of the young. Calling on the Birmingham congregation to renew its support for the communal school—'so sunken as to be scantily supported and seldom frequented'—he asked: 'What work could be more God-pleasing than the education of youth?' Early in September, shortly before the Day of Atonement, he made his way to Manchester, where, like Hirsch Lanker, who had arrived a little earlier in less favourable circumstances, he offered his services as teacher of 'the Hebrew language, Biblical and Rabbinical Literature and History' from an address in Cheetham Hill. The reasons for his movements are not on record, but it seems likely that he was in search of a permanent ministry, and perhaps for one which offered greater scope for independence than would have been possible under the shadow of Dr Adler in London.

The impact of two sermons delivered at Halliwell Street in German on the Day of Atonement is described in a report by the congregation's secretary, M. H. Simonson:

During the New Year Holydays a Gentleman the Revd Dr Schiller appeared in this town when the attention of the Jewish community was attracted by two beautiful discourses delivered by him on the Day of Atonement. So great was the delight felt by the hearers that the Executive were immediately waited upon by some influential Gentlemen to request the Revd Dr to prolong his visit over the Feast of Tabernacles in order that he might again delight his audience by his thrilling eloquence. With this application, the Revd Gentleman was pleased to comply and your committee were rejoiced to see a large amount of Enthusiasm created among their German Co-religionists which ended in one feeling viz. the desirableness [sic] of Securing the Revd Gentleman's permanent services to the community.[99]

A correspondent from Manchester wrote to the *Jewish Chronicle*,

Men whose minds had long been seemingly benumbed by religious indifference, awoke, at the touch of his manly eloquence . . . Here, as elsewhere, the fire of devotion burns in the hearts of many, many sons and daughters of Abraham, erroneously taxed with a want of spiritual susceptibility; it needs but the breath of a pure and judiciously-directed religious inspiration to fan the latent element into a bright and cheering flame.[100]

The *Chronicle* itself pressed Dr Schiller upon the Manchester community as the man who, by his pulpit oratory, would 'regenerate' its religious life, 'restore many who hitherto were altogether indifferent to the synagogue', and effect a 'cordial union' between the warring synagogues.[101]

Dr Schiller had everything to recommend him. He was a Hebrew scholar, deeply concerned with the education of the young, just as the Hebrew Educational Association was planning a new school for which it had not yet found a suitable Superintendent. He was a fluent lecturer in German, and was beginning to master English, when the congregation was 'entirely destitute of pulpit instruction' and England was notorious for its 'lack of efficient men' to lecture in the vernacular. Here was a man whose western scholarship, fluent oratory, and rabbinical *semikhah* of undoubted authenticity, would place Manchester on a par with any congregation in London. Testimonials obtained from continental referees confirmed not only his orthodoxy, but also his 'high character for learning, piety, morality, and Religion'.[102] He spoke as a revivalist when Manchester's religious life was at a low ebb. He was free from the taint of Reform. Although the endorsements to his rabbinical diploma included one from a rabbi of Reformist leanings, the orthodoxy of Dr Schiller's own practice and opinions was beyond suspicion. At Eperies his single innovation was the institution of elaborate confirmation services for girls as well as boys, while earlier he had launched a personal attack upon the radical, and, he believed, 'destructive', resolutions of the conference of Reform rabbis which met at Frankfurt in July 1845. The keynote of all his early sermons in England was upon the need for a strict observance of traditional Judaism.

On 14 October, after the Senior Warden at Halliwell Street had 'dilated at some length on the benefit to be derived from having a Gentleman of Dr Schiller's attainments resident in the community',[103] the congregation set up a sub-committee, consisting of Simon Joseph, J. M. Isaac, Eleazer Moses and Louis Behrens, to communicate with Dr Adler and Dr Schiller, and to conclude an arrangement satisfactory to both.[104] The matter was one of very serious concern to the Chief Rabbi. What Manchester was proposing was the appointment of a man whose qualifications equated to Dr Adler's own and who had the power, in religion, if not in the administrative structure of Anglo-Jewry, to make independent judgements and pronouncements on religious questions. In the past, Manchester had no alternative to the jurisdiction of London on all religious issues: when a case of 'attempted *makadesh*' had arisen in Manchester early in 1850, the Chief Rabbi sent down Dayan Aaron Levy to deal with it, at the request of Halliwell Street.[105] Now the possibility existed of religious independence, and with it the still more important danger of a movement in the direction of Reform which the Chief Rabbi might be powerless to check. There now existed, for the first time in England, the serious possibility of the kind of religious fragmentation which, in the absence of central control, was already beginning to characterise the American scene.

Only a little earlier, Dr Adler had been compelled to deal with the symptoms of revolt in Liverpool, where in August 1849, even without the backing of a rabbinical guide, the Congregation at Seel Street had introduced 'a division in the Sabbath Morning Service' without his consent.[106] His prompt intervention brought a retraction and an apology, but the Chief Rabbi had been made aware both of Liverpool's belief that 'a general desire for reforms in our divine service prevails throughout the congregations of the provinces' and of the danger of independent action, even when local rabbinical authority was absent.[107] He had made the point in Liverpool that the congregation had no right to act in such important matters on the advice of its 'local officers' rather than that of the *Beth Din*.[108] Now he faced the more serious prospect of a qualified and forceful local rabbi, whose influence and prestige might conceivably be harnessed by those who sought ritual change. And his determination to contain change within the national framework he had laid out in 1847 was strengthened by fear not only of a radical secession such as Margaret Street represented but of a more conservative defection. He wrote to Liverpool:

there exists a large and important party, who are so attracted to the established order of service, that any precipitate interference might drive them to secede and thus lead to the deplorable consequence of splitting our religious brotherhood in this Kingdom into scismatic [*sic*] divisions instead of affecting that most beneficial conformity which you so strenuously desire.[109]

With these thoughts in mind, the Chief Rabbi arranged a conference in London in December, to obtain from the Old Congregation's delegates some assurances on the question of Dr Schiller's powers.[110] There he sanctioned the appointment of the new 'minister', but only

under [*sic*] the understanding that he would not assume for himself any decision on rabbinical questions . . . [nor] introduce any new measure affecting the spiritual position of the Congregation

without the consent of the Chief Rabbi.[111] At a later date, the Chief Rabbi agreed that Dr Schiller might be called to the Law under the rabbinical title *Morenu*, but not without his approval.[112] The lay delegates (J. M. Isaac and Louis Behrens) were made to promise 'to watch over the conscientious adherence to those conditions', and subsequently obtained from Dr Schiller his 'positive declaration' to be bound by them.[113] On this basis, on 5 January 1851, Dr Schiller signed a 'resume of functions' with the Old Congregation. In return for an annual payment of £250 (nearly twice the amount offered to the Reader), he undertook

to deliver a sermon once a fortnight, at least alternately in the English language, to preach on Festival Days . . . to deliver addresses on other occasions . . . in German or English; to officiate as Minister within the Congregation and outside the synagogue . . .; and to superintend the Education Department generally as may be arranged by the School Committee . . .[114]

V

When Dr Schiller was installed on these terms on 18 January 1851, the event was described at Halliwell Street as

all important to the future interest of the Jewish community of this town . . . fraught with good to the congregation and . . . full of promise to the rising Generation now before them.[115]

More obviously, it was the final link in a chain of events which was drawing the two Manchester congregations closer together. According to Margoliouth, who was in Manchester shortly afterwards, the appointment 'had the effect of throwing the Long Millgate Synagogue completely in the shade',[116] but at the same time, it provided the Old Congregation with a means of political retreat without loss of face, and both congregations with a convenient rationale for a reunion motivated chiefly by social and economic expediency. There was about it, too, an element of the German bond. Dr Schiller was a German-speaking liberal; his sermon in September had brought to Halliwell Street a handful of German Jews—including, for example, the music teacher, Carl

Engel, and the commission agent, Alexander Hess—who had not previously seen the inside of a Manchester synagogue. His special appeal was to the German groups in both synagogues whose social and political solidarity was already pronounced. His association with European liberalism also exercised a strong appeal to men like Hesse and Beaver, both of whom had paid heavy offerings to hear him speak. There was no hint from any quarter that the 'future interest' of the community involved anything more than its permanent reintegration and the recovery of the national standing it had enjoyed at the time of Theodores' Damascus letter. Dr Adler had obtained the undertakings he required, and there seems no further reason to suppose that he now feared, or that others anticipated, radical ritual innovation or a movement towards religious autonomy. In all probability he shared local hopes that Dr Schiller would serve as a strong communal nucleus and so finally put an end to a bitter dispute which threatened the repute of Judaism and the welfare of the Jewish poor; he had already accepted the invitation of the Hebrew Association to open their school later in the year, and no doubt he expected to find the community reunited around it.

The formalities of reunion were, in fact, very rapidly concluded. An exploratory letter from Philip Lucas to David Hesse in March 1851,[117] opened the way for conversations between them on the neutral ground of the (old) Jews School in Hanover Street.[118] Talks which took place, appropriately enough under the mediation of Dr Schiller, resulted in the setting up of a joint committee to arrange the terms of reunion.[119] Four 'principles of amalgamation', which covered administrative problems and ensured that the members of the New Congregation did not lose their privileges, nor its officials their status, were quickly drawn up and agreed, and on Sunday 6 April, at the synagogue chambers in Halliwell Street, the two synagogues were formally reunited.[120] Seventeen former members of the New Congregation attended Passover service at Halliwell Street six days later. Accustomed perhaps to Manchester's vacillating moods, Sir Moses Montefiore was unwilling to accept Simonson's statement of the fact of reunion, and sought confirmation from Louis Beaver, which was recorded by the Board of Deputies in September.[121] Meantime, in Manchester, the volcano at Ainsworth's court had been officially pronounced 'extinct'.[122]

Although the Old Congregation took over the members, the assets, the building, and the Burial Ground of the New, the terms of amalgamation represented a substantial victory for David Hesse and the party of democratic reform. A committee of six appointed in June to revise the laws of the congregation included Hesse and Louis Beaver from the former rebel party and effected a major, if not a total, liberalisation of the synagogue constitution, 'in order to carry out fully and efficiently' (according to the Select Committee) 'the system of representation with taxation'.[123] In a new system of classification, proposed by Hesse, the assessment of individuals on a basis of their wealth was replaced by a less invidious pricing of seats according to their eligibility. Any person who occupied a seat at a rental of 26s or more for at least one year became entitled to be 'balloted for' at a General Meeting and, on the receipt of a majority of the votes cast, became a full member with the right to vote at General Meetings. Those who subscribed at least 52s a year were further entitled to hold honorary office and to become members of a Select Committee of thirteen members. This 'remodelling' of the laws 'on the most liberal principles' (according to Hesse) was said to

hold out the Example of an Institution comparatively free and untrammeled by laws grown into desuetude and which your Committee believe in this Enlightened Age only serve to obstruct many good and useful purposes,[124]

but although the franchise was certainly extended, democracy was far from complete. The compromise of 1851 was a triumph of middle-class radicalism within a Jewish milieu: only a fraction of the adult male population (perhaps 149 persons in all) could afford the level of taxation to which representation was attached.

The settlement of 1851 expressed in constitutional terms the narrowing of what in 1844 had appeared a wide economic and cultural gulf within the Jewish middle class. There were no religious differences to sort out, since none had ever existed, and it was for this reason also that the issue had been decided more by events which stressed the ties of class than those which emphasised the bonds of religion. Time and economic change had themselves served to narrow the gap. The German members of both congregations had united in sympathy with middle-class Germany. The romance of middle-class liberalism in Europe had given the ideas of Hesse an air of respectability. But, most of all, the pauper immigrants of the later 1840s, and particularly of 1848–51, had changed the whole frame of reference, since they had created a new group, and new standards, against which the Jewish middle-class as a whole needed to defend itself, and the community. The terms of reunion were for this reason, also, class terms, excluding the immigrant in Red Bank as surely as they admitted the shopkeeper from Shudehill. This was not simply a matter of cost. The admission of new members still depended in the last resort on the recommendation of the Committee and a general ballot and this process of selection was quite as liable to social bias after 1851 as before 1844. However dynamic a personality, Dr Schiller was neither more nor less than a convenient symbol of the identity of interests and growing local pride of the communal middle class, as in succeeding years he was seldom more than a symbol of the community's other changing moods, values and emotions.

8 A spirit of independence, 1851–53

The reunification of the community raised quite as many problems as it solved, since it was by no means certain that those who now reconciled their political differences were agreed on other matters. Most obviously, reunion seemed to set the seal on Manchester's progress over the previous two decades. Simonson wrote:

Powerful for good, united in feeling, strong in purpose, banishing selfishness, what is there that the Manchester congregation could not achieve?[1]

David Hesse, who believed, probably wrongly, that Manchester was 'the first and largest provincial congregation', was even more emphatic:

The Manchester [community] of today is counted by hundreds and has progressed alike in number, intelligence, wealth, and all those qualities destined to raise men in the Social Scale, hence what suited a community of 20 or 30 individuals will no longer adjust itself to the present time . . . the tide cannot be stemmed, and happy he who by foresight and judgement can understand the requirements of his Day, and gracefully confer what necessity demands.[2]

But what were the requirements of the day? It was easy enough to see that the community was now in a position to consolidate its achievements in the field of education, and to tackle the difficult problem of itinerant poverty; but beyond these immediate objectives it was not easy to see how the community could adjust its religious life to suit the tastes of those who were rising on the social scale. The *Jewish Chronicle*, which drew particular attention to the large number of Jews in Manchester who were not 'connected with the synagogue', believed, with many local leaders, that Dr Schiller's pulpit would become 'the focus whence light and fervour are to be shed on the benighted as well as the torpid portions of Israel',[3] but it was not clear what adjustments to traditional Judaism might be required to win back lost souls from a highly assimilative and secular mercantile milieu. Hesse himself, and probably most other members of the former New Synagogue, believed the first requirement to be a sufficient measure of autonomy for the community to determine its own religious future, but it was not clear to what extent others in the community, or indeed, Hesse himself, were prepared to jettison the central control of the Chief Rabbi and risk the possibility of local independence becoming the basis of religious heresy, as it had in many communities in the United States.

Dr Schiller was in an equivocal position. How would he adjust to the centralised structure of Anglo-Jewry in which his own *halakhic* authority was subordinated to that of Dr Adler? To the Census enumerators of March 1851 he described himself as 'Local Rabbi of the Hebrew Tongue', and it may be that in assuming a title which was not justified by his agreement with the Chief Rabbi, he already had in mind an independent jurisdiction such as it would have implied in Europe. He knew little of the historical background of the English system, and probably regarded his subservience to Dr Adler as no more than a temporary inconvenience. On his religious outlook, the *Jewish Chronicle* had written, in 1850:

His classical and scientific culture places him above the suspicion of being an obstinate stabilitarian, while the fidelity with which he has served the Jewish cause . . . no less than the manifest sincerity of his firm religious conviction, offers every guarantee for his steadfastness in upholding every title of what is essential to Judaism in form and spirit.[4]

But this again begged the question of what *was* essential to the form and spirit of Judaism. In trying to accommodate the tastes of his most sophisticated congregants, what degree of ritual innovation was Dr Schiller prepared to countenance?

Theodores almost certainly saw him as the harbinger of Reform, but there was little in Dr Schiller's record to suggest that this is what he might become. In a sermon preached to the Hardman Street congregation in Liverpool on 21 September 1851 he used the term 'reform' to suggest not change, but revival:

I beseech you to regulate your Divine Service methodically, to reform it—not in a destructive manner, not on the plan of those who remould holy things till no part of the original is left, and there is nothing more to be remodelled! This is no reform, it is rather a new creation. But reform your Divine Service: that is, first reform yourselves. Bring hither, whenever you enter these sacred courts, the original spirit of the Jews, the spirit of earnest piety, the spirit of devotedness to Divine commandments, the spirit of adherence to well-approved customs, doubly sacred in our sight by their meaning and their antiquity. Reform your Divine service; that is, secondly, take heed that the life-giving word of instruction may never fail here . . . Reform your Divine Service; go back to the original duty of Israel.[5]

There was no comfort for Theodores in a sermon which insisted that 'light and truth' were to be found not by 'dabbling in philosophy' but by prayer and willingness to know God.

More realistically, Hesse regarded Dr Schiller as providing the necessary basis for religious autonomy, but it remained to be seen whether or not the new minister would allow himself to be set on such a collision course with the Chief Rabbi.

Almost everyone in the community was prepared to accept that a further degree of change was necessary in the form and decorum of the service in the synagogue, to keep it in line with the increasing cultural sophistication of its members. When the first open debate on ritual took place at Halliwell Street in 1853,

> ... the gentleman, Mr Simon Joseph, said, 'We who are regular in attending the syna-gogue every Sabbath are satisfied with things as they are'. But the remark was met with an electric shout of 'No! No! No!' in which shout every other orthodox member joined.[6]

But the degree of change was a matter for dispute, in which the judgement of the Chief Rabbi was as likely to decide the issue as individual conviction. The issues of local independence and Reform were very closely linked, not necessar-ily in the minds of those who sought greater freedom of action for Manchester, but in any final reckoning, since the Chief Rabbi was likely to oppose auton-omy as a potential basis for Reform, while Reformers were likely to press for it as a possible vehicle for radical change.

Dr Adler saw himself as the rock upon which Jewish orthodoxy rested. To some extent Judaism in England reflected the centralisation of the Established Church implied in the close association of Church and State, just as in America their separation had encouraged the growth of independent communities and a 'regime of free option' which opened the way to many variations of the ortho-dox Jewish canon.[7] At the same time, the Chief Rabbi's power reflected both the need for a central jurisdiction to preserve the framework of Jewish life in eighteenth-century England, and the unique position of the secular plutocracy in London from which the Chief Rabbi's powers emanated. The Chief Rabbin-ate was as much the ecclesiastical arm of the plutocracy, as the president of the Board of Deputies was its secular representative. It is significant, for example, that when religious controversy began in Manchester in the early 1850s, Dr Adler and Sir Moses Montefiore not only thought alike, but acted in concert, as they did also in their relations with the Reform Synagogue in London. Both feared in the early 1850s that the notions of ritual innovation which had taken congregational shape in London in 1840 might spread to the provinces and there flourish within the confines of autonomous congregations, and this fear was focused upon Manchester as the only provincial congregation with a rab-bi of its own. The questions in Manchester concerned the extent to which Dr Schiller was prepared to push his rabbinical claims, Hesse his desire for local freedom, the rest of the congregation its hope for ritual improvement, when faced with the opposition of the Chief Rabbi. Could all three aspirations find satisfaction without destroying the unity of the congregation and initiating the religious fragmentation of Anglo-Jewry?

I

Manchester Jewry of the 1840s and 1850s was a community in search of an identity. At a time of continuous immigration, and rapid social change, could a set of values be devised which was acceptable to the community as a whole and tolerable to the Chief Rabbi? Or was it inevitable that, with expansion, there should take place a division into separate congregations, each of which expressed a different facet of religious, social and political need? These questions were answered in the political sphere in 1851, when the Hesse–Lucas settlement suggested that the community might base its unity on the foundations of a propertied democracy not unlike that which gave a measure of stability to the nation. In matters of religion, which became the issue of the 1850s, the problem was less easy to resolve. Differences were less clearly defined and less obviously linked to social class or length of residence. During the 1840s a man's view of 'privilege' had tended to depend on the level of his wealth and the time of his arrival in Manchester, but on the burning issue of religious change, the cultural preferences and intellectual convictions of individuals cut across class boundaries, dividing upper-class and middle-class families both from each other and within themselves. There were no 'parties' in Manchester during the period 1851–53, no well-defined 'interests', only a small minority with fairly specific objectives trying to make what they could out of the vague aspirations and inhibitions of the remainder.

The only unequivocal advocate of Reform in Manchester in 1851 was Tobias Theodores. In describing the reunion of the Manchester congregations, the *Jewish Chronicle* had referred to 'the conservative and progressive portions (into which, as by a law of nature, every political and religious corporation is now-a-days divided)',[8] but the terms had meaning within a political, not a religious context. The New Congregation was not in any sense a movement towards Reform, nor is there any evidence that reunion was achieved by embryonic Reform groups in both camps coming together in the hope of radical change under the aegis of Dr Schiller. For Theodores, Reform was a matter of deep conviction, an integral part of his outlook, as well as a rationalisation of his hopes for the social and political future of Anglo-Jewry. In March 1851 he was appointed teacher of German at the newly-founded Owens College,[9] and in his inaugural lecture in the following October he offered a liberal view of cultural interchange with unmistakable implications for the Jewish community.[10] He commented, in particular, upon the unjustifiable arrogance of those national groups which claimed to be the 'sole depositaries of antique virtue and wisdom . . . amid a degenerate world', and cast himself, in his capacity as a language teacher, as 'a modest hand maid of the establishment of a cordial

FIGURE 8   Tobias Theodores (1808–1886).

exchange of moral and physical benefits between race and race'. This was the role, too, he hoped to play in the Jewish world: to draw traditional Judaism out of its cultural isolation and expose it to the full glare of critical reappraisal. A House of God 'hung over and around with the cobwebs of superannuated incongruities' might then be 'renovated and brought into harmony with the spirit of the times',[11] or, in practical terms, a form of service adopted similar to that in use in Germany's Reform Temples. If this objective, when subsequently translated into terms of specific ritual innovations for the Manchester synagogue, seemed less than revolutionary, this was because Theodores was acutely aware that he was pulling against a deeply embedded anchor of orthodoxy when others were deeply concerned at the consequences of the boat being set adrift. The powers of the Chief Rabbi concerned Theodores in both theoretical and strategic terms. Dr Adler was a declared opponent of Reform and must be circumvented, but the wide pretensions of the Chief Rabbi—such, for example, as he had exercised at the expense of the London Reformers—

were also as intellectually suffocating as the 'rabbinism' of the Talmud. Even in Jewish tradition, Theodores could find no justification for the exercise by rabbis of powers other than those conferred upon them by the congregations which had appointed them. Dr Adler ought properly to confine his jurisdiction to Duke's Place.

Fundamental to Theodores' thought was the great store he set by western culture, not for its own sake alone, but as the means by which Jews and Judaism would find acceptance as equals in the modern world. The inherited tradition of the Talmud must be re-examined to bring Jewish observance and ritual practice into line with cultural standards acceptable in the West. By means of a secular form of education

there should be a fusion between the Jew and the Christian, with the one exception of conscience . . . not . . . like the passage of the Rhine through the Lake of Constance, which could be followed from its ingress to its egress, but like the combination of life and matter, discernible to the eye of God alone . . .[12]

Only by closing the personal and institutional gap between Judaism and western culture could Jews expect to obtain the equality 'not only before the law, but in the estimation of their countrymen'[13] upon which political equality depended. It was only yesterday, Theodores wrote, that the gates of the Ghetto had been thrown down and the Jew allowed into a western world 'upon which he had formerly been only allowed to peep over prison walls'. As yet, Jews had 'contributed nothing to the intellectual glory of England'.[14] Now the time had arrived for Judaism to accommodate itself to its new and more open environment, and for Jews to fit themselves by education for a greater participation in the intellectual life around them. Of this total philosophy, the introduction of modifications into the service of the synagogue played only a small part, although it was the part most visible to his opponents.

Although Theodores probably had little or no following in Manchester in 1851, there were social groups from which he might in due course expect support, since their cultural orientation approximated to his own. This was true, in particular, of German-Jewish mercantile and professional families which had been subjected to strong assimilatory pressures in Germany or Holland before their arrival in England, and to which Theodores was linked by strong ties of national and liberal feeling. Some, like Salis Schwabe, James Hertz or Henry Leppoc, had abandoned Judaism completely; others, like Harry Lazarus, attended synagogue only on the High Holy days: a few, according to a contemporary, were 'hesitating between Unitarianism and Judaism'.[15] In Bradford, where the Jewish community consisted entirely of men of this stamp, religious life was almost totally corroded, circumcision was rare, Christian marriage and burial common, and 'they do not wish to pass for Jews, although every child in Bradford knows them to be Jews'.[16] In Manchester, this was the group which the *Jewish Chronicle* expected Dr Schiller to attract back to the synagogue. Other mercantile families already had connections with the London Reform congregation. Sigismund Schloss of Frankfurt, who arrived in Manchester in or about 1852, was one of four brothers engaged in trade with South America, one of whom, Leopold, was a member at Margaret Street, where in 1851 he had married the daughter of Horatio Montefiore, one of the founders of English Reform. The marriage of Schloss' sister to Horatio Micholls of Shakespeare Street, Ardwick, Henry's younger brother, and a partner in Lucas & Micholls, brought two of Manchester's leading commercial families into close touch with the metropolitan Reform circle. Two German-Jewish forty-eighters in exile in Manchester were in the substantial group which hovered between faith and apostasy. Dr Louis Borchardt[17] of Landsberg in East Prussia, who had spent two years in prison in Glatz for revolutionary activities, arrived in Manchester in 1852 from Bradford, where he had been befriended by a German Unitarian family, the Steinthals. In the following year he began a distinguished professional career as consulting physician to the Manchester Children's Dispensary. Leopold Dreschfeld[18] of Bavaria, a dentist, and also a former revolutionary activist, settled in Cavendish Street, Chorlton-on-Medlock, in 1852. The opportunity existed for Theodores to enlist the immediate sympathy of the Straus brothers, Schloss, and others who, like himself, remained within the synagogue in the hope of introducing changes from within, and the subsequent allegiance of those, like Borchardt and Dreschfeld, whose return to Judaism depended upon its 'renovation'. It was one of the tragedies of the situation that while to their conservative opponents Reformers appeared to be devising an effective way out of Judaism, they saw themselves as seeking a way only of remaining within it, and of recovering the allegiance of those whose Jewish identity might otherwise be irretrievably lost.

Hesse was not overmuch concerned with ritual change, nor with the general objects of Reform, except in so far as they involved a condemnation of rabbinical despotism in England. As in 1844, his hopes for the congregation were political rather than religious, although now they concerned not democracy within the synagogue but the right of each congregation to determine its own future within Anglo-Jewry. He had already expressed Manchester's independent voice at the Board of Deputies and he was now ready to believe that the community had a role to play within Anglo-Jewry quite as important as that which Manchester had assumed in the affairs of the nation. Manchester had become, according to the *Spectator*, 'the political, intellectual, and practical metropolis of the Empire'.[19] Men of the 'Manchester School' were educating the

nation and, less obtrusively, the town was setting new standards of urban development. A movement was initiated in 1850 towards the establishment of
the first rate-supported public library in England. In March 1851 the founders of
Owens College rejected the Oxford and Cambridge pattern and struck out
into a new style of university education. In 1847 the first Bishop of Manchester
was appointed, only four years before the first rabbi, and six years later a
Royal Charter endorsed Manchester's right—already widely assumed—to describe itself as a city.[20] The Queen visited the town in 1851, expressed her satisfaction at 'the quiet and orderly behaviour of the people', and knighted the
Mayor,[21] and when Louis Kossuth arrived, unofficially, a few months later,
the only echo of popular radicalism was the ceremonial burning of *The Times*
in Market Street.[22] Manchester had achieved an economic maturity which produced years of unequalled prosperity in the early 1850s. It seemed to Hesse that
in the Jewish context Manchester had come of age with the appointment of Dr
Schiller, no longer required metropolitan tutelage, and might set its own standards of congregational life which would serve as a model for other provincial
communities, as they, in their turn, became ready for independence. The central jurisdiction of the Chief Rabbi may well have been necessary to the eighteenth century, but it did not suit the conditions of the mid-nineteenth, when
provincial congregations had the means to supply all their own religious
needs. With Dr Schiller at Halliwell Street, there was no longer any need to
look to London for guidance for decisions on ritual issues, for the authorisation
of marriages, or the licensing of *shochetim*. Hesse probably had no preconceptions about Manchester's future ritual arrangements, so long as it was Manchester who decided them.

Civic pride was only one of several factors which influenced Hesse and
which made localism the dominant current of feeling in the Manchester Jewish
milieu of 1851–53. Even more important, perhaps, was the expansion of the
community itself in the later 1840s, when it overtook Birmingham in size and
became second only to Liverpool in the provinces.[23] In November 1851, 'having now experienced the advantages arising from unity of interests', Manchester was bold enough to offer its mediation to the warring factions in
Liverpool,[24] only to be told by the authorities at Seel Street that they were
'fully capable' of looking after their own affairs.[25] Hesse himself had
spoken of the community's movement up the social scale, and this was in
fact marked by personal and communal achievements which made 1851 the
Annus Mirabilis of Manchester Jewry. Theodores' inaugural lecture at Owens
College was attended by many Jews, including Louis Behrens from within
the synagogue and Leopold Amschel from beyond it.[26] Horatio Micholls
was elected to the governing council of the School of Design.[27] In November

Philip Lucas was returned unopposed to serve Cheetham Ward on the City Council, with the approval of the *Manchester Guardian*, which commented upon his superiority to his Gentile predecessor.[28] William Berlack, a seat-holder at Halliwell Street, was salaried secretary to the Society for the Relief of Distressed Foreigners. There was a Jewish attorney in Manchester—Michael Cohen De Lara (of De Lara & Fogg, Tib Lane)—who in January 1853 success-fully cleared Louis Beaver of a charge of obstructing the highway with the two lamps suspended outside his shop in Cross Street.[29] Edward Salomon,[30] son of the cotton merchant H. M. Salomon of Plymouth Grove, played a conspicuous part, as an architectural student at the School of Design, in creat-ing an elaborate *Cosmorama* of scenery and sculpture at the Free Trade Hall in 1850—the first attempt, according to the *Guardian*, 'to render a place of amuse-ment attractive to the higher and purer resources of genuine art'.[31] Salomon graduated in 1852 and began a distinguished local career from an office in King Street. He was also a prominent member of the Royal Manchester Institution, and subsequently its honorary secretary.[32]

In commerce, Jews remained outstanding in the retail clothing and jewel-lery trades, and sustained a high level of integrity and success in the textile trade. Louis Behrens was called in by a Rochdale cotton manufacturer in De-cember 1849 to act as an independent arbitrator in a bankruptcy case.[33] Others explored the import of miscellaneous 'fancy goods', rendered increasingly prosperous by the expansion of luxury retailing. William Danziger, and his brother, Isidore, both from Danzig, set up an import agency in the Old Town in 1851. Hesse, who by 1851 owned a linen factory at Dundalk in Ireland, also imported 'French and German goods' and distributed them through a 'repository' in Albert Square. Julius Arensberg, who was prominent also in Freemasonry, imported and retailed tobacco and cigars. Joel Aaron Kohn of Brodie and Lasar Barsam of Odessa used a warehouse in Church Street to store Russian goods imported from the Black Sea ports.

The growth of the community, its economic prosperity, the civic achieve-ments of its leaders, its reunion, the appointment of Dr Schiller, the extension of the Jews School, and the sustained support of the *Guardian* for Jewish emancipation, all contributed to the growth of local pride which Hesse ex-pressed as a desire for a greater degree of congregational freedom than that which existed within the traditional framework of Anglo-Jewry. At this point Hesse's pragmatism and Theodores' philosophy converged, although, as yet, they did not see themselves as part of the same movement. Their objectives were markedly different, and while Hesse had wide, perhaps almost unani-mous suppport for a movement which involved no religious issues, Theodores possessed, at most, a handful of passive sympathisers with Reform. It re-

remained open to the Chief Rabbi to keep them apart, and to deal with each separately. Dr Schiller's role is difficult to assess. Both Hesse and Theodores looked to him for a measure of support, and it seemed certainly to be in his own interests to encourage a movement towards greater autonomy. On the whole, however, it does not seem likely that he had any choice in the matter. In 1851 he symbolised class unity, and thereafter he was caught up in a turbulence which was not of his making. The question was the extent to which he was prepared, from conviction or ambition, to lend his weight to the forces which were taking shape, since it was in the minds of all those who wanted change that Dr Schiller might help them to accomplish it. During the years 1851–53, when his own personality and ideas had not yet clearly emerged, he was all things to all men.

Between Theodores, the convinced Reformer, and his mercantile sympathisers, and Hesse, the convinced liberal, the core of whose support came from his former colleagues of the New Synagogue, lay a powerful body of shopkeepers, whose families were chiefly of eighteenth-century pedlar origin, and out of whose activities the communities of provincial Anglo-Jewry had in the first instance taken shape, and who in the past had kept them on strictly orthodox lines under allegiance to the Chief Rabbi. The currents of Reform prevalent on the Continent had followed their departure to England, they had received little or no western education, and although inclined to believe that a more decorous synagogue was a fitting compliment to their improving social status, they had been brought up to believe that the preservation of Jewish tradition far exceeded the importance of its modification. They saw Dr Schiller as an eloquent firebrand, who might certainly 'improve' the ritual with minor adjustments acceptable to the Chief Rabbi, but whose main task would be to revive religious enthusiasm, to strengthen religious education and to stem the tide of religious assimilation. They liked the assertiveness of Hesse, since it boosted their own importance, but most were probably not prepared to back him to the extent of undermining the Chief Rabbi. They favoured moderate improvement and a measure of autonomy, but it seems unlikely that in 1851 they had given very serious consideration to the full religious or political implications of either. They had no spokesman, and their opinions ranged from the enlightened tolerance of Isaac Franklin to the blind conservatism of M. H. Simonson, the querulous Second Reader and occasional *shochet*, who, between complaints of his long hours of arduous labour and low pay, wrote a pamphlet in April 1851 in which he sought a 'philosophical explanation' of Joshua's command to the Sun and Moon (Joshua x. 12–14).[34] Although addressed to 'the truly conscientious but scientific man',[35] it was credulous to a degree and, more significantly, intellectually subservient to the Talmud. 'The opinions of the Rabbies . . . our Doctors of old, the Rabbins of blessed memory' were quoted as incontrovertibly true,[36] when the Reform controversy turned upon their acceptability. In the long run, if Theodores was to convert the congregation as a whole to Reform, he could do so only by arousing a critical spirit in those whose natural predisposition was conformity.

Finally, there were the immigrant poor of Red Bank, for whom Reform was as unthinkable as Christianity, who were only now 'peeping over the walls of the Ghetto', and to whom the orthodoxy of Halliwell Street was itself suspect. In Verdon Street were men and women whose strictness of observance had been refined by persecution and insularity. They were not Free Members at Halliwell Street, where even those who could afford the entrance fees were socially unacceptable, so that they were not expected to play any part in debates on religious or political matters, and in so far as they had any effect on the course of events, it was to interrupt the proceedings of controversy with their clamorous material needs. The Jewish middle class hoped most of all that they would leave, and did what it could in the way of private benevolence and concerted deterrence to bring this about. In June 1851 the Select Committee thankfully accepted a donation from A. S. Sichel

for the purpose of affording many poor but industrious families of the town to seek their fortunes on the other side of the Atlantic, whereby a great saving to this Congregation was affected.[37]

But the influx continued, and when in July Simon Joseph spoke

at great length . . . of the inefficient system of relieving the casual poor, and urged upon the Meeting [of the Select Committee] to devise some plan how to act that the deserving only be relieved,[38]

the Congregation turned, on 9 July, to a fierce policy of deterrence as 'the best means of dealing with the itinerant poor'.[39] All help was refused to 'young, healthy, and able-bodied mendicants'. The sick and the old were still to receive support, but the rest were to be referred to

the Industrial Institution of the Manchester Poor House, thereby securing for the Wanderer and Wayfarer a Supper, Night's Lodging and breakfast, for which they will be compelled to perform some labour.

A notice to this effect was pinned on the inner door of the synagogue, and the decision communicated to Jewish congregations in Hamburg, Hull, Liverpool, Birmingham and London. Jewish lodging-house keepers in Manchester, of whom there were at least six in 1851, were warned against 'harbouring young persons who have no visible mode of gaining a living' on pain of being excluded 'from any Funds during Sacred Festivals, and Passover Cakes'.

These measures were more an indication of panic than a serious attempt to cope with the itinerant poor. Since it was not possible to reach the economic roots of the problem either in England or in Europe, a stemming of the tide was not to be expected. To categorise all able-bodied transmigrants as 'undeserving' was neither just nor effective. Most paupers refused, on religious grounds, either to enter the workhouse or accept its meals, and since they could not be left to starve or beg, the experiment failed within the six-week trial period allotted to it. The congregation returned to the methods devised during 1847–48, which seemed to offer as great a degree of deterrence as the circumstances would allow. At the same time, Eastern European settlement was a cumulative problem once an original nucleus had been created, as it had by 1851, with a pattern of life and work capable of absorbing new immigrants. A majority of those who left Eastern Europe travelled on to the United States, but the small colony increased in size from twenty-one households in 1851 to forty-seven in 1853, and during the decade of the 1850s increased as a proportion of the community from 11 per cent to 22 per cent. The number of children at the Jews School had risen to 150 by 1855, an increase of 40 per cent over the year 1851–52. With some insight into the potential of the situation, Beaver bought five houses in Red Bank, Hesse four, all occupied by immigrants at the time of the Census of 1861.[40] Dr Schiller's role was again equivocal. He was brought into close contact with the immigrants through the Jews School, of which he became Superintendent and religious teacher; he sympathised deeply with their needs, and respected their religious instincts, to the point of providing his guidance to an immigrant conventicle, the *Chevra Tehillim*, founded in 1854.[41] But his ambition as much as the terms of his appointment bound him to the Jewish middle class, and it was their objects he was expected to achieve. In the web of controversy and intrigue which occupied the succeeding decade this duality of interest was another of the tensions to which Dr Schiller was subjected as the community passed through its many moments of decision. The immigrants had already played a major part in determining the future of the community, by emphasising the common interests of the middle classes during the period 1848–51, and they continued to do so for the rest of the decade, not only by occasionally posing problems which necessitated a truce in religious hostilities but also by sustaining the class-consciousness of the assimilated élite which was one of the factors making for Reform.

The changes taking place within the community were scarcely visible outside it. The small body of Jewish immigrants in Red Bank was massively overshadowed by the great 'Celtic *incubus*'[42]—'the enormous shoal of paupers' from Ireland who 'quarter themselves on our local poor rate for life'.[43] By throwing the onus of proving the absence of legal settlement on to the local overseers, the so-called 'Irremovable Act' of 1846 had aggravated the 'almost normal condition of Irish pauperism', since in their 'notorious unscrupulousness', according to the *Guardian*, the Irish compounded poverty with perjury.[44] The successive failures of the potato crops in the later 1840s created a wave of sympathy—including a prayer composed by the Chief Rabbi, read at Halliwell Street in March 1847[45]—and tens of thousands of emigrants, many to Manchester. If Red Bank was drab, cramped and insanitary, Little Ireland was a 'pestilential place' compared by a contemporary to the Black Hole of Calcutta.[46] Jewish settlement passed without comment, and the only recorded instance of anti-Jewish violence—if this is what it was—dated from September 1850, when Laurence McKay, 'a rough looking young fellow', made an unprovoked attack upon Morris Levy, a traveller, and four or five other Jews who were standing in conversation at the corner of Miller Street.[47] Otherwise, the bulk of the middle class stood by its stereotype of the respectable Jewish trader, and the *Guardian* sustained its support for Jewish emancipation. When, in April 1853, in a railway carriage on the Liverpool–Manchester Railway, Richard Beswick, the Chief Superintendent of Police, was heard by Joseph Slazenger Moss to refer to 'the generality of the Jews' as receivers of stolen goods, an apology was sought by Philip Lucas through the Town Clerk,[48] and Beswick wrote formally to confirm that in his twenty-one years in the police force he had formed the 'highest opinion' of the Jews.[49] Even amongst the conversionists, the edge of prejudice had been blunted.

Depraved [the Jews] undoubtedly are [wrote Rev. A. E. Pearce] but not more so than thousands who have been converted . . . if they are mercenary, is it not because they have been so often plucked and spoiled of their possessions, that it has taught them to hold with a tenacious grasp, and driven them to unjust methods of accumulation?[50]

Equality was sometimes double-edged. When Nathan Kantrowitz, a Polish tobacconist in Chapel Street, Salford, in court in 1850 for opening his shop on the Christian Sabbath, claimed that his business depended on his Sunday trade, the local magistrate (H. L. de Trafford) commented: 'If you choose to shut up on Saturday, in obedience to your own religion, you must close on Sunday for ours.'[51]

The conversionists took note of those religious changes which might have affected their strategy or chances. The most perceptive analysis was that of Israel Napthali, who divided Manchester Jews into three categories.[52] First, there were those, amongst whom he classed 'a great nucleus of English Jews', whose religion was based upon a blind acceptance of tradition: 'with them we have little success, as they are extremely ignorant and excessively bigoted'. Then there were the 'Talmudic Jews' (that is, one may suppose, the immigrants from Eastern Europe) of sterner frame of mind, profound in subtlety, versed in abstruse questions, philosophically cautious, and hard to convince, but if convinced at all, the most valuable converts to the Christian faith;

and finally the Jews whose knowledge of Judaism was confined to the five books of Moses, who were 'generally open to conviction, and promise good success to our endeavours'. A recurrent theme, which did little good to the cause of Theodores in Manchester, was the suggestion that those Jews who embraced Reform were on their way to Christianity. Margoliouth told a public meeting in Manchester that since Jews were 'rejecting oral tradition', it was to be expected that 'they would study Moses and the Prophets', at which point, 'they would not be far off from Him of whom Moses and the prophets wrote'.[53] Stowell compared Jewish 'rabbinism' with 'the rabbinical traditions of Oxford' and rejoiced at what he took, in 1848, to be the collapse of both.[54]

II

The first fruits of unity, as well as the first explicit indication of the assertive mood of the Manchester community, were both in the field of Jewish education. The new school building on Cheetham Hill Road was completed soon after the formalities of reunion, and opened by the Chief Rabbi on 22 May.[55] Within a few months its governing committee, led by Lucas, had taken issue with the Board of Deputies on the form of relationship with the State best suited to the interests of Jewish education.

Built to the 'Italian' design of J. E. Gregan, the new school was situated near the junction of Lord Street and Cheetham Hill Road, where the ground sloping down into Red Bank provided space for a 'covered playground'.[56] A square tower, 45 ft high and faced with white firebrick in Romanesque patterns, stood, as if symbolically, at the boundary of the middle-class districts of Strangeways and Cheetham Hill, and the immigrant quarter below. A collection made at a dinner held in the evening of the consecration, at the Albion Hotel, raised a final sum of £360, more than enough to cover the remaining deficit in the building fund.[57] In the final analysis, the total cost of the land, buildings, fittings and furniture amounted to £1,912,[58] nearly three times the annual expenditure of the congregation and around eight times the cost of casual poverty in the period 1848–51. Dr Schiller, became the school's honorary superintendent and religious teacher, Joachim Levy continued to provide lessons in the Hebrew language and literature, Mrs Sophia Solomon stayed on as governess for the girls and teacher of needlework, and secular instruction—'in reading, writing, grammar, history, etc.; in arithmetic, geography, and all the other branches of an elementary and a general education'[59]—was provided by the headmaster, Mr Millar, to the school's eighty pupils, all between the ages of five and fifteen.

It was in fact secular education which provided the school's chief *raison d'être*. Although Isaac Franklin was to insist year after year, once to the point of resigning his honorary secretaryship, upon the high standard of Hebrew teaching, the school's main object was seen to be the social and cultural integration of the immigrant poor. Franklin wrote, in his annual report for 1851–52,

It is gratifying to record that these [pupils] are not limited to the indigent members of our community, but that those amongst the most prosperous classes are equally availing themselves of the institution,[60]

but his optimism made a poor showing on the balance sheet. The school's annual income from fees was £55 7s 9d as against subscriptions and donations totalling £300. Most children attended free, and many required the free suits and dresses provided by the School Clothing Society which was formally constituted, under the presidency of Mrs S. L. Behrens, in May 1853.[61] The Society met twice a year to provide decent attire to children 'whose parents are *proved* to be unable to afford getting them', whose families had resided in Manchester for at least six months, and whose attendance had been regular and punctual.[62] It was, in effect, a wheel within the wheel of assimilation. At the ceremonial half-yearly distributions—each mother standing beside her child—'careful and diligent enquiry' was made

into the habits, character and circumstances of the *parents* of the children as are to be included in each half year's list of candidates,[63]

and the subsequent misconduct of a parent was sufficient to disqualify his or her child. Two members of the society visited the school at least once a fortnight 'to superintend . . . the state and conduct of the recipients of the charity', and those whose record of attendance was poor, or who returned their suits or dresses 'in bad condition', forfeited any future benefits.[64] The result, according to Franklin, was to induce

a degree of order, cleanliness and steady application to the studies of the school, among a class of children that might otherwise have groped continually in the darkness of ignorance and destitution.[65]

The degree of the school's success as an agent of integration is difficult to gauge, but, on the whole, it was probably more effective in breaking down the immediate linguistic and social barriers to assimilation than in overcoming the economic limitations of the immigrant milieu. Lucas claimed later that several seventeen-year-old boys educated at the school had been found 'situations as clerks', some on salaries of £50 to £75 a year, and many of the girls had been 'placed in service' as housemaids and needlewomen,[66] but a more evident trend was for children to drift into the 'immigrant trades' as soon as they were free of the school's influence.

Although several shopkeepers sent their children to the school, the suburban rich made other arrangements. Benjamin Hyam employed a private tutor, Michaelis Silverstein, who also collected the firm's debts.[67] Abraham Franklin's youngest son, Henry, was educated at Mr Neumegen's private school at Kew,[68] Philip Lucas' son, Arthur, at University College School,[69] the daughters of Esther Segré at 'the distinguished seminary of the Misses Belisario at Clapton'.[70] The eldest daughter, Theresa, opened her own private school on 9 May 1853 at 132 York Place, Cheetham Hill, where, with her sisters, she offered to

devote herself to the instruction of young ladies in all the approved branches of a useful education and of elegant accomplishments, combined with the needful study of Hebrew, and the inculcation of religious knowledge.[71]

The school flourished until 1859, when Theresa Ségre married her cousin, Isaac Franklin. There was also a German Day and Sunday School—another indication of German solidarity—which was opened in rented rooms in Brewery Street, Strangeways, in September 1852, and which offered a general education (up to the age of sixteen) to the children of German parents 'without distinction of religion'.[72] At the beginning of 1853 the school began to send some of its older children out to work, to accustom them to 'industry and activity'.[73]

It was partly because the Jews School was, in effect, a charity school, dependent upon private subscriptions, that the question of State aid assumed such importance. It was not the money itself which mattered at first—the earliest government grants amounted to only £10 a year—but the establishment of the principle that Jewish elementary schools were quite as much entitled to State assistance as voluntary Christian institutions. Neither party nor public opinion in the early nineteenth century had favoured the provision of nondenominational State schools, so that when State aid had commenced, on a very meagre level, in 1833, it had taken the form of subsidies to voluntary organisations of the Christian communion. Jewish schools were effectively excluded by a provision which insisted that in State-assisted schools 'the Holy Scriptures' should be daily read. The Manchester Hebrew Education Society (the former Hebrew Association) had taken the matter up with the Privy Council in 1849, only to have it confirmed that its school, since it could not use the Holy Scriptures in their full Christian sense, was 'not eligible' for a State grant.[74] Philip Lucas, the Society's president, was amongst the influential Manchester men who in 1849 petitioned Parliament for a national secular system[75] into which Jewish children might have been absorbed, but since this way forward seemed likely to be blocked by interdenominational bitterness it was important that the Manchester Jews School should establish its eligibility for aid as a voluntary body. With the help of a sympathetic local inspector, J. D. Morrell, the new school on Cheetham Hill was built 'in conformity with the requirements of the government plan',[76] and the 'secular part' of its instruction was opened to children 'of every denomination', not simply, as Isaac Franklin put it, 'to spread the blessing of education to all creeds', but even more to place the school on a par with those which received State aid.[77] The matter then became, beyond doubt, one of discrimination, since it was the religious disqualification alone which was the excluding factor. In June 1851 the Society put pressure on the Board of Deputies to take the matter up with the government,[78] and on 14 July the Board was awoken from its lethargy to the extent of appointing a sub-committee of six, chaired by Baron de Rothschild, 'to exercise its best endeavours' with the Education Committee of Privy Council.[79] For the first time since the debates of 1847–48 Manchester had used its influence to promote national Jewish interests through the Board of Deputies, and its own deputy, Jacob Franklin, who had helped to press the case for State aid, was a member of Rothschild's sub-committee.

In Manchester, meantime, the situation was complicated by the promotion of a private act for raising a compulsory rate in aid of local voluntary schools. The act was devised by the Manchester and Salford Committee on Education, the powerful protagonist of denominational schools, and its clauses would have excluded Jews from assistance on the same grounds which disqualified them from State aid. When the Hebrew Education Society pressed for clarification of the 'fatal ambiguity' concerning the 'Holy Scriptures', the Committee refused to insert a saving clause

that in the case of the Jews the term 'Holy Scriptures' should be deemed to imply such portion of the Scriptures as that denomination acknowledge and make use of.[80]

Faced with the prospect of Jews paying 'their proportion of a tax for educating all other denominations',[81] the Society set up its own sub-committee—Dr Schiller, Lucas, Theodores, A. S. Sichel, J. M. Isaac, and Isaac Franklin—in November 1851,

with full power to adopt such measures as they deem expedient for making known to the Jewish community in this town the facts of the case, and for strenuously opposing the success of the Bill, in its present form, when presented to parliament.[82]

The Committee's services were not required. At the end of 1852 the Society was able to report that the negotiations of the Board of Deputies had proved successful, and that the government had conceded, at least 'in principle', the admission of Jewish schools to participation in State grants.[83] The only statutory requirements were that the average attendance at a Jews School should reach the required level (fifty boys and forty girls in the case of the Manchester school), that part at least of the Holy Scriptures should be daily read, and that the secular elements of instruction should be opened to government inspection. The local act, meantime, was first delayed, and finally destroyed, by interdenominational rivalry.[84] When, in March 1853, the Manchester Jews School received £10 towards the salary of a pupil-teacher, Samuel Goodheim,[85] it became the first Jewish educational body in England to receive State aid, a fitting climax, as the *Jewish Chronicle* commented, to Manchester's role in insisting upon Jewish rights.[86]

Manchester was prepared not only to chivvy the Board of Deputies into a more active pursuit of Jewish interests but also to resist the Board's attempts to tamper with the autonomy of local communities. When, in 1852, the Board's legal advisers drew up a 'model deed' for Jewish schools which would have placed them under the supervision of the Chief Rabbi, the Hebrew Education Society in Manchester, through Lucas, objected to 'the assumption on the part of the Deputies of powers not vested in them by the sanction of their constituents'.[87] Manchester rejected the deed in part because it believed that the secular education of Jewish youth should be free of inspection by the ecclesiastical authorities, but also because it believed each Jewish school in the provinces should be managed entirely by its own committee. Lucas' letter ended

the Committee of the Manchester School confidently trust that they will be spared the necessity of taking further steps for the purpose of maintaining the independence and free action of Jewish School Committees in the matter of Education which in their view ought to be entirely free from Ecclesiastical interference.

It seems likely, since Dr Schiller was Superintendent of the Jews School, that the objection was not to 'ecclesiastical interference' as such, but to the interference of the Chief Rabbi in particular. The mood communicated by the letter is one of resentment at external restraints imposed by either the Board of Deputies or the Chief Rabbi's Office. It is not clear what 'further steps' were contemplated, since central authority was not in fact imposed, but the threat was one which hinted at a desire for greater independence. Since the Manchester School was open to non-Jewish children, part of Lucas' objection was to the 'sectarianism' of the model deed; but the greater objection was to the attempt of London to tell Manchester how to manage its educational affairs.

III

The education question did not raise fundamental issues, since Manchester could, and did, run its school independently without violating in any way the traditional ecclesiastical jursidiction of the Chief Rabbi. Nor was any religious principle or practice involved, since there was no hint that Dr Schiller was involved in activities more radical than the preparation of children of both sexes for confirmation. Other matters, however, raised more serious problems. With Manchester in a mood for independence, and equipped with its own rabbinical guide, what was to happen to the Chief Rabbi's powers to authorise marriages, for example, to examine and license *shochetim*, and to decide on ritual matters? To what extent would matters formerly within the exclusive province of the Chief Rabbi in London now be decided by Dr Schiller in Manchester?

Soon after David Hesse's election as one of the two wardens at Halliwell Street, in the autumn of 1851, the question assumed concrete form over a relatively trivial matter. At that time a certain Abraham Shienfeld, a young Polish cap maker living at 10 Fernie Street, announced to the Select Committee his intention of marrying a woman of Christian birth, Annah Williams, who claimed to have been accepted into Judaism in Holland. The Committee examined the documentary evidence of the woman's conversion, accepted its validity, and in November wrote to the Chief Rabbi for his authorisation of what they chose to regard as an ordinary marriage.[88] It is hardly likely that they were unaware of the implications of the request: as the Chief Rabbi pointed out to Hesse, it had been the custom 'as far back as the records of the Jewish Congregations of this country go' for a convert who had undergone the ceremonies of acceptance in Holland 'to come to London for her final reception into the bosom of our faith'.[89] It was a custom 'which [according to Dr Adler] the length of time has proved admirable and necessary', especially in view of the lack of proper witnesses to the performance of the ceremony, and one from which Solomon Hirschel had deviated only in very exceptional circumstances.[90] Sensing the small beginnings of a challenge to his authority, he demanded the appearance of Annah Williams in London (even offering £1 towards the cost of her rail fare), at the same time extracting from Dr Schiller a promise not to act independently in the matter.[91] The Select Committee was equally stubborn, refusing to accede to the request and claiming 'a right to judge . . . the Evidence on this as in all other cases where the parties concerned are resident in our town',[92] and when Dr Adler reiterated his demand, Simonson replied that the wardens had decided to go ahead with the marriage 'without the order or leave from the Rev. the Chief Rabbi if such leave can

not be obtained', again claiming for the Select Committee the right to judge
for themselves 'what is, or is not good Evidence'.[93] Hesse and Dr Adler had
quickly taken up unequivocal positions; it remained to be seen how far each
was prepared to push his case.

In the event, Dr Adler decided not to force the issue. In his reply to Hesse
on 5 December[94] he pointed out that the Old Congregation's stand not only
placed his own authority in jeopardy, but was 'even entirely at variance with
the civil right of this country'. At law, he argued, it was essential to the validity of a Jewish marriage that the 'proceedings' had conformed 'to the usages
of the Jewish religion', which they had not in this case since Annah Williams'
conversion had not been fully attested. None the less, he agreed by way of
concession to send Dayan Aaron Levy to Manchester to act with Dr Schiller,
and with a third person of their choice, to ensure that the proselyte underwent
the 'final ceremonies' of acceptance; 'but in all future cases [he wrote] I must insist on the procedure hitherto observed'. From this ambiguous outcome both
parties believed they had advanced their cause: Dr Adler that he had asserted
his supremacy without pushing the Manchester congregation beyond a point
of no return, Hesse that a degree of local autonomy had been acknowledged.
In a carefully phrased letter to the Chief Rabbi, Simonson thanked him for
transferring the matter to Dr Schiller 'from whom it ought never to have been
taken'.[95] The Chief Rabbi believed that he had curtailed Dr Schiller's powers,
Hesse that they had been partially enhanced. Dr Schiller himself remained
silent and it seems likely that the whole train of events was set in motion by the
warden rather than the minister; its outcome confirmed not Dr Schiller's ambition, but the strength of local feeling. It was a matter of more than local interest, however. The issue was whether Anglo-Jewry should develop on the
European and American pattern of independent congregations which established rules as they wished, sharing only a common tradition and associating
only occasionally for specific purposes of limited duration, or continue along
the lines already laid down in the late eighteenth century towards the consolidation of a central and coercive ecclesiastical authority in the person of the
Chief Rabbi. Manchester was the provincial test case.

In this context, Hesse decided to move on from a partial to a complete victory. On 16 December, less than ten days after the decision on the marriage
case, the Select Committee recommended to the congregation the election of
Dr Schiller as 'Local Rabbi' for a term of three years, 'subject to the jurisdiction of the Chief Rabbi'.[96] What followed is a clear indication of the assertive
mood of the whole of middle-class Jewry. At a General Meeting chaired by
Hesse on 25 December, at which the new seat-holders exercised their franchise
for the first time, Dr Schiller was unanimously elected to an office which was

without precedent in England.[97] Immediately after the vote, he was called into the meeting and notified of the result, 'which was followed by cheers'.[98] Since the functions of a Local Rabbi were not defined, the status of the office depended upon whether emphasis was placed on the title or on its limiting clause. It is clear, however, that Hesse hoped to outmanœuvre the Chief Rabbi by presenting him with a *fait accompli* difficult to reverse without hardening local feeling: Dr Adler was not consulted until after the event, and then only as a matter of report. His reply, written on 29 December,[99] opened a controversy which lasted a little over four months. As to Dr Schiller, it seems likely that although he was carried into office by what Hesse described as 'a spontaneous act' of the congregation,[100] he welcomed the appointment both for the status attached to it and because he regarded it as a move in the right direction for provincial Anglo-Jewry. There were, he believed, 'two parties' in the country as a whole,

the one endeavouring to find fault with what had been done, and regarding us with a jealous eye, and the second looking to Manchester as its model.

It was the duty of the officers of the Old Congregation, he argued, to be 'careful to disappoint the former, whilst [to] the latter we should always be as an example'. Although

. . . the steps had not been made without opposition, still he maintained it was only consistent with what was right and according to *the example of our continental brethren,* care always being taken that the party so appointed should be legally qualified . . .[101]

The *Jewish Chronicle* endorsed these views:

It is high time the Jews in England should bestir themselves, and not appear dormant to the proper attainment of spiritual aid in the provinces; the idea of a [local] Rabbi is common on the continent, and why should we be backward? . . . A lay body are not qualified to make a Rabbi, but have a perfect right to elect one.[102]

At the beginning of January 1852 the Select Committee began a delicate exercise in appeasement. Although Hesse and a handful of extremists close to him, chiefly former rebels like Saul and Nathan Mayer, were prepared to jettison the Chief Rabbi altogether if need be, they calculated that to carry the whole congregation with them a more cautious approach was required. Others were anxious that no event in Manchester should undermine the structure of the Chief Rabbinate. On behalf of the Select Committee, Simonson explained to Dr Adler that Dr Schiller's new title implied

that he should do and exercise all rabbinical functions in this town, or in other words, that he has to perform all the *ordinary* duties of a Rabbi to the congregation, while 'subject to your jurisdiction' leaves all *extraordinary* matters to yourself.[103]

The Local Rabbi, he explained, was 'strictly to confine his rabbinical authority to the Manchester Congregation alone'. The appointment was in fact, he continued, a mark of respect to the Chief Rabbi, 'as by the appointment the dignity of the Ecclesiastical Office is much enhanced'. Such equivocation was too much for Dr Adler. He wrote to Hesse on 5 January to express his regret

that you should have finally decided on so important an ecclesiastical matter as the election of a Rabbi without previously requesting my sanction thereto,

and emphasised that such actions 'set a precedence [sic] more dangerous in this country where an overall control is more difficult than anywhere else'.[104] He did not question Dr Schiller's paper qualifications, but ruled that recognition of his office depended upon his appearance in London for an examination of his competence to exercise rabbinical functions. Press support for local Rabbis on the continental pattern, and for the right of pcovincial congregations to elect them, strengthened the Chief Rabbi's fear that events in Manchester might produce centrifugal forces difficult to restrain, especially at a time when fugitives from Eastern Europe included rabbis of varying quality, any one of whom might be persuaded to remain in England. This would explain his concern to emphasise that a man who had exercised rabbinical functions on the Continent possessed no automatic right to discharge them within an English congregation.

When the Select Committee replied to his letter on 11 January to the effect that

they do not feel themselves justified in recommending the Rev Dr Schiller to undergo another rabbinical Examination as to his fitness for the performance of rabbinical functions,[105]

and proceeded to install Dr Schiller in office on 31 January,[106] Dr Adler launched a comprehensive attack upon the integrity of the Local Rabbi and the judgement of the Manchester executive.

Gentlemen [he wrote on 5 February], I can now . . . not longer with justice to my responsible duties or with deference to the dictates of my conscience, postpone the unreserved expression of my views . . .[107]

The distinction made in Manchester between 'extraordinary' and 'ordinary' rabbinical duties he declared to be 'too precarious and uncertain for any practical purpose'. Since Dr Schiller had given his word in December 1850 not to exercise any independent powers, his acceptance of office was a 'breach of faith' which his election had compounded: on this 'moral ground' alone the Chief Rabbi felt justified in expressing his 'unqualified regret', since without morality 'a Minister as well as a Community are nonentities'. But this was not all, since it was contrary to Dr Adler's policy

to allow the performance of rabbinical functions in the Congregations under my charge to any gentleman, however he might be supplied with foreign Diplomas, without my previous examination . . . [to ascertain] his capability of exercising such responsible duties . . . In a country like this, when there exists no government control of qualifications whatever, such measure of precaution appears to me an absolute necessity.

In these circumstances, he claimed the right to decide upon 'the fitness of rabbis for office' in the way 'most advisable to my judgement', and in the case of Dr Schiller by a personal examination in London.

If this right be denied to me, I cease virtually to exercise a spiritual control over such Congregation. But it was one of the principal conditions under which I accepted the office of Chief Rabbi, and to which you have given your assent, that I should have the spiritual guidance of *all* the United Congregations.

Gentlemen, if you desire therefore not to be instrumental in the breach of promise on the part of the Rev. Dr Schiller, if you desire to be yourselves faithful to the spirit of your own promises [of 1850], if lastly you desire to keep up the bond of spiritual union which now exists among our Congregations throughout the British Empire: I repeat my urgent request that you recommend to Rev Dr Schiller to present himself before me for the purpose of an examination in the functions of a Rabbi . . .

On 18 February, David Hesse replied in person.[108] Although confessing an 'error of judgement' in not informing the Chief Rabbi of the congregation's intentions, he advanced the mitigating plea of an overflow of local pride at a time of expansion and reunion. Manchester, he argued, could no longer be treated as an insignificant community on the periphery of Anglo-Jewry. It was increasing rapidly in size and prestige, and required new ecclesiastical arrangements in keeping with its status. While the Chief Rabbi's 'privileges' were 'sacred and untouched', the Manchester community had acted

in the zealous feeling for our rights because the right to do what we have done can not be impunged, and can never be surrendered.

As to the alleged 'breach of faith' on the part of Dr Schiller, he had sought neither the appointment nor the title which the members of the congregation had chosen to confer upon him. Nor had the congregation broken its word, since the agreement made in 1850 was for a year's duration only and did not apply to the new appointment. Finally, on a conciliatory note, Hesse sought the Chief Rabbi's confirmation of Dr Schiller's position without a 'humiliating examination'. In substance, however, the letter yielded nothing. It acknowledged an excess of zeal and apologised for undue discourtesy, without conceding that the congregation had in any way infringed the jurisdiction of the

Chief Rabbi. It implied that the rights of a Local and a Chief Rabbi might be reconciled, without defining either.

Although gratified by the 'reconciliatory spirit' of the letter, Dr Adler doubted the validity of its arguments. On 3 March he wrote that Manchester's failure to seek his guidance involved not only

a want of courtesy . . . but an encroachment of [*sic*] the privileges conferred on the spiritual head of this country with the consent and co-operation of your Community.[109]

He agreed that in 1850 he had intimated that he

might in the course of years sanction Dr Schiller's taking the title of 'Morenu', but in this I could certainly not mean the assumption of that dignity without the least communication to me. If Dr Schiller's testimonials were sufficient to acknowledge him as 'Minister', without any further examination; it does not follow that they are equally satisfactory for an engagement as 'Rabbi'.

The examination in London would involve no 'degradation' of Dr Schiller, who was given the choice of an examination by the *Beth Din* or by the Chief Rabbi in his private residence. Not wishing to precipitate a crisis, however, Dr Adler agreed—'for the sake of peace'—to sanction the immediate use of the title on condition that all questions of religion and ritual were referred to London for decision and that Dr Schiller 'do not introduce any alteration in the religious affairs of the Community without my previous permission'. Pointing out that Dr Schiller would still have 'ample' and 'extended' scope for the exercise of his ministerial functions, he emphasised the 'dissension' and 'strife' which might follow 'a protracted difference of opinion . . . within your community'.

There matters rested for two months. The Chief Rabbi was not anxious to adopt such extreme measures as would only strengthen local feeling in favour either of autonomy or of Reform; Hesse was persuaded that a premature rebellion might alienate influential members of the community whose support his cause required, but whose loyalty to the Chief Rabbi was, for the present, above suspicion. For the time being, he accepted a title as all that could be obtained.

The affair acquired a new significance, however, as soon as Dr Adler sensed that the community was moving on from a desire for autonomy towards measures of Reform. At first Dr Schiller had remained content with the performance of routine ministerial functions and the delivery to crowded congregations of long, erudite sermons which contained no hint of radical intentions, but during April he initiated minor changes which, although not in themselves fundamental in character, were regarded by the Chief Rabbi as a breach of the conditions he had imposed on 3 March and therefore as the possible beginnings

PLATE I   Jacob Franks (1781–1846).

PLATE II   Louis Beaver (1822–1879), by Philip Westcott, *c.* 1856.

of a more serious movement towards innovation. The first was the introduction of a regular choir, which was commented upon favourably by the *Jewish Chronicle* on 9 April.[110] The second, and more significant, was the organisation of a ceremony of confirmation for eight girls and one boy who had been under his personal instruction at the Jews School for almost eighteen months.[111] On 28 April the Select Committee set up a small sub-committee to ensure that the ceremony was arranged according to Dr Schiller's views.[112] Aware of the general desire in Manchester for ritual change and probably of the growing support for the views of Theodores, Dr Adler adjudged the situation to be sufficiently serious to require his presence, and that of Sir Moses Montefiore, in Manchester to arrange a permanent settlement. At short notice, on 2 May, the lay and ecclesiastical heads of Anglo-Jewry arrived at the Queen's Hotel in Piccadilly to bring their errant provincial child under proper control, Sir Moses by private persuasion, Dr Adler by open negotiation.[113]

An informal meeting between Dr Adler and the Committee at the Queen's Hotel in Piccadilly on the 2nd[114] was followed by a private discussion between the two rabbis on the following day and a full meeting of the Select Committee in the evening.[115] Ten minutes after the committee had assembled at Halliwell Street, Dr Adler entered the room with Dr Schiller and with the two wardens, Ansell Spier and David Hesse, who had been to the hotel to fetch him. Following a formal introduction, Hesse took the chair, with Dr Adler on his right side and Dr Schiller on his left, and 'after much argument and discussion' (the details of which were not recorded) an agreement was reached which went some way towards satisfying local and London feelings. Dr Schiller's title was again sanctioned, along with his right to be called to the Law with the title *Morenu*, but on condition that he introduced no innovations, that he allowed no marriage and granted no divorces without the sanction of the Chief Rabbi, that he notified the Chief Rabbi's Office of any marriage he intended to solemnise 'a few days' before its celebration, and that he made decisions on religious questions only in cases of emergency. By way of concession, Dr Adler ruled that in future proselytes might 'undergo the second ceremony in Manchester' and that the ceremony of confirmation might be allowed to proceed 'under a formal protest'. In the event of any vacancy occurring in the *Beth Din* in London, Dr Schiller would be called upon to serve as *Dayan*. The agreement, which was signed by the two rabbis and by the congregational executive, went only a little way beyond that of March. Dr Schiller was allowed to retain his title, with the honour and duties attached to it, in return for recognising the subordinate and dependent status of his office. He salvaged his prestige, the congregation its pride, Dr Adler his supremacy. Later in May, on the First Day of the Feast of Weeks, the ceremony of confirmation

was performed for the first time in Manchester, the Select Committee expressing to the 'worthy Local Rabbi . . . their entire and unqualified approval'.[116]

The agreement naturally failed to satisfy those extremists in Manchester
who wanted full local autonomy, ritual reform, or both. Criticism centred on
plans then being drawn up by the Chief Rabbi, without consulting the provincial communities, for a college to provide training for candidates for the
Jewish ministry. Partly with the danger of local independence (and possible
Reform) in mind, the Chief Rabbi had failed to make any provision for
rabbinical training. It was enough that rabbis appeared from overseas without
producing any in England. A 'Manchester Man' wrote to the *Jewish Chronicle*
on 10 May, regretting Dr Adler's failure to take provincial advice and expressing the hope that he would encourage other congregations to follow Manchester's example in the appointment of local rabbis

instead of the system hitherto existing, of a class of Gentlemen officiating, called ministers or lecturers . . . who are incapable of the great task of carrying out the regeneration of our holy religion, having neither functions nor independence; neither do they
command sufficient respect of the congregation, in consequence of being simply LAY-
MEN, through want of proper clerical titles.[117]

It was, of course, just this link between local rabbinical independence and religious 'regeneration' which Dr Adler most feared, and a continuation of the
correspondence in the press did nothing to reassure him that the issue was
dead. In a letter published on 25 June, Saul Mayer wrote:

I confess my regret that, at present, his [Dr Schiller's] jurisdiction does not extend
further than this locality; for we cannot deny . . . that spiritual destitution is so manifest in the provinces that something must be done shortly to arrest this crying
evil . . .[118]

Mayer implied that Dr Schiller might fill a role of religious leadership
throughout provincial England until such time as other communities recognised their 'imperative duty' of appointing local rabbis, 'who shall dwell
amongst them', by drawing on the pool of qualified talent which existed on
the Continent. He acknowledged that a Chief Rabbi might retain an overall
supervision, but with the help of 'a consistoral court' of local rabbis on the
French pattern, since one individual, he argued, 'cannot command sufficient
authority alone'. Although this 'Manchester pattern', in its several variations,
was not of Dr Schiller's making but a product of growing local consciousness
on the one hand and perhaps of the reasoning of Theodores on the other, his
talk of 'two parties' leaves little doubt that he would have welcomed a widening of his authority. Already his letters were headed 'Office of the Local
Rabbi' on the model of those of Dr Adler, and he had taken over the

function, formerly exclusive to the Chief Rabbi, of examining *shochetim*.[119]

For the time being, however, local feeling was largely satisfied by the May agreement, while the leading radicals preferred to consolidate such slight gains as they had made before pressing on to a fresh stage. When in June the Chief Rabbi finally sought local opinion on the plan for Jews College, the Select Committee decided

it would be useless to call a general meeting upon the subject, in consequence of the plan not being approved of in this town, although such an institution is considered desirable.[120]

The question of Dr Schiller's status flared up again briefly in the autumn of 1852 when, on a visit to London, the Local Rabbi was not accorded the title *Morenu* when called to the Law in the Great Synagogue. The *Jewish Chronicle* received fourteen letters on the subject, in which Dr Adler's oversight was described variously as an affront to the dignity of the Local Rabbi, a snub to the Manchester community and

an unqualified breach of the contract [of May] . . . It must be obvious that the Manchester congregation cannot be considered as being any longer bound by a treaty which has been set aside in so public and decided a manner by one of the *principal* contracting parties, and no doubt they will know how to make use of this act when a proper time shall arrive, when it will be shewn that a contract broken and set aside by one party is no longer binding on the other.[121]

While the Chief Rabbi was anxious that the honour attached to the title should be confined to Manchester, there was a strong local feeling that it should 'carry its dignity over the United Kingdom'.[122] A diehard conservative like Simon Joseph was sufficiently moved to write a strong letter of protest to the Chief Rabbi, whose authority he had shown no previous inclination to question.[123] John Michael Isaac, hitherto a moderate in the mould of Isaac Franklin, tabled a motion condemning Dr Adler for his insult to the Manchester Hebrew Congregation. When it was refused by the Select Committee, he resigned from the synagogue and was only with great difficulty persuaded to return.[124] Again, neither side pushed the confrontation to the point of crisis. Dr Adler disclaimed any intention of insulting the Local Rabbi or his flock.[125] In Manchester, moderates allowed the agitation gradually to die away, while Hesse was satisfied with a further strengthening of his following. It was suggested that Dr Schiller himself was

too wise to require a disputed title. He is no doubt content; at least his good sense will tell him not to be offended at what has happened in London, a place not belonging to his Rabbinical authority.[126]

IV

At all events, political dispute was broken off, as it had been in 1847, and again in 1851, by the pressing problems of the itinerant poor, whose movement through Manchester was the drab backcloth against which the jurisdictional debate was staged. Writing of the country as a whole, the *Jewish Chronicle* commented at the end of 1852:

There is no defined system or principle to guide the dispensers [of relief], except the one which appears generally to be acted upon, viz. to induce the poor who apply for relief to go to another town or city; and thus many are induced to go, say from London to Birmingham, from thence to Manchester, next to Liverpool, and perhaps back to Manchester; and so on, from town to town, each congregation in some shape or other assisting to pay a portion of the dividends on railway stock, under the name of that much abused word, charity.[127]

In June 1852 a number of private persons within the community had considered setting up a 'Mendicity Society' to which the congregation agreed to donate £150 a year 'under the condition that the Society undertake the relief of all Jewish poor',[128] but those behind the scheme either thought better of it or failed to obtain the financial support to render it viable. In the absence of any organisation or funds beyond those of the congregation, the problem had again reached crisis proportions by the winter of 1852–53. At a meeting of the Select Committee on 16 December the two Relieving Officers, David Falk and Abraham Franks, opened 'a very warm discussion' on the inadequacies of the synagogue's arrangements, in the course of which Falk resigned, apparently in disgust at the committee's lack of urgency.[129] Three days later, Ansell Spier, the presiding warden, reopened the discussion and 'urged upon the Committee the necessity of adopting some stringent means relative to the relief of the poor'.[130] Congregational expenditure on poor relief which amounted to £253 in 1851–52, was moving towards a record total of £305 for 1852–53.

What Spier now proposed, and the Select Committee accepted, was a return to the drastic measures taken in July, 1851. It was first resolved

That in consequence of the alarming increase of Itinerant Poor visiting Manchester, which has been found to exhaust every mode devised for their relief, the Committee find after expending large sums of money for many years, it has only tended to increase a great social and moral evil, not benefiting in any degree the position of the recipient and causing a great outlay of funds of the Congregation, they are necessarily compelled as ratepayers of Manchester to refer all such itinerants (except in cases of sickness) to the Manchester Board of Guardians as the only means they can devise for checking the alarming increase of vagrancy. All sick poor applying for relief shall be referred to a Medical Officer to be appointed by the executive for that purpose and relief be granted only upon the relieving officer receiving a certificate by such Medical referee.[131]

Although not granted an official title (or an official salary) until 1855, Isaac Franklin served as Medical Officer from his surgery in Long Millgate. A second resolution, announcing the closure of the congregation's relief services and the discontinuance of weekly payments of aid to the able-bodied, was translated into Hebrew and German and posted on the synagogue doors.[132]

Within a month, however, these new expedients were revealed to be as unworkable as those of 1851, and for much the same reasons. Since they failed to touch the causes of itinerant poverty, they had little effect except to deepen still further the miseries of the itinerant poor. Jewish paupers continued to arrive, and since most of them lacked the means of earning a livelihood in a strange city, they faced an invidious choice. Either they starved to death, or they went begging into the streets, or they were forced back upon the workhouse, where their religious observance was placed under a severe strain. Whichever way the decision went, the community could only lose. Either its reputation was darkened by mendicants and corpses, or it was party to the erosion of its own religious integrity. On 9 January 1853, Simon Joseph, notable as one of the more humane Relieving Officers, tried to have Spier's resolution rescinded, but could find no seconder within the Select Committee.[133] A week later David Hesse reported to the committee that 'notwithstanding the relief board being closed' he had distributed 40s 3d to the 'really exigent poor', including 7s 6d 'to one poor woman with five children (who were dying from starvation)'.[134] The prestige of Hesse was sufficient for his generosity to undermine the decision of the committee, 'exceptional' relief payments gradually became more frequent, and by the beginning of March the Relieving Officers were back at work, in fact if not in name, with all their accustomed inefficiencies. Apart from the institution of an Honorary Medical officer, the only effect of the experiment was to distract the congregation from its political tussle with the Chief Rabbi, to which it returned as soon as the immediate crisis had passed.

V

By the spring of 1853 a series of sharp clashes with the Chief Rabbi had hardened sentiment in Manchester which favoured at least a measure of religious autonomy. Hesse regarded the community as the largest in provincial England, intelligent, wealthy and socially reputable, and on this basis he had constructed a policy of local independence. He had been carried forward by the momentum of reunion and middle-class liberalism into an ascendant position from which he was able to rally the congregation behind his views. In 1851 he and Ansell Spier had been elected wardens at Halliwell Street and respectively vice-chairman and chairman of the committee for the revision of the laws. In a partnership which the congregation retained in office for the unusual period of two years, Hesse was the dominant partner, although through Spier he was able to exercise an influence over longer-established and more conservative families. On at least two occasions clashes with the Chief Rabbi had threatened to polarise the community on the issue of ecclesiastical jurisdiction, but on both Dr Adler had conceded just enough to satisfy the leading radicals, who in turn had stopped short of demands which might have alienated more conservative souls. The chief effect of these disputes was probably to weaken the local standing of the Chief Rabbi. In the new code of laws, which was published in March 1853, the 'general religious direction' of the congregation was vested in the Local Rabbi 'for the time being in conjunction with the Chief Rabbi'.[135] Reform had not yet become the overt issue. Most of those who sought local independence favoured it as an expression of local progress. Only a very small minority regarded it as a prelude to ritual change on the Margaret Street pattern, and for the time being they were prepared to encourage localism in the belief that at a later stage they might turn it to their advantage. Dr Schiller they regarded as an asset, since at the very least they might use his local power to ward off any blows of the Chief Rabbinate. At best, he might become a convert to Reform.

With the revision of the laws complete in March 1853, Hesse and Spier were ready to hand over to a new executive which would have to implement them. As they did so, in May, the issue of local independence acquired a deeper significance as it became narrowly focused upon the validity in Manchester of the *cherem* imposed on the West London Synagogue of British Jews.

The pressure for a greater degree of local independence which had produced the sporadic conflicts with the Board of Deputies and the Chief Rabbi during the years 1851–53 was an assertion by Manchester's middle-class Jewry, recently reunited, prosperous, and excessively self-confident, that it was no longer prepared to accept without question either the tutelage of the London plutocracy or the authority of a metropolitan rabbi. In some respects it was a translation into political terms of the enhanced status of Jewry within Manchester, and of Manchester within England. Although it is tempting in the light of subsequent events to regard it as the first stage of a movement devised by an inner clique of conspirators around Hesse and Theodores to lead the Manchester congregation in the direction of radical religious change, such an interpretation is not justified by the evidence. The appointment of a Local Rabbi and the defence of local rights was undertaken by the middle class as a whole, not by a minority of Reformers with designs upon the Oral Law. Notwithstanding the morbid fears of Dr Adler, the motivating forces were neither theological nor ritualistic, but social and secular. The key figure was neither Theodores, who had played little part in the events, nor Dr Schiller, who was essentially the creature of his congregation, but Hesse, the ingenious, liberal-minded entrepreneur. From his new house in Temple Terrace on Cheetham Hill, next door to Louis Beaver and David Falk, and near the mansion of Philip Lucas, Hesse had directed affairs with such tactical skill that the community had remained united behind his policies in a way which would not have been possible had the dispute turned on questions of ritual and belief. The result was the Local Rabbinate, not as independent as Hesse would have wished, but conferring upon Manchester as great a measure of local prestige as could be obtained within the framework permitted by the Chief Rabbi.

The Local Rabbinate may also be taken as a culmination of the forces of improvement which had been at work within the community since the early 1820s and which had given rise, successively, to the synagogue and Philanthropic Society during 1825–26, the Hebrew Association in 1838, and the first Jews School in 1842. A prosperous and coherent Jewish middle class had expressed its growing wealth and confidence in communal terms, in an urban environment which placed no serious restriction on Jewish aspirations. Communal ambitions were, in fact, strengthened by class consciousness as Jewish merchants and shopkeepers were accepted into the wider society. The gentle process of improvement was interrupted in 1844 only because an established oligarchy which had come to regard itself as the sole arbiter of communal progress was challenged by immigrant entrepreneurs, who, although achieving economic success within the town, were denied privilege within the synagogue. The demand of the rebels was never, in reality, for 'perfect equality', but for an enlargement of the oligarchy such as was achieved by the terms of reunion in 1851. It was the pooled energy and resources of the entire Jewish middle class which Hesse harnessed during the period 1851–53 to create and sustain the Local Rabbinate, which, in this sense, was only the latest stage of the desire of the middle-class community for an institutional progress which matched its social development. But although united in local pride, the Jewish middle class was made up of disparate elements, as widely different in their origins and cultural ambience as in their levels of wealth. In moving on from the Local Rabbinate to a 'renovation' of the liturgy which all but Simon Joseph deemed essential, could these elements remain united behind a common programme, or would they assert themselves as congregational divisions?

The question assumed concrete form on 23 May 1853, when fifteen prominent members at Halliwell Street petitioned David Hesse, in his last days as presiding warden, to call a meeting 'for the purpose of taking into consideration the desirability of altering the present form of worship in the Synagogue'.[1] Apart from Theodores, the signatories were cotton merchants living in Manchester's outer suburbs who, with one exception, had come to Manchester from London, Holland or Germany since 1834. They were all leading members of the plutocracy which had guided the destinies of the community before 1844: Philip Lucas, A. S. Sichel, S. D. Bles and his son David, and Louis and Rudolph Behrens, from north Manchester; Henry and Horatio Micholls, S. L. Behrens, Henry and Ralph Straus, Benjamin Jonas, Nathan Hess and H. M. Salomon from the south. When, in answer to the petition, Hesse called a special meeting at the Jews School on 5 June, it was Theodores who acted as their spokesman.[2] In what was described by Simonson, without further detail, as an 'elaborate address', Theodores spoke for forty-five minutes to a proposal that a committee be set up to consider the 'best means' of introducing 'beneficial and essential' (but unspecified) improvements. The motion was carried unanimously by a meeting attended by nearly a hundred persons and a representative committee was set up to put it into effect. Apart from five of the original petitioners—Theodores, Salomon, Horatio Micholls, Louis Behrens and Ralph Straus—the committee included two general merchants of more recent arrival, Keppel Simon and Joel Aaron Kohn; Isaac Franklin,

David Hesse; and six shopkeepers, Abraham Franks, Ansell Spier, David Falk, Michael Goldstone, Saul Mayer and Henry Leveaux, of whom only the last three had been members of the defunct New Congregation. The absence of any of the former rebels of Ainsworth's Court amongst the original petitioners again rules out any suggestions that the New Congregation had once served as the reservoir of religious radicalism.

Although the *Jewish Chronicle* saw the Manchester meeting of June as 'the most important in the annals of Jews in this country',[3] implying that the community was on the point of defining its attitude to Reform, its significance is not easy to assess. The names of the petitioners suggest that the suburban élite which had ruled at Halliwell Street before 1851 was attempting to reassert its right to lead the whole community in the direction of its own tastes, as if the rebellion of 1844 had never occurred. This was probably part of the truth. If the plutocracy had lost its political powers, it might still attempt to lead by persuasion. But the presence of Theodores, and his prominence at the meeting, suggest that he provided some, perhaps most, of the impetus. The most logical explanation of the whole train of events is that Theodores was attempting to channel a general desire for change into a specific demand for Reform. The alliance of the suburban élite with Theodores was natural enough at this stage, not because they shared a programme of radical change but because his intellectual position came closest to reflecting their cultural inclinations. The committee of improvement was probably a disappointment to them because it was composed, in the main, of men of more orthodox and conformist dispositions than their own. It represented the full spectrum of opinion in Manchester and demonstrated the difficulty which lay ahead of Theodores if he hoped to achieve a consensus on the issue of Reform. And this was, in fact, the issue which had been raised. Could the community achieve unanimity on ritual matters, or was the congregation to divide after the manner of the metropolitan community? The *Jewish Chronicle* was right in believing that a moment of decision had been reached, but it was one which stretched over the succeeding five years, as everyone in the community decided how much his conscience would allow and found out how much the Chief Rabbi would permit.

The process of decision-making passed through two main stages, of which the first lasted from May 1853 until the winter of 1855–56. The main issue during this period was not Reform as such but the authority of the Chief Rabbi, and particularly the validity of the *cherem* upon the West London Synagogue of British Jews which Dr Adler had enforced with special vigour and which most obviously symbolised his central jurisdiction. The *cherem* question overrode all others because it was the point at which the views of Hesse and Theodores converged. Theodores knew as well as Dr Adler that rabbinical jurisdiction and ritual change were closely related, since the solution of the one would serve to determine the extent of the other. Dr Adler's views were well known. Unlike Theodores, he believed that the survival of Judaism depended upon the retention of traditional ways within a centrally defined and uniform ritual framework. He wrote:

... religion is not a matter of fashion, changeable according to the whims of the multitude; nor is it a science, which has a time to build up, and a time to break down; nor is it an art, which is influenced by the taste and atmosphere of the time;—no, religion is consistent amongst the changes, immutable amongst the vicissitudes—is divine and therefore eternal.[4]

And the Chief Rabbi had the upper hand in Manchester because a large body of established middle-class families, whose English origins lay in a less secure age, were predisposed to accept his definition of the boundaries between orthodoxy and heresy. If Theodores was to persuade the Manchester congregation to adopt his advanced views, then he had first to persuade it to renounce the Chief Rabbinate. If the jurisdictional victory was won, ritual change would follow. Hesse, on the other hand, saw the problem in political terms. He was not yet interested in specific religious innovations, but he saw the Chief Rabbi's power as an unjustifiable restraint upon congregational freedom. Opposition to any coercive exercise of central authority was a logical projection of the objectives he had pursued in creating the Local Rabbinate. When the *cherem* question came up for debate in London during the summer and autumn of 1853, Theodores and Hesse were drawn into an alliance of convenience in Manchester.

I

The *cherem* imposed upon the West London Synagogue by Solomon Hirschel in 1841, never popular in the rest of Anglo-Jewry, excited strong orthodox opposition once Dr Adler began to impose the full penalties involved, including the prohibition of marriages between orthodox and heterodox families.[5] Even those who felt as Dr Adler did about the ritual of Margaret Street did not believe that it justified penalties which divided Anglo-Jewish families just when their unity was most necessary to the struggle for emancipation. Nor could religious schism break the strong ties of friendship, family and commerce which bound members of orthodox congregations to their co-religionists in Reform. The pressures exerted for these reasons had resulted, in March 1849, in the lifting of the pains and penalties of excommunication from the shoulders of individual Reformers. But while Dr Adler was prepared to make this gesture in the interests of solidarity, and possible reconciliation, he was still not prepared to accept the congregation as a whole as Jewish, nor to withdraw his ban upon its ritual. For this reason, there existed, from 1849, the anomalous situation of a *cherem* lying upon a congregation, but not upon its members. This in itself, how- ever, involved the Reformers in severe disabilities. Since it was not a 'congre- gation recognised by the Chief Rabbi', Margaret Street was denied by the Board of Deputies a certificate which would have enabled its minister to solem- nise marriages under the Marriage Registration Act. Reformers were thus 'disgracefully compelled . . . to marry in the first instance before or in the presence of a magistrate' before proceeding to the religious ceremony in the synagogue.[6] More seriously, and for the same reason, the Reformers were denied representation on the Board of Deputies, whose President, Sir Moses Montefiore, accepted and reinforced the Chief Rabbi's ban.[7]

In the demands which arose during 1853 for the admission of Reformers to the Board of Deputies, a number of different viewpoints were represented. Some Reformers saw it as the thin end of a wedge which would secure the ad- mission of Margaret Street into the orthodox communion. Since the Chief Rab- bi was clearly intractable, the Reformers would first secure a political lever- age within Anglo-Jewry which they would then use to undermine the uniform pattern of Anglo-Jewish orthodoxy, and the rabbinical power which sustained it. Others hoped simply that religious differences could be sunk in a political solidarity necessary to the solution of 'the question of questions . . . the re- moval of our disabilities'.[8] The orthodox were similarly divided, some hoping for religious reconciliation, others for nothing more than political union. It seemed inconsistent for the Anglo-Jewish community to exercise a discrimina- tion on religious grounds which it was seeking to eradicate from the political life of the nation. Hesse wrote: 'How can I ask Christians to accord me reli- gious freedom if I deny the same to my Jewish brother?'[9] On the other side, Dr Adler and Montefiore were not disposed to make concessions which might re- duce the premium on orthodoxy and so shatter the unity of Anglo-Jewry. When, in May 1853, the three-year term of the Board of Deputies ended, and preparations were made for elections throughout the community, the Re- formers gave religious dispute a political dimension by making their disabili- ties a major election issue, particularly in the provinces, where more freedom of expression was expected. As a result of the Board's decision to widen its representation,[10] it was increased by sixteen provincial deputies, and it was from these that the Reformers hoped for most support. Elias Davis wrote:

It is mainly to the enlightenment and independence of the provinces, that the commun- ity will be indebted for those ameliorations and improvements which the Jewish body stands most in need of.[11]

Four Reformers had put themselves forward successfully as candidates for provincial congregation—Jacob Elkin at Portsmouth, David Jonassohn at Sunderland, Samuel Ellis at Chatham and Elias Davis at Norwich—and elsewhere pressure was exerted to secure the election of men liberally disposed towards Margaret Street.

In Manchester the way to a new expression of local feeling was opened by the retirement of Jacob Franklin. When pressed by delegates from Halliwell Street to renew his candidacy, he wrote to Ansell Spier on 8 May:

Under the existing constitution of the Board of Deputies, so little comparatively can be effected by an individual member, who advocates a timely origination of useful measures, instead of a mere waiting for emergencies—who strives to maintain moderate and safe courses between our conflicting parties—(on the one extreme imputed zealotry, on the other avowed rationalism)—and who has moreover to strive, within closed doors, against the intolerance of both extremes alternatively, that I see no such prospect of future usefulness as might dispose me to renew my responsibilities . . .[12]

An effort to secure government recognition of Jewish rights in public education was, he continued, no longer necessary. The legal rights of the synagogue had received specific confirmation. For six years no legislative encroachment on Jewish rights had been sanctioned by parliament. Complete political emancipation was in sight.

What remains to be overcome are the religious scruples of high-minded men, scruples which in my humble opinion claim respectful consideration from every conscientious Jew, and which may best be met by reasons and evidence, appropriately brought to bear.

He had no stomach for a political wrangle centring upon Reform, and, at all events, he believed that on so sensitive an issue 'the view of the Manchester Synagogue should hence forward be more directly represented'. After Benjamin Hyam had declined to stand,[13] perhaps because he feared a more radical mandate than his conscience would permit him to honour, on 22 May David Hesse, Horatio Micholls and J. M. Isaac were elected to represent Manchester on the Board of Deputies.[14] Amongst the many reasons for believing that at this stage Hesse was not identified with Reform was his nomination by so strictly orthodox a member as Joseph Slazenger Moss.[15] The three Manchester deputies reflected the three major social segments of the community—the mercantile élite, the immigrants of the early 1840s and the longer established shopkeeping bourgeoisie—rather than any religious grouping.

It is clear, however, from the tenor of the meeting at which they were elected that they were expected to support the admission of Reformers to the Board of Deputies. Simon Joseph, conservative though he was, hoped that the Manchester deputies might be instrumental 'in re-connecting the several links of the Jewish body', and described the *cherem* as 'inconsistent with the spirit of progress and enlightenment'.[16] Theodores, in proposing Micholls, dwelt 'on the necessity there existed for infusing a more active and liberal spirit in the Board of Deputies'.[17] The three deputies were expected to act as 'advocates for a thorough reform of the laws constituting the Board',[18] particularly the rule which excluded the Jewish press, but their chief mandate was to secure the removal of the *cherem* and to work towards the religious reunification of Anglo-Jewry. The meeting was pervaded by a 'cordial feeling and liberal spirit'[19] and presumably represented the general sympathy of the Manchester community, not for Reform, but for Reformers. This attitude, and the events at Portsmouth, Chatham, Norwich and Sunderland, encouraged the Reform congregation to believe that there was strong sympathy, not only for their political plight, but also for their religious principles. One member wrote:

if all the members of the various congregations were called upon to give their vote for or against a reform of our synagogue worship . . . at least two to one would vote in the affirmative.[20]

Another added:

some measure of reform is universally considered necessary, otherwise so many of the extreme party would never have been chosen.[21]

Although the support they received was more limited and less enthusiastic than they were prepared to admit, the Reformers had some reason to hope that when the Board reconvened in August it would deal more sympathetically with their case. Hesse wrote to the *Jewish Chronicle*: 'the groundwork has been laid for the establishment of that peace in our community for which you have often appealed'.[22]

These hopes were badly disappointed. When the old Board met on 18 August to confirm the elections of June, Louis Cohen proposed the exclusion of the four Reformers on the grounds that they were members of a congregation 'which does not conform in religious matters to the ecclesiastical authority'.[23] In the teeth of a bitter opposition led by Baron de Rothschild, Montefiore ruled that the Reformers could not take their seats until the new Board had voted on Cohen's motion. The meeting which followed at Duke's Place on 31 August, and attended by thirty-two deputies, including the three from Manchester, was a notorious disaster.[24] Montefiore refused to read letters received from those who opposed the exclusion of the Reformers, he signed the minutes of the previous meeting in the face of vigorous protest, and when three of the excluded members attempted to take their seats, he ordered the 'strangers' to withdraw. An 'indescribable uproar' followed. A constable called in to eject the Reformers was tactfully refused entry by the wardens of the Great Synagogue.

Montefiore vacated the chair, David Salomons declined to preside in his place, and the meeting broke up in disorder. When the Board reconvened on 8 September, for the first meeting to which the Jewish press was invited, the Reform deputies were again excluded, after an even split, by the casting vote of the president.[25] A cooling-off period of two months was decreed, during which a sub-committee of five deputies sought to effect a reconciliation between Margaret Street and the Chief Rabbi,[26] but since neither party was prepared to change its religious position, this again was abortive. On 23 November the matter concluded when the Board resolved, on a motion originating with the Hambro Synagogue, that the admission of Reformers was 'calculated to endanger and undermine our established Faith'.[27]

Manchester sided throughout with the excluded Reformers. According to Hesse, the 'snake of persecution' had reared its head in London.[28] He regarded Louis Cohen's motion as 'one of the most ill-timed and ill-advised resolutions it has ever been my lot to have heard of',[29] and he had played an active role on behalf of the Reformers in the debate of 31 August.[30] Acting on a report which he presented to Halliwell Street on 6 September, the Select Committee confessed, after paying lip-service to the good works of Montefiore,

its regret and astonishment at hearing of the singular and as it appears illegal proceedings on the part of the Honourable Chairman.[31]

The whole proceedings were a matter for regret, since their only effect

was to nullify the purpose of the meeting to attend which many gentlemen had put themselves to much trouble and inconvenience.[32]

The committee voted its thanks to the three deputies, and mandated them to oppose Louis Cohen's motion on 8 September, when, in fact, Montefiore secured its passage. Isaac was prevented by illness from attending—an accident with more significant effects than could have been foreseen—but Hesse and Micholls both spoke in favour of the admission of the Reformers, and voted on the losing side.[33] Manchester kept up the pressure even after the Board's decision in November. A petition from the community calling on the Board to admit the Reformers was defeated on 7 December, again only by the casting vote of the president.[34]

The main effect of the episode was to cement the alliance of a small group of men—led by Theodores, Hesse and Horatio Micholls—in uncompromising opposition to a centralised ecclesiastical authority. For Theodores the matter was the more urgent because the committee of improvement appointed in June had broken up without reaching agreement.[35] Even those established members who sympathised with Reform were reluctant to make any move in defiance of the Chief Rabbi, and it seemed clear to Theodores that it was this inhibition which most obstructed the path of radical change. For Hesse, the events only confirmed the illiberality of the metropolitan leadership and the ill effects of central rule. The rest of the community, while united in their sympathy for the Reformers, was undecided on the issue of Reform. Many hoped that the Chief Rabbi would be persuaded to reinterpret orthodoxy in a way which would embrace the practices of Margaret Street. Even Simon Joseph professed to believe that the Chief Rabbi would, in time, relax the *cherem*.[36] The community divided on the *cherem* question only when it became clear, as it did during December 1853, that Dr Adler's position was immutable. Each member had then to decide whether or not he could continue to pledge his allegiance to the Chief Rabbinate.

II

The decision was forced upon the community by a motion presented by Hesse to a General Meeting of the congregation on 18 December 1853:

That the *cherem* or excommunication upon the synagogue in Margaret Street, London, promulgated in this congregation some years since is hereby repealed and declared null and void so far as regards this congregation.[37]

The response of the Chief Rabbi was unequivocal. In reply to a letter in which Eleazer Moses had sought his advice he described Hesse's motion as 'an open rupture' with his authority, an attribution to a local congregation of powers it did not possess, and a danger to the religious uniformity, and therefore the orthodoxy, of Anglo-Jewry.[38] His call to Eleazer Moses and his 'friends' to resist the resolution had the effect of shattering Manchester's unanimous opposition to the *cherem* and turning the question, instead, into the centre of partisan dispute.

The rift opened up in the course of a general meeting of the congregation which lasted, with two adjournments, from 18 December 1853 until 16 April 1854. The first session, on 18 December, set the scene.[39] The chief protagonists emerged, the central issue was defined, and the mask of cordiality which had characterised the community during the period 1851–53 was set aside to reveal the even balance of conflicting opinion, and its bitter edge. After Hesse's motion had been pressed by Theodores and Micholls, it was Benjamin Hyam who lead the opposition with an amendment which would have referred the question to the ecclesiastical authorities in London 'who alone are competent to pronounce a decision'. The amendment was seconded by Eleazer Moses, and supported by Michael Goldstone, Henry Mendleson, Simon Joseph and

Adolphus Sington, presumably some of the 'friends' whom Moses had mustered at the Chief Rabbi's bidding. Recognising that the immediate issue was not yet Reform, but the extent of the Chief Rabbi's power as symbolised in the *cherem*, a perceptive observer described the parties which now began to take shape, not as Orthodox and Reform, but as 'Cheremite and Anti-Cheremite'.[40] It is significant that they cut across class divisions. Eleazer Moses, a textile merchant, had more in common with Micholls, whose London background he shared, than Michael Goldstone, a steel pen manufacturer and former hawker of Polish extraction. Former members of Ainsworth's Court were to be found on both sides. This was a new division in which individuals made their choice largely according to the degree of their conservatism and the extent of their deference to rabbinical authority. It was also a preliminary trial of strength in which neither side was prepared to concede defeat. Hyam's amendment was carried by thirty-six votes to thirty-five, but when the chairman, Abraham Franks, himself a Cheremite, attempted to put it to the meeting as a substantive motion

a strong and tumultuous discussion took place between all parties present. The chairman not being able to obtain silence or order then adjourned the meeting.

When Hyam's motion was put to a reconvened meeting on 1 January 1854, Hesse in turn proposed an amendment to the effect that, since the *cherem* was

fraught with injury to our co-religionists of their [i.e. the Reformers] community . . . and injurious to the Jews of the Empire . . . we do hereby declare that we do not recognise its existence in this congregation.[41]

When this amendment, which was, in effect, a rephrased version of Hesse's original motion, was carried by thirty-nine votes to thirty-four, so turning the tables on the Cheremites, Franks put an end to the discussion by adjourning the meeting *sine die* on the strength of an undisclosed motion handed to him by Adolphus Sington.

What followed was a cooling-off period similar to that which followed the September meeting in London, during which the leaders of both camps attempted to whip up support and to jockey for position. On 10 January Hesse wrote a carefully-worded letter to the Select Committee, in which he introduced an anonymous friend, supposedly a subscribing member of the West London Synagogue, who was presently residing in Manchester, and

wishes to become a member of your sinagogue [*sic*] . . . previous to doing so he wishes to know whether he can be accepted . . . I told him I had my doubts about it in consequence of the resolution come to by the Board of Deputies. I now submit the question officially to you, and requesting your answer with as little delay as possible.[42]

While the existence of the friend may perhaps be doubted, the issue was clear enough. Hesse faced the Select Committee with the question posed to Montefiore and the Deputies in the previous September. Could a member of the West London Synagogue, a congregation under *cherem*, be accepted as a member of a synagogue which acknowledged the Chief Rabbi's supremacy? If the answer was yes, then this was tantamount to an admission that the Chief Rabbi's writ did not run in Manchester; if no, then the Select Committee was exercising in Manchester the kind of discrimination to which, through its Deputies, it had objected in London. In the absence of a democratic decision, Hesse was seeking victory by default. Again, however, the issue was shelved. Although Hesse pressed hard for an unequivocal reply, the Committee simply set the letter aside for a 'future consideration'[43] which it never, in fact, received.

A greater impact was made by Theodores in a public lecture at the Jews School on 'The Rabbinical Law of Excommunication' on 29 January.[44] An audience of around 170 persons, chaired by Horatio Micholls and including most of the wealthier members of the community, was 'electrified and rivetted [sic]', according to the *Jewish Chronicle*,[45] by an exposition of the Reform position which lasted for over one and a half hours. The powers of the Chief Rabbi and his proclamation of the *cherem* were subjected to a relentless 'historical criticism'.[46] Since the expulsion of the Jews from Babylon, he argued, no authority had existed within Judaism with the power to bestow the rabbinic *semikhah*. Some congregations had found it convenient to appoint teachers whom they called 'rabbis', to interpret religious law and arbitrate in matters of local dispute, but such persons were not genuine rabbis, and had no powers beyond those bestowed by the congregations which appointed them. 'The law of one congregation' was, for this reason, 'not obligatory on any other'.[47] The limited mission of the modern Jewish rabbi, with no intrinsic authority arising from his office, was that of 'explaining what is conformable or discordant to the laws of Judaism' to the congregation from which he derived his authority.[48] In England, the nation-wide jurisdiction claimed by the Chief Rabbi was 'fictitious' and the *cherem* which he had enforced was a 'mythical excommunication'.[49] Even if Dr Adler had been endowed with real rabbinical powers, the *cherem* would have been invalid, since its imposition demanded a procedure which, in modern conditions, was impossible.[50] Furthermore, if the Chief Rabbi argued that a congregation was excommunicate if it failed to observe the letter of the Talmud, then he must prepare 'never-ending bulls for by far the vast majority of the flock in all the synagogues of the Empire', since many Talmudic regulations were widely abandoned in congregations which the Chief Rabbi chose to regard as orthodox.[51] And yet, for all its lack of historicity and inconsistencies, the central authority of the Chief Rabbi lay heavily on the London Reformers:

let us, at the bidding of Truth [say] that we know of no excommunication in existence against any one of our brethren in the land; and let us manfully protest . . . against the infliction of offensive penalties under the fictitious plan of an impossible excommunication.[52]

In a speech which reached a wider audience in pamphlet form, Theodores added a philosophical dimension to his strategic attack upon the Chief Rabbinate.

There, for a time, the debate rested, partly because members of the congregation needed time to make a decision and partly because their attention was again temporarily diverted by the problem of itinerant poverty. Throughout 1853 the congregation faced a mounting number of transmigrants, some of whom settled in Red Bank. In March forty-seven families, comprising 196 persons, applied successfully for Passover Relief, and the synagogue laid out a record sum on 1,400 lb of *matzoth* and 150 lb of meat. A month later a 'disgraceful disturbance' at Halliwell Street, in which fighting broke out between members of the congregation and ushers at the main entrance, was put down to 'overcrowding'.[53] For the first time, in September 1853, the congregation organised overflow services for the poor in the Jews School.[54] Methods of relief remained haphazard and only partially effective. After laying out over £8 in the first eight months of 1853 to assist six poor families to reach America,[55] the Select Committee decided that, in view of the increasing demand, 'all such applications for assistance in [*sic*] Emigration shall be refused',[56] a policy which was itself reversed during the succeeding twelve months to rid the community of 'deserted' families.[57] In August 1853 the secretary wrote to the main London synagogues for details of their methods of relieving strangers, only to learn of expedients no less pragmatic than their own.[58] In March 1854 Louis Behrens suggested that the congregation establish its own 'Room or workshop for the employment of the able-bodied poor', which might apply a communal 'labour test', and so 'relieve the Congregation from the heavy disbursement at present on the poor'.[59] The Select Committee pledged £20 to the project, but Behrens was unable to raise the voluntary subscriptions which alone would have made it possible.

The cost—social and financial—of itinerant poverty was one reason for the suspension of religious hostilities in Manchester in the spring of 1854. The other was a strong current of feeling, emanating from London, that Anglo-Jewry should close its ranks to complete the struggle for emancipation. In his most conciliatory mood, Dr Adler called for an end to party bickering 'which must disgrace us in the eyes of our neighbours'.[60] It was the duty of every orthodox Jew to attract those 'who have gone too far, and have, intentionally or not, made organic changes . . . back to the bosom of our established religion', but in the event of reconciliation proving impossible, 'let us agree to differ, and let us have peace in our camp'.[61] Manchester responded with moves towards a truce which also suited its material needs. Hyam hoped that 'the reconciliation of the two parties which we regret to say exist in our community may be speedily and perfectly effected'.[62] But it was Lucas who formulated peace terms, in a carefully worded motion submitted for discussion at the general meeting which was due to reconvene on 16 April:

That having examined the minutes of our Congregation and finding no record therein of a 'cherem' existing against the Margaret Street Congregation it is hereby resolved that the adjourned meeting intended to be holden for a consideration of the 'Cherem' is hereby postponed sine die.[63]

By the time the meeting took place, Lucas was in Southport recovering from an attack of gout, but the resolution was presented in his absence by David Hesse and passed unanimously.[64]

Looking back four years later for the origins of a Reform Party in Manchester, Theodores found 'the most active impulse' to have come from the *cherem* imposed by 'overweening ecclesiastics' on Margaret Street.[65] The original Reformers were those who wished to oppose 'a plain everlasting inflexible "No" to every attempt at intolerance or oppression'.[66] This was something of an overstatement. What the events of 1853–54 had succeeded in doing was to divide the community on the issue of the central jurisdiction of the Chief Rabbi; it remained to be seen how many of those who opposed the *cherem* were also willing to accept Reform. A large body of moderate opinion, perhaps a majority, still hoped for compromise on matters of ritual in which both Theodores and Dr Adler would yield ground. As Henry Leveaux wrote to the *Jewish Chronicle*: 'Let all *extremes* give way—the extreme orthodox and the extreme liberal . . .'[67]

Meantime, the poor were given short shrift, as their relief was subordinated to considerations of economy. On 1 July 1854, acting on the advice of Hesse, the Select Committee again decided to refer all able-bodied casual paupers to the local Unions, while at the same time setting a limit to its expenditure for the deserving resident poor.[68] The annual ceiling was fixed at £250: £40 for Passover Relief, £30 for payment on other Holy days, £2 a month for 'general relief', and £56 as an emergency reserve. It is a measure of the congregation's determination to cut back on payments to transmigrants, that this system, with all the hardships, religious as well as material, which it involved, was enforced rigidly for the succeeding five years. The heaviest burden of Jewish poverty was passed on to the State, while the immigrant families of Red Bank were, for the most part, left to fend for themselves. During an outbreak of cholera in the autumn of 1853 Dr Schiller read 'propitiatory prayers' in the synagogue and urged the poor to observe the sanitary regulations of the town as much as those enjoined by Mosaic Law,[69] but no further attempt was made, except in a small way by the Clothing Society, to improve their living conditions.

III

The debate on the religious future of the congregation took a new turn when Dr Schiller's contract as Local Rabbi came up for renewal, as it did on 17 April, the day after the passage of Lucas' motion. So far, the members of the congregation had been asked to decide directly on the powers of the Chief Rabbi and had somehow managed to evade the issue. Now they were called upon to examine the same question, but from a different standpoint, by defining those of Dr Schiller. Having failed to persuade the congregation to curtail the authority of the Chief Rabbi, Hesse, Micholls and Theodores now hoped to effect its *de facto* limitation by consolidating that of the Local Rabbinate.

Dr Schiller had remained silent throughout the *cherem* controversy, and, although he had a good deal to gain from a victory of the Anti-Cheremites, there is no reason to suppose that he was actively involved in their tactics of 1853–54. Rumour in the Jewish press twice linked him with nonconformist tendencies, but on neither occasion did the reports have any substance.[70] On the second, when he was said, among other matters, to have allowed a relaxation of the laws relating to the seven days of mourning, he was defended by Theodores, who can hardly be supposed to have anything to gain by dissociating Dr Schiller from Reform.[71] Theodores rejected any suggestion that the Local Rabbi had made any radical changes in the past or that he had any future intention of 'effecting a Reform' or of breaking his agreement with the Chief Rabbi which bound him to introduce no changes without Dr Adler's consent. The truth would seem to be that he fulfilled his pastoral and educational duties conscientiously, and to the satisfaction of the community's most conservative members. The only criticism of his religious teaching was that it was 'much too metaphysical' for the children of the poor.[72] If in fact he had been guilty of Reformist transgression these would not have passed without comment either in the Select Committee or in the Chief Rabbi's Office. On the only occasion when Dr Schiller spoke up for himself before April 1854—in a minor confrontation with an eccentric congregant who described him as 'a Hypocrite and an Epicurean'—he expressed his wish 'to be at peace with everybody'.[73] This included Dr Adler. In defining the Local Rabbi's powers, the revised Code of

Laws published at Halliwell Street in March 1853, altered the phrase 'under the jurisdiction of the Chief Rabbi' to the more equivocal 'for the time being in conjunction with the Chief Rabbi',[74] but at that time neither Dr Schiller nor his Select Committee read into the change any modification of the compromise arranged in 1852.

The terms of reappointment for 1855, which were drawn up by the Select Committee on 17 April 1854, not only showed the congregation's concern for 'retrenchment' but suggested also that the Cheremite party was on its guard against the Local Rabbi being used by those within the community who wanted religious autonomy or ritual change. The arrangement of Divine Service was taken out of his hands and entrusted to a committee, of which he was chairman, consisting of the two wardens and two treasurers of the congregation.[75] The exercise of his authority, and his relationship with the Chief Rabbi, were to be 'at all times in accordance with and subject to the Laws of this congregation'.[76] Like the poor, he was also a victim of the congregation's parsimony. The congregation was no longer willing to guarantee his salary and tax, as it had done since 1851, when the donations received towards a Minister's Fund had been made up to a total of £250. Now the congregation limited its contribution to a maximum of £50, so that Dr Schiller became dependent for his full salary on the good will of the community.[77] These terms were endorsed by a General Meeting on 30 April:

The meeting then proceeded to the Election of the Reverend Dr Schiller-Szinessy as Local Rabbi of Manchester, when every gentleman present held up both hands.[78]

The enthusiasm and unanimity of the reappointment, whatever the limitations on its terms, is proof enough of Dr Schiller's acceptability to orthodox members. What they really feared was that he would become a pawn in the hands of those who opposed the Chief Rabbi.

In taking steps to prevent this, however, they had made one serious miscalculation. It seems that in making the exercise of Dr Schiller's authority subject to the laws of the congregation, they were under the misapprehension that the rules still placed him explicitly under the Chief Rabbi's direction. When they found that this was not, in fact, the case, they hurriedly backtracked on the terms of appointment, to have them changed before they came into effect on 1 January 1855. At a general meeting on 7 May Eleazer Moses, the leading spirit of the Cheremites, spoke wildly of 'deception'[79] on the part of those on the Select Committee who knew well enough what the rules decreed since, like Hesse, they had been concerned with their revision. When his 'heated' remarks were ruled out of order, he replied

that he felt so warm on the subject that he considered he could not do justice to the question therefore would feel obliged by the chairman [Abraham Franks] permitting him to leave the meeting . . . to which the chairman politely acquiesced.[80]

In a more temperate mood, on 25 June, he challenged the minutes of the Select Committee meeting which had drawn up the terms of reappointment because they made no mention of the phrase 'under the jurisdiction of the Chief Rabbi', only to be told by the chairman that minutes could not be altered to include words which, however desirable, had not been used.[81] Finally, however, the Cheremites made their point. On 8 July Franks, now free from the neutrality of chairmanship, proposed an alteration of the laws to include the vital codicil, so that at the time of his appointment the Local Rabbi would be bound by it.[82] Hesse protested that a congregation which had already 'taken nine-tenths of his [Dr Schiller's] prerogative away from him . . . now intended to take the last tenth', but the meeting passed the motion by eighteen votes to twelve. Perhaps the vital speech was made by Isaac Franklin, the respected moderate, who came forward 'as a strong friend of Dr Schiller'. Franklin argued 'that Dr Schiller would not be compromised in the least, but best secured by the passing of the resolution', since some of those who opposed it, like Theodores, were opposed to any form of rabbinical jurisdiction. If the whole episode, as seems likely, was another stratagem of the Anti-Cheremites designed to throw off the community's allegiance to the Chief Rabbi, it revealed only the degree of loyalty which remained, perhaps even the growing strength and determination of the Cheremites. The conservatives were digging in their heels as they became increasingly aware of the direction in which Hesse and Theodores were moving. As to Dr Schiller, although no doubt aggrieved at the curtailment of his authority and the uncertainty of his salary, he

protested against the alteration in the terms of the original Agreement [of 1851] . . . but nevertheless acquiesced in the Terms of the Agreement for the Year 1855.[83]

Acquiescence was perhaps too strong a word. The *Jewish Chronicle* hinted that the 'seeds of discord' had been sown between the Local Rabbi and the wardens, and, although the paper decided against any further comment as 'being only calculated to aggravate matters',[84] the disenchantment of Dr Schiller soon made its impression on the minutes of the congregation. Joseph Hyman, Frank's successor as presiding warden, put the question to a general meeting:

Whether they approved or disapproved of the Local Rabbi of their congregation refusing to marry Free Members . . . without being paid; refusing to attend the Dead to the Grave when requested to do so by members; also refusing to attend the Circumcision of members children, because in such instances the members do not subscribe individually to the Local Rabbi Fund?

Secondly, Have not the members of the Congregation a claim for such services by virtue of the payment of £50 per annum to the Local Rabbi, out of the Congregational Funds?[85]

Dr Schiller took the position that since his salary was now dependent on private donations, then only those who made donations were entitled to his services, and since the congregation had altered its obligations towards him, then he was no longer bound by the terms of the original agreement. When approached by a small deputation from the Select Committee, led by Frederick Eskell, he told them bluntly that since his £250 was no longer guaranteed,

it was his intention to charge all non-subscribers to his Fund for any services they may require from him.

The Deputation then enquired of him, if he chose, could he charge £20 for giving 'Kedusha' to any non-subscriber to his Fund, he replied Yes![86]

Although he intended to charge marriage fees, he claimed the sole right to perform marriages as 'one of his privileges'.

The Rev Dr also informed the Deputation that if he thinks fit to Lecture only once in three months, he was not bound to Lecture oftener.

If, however, the congregation once more guaranteed his salary and tax 'he would then willingly perform all the duties required of his office'.

Differences were patched up because the Local Rabbi's services were regarded as indispensable, and because it was hoped that in time he would become more amenable to reason. After a 'protracted discussion', a general meeting on 8 August resolved, on the motion of Saul Mayer,

That this meeting having listened to the explanation of the Revd Dr Schiller, feel fully satisfied with the same and do now adjourn.[87]

But the Local Rabbi had moved on to uncertain ground. Of the sixty-one new seat-holders who joined the congregation between 1851 and 1854, a handful were Eastern European immigrants of the late 1840s who, like the Polish master cap maker, Abraham Grabowsky, had attained the financial and social status required for entry, but most were newcomers, chiefly from London and the English provinces. They had not been party to the upsurge of local pride of which the Local Rabbi was a symbol, and in the case of his position coming into question they could not be expected to set great store by it. If the Local Rabbi intended to persist in disregarding the feelings of influential members of the community, he risked the erosion of the support upon which his position in the congregation depended.

IV

There were in fact two quite separate conflicts in the making during 1854–55, one between the Local Rabbi and the congregation, the other between the parties which supported and opposed the supreme authority of the Chief Rabbi. It was still accurate to speak of these parties as Cheremite and Anti-Cheremite, since the central issue was still one of jurisdiction, not ritual—the *cherem* itself, not the opinions which the *cherem* condemned. At the same time, it is clear that Theodores and his handful of supporters had tried to use the *cherem* issue to break down the resistance of those whose only objection to radical change was that the Chief Rabbi had condemned it. They had tried to convert local pride into a revolt against the Chief Rabbi which would open the way to Reform. But the conservatives, alerted by the Chief Rabbi to the far-reaching effects of local independence, had refused to be persuaded or deceived into the renunciation of a jurisdiction they believed to be essential to Anglo-Jewish orthodoxy. The result was to bring the Reformers into the open. Now their only hope lay in a convincing presentation of their case which would overcome the prejudices and inhibitions of the orthodox.

At first, the cracks were papered over in the interests of solidarity in other spheres. Hesse and Micholls were unanimously re-elected to the Board of Deputies.[88] Cheremite and Anti-Cheremite co-operated in the routine business of the synagogue, in the field of charity, and during 1854–55 on a Jerusalem Fund Committee set up to channel support to the Jews of the Holy Land whose main sources of support in Russia had been cut off by the Crimean War.[89] But a clash was inevitable, and, in the event, the occasion for it was provided by an almost accidental intrusion of the town into the inner life of the community. In July 1855 the Select Committee received formal notice that the synagogue was to be compulsorily purchased by the City Council under the terms of the Manchester Streets Act of 1853[90] to make way for the completion of Corporation Street, which was gradually, so it was said, bringing light and air into the nooks and crannies of the Old Town. There was little point in protest, and perhaps little reason, for the community had, in fact, outgrown both the synagogue and its site. In August the three trustees—Ansell Spier, Philip Lucas and Abraham Franks—were empowered to negotiate the sale on the best possible terms,[91] and in January 1856 it was sold to the corporation for £1,500—£200 less than it cost to build a quarter of a century earlier.[92]

An anonymous Manchester correspondent wrote to the editor of the *Jewish Chronicle*:

Now, Sir, here will commence the great struggle which has been preparing in the minds of many for a long time: for as the countenance of man is the index of his mind, so is the synagogue of a congregation the index of its worshippers; and the two parties, orthodox and reformers, will now fight for ascendancy, whether the divine service shall be performed according to the notions of one party or according to the notions of the other, and of course, the synagogue will be constructed accordingly.

Now as Rev Dr Schiller is the head of both parties, it is hoped that the two parties will yield a little to one another, namely to have a moderate reform in an orthodox synagogue so as to keep both parties together in one field; otherwise there is very little doubt there must and will be two synagogues, which will destroy Manchester as a respectable Jewish community; for there will be continual strife, contention and animosity, each party will speak against the other . . . and both parties will consequently appear wrong in the eyes of the stranger.[93]

10 The emergence of Reform, 1856–60

The otherwise perceptive analysis of 'Manchester Man' omitted to take into account Dr Schiller's deteriorating relationship with the wardens at Halliwell Street. He was certainly neutral in the political battle in the synagogue, but he was no longer an entirely disinterested party in other ways. The events of 1854–55 had revealed the insecurity of a Local Rabbinate which was entirely dependent for funds and moral support upon a single penny-pinching congregation. In 1851 Dr Schiller had served the purpose of the Manchester community, but there was no reason why he should not be rejected as soon as that purpose was fully achieved. No doubt the Local Rabbi was concerned that sooner or later he would have to declare himself unequivocally on matters of ritual and theology, but his actions during 1856–58 were also guided by two strategic considerations: the need to secure his financial position, and the desire to strengthen, and perhaps extend, the basis of his rabbinical jurisdiction in the provinces. In achieving either he was as likely to be involved in a clash with the Select Committee as with the Chief Rabbi's Office. His relationship to the Reform Party, which had acquired form and substance during the winter of 1855–56, and the allegiance of the leading localists, David Hesse and Horatio Micholls, is difficult to define. There is no doubt that the support of a party which included some of the wealthiest and more influential members of the community would have shored up his Local Rabbinate, but to have joined it would have involved a substantial alteration of his religious outlook. Another possibility, and one which was perhaps more consistent with his background and earlier sympathies, was an extension of his rabbinate beyond Manchester to embrace the Eastern European groups which were emerging along the line of transmigration. It seems likely that at the beginning of 1856 he had considered both possibilities, and rejected neither.

Although the Cheremite controversy had probably strengthened both Reformists and ultra-orthodox tendencies within the congregation, few of the participants had taken up precise or irreversible positions, and there was a large body of uncommitted opinion. Two of the most militant conservatives, Benjamin Hyam and Simon Joseph, had left Manchester during 1855–56 to establish their commercial headquarters in London. Only Theodores in Manchester was ideologically committed to Reform. The other members of the Reform group at the beginning of 1856—Micholls, Hesse, David Falk, Louis Behrens, Sigismund Schloss, Joseph Goodman and Ralph Straus—differed in background and were ready to accept varying degrees of compromise. Few would have been deaf to timely concessions on matters of ritual; some, like Hesse, might have been content with a strengthening of local autonomy. There were influential moderates whose family ties and conciliatory dispositions might have averted a crisis. Of the Reformers, John Michael Isaac was struck down by an illness to which he finally succumbed in 1858,[1] but his wife, the former Sarah Arayne, was closely related to the most orthodox families and throughout the dispute tried to bridge religious differences by personal contacts.[2] Alexander Jacob, once the leading defender of Jewish rights, emerged from retirement and disgrace to urge the congregation to 'expunge' from its code only such practices as 'may weaken our faith'.[3] Amongst the orthodox, Isaac Franklin, in particular, hoped most of all for unity. No one on either side looked forward to schism. In these circumstances, Dr Schiller might well have served as the focus of solidarity had he not been preoccupied with his own concerns. The tragedy was that two different situations worked themselves out together in a relatively short span, occasionally overlapping to obscure central threads in what was, in any case, a complex web of attitudes and opinions. The Local Rabbi attempted to define for himself a secure and permanent jurisdiction. The Reform Party tried to lead the whole Manchester community into religious nonconformity.

I

The power of the Local Rabbinate was effectively destroyed as a result of a relatively minor incident during January 1856. When Dr Schiller refused to perform a marriage within the congregation until he had received a guinea as a 'special fee' from the bridegroom, Nathan Israel, a non-subscriber to his Fund, the Select Committee took the extraordinary step of making direct application for a licence to Dr Adler in London.[4] The Chief Rabbi was asked not only to sanction the marriage without reference to Dr Schiller, but also to authorise its performance by Philip Dessau, the Reader. In effect, they invoked the authority of the Chief Rabbi to put the Local Rabbi in his place. No doubt anxious to avoid a public show-down, Dr Adler pleaded for a 'peaceable solution',[5] but while the Select Committee went through the motions of persuading Dr Schiller to give way, they seemed more anxious to force the issue. As the time for the marriage approached, they insisted in a telegram to the Chief Rabbi that it could not be delayed,[6] giving him time only for a telegraphic reply in which he was able to convey his acceptance of their arrangements, but not his equally important reservations.[7] The marriage had already been performed by Dessau on 23 January when the Committee received Dr Adler's considered reply, which ended:

At the same time, I must respectfully request that for the purpose of avoiding any unpleasant feeling, you will before handing the Licence to the Rev Mr Dessau once more solicit the Rev Dr Schiller to relinquish his determination not to sanction the marriage in question.[8]

The chain of events leaves little doubt that the Committee had used both the occasion, and Dr Adler's supreme authority, to underline, beyond question, the subordination of Dr Schiller to the lay authorities of the synagogue.

The most logical explanation of so extreme a measure was the fear of the orthodox that the Local Rabbinate would become the vehicle of Reform. It is clear that Dr Schiller's own orthodoxy was not in question, since the Chief Rabbi would hardly, in that case, have adopted so conciliatory an attitude. What concerned the Select Committee—on which the orthodox were temporarily predominant—was the possibility that the Reform Party, which was then known to be concerting its plans, would use the protective shield of the Local Rabbinate to ward off the intervention of the Chief Rabbi. The dispute on the *cherem* question had linked the issues of Reform and local autonomy so closely that neither could be independently resolved. Local autonomy was now regarded in orthodox circles in Manchester, not as the legitimate expression of local pride but as the foundations upon which Reform might be built. It is clear, too, from Dr Adler's reactions that he was not yet aware that the Reformers were preparing to move into the open. The effect of the incident was to place him on the alert, and in Manchester both to convince the Reform Party that it had nothing to gain from further delay and to demonstrate to Dr Schiller that if he hoped to place his provincial jurisdiction on a lasting basis, then he must look for it elsewhere than in the Old Congregation.

The first alternative was posed by events in Hull, where in the early 1850s immigrants from Central and Eastern Europe took their place beside an established community of some two hundred persons.[9] It appears that soon after the rebuilding of the synagogue in Hull, during 1855, a small body of 'foreign Jews' formed themselves into a society for the purpose of reading the Psalms in the synagogue every Sabbath.[10] Far from beginning as a subversive group, they met with the blessing of the warden, Bethel Jacobs, who encouraged them to purchase a *Sepher Torah*.[11] Instead of being placed in the Ark, however, the scroll was retained by Meyer Levy—'a poor man who obtained his living by hawking jewellery'—who persuaded a few others—'three or four of the lowest order of travelling Jews who lodge in this town', according to Jacobs—to meet in his house for the regular celebration of Divine Worship.[12] The group, which now described itself, on the model of a group which met in Manchester under Dr Schiller's guidance, as the *Chevra Tehillim*, or Psalm Society, went on to rent a room for *2s 6d* a week, and to attract to itself 'men of the humblest grades of Society . . . not four rated householders amongst them'.[13] They also received more influential backing from Henry Franks, an optician in Whitefriar's Gate, the younger brother of Abraham Franks of Manchester and the son-in-law of David Hesse, whose daughter, Louisa, he had married at Halliwell Street in 1852. The *chevra* also derived what Jacobs described as 'new impetus' from the accession of a 'Mr Barnett', a former *shochet* of the Birmingham congregation.[14] Although inevitably spoken of contemptuously by Bethel Jacobs and the secretary of the Hull synagogue, Simeon Moseley, the *chevra* probably represented the earliest attempt of Hull's immigrant community—the equivalent of Manchester's Red Bank—to organise a separate religious life. Its members began to speak of themselves as 'Seceders from the Old Congregation' and, finally, in February 1856, as the 'Hull New Congregation'.[15] One of the many indications that the *chevra* was anything but Reform was the failure of Bethel Jacobs to use this as a means of condemning the 'three or four malcontents'[16] who·led it.

None the less, the leaders of the New Congregation, faced with the intransigent opposition of the wardens of the Old, were unable to secure official recognition from the Chief Rabbi's Office. It seems likely that during the winter of 1855–56 Dr Adler had already expressed his unwillingness to give the congregation a sanction which would have provided it with his own rabbinical services and with a certificate from the Board of Deputies for the registration of marriages, and it was in these circumstances that Dr Schiller was approached, perhaps through the good offices of Henry Franks and David Hesse. On 10 February, when rumour reached Bethel Jacobs that Dr Schiller intended to visit Hull, and to perform a marriage which Dr Adler had refused to authorise, he wrote to Halliwell Street:

I have the pleasure of knowing Dr Schiller and can scarcely believe it possible that one ever anxious for peace as he has always been would rashly do any act which would widen rather than close the breach at present existing between the authorised Congregation and a few discontented persons.[17]

On 13 February, after the rumour had been confirmed, he added:

I sincerely hope that Dr Schiller will ponder well before he takes so fatal a step (as far as his reputation and character are concerned) as to come to Hull to act as the *tool* of despicable men who boast already of their success in inducing him to come to perform the marriage ceremony in Hull despite the Law of the Country or his courtesy and engagements to Dr Adler.[18]

There was in fact no question of illegality, since what was planned was a marriage in the office of the Hull Superintendent Registrar which would be *followed* by a ceremony in accordance with Jewish rites, but there is no doubt that the procedure involved a breach with the Chief Rabbi. In sanctioning the marriage Dr Schiller would have assumed powers which were customarily reserved to the Chief Rabbi.

This he was no longer reluctant to do. Between them the Chief Rabbi and the Select Committee had robbed him of most of his authority, and he was prepared to look elsewhere for compensation, particularly to a group which might conceivably form the first of a chain of immigrant congregations. On arriving in Hull on Thursday 14 February, he requested Bethel Jacobs to 'wait upon him' to discuss local communal affairs, 'as certain persons resident in this town' had invited him to become their 'Chief Rabbi'.[19] When Jacobs declined, he publicly announced his intention of proceeding with the marriage on the following Tuesday, without the sanction of Dr Adler and the Hull wardens, and without reference to the Manchester authorities,[20] whose failure to warn him of the consequences was consistent with their indifference to his fate. At midday on 19 February, after a civil ceremony in which he acted as one of the witnesses, Dr Schiller solemnised the marriage according to the Jewish rite in a room hired by the New Congregation.[21] According to a report sent to Manchester by Bethel Jacobs, the secessionists signed a document dictated by Dr Schiller in German (and translated into English by Henry Franks) in which they acknowledged him as Chief Rabbi, while, for his part, Dr Schiller promised the supply of 'ample means' from Manchester, the immediate sum of £30 towards the purchase of a Burial Ground, the services of a religious teacher, and a facility for the authorisation of marriages at a cost of half a guinea each.[22] 'Mr Barnett' of Hull—'a dangerous fellow', according to Jacobs—supposedly acted as intermediary between the Hull New Congregation and Dr Schiller's 'friends' in Manchester.[23] Who these friends were must remain a mystery. The Reform Party had nothing to gain, and everything to lose, from becoming involved in remote communal politics in which it had no stake. It is possible that Hesse, linked through Franks with the Hull community, was prepared to take a stand for the notion of congregational freedom even if it was not exercised in a radical cause. But what seems most likely is that Dr Schiller banked upon a support in Manchester which did not, in point of fact, exist. He remembered too well the euphoria of 1851–53 and the unanimity of his re-election to the Local Rabbinate, and he was not yet sufficiently aware of the effects of the congregation's division of other issues. In particular, he did not yet realise that neither party regarded him as indispensable.

He was, in fact, almost completely isolated. Dr Adler wrote to Manchester to express his amazement at the 'extraordinary proceedings' in Hull and called upon the Select Committee to provide good reasons why he should not cease to recognise Dr Schiller as Local Rabbi.[24] The Select Committee, of course, had no such reasons. On 20 February, on the motion of the wardens, Frederick Eskell and Ansell Spier, Dr Schiller was suspended from all his official duties pending an enquiry into the 'commission of . . . illegal acts' in Hull.[25] The Local Rabbi then fell back upon the mercy of the congregation as a whole, to which alone he held himself accountable. He wrote to the Select Committee:

I solemnly protest against the usurpation by them of an authority not belonging to them. Although the Committee may be the organs of Correspondence between me and the Congregation, I will not acknowledge the competence of the Committee to decree against me a suspension of those functions with which I have been solemnly invested by the whole body of Manchester Hebrew Congregation, whose authority alone I recognise. I shall continue to perform my duties towards the Congregation from doing which nothing shall ever deter me, save my fear of giving an occasion to see the sanctity of the House of God profaned by the violence of the evil disposed, which the Lord, in his mercy forbid![26]

When the Select Committee called on him to provide a full explanation of events in Hull, he declined to provide one, but added: 'I shall, however, be most happy to do so in a General Meeting convened for that purpose.'[27] It seems clear that in spite of his bid for power in Hull he still regarded himself as the servant of the Manchester Congregation, whose substantial backing he now expected to receive. The episode again illustrates his lack of familiarity with the 'select' system of congregational government and the centralisation of rabbinical authority, as much as his failure to read the political situation correctly.

In response to the Local Rabbi's second letter, the Committee called a General Meeting, 'for the purpose of giving notice of dismissal to Dr Schiller', at which he was called upon to answer three charges: that he had 'openly violated' his agreement with the congregation by refusing to marry persons without the payment of a fee, or to allow other salaried officers to perform them in his place; that he had broken his agreement with Dr Adler and the congregation by proceeding to Hull; and that he had attempted

to undermine the foundations and best interests of the Congregation by sowing the seeds of disunion amongst the Members, which have already proved prejudicial to the peace of the community, through his secretly canvassing the members to subscribe to a place of worship which he contemplated establishing.[28]

Dr Schiller was not given the opportunity of attending, but he was invited to submit a written reply, which might be read by a person of his choice. Although the first two charges were clear enough, and probably justified, the accuracy of the third is difficult to assess, particularly since, in the event, Dr

Schiller chose not to defend himself. If he was, in fact, planning a new place of worship, it was not in the Reform interest. The thirteen members at Halliwell Street who on 3 March intervened to question the legitimacy of Dr Schiller's suspension[29] represented a wide spectrum of opinion, including Hesse and the Mayer brothers from the Reform wing, but also shopkeepers of undoubted orthodoxy such as Alexander Leveson and Saul Isaacs, and the immigrant entrepreneurs Joseph Rosenthal and Saul Oppenheim. When the General Meeting was convened, on 12 March, to consider Dr Schiller's position, Isaac Franklin proposed a motion which would have lifted the suspension until such time as the Local Rabbi had been given an opportunity of vindicating himself in person.[30] What, perhaps, seems most likely, is that Dr Schiller had in mind a congregation which was based on a compromise on matters of ritual acceptable to the whole community. But in seeking a new power base, whether in Hull or Manchester, or both, he had alienated a substantial body of opinion which now regarded him, not without justification, as chiefly preoccupied with his own future. Franklin's motion was voted down by forty-seven votes to twenty-seven, the suspension was confirmed, and a date was fixed for the congregation to decide finally on the question of a dismissal.[31] Dr Schiller did not await the formalities. On 25 March he submitted his resignation on the grounds that an unbiased judgement was no longer to be expected from the Special General Meeting which was due to meet five days later.[32] The congregation accepted it, adding only its 'disapprobation . . . at his impropriety in impunging the impartiality of the meeting', and on 30 March the Local Rabbinate was officially concluded.[33]

Although Dr Schiller had contributed to this result by his own recklessness and misjudgement, it is arguable that the Local Rabbinate was already doomed as a result of the *cherem* question which had identified local independence closely with Reform, and so undermined the consensus of 1851–52. The events of February and March were no more than a logical extension of the marriage issue of January 1856, when the Select Committee brought Dr Schiller to heel with the help of the Chief Rabbi. The support of his older admirers, not all of them Reformers, was insufficient to save the Local Rabbi. His position after 30 March is obscure. When approached by his friend Isaac Franklin with regard to his position as superintendent of the Jews School, he wrote:

whatever my position may be towards the Halliwell Street congregation, the interests of the poor and of the children of the Israelite community of Manchester will never cease to be dear to my heart.[34]

He continued to work for school governors, some of whom were members of the Select Committee which had suspended him. It is clear also that he served a

PLATE III   The Manchester Great Synagogue, 1858.

private *minyan*, for whom he issued divorces and licensed *shochetim*, in spite of the Chief Rabbi's public declaration that his rabbinical functions were 'altogether terminated'.[35] On 2 May he advertised in the *Jewish Chronicle* for

A Gentleman competent to perform the duties of Shochet and Assistant Hebrew Teacher. Testimonials to be sent, prepaid, to the Rev. Dr Schiller–Szinessy, Chief Rabbi of the New Congregations of Manchester and Hull, whose approbation will be required previous to engagement, and from whom further particulars may be learned.[36]

Again one may doubt whether either of these congregations subscribed to Reform principles. In Manchester the Reformers had made known their intention and were perhaps holding an occasional *minyan* in Horatio Micholl's home in Shakespeare Street, Ardwick, but they had not at that time decided on a separate congregation, nor had they negotiated with Dr Schiller to ascertain his views. What Dr Schiller had in mind, in so far as his objectives were clearly defined, was an independent group of congregations bound together not by common ritual observance, but by common acceptance of his authority. It was not until 3 May—perhaps when the Reformers became aware through the press that Dr Schiller was planning his New Congregation—that he was invited to Horatio Micholls' house to discuss the terms upon which he was prepared to serve as the minister of a Reform synagogue.[37]

II

The exploits of Dr Schiller had by that time been overshadowed by the drama of Reform. On 17 February, the Sunday before the Local Rabbi had performed the fatal marriage at Hull, members of a newly-established Reform Association met at the house of Horatio Micholls and adopted three resolutions:

That this association adopts for its Synagogue the Prayer Book now in use at the Margaret Street Synagogue of British Jews.
That the mode of reciting the Prayers, and the Ceremonial of Public Worship now in operation at the Margaret Street Congregation of British Jews be likewise adopted.
That it is highly desirable to introduce the formation of a Choir, to heighten the solemnity of the worship.[38]

The Association elected a provisional committee—Horatio Micholls, David Hesse, David Falk, Louis Behrens, Tobias Theodores, Sigismund Schloss, Joseph Goodman and Ralph Straus—

for the purpose of laying before the officers of the Hebrew Congregation now existing the Resolutions passed at the meeting and to take such further steps as they may deem necessary, in order to combine with the general body of the Jews of Manchester with a view to carry out the purposes of this Association.

It is at the same time resolved that if the Committee fail in obtaining the co-operation of the general body, the members of this association pledge themselves separately to prosecute the objects now proposed until they are effectually secured.[39]

The events of January, which had finally undermined the Local Rabbinate, had persuaded the Reformers that they could not proceed gradually towards Reform through an intermediate stage of local autonomy. The alternatives were now persuasion or schism. At the beginning of March the three resolutions were sent to the Select Committee with a covering letter inviting the congregation 'to declare their adherence to the same, a result which we would hail with the greatest satisfaction'. If they failed to do so, 'we may then proceed for ourselves'.[40] On 16 March, the Select Committee responded by appointing three delegates—Frederick Eskell, Ansell Spier and David Cowen—to meet a deputation of three Reformers at the Jews School on 6 April.[41]

In the negotiations which then began it is clear that the hopes of the orthodox for compromise were, if anything, greater than those of the Reformers. The Reform Association pursued an existing model from which it would deviate in only one particular; the object of the orthodox was to approach as nearly to this model as the Chief Rabbi would allow, in the interests of unity. Although the Chief Rabbi was regarded by the orthodox as the final arbiter, he was pressed to avoid schism by 'timely providing for the emergency by moderate concessions'.[42] It was suggested to him tactfully that a compromise might not only preserve the integrity of the congregation, but also recover the religious allegiance of the many Jews in Manchester who had 'studiously avoided' the synagogue. Some, so it was said, 'even state their intention of closing their warehouses on the Sabbath day'.[43] The declared intention of Eskell and the Select Committee was to meet the conscientious objections of the radicals, while 'at the same time preserving inviolate the Religion professed by the Congregation',[44] a bargain to which only Dr Adler could affix the precise terms. On the other hand, it was clear from the first meeting, on 6 April, that the Reformers were prepared to modify the 'worship and decorum' of Margaret Street only by retaining the Second Days of Festivals. They were prepared to consult Dr Adler on the licensing of *shochetim* and the authorisation of marriages, but they were not willing to accept his authority in matters connected with 'the mode of public worship' or the 'internal management' of the synagogue.[45]

In a letter to the Congregation on 29 April, in which he defined the limits within which a compromise must be effected, the Chief Rabbi took up a familiar position. He accepted the 'expediency' of avoiding a schism, but not at the expense of what he chose to regard as the 'organic changes' introduced in the

Reform Prayer Book. Nor could he surrender to Manchester any of the authority on matters of public worship which sustained its uniformity. He agreed to sanction further precautions against noise and disturbance in the synagogue, including the use of fixed rather than movable desks. He agreed to the curtailment, even to the abolition, of *misheberachs*. He encouraged the delivery of sermons in English by a suitable successor to Dr Schiller. He agreed to a pause of five or ten minutes between the Morning Prayer and the Reading of the Law 'so that all members may then enter and assemble at the same time'. But he ruled out Eskell's suggestions that the *Aliyoth* might be dispensed with and that an 'entire division' might be instituted between the Morning Service and the Additional Prayers.[46] When pressed in a further letter to delegate some powers of discretion to the local congregation,[47] he replied that he could not allow the local authorities to make any alterations in the Prayer Book 'however slight or trivial' without his sanction.[48] His advice was characterised by the usual circularity. He spoke of 'the paramount necessity of upholding concord and unity among our Community',[49] but he would not sanction the concessions which alone would make it possible. Both sides wanted unity, each on its own terms. The position adopted by each was logical within its own terms of reference. Dr Adler believed that the integrity of Judaism required a uniform pattern of ritual supported by a strong central control. He was reluctant to modify the agreed pattern in the case of a single congregation, not because each detail was in itself inviolate but because deviation invited an anarchy in which the essence of Judaism might be lost. For the same reason the delegation of discretionary powers was out of the question. His opposition to the Reform Association's demands was perfectly consistent with his anxieties about the Local Rabbinate. Nor was his attitude unduly swayed by the threat of schism, since the secession of a single congregation was preferable to general chaos. The position of the Reformers was equally logical. The vitality of Judaism depended upon an adaptability which was hampered by excessive reliance upon fixed tradition and central authority. Although their demands in 1856 were made within the gentle context of English Reform, and were far short of the most radical developments in Germany and the United States, the insistence of the Reformers upon congregational discretion in fact opened the way to a full exploration of the variety of possibilities inherent in Judaism. The Reformers were not prepared to accept restrictions which the Chief Rabbi believed to be essential.

By 3 May the Reformers were sufficiently convinced that agreement was beyond hope to begin negotiations for the services of Dr Schiller.[50] At first these negotiations did not proceed smoothly. When asked if he was prepared to accept the Margaret Street Prayer Book, he replied that he would do so only after his acceptance as 'Chief Rabbi'.[51] The placing of an advertisement by the Reform Association in the *Jewish Chronicle* of 8 June for a 'minister to officiate as Lecturer and Reader', suggests that it would have preferred a man of greater modesty, and perhaps more advanced views, than Dr Schiller had demonstrated, but, since no suitable candidate appeared, Dr Schiller's services were accepted, probably at some time in July. Meantime, during the second week of June, Louis Behrens and Sigismund Schloss opened negotiations with Halliwell Street for a share of the congregational burial ground and the services of the orthodox *shochet* in the event of a secession.[52]

Although these events determined the new warden, Joseph Spier, to make one final attempt at compromise, by again pressing Dr Adler to extend the acceptable boundaries of orthodoxy,[53] the only effect of his argument was to draw from the Chief Rabbi his most comprehensive defence of the orthodox position.[54] He wrote to Spier:

In reply to your letter of 16th [June], I have the honour to state . . . that it is a difficult task to give you reasons for the religious ceremonies in our public worship because our prayers are the expression not of individuals but of the *whole nation* and therefore words and actions which might appear to you strange from your point of view are full of meaning with regard to other countries and Israel at large. It cannot be denied that our present prayer book has contributed largely to the preservation of our nation. While in former time one ritual was sufficient for every Synagogue in different quarters and countries which strengthened the ties of brotherhood[,] at present there are countries where every Synagogue requires a different Prayer book[,] and on the other hand while our present Prayer book has the dignity of age and has been introduced in all congregations, the prayer book of Margaret Street has not been adopted by any village, even not in America where all kinds of experiments are exercised. Therefore everyone who has the future welfare of Israel at his heart ought to maintain *uniformity* and not be over anxious in introducing changes which as experience teaches leave the Synagogue [as] deserted as before when the charm of novelty has subsided.

He went on to deal in turn with each of the points raised by Spier. The *Aliyoth* were indispensable, although the wardens might exercise their discretion in calling up only 'those who are respectable'. It seemed reasonable that only the Minister, Reader 'or other fit substitutes' be called to the coveted reading of the *maftir* and the *haftorah*. A division of the Divine Service he still regarded as 'objectionable' and pressed that his proposals for an interval be given a fair trial. The priestly benedictions were of 'very great importance' and could not be omitted:

It is a false notion to object to the *Cohanim* because the congregation do not consider them worthy enough to pray for them. The Lord said (Num. vi, 27) 'They shall put my name upon the children of Israel and I will bless them.' The Priests have but to express His name, the blessing comes from the Lord.

The intermediate prayers concerning dreams

are *private* and are to be said silently . . . If we be liberal we must have due respect also to opposite opinions and not interfere with private feelings.

Celebration of the Second Days of Festivals was essential:

It is impossible to exhaust in a letter the reasons for the second days of festivals which is connected with the whole system of the Jewish calendar . . . It is sufficient to know that the solemnisation of the second days is adopted throughout the globe and those who acknowledge the system of Calendar [sic] as a fact of historical Judaism and deny the second day which is also such a fact commit the greatest inconsistency.

In calling upon Spier to 'settle this important matter to the satisfaction of the majority without injuring established customs and rites', he made it clear that the price offered for the avoidance of a schism was too high. He was now reconciled to the possibility of a dissident minority lying beyond the scope of a consensus in Manchester as well as London, since he saw this as preferable to a form of accommodation which would undermine the fundamental unity of Judaism.

On 30 July, after carefully weighing its loyalty to the Chief Rabbi against the urgent need for local integrity, the Select Committee came up with the most radical programme it was prepared to countenance in the interests of reunion.[55] All *mishaberachs* would be abolished—'the deficiency in revenue arising therefrom to be made up from other sources'. Although *Aliyoth* must continue, persons would be called up 'by the number of the portion, instead of by name'. On Sabbaths and Festivals, the morning service would be divided

Early service at eight o'clock to conclude with *Kaddish* after *Shemona Asra*. The second service to commence at Ten o'clock by the Choir chanting [the appropriate Psalm] . . . the Reading of the Law then to take place, sermon, additional service, and conclusion.

The prayers would be 'recited solemnly' by the Reader, the responses by an efficient choir, 'the congregation to pray silently, until enabled to chant in unison with the choir'. A modification might be made in the chanting of the *Cohanim*. Decorum would be strictly enforced. No offerings for departed relatives might be made in the synagogue without written notice given three days before a Festival. Finally, four members—M. H. Simonson, Joachim Levy, Joel Kohn and S. L. Meisels—were deputed to advise the committee on other modifications which might be made to the Prayer Book, and on 4 August, at their suggestion, it was proposed to dispense also with the *Piyyutim*, except on Rosh Hashana, Yom Kippur and Hoshana Rabbah.[56]

When these terms were put to the delegates of the Reform Association— Micholls, Hesse and Theodores—at a conference held at the Jews School at 10 a.m. on 17 August,[57] it soon became clear that the time for compromise had passed. In their own words, the Association had already 'finally decided' to adopt the Prayer Book of Margaret Street and to reject, without reservation, the authority of the Chief Rabbi. Micholls commended Spier on his 'sincere manner' in devising proposals which, he believed, 'at an earlier period would have settled the question', but he now declined to accept reunion on any terms but his own. The only concession the Reformers were prepared to make was the retention of Second Days, 'purely and professedly as ancient institutions upon which many of our members look with a feeling of reverence'. The secretary at Halliwell Street wrote: 'the meeting terminated in a final rejection of the peaceful overtures made by them'.

III

With peaceful negotiations over and a break certain, relationships between the two groups became more abrasive, particularly since the minister of the one was the errant rabbi of the other. As both congregations acquired sites and commenced building separate synagogues, each of which was regarded as a more reputable and convenient alternative to Halliwell Street, a bitter dispute developed as to the terms upon which facilities for burial and *shechita* might be shared. When the Old Congregation turned down an initial request for 'friendly arrangements',[58] Micholls, Hesse and Ralph Straus lodged a formal protest at receipt by the orthodox of the total proceeds from the sale of the old synagogue building.[59] They argued that the Reform Association was as much entitled to a share of the proceeds, since the Trust Deed made no mention of any restriction on the form of service or the nature of the ecclesiastical authority. Since they were not in need of the money, however, they made it known in private that they might be persuaded to waive their claim in return for a share of the Old Congregation's cemetery and *shochet*.[60] In the meantime, to the scandal of the community, the Town Clerk lodged the money in the Court of Chancery, out of reach of both parties.[61] Since the Old Congregation, with a larger but poorer membership, was most in need of funds, however, some form of compromise was inevitable. Following an extensive private correspondence and a barrage of abusive letters in the Jewish press,[62] the Old Congregation swallowed its pride and in October 1856 sought permission from the Chief Rabbi to come to terms, since

it may be the means of effecting a peaceful separation, which separation must inevitably take place, whether peacefully or adversely.[63]

More difficulties followed when an attempt was made to work out the conditions under which the Reformers might use the burial ground at Prestwich.

The Chief Rabbi's insistence upon a division of the plot into two exclusive parts, and his refusal to countenance the use of the Reform Prayer Book in either, complicated local negotiations, which dragged on until September 1857.[64] Finally, the Reform Association agreed to receive £500 in lieu of any further claim upon the property or services of the Old Congregation.[65]

Both congregations then pushed forwards, with an air of competition, with the erection of buildings which suitably enshrined their differing ideals, and which ultimately took shape within a few hundred yards of one another on Cheetham Hill Road. There was no sense in which Reform in Manchester fulfilled the special needs of those who had moved into a new district which lacked synagogal accommodation, as in London it was to some extent associated with the movement of Jewish families into the West End. The sites chosen for both Manchester synagogues reflected the changing pattern of Jewish settlement as a whole, and particularly the northward movement of middle-class families into Strangeways and Cheetham Hill. Both lay near the heart of the middle-class residential districts of north Manchester. In January 1856 the Old Congregation—which had vacated Halliwell Street during the autumn and moved into temporary premises in Miller Street—purchased 1,200 square yards of land opposite Cheetham Town Hall from the agent of the Earl of Derby at $8\frac{1}{2}d$ a square yard, with an option on as much more as they required.[66] The Reformers began to build rather closer to town, at the junction of Cheetham Hill Road and Park Place. Families living in central and south Manchester were equidistant from both and, in fact, chose between them. Of the merchants of Plymouth Grove, H. M. Salomon opted for Reform, S. L. Behrens for orthodoxy, Ernest Reuss for Unitarianism. In the final analysis, twenty-one of the founder-members of the Reform Synagogue lived in south Manchester (eleven in Chorlton-on-Medlock, four in Greenheys, two in Ardwick, two in Victoria Park, one in Old Trafford and one in Bowdon), eighteen north of the Irwell (three in Strangeways, eight in Cheetham Hill, seven in Higher Broughton), and the remaining seven in the central commercial districts of Manchester and Salford. Nor was Reform, in a general sense, an attempt by suburban families to rationalise a breach with traditional observance which would have enabled them to move even further from the centre of town. The intent to move was not confined to Reformers. During the years 1858–60 Louis Behrens, Horatio Micholls and Giuseppe di Moro moved to Bowdon, some seven miles south of Manchester, which in due course was to become an important centre of residence for Reformers, but S. L. Behrens moved equally far to Alderley Edge, while his sons, who also remained within the orthodox communion, acquired Worleston Grange, a Georgian mansion near Nantwich, with a substantial acreage and four home farms, where they held hunting parties occasionally attended by the Gaskells.[67] What the sites of the new synagogues did confirm was the staking out of north Manchester as the major area of Jewish settlement in the later nineteenth century.

Of the eleven plans submitted to the Old Congregation during January 1857—including one from the London Jewish architect, N. S. Joseph—the Building Committee chose that of Thomas Bird of Manchester, the architect of Cheetham Town Hall, whose design and specification were accepted by the Select Committee, with only minor modifications, on 10 February.[68] The Reform Association chose the plan prepared by one of its own members, Edward Salomon. Both buildings cost between £3,500 and £4,000, although, with the cost of land, architects' fees, legal charges and internal fittings, both congregations were committed to a total outlay of around £5,500.[69] Long before the money had been raised, foundation stones had been ceremonially laid, by Horatio Micholls in Park Place on 11 March, and by Dr Adler, for the Old Congregation, on 29 April 1857, each accompanied by a procession of children from the (same) Jews School. As Dr Schiller remarked, the operations resembled the building of the Second Temple:

They were both built by a part only of the Jewish community, and in spite of the virulent opposition of disaffected co-religionists; the weapon was wielded with one hand while the building was builded with the other.[70]

As the buildings arose during the winter of 1857–58, the Old Congregation, having already lost a third of the proceeds from Halliwell Street, faced the uphill task of raising more money than its reduced membership was able to subscribe. Its canvass was extended to embrace Jewish families which had long since lost their religious identity.[71] John Peiser, the coach-lace manufacturer from Posen, who had not once attended synagogue since his arrival in Manchester in the mid-1820s, contributed five guineas and appeared first on the list of subscribers. Harry Hiller, the commission agent from Hanover, who had on very rare occasions rented a seat for the Holy days, donated three guineas, and other 'lapsed' Jews who contributed were Bernard and Henry Hahn, and the cigar dealer and insurance agent Bernard Goldschmidt, who soon afterwards was pressed by the Chief Rabbi to provide as generously for the wife he had deserted in London.[72] The house of Rothschild and Sir Moses Montefiore each contributed £25, and there were eighteen other donations from London; 10s was given by Henry Franks, so recently involved in the mysterious affair in Hull, of which the main effect, according to one commentator, was the closure of his shop on the Sabbath.[73] B. L. Joseph, the former democratic rebel in Liverpool, sent two guineas, and other sums arrived from Birmingham, Coventry, Bristol, Glasgow, Sheffield, Yarmouth, Truro, Warrington and

Falmouth. Two contributors lived in Australia, one in Toronto. The Mayor of Manchester gave ten guineas; of Salford, ten shillings. But the £1,655 got together by an active Building Committee chaired by Ansell Spier was not enough. In May 1857 an anticipatory loan of £250 at 5 per cent was negotiated with the Hebrew Philanthropic Society, and finally the Old Congregation paid its bills only with the help of a mortgage of £2,700.[74] With extravagant pride the Reformers boasted that they had raised all the money required within their own small, but affluent membership.[75] None the less, they lost the race to completion. The Great Synagogue, as the Old Congregation called its new house of worship, was consecrated by Dr Adler on 11 March 1858; the Manchester Synagogue of British Jews, by Rev. Professor David Woolf Marks, on 25 March. Although Marks was unwilling to accept the Manchester congregation as a 'branch' of Margaret Street, chiefly because it had chosen to retain Second Days,[76] he was happy enough to place his seal of approval upon the emergence of Reform in the provinces.

The two buildings presented a sharp contrast in concept and style. The Reform Synagogue—a 'Saracenic modification of the Byzantine', according to a reviewer in *The Builder*[77]—was a simple, restrained, slender building of classic proportions, 100 ft long and 50 ft wide, which relied for dramatic effect chiefly upon the arabesque patterns picked out by red and white ornamental brickwork, which was regarded as 'perhaps the most elaborate yet executed in the city', and two tiers of 'Byzantine' windows, one above, one below the Ladies Gallery. Internally, the main body of the synagogue was divided, church-like, into a nave and two side-aisles, the lines of which were picked out by deep horseshoe arches resting on iron columns with foliated capitals. Accommodation was provided in the nave for 400 men, and, in two lateral galleries, for 250 women. The separation of the male and female members of the congregation was again characteristic of the reticence of English Reform. At the east end, a simple Moresque arch framed an octagonal apse in which were placed the Ark, and, before it, the Reader's desk. A simple wooden pulpit, embossed with miniature arches, stood on a platform extending from the apse into the nave. The 'highest aim' of the architect, according to Theodores, 'was to blend in the . . . institution the antique gravity of the faith with . . . modern beauty of form'.[78] The absence of imposing display, the external simplicity of line, the organ in the west gallery, and the internal similarity of the nave to the layout of a church, all symbolised their attempt to 'blend' with the dominant culture. At the laying of the foundation stone, Theodores spoke of the cultural significance of Reform. Reformers, he said,

while cheerfully acknowledging the indissoluble ties which connected them historically with the remote east, and the epoch of the dawn of human civilisation . . . proclaimed themselves, as loudly, the children of the Occident and willing partakers in the glorious Occidental enlightenment and civilisation.[79]

The synagogue's link with the unique tradition of Judaism was symbolised by the burial in the foundations of a fragment of rock from Mount Sion.

The Great Synagogue was as flamboyant and ornate as Park Place was simple and restrained.[80] In an extravagant western façade, described by its architect as possessing an 'Italian character', a flight of twelve steps, 40 ft in length, led up to a row of columns of polished stonework which formed the entrance to a covered loggia, 24 ft wide and 12 ft deep, supported by an elaborate Corinthian balustrade. The wings of the loggia, which enclosed the staircases to the Ladies Gallery, were each surmounted by an ornate cupola of green lead. All the external interest was concentrated on the frontispiece facing Cheetham Hill Road. The north and south sides, and the east end, were of 'patent pressed' red stock bricks, relieved only by drab stone dressings around the windows. The interior—with space for '372 gentlemen, 9 boys or pupils, and 60 free sittings'—was arranged in traditional style around a central reading desk, with the seats arranged laterally below the Ladies Gallery. The Ark stood alone in a recess at the east end, approached by five steps and flanked by wooden pedestals supporting bronze candelabra. The pedestals, the curved doors of the Ark, an imposing pulpit, the desk, and the praesidial box, were all beautifully carved out of polished Spanish mahogany by a local carpenter, Thomas Tully. Extravagant gilt chandeliers and Persian carpeting from the warehouse of a Free Member, Samuel Phillips, added to a rich and colourful interior. Unlike Park Place, the Great Synagogue was an exercise in conspicuous display, not an attempt to blend, but an assertion that the unique had its proper place in the English setting.

The movement of synagogal accommodation of both varieties out of the Old Town into a respectable inner suburb, and the building of stylish places of worship, however different in character, marked yet another stage in the community's advancing status, of which there were many other indications. In February 1858 Philip Lucas, who had already served a term as City Councillor, was elected to the Board of the Manchester Chamber of Commerce, probably the most important economic pressure group in England.[81] When Manchester emphasised its role as a cultural centre by staging an elaborate Art Treasures Exhibition in 1857, the 'palace' at Old Trafford in which the exhibition was housed was designed—although with an obvious debt to Crystal Palace—by Edward Salomon,[82] who went on to become a major architect of civic buildings, some in a 'Saracenic', others in a Gothic style.[83] Jacob Casper marketed an 'Art Exhibition Suit' at 43s. Isaac Simmons advertised his jewellery, Abraham Franks his spectacles, in a special edition of *Bradshaw's Guide*.[84] Jewish traders held the vice-consulships in Manchester for Austria (Julius Sichel), Sweden and Norway (Edward Nathan), and the Netherlands (H. S. Straus), and the consulship of the New Granadian Republic in South America (a former resident there, Sigismund Schloss). There was a Jewish tailor, jeweller or tobacconist in every major commercial district of the town, and Jewish families in suburban districts from Prestwich and Sedgley Park in the north to Bowdon and Alderley in the south. As a symptom of the community's prestige, the Dress Tea and Soirée held in the Assembly Room of the Free Trade Hall to mark the opening of the Great Synagogue was attended by the Mayors of Manchester and Salford, and a coterie of aldermen and councillors from both sides of the Irwell.[85]

The community also basked in the reflected glory of political emancipation. during 1858 the City Council endorsed—'almost unanimously', as Godfrey Levi wrote tactfully—a final petition for the removal of Jewish disabilities.[86] A Bill sanctioning the admission of Jews by resolution, without any obligation to subscribe to the words 'On the true faith of a Christian', passed rapidly through both Houses, and on 26 July 1858 Baron de Rothschild legally occupied his seat in the House of Commons. Emancipation finally took the form of a 'special indulgence'. To meet the susceptibilities of the House of Lords, the Parliamentary oath remained intact, but either House was authorised to admit Jewish members by exempting them, by special resolution, from the part which they found objectionable. This was less than the religious equality for which the *Guardian* had hoped,[87] but it served Jewish purposes adequately enough. Like the Great Synagogue on Cheetham Hill Road, it was an emphatic confirmation of half a century of social and economic improvement, and it was fitting that the congratulatory address sent to Rothschild by the Manchester community was drawn up by a committee under the chairmanship of Joseph Slazenger Moss, himself a descendant of the itinerant dealers of eighteenth-century England.[88]

IV

The meaning of Reform at Park Place was summarised by Dr Schiller on the day of its inauguration:

... with respect to our Divine Service within the synagogue, we proceed on this principle, on the one hand strictly to avoid all that was unseemly or calculated to damp devotion at the late synagogue of Halliwell Street: to avoid all that is detrimental to the dignity and decorum of the Divine Service, or that destroys the awe that ought to be felt in a house of God; and, on the other, to encourage all that is deservedly dear to the thinking and religious Jews; to cause the whole congregation to participate in the hymns sung to the glory of God; to cause these hymns to be accompanied by instrumental music, so powerful in its inspiring effects; to reintroduce, instead of insipid compositions called *Piyutim*—many of them are the efflux of ignorance, superstition, and a love of solemn trifling with our sacred language—the Psalms of David . . . which have been almost neglected by us while they have been eagerly received into the worship of non-Israelites all over the civilised world; to introduce a prayer book . . . which [contains] the best prayers of the two principal rituals; and finally, to preach the word of God in the vernacular . . .

As to belief,

we laid down the general principle that we would return to biblical truth, and that we would admit only such post-biblical usages in our synagogue teachings and domestic practices, as are not contradictory to the law of the bible.

Now, is this an innovation to be dreaded by Jews? Have not the learned and the good of Israel, in all ages, upheld the doctrine we advocate? Was not this the ideal of many of the greatest and most pious teachers of the Talmud?

Still, for this we were driven to separate ourselves, and to divide the feeble strength of the community in this city. Indeed, not limiting ourselves to a mere apology of our position, we confidently proclaim our right and title to the denomination of the truly orthodox Manchester congregation.[89]

Attempts to minimise the differences between the two synagogues, either by contemporaries like Dr Schiller or by historians, overlook the extent to which each put itself forward as a distinct ideal and the difficulties which overcame the genuine efforts to arrive at a compromise during 1856. The innovations demanded by the Reformers may certainly be regarded as an extension of changes sought by many who remained orthodox, but they were an extension of a qualitative as well as a quantitative kind, which involved a critical reappraisal of the development of Judaism and the place within it of rabbinical authority. In his refusal to sanction concessions during 1856 Dr Adler made it perfectly plain at what points he believed this qualitative change to begin. It may be argued that he was inflexible in his attitude towards Reform, but it was an inflexibility which arose not so much from rigidity of outlook as from a determination to preserve what he saw as the essentials of Judaism by insisting upon a framework of ritual uniformity and central control. He upheld a view of Judaism in which the emphasis was upon tradition, uniformity and authority against those who, however modest their immediate aims, stood for adaptation, variety and experiment. The assessment of English Reform as 'in no sense a revolution in Jewish theology but merely an adventure in Jewish aesthetics'[90] begs this question, with its underlying implications for the status of the Oral Law, and fails to account for what otherwise might appear to be an inexplicable obstinacy on the part of Reformers in London and Manchester. When Joseph Slazenger Moss, at an early stage in the negotiations, had called upon the Reformers to rest content with the ritual and decorum of the West London Branch of the Great Synagogue, the orthodox alternative to Margaret Street, Micholls turned down the offer with 'sincere regret'.[91] Some Manchester Jews may have made their choice between the two synagogues on 'aesthetic' grounds, but aesthetics do not account for the choice which had to be made.

Other factors closely associated with the rise of Reform in England may be distinguished from its causes. In London some of the early momentum of the movement arose from the lack of synagogal accommodation in the West End and the inadequate decorum of services at Duke's Place and Bevis Marks, but that these provided the occasion rather than the cause of Reform is suggested by events in Manchester, where the absence of a suburban synagogue clearly played no part, and the need for greater decorum was generally acknowledged and universally sought. Neither the power of the Chief Rabbi nor the proclamation of the *cherem* explains the rise of Reform in Manchester, where a near-unanimous desire for local autonomy and a general sympathy for the disabilities of the Reformers was in fact destroyed by the emergence of Reform as the major issue. In London Montefiore saw Reform as an attempt to render Judaism more acceptable in Gentile eyes during the struggle for emancipation, but this stimulus scarcely applied in Manchester, where the emergence of Reform nearly coincided with the attainment of political freedom. Theodores once described English Reform as the *via media* which would indicate by its approximation to the externals of Anglo-Christian worship that Jews were committed equally to the divine destiny of the House of Israel and to the British nation, 'whose equally Divine mission is to carry civilisation, liberty and prosperity to the uttermost bounds of the earth'.[92] This may well have been so, but what Theodores was speaking of were the consequences of Reform, not the causes. What Reform represented, in Manchester, and probably elsewhere in England, was the impact of currents of thought emanating from Germany.

This is not to rule out the probability that many individuals made their choice from social, political, and cultural considerations which were often confused and inconsistent. What it does suggest is that the form of choice available had its origins in Germany. In 1845 Abraham Rice, perhaps the first American orthodox rabbi, wrote from Baltimore: 'the sparks from the burning [in Germany] are already kindling a flame in our dwelling',[93] and it was these same sparks which set Manchester alight. In Manchester Reform was first publicised by Theodores, in whom the ideological links with Germany were at their most explicit, and who provided the movement with such continuity as it possessed. Other factors—localism, the 'pretensions' of 'overweening ecclesiastics', associations with London Reform, cultural sophistication—explain chiefly why, at various stages, individuals and groups pledged their allegiance to Theodores.

In the last analysis, it was Theodores' German following which decided the issue. Of the forty-six founder members of Park Place, twenty-nine were of German birth, and, of these, sixteen were drawn from the urban centres—Hamburg, Frankfurt, Leipzig, Cologne, Essen and Berlin—in which religious modernism was at its strongest. All twenty-nine had been brought up in the highly assimilative milieu of post-war Germany, and arrived in Manchester only after 1834. With the exception of the Micholls brothers, and John Michael Isaac of Salford, Jewish families which had their English origins before 1820 played no part in Reform, and those of English birth—Benjamin Hyam, Simon Joseph, Joseph Hyman (born in Plymouth in 1821), Eleazer Moses and Joseph Slazenger Moss, for example—were amongst the most conservative members of the community. It was certainly not the case that Reform followed logically and inevitably from a process of social and cultural acclimatisation. On the contrary, it might be argued with greater force that Reform in Manchester was an expression within the Jewish milieu of the growing national consciousness and social solidarity of German immigrants which found its secular expression in the opening of a German newsroom, library and cultural centre —the *Schiller Anstalt*—in Cooper Street, in July 1860.[94] It is perhaps not without significance that the first chairman of the *Anstalt* was an assimilated Jew, Dr Louis Borchardt, the second a Reformer, Louis Behrens, and that there were altogether too many Jews in the society for the mildly anti-Semitic taste of Friedrich Engels.[95]

But although Reform in Manchester is perhaps best regarded as a foreign import which subsequently gained adherents from local causes, it also has a place in the internal history of the community. The process by which Manchester Jews devised institutions to reflect what Hesse described as their advance on 'the Social Scale', and which began in 1825, or even earlier, three times encountered situations in which the direction of its development became a matter of doubt. In 1844 the question posed was whether the community should submit to the guidance of a plutocracy or rest its congregational structure of privilege and power upon a more representative base. The issue was a fairly clear-cut one of class interest, and it was settled as soon as it became clear that the middle classes as a whole had most to gain from an extended oligarchy. Matters of religion were not at stake. The second moment of decision came during 1851–53, when a feeling gained ground that the community's interests might be better served by an autonomous rabbinate than by continued subjection to the Chief Rabbi in London. This feeling may well have achieved a measure of religious independence for Manchester, and so altered the course of Anglo-Jewish history, had the issue not been complicated by the apparent inseparability of local autonomy and Reform. It became clear that a decision on local independence could not be reached before the community decided the quesion of whether its religious life should proceed into Reform, or remain within the framework of orthodoxy defined by the Chief Rabbi. During 1856 Theodores and Dr Adler posed the ideological and ritual alternatives very precisely, and it was then left to every individual to make up his mind between them. The divisions, even the friendships, of 1844 became irrelevant, as former radicals like David Cowen, Michael Goldstone and Louis Beaver opted for orthodoxy, while their old leader, Hesse, finally threw in his lot with Reform. The unanimity which had brought the Local Rabbinate into existence was also shattered.

Some of those who opted for Reform, like the Straus brothers from Frankfurt, were already under its influence before they left Germany during the 1830s, but there were others, of English origin, who made their choice on the basis of cultural, social, political, and even aesthetic considerations, and it was for this reason that families were divided within themselves, often tragically, in a way which would not have been possible in 1844. In December 1858 Elizabeth Isaac, a kinswoman of the Franklins and sister-in-law of J. M. Isaac, who became a member at Park Place, wrote to her mother, sisters and brothers, who remained within the orthodox communion:

. . . nor have I had cause to regret the step as I never became a reformer (in the true acceptance and *groundlessly* dreaded title of the word) but have always maintained unaltered the pure religious ideas of our 'Holy Faith' inculcated by you from my earliest infancy . . . I have fully enjoyed that pure devotional spirit which characterises the well-conducted service [at Park Place].[96]

Although she would not turn her back on Reform, she wrote that she wished to be buried near her brother in the orthodox burial ground at Prestwich: 'still if such a movement be repugnant to you my loved ones, is left for you to decide'.[97] Dr Adler's insistence on the exclusiveness of the orthodox cemetery divided the community even in death. Other families were also ripped apart by conscience. S. L. Behrens remained orthodox (though remote) while his cousins, Louis and Rudolph, chose Reform. Horatio Micholls was the first president of the Reformers; his uncle and senior partner, Philip Lucas, although vacillating, remained orthodox. The Segré sisters, one of whom was married to Isaac Franklin, were orthodox; their aunt, Sarah Isaac, widow of John Michael Isaac, was a moderate Reformer. Others wavered between the two congregations. In October 1859 three Reformers returned to the orthodox fold, two founder members of the Great Synagogue moved to Park Place, and one member of the community opted to rent seats in both.[98] In November 1859 it was reported that 'the two congregations are on amicable terms, with few exceptions, and both are increasing in numbers'.[99]

Many who joined Park Place during the years 1858–60 saw Reform, like David Einhorn, an American rabbi, as 'the liberation of Judaism for the sake of preventing an estrangement from Judaism',[100] and as the means of recovering lost Jewish souls. Their hopes were only partially realised. When, in April 1859, a leader in the *Jewish Chronicle* attacked 'prosperous foreign-born' Jews in London, Manchester and Liverpool for cutting themselves off from the synagogue and the community,[101] 'A Foreign Resident' of Manchester replied:

It is quite true that the educated classes kept aloof from the synagogue till lately, but this was equally true in the case of English and foreign Jews, but since a synagogue worship has been introduced more in harmony with their ideas they subscribe money freely, and to a considerable extent attend public worship.[102]

The editor of the *Chronicle* commented that he was pleased to hear that foreign Jews were playing a greater part in communal life in Manchester than in London, but that he still believed 'there are numbers of German Jews at Manchester who are not even known as co-religionists'.[103] This was true enough. Reform had little effect upon the many German-Jewish mercantile families which had arrived in Manchester prior to 1830 and whose cultural and religious assimilation was far advanced. Many later arrivals—H. J. Leppoc, Dr Louis Borchardt and Harry Hiller, for example—were not attracted back to the fold. But Reform opened the door to others—Leopold Amschel, Harry Lazarus, Marcus von Raalte, Leopold Dreschfeld, Jacob Da Costa—whose allegiance to Judaism would otherwise have been irretrievably lost. But its most important effect, in this context, was to provide the community with a religious safety-net for the future—a means of retaining the loyalty of assimilated families whose subsequent distaste for traditional Judaism might otherwise have entailed their departure from the faith. In the generation which followed the initial controversy, the families of Joseph Salzenger Moss, Abraham Franks and Eleazer Moses, amongst others, made the short journey from Derby Street to Park Place. Perhaps the greatest service of Reform was that, in this sense, it retained within the community the expertise and resources of assimilated suburban families—like the Lazarus-Langdons[104] and the Hesses—whose contacts, wealth, civic knowledge, and experience of Gentile institutions were thus made available to serve Jewish causes. In succeeding years, as even Nathan Laski was prepared to concede,[105] Jewish charitable and educational agencies in Manchester owed much of their character, and some of their effectiveness, to the experience and predilections of the Reformers.

In so far as the Manchester Reform controversy had a victor, it was the Chief Rabbi. First by limiting the power of the Local Rabbinate, and then by laying down in uncompromising terms the only possible pattern of orthodoxy, he had undermined a strong movement towards local independence and so consolidated the foundations of a centrally controlled uniformity upon which the United Synagogue was subsequently built. It has been suggested that a centralised system in English was secured by the outcome of a conflict in the Portsmouth Community in the 1760s which vindicated the primacy of the Rabbi of Duke's Place, but equally important was the outcome of the crisis of the 1850s, when the Chief Rabbi was called upon to deal with the threat of local autonomy. In Manchester those who wanted independence were skilfully isolated and contained within a relatively small Reform Congregation.

V

What is to be made of the enigmatic Dr Schiller-Szinessy? By 21 October 1856, when he preached at Margaret Street, he believed that David Marks' radical views on the Oral Law were

nothing more than I have invariably taught in public and private . . . a doctrine from which I have seen no occasion to swerve in mature years.[106]

With equal self-deception, he spoke to his Manchester flock of the way in which his attempts to lead Halliwell Street along a path of '*moderate improvement*' had been frustrated by men of questionable motives.[107] He credited himself with changes,[108] two of which—the introduction of sermons, and of religious instruction at the Jews' School—preceded his arrival in Manchester, while another—the partial abolition of the *Piyyutim*—took place after his departure from the Old Congregation and on the initiative of men who remained well within the orthodox fold. Of the remaining innovation—'the institution of an English service on behalf of departed souls'—there is no evidence either way. Such changes as are known to have been made at Halliwell Street owed little or nothing to Dr Schiller. At the same time, he suggested to the Reformers that it was on the initiative of their own 'active members' that he had been first appointed to the position of Local Rabbi, implying that he had remained loyal to those—'of a *progressive* turn of mind'[109]—whose interests he had first been called upon to serve. This ignores, amongst other matters, the part played in the initial negotiations by such conservatives as Eleazer Moses, Simon Joseph and Isaac Franklin, and, even more, the unanimity which had characterised both his appointment and his re-election. No doubt this interpretation suited the Reformers themselves, who might now characterise themselves as the pressure group which, through Dr Schiller, had sought an enlightened improvement of the forms of public worship in face of diehard resistance of dubious integrity, but it does not fit the facts of the case, which indicate not a small group exerting pressure but a general desire for improvement which only gradually narrowed itself down to a minority demand for Reform. The relations between Dr Schiller on the one hand and Dr Adler and the Select Committee on the other until after the Hull affair suggest that he was not associated with Reform until the exploratory meeting in Micholls' house on 3 May 1856. Even then, his subsequent appointment as minister at Park Place has all the appearance of a compromise forced upon the Reformers by the absence of more committed candidates.

His account of himself as the conciliatory guide whose only regret was that 'the Israelites in the city could not agree on one superior principle in which all difficulties might have been merged'[110] plays down the soaring ambition and political ineptitude which provoked his first clash with the Select Committee, and which led him to seek a basis of rabbinical power beyond Halliwell Street, even in Hull, and finally in Reform. He once complained that he had been wrongly portrayed at Halliwell Street both as a radical who hoped for 'extraordinary' innovations, and as a conservative who 'mainly laboured to replunge the congregation . . . into the religious barbarism of the Middle Ages',[111] but such views were understandable in the light of his flirtations first with an immigrant *chevra* and then with the Reform Association. Perhaps he did want moderate change, but if so he proposed no programme which would have achieved it. But if he seemed to latch on to any movement which might serve his own ambition, it was also true that each movement in turn used that ambition for its own ends—the Old Congregation, in 1851–52, to symbolise communal pride and cement communal reunion, the 'New Congregation' in Hull, to substantiate its official standing, the Reformers, to obtain ministerial guidance. The group at Hull disintegrated during 1856. In Manchester, the Old Congregation dispensed with his services as soon as it sensed the religious danger of a Local Rabbinate, Reform as soon as a minister of more radical disposition became available.

The settlement of 1858 did not satisfy everyone's taste. On Red Bank the *Chevra Tehillim* continued, even without Dr Schiller's services.[112] In the Great Synagogue there were some who believed that the congregation had leaned too far in its attempt to appease the Reformers. In December 1859 a group of about thirty members—calling themselves the 'United Brothers'—seceded to set up a rival congregation, 'upon ultra-orthodox principles',[113] which remained apart until September 1860, when it was agreed that

the building at present occupied by the dissatisfied members for the purpose of worship shall for the object of peace forthwith be closed, and entirely discontinued, and each member [shall be] expected to pay his arrears on his return.[114]

Even then, 'ultra-orthodoxy' remained a source of instability. The composition of the Reform Congregation, on the other hand, reflected the diversity of its origins. Those, like Theodores, who were ideologically committed to advanced Reform on the German pattern chafed at the concessions—particularly the observance of Second Days—which had been made to the more conservative English families in order to secure their initial support. When, in the spring of 1860, this advanced group moved into the open and carried a resolution abolishing Second Days, an internal storm ensued, of which the only external evidence was the resignation of Dr Schiller. There was a limit to the changes which even he could countenance, and, to meet his reservations, the committee agreed not to make the change until after the appointment of his successor.[115] Good relations were apparently maintained. At a confirmation service in May, an address by Dr Schiller

contained several feelingly-expressed allusions to his approaching departure from Manchester, and to the kindly relations that had subsisted for years between the pastor and the majority of the flock.[116]

At the Great Synagogue, however, he had left a legacy of bitterness. When, in September 1860, he sought an open testimonial to his former ministry at Halliwell Street, the Select Committee sent a note:

This is to certify that Rev. Dr Schiller-Szinessy officiated in the capacity of Minister to this Congregation from the year 1851 to the year 1856, during which time his religious and moral character was unexceptionable.[117]

When he protested at so perfunctory a reference, the wardens at first replied curtly that 'the Certificate having been furnished to him, the Committee cannot provide him with any other',[118] but, on reflection, they noted that 'some Gentlemen have volunteered to form themselves into a Committee for the purpose of carrying out his views'.[119] Dr Schiller's services to the Jews School, where he remained superintendent until his departure, won him the firm friendship of men like Isaac Franklin, who found his religious views and political pretensions unacceptable, and it was they who now rallied to his support. Horatio Micholls, as president at Park Place, added a testimonial to his Reform ministry, on 3 October 1860,[120] and with these secured Dr Schiller retired to the Cheshire countryside, where he supported himself by taking private pupils before embarking on an academic career in Cambridge in 1863.[121] Margoliouth concluded: 'Manchester soon became too little for his speculative mind.'[122] His successor at Park Place, in keeping with the forces which had become dominant there, was Gustav Gottheil, a young man of advanced views, who was then assistant rabbi at the Reform Congregation in Berlin.

At the Great Synagogue, meantime, the orthodox recalled David Meyer Isaacs of Liverpool, at first on a basis similar to that on which he had been engaged by the Manchester Hebrew Association during the period 1838–42. At Seel Street, where his services had been retained, according to a Manchester critic, chiefly 'for Pride and show',[123] Isaacs had become the centre of dispute during 1849–51 after he had resigned on the grounds of the inadequacy of his salary and the insecurity of his tenure, and the congregation had divided on the issue of whether or not to reinstate him.[124] Pride proved decisive. Since the Chief Rabbi could not persuade Isaacs to request his own re-engagement, nor the Select Committee to invite his return, the position reached stalemate, and in 1851 Isaacs resolved his own future by accepting the ministry of the New Liverpool Congregation, then in Pilgrim Street.[125] He took with him a small group of supporters led by Godfrey Levi, a bookseller, accountant and optician, who settled in Manchester in 1852, and in 1855 accepted the post of salaried secretary at Halliwell Street. Levi was amongst the members of the Old Congregation who in March 1858 pressed the Select Committee to invite Isaacs to deliver a sermon at the Great Synagogue on the first Sabbath after its inauguration.[126] In the following month, he was offered a contract to deliver sermons on alternate Sabbaths for one trial year, at £150,[127] and when Philip Dessau resigned to return to Hamburg in January 1859 a deputation from the synagogue went to see him in Liverpool 'to ascertain whether he would officiate as Resident Minister and Reader, and give Religious Instruction'.[128] Terms could not be agreed, since Isaacs held out for a salary (£350) which would have entailed a 15 per cent increase in seat rents which the members would not sanction, and, instead, his contract was extended for three years (to 1862), to include religious instruction on Sundays, at an increased retainer of £200 a year.[129]

Isaacs was perfectly suited to the subdued mood of the orthodox community following five years of stormy controversy. There was no question of another Local Rabbinate. Although occasionally overbearing towards his colleagues, he was never anything but deferential to the Chief Rabbi, and, at all events, he lacked the rabbinical qualifications which had sustained Dr Schiller's hopes of independence. He had interested himself in Hebrew literature in Liverpool, where he had acted as founder president of a Literary Hebraic Society in 1844,[130] collaborated with Moses Samuel in producing a short-lived literary periodical, the *Cup of Salvation* (1846–47),[131] and taught Hebrew at Queen's College.[132] Picciotto wrote of him: 'Though not an Englishman, his accent and fluent acquaintance with the English language would proclaim him of English birth.'[133] Dignified, scholarly, urbane, sophisticated, anglicised, he provided the Great Synagogue with the 'Pride and show' it required after an important movement of secession, and with a period of religious calm based upon the enlightened orthodoxy which had evolved during the negotiations of 1856–57. In June 1862 the Old Congregation finally found the means to finance his permanent appointment, and in August he left Liverpool after serving the two congregations there for over twenty-seven years.[134]

11   The immigrant poor, 1861–74

The dominating feature of communal history in the decade which followed the Reform schism was the very rapid expansion of Eastern European settlement in Manchester and the consequent emergence on Red Bank of an immigrant 'colony' which by 1871 embraced well over a third of the total Jewish population. This represented more than a change in scale. In creating a distinct pattern of culture and generating poverty of an unprecedented kind, the immigrants posed a direct threat to the values and image of the Anglo-Jewish community. The nature of this threat, and the form of the Anglo-Jewish response, provide the 1860s with their central themes.

I

The strong, and finally deterrent, reactions of Anglo-Jewry to the growth of casual poverty in the years 1851–52, 1854–55 and 1857–58, suggest that immigration was a continuous process during the decade. Certainly, the population of Red Bank tripled during 1850s to a total of 430 by 1861. But it was the 1860s which proved crucial in the creation of a new style of Anglo-Jewish community, in other centres as well as Manchester, in which Eastern Europeans constituted a major, and sometimes a predominant, element. The increasing concentration of provincial Anglo-Jewry in the larger industrial towns during the second half of the nineteenth century is often treated as if it involved no more than a reshuffling of the existing population.[1] In fact, this was only part of the case. Equally important—in the long run, perhaps more important— was the settlement of new Eastern European immigrants in those growing centres of industry which seemed to hold out the best economic prospects.

The turning point was perhaps the outbreak of the American Civil War in April 1861.[2] As the attractions of the New World were temporarily dimmed—'suspended' was the word used by the *Jewish Chronicle*[3]— the government's Commissioners at Liverpool reported, in July 1861, that emigration to the United States had 'decreased to an enormous extent'.[4] In June alone 5,490 fewer persons crossed the Atlantic than in the same month of the preceding year, and the slump continued at least until May 1862. Although the pace quickened during 1862–63, conditions in America in 1864 again persuaded many who had set out hopefully for New York to settle for destinations in England, particularly those, like Manchester, in which an Eastern European nucleus already existed.[5] The effects were cumulative, for the larger the immigrant settlements in England became, and the more organised the Anglo-Jewish agencies for their support, the greater was their appeal to later passengers. By the time the full flow of migration to America was renewed during 1865, English centres of Jewish population had begun to exercise a strong independent appeal. Towards the end of 1866 the *Jewish Chronicle* wrote of the

vast numbers of foreigners who, to escape the hardship of a military service at home, have sought asylum in this hospitable country, many of whom have taken up residence in this northern metropolis, whose wealth and charity seem to have gained a continental reputation.[6]

Developments in Eastern Europe increased the urgency of emigration. The defeat of the Polish uprising of 1863—itself the climax of a long 'state of effervescence' and unrest in Russian Poland[7]—was followed by the severe punishment of Jewish participants. Famine struck Lithuania in 1866, cholera spread through the Russian Pale of Settlement during 1868, and in the following year the whole of Western Russia and Eastern Prussia was submerged by 'pinching want and commercial stagnation', with typhus 'completing what the ravages of hunger had initiated'.[8] Manchester experienced an 'unforeseen influx of Jewish poor' during 1869–70,[9] and a Liverpool relief agency spoke of 'the casual poor, principally Poles . . . driven from their unhappy country, either through political causes or the scarcity of food' who begged their way to England.[10] Anti-Jewish outrages in Odessa and other towns in South Russia during 1871 added to the many incentives for departure. By 1873–74 Manchester was experiencing 'a continuous immigration from Poland, Russia and the Principalities'.[11]

The overall effect of the migrations of the 1860s and early 1870s was to consolidate Jewish life in the growing urban centres of the north-west, the north-east, the industrial Midlands, South Wales, and the West Riding of Yorkshire. In Leeds, where an organised congregational life had been developing very slowly since the 1820s,[12] the migration of the 1860s took the Jewish population to over sixty families, mostly very poor, 'strict in their observance', and concentrated even then in the Leylands district.[13] By 1866 'great numbers' of immigrants had settled in Hull.[14] Elsewhere in the north-east, the 'backlog' effect caused by the American Civil War had given rise to thriving communities in Newcastle, West Hartlepool, North and South Shields, Sunderland and

Middlesbrough.[15] In Middlesbrough, the number of Jewish families rose from only one in 1862 to fifty (or about three hundred persons) in 1873, when the congregation built a new and larger synagogue in Bretnall Street.[16] The new settlers were spoken of as 'really hard-working men, striving by dint of toil to obtain a livelihood'.[17] Of the thousand Jews in Newcastle by 1873 the majority were poor immigrants who had arrived within the preceding decade direct from Poland via Hamburg and Hull.[18] It was this influx which completed the eclipse of the older communities of the southern sea-ports and market towns. The congregations at Bedford, Ipswich and Colchester disappeared during the 1870s, and others which suffered a drastic reduction in size included Norwich, Exeter and Falmouth, as the settled population gravitated (with the immigrants) to newer industrial towns.[19] In these the immigrant presence was so pronounced by 1872 that the *Jewish Chronicle* could claim that provincial communities in general were distinguished from London by the predominance of their 'foreign element'.[20]

This was certainly true of Manchester, which, as the largest industrial town on the northern route of transmigration and the last before the port of embarkation for America, probably received the most substantial access of immigrant settlers during the 1860s. The number of persons of Russian or Polish birth rose from 325 in 1861 to 1,200 in 1871, or from 19 to 35 per cent of the total Jewish population,[21] and these figures do not include the English-born children of immigrant parents. In 1861 27 per cent of Manchester's Jewish population was of Polish birth or parentage, and the proportion had risen to over 50 per cent by 1871. The number of pupils at the Jews School rose from 217 in 1859 to 379 in 1868 and 609 in 1873,[22] and so great was the proportion of immigrants that in 1872 the school committee put pressure on the new Manchester School Board to appoint a special officer to enforce their attendance.[23] The population of Red Bank again trebled during the 1860s, to a total of 1,153 persons, as most immigrants were drawn to the cheapest housing within easy reach of the communal facilities,[24] and to a district already settled by their *landsleit* of an earlier period. In the three Censuses of 1851–71, the proletariat on Red Bank comprised successively 12, 24 and 33 per cent of Manchester's growing Jewish population.

II

Until the early 1860s Red Bank was regarded by Manchester's Anglo-Jewish leaders as a peripheral slum district, the home of Eastern European families certainly, but not in sufficient numbers to provide a viable basis for a separate social and religious life. Although the immigrants of the later 1840s and early 1850s had created a distinctive economy based upon the small domestic work-shop, they had tended to seek their social fortunes within the established Anglo-Jewish community. Most had worshipped at the Old Congregation, where by 1860 many had become seat-holders and a few of the more ambitious were seeking the privileges of Free Membership.[25] Successful immigrant entrepre-neurs had married into established families, sent their children to the Jews School, and moved upwards from the Irk Valley into the middle-class residen-tial districts of Cheetham Hill and Strangeways. The immigrants lacked the coherence to think in terms of their collective interest, and, even if they had done so, would have lacked the means to achieve it. The effect of the more ex-tensive settlement of the 1860s was to make corporate existence a viable propo-sition, particularly since newer immigrants could count at least upon the finan-cial support of the *nouveaux riches* of an earlier generation. The result was a 'moral Poland'[26]—a distinct and strictly observant Jewish society based upon the exclusive *Yiddishkeit* of the Eastern European ghetto and sustained both by an expanding galaxy of *chevroth* and by an informal network of close personal, family and economic connections. For the most part, the immigrants spent their days together in cramped workshops, returned late in the evening to the densely crowded tenements of Fernie Street, sent their children to private *chedarim*, and worshipped together in their 'chapels-of-ease'.[27]

It was in the 1860s that the *chevra* became established as an integral part of immigrant life. There the Polish newcomer found a familiar warmth and infor-mality lacking in the decorum and English rhetoric of the Old Congregation; respect, friendship and advice in a strange environment; seats and honours at low cost, when membership of the Great Synagogue was expensive, and often unattainable at any price. The first *chevra* in Manchester, the *Chevra Tehillim* of 1854, revived during the 1860s and was still a going concern, with thirty members, in 1872, when its representatives attended a meeting at the Old Congregation.[28] The foundation of new bodies kept pace with immigration and often reflected its origin. On the First Day of the Feast of Tabernacles, 1865, immigrants from Kovno in Lithuania founded the *Chevra Torah* (the Society of the Holy Law) in a private house in Park Place where seats were priced at 3*d* a week.[29] By 1872 there were sixty members, but since only half paid their subscriptions regularly, providing a weekly income of 15*s* against an expendi-ture of 27*s* 6*d*, survival was made possible only by voluntary offerings.[30] The same was true of the *Cracow Chevra*, founded at 6 Dale Street, Red Bank, in 1868 to provide its members with 'divine service and good actions'.[31] In 1872 it had thirty members—including some of the community's leading water-proofing entrepreneurs—and its own salaried Reader, Joshua Passelchawski.[32]

The *Chevra Walkawishk* was founded in 1871 by Lithuanians from the neighbourhood of Walkawishk who, according to tradition, knocked away a wall separating two back yards in Fernie Street and worshipped under corrugated metal sheeting.[33] The *Warsaw Chevra*, founded at about the same time, had thirty-five members by 1872, when each paid 3*d* a week.[34] The secretary of the Old Congregation calculated that there were at least fifteen *chevroth* in Manchester by 1876, with a total membership 'alarmingly large'.[35]

Although no indigenous record of their inner life survives, it is clear from external sources that they served as the social and religious centres of immigrant life. A report in the *Jewish Chronicle* of the consecration of a new scroll at the *Cracow Chevra* in December 1868,[36] provides some insight into the order of priorities, of which the first was divine worship, the second charity, and the third study:

It may be that the study of the Law is much neglected in England and America, but nevertheless the principles of the Thora are professed by our brethren everywhere.

In his speech to invited guests, Simon Weiss, the President, stressed the relief work of the *chevra*'s auxiliary organisation, the Cracow Hebrew Friendly Society (later the Cracow Benevolent Society):

. . . if a countryman of ours comes to Manchester, and is in need of charity, our society relieves him as quickly as possible, in order that he may not go about half-starved, until he collects a few shillings for a new start in life, and for this new start in life we assist him with money and good advice.

I think everyone of us ought to feel the necessity of visiting the sick, for we are here in a foreign country, having few or no relatives and scarcely any friends. When we are sick in bed, and even not in want of relief, we would give anything to have somebody to talk with. All of us are hard working for our daily bread. While we are in health and can move about, we may meet with some friends; but when we are confined to a sick room, nobody would know what has become of us but for this society. In our native places we have relations and friends to visit us during sickness; but in England, some of us have wives, but many of us are single, often lodging with persons of a different religion.

The room in Dale Street was a temporary expedient. It was hoped 'that our society will prosper, and that we shall be able in a short time to lay a foundation stone of a synagogue'.

It was this ambition of each *chevra* to remain independent and become permanent which hardened opinion against them within the Anglo-Jewish community. First and foremost, they were seen as serious obstacles to a process of cultural assimilation upon which the future repute of the community was believed to depend. By promoting an insular religious and social life they delayed indefinitely 'the transformation of Polish into English Jews'.[37] They provided the kind of advice and material support which kept the immigrant out of reach of the assimilatory influences of established charities. They projected the wrong kind of image. Their buildings—like that of the 'Tin Schule'—were frequently makeshift and squalid, their proceedings often disorderly and occasionally turbulent. They were a financial threat to the Old Congregation, since their members took advantage of congregational facilities (*shechita*, for example), looked to the synagogue for *matzoth* at Passover, and attended its overflow services on the High Holy days, without contributing to its funds. Occasionally they provided cheap illicit services such as the *Shtille Choopah*, or secret marriage, correctly performed according to Jewish rites but not registered by the State. Such a marriage might satisfy an immigrant family, particularly since it evaded the official charges and the strict investigatory procedures of the Chief Rabbi's Office, but it was quite unacceptable to the Old Congregation. According to one official, secret marriages were 'surely not different from co-habitation practised by only the lowest classes of the other sects'.[38] They represented another loss of revenue to the synagogue. They increased the difficulty of fixing upon the head of the family the legal obligation of supporting his wife and children, particularly if he had deserted them. To the middle-class English Jew, the semi-autonomy of the *chevroth* was presumptuous, its cultural isolation dangerous, its ethos unacceptable.

III

The material condition of Red Bank was as sharply distinguished from that of neighbouring Anglo-Jewish districts as its pattern of culture. In 1866 one observer, himself Jewish, spoke sadly of the 'overcrowding of the miserably furnished houses' in which the immigrants were 'compelled to seek shelter',[39] in streets where, even under communal pressure, landlords undertook only the minimum of work required to render their houses habitable. It was a densely populated working-class district of 'close, dirty, ill-ventilated and ill-drained habitations', according to Isaac Franklin, who spoke in 1870 of the high rate of infant mortality and the rapid spread of infectious diseases.[40] Other evidence suggests that immigrant Jews took to cellar-dwellings as readily as the immigrant Irish.[41]

For the most part, the new immigrants drifted into the narrow range of trades established by their predecessors. The *Jewish Chronicle* pressed the advantages of diversification,[42] but other opportunities were restricted by the real difficulty of discovering new unskilled openings in industries in which Jews could work together without placing their religious observance at risk. The 'immigrant trades' also continued to offer a fairly swift upward mobility to the more enterprising. Early in 1860 Edward Marcuse, a cap maker, paid 8s a week for an upper room in Shudehill, where he worked up material supplied on credit by wholesale warehouses. The work was done by hand, and on too small a scale for Marcuse to buy in cloth and deal directly with retailers, until the owner of the property was persuaded to provide two sewing machines on a weekly rental and to purchase material on Marcuse's behalf for a 15 per cent interest on his costs. By March 1861 Marcuse was supplying retailers direct. He had taken a second room, at an additional rental of £30 a year, and owned stock to the value of £600.[43] Finally, the rambling houses of Red Bank lent themselves to the workshop trades. A family in Fernie Street, and its lodgers, was a domestic work-force in which there was a place for the women and children, as well as for the men. By 1871 almost a quarter of all piece-work tailors, and over a third of all cap makers, were women. On several occasions during the 1860s the committee of the Jews School complained that the education of immigrant children was 'interrupted and irregular', since they were 'taken away capriciously from school at an early age' by parents eager to put them 'as soon as possible to profitable use'.[44] The immigrant trades—tailoring, cap making, waterproofing, shoemaking, slipper making, glaziery and cabinet making—accounted for 57 per cent of Manchester's employed Jewish population (or 617 persons) in 1871, as against just over 34 per cent ten years earlier.

Although the workshop trades suffered from the disadvantages of fluctuating demand, there was usually scope for the temporarily unemployed in glaziery or some other form of street hawking. An observer of 1871 wrote:

Of the poor foreigners we find in our streets, the glaziers and sponge and wash-leather dealers are mostly Jews, and generally either Austrian or Polish. The men with organs and the image men are Italians, the bagpipe men and the marmot boys are either Savoyards, Neapolitans, or Tyrolese; so that in other words commerce is represented by Jews, and music and the fine arts by Italians.[45]

The 618 Jewish persons in full-time employment at the time of the Census of 1861 included sixty-eight itinerant dealers, and in 1871 the ninety hawkers and travellers still comprised 8 per cent of the employed population. But they were neither country traders nor even urban pedlars on a permanent basis. Some were the well-paid travelling representatives of established firms; most were recent immigrants seeking temporary support, many before finding their economic feet in the workshop trades. In 1871 one Polish waterproofer survived in the off-seasons by travelling in jewellery during the winter and by photography during the summer months;[46] another described himself evocatively to the Census enumerator as a 'waterproofer and glazier'. Glaziery, in particular, emerged as a common form of subsistence during periods of unemployment, particularly during the later 1860s, when Lazarus Caro, himself a Polish immigrant, established a glass warehouse in Long Millgate, where he was prepared to advance credit of up to £4 for the completion of small contracts.[47] By 1871 glaziery was said to be attracting at least two new immigrants every week. The number of hawkers applying for Passover Relief between 1864 and 1870 fell from twenty to two, while the number of glaziers increased from ten to seventy-three over the same period.[48]

The thrift of the immigrants became well known. They were seen by the Manchester public as essentially 'sober and economical, hard-working and uncomplaining'.[49]

When once a poor foreigner obtains a start he is almost sure to succeed, especially if he be a Jew. He lives, thrives and saves money where an Englishman . . . would starve. I have known these men when not earning more than a shilling a day saving never less than six pence, and sometimes as much as ninepence of it. Two-pence or three-pence for lodgings and two pence for bread would be the sum total of their disbursements for the day . . .[50]

But even at times of fullest employment (from April to July, and from October to December), the workshop trades provided the majority of immigrant workers with no more than the barest means of support. Early in the 1870s it was said of the 'poorer class of Jewish tailors and needlewomen' that 'by working hard and late' they earned 'at best a scanty subsistence'.[51] The threat of legal action against Sunday working in domestic workshops—after complaints of disturbance from their Gentile neighbours—caused panic in the Manchester tailoring trade in 1871, since it would have entailed the loss of a day's earnings in the summer and one and a half days during the winter, when only 'the very hardest work' for six days a week provided a living wage.[52] The 'Manchester Grievance' was taken up by the *Jewish Chronicle*; the chairman of the local Poor Law Union expressed his sympathy; and the Town Clerk was finally persuaded to take no further proceedings.[53]

The growth of the immigrant population was accompanied by a substantial increase of resident poverty. Passover relief from the Old Congregation—in the form of *matzoth* and provisions for anyone in genuine need—was given to ninety-four families (318 persons) in 1860, 167 families (431 persons) in 1866, and 283 families (707 persons) in 1869, and expenditure on winter relief rose from £101 in 1860–61 to £190 in 1862–63 and £239 in 1865–66.[54]

There were also special problems related directly to the processes of immigration. Those who arrived without capital and skill—probably the large majority—required some form of support until they had accustomed themselves to the 'language and trading customs' of England,[55] so that by the later

1860s and early 1870s each high-water mark of immigration was accompanied by a substantial increase in the number of applications for relief. There was also the 'crying evil'[56] of deserted families, left behind in Manchester for the most part by menfolk who had gone ahead to establish a secure means of livelihood in the United States. Although most frequently a form of temporary collusion, in which a man expected his wife and children to seek relief until such time as he could send for them,[57] the deserted family presented the community with one of its 'most difficult subjects',[58] particularly when the father disappeared, and one which at times of especially heavy immigration was likely to increase 'in an alarming ratio'.[59] When conditions on the Continent made repatriation impracticable—during the Franco–Prussian War, for example—the community was particularly 'severely taxed both for means and ways how to act' towards helpless women and their starving children.[60]

Moreover, beyond the special conditions closely linked to the flow of immigration was the special form of poverty associated with Eastern European settlement. The resident poverty of the 1860s and 1870s was not for the most part that of occasional individual misfortune such as overtook the country hawker, the old or the infirm, but a regular condition of need which arose out of the very nature of a working-class industrial economy resting upon uncertain and seasonal demand and highly sensitive to the fluctuating fortunes of the cotton trade. This lesson was first brought home during the years 1862–64 by the distress of the Lancashire Cotton Famine in which poorer Jews were said to have shared 'to the fullest extent'.[61] At least five Jewish cap makers failed during 1861–62 alone,[62] and no doubt other workshops cut down on their labour costs, as even the largest mills had been forced to do. Another cap maker, anticipating disaster, sold off his credit stock, absconded with the proceeds, and was 'not known to have been seen since in England'.[63] A Polish Jew who arrived from Le Havre in the autumn of 1862 found conditions so 'miserable' that he attempted suicide after writing a letter to the Mayor, bemoaning his 'exile' and requesting burial in a Jewish cemetery.[64] Although it took some time for the full implications of the message to sink in, the Cotton Famine gave notice to the Anglo-Jewish middle class that they now faced, for the first time, the endemic poverty arising out of the inadequate and irregular earnings of an industrial working class. By the later 1860s it was taken for granted that the extent of resident poverty would be directly related to the 'state of trade'.[65] In the long run, it was not simply the increasing scale of poverty which caused the community to reassess its structure of poor relief, but equally its changing character in an age of immigration. Most applicants for relief in the 1860s were not displaced hawkers, destitute transmigrants or resident pensioners. They were new arrivals who lacked 'mechanical knowledge'[66] or workers in the immigrant trades; 90 per cent lived in Red Bank, over half in Verdon Street and Fernie Street.[67] There again, the 'meagre condition' of immigrant parents, overcrowding and pollution provided the physical context for an unprecedented rise in the incidence of infant mortality and epidemic disease.[68]

The growing distress of the early 1860s threw into relief all the old deficiencies of the traditional mechanisms of communal welfare—its dependence upon the general and precarious income of the synagogue, the absence of a permanent and efficient system for assessing need and detecting fraud, its excessive emphasis upon the temporary and largely pragmatic relief of immediate need, its tendency to vacillate between costly generosity and harsh deterrence. There had always been individuals who had foreseen the need for reforms. Isaac Franklin had suggested a Strangers Aid Society as long ago as 1841. During 1847 Hesse and his New Congregation had sought without much success to apply the harsh principles of the New Poor Law. In 1849 the suggestion was mooted of 'a well-organised Association with an active paid Secretary under the superintendance of Gentlemen willing to give their money and time to the public good'.[69] In 1854, at Hesse's suggestion, the Old Congregation had placed a temporary financial ceiling on casual relief. In the same year Louis Behrens had canvassed the possibility of a communal workshop applying its own Benthamite test.[70] In 1855 Dr Schiller made the first public appeal on behalf of a congregational Benevolent Fund designed to provide bread, coal and other emergency supplies during the winter months to resident poor whose 'moral conduct . . . was satisfactory'.[71] It is possible that such initiatives would have given way in the later 1850s to structural changes, had not the Reform controversy intervened. A 'Joint Relief Board of the Jewish Poor of Manchester'—'composed of an equal number of gentlemen of each respective congregation'—was established during 1857 to 'concert' charitable work in the event of religious reconciliation proving impossible,[72] but the effort foundered on the ill will of the final schism. Horatio Micholls could not be persuaded to renew his support of the Board in the spring of 1858 in spite of polite reminders from the Old Congregation 'pointing out the severe distress' and stressing that funds were 'nearly exhausted'.[73] Faced with the task of solving the problem alone after the loss of many of its wealthier members to Park Place, the Old Congregation fell back on an old (but temporary) expedient:

in consequence of the present state of congregational affairs . . . it is deemed necessary . . . to suspend Relief of the Poor from the Funds of the Congregation until future events shall warrant its resumption, exceptional cases to be left to the discretion of the Treasurer.[74]

At the same time, it was said that there were between 100 and 120 Jewish families in Manchester who were 'deserving of relief'.[75] Communal charity now suffered from the additional disadvantage that it was based on only one of Manchester's major congregations, and that the least affluent.

No private charity in the Manchester community was sufficiently large or well-organised to make up for the defects of the synagogal structure. The Hebrew Philanthropic Society came nearest to doing so. To its pension fund for widows, orphans and the aged, and its scheme of assisted emigration, in 1857–58 the society added a loan service to provide selected immigrants with the basic stock or equipment required for economic independence.[76] During 1858 forty-six persons were relieved or assisted to emigrate, and twenty-three loans were granted, to be repaid in up to 179 instalments.[77] The maximum loan available was £10 and the repayments varied from 1s to £1 a week, the majority paying between 2s and 3s.[78] During 1861 the society loaned £135 in sums of between 10s and £10 and voted £65 to pensioners and intending emigrants.[79] After the Reform Schism, it was, according to the *Jewish Chronicle*, 'the only charity in which the members of the two congregations unite heartily, co-operating in the work of benevolence';[80] for the sake of peace, it was decided (on David Hesse's advice) that the president should hold office in neither congregation.[81] The society performed useful functions, some of which might well have served as models for a more far-reaching charity, but it lacked the resources and the permanent staff to investigate and handle the substantial and regular poverty of the 1860s. Other private organisations were more limited in scope. In 1853 the United Sisters Society (otherwise the Lying in Charity) helped fourteen cases of childbirth and convalescence at a cost of £13 8s 'besides the loan of clothing to mothers and infants' and the occasional provision of a trained nurse.[82] At the Jews School, the Ladies Clothing Society provided free clothing to selected applicants, and the women's committee offered 'soup and nourishment' four times a week to children of the poor 'in regular attendance'.[83] The Reformers, who were involved in all these private enterprises, had their own Winter Relief Fund designed for the (very few) needy members of their own congregation.[84] Each voluntary body had its own small coterie of subscribers, while all were entitled to a share in the proceeds of an annual Charity Ball, held for the first time in 1852.

There was also Manchester's first Jewish Friendly Society, the Hebrew Sick and Burial Benefit Society,[85] founded, probably by Joseph Slazenger Moss, who became Life President, in 1860. Unlike later Friendly Societies, this was not an essay in immigrant self-help. Essentially it was an attempt by a few Anglo-Jewish leaders—Moss, Louis Cobe, Michael Goldstone, and Ezekiel Casper—to promote a form of contributory insurance amongst 'those whose income was not adequate to meet the contingencies of sickness and death', and who might otherwise become a serious charge on synagogal funds. It was almost certainly an attempt, too, to wean the immigrants from the relief agencies of the *chevroth* towards the protective custody of their cultural betters. Members paid an entrance fee varying according to age from 4s 6d (between the ages of fifteen and thirty) to 9s, and a subscription of 4d a week, which entitled them to weekly allowances in times of sickness, to the services of the society's medical officer, to *shiva* benefits, and to free burial. Weekly allowances were paid to the sick at a rate of 8s for the first five weeks, 6s for the second, and 4s thereafter. The Society helped some immigrants to guard against special misfortune—by the mid-1860s it had about sixty members[86] —but it did nothing to alleviate more general need.

IV

During the 1850s the failure of the Anglo-Jewish leaders to revise their attitudes to poverty, although serious, did not prove fatal. Following the crisis of 1862 and the increasing pace of immigration, the problem could no longer be shelved. The community faced the prospect of poverty running out of control unless some systematic attempt was made not simply to treat the symptoms but to absorb immigrants into the economic and social fabric of communal life. This again turned on the need for an efficient and permanent administrative mechanism backed by the combined energies and resources of both Anglo-Jewish congregations. The alternative was Jewish pauperism on a scale which would endanger not simply the material and spiritual welfare of the poor themselves but the reputation and financial viability of the Anglo-Jewish community. The poor of Red Bank were potentially open to all the physical dangers and disrepute of the Gentile rookeries in Little Ireland and Angel Meadow. Cases had already been reported of immigrants being lured by promises of money and presents into conversionist meetings and workshops,[87] and an agent of the Anglican Society in Liverpool, more candid than most, wrote: 'the most persuasive missionary to the Jews is starvation'.[88] Jewish beggars were becoming so numerous on the streets that 'a class of begging-letter writers' had grown up to support them.[89] Theodores wrote:

pauperism amongst the Jews assumed too often the very worst aspects of beggary. It was heartrending to see them crawling from door to door to obtain assistance.[90]

Moreover, the unacceptable 'foreign' culture of the immigrants tended to be regarded by Anglo-Jewry as a facet of their poverty, so that the removal of the one was regarded as a prerequisite to the disappearance of the other.

Models for action existed in both the ideas and the methods of progressive English philanthropists like Mrs Louisa Twining or William Rathbone of Liverpool, who in the 1850s were beginning to seek a more informed and scientific approach to the poverty of the growing industrial town,[91] and in the attempts being made in Liverpool, London and Portsmouth to adapt such attitudes to the treatment of the Jewish poor. In Liverpool the Hebrew Mendicity Society was revived, although again only briefly, in 1853.[92] The most significant developments were in London, where, following a series of strong leaders on the subject of immigrant poverty in the *Jewish Chronicle* during the year 1857–58,[93] Lionel Louis Cohen and Ephraim Alex established the London Jewish Board of Guardians in 1859.[94] In many ways the London Board represented a new departure in Jewish poor relief. It fused the charitable functions of the three City synagogues into a single communal agency with a permanent staff of salaried officials. It employed a careful investigatory machinery both to detect fraud and to distinguish the particular deserts of each applicant. Its aim was not to provide temporary palliatives, but to find the best means of raising the poor to permanent independence. Working at first through the medical officers of the synagogues, it sought to exercise a degree of control over the sanitary condition of the immigrant quarter. The same thorough and discerning approach was adopted by the Portsmouth Hebrew Mendicity Society, founded in 1860.[95] According to the Society's founders,

Every case of poverty has its own special circumstances, and the intelligent giver has to discover how the means at his disposal may be made available to the best and most lasting advantage. Then again it is occasionally a duty to withold rather than to give.[96]

In their emphasis upon the need to examine professionally the specific needs and merits of each case, in their avoidance of indiscriminate charity in favour either of deterrence or curative relief, and in their explicit concern for the physical condition of the poor, the new initiatives in London and Portsmouth were in keeping with the most advanced thinking in the world of English philanthropy, and in this sense they were a reflection within the community of developments outside it. But they were also the first concerted attempts to cope with the new communal problems raised by extensive immigration, and it was for this reason that they had a particular relevance for other Anglo-Jewish communities.

By the early 1860s such attitudes were beginning to exercise an influence in Manchester both amongst the orthodox of the Old Congregation and at Park Place, where the external image of the community was a matter of particular concern. The Reform merchant, Philip Falk, argued that the existing 'charitable labours' of the community resulted in alleviating in a temporary manner the most pressing wants of some 80 families, without taking sufficient effectual means to encourage those who are willing to make efforts of their own to free themselves from the trammels of poverty, and to discourage that feeling of abject poverty which characterises the mere pauper.[97]

What was required, he believed, was

an efficient system of dispensing charity in a liberal, and at the same time judicious manner—protecting the public from fraud and imposition, and promoting that feeling of self-dependence and self-reliance among the poor which alone can elevate them in the social scale.[98]

But the key figure in promoting new attitudes in Manchester was Samuel Landeshut,[99] a young, ambitious and serious-minded minister of German origin, who came to the town from Bristol in June 1859 to serve as the new Reader of the Old Congregation.[100] Landeshut shared both the philosophy of the London Jewish Board of Guardians and the general outlook of the Anglo-Jewish middle class in Manchester. A systematic attack on poverty was in itself important, but it was also part of a wide-ranging assault which he launched upon the insularity of immigrant religious and cultural life. Although his methods sometimes appear piecemeal and pragmatic, at his most far-sighted he sought to reunify the whole community, drawing the Reformers as well as the *chevroth* towards the orthodox centre, and building upon it a model relief agency which would direct the combined skill and resources of community to the social and economic integration of the immigrant poor.

His earliest effort began during the Cotton Famine with an attempt to convert the Old Congregation's Benevolent Fund, which provided only temporary relief in kind during the winter months, into a communal charity on the style of the London Board. When a special appeal during the winter of 1862–63 raised more than enough to meet 'the increased misery' of the poor, the surplus of £52 was placed in a reserve fund to be applied, at some future date, 'to some institution that will have for its object the raising of the more industriously inclined to a state of comparative independence'.[101] It was with this aim in mind that he arranged a 'Conference of Gentlemen' from both congregations, which in February 1863 arrived at 'certain resolutions having a tendency to amalgamate all the Jewish charities in this City under one Head, and controlled by an efficient Board of Guardians'.[102] These resolutions received sufficient support from the general bodies of both congregations for negotiations to proceed into 1864. The Reformers expressed their desire 'to carry out the recommendations of the Conference in the spirit in which they are conceived',[103] while at the Great Synagogue the proposal of Isaac Franklin (then president of the Benevolent Fund) that the congregation should act upon them was carried, if only by twenty-six votes to twenty-four.[104] Negotiations broke down, however, ostensibly over the question of the burial of paupers, for while both congregations could agree to receive paupers into their cemeteries, and alternately to bear the cost of their burial, the Great Synagogue would not sanction the use of the Reform Prayer Book in the (unlikely) event of a Reform pauper being buried at Prestwich.[105] More fundamentally, perhaps, the bitterness of 1856–58 was still too recent to allow for co-operation even for limited objectives.

With little immediate hope of inter-congregational co-operation, Landeshut reverted to extending the scope of the Benevolent Fund within the orthodox community. A further surplus of £77 following the distribution of 1863–64 was used to establish an 'industrial committee' (based upon the practice of the London Board)

to supply artisans of known industrial habits with sewing machines or tools necessary for their trade, and well conducted hawkers with sufficient goods to enable them to obtain a livelihood; to assist parties desirous of emigrating; and to set up in business such of our poor as might be deemed deserving of such a boon.[106]

The immediate extent of these services is not known. Few cash loans were granted—only four during 1864–66—but twelve families were assisted to cross the Atlantic during 1864–65 and nineteen during 1865–66.[107] In November 1865, on the strength of a £10 donation from the Old Congregation and the free services of Isaac Franklin, it was decided that the Jewish poor should receive 'gratuitous advice and medicine' at the expense of the Fund.[108] In the following year,

the prevalence of various kinds of distress amongst our poor, the result no doubt of want, together with . . . overcrowding . . . called the services of the Medical Officer into greater requisition.[109]

From December 1865 money was raised to extend the services of the Fund throughout the year.[110] Finally, on 12 August 1866, a 'sanitary committee' was set up (again on the London model) 'to visit the habitations of the poor with regard to their cleanliness and to report thereon to the General Committee'.[111] Two of Landeshut's letters survive, one to Louis Beaver, who owned houses in Fernie Street,[112] the other to the Gentile slum landlord, James Craig.[113] Each expressed the hope of the sanitary committee

that, considering the prevalence of epidemic diseases in a neighbouring town and other parts of the kingdom, which, under Providence, cleanliness is calculated materially to prevent, you will perceive the necessity of having [your houses] white-washed without delay.

Meantime he continued to work for co-operation between Manchester's two Anglo-Jewish congregations. In answer to criticism of the Benevolent

Fund in the *Jewish Chronicle* in November 1864 he wrote:

much more might certainly be done by a united Board of Guardians. Let both parties
. . . show their earnestness in the matter by making charity independent of congregational affairs and that most desirable object will be speedily obtained.[114]

Much of the following two years was devoted to laying the basis at least of
common action, and possibly of religious reconciliation.[115] In negotiations conducted on 25 March 1866, in such secrecy that only the chance survival of
rough notes in Landeshut's hand in a Passover Relief Book reveal that they
ever took place, three representatives of the Old Congregation (Abraham
Franks, Adolphus Sington and Isaac Franklin) met three Reformers (David
Hesse, Louis Behrens and Adolph Kauffman) to consider a 'plan for
amalgamation', whose authorship (although its details are not known) may
logically be attributed to Landeshut.[116] As an attempt to fuse Orthodoxy and
Reform, the meeting was a disappointment. The Orthodox delegates laid down
conditions for unity—a fundamental revision of the Reform Prayer Book, the
exclusion of uncircumcised seat-holders from a reunited congregation, and the
strict enforcement of a single system of *shechita*—which the Reformers found
totally unacceptable, particularly since at Park Place Gottheil was at that very
time contemplating a further movement in a radical direction.

But if religious unity was out of reach, Landeshut's negotiations built up a
sufficient body of good will at Park Place to lay the basis for co-operation in
more limited endeavours. There is some evidence to suggest that, although the
Benevolent Fund remained tied to the Old Congregation and subject to the
direction of the Select Committee, individual Reformers were contributing to
its funds and participating in the work of investigation.[117] Moreover, the increasing use of the Benevolent Fund's services and their increasing cost (from
£101 in 1860 to £239 in 1866), as well as the growing expenditure on Passover Relief from congregational funds, reflected a substantial extension of immigrant poverty which could not be ignored in either congregation. At the
same time, the Benevolent Fund's work suggested the real possibility of adapting London methods to Manchester needs. Serious negotiations to this end
which began during the autumn of 1866 made rapid progress. In November
Landeshut wrote to the *Jewish Chronicle*: 'a permanent Board of Guardians will
be established, taking as its prototype the kindred institution of our brethren in
the metropolis'.[118] A provisional committee representing both congregations
convened a public meeting on 12 May 1867, under the chairmanship of Philip
Falk, at which the foundation of a Board of Guardians was formally approved.[119] A Relief Committee of twenty-one was elected at the end of

June,[120] and on 1 July, at the Jews School on Cheetham Hill Road, the Board held its first official meeting.[121] Falk served as the first president and the joint secretaries were Landeshut and the Reform merchant, Henry Samson, partner in the cotton firm Samson & Leppoc and secretary–librarian of the *Schiller Anstalt*.

V

The constitution of the Board[122]—modelled upon that of London 'almost in every respect'[123]—devised an administrative means of shifting the responsibility for poor relief from the synagogue to the community. Control was taken out of the hands of congregational officials and vested in a Board of twenty-one members, elected annually by half-guinea subscribers; funds were raised by private subscription both from individuals and from corporate bodies, which were entitled to nominate one additional delegate for each £50 subscribed. In practice, this last provision applied only to the Old Congregation, which, in return for shedding most of its burden of relief work, provided an annual subsidy of £200. In the event, the Board represented all shades of religious opinion except that of the poor themselves; of the first twenty-one elected members, eleven were Reformers, and those included the president, vice-president, the treasurer, and one of the honorary secretaries. The Reform Congregation made no corporate contribution—on the grounds that it received only a very small proportion of the taxes arising from *shechita*—but individual Reformers accounted for the most substantial part of the privately subscribed funds and played the leading role in administering them. In effect, the two Anglo-Jewish congregations pooled their resources and assumed joint responsibility for all relief work other than the distribution of *matzoth* at Passover, the arrangement of overflow services for the poor on Holy days, and the burial of paupers (all of which remained the sole responsibility of the Old Congregation)[124] and the specialised functions performed by such agencies as the United Sisters. The relief of the poor was placed beyond the influence of religious dispute (as it had not been, for example, in 1847 or in 1857–58), provided with independent funds, and underpinned by a degree of administrative continuity.

The Board aimed at being both comprehensive and consistent. Private almsgiving was actively discouraged and subscribers were given tickets describing the Board's work to hand out to all applicants for relief. The eclectic basis of congregational relief was replaced by centrally directed policies designed to discourage new pauper settlement whenever this was possible, to detect and expose fraud, and to provide those who could not be persuaded to move on, and whose needs were 'genuine', with the means of achieving economic independence. The basis was a strict investigatory procedure in which the key role was played by the Board's salaried clerk (in the first instance, Samuel Landeshut). With the help of a Relief Committee composed of three members of the Board, the clerk weighed the justice of every claim, determined the amount and nature of the relief required, and made the necessary arrangements for its administration. If the applicant was new to Manchester, he was eligible only for a single payment of 2s 6d during his first month in the City; if he could then be persuaded to move on, assistance might be given towards his emigration, or, less frequently, his repatriation. The Board inherited the Old Congregation's arrangement with the Society for the Relief of Distressed Foreigners, by which the society provided cross-Channel tickets to those helped by the Board as far as Hull. During 1868–69 the Board laid out £40 15s 8d to help 107 emigrants to reach America, and a further 143 received £65 9s 11d during 1869–70;[125] ninety-six others took advantage of an arrangement made by the Board with a Liverpool steamship company 'for the transport of emigrants at the charity rate, whether they be recipients of charity or merely deserving poor recommended by the Board'.[126] Those who opted to remain in Manchester beyond a month were provided with such temporary assistance as they required, usually in the form of 'stamped and authenticated' tickets exchangeable for fixed amounts of food, fuel, clothing or accommodation, and with the means of obtaining an immediate livelihood: at the very least, advice or employment; at most, a loan or gift of stock or equipment (a glazier's diamond, perhaps, a shoemaker's last, or a sewing machine), a cash grant (of up to £1) or an interest-free loan (of up to 10s). A register was kept of 'industrious and respectable persons of both sexes . . . desirous of obtaining situations as domestic servants or other employment', which was available for inspection at the Board's offices (in the Jews School). The Board was, of course, concerned with the many cases of exceptional need and with the support of 'the halt, the lame, the blind, and the aged' with fixed allowances, but its best efforts were directed towards recent immigrants. By far the largest proportion of all recipients of relief (83 per cent, or 2,289 persons between 1873 and 1881) were of Polish birth, and, of these, 58 per cent had resided in Manchester for under a year; 11 per cent were born in Germany, and only 3 per cent (ninety persons) in England.

Beyond the explicit aim of economic integration lay the implicit hope for cultural assimilation. From the beginning it was made a condition of relief that applicants sent children between the ages of five and thirteen to the Jews School. At first, parents were asked to present the Board's clerk with monthly certificates, signed by a teacher, as proof of the regular attendance of their children,[127] and when this did not prove sufficient a check, the Board began to keep attendance registers of its own.[128] As a result, it was believed,

though the parents on account of their ignorance of the language and customs of the country often continue to be the objects of charity, the children by the end of the education afforded by our excellent schools are brought up to be useful members of society.[129]

Soon after the foundation of the Board—on 15 October 1868—the community laid the corner-stone of a new and larger school building in Derby Street which opened in October 1869 with accommodation for seven hundred children.[130] The two organisations may be seen, perhaps, as the community's cultural earthworks, and it is significant that both were commanded by Reformers, with their special commitment to bridging the cultural divide between Jew and Gentile. Theodores wrote (in 1868): 'We wish never to be reminded of any difference between us and our fellow subjects save and except within the precincts of our house of worship.'[131] Falk's equivalent at the Jews School was the Reform merchant Edward Nathan, who had succeeded Philip Lucas as president in 1865. The Board also took such occasional measures as lay within its power to attack the more insular elements of immigrant life. On at least one occasion, relief was refused to an applicant on the grounds that he was an official of a 'clandestine society', a *chevra*.[132] Secret marriages were discouraged, partly because they increased the potential severity of desertion cases, but also for their supposed 'immorality'.[133] Those who performed secret ceremonies were threatened with an appearance before the local magistrates, who were confidently expected to hand down sentences of imprisonment with hard labour.[134] Landeshut personally saw a close link between material and cultural objectives. As Secretary of the Old Hebrew Congregation he waged a bitter war against immigrant conventicles,[135] and he tried unsuccessfully to enlist the support of the Board of Deputies in the suppression of both the *chevra* and the *Shtille Choopah*.[136] As Clerk to the Board of Guardians he sought to undermine the physical basis of immigrant isolation.

These wider objects help to explain the degree of the Board's concern for the living conditions of the poor, for their 'foreign' ways tended to be regarded as part of the culture of their poverty. A Medical Officer was appointed whose duty it was to concern himself with public health and sanitation, upon which he was to provide the Board with monthly reports. He was to establish a surgery 'near the area where the poor live' and there he was to make himself available at fixed times for consultations, to supply medicines, 'stimulants and nourishments' (including wine and brandy) at the Board's expense, and to keep a register of his patients. Whenever necessary, he was to visit the sick poor in their homes to provide whatever treatment was required. Even here, however, charity was accompanied by the 'greatest circumspection'.[137] In 1869, the Medical Officer (inevitably, Isaac Franklin) wrote that the number of his patients was swollen

by the tendency of our poor to avail themselves on the slightest grounds of this facility for professional aid, especially as when placed on the sick list, they have better hopes of profiting by the sympathies of the charitable; much caution is needful and I endeavour to exercise it so that the truly worthy and helpless shall not be confounded with the habitually idle and falsely complaining.[138]

The Board subscribed, on behalf of the poor, to a number of local hospitals, including the Royal Infirmary, where Landeshut was able to arrange for the regular provision of kosher food.[139] Another sub-committee of the Board called regularly at the homes of the poor, advised on matters of sanitation and personal cleanliness, and, in urgent cases, was empowered to make cash grants of up to 5s.

Few of the Board's methods were novel. The Hebrew Philanthropic Society had been providing interest-free loans since 1858 and medical relief since the 1830s. Visits to the houses of the poor were a regular part of the work of the United Sisters, the Manchester Hebrew Sisters Society (founded in 1866 to provide women and children with medical attention),[140] and the Ladies Clothing Society. Assisted emigration, fixed pensions and casual relief had all been part of the Old Congregation's routine work since the 1820s, medical relief since 1854. The achievement of the Board of Guardians, following on the work of the Benevolent Fund, was to bring these functions together, to provide them with a clearly-defined sense of purpose, and to focus them upon the problems of immigrant poverty, without interfering with the more specialised charities. Although in theory it was a voluntary charity like any other, within the community it acquired, in practice, a semi-official status. It was, in effect, the community's own Poor Law Union, with a constellation of voluntary organisations such as surrounded the State system.[141] But the community was fortunate enough in its freedom from the restraints and preconceptions of the New Poor Law. The rise of a new form of Jewish poverty, and of Jewish poverty on an unprecedented scale, coincided with the emergence of a new outlook in the English world of private philanthropy particularly applicable to the community's needs. This outlook was adapted to Jewish purposes in London in 1859, and in Manchester in 1867. It 'marked an important development in charity practice in England'[142] which came to full fruition in the Gentile milieu only with the foundation of the Charity Organisation Society in 1869.[143]

Apart from strengthening the internal mechanism of communal relief,

Landeshut was anxious to establish the eligibility of Jewish paupers for relief by the State on terms acceptable to the Jewish conscience. It seemed a matter of principle

to take at all times the steps which may be deemed available in order to insure to the Poor of the Jewish faith the full benefits of the Poor Laws of the Empire.[144]

This did not mean that Jews should take advantage of those laws in the normal course of events; on the contrary, it seemed politic that the community should, wherever possible, 'support its own'. In part, it was another phase in the community's long search for equality before the law, which three years later took the additional form of a public protest in Manchester at the remaining disabilities suffered by Jews in the older universities. There were also real practical advantages. It was foreseen, for example, that the Board would occasionally be faced with immigrant poverty or local distress on a scale which lay beyond the scope of its limited financial means. At such moments of crisis, the Poor Law Union offered an additional source of relief, however unsatisfactory.[145] The New Poor Law might also provide the Board with a further means of discouraging immigrant settlement, since particularly 'undeserving' cases might be refused even minimal relief and referred instead to the local workhouse, without the Board having to feel that it had placed their religious observance in jeopardy.[146] The same was true of persistent, 'incorrigible' cases. The referral of deserted wives to the workhouse was also the only way of establishing a legal means of finding and punishing their husbands, should they still be in England.[147] Finally, a significant gap in the provision of the Board was the absence of residential facilities for orphans, deserted wives, the aged and the chronically sick. Ideally, Landeshut would have wished for a Jewish hospital,[148] but in fact the Board's limited resources placed this and other forms of welfare accommodation beyond its reach. It seemed necessary, therefore, to establish Jewish claims to the services of the State, particularly when many large urban Unions were beginning to establish separate infirmaries for the sick poor in the wake of the Metropolitan Poor Act of 1867. With these ends in view, in November 1868, the Board set up a Poor Law Committee to explore the whole position and to act as the community's channel of liaison with the local Poor Law Unions and the national Poor Law Board.[149]

When, in January 1869, the Poor Law Committee met representatives of the Manchester Union for the first time to discuss the terms upon which the Jewish poor might enter the local workhouse, the Union went a long way towards meeting Jewish requirements.[150] No objection was raised to Jewish inmates abstaining from labour on their Sabbath. The festivals created more of a problem, since it was felt that any privileges accorded to Jews would inevitably be claimed by the far more numerous Roman Catholics

who had so many high festivals in the course of a year . . . moreover . . . many Protestants might for that purpose declare themselves Catholics, although they would have some difficulty in proving themselves to be Jews.

But an agreement on the point was finally reached, by which all Jewish inmates would be temporarily discharged during the festivals, when their relief would be borne by the Jewish Board. The Union further agreed to allow kosher food to be taken to the workhouse, although at first only as an experiment, and at the Jewish Board's expense. When it was pointed out that the provision of food for Jewish paupers in Crumpsall Workhouse could be achieved only 'with great cost and considerable inconvenience', the Union agreed— 'for the time being'—to send all Jewish paupers to the workhouse in New Bridge Street. Jewish ministers of religion were given access to the workhouse, while orphans and 'deserted' children might be 'draughted'—after an investigation of the merits of each particular case—not to a parochial school but to a Jewish residential school. Further negotiations in London in February 1868, between G. J. Goschen, the President of the Poor Law Board, and representatives of the Jewish Boards of Guardians of London and Manchester made the necessary provision for the placement of Jewish orphans 'in a certified school of their own creed'—at first, either the Jews Hospital at Lower Norwood or the Jews Orphan Asylum in Goodman's Fields—and for their maintenance there at the public expense.[151]

The marked success of these local and national negotiations redounded very largely to the credit of Landeshut, who took the initiative in defining the relationship between Jewish voluntary charity and the State,[152] much as Lucas and Micholls had taken the lead at an earlier period in establishing the eligibility of Jewish voluntary schools for State grants. His name and achievements were brought to the notice of London's Anglo-Jewish leaders, and in January 1869, on the recommendation of Jacob Franklin, who had accompanied him in the negotiations with Goschen, he was invited to become Secretary of the metropolitan Board of Guardians.[153] During February, the committee of the Old Congregation offered him a 'considerable advance in salary' if he would remain in Manchester, but they could not meet his condition of 'an engagement for life',[154] and in the early summer of 1869 Landeshut left for London.

What is to be made of Landeshut's career in Manchester? Little is known of the man himself. He lived with his family in Elizabeth Street, then in the higher and 'most salubrious' district of Cheetham Hill—'within two minutes walk of the open fields'—and there he supplemented his salary by taking in four young boarders who received their English and general education at the

Jews School and their instruction in Hebrew, German and religion 'under his own immediate care'.[155] He was a methodical man with 'eminently a statistical mind', according to his obituarist; sometimes severe in his attitudes to poverty, but never harsh towards the poor.[156] He shared the cultural inclinations of the Anglo-Jewish middle class, whose outlook he reflected in his attitude towards the *chevroth*. He was ambitious enough before coming to Manchester to canvass his candidacy for the Readership of Duke's Place in the *Jewish Chronicle*,[157] and while in Manchester to apply for a similar vacancy at the new and important Bayswater Synagogue.[158] Apart from his work at the synagogue and the Board of Guardians, he played the major role in founding a Manchester Jerusalem Society, possibly modelled on a similar organisation in Liverpool, to channel funds to the Jews of the Holy Land.[159] Perhaps his major overall contribution to communal life was to widen its horizons after the comparative introversion which accompanied the Reform controversy. In seeking means of dealing with the *chevroth*, it was Landeshut who renewed Manchester's representation on the Board of Deputies,[160] which had lapsed since the culmination of the Cheremite dispute. In the field of poor relief he kept Manchester abreast of national developments. It is arguable that a Board of Guardians or its equivalent would have emerged before 1860 had not the Reform schism intervened, and that its subsequent creation was made inevitable by the foundation of the London Board and the increasing pace of immigration during the 1860s. But it was Landeshut who turned probability into reality, first by experimenting with London methods through the Benevolent Fund, and then by working for co-operation across sensitive religious boundaries.

VI

The Board he had helped to create was not at first a total success. There was general agreement that 'the begging system so much practised prior to the establishment of this institution' had 'considerably decreased' since the Board had begun to monitor all applications for relief,[161] and that the 'street mendicancy' of which Theodores had complained had 'sensibly fallen off'.[162] Many intending immigrants were said to have been frightened off by the threat of refusal,[163] and many passing strangers had been encouraged to move on. The bulk of the Board's expenditure, as it repeatedly told its subscribers, was concentrated upon the relief of the 'deserving poor' who had resided in Manchester for at least a year, and 'the least possible encouragement had been extended to casuals and tramps'.[164]

But while the Board's methods of relief and deterrence were a substantial success, it was becoming increasingly difficult to conceal the failure of its mechanism of integration. The loan service which had been intended to provide the newcomer with the means of achieving economic independence had begun badly. No special fund had been set aside, little attempt had been made to publicise its existence, and no proper system had been devised for judging the merits of applicants. In 1871 'the dictates of policy as much as the fears of incurring the expenses and onus of legal proceedings' induced the Board to write off £9 in bad debts.[165] And yet the Board could not operate successfully without some means of absorbing immigrants, particularly as the pace of immigration began to quicken in the early 1870s. It was necessary to prevent the emergence of a permanent reservoir of poverty which would grow deeper with every fresh wave of new arrivals. As the Board grimly told its subscribers, 'something effective must be done to reclaim the poor immigrants from the helplessness which now afflicts them'.[166]

The means chosen was a reinvigorated loan scheme backed by a substantial reserve fund and a proper means of close surveillance. Two separate funds —one opened in April 1873 for the 'granting of loans and the purchase of tools, sewing machines and other implements',[167] a second in May (on the initiative of Theodores) 'for the encouragement of Industrial pursuits among the deserving poor'[168]—were amalgamated in June, when a total of £960 had been raised, and on 5 November an Industrial Committee was set up to supervise their management.[169] The declared aim of the committee, modelled on an experiment being conducted by Landeshut in London, was to arrange the loan of cash or equipment to 'deserving traders' and to organise the apprenticing of poor Jewish children 'to divers appropriate trades';[170] its objectives were, in the short term, to assist inexperienced newcomers to find an initial source of independent support, normally in one of the immigrant trades, and, in the long run, 'to distribute over a wider field the industry of the Jewish working class'[171] by persuading younger immigrants to seek economic outlets beyond the traditional Jewish occupations. The immediate economic support of one generation would be followed by the total integration of the next.

An attempt was now made to hedge about the Board's work with proper safeguards. Each person wishing to borrow a machine had first to find two sureties who would guarantee its safety and the repayments for its hire. He had then to undertake to repay the Board at the rate of 4s a week during the 'busy season' and 2s a week for the rest of the year, to 'keep the machine continually in his own house or apartments' (an incidental stimulus to outwork in the tailoring trade), and to return it to the Board on request:

Where the stipulated hire of the machine shall have been regularly paid to the agreed value thereof [10 per cent above the cost price] it shall become the property of the borrower.

Interest-free cash loans of up to £2 might be granted without security; loans above £2 to a maximum of £10 required the guarantee of two householders. Since the loans were granted for the express purpose of enabling an applicant to earn an independent livelihood, no borrower was entitled to any other form of relief. Early in 1874 a further cautionary 'by-law' limited the granting of loans to those who had resided in Manchester for at least six months.[172] Occasionally, beginning in January 1875, loans took the form of 'guarantee notes' to wholesale or retail clothiers, who were asked to supply poor Jewish tailors on credit with sufficient cloth to fulfil small contracts.[173] Loans towards the apprenticeship of suitable young applicants to 'appropriate' occupations (those, that is, which offered more stable prospects than the 'immigrant trades') were to be repaid out of subsequent earnings. The Board undertook to seek out willing masters, to arrange satisfactory contracts, to watch over their observance, and to advance the initial premium.

In the event, the whole scheme very nearly collapsed. After eighteen months, the committee confessed that few loans had been granted 'for purely industrial purposes' and that most applications had come from 'people who under any circumstance are not likely to be permanently benefited'.[174] One applicant sought to redeem clothing from pledge;[175] another had already obtained his ticket to Hamburg from the Society for the Relief of Distressed Foreigners;[176] a third (the former Reader of a *chevra*) wished to travel in tea; a fourth to patent 'a substitute for umbrellas'. More deserving cases were said to be too proud to appear, even for a loan, 'before men known as public distributors of charity'.[177] The committee had also exchanged the haphazard character of the old system for an excessive caution: 'they required more than ample security, and frightened the poor away'.[178] The apprenticeship scheme met with even greater disasters. Parents were naturally reluctant to have their children apprenticed to 'useful and honourable trades', when 'during the first years the scale of payment is necessarily lower than could be obtained by tailoring or glazing'.[179] Neither the offer of subsidies to parents of 5s weekly during the early years of an apprenticeship nor extensive propaganda in 'the Jewish district' served to make the scheme any the more popular.[180] Another difficulty was that of finding 'honourable traders' who were willing to accommodate the religious needs of Jewish employees. The Post Office, for example, rejected the committee's suggestion of 'giving employment to Jewish youths, allowing them to take the place of Christian employees on Sundays instead of working on Saturdays', on the grounds that it could offer no special exemptions to any of its employees.[181] A handful of Gentile employers accepted Jewish apprentices on suitable terms, but young and observant immigrants found it difficult to work in occupations which cut them off from their co-religionists, even when their scruples were respected.[182] A few so-called 'masters' were workshop entrepreneurs in search of cheap labour.[183] The 'migratory habits' of Jewish families also created problems; on at least one occasion an apprentice left with his family for America before the completion of his term.[184] When disputes developed between employers and parents, as they frequently did, the Board found that it possessed no ready means of intervening, however careful the contract.[185] By the end of 1876 only five Jewish children had been placed with any degree of success, and the apprenticeship scheme was allowed to run down until it was replaced by loans to parents to enable them to make their own arrangements.

In the long run, all that was salvaged from the whole programme was the systematic issue of cash loans. The loan of equipment met with insuperable risks, and was terminated in 1874;[186] instead the Board decided to *give* cash grants to selected applicants 'to purchase tools before starting them on work', and even on occasion to give equipment to applicants who might subsequently apply for a loan to supply themselves with raw material.[187] Once a less humiliating and more generous approach had been adopted, however, as it was in the later 1870s, cash loans gradually established themselves as a regular part of the Board's work, and perhaps its most successful and distinctive characteristic. They solved the Board's immediate problem of effecting the immigrant's economic initiation, if only at the expense of driving successive generations towards the immigrant trades. Two years, nine months, according to Max Hesse,[188] was the time required to establish a new immigrant firmly in a position of total independence. Loans were the most explicit symbol of the Board's intention to avoid temporary, piecemeal relief, in favour of curative charity, and of its basic confidence in the recuperative powers of the immigrant poor. Landeshut had once written of the Board's recipients that they were 'for the most part above the class of mere paupers'; the loan service, in particular, bespoke a greater communal faith in the poor than most Gentile charities were prepared to profess, and with every justification.

VII

The increasing communal poverty of the 1860s and the early 1870s arose in part out of the pressing immediate needs of successive waves of destitute newcomers; in part out of the close dependence of settled immigrant life upon the fluctuating fortunes of a narrow range of workshop trades. It was the coming together of these two elements in Jewish poverty which necessitated an urgent reassessment of existing communal attitudes to poor relief.

In London, the severity of the problem had been brought home by the trade depression of 1857–58, which provided the final impulse towards the formation of the London Jewish Board of Guardians;[189] in Manchester, by the impact of the Cotton Famine. Although its Board was closely modelled upon that of London, and tended to follow the metropolitan example, the Manchester community faced the same problems and would have been compelled to work out radical solutions even if no London precedent had been available. The problems posed were those of keeping pauper settlement to a minimum, of reducing endemic industrial poverty to manageable financial proportions, and of providing an efficient means of absorbing immigrants into the settled community. The language in which they were debated in the Jewish press was that of the contemporary Gentile discussion of the deficiencies of the national system of poor relief, and the means chosen for their solution were ultimately those favoured by the more advanced Gentile critics of the New Poor Law. But the conditions out of which they arose were unique to the community. Whatever the debt to Gentile models, the foundation of Jewish Boards owed less to new theories outside the community than to new problems within it. The chief effect of external influences was to provide convenient means to necessary ends.

These means were not altogether successful. In consolidating the immigrant trades, the Board reinforced the social solidarity of immigrant life upon which its dreaded cultural isolation was based. The Board was also rather less deterrent in its effects than it sometimes made itself out to be. This was partly because humanity sometimes confused its more severe intentions, particularly in dealing with such problems as the deserted family. Already, in 1870, members of the Board were 'severely taxed both for means and ways how to act in accordance with true charity towards the poor, and justice to the subscribers'.[190] A pragmatic approach to such cases occasionally left the Board with more dependent families than it could readily support.[191] Then again, since the community could not risk the ill repute of pauperism or mendicancy, on however small a scale, those who refused to leave the community, whatever their 'deserts', had ultimately to be accepted into it, whatever the cost. Nor was it realistic for the Board to believe, as it sometimes professed to do, that its methods served to dissuade immigrants from crossing the Channel. Certainly, it offered no inducement, but it was in no position to stem a tide which for the most part washed over Manchester on its way to more distant shores. Nor was the immigrant entirely at the Board's mercy. 'Secret charity' was often available from prominent individuals, like William Aronsberg,[192] the eccentric Russian optician, who once urged it upon the Board.[193] The agents of the *chevroth*—of which there were more than a score in Manchester by the later 1870s—were always prepared to offer a few shillings and some good advice to provide their *lansleit* with a 'new start in life'.

Moreover, the Board's problems were inevitably recurrent until the pace of immigration was slowed by the Aliens Act and the outbreak of the First World War. A member of the Board wrote:

> as soon as the people learn to maintain themselves, and cease to take relief, their places are filled by new arrivals who weigh on the resources of the institution.[194]

In much the same way, the efforts of the Board's medical service and Visiting Committee were offset by the increasing density of population in Red Bank (and in lower Strangeways during the later 1870s). In spite of notices served by the Medical Officer for the 'cleansing and whitewashing' of houses, and the regular distribution of 'disinfectives', the spread of an acute form of scarlatina through the 'Jewish streets' in November 1875 was attributed by Franklin to 'the defective sanitary condition' and overcrowding of immigrant homes.[195] Fears that smallpox would take a similar course in August 1876 led the Board to issue warnings that no relief was to be given to any person who refused to be vaccinated or revaccinated,[196] and in the following year, after the issue of 350 summonses against the owners of insanitary dwellings in Red Bank, William Aronsberg lectured a large audience in the *Chevra Walkawishk* on the importance of domestic cleanliness.[197] Each new generation of immigrants served also to reinforce the distinctive cultural ambience of immigrant life and to multiply, apparently indefinitely, the number of *chevroth* and *chedarim*. The achievement of the Board was to contain immigrant poverty within the limits set by the community's financial resources at a time of mounting immigration,[198] to operate a mechanism of integration so effective that it required only minor adjustments to meet the more exacting demands of the 1880s, and to lay the younger generation of immigrant families open to the powerful assimilatory pressures of the Jews School.

A significant side-effect was the promotion of cordial relations between the Old Congregation and the Reform Synagogue at a time when religious differences were being accentuated by radical changes at Park Place. The new Reform minister, Gustav Gottheil, suffered from none of the conscientious inhibitions which had restrained Dr Schiller. In Berlin, he had served as third minister to the advanced Reformer, Dr Samuel Holdheim, and it was his declared intention to preach in Manchester the theories he had heard expounded in Germany.[199] Moreover, he owed his appointment to Theodores and the 'German' group which set little store by the gentle compromises of English Reform, and no doubt he was expected to meet their ideological demands. Although the archives of the synagogue were destroyed during the Blitz, occasional notices in the Jewish press plot the general course of the congregation's religious movement during Gottheil's ministry (1860–73). In December 1864, it was reported that pews had been set up in the synagogue

so that husband and wife might not be separated during their worship . . . as has hitherto been the case, contrary to the spirit of the century.[200]

In 1862 it was noted that the Manchester Reformers had 'expunged from their liturgy every passage which the orthodox have taken from the Mishna and the Talmud', and that a large part of the ritual was then read in the vernacular.[201] Bibles in English had been provided for every congregant before 1869, when Gottheil reported the fact to the Reform Synod in Leipzig.[202] Other changes included the introduction of an organ, the institution of a special Memorial Service for the Dead on the Day of Atonement, and a seven-year cycle for the reading of the Law.[203] By the early 1870s, Park Place was reported to have 'drifted much farther away from the old minhag' than the London Reform congregation, and to bear a closer resemblance to the Reform Temples of the United States.[204]

In 1861 relations between the Old and the Reform congregations were sufficiently strained for both to air their differences on matters of *shechita* in the local press.[205] By February 1870, notwithstanding a widening religious gulf, so great an improvement had taken place that it was possible to arrange a joint service at the Great Synagogue,[206] and for Samuel Montagu to believe (wrongly as it turned out) that 'there was a probability that a union would shortly be effected between the Old and the Reform Congregations in Manchester'.[207] Further joint services were held at Park Place in the following December, and at the Great Synagogue in 1871, and it was only the forceful intervention of the Chief Rabbi which kept Dr Gottheil from entering the pulpit at the Great Synagogue in 1872. Dr Adler bluntly refused his permission, and the pleading of a delegation from the Old Congregation which went down to London and 'argued with him for hours' only increased his obstinacy.[208] The Select Committee wrote indignantly of its regret that he had obstructed 'the anticipated union of cordiality and feeling . . . so much to be desired',[209] but in Manchester all it could do was indicate the absence of local ill will by accepting Theodores' invitation to a special service for the consecration of a new organ.[210]

The healing of the religious wounds of 1856–58 was not entirely incidental. Landeshut had worked quite consciously to 'cement' the various sections of the Anglo-Jewish community 'into one solid compact brotherhood for the furtherance of charitable objects',[211] and it was part of his achievement to devise an administrative framework which made this possible. A warmth of feeling was also to be expected as the immigrant threat to the social values and status of the community underlined once again the common interests of the Anglo-Jewish middle class. The Board of Guardians both expressed this sense of solidarity and confirmed it. In London, a Board had been preceded by co-operation between the three major orthodox congregations in a Conjoint Board of Relief since 1834. But in Manchester, the religious division of a relatively smaller Anglo-Jewish middle class was not between several orthodox synagogues but between a single orthodox congregation on the one hand and a Reform congregation on the other. The mobilisation of Anglo-Jewish resources demanded co-operation across this religious frontier.

12　A pattern of synagogues, 1869–74

Quite as important as the consolidation of an Eastern European working class on Red Bank during the 1860s was the creation of a new and substantial Jewish *petite bourgeoisie* in the inner suburban districts of Strangeways and Cheetham Hill. As many of the established merchants and shopkeepers of an earlier period pressed northwards along the Bury New and Cheetham Hill Roads towards the semi-rural areas of Higher Broughton, Elizabeth Street and Smedley Lane, the residential districts closer to town were taken over by a new wave of petty retailers, travelling salesmen and workshop masters. Most were Polish and Russian immigrants, like Jacob Rothband, Joseph Mandleberg or Philip Frankenstein, who had made their way fairly rapidly from humble beginnings as glaziers or sweated workers into entrepreneurial positions in cap making, tailoring and waterproofing. A few were newcomers to Manchester from Germany or from other English towns, who arrived with a little capital and expertise to invest in tailoring, pawnbroking, or one of the other traditional Jewish retail trades, but without the substantial wealth which would have carried them directly to the outer suburbs. While the élite of Higher Broughton and Chorlton-on-Medlock grew only very slowly during the 1860s, the Jewish population of Strangeways and Cheetham Hill more than doubled, from 610 in 1861 to a total of 1,419 ten years later. In economic terms, the entrepreneurial class in the workshop industries expanded rapidly during the 1860s, while Jewish involvement in retailing and overseas commerce, although substantial, remained relatively static.

If a large part of the history of the 1860s and early 1870s may be regarded as a response to the challenge of pauper immigration, much of the remainder may be seen as a reaction of established Anglo-Jewry to the threats implicit in the growth of a new Jewish lower middle class, chiefly of Eastern European origin. One of these threats was to the social tone of the residential area immediately around the Great Synagogue; another, of greater political moment, was to the exclusive character of the synagogue's Free Membership. In effect, the political wheel of congregational life had turned full circle since the successful outcome of David Hesse's democratic rebellion, in 1851. By the later 1860s a new generation of immigrants had acquired seats in the synagogue and were pressing for acceptance into a privileged élite of which some of Hesse's former companions were now leading members. The stage was set for a new phase of the dialectic which had begun with the foundation of the first New Synagogue in 1844.

I

The secession of the 1840s had led to an amendment of the laws of the congregation which enabled seat-holders to obtain the privileges of Free Membership (including the franchise) by paying a seat rent of 26s for only one year, securing election by a General Meeting, and paying an entrance fee of 21s. Free Members who subscribed at least 52s a year were further entitled to hold honorary office. It was a middle-class compromise which had produced a constitution sufficiently egalitarian to admit Hesse and his friends to Free Membership without making privilege available on too general a scale. Thereafter, a further reaction set in, stimulated both by the removal of some of the more liberal Free Members, including Hesse himself, to the Reform camp during 1856–57, and by the rapid expansion of a lower-middle-class Jewry during the following decade. The established middle-class families closed their political ranks to maintain the undiluted leadership of an anglicised élite. A revised code of laws published in February 1858,[1] restricted application for Free Membership to those who held seats valued at £2 12s a year, insisted that applicants should provide the names of two Free Members to act as referees, and limited the subsequent exercise of full privileges to those who paid seat rents of at least three guineas. The entrance fee to Free Membership was raised in December 1860, from one guinea to three guineas in the face of a more extreme proposal for setting it at £5.[2] From May 1865, nominations for the Presidency were limited to those who paid at least five guineas a year, and for the office of Treasurer to those who paid four.[3] Early in 1869, in a move distinctly reminiscent of the 1830s, a 'burial tax' was imposed upon seat-holders, while Free Members remained entitled to free burial.[4] The evidence also suggests that even qualified applicants for Free Membership were subjected to an increasingly intensive screening by the Select Committee.[5] Meantime, beyond the barriers of privilege, the number of seat-holders increased rapidly during the 1860s as new English and German immigrants arrived in Manchester, and Eastern European entrepreneurs sought to confirm their economic and social progress by abandoning the *chevroth* for the Great Synagogue. Under this pressure, the number of seat-holders and members quadrupled during the period of office of Godfrey Levi as secretary (1854–65)[6] to a total of over three hundred, of whom less than a quarter were Free Members.

The dangers of this situation were intensified by the concern of new seat-holders at what they regarded as the excessively 'English' character of services in the synagogue. In particular, D. M. Isaacs, who had already been taken to task for trying to lead the congregation 'from the ceremonies of the dark ages . . . into modern life',[7] was under criticism for laying more stress on 'long lectures' in English than on 'devotional prayer' in Hebrew.[8] It was suggested, amongst other matters, that his sermons 'would admit of being much shortened'.[9] That these comments came chiefly from new immigrants is suggested by a letter to the *Jewish Chronicle* in Isaacs' defence by A. F. (Abraham Franks?) of Manchester:

There are . . . some people who on account of their limited knowledge of the English language do not quite understand a lecture, but who are nevertheless very prone to giving their opinions,[10]

a comment which also hints at the kind of cultural snobbery which had already produced tougher obstacles to Free Membership. Ill at ease in an Anglo-Jewish Synagogue, as yet struggling to adjust to Manchester's economic life, and excluded from congregational power, the seat-holders built up a strong sense of collective resentment against those who denied them equality. The physical limitations of the Great Synagogue, which created severe problems of overcrowding, particularly at Festival time, exacerbated the social tensions within it.

An explosive situation reached critical proportions soon after the resignation of Samuel Landeshut as Secretary and Reader, in February 1869, leaving vacant a combination of posts which in his hands had become key positions in communal life. It was from them that Landeshut had taken the earliest steps towards the creation of a Board of Guardians. This being so, the seat-holders particularly resented their exclusion from the selection of his successor, especially when the choice was seen to lie between candidates with continental qualifications and experience and Henry Davis Marks, the young English-born and London-educated Reader of the Cardiff Hebrew Congregation.[11] The long electoral procedure provided the seat-holders with an opportunity for voicing all their grievances. On 29 June, forty-seven of them sent a 'memorial' to the Select Committee seeking a vote in the election, the abolition of the new burial tax, and a more egalitarian constitution.[12] They proposed an amendment to the laws which would have made anyone holding a seat at an annual rental of two guineas for three years eligible for Membership and full exercise of rights, on payment of an entrance fee of a guinea. The dissidents had clearly been considering the matter for some time, since they made it clear that, in the event of their proposals not being accepted, they intended to establish a 'New

Congregation' of their own. It may be suggested that if the congregational rebellions of the early nineteenth century in Liverpool and Manchester
owed something to the democratic feelings generated by the Reform Act of
1832, that of 1869 acquired some of its inspiration from the Act of 1867,
although communal tensions were clearly paramount at both periods. In
another parallel with the revolt of 1844 the Select Committee decided on
1 July that the new petition 'could not at present be entertained, the time for
election being short'.[13] Again, these tactics of delay only increased the
determination of the rebels.

The militancy of the malcontents may be judged by their arrival, without
notice, at the Special General Meeting convened on 4 July to elect Landeshut's
successor, 'to enforce their demands'.[14] Not being eligible for admission,
however, they were there treated to the additional indignity of waiting in an
anteroom for the outcome of the debate. After a prolonged discussion, the presiding warden, Alexander Leveson, emerged to inform them that their requests
could not be considered since they were contrary to the spirit as well as to the
letter of congregational law. All Leveson could do was promise a further meeting, at some indefinite future date, to give the matter further consideration.
The seat-holders then departed, while within the meeting Marks was elected
Reader and Secretary by a substantial majority. From the beginning, however,
his position was equivocal. While he clearly had the backing of the Anglo-
Jewish élite, in the eyes of the discontented seat-holders the limitations of his
English background were compounded by his irrevocable association with an
exclusive system of congregational government and those who upheld it. The
exclusion of the seat-holders from his election was also the immediate cause of
their secession. During August 1869 twenty-three resigned and established
their own synagogue—the second New Congregation in Manchester's
history—in a room 'fitted up temporarily for Divine Worship' in Robert
Street, Cheetham Hill.[15] Within a year the membership of the New Congregation had grown to over forty-five.[16]

The composition of the new synagogue, in so far as it can be reconstructed,
provides the clearest evidence of its rationale.[17] Of the thirty-two members
whose origins are known, fourteen were born in Poland, five in Russia, three
in Austria, seven in Germany, and three in English towns—David Hyams, a
watchmaker, in Newcastle upon Tyne, Solomon Raphael, a 'salesman', in London, and Godfrey Levi, of whom more later, in Birmingham. At the time of
the secession twenty-two were living in Cheetham Hill, six in Strangeways,
two in Lower Broughton, one, Godfrey Levi, in Higher Broughton, and one,
Israel Kersh, a master tailor from Russian Poland, in Fernie Street, Red Bank.
The rebels included nine tailors (seven workshop entrepreneurs and two re-

tailers), four travelling salesmen, five watchmakers, two shoemakers, an accountant, a merchant, a commercial clerk, a fishmonger, a tobacconist and Lazarus Caro, the master glazier. Most had lived in Manchester between five and fifteen years, the longest established being two waterproofers, Philip Frankenstein of Prussian Poland and Joseph Mandleberg of Cracow, both of whom had arrived in the mid-1850s. The chief momentum clearly came from Eastern European immigrants who had resided in Manchester for long enough—eight and a half years on average—to establish themselves as independent retailers or as entrepreneurs in the workshop trades and to move from Red Bank into the lower residential districts of Strangeways and Cheetham Hill. Their movement out of the *chevroth*—Mandleberg, for example, was a founder of the *Cracow Chevra*—and their demand for synagogal privilege were both the logical outcome of their modest socio-economic success.

Articulate leadership was provided, however, by a few men of English birth or background, and particularly by the former secretary of the Great Synagogue, Godfrey Levi, who became the New Congregation's first president. After holding the office of salaried secretary for over ten years, Levi had retired in January 1865, to set himself up as an independent 'professional accountant, public auditor, financial agent' and insurance broker at 50 Princess Street.[18] In a letter to the *Jewish Chronicle* announcing his retirement, he thanked the members of the Old Congregation for their generosity, and assured them 'of his continued aspirations for their future welfare and happiness both individually and collectively'.[19] The congregation reciprocated by granting him all the privileges of Free Membership, and in April 1865 he was elected to the Select Committee.[20] In May 1866, however, the validity of his election was called into question on the legal technicality that he had not occupied a seat in the synagogue with an annual seat rental of at least three guineas, and a subsequent General Meeting thereupon declared his election null and void.[21] Although Levi was pressed by the meeting to take a three-guinea seat and so qualify for office, his pride had been too badly hurt. He refused the offer, and instead

addressed the meeting vehemently defending his right to act as a committee man after having been elected as such by the general body . . . [finally] demolishing the testimonial on which the presentation of the Free Membership by the committee was engrossed.[22]

For this act of 'misconduct', he was at once deprived of all his privileges.[23] Thereafter he carried his resentment out of the synagogue, and he did not reappear on the communal stage until August 1869, when he emerged as titular leader of the secessionists. He and they had little in common beyond a sense of grievance towards the entrenched Free Members, but his English background, political skill, and knowledge of synagogal organisation provided the New Congregation with a secure base. The secretary of the New Congregation was Albert Hart, a young commercial clerk who earlier in the year had played a major part in the creation of the Manchester Hebrew Young Men's Literary Society.[24] The early months of the society's existence had included a power struggle in which Hart was the loser, and he may well have seen his post as secretary to the secessionists, with whom he had little in common, as a means of restoring his communal prestige. Like Levi he shared the frustrations of the rebels rather than their aims.

Although the Select Committee of the Old Congregation informed the Chief Rabbi that they intended to deal with the grievances of their seat-holders 'in a truly liberal spirit',[25] it soon became clear that the only liberal step they were prepared to take was the abolition of the burial tax.[26] Otherwise, as Marks wrote to Dr Adler

a great conservative spirit has sprung up and so far from giving way a determined intention is evoked to conserve the privileges of the congregation.[27]

A proposal of Joseph Harris, a new Free Member, at a General Meeting of 12 September, that seat-holders 'should possess an unconditional vote in the election of salaried officers' met with such concerted opposition that he withdrew it.[28] W. F. Bernstein, a prominent woollen merchant of German origin, underlined the socal character of the rift when he 'spoke at some length on the great desirability of passing measures which would ensure the thorough respectability of members',[29] as if to suggest that, far from being illiberal, the constitution already leaned too far in a democratic direction. Others in a powerful group of Free Members—chiefly well-established retail tradesmen—who set their faces against any form of compromise were Alexander Leveson, an English-born manufacturer of perambulators and invalid carriages who had settled in Manchester in the mid-1850s; the jewellers, David Cowen, Isaac Simmons and Michael Goldstone's eldest son, Sampson; the clothiers, Adam Casper, Joseph Hyman and Michael Lipman; and the Dutch cigar dealer, Joel Themans. The common factor was their membership of the richest and most assimilated families outside the Reform Congregation. Marks acted as their spokesman when he attributed the secession to 'a few isolated and unimportant seat-holders', a 'factious minority' which lacked the means and the experience to establish a separate congregational life.[30] He wrote:

There is without exception not one among them of any weight or social standing in the Community. When we come to reckon the amount lost to the cogregation by all the resignations [it] is between £40 and £50: a mere bagatelle to this wealthy and increasingly influential body.[31]

Leveson spoke for the whole group when he announced 'that they did not think the other body could exist much longer'.[32] What was expected was a swift and unconditional surrender.

The Chief Rabbi was called upon to speed this result by witholding his official approval of the New Congregation, on the grounds of its lack of resources and supposed Reformist leanings.[33] The grievances of the seat-holders, as put to Dr Adler by Godfrey Levi, were described by the Select Committee as 'a tissue of gross exaggerations' and 'direct and impudent falsehoods'.[34] But the Chief Rabbi was by now wary of personal intervention in local controversy, particularly when it became clear that religious principle and practice were not in fact at stake. Nor was he prepared to allow party bickering to reach the scandalous proportions of the 1850s. Recognising the real inadequacy of synagogal accommodation in a growing community, he was prepared, in February 1870, to give the New Congregation his formal blessing without pronouncing judgement on the issues in dispute.[35] In the following month, the rebels appointed their first official Reader.[36] By August 1870 they had purchased part of the new Philips Park Cemetery from the Corporation 'on satisfactory terms', with the privileges of fencing the land and building a mortuary house.[37] By that time the expenses of fitting out a temporary synagogue had been covered, and the congregation's annual expense of £277 was matched by an income of nearly £300.[38] Notwithstanding the allegations of the Old Congregation, services were conducted on an orthodox basis. In September 1869, an observer from the *Jewish Chronicle* had found the 'order and decorum' already 'unexpectedly good', and praised the strictness of regulations, one of which kept all members in their seats until the conclusion of the service.[39] It was perhaps inevitable that rebels in search of prestige which had been denied them at the Great Synagogue should place emphasis on the orderly respectability of their own place of worship. In October 1870 the congregation agreed on minor ritual changes—including the abbreviation of the *Piyyutim* and *Selicoth*—in the interests of greater decorum, and the alterations were carried into effect on Yom Kippur and the Feast of Tabernacles before crowded congregations.[40] It would seem that under Levi's guidance the Eastern European *nouveaux riches* had created a synagogue which might adequately and permanently reflect their economic status and social aspirations.

And yet a point had been reached by the autumn of 1870 at which the New Congregation was prepared to reassess its future. The original intention, after all, had been to gain admission to the privileges of the Great Synagogue, and the point had now been made that the alternative of secession was available. Was it necessary to continue into permanence by creating a new synagogue building and a separate communal service of *shechita*, or might it not use the bargaining power of secession as a basis for achieving reunion on acceptable political terms? For its part, the Old Congregation had nothing to gain from prolonging a financially damaging schism. When, therefore, at the end of 1870, the leaders of the New Congregation 'expressed a wish to return upon certain terms', Leveson welcomed the move, and called on his members to act 'in as temperate and conciliatory a manner as the occasion demanded'.[41] Levi was seen by all as the key to successful negotiations. Leveson saw in his personal rehabilitation the means of securing a bargain which would involve no serious political concessions; the rebels saw him as the only man powerful enough to arrange their admission to Free Membership. Levi himself was anxious only for readmission without loss of face and in a manner which marked him out as a figure of importance within the community. For all these reasons, on 15 January 1871, Levi was readmitted to Free Membership after making an 'ample apology' for the offence of 1866, on condition that he arranged for the return of his members.[42] To some extent, it was a sell-out. Levi's status was assured, and in return he used his influence to secure the return of the seat-holders without any alteration of the synagogal constitution. All that was held out to the rebels was a promise of nomination for Free Membership (without even the assurance of election) for those who had occupied seats in their new synagogue at rentals of at least £2 12s.[43] Levi could not promise the Old Congregation that his seat-holders would accept 'peace and unanimity' on these terms, 'but he would say on the honour of an Englishman that such would be the result'.[44]

In the event, however, the attempt very nearly foundered on the reactionary tendencies of the more die-hard members of the Old Congregation. At the first ballot, held on 5 February 1871, thirty-eight secessionists were elected to Free Membership and four rejected, while three others had their applications held over pending the receipt of 'proper references'.[45] When four more were elected a week later, however, Leveson and his more conservative friends were shocked into action to preserve what they could of the élitist structure of the synagogue. On their initiative a motion was passed which barred Free Members of less than three years' standing from holding congregational office or serving on the Select Committee.[46] Since its effect was to exclude from power all new seat-holders, including himself, the new rule was unacceptable to Levi, who announced his opposition to it at a General Meeting on 9 April. 'After a very protracted discussion proceeding over two hours', Levi proposed the rescinding of the motion to a meeting which, with an attendance of eighty-seven, was the largest ever held at the Great Synagogue:

at this juncture such a noise and disturbance ensued that after several ineffectual attempts the tellers reported that they could not properly perform their duty. No reliable result being likely to accrue, as the chairman could not obtain order, the meeting was summarily adjourned . . . amidst much tumult and disorder.[47]

Levi now dug in his heels, refusing to wind up the new synagogue or to resign his presidency until, as he put it, 'satisfactory arrangements were completed with the Old Hebrew Congregation so as to secure a permanent peace in the community'.[48] A total of 104 members attended the meeting on 23 April at which he intended once more to put forward his case against the three-year rule, and a renewal of open conflict was avoided only by the intervention of Isaac Franklin, as always, in the interests of conciliation. His resolution that the new law regarding eligibility for office should be 'left for confirmation or otherwise until a further opportunity' was carried with only one dissentient, and with some relief the terms of reunion were completed.[49] On the same day, Marks wrote to the Board of Deputies:

the members of the New Hebrew Congregation have again united themselves fraternally with the members of the Old Hebrew Congregation and . . . from this date the Manchester New Hebrew Congregation will cease to exist.[50]

The democratic movement of 1869–71 resembled that of 1844–51 in that it was the political expression within the synagogue of deep social differences within the community: it differed from the earlier secession chiefly in its comparative lack of idealism. Although he demonstrated a keen tactical sense and displayed some skill as a negotiator, Godfrey Levi was no David Hesse. While Hesse was moved by genuine liberalism, Levi acted largely out of personal pique. As a result he was ready to surrender the new congregation once his personal position had been clarified and without holding out for a more comprehensive restatement of the laws governing membership. This is not to say that he did not believe in a more egalitarian system—in Liverpool he had been involved in the seat-holders' revolt which had taken David Meyer Isaacs to the New Synagogue in 1852—but simply that expediency acted as a stronger force than principle. The secessionists as a whole acted from similar motives. They were more concerned about sharing power themselves than they were about creating a democratic structure which would open power to their successors. As a result, they settled for their own admittance to Free Membership and left the future to look after itself. The secession emphasised the advantages of the then new Board of Guardians in that, unlike the earlier dispute, which had undermined a structure of relief based upon the synagogue, it had no ill effects upon a welfare system based upon the community as a whole. Dr Adler's intervention was not necessary, either to organise co-operation in relief work (as he had in 1847) or to deal with the problems of religious jurisdiction (as in 1851). Neither the Chief Rabbi's authority nor Anglo-Jewish orthodoxy was at stake; the only suggestion of religious rivalry between the two congregations of 1869–71 had been in the attempts of each to outdo the decorum of the other.

While giving their general support to the settlement of 1871 as the necessary price of reunion, many established Free Members regarded it with ill-concealed regret as the first stage of the Old Congregation's social decline. They believed, with Henry Mendleson, that 'in the new seat holders they had acquired quantity and not quality'.[51] Louis Cobe spoke sadly of a Great Synagogue now 'chiefly supported by the industrial class'.[52] Even a moderate like Isaac Franklin attributed 'the anarchy which had crept into the Congregation' to 'the privileges being obtained for a small amount'. He added: '. . . but that was a circumstance of the past and could not be remedied. No doubt matters would come right in the end.'[53] But this was not necessarily the case. The immediate constitutional issue had been shelved; the deep social division remained.

II

A further and more critical phase in the relationship between the Anglo-Jewish élite and more recent middle-class immigrants was reached during a long and acrimonious debate, of which only the barest details survive, and which centred upon the person of the new Secretary–Reader, Henry Davis Marks. The earliest days of his ministry had received wide acclaim. The *Jewish Chronicle* commented in September 1869:

Mr Marks gained golden opinions from all members of the congregation for his very clear and distinct intonation, and for the harmonious strains in which he chanted his magnificent liturgy of the day; his delivery being free from all meretricious accompaniment likely to jar on the sensitive ear of the discriminating audience.[54]

But to the former rebels of the New Congregation, of whom he had spoken in the most contemptuous terms, he was the protégé of the Anglo-Jewish establishment and a symbol of their former lack of rights. He was also personally vulnerable. During his term as Reader at Cardiff he had been accused of unspecified moral misdemeanours, and although he had cleared himself of the charges, the scent of scandal remained. When he had first applied to Manchester in 1869 the wardens had

fully and minutely examined all the charges brought against him in full Committee, whose unanimous opinion (backed by Rev Dr Adler) was that all the allegations affecting his moral character were false and unworthy of credence.[55]

But the allegations themselves were apparently sufficient to bar him from the short list when he applied for the Readership of the Great Synagogue in London in March 1871. He wrote to his London supporters:

Holding the high and important office as I do in this wealthy and most influential congregation (the largest and most powerful out of London), I had not the slightest idea but that I should have been admitted as a candidate without the least hesitation.[56]

In the autumn of 1871 the question of his moral character became the *casus belli* of a final and disastrous clash between rival groups within the Great Synagogue.

This new chain of events was set in motion, perhaps accidentally, by the Rev. Professor Isaacs, who on 30 October 1871 was reported in Select Committee as having said that 'he could state something which would cause the Rev. H. D. Marks to receive 5 minutes notice from the congregation'.[57] The details of what followed may be passed over briefly. After a sub-committee appointed to investigate the matter reported on 5 November that there was 'no foundation for the charge so foully brought against the Rev. H. D. Marks',[58] a General Meeting declared him to be 'worthy of the full confidence' of the congregation.[59] There the matter rested until the following March, when a determined move to discredit Marks and to deprive him of at least one of his offices was led by Elkan Davis, a pawnbroker of Polish origin who had settled in Manchester during the 1860s, and one of the secessionists of 1869. Feelings ran high as the congregation divided on the issue. When, on 17 March, Davis first proposed that the offices of Secretary and Reader should be separated (and therefore Marks deprived of one of them), the presiding warden was sufficiently aware of 'the excited state of the congregation' to open the discussion with the hope that 'members would calmly discuss the question and that, whatever result was arrived at, harmony and peace would result'.[60] None the less, the meeting rapidly deteriorated to a point of noisy disorder at which he was compelled to dissolve it. Subsequently he was granted the power to eject from meetings anyone causing a disturbance.[61] When the indirect move to curtail Marks' power failed, Davis went on to press for his outright dismissal on the grounds of yet more unspecified blemishes on his moral character. A series of bitter arguments and close votes revealed the even balance of opinion. On 4 August a move to give Marks notice of dismissal was defeated by fifty-two votes to thirty-nine;[62] a week later, a further attempt to divide his offices was defeated by forty-one votes to thirty-seven.[63] Finally, after a series of requisitions and counter-requisitions and further, increasingly acrimonious, debate, a Special General Meeting on 8 September decided by fifty votes to forty-four to give Marks six months' notice and a testimonial payment of £150.[64] The nature of the meeting may be judged from Isaac Franklin's departure from it in disgust and his subsequent refusal to participate further in the affairs of the congregation. To avoid further warfare, Marks agreed to surrender his offices immediately,[65] and on 17 September Isaac Asher Isaacs of London was appointed to replace him.

Marks' fate is of less interest than the forces which determined it, for his dismissal had in fact less to do with his inadequacies than with a more fundamental struggle for synagogal supremacy. Although personal animosity and ambition clearly played their part, there can be little doubt that the debate on Marks' future was in essence a final trial of strength between the English and foreign elements within the Old Congregation. The attacks upon him came chiefly from the former secessionists, while his defence was organised by the political diehards of 1869–71, and particularly by Alexander Leveson. Seen in this light, his dismissal amounted to a shattering defeat for the Anglo-Jewish élite which had controlled the affairs of the synagogue since the Reform schism. This élite had now to reconsider its future. Was it prepared to remain within a congregation now guided by immigrant hands, or was there some way in which it might preserve its coherence and prestige beyond the Great Synagogue? There is some evidence to suggest that this question had already been considered during the spring of 1872. At the meeting of 10 March at which he had proposed the separation of Marks' offices, Elkan Davis had pointedly asked Leveson why he had recently convened two 'private meetings', and why Marks had supplied those meetings with a complete list of seat-holders. The answers were equivocal and, in context, scarcely convincing. Leveson explained that the meetings had been called

simply as an outdoor agitation of various questions he and others had desired for the welfare of the Congregation which, although carried in committee, the presidents had persistently shelved,

while Marks replied that the list was necessary to invite everyone 'to an entertainment to be held at Cheetham Town Hall'.[66] Even allowing for Davis' powers of innuendo, its seems reasonable to suggest that, in the light of his sharp reaction, the 'outdoor agitation' and the 'entertainment' were, if not entirely fictitious, then at least irrelevant. What seems much more likely is that, under Leveson's guidance, the older-established members were meeting to assess the degree of support which they might expect both in their defence of Marks' position and in any attempt to determine their separate future should that defence fail, as indeed it did in September 1872. Was there a body of seat-holders who might, in the last resort, provide the basis of a new Anglo-Jewish congregation?

The debates of the summer suggested that there was. In August 1872 sixty-nine members had signed a note of protest at the·attempts to remove Marks from office,[67] and early in the following month forty-four actually voted against his departure. Looking back over the course of the ten months' debate which culminated in Marks' dismissal, it is possible to identify a growing body of Free Members who acquired a new coherence in rallying to his defence. The nucleus was provided by the group which had opposed political compromise during 1869–71—Bernstein, Leveson, Cowen, Isaac Simmons, Sampson Goldstone, Adam Casper, Joseph Hyman, Joel Themans and Michael Lipman—but each new twist in the Marks debate added new supporters. This was particularly true after the annual synagogal elections of 28 April, which put beyond doubt the power of the new immigrants to control congregational affairs through their nominees. Elkan Davis and Isaac Wolstone, both immigrants of the 1860s, became joint treasurers, and the committee included the immigrant entrepreneurs Adolph Shiers and Benjamin Wansker, and the former leader of the New Congregation, Godfrey Levi. The defeated candidates included Morris Sykes (who, as Morris Friedlander, had arrived in Manchester as the first Jewish waterproofer in 1848), Louis Cobe, Jacob Casper, Joseph Franks and Solomon Themans (Joel's brother), all of whom participated in subsequent debates on Marks' behalf. The bias of the new Select Committee against Marks inclined other established Anglo-Jewish members, including Israel Levy (son of Joseph Levy, the tailor), Henry Mendelson and Samuel Isaac (the furrier), in his favour. The defeat of what had become a substantial party in the debate of 8 April precipitated the final decision to seek a new centre of congregational life. The only questions was—where?

III

This in turn focussed attention upon another problem.[68] Throughout the 1860s, as immigration had depressed the social standing of Strangeways and the lower parts of Cheetham Hill, a number of established Jewish residents who could scarcely afford the luxuries of the outer suburbs in Higher Broughton had sought a cheaper refuge in the fashionable residential district around Grosvenor Square, just to the south of the city centre, in Chorlton-on-Medlock. There, in what one contemporary Jewish writer described as 'the West End of Manchester',[69] a small colony of Jewish families settled in town houses to the south of St Peter's Square, along Oxford Road and Upper Brook Street, and in the streets radiating from All Saints Church. By 1871 this group of cultural refugees included David Cowen (in Portland Terrace), William Aronsberg (in Holywell House, Oxford Road) and W. F. Bernstein (in Acomb Street), and the evidence suggests that others were on the point of departure. Their movement was no more than the social equivalent of the political stand they had taken during the years 1869–71. They joined a handful of Jewish professional men who had made Chorlton-on-Medlock their first point of settlement in Manchester, some of whom, like Leopold Dreschfeld, the dentist, had lived near All Saints since the 1850s: others were Dr Henry Zirndorf, a German poet, theologian and private teacher of languages,[70] who during the 1850s had served briefly, and none too successfully, as Hebrew teacher at the Jews School in Cheetham Hill,[71] and Dr Adolph Wahltuch, a newly settled German doctor, later to be president of the Manchester Clinical Society.[72] Dreschfeld's son, Hugo, and nephew, Julius, both brilliant graduates of Owens College,[73] were making their way in the Manchester professional world, the former as a dentist, the latter as a physician,[74] while Dreschfeld himself, apart from his private practice, had been one of the founders of the Dental Hospital.[75] A number of other Jewish residents in the area were shopkeepers or professional men who, like Frederick Eskell, the dentist, and Julius Arensberg, the cigar dealer, had moved across the town towards a growing retail centre in and around St Peter's Square. By the autumn of 1872, as Leveson and his defeated colleagues assessed their future, Grosvenor Square was the hub of a Jewish social wheel, including perhaps twenty families in all, in a fashionable area of English and German settlement, and already thought of by contemporaries as 'in some eyes more aristocratic' than the Jewish settlement in the north.[76] It was natural enough that the district should be seen, even by families with their homes in Cheetham Hill like the Levesons or the Caspers, as an appropriate centre for a new and more culturally sophisticated congregational life, particularly since it might be claimed (in defence of secession) that the southern families were badly in need of synagogal accommodation within walking range.

This claim had first been made on 10 May 1872, in a letter to the *Jewish Chronicle* from 'Mauricius' of Oxford Street, Manchester (perhaps David Cowen's son, Morris), who laid stress on the distance—a liberally estimated three miles—between the Great Synagogue and 'Oxford Street and its environs . . . a district . . . largely inhabited by our co-religionists'. 'On wet and sultry days', he wrote, 'as well as for aged and infirm people, it is quite inaccessible.' He went on to suggest a

branch synagogue . . . not, let it be understood, a secession, but a branch, solely for the convenience of residents who would retain their membership in the parent synagogue.

At this stage, with the fate of Marks still in the balance, the idea of a branch was perhaps genuine enough, although even then it is possible to interpret

'Mauricius' as opening a tentative canvass for a more independent south Manchester scheme. This would perhaps explain the reply of 'Veritas', who regarded the idea of a southern synagogue as 'inadvisable' and 'impractical' in view of the ample accommodation in north.[77] He accused the residents of the south of wanting 'religion made easy' in refusing a half-hour's walk 'which many ladies in the Bayswater and Maida Hill districts perform every Saturday'.

It is significant that the matter was not taken up again until after Marks' fate had been virtually sealed. On 27 August 1872 the Select Committee decided unanimously to recommend his dismissal to a Special General Meeting; five days later, on 1 September, David Cowen convened an open meeting at the Temperance Hall in Grosvenor Street, 'to consider the desirability of establishing a synagogue in the thickly populated district of the southern part of the city'.[78] Cowen again stressed 'that there was not to be a secession from any existing synagogue' and that the new congregation was 'for the sole convenience of those residing in the southern portion', although there could have been little doubt locally of his wider purpose. 'An Englishman' provided the *Jewish Chronicle* with a rather more accurate version in describing the members of the Old Congregation as

individuals who, though of a very respectable social class, are not always distinguished by their amenities [*sic*]. Hence their debates are never conducted in a very parliamentary manner . . . Lately these gentlemen have had a fearful quarrel . . . The consequence is that many of the conquered party have left the Synagogue . . . Mr Cowen, a gentleman living in Oxford Road, has taken advantage of the circumstances, and hence this movement.[79]

Cowen's project was endorsed by his audience, and a sub-committee of five was appointed to prepare a code of laws for submission to a further meeting on 8 September,[80] a timetable which itself suggests a greater degree of preparatory planning than the bare events reveal. The laws were accepted, and during October the South Manchester Congregation held its first services in a rented room in Chorlton Town Hall.[81]

Retrospective accounts of these events suggest the same duality of purpose. In the official version composed for the South Manchester Synagogue, Cowen figures as

an active and intelligent member of the community prompted by true brotherly and religious motives for the welfare of his co-religionists [of the south] who had long been estranged from regular attendance at Divine Worship

by their distance from Cheetham Hill.[82] The sole object was to create a congregation which would encompass all southern residents, whatever their former allegiance—a 'fusion of all sections of opinion . . . orthodox, Portuguese and Reform'—in a single and convenient synagogue in the area of All Saints after 'years of inconvenience . . . silently suffered'. Isaac Asher Isaacs, Marks' successor at the Old Congregation, took a more cynical view.[83] The South Manchester Synagogue, he wrote, was

an offshoot of the parent synagogue . . . called into existence not through the actual want of a Synagogue in the southern part of the town but merely through a schism which occurred amongst the members of this Congregation, the result of an angry difference of opinion,

and he underlined the point by complaining of the orthodox Jews who passed the front of the Great Synagogue on their way to the 'more convenient' place of worship in the south. There was some truth in both accounts. By 1872 there was certainly room for a southern synagogue, although the need was neither as desperate nor as long-standing as Cowen implied. There can be little doubt that the immediate cause of the synagogue's foundation was the dispute within the Old Congregation and the need of Leveson's 'conquered party' for a new synagogal base. In this sense, the foundation of the South Manchester Synagogue was a continuation of the political battles of 1869–72 within the Old Congregation, and the indirect consequence, therefore, of the growth of an immigrant middle class. This being so, and taking into account the fact that most Jewish families who had 'silently suffered' in the south before 1872 were there to distance themselves from their social inferiors, it is arguable that in its origins the South Manchester Synagogue owed more to snobbery than to geography.

Other features emphasise the link between events in the north and the foundation of a synagogue in the south. One was the composition of the new congregation.[84] Of a total of forty persons who enrolled in September 1872, and eleven others who joined during the succeeding twelve months, twenty-six lived in the south (nineteen in Chorlton-on-Medlock, three in Greenheys, and one each in Whalley Range, Longsight, Old Trafford, Ardwick and Hulme). Of the remainder, six lived at their places of business in central Manchester, equidistant from both congregations, fourteen in Cheetham Hill, and five in the northern regions of Strangeways. What gave the group coherence was not residence in a single compact district but the discovery of common and distinctive social standards and aspirations, of which life in southern suburbia was only one possible symptom. The decisive factors in emphasising these common standards were the social decline of the inner suburbs of north Manchester and the reflection of this decline in the composition of the Old Congregation. No rapprochement was likely, since there was no way in which these developments in the north might be reversed; unlike Levi's New Congregation, the south Manchester movement represented a permanent secession. Another significant feature of developments in the south was the rehabilitation of Henry Davis Marks. On 12 October 1872 the executive of the South Manchester Congregation accepted his offer to officiate on a voluntary basis at the Holy Day services in Chorlton Town Hall,[85] and shortly afterwards he was appointed 'with acclamation' as 'Reader, Stipendiary Secretary and Minister' at a salary of one hundred guineas a year.[86] It is logical to attribute his appointment in the south to those who had earlier defended him in the north, when he had served as the symbol of the power (and then the declining power) of the Anglo-Jewish élite. It may well be, as the mysterious meetings of Leveson suggest, that in the spring of 1872 the 'English' group already had Marks in mind as their minister in the event of a secession. And the South Manchester Congregation was a secession, in spite of Cowen's claim that it would be no more than a 'branch' of the 'parent' body. All but three of its members—Louis Cobe, Michael Lipman and William Aronsberg—severed their personal connection with the Old Congregation by resigning their seats within it,[87] and there was never any suggestion that the new congregation would either recognise the suzerainty of the Old or adopt the attitudes of deferential respect appropriate to an offspring. Far from it: such attitudes would have run exactly contrary to the social ethos of the south Manchester group.

In truth, the South Manchester Congregation figures in the records of the Great Synagogue not as a friendly branch, but as a deadly enemy. Those who had resigned without paying off all their arrears were threatened with legal prosecution, beginning with Leveson as a test case.[88] The subsequent attempts of the South Manchester Congregation to win the approval of the Chief Rabbi and to secure facilities for *shechita* and burial met with strong opposition. Delegates from the south who, in November 1872, tried to negotiate for the use of the Old Congregation's burial ground at Prestwich were received 'very uncourteously', according to David Cowen,[89] and their request was turned down, first as 'too premature to admit of consideration', and then unconditionally.[90] Finally, the southerners, like Levi's rebels, purchased from Manchester Corporation 'a plot of land, part of the Dissenters' Burial Ground' in Philips Park.[91] When in July 1873 Dr Adler announced his intention to recognise the new congregation and to consecrate the new synagogue then under construction in Sydney Street, the Select Committee of the Old Congregation registered a protest that they had not been consulted, particularly since the new congregation had

been started and is being supported in opposition to ours, principally by members who have seceded from us and who are inducing other of our present constituents to leave our congregation and join theirs.[92]

Social bitterness was compounded by loss of seat rents.

It was the strength of the Old Congregation's feelings which persuaded Dr Adler that his personal intervention was necessary. Although he correctly judged religious division to be inevitable, his hope was that it would be accepted without animosity on either side and without undermining the facilities—for *shechita* and poor relief—upon which the general well-being of the community depended. Communal projects must not be allowed to founder either through lack of co-operation or because the Great Synagogue, following a substantial loss of wealthier members, no longer possessed sufficient income to sustain them. Accordingly, he suggested that each congregation should appoint three delegates to a joint committee which would try to arrange an amicable settlement, first by conferring alone and finally by reaching a formal agreement under his own chairmanship. This was not as easy as it sounded, and it seems likely that in suggesting it Dr Adler both misinterpreted the origins of the division and, for that reason, underestimated the social differences upon which it was based. Both congregations proved reluctant to appoint delegates, and, when they finally did so, neither was disposed to make concessions. When delegates from the Great Synagogue turned up 'at the appointed time and place', they were greeted only by a curious letter from the south 'alleging that as two of their Delegates were absent the meeting could not take place'.[93] When the two sides finally came together on 14 September, only two days before Dr Adler's arrival, and three before the consecration of the South Manchester Synagogue in time for the High Festivals, it was decided only 'that as the Delegates had not finally concluded their arguments, the subject be further postponed'.[94] Meantime, after holding temporary services at 58 Upper Brook Street,[95] the South Manchester Congregation had purchased a three-storey dwelling house in Sidney Street for £930 and spent a further £800 in fitting it out as a synagogue in the 'incredibly short period of six weeks'.[96] Could Dr Adler effect an agreement before the consecration of the new building on 17 September?

In opening a final conference under his own chairmanship at the Palatine Hotel on 16 September, Dr Adler spoke

in very affectionate terms exhorting everyone to use his best endeavours to bring about peace . . . as it was essential above all that there should be peace.[97]

It was a matter for regret, he said, that there should be in Manchester a 'divided house at this season of the year when each should forgive and be forgiven'. Although the meeting was conducted in absolute secrecy and no minutes have survived, a report in the *Jewish Chronicle* suggests that provisional agreement was reached on two points.[98] The first decreed the use of a 'common burial ground', although on what terms is not known; the second, and more important, that members of the South Manchester Congregation should make an annual *pro rata* contribution to the funds of the Great Synagogue. This was intended, in part, to emphasise the dependent status of the new congregation, in part to compensate the Old Congregation for the loss of seat rents upon which, amongst other matters, its substantial contribution to the communal Board of Guardians was based. If these terms were ratified by both congregations, then it was further agreed that 'the two congregations should act in concert in general communal action'. On the basis of this tentative agreement, the Chief Rabbi felt justified in proceeding with the consecration on the following day. A banquet followed in Hulme Town Hall, at which Leveson presided, and which was attended, amongst other dignitaries, by the Chief Rabbi and the Mayor of Salford.[99] In the main speech Dr Adler expressed his satisfaction that 'he had done his duty in laying down the basis of union' and voiced the hope

that the members of the Old Congregation would bear towards members of the South Manchester Congregation the same kindly feelings as they bore to them.

Thereafter, according to the main press report,

Dancing was kept up with much spirit until an advanced hour, and the evening's happiness was not marred by the slightest drawback.

This was not quite true. Isaac Franklin introduced a sour note when he remarked upon the absence of the officers of the Old Congregation.

The spirit of the agreement of 16 September had not in fact survived, even until the following day, and the letter of it was destroyed very soon afterwards. Early in October, Isaac Asher Isaacs wrote to the Chief Rabbi that

the minutes of the conference . . . as noted down by A. Leveson, the Honorary Secretary of the Delegates of the South Manchester Synagogue do not correspond with my entry, which is a full and complete record of the proceedings.[100]

A discussion of this discrepancy 'elicited a lengthy argument' in the Select Committee of the Old Congregation,[101] which finally decided to abandon the agreement and to postpone the whole question *sine die*.[102] The Chief Rabbi did not feel inclined to risk his prestige by further intervention, and, in the absence of any local movement of rapprochement, bitter ill-feeling between the two congregations persisted for the remainder of the decade.[103] It flared up again, for example, when in July 1876 the South Manchester Congregation sought from the Chief Rabbi the right to appoint its own independent *shochet*, and again, in March 1878, when the South Manchester executive took the initiative in suggesting a joint charity service. On the first occasion, the Old Congregation coupled a general defence of its monopoly of *shechita* with a pointed attack upon the supposed illiberality of the South Manchester Synagogue;[104] on the second, the desire for a joint service was put down to an attempt 'to get the Rev. Mr Marks acknowledged as a preacher and colleague of the Rev. Professor'.[105] Reconciliation was not effected until the mass influx of Eastern European refugees after 1881 emphasised the logic of a united front, not only in the interests of humanity but still more to preserve the identity and interests of a middle-class Jewry which stretched over both congregations against the inroads of a fresh horde of pauper immigrants.[106]

IV

During the clash of 1876 Isaac Asher Isaacs informed the Chief Rabbi that the Great Synagogue

would willingly bury the past in oblivion and fain would believe as much of South Manchester but that there is a *lever*, which probably you are aware of, and which is *continually at work* against the welfare of *this* House of Worship.[107]

He urged Dr Adler to turn down the request for a *shochet*

until the time is ripe for a general amalgamation, which, however, cannot take place so long as the *lever* continues to act.[108]

Why was Isaacs so cryptic in identifying the source of dissension? It seems reasonable to suppose that the 'lever' was a living person, the use of whose name would lay Isaacs open to accusations of libel. But what person? Only one name fits. Using a play on words, Isaacs was laying the charge of conspiracy at the door of Alexander Leveson. This seems reasonable enough. Leveson, who settled in Manchester in the early 1850s, had been one of thirteen signatories who in March 1856 had protested at the 'extraordinary and unprecedented' dismissal of Dr Schiller-Szinessy as Local Rabbi. Of the thirteen, nine, including David Hesse, had subsequently joined the Reform Association, which places Leveson in a highly assimilated group, most of whom ended up at Park Place. It was natural that Leveson should subsequently emerge as one of the leaders of the anglicised élite which remained in the Old Congregation. In this capacity he had opposed the demands of the new seat-holders in 1869, and it was he who chaired the meeting which elected Marks, and from which the seat-holders were ignominiously barred. Thereafter he had opposed political concessions to the rebels. During the debates of 1871–72 he organised Marks' defence and apparently prepared the way for a possible secession. What more natural than that with the victory of the immigrant group and the dismissal of Marks, he should take it upon himself to organise the rump of Anglo-Jewry? It is quite possible, indeed, that it was Leveson's ability and force of character which did most to create the South Manchester Synagogue, and that Cowen's chief contribution was to provide a dignified and civilised front. It was again logical, as Isaacs' letter suggests, that Leveson should persistently oppose reunion and should welcome any move—such as the appointment of an independent *shochet*—which emphasised the congregation's separate identity. If the group which founded the South Manchester Synagogue might have achieved social solidarity without him, it was Leveson who provided it with political unity.

He would have liked also to determine its religious character. In a crucial debate in May 1873, in which the committee of the South Manchester Synagogue had discussed their future relationship with the Chief Rabbi, Leveson was amongst those who pressed for absolute autonomy.[109] This is not to suggest that he was a Reformer. Leveson was still committed to the original idea of a congregation open to 'all sections of opinion', and he was anxious not to adopt a measure, such as the acceptance of the orthodox Chief Rabbi of the Ashkenazim, which would effectively exclude Reform and Sephardi Jews living in south Manchester. Leveson's concept was of a congregation in which the bonds of cohesion were exclusively social, and in which religious differences counted for nothing, While sharing his social bias, however, the committee was not inclined to take it to the point of seeking a ritual common denominator. His view was not accepted, and the congregation opted to accept the spiritual guidance of the Chief Rabbi.[110] Effectively, the basis of the congregation's support was limited to the Ashkenazim and its ritual future restricted within the boundaries of Adlerite orthodoxy.

General matters of ritual and decorum had first been discussed at the open meeting of 8 September 1872, when it was accepted that the new synagogue's affairs should be

marked by that thoroughly conciliatory and inaggressive spirit, which at all times has been the standard of a truly Jewish movement,

and that its ritual should be

conducted upon the same principle as the Bayswater Synagogue of London, which has proved a success amongst the suburban synagogues of the metropolis.[111]

A letter from Dr Hermann Adler, the Minister at Bayswater (and son of the Chief Rabbi), provided the necessary information and promised further support, and in the following month Marks was sent to London to familiarise himself with the 'Bayswater liturgy'.[112] This provided for a strengthening of decorum and a simplification of the service which, while recommending itself to the assimilated families of suburbia, involved no commitment to radical ideology or practice. In June 1873, following the discussion of the Chief

Rabbi's role, the Council of Administrators (the executive organ of the congregation) pledged itself

to carry out in the congregation due decorum in the service and whilst adhering most strictly to the principles of orthodoxy a gentle reform in the service should take place.[113]

In immediate terms, 'gentle reform' meant nothing more than the Bayswater ritual, and in the long run it involved no greater changes than a reordering of the internal layout of the synagogue and the promotion of English as the language of prayer, the latter at the instigation of the German woollen merchant, W. F. Bernstein. According to the *Jewish Chronicle*

it was chiefly on his initiative that the 'Ten Commandments' and other portions of the service were read in English at their synagogue long before such practice was adopted at any other orthodox synagogue.[114]

There was, in fact, no one amongst the original founders to provide the congregation with any radical intellectual momentum. The only Hebrew scholar was Henry Zirndorf, who had served as rabbi of a congregation in Hungary, but he had no new ideological preconceptions and, at all events, exercised little influence. In May 1874 he left Manchester to become minister of the Jewish congregation at Munster in Westphalia and Principal there of the Ecclesiastical College School.[115] It was the social quality of the new congregation, not its religious novelty, which accounted for its distinctive features. It expressed the ambitions and fears of an Anglo-Jewish élite in 1872, and in later years provided a nucleus for the settlement of assimilated Jewish families in the southern suburbs.[116]

V

The foundation of the South Manchester Synagogue was only one of the consequences of the political storms which swept through the Old Congregation during the years 1869–72. They also provided the occasion, although not perhaps the cause, for the foundation of Manchester's first Spanish and Portuguese Synagogue.

Few Sephardi Jews had found their way to Manchester before the middle of the nineteenth century. The first was perhaps a Joseph Mendez, of whom nothing is known beyond the fact that he lived at 15 Cross Street and occupied a seat in the Halliwell Street Synagogue for a few months during 1827–28. Manchester residents of the early 1830s included Hyam De Costa and Joseph Raphael, both quill dressers in the Old Town, neither of whom stayed for more than two years. The first permanent Sephardi settler was Samuel Hadida, a commission agent of Gibraltese birth, who arrived early in 1843, acquired an office in Mosley Street and rented a house in Moreton Street, Strangeways, then emerging as a middle-class suburb. On 7 May 1844, at the synagogue in Halliwell Street, he married Charlotte Solomon, daughter of the *shamash*. Hadida was apparently at the centre of a small group of Sephardi merchants—not more than eight in all—who settled in Manchester during the 1840s. On Census night, 1851, when he was living at 35 Great Ducie Street, his lodgers included Abraham Nissim Levy of Constantinople, a visitor to Manchester since 1843 and a seat-holder at Halliwell Street from 1844–45; Isaac Pariente, a young general merchant from the African 'Barbary Coast', who first appears in congregational records as a 'stranger' in 1845–46; and Joshua Padr of Constantinople, nineteen years of age and an 'assistant at a foreign house' (probably Hadida's), who first rented a seat at Halliwell Street for the Holy days of 1847–48. Padr was known to the congregational treasurers, perhaps in mock Ashkenazi deference, as 'Deo Padro'. Others who appear briefly in the synagogue's records as the donors of offerings were Moses Ben Messulam, also of Constantinople (from September 1847, when he was described as being 'with A. N. Levy'), Myer Hadida (1847–48), Samuel Ventura (1850–51) and Joseph Azula (1851–52). Other Sephardim in the Census of 1851 were Samuel Kutura, a confectioner and the first Jewish settler from Corfu; Moses Benzieri of Gibraltar, an interpreter (perhaps for Sephardi traders), lodging in Moreton Street; and Nathan B. Lyons, a sixty-year-old Hebrew teacher of Turkish origin living in a crowded lodging house at 66 Long Millgate. Lyons apart, it seems reasonable to see in these early settlers, a group of closely-associated immigrant entrepreneurs, the younger members of established commercial families in the Sephardi world, seeking to breach the Greek monopoly of Manchester's textile trade with the Mediterranean littoral by setting up agencies at the source of supply.[117] The immediate incentive was perhaps provided by the development of a regular steamship service between Britain and Mediterranean ports from the later 1830s and the development of overland links between the Mediterranean and the Indian Ocean, through Syria and Egypt, early in the following decade.

The compounding of these advantages by the completion of the rail link between Alexandria and Suez during 1856–57, and the gradual opening up of the Mediterranean hinterland, brought a fresh wave of Sephardi commercial agents to Manchester during the later 1850s, from Greece, Egypt and the Levant. The first were perhaps Mardocheo Besso, and his son Haim, of Corfu, whose commission agency in Bond Street was founded in 1857.[118] Four years later, a colony of at least fifteen Sephardi families included Ezra Sharim and

Joshua Cohen, both of Aleppo; S. G. Besso and Sabbato Levy of Corfu; Felice Naggiar, from one of the wealthiest Sephardi families of Cairo; and Isaac David Belisha,[119] whose family traced its origins to the Jewish intellectual aristocracy of medieval Spain. Their settlement was only very recent, and perhaps still tentative at the time of the Census of 1861, when most were living in lodgings with Jewish families in Strangeways and Cheetham Hill, Haim Besso, for example, in the household of M. H. Simonson, the former Secretary–Reader and then a private teacher of Hebrew, on the Bury New Road. In so far as the group had a leader it was Belisha, who settled with his wife and five children in the fashionable Bloomsbury district of Chorlton-on-Medlock. Born in Paris in 1825, Belisha had spent his early years in London before setting up a commission agency in 1852 in the newly-founded city of Melbourne, where he played a leading part in creating the first Jewish congregation. He moved to Gibraltar in 1855 and settled in Manchester four years later. His outstanding wealth, knowledge of English and experience in the organisation of communal life equipped him to provide the nucleus of a Sephardi congregation, while the failure of several Greek houses in Manchester with the collapse of Turkish credit during the winter of 1860–61[120] increased the likelihood of a permanent and expanding Sephardi settlement. By the middle of the decade some twenty Sephardi families, including Belisha's, were clustered around Elizabeth Street and Heywood Street in the upper, and more salubrious, regions of Cheetham Hill.

Although the evidence is fragmentary, it seems likely that during the early 1860s the Manchester Sephardim combined membership of the Great Synagogue, which assured them of communal facilities for marriage, burial and *shechita*, with occasional attendance at a private *minyan*, in which services were conducted according to the distinctive Sephardi ritual.[121] During 1864–65 they conducted negotiations with the Select Committee, apparently to agree terms upon which they might retain the privileges of membership without losing the right of private worship.[122] Subsequent admissions to the Free Membership of the Old Congregation included Sabbato Besso, Isaac Azula, Elia Levy and Isaac Belisha (1865), Felice Naggiar (1868), Saul Bigio (1869), Moses Messulam (1870) and Raphael Besso (1871), and marriages in the synagogue included those of Moses Bianco of Aleppo (to the daughter of Ezra Sharim, in 1867), Isaac Zaguri (1868) and Felix Sahal (1869). At the same time, the Sephardi *minyan* was centred successively in a house in Southall Street (on a site subsequently occupied by the Woolpack Hotel), 59 Cheetham Hill Road (the celebrated 'Hayshop Shule', above a provender shop) and the old building of the Jews School at 78 Cheetham Hill Road.[123] In August 1868 they were said to be 'talking of building a synagogue of their own',[124] but nothing came of the idea, perhaps because the multinational character of the Sephardim militated against unity. Four years later, when the number of Sephardi families in Manchester had risen to thirty-five, a reporter from the *Jewish Chronicle* was

delighted with the good order . . . maintained in their private prayer room . . . it speaks well for a community that is formed of so many different nationalities.[125]

The ten Corfiote families possessed sufficient cohesion to contribute collectively in 1872 to the languishing Talmud Torah of their home town,[126] but no group was as stubbornly independent as the merchants of Aleppo, who looked for leadership to Ezra Sharim and found a social centre in a coffee house attached to the warehouse of Moses Bianco in Bootle Street.[127] It seems certain that by the beginning of 1872 there were several Sephardi prayer rooms, including one at the house of Sharim in Petworth Street.[128] The main Sephardi *minyan* possessed no separate religious organisation, the senior members acting in turn as 'principal readers' on Sabbaths and Holy Days, to the accompaniment of a small choir.[129]

What almost certainly provided the Sephardim with the final impetus towards the creation of their own place of worship was the political and social deterioration of the Old Congregation during the stormy debates of 1869–72. After occasionally attempting, none too successfully, to exercise a moderating influence, the Sephardim became convinced of the disadvantages of being 'swamped in the German ocean',[130] and of the need to unify their own congregational life and to place it on a more permanent and respectable basis. Although social considerations were perhaps not so pronounced, and certainly not as explicit, as in the south Manchester movement, there was a sense in which a Sephardi commercial aristocracy was no longer prepared to accept the noisy company of German shopkeepers and Eastern European entrepreneurs. On 4 February 1872, as the debate surrounding Marks reached its climax, thirty-one Sephardim met at 78 Cheetham Hill Road, under the chairmanship of Elia Negrin

in order to bring forward a discussion as to the mode of improving the present place of worship, the better organisation of conducting it, with the view of erecting later on a more suitable place of worship.[131]

Negrin provided no more than the advantage of a neutral chair; the prime mover was Belisha, who was made chairman of a steering committee of fifteen.[132] Proceedings were held up briefly by the dissent 'of some of the Aleppo gentlemen', described bitterly by Belisha as '*Karaites*',[133] but once Sharim was won over there was no further obstacle, either social or financial. At the initial meeting, donations were promised to a total of £910. A delegation which travelled to London to seek the support of Bevis Marks received a friendly welcome, and financial support, on the sole condition that the Manchester Sephardim accepted the religious guidance of the Haham.[134] A site was chosen on Cheetham Hill Road, the land purchased from the Earl of Derby, and on 11 June 1873 the corner-stone was laid of a new building (see Figure 9), designed—again in a 'saracenic' pattern—by Edward Salomon, the architect of Park Place.[135] In the following March the Sephardim found a suitable minister in the young Henry Pereira Mendes, son of Rev. A. P. Mendes, the Principal of Northwick College and grandson of Haham Dr Meldola.[136] The building was completed soon afterwards at a total cost of around £3,000 and was consecrated by Haham Dr Artom on 6 May 1874.[137] With the exception of the family synagogue of the Montefiores at Ramsgate, it was the first Sephardi synagogue in provincial England.[138]

Its foundation was accompanied by none of the unpleasantness of the south Manchester secession. This was chiefly, perhaps, because it was explicable at the Old Congregation in terms which implied no criticism of its standards.

FIGURE 9   The Spanish and Portuguese Synagogue, 1874.

The south Manchester movement was construed, probably correctly, as a snub; the exodus of the Sephardim was regarded as the inevitable consequence of real ritual differences, which implied no inferiority on either side. Both represented a loss of seat rents; only south Manchester implied a loss of dignity. Two years later, therefore, Isaac Asher Isaacs was willing to draw a sharp contrast between the 'antagonistic' congregations at Park Place and Sidney Street, and the 'friendly Synagogue of Portuguese Jews'.[139] The Sephardim had in fact gone out of their way to retain the good will of the Old Congregation, not least because they wished to share the burial ground at Prestwich. When, on 19 September 1872, the south Manchester group invited them to join forces in the creation of a single new congregation, Belisha replied, with significant exaggeration, that 'the progress of our present object was so far advanced, that it is impossible to annul the whole by entertaining their proposal'.[140] In June 1873 Belisha pointedly refrained from inviting representatives from Sidney Street to the corner-stone ceremony, a matter of 'deep regret' in south Manchester.[141] In March 1874, as part of the terms by which they were given access to Prestwich, he agreed to remain independent of any other Manchester congregation,[142] a matter which at all events had become academic once south Manchester had accepted the jurisdiction of the Chief Rabbi. Subsequent relations were not improved by the attempt of the south Manchester committee to secure the allegiance of disaffected Sephardim.[143] In fact, however, the Spanish and Portuguese Synagogue did not exist in opposition to any other; rather it provided the opportunity for a separate religious life on the basis of the ritual and traditions of the Sephardim.[144]

VI

The opening of the Spanish and Portuguese Synagogue completed the basic pattern of Manchester's religious life. In possessing Reform, Sephardi and Ashkenazi places of worship, it was, as the *Jewish Chronicle* commented, 'the only provincial city which contains congregations representing all three sections of the Jewish community'.[145] Since the orthodox Ashkenazim were divided in their synagogal allegiance, the division was in reality fivefold. The Old Congregation was the centre of traditional Anglo-Jewish orthodoxy, veering slightly in a more conservative or more radical direction with the changing balance of its membership, but always falling back on the even keel of moderation. In adopting the Bayswater liturgy south Manchester had set the predominant style of suburban orthodoxy in a 'gentle reform' of ritual, acceptable equally to the Chief Rabbi and to a self-conscious middle-class élite. It was a style which later recommended itself, in various forms, to other suburban groups in north as well as south Manchester, which wished to express the degree of their assimilation to English middle-class norms without entertaining the extreme of Reform.[146] In its origin, it made the point that a 'suburban synagogue' was not one simply which met the needs of well-to-do Jewish families which had colonised a new district; the crucial matter was a sense of corporate class identity which was expressed not only in topographic terms. Finally, there were what Isaac Isaacs described as 'the various opposing influences' of at least twenty *chevroth*,[147] varying in the precise form of their religious life, but dedicated as a whole to the strictest religious standards of the Eastern European ghetto. Although vulnerable to the overwhelming forces of social assimilation, directed towards them in part by the Jews School and Board of Guardians, the *chevroth* were sustained by a flow of immigration which kept up until the First World War and by a line of the most uncompromising Polish rabbis, of whom the prototype was Susman Cohen of the *Chevra Walkawishk*. Despised by leaders of Anglo-Jewry, the *chevroth* served in many ways to underpin the whole religious structure of the community by providing a constant source of fresh inspiration from the fount of Jewish orthodoxy.

Within the Great Synagogue, the loss of members by secession was the cause of considerable distress. Isaac Asher Isaacs, in particular, believed the Manchester experience of rebellion and dissent to have been 'sad indeed'. He wrote in 1876:

It will take a long time for this Synagogue to recover [from] the keen effects of the blows it *has* received and *under which it still reels.* Should any further blows be dealt at it the consequences may be more serious than can—on the surface—be surmised.[148]

The blows had been to the pride and reputation of the Old Congregation as much as to its wealth. Louis Cobe told a communal conference that

. . . other Synagogues had arisen, secessions had taken place and the whole character of this Synagogue had altered, until now it was composed of working men and small shop keepers. The other Synagogues . . . had taken their wealthiest members.[149]

These were overstatements. In spite of the very real losses of 1872–74, the Old Congregation survived not only as the centre of gravity of Manchester orthodoxy but as the largest and collectively the wealthiest of Manchester synagogues. A monopolistic control over *shechita*, in particular, provided the congregation not only with an unassailable sphere of religious influence but with a steady and substantial source of income. Moreover, however many the dissentients, the Old Congregation continued to regard its ritual as the religious norm. As one member commented during one of the perennial battles with the immigrant rabbis of the *chevroth*: 'We are looked upon as *the* Congregation and must not humble ourselves to others.'[150]

Conclusion

The period of Anglo-Jewish history which opens with Rothschild's entry into the House of Commons in 1858 and ends with the Russian pogroms of 1881–82 is often treated as something of a hiatus between the social and political establishment of Anglo-Jewry on the one side and the flood tide of Eastern European immigration on the other. Many loose ends were tidied up, but the really significant movements within the English community are taken to have fallen on either side of the period. Preceding it was the development of an anglicised middle-class community, the struggle for social acceptance and political freedom, the Reform controversy, and the creation of three great metropolitan institutions—the Board of Deputies, the Chief Rabbinate and the Board of Guardians. Following it was the 'mass immigration' of 1881–1914, a period of critical tension between immigrant and Anglo-Jew, the political awakening of working-class Jewry in the sweat-shops and the slums, the venom of the 'Alien Question', and the origins of Zionism. The years between often appear, by contrast, to constitute a plateau between two periods of substantial and fundamental change. Even those who see continuous Eastern European settlement as having begun in the 1870s, or the middle 1860s, or even earlier, seem reluctant to admit that its impact was anything but peripheral before 1881.[1]

I

This was not true of many provincial communities, particularly in the north of England, South Wales and the industrial Midlands. The Manchester evidence, taken at a strategic point on the main route of transmigration, suggests that the influx of 1881–82 may be regarded not as a new beginning but as the culmination of a process which can be traced back to the mid-1840s, and possibly earlier, and which owed its origin to deteriorating economic conditions in the overpopulated Jewish districts of Russian and Prussian Poland, aggravated in the former by constant discrimination and occasional persecution. The account book kept by the Old Congregation's Board of Relief during the period 1848–52 establishes beyond doubt that, notwithstanding the political upheavals in Western Europe, a majority of transmigrants had travelled from towns and villages in the districts around Warsaw and Posen, aided by improving rail services converging on Berlin and Hamburg. It was the 'residue' of this trans-migration which by the time of the Census of 1851 had laid the social and economic basis of Eastern European life on Red Bank. The early 1860s were an important turning point, not so much, as has been suggested, in the nature of Jewish migration (from German and Dutch to Polish and Russian),[2] but as a point at which many immigrants, deterred by Civil War in America, elected to remain in English towns, including (perhaps especially) Manchester, rather than proceed across the Atlantic. Unlike the pedlars of an earlier age they elected to settle not in seaports and market towns but in some of the more buoyant centres of England's industrial life and, in so doing they served, at the very least, to confirm a new pattern of Jewish settlement in the provinces. Further research may perhaps confirm that Eastern European settlement itself, beginning as it did in the later 1840s, was the main factor in establishing the numerical predominance of industrial centres in Anglo-Jewish life in the second half of the nineteenth-century.[3] However that may be, Eastern Euro-peans formed a steadily increasing proportion of Manchester's expanding Jewish population, until by 1875 they comprised at least half, and possibly as much as two-thirds, of an estimated total of 7,000.[4]

This was of more than demographic significance. It is clear from a variety of sources that the pattern of immigrant society usually associated with the 1880s—closely-knit slum settlement, a narrow range of workshop trades, and a distinctive cultural and religious life centred upon the *chevroth*—was al-ready evolving during the 1860s and 1870s, and by 1875 had already achieved a form which did not alter in its essentials for the succeeding forty years.

Again, Manchester shared the common experience of English urban com-munities of the 1860s. Wherever the immigrants went they developed an econ-omic life which owed more to their own prior experience and religious scruples than to the characteristics of the host community. The *Jewish Chronicle* saw the extension of Jewish settlement to new centres of industry as a means both of decentralising the working-class community and of easing it away from '2 or 3 ill-paid trades'[5] towards more stable occupations.

Is it written in the Book of Fate that all poor Jews who come to England shall reside in London—in a few squalid, unhealthy streets in the metropolis, and shall eke out a miserable existence in two overstocked and unhealthy trades, aided by almost contin-uous assistance from the Board of Guardians? . . . The more channels of labour that are opened in the provinces the better for the metropolis.[6]

The coal mines of Newcastle and the iron industry of the North Riding were amongst several well-publicised alternatives.[7] But, in fact, while London Jewry's East End continued to expand, Jewish immigrants in provincial towns did little more than reproduce the metropolitan pattern, at least in the first generation. The thousand Polish Jews living in Newcastle in 1873 earned their living, like their *landsleit* in Manchester, as 'slippermakers, tailors, itinerant glaziers and travelling jewellers'.[8] The foundations of the wholesale tailoring industry of Leeds were laid in the workshops of immigrant entrepreneurs, like that of Herman Friend in Templar Street, in the 1860s.[9] Everywhere, too, the immigrants moved into down-at-heel areas recently vacated by English working or lower-middle-class families, clearly distinguished from the residential districts of Anglo-Jewry,[10] and established a separate religious life, distinctive, devout, and usually torn by personal and sectarian dispute.[11] Variations from town to town were matters only of balance and degree.[12]

By posing what were regarded as serious threats to the repute and financial viability of the established community, Eastern European immigration and settlement had also begun to shape the institutional structure of Anglo-Jewish life in Manchester long before the 1880s. It was the beginning of extensive transmigration in the later 1840s which, more than any other single force, brought together the two warring segments of the Jewish middle class in a defence of their common prestige.[13] Subsequent immigration and settlement served as the final catalyst in the community's erratic attempts to adjust traditional methods of congregational relief—well-intentioned, but pragmatic and paternal—to the new and growing demands of a large urban community. The emergence of more deterrent attitudes, however ineffective, gave rise to the Board of Relief during the years 1847–52, to the occasional suspension of all relief operations during the 1850s, and to the severe measures of retrenchment suggested by David Hesse. At this stage, while it was still possible to believe that Polish immigration was a temporary phenomenon which might be discouraged, or at least diverted, Hesse saw the answer to the community's problems in the application of the harsh Utilitarian principles of the New Poor Law. The increasing settlement of the 1860s shattered this illusion and brought a new sense of urgency which Landeshut was able to convert into a local board of Guardians. It is not enough to see the foundation of Jewish Boards of Guardians in Manchester, and in other provincial centres,[14] as part of the 'reflected light' of London Jewry.[15] Certainly London provided a model; but other urban communities faced similar problems and were beginning to feel their way, in the 1850s and 1860s, towards structural solutions which required a similar range of components. Processes of integration, as much as policies of 'anglicisation', were a product not of London, or of the 1880s,[16] but of an earlier period, when they emerged as part of a common Anglo-Jewish response to pressures from the Eastern European poor. If Manchester reacted earlier, and more strongly than most other communities, it was because she lay directly in the path of immigration.

The growth of the immigrant community, although it was not responsible for the foundation of the Manchester Jews School, promoted its expansion and determined its character as an explicit agency of assimilation. During the 1860s the school abandoned the last vestiges of the early pretence that it served the needs of the upper and middle as well as the lower classes. It was characterised rather by an 'immensely large element of foreign children' who spoke little English and heard none at home.[17] It became quite openly an institution 'to afford to the children of the indigent the best means of raising themselves from the abject and dependent condition of their parents'.[18] The character of the school was also reflected in the style of its curriculum, which, apart from the introduction of drawing (1857–58)[19] and vocal music (1867–68),[20] reflected working-class needs. 'Able and deserving' girls were encouraged to 'cooperate' with the school charwoman 'with a view to their imbibing useful knowledge of an essential branch of domestic economy';[21] sewing, in which the instruction was made more 'practical' after 1861,[22] was described by the school committee as 'woman's chief resource';[23] in 1871 a 'drilling master' was appointed to instil greater 'decorum and discipline' into the children,[24] whose rowdiness broke one Hebrew master after another.[25] Boys who had passed the Sixth Standard were eligible for the apprenticeship scheme organised by the Board of Guardians,[26] while their parents were invited to a Mothers Meeting at which they were taught the art of mending clothes by middle-class ladies of leisure.[27] So proletarian had the school become by the mid-1860s that a powerful movement developed to provide a suitable alternative for the middle classes. In October 1864 D. M. Isaacs, minister of the Old Congregation,[28] chaired a meeting at which 'sixty gentlemen' each pledged £5 towards the venture,[29] and three years later sufficient had been collected to open the 'Manchester Classical and Commercial Schools' under the presidency of Abraham Franks.[30] The *Jewish Chronicle* commented:

a seminary for the children of the wealthier classes had long been a desideratum of this rapidly increasing congregation. It was felt almost a reproach that whilst so much was done for the instruction and amelioration of the indigent, chiefly by the patrons of the Manchester Jews School, no attempt has been made on a large scale to provide a special Jewish education for the rising generation amongst the more fortunate Israelites,[31]

sentiments reiterated by Dr Adler when he came down to Manchester to consecrate the new South Manchester Synagogue.[32]

The overall effect of Eastern European settlement was to emphasise the collective self-interest of the 'more fortunate' Anglo-Jewish families. It gave new edge to the recurrent, and usually abrasive, interaction between established families and newcomers of all kinds which provided communal history with its basic dialectic. It is possible to read such a clash into the relations of the Jacob and Franklin families in the 1830s, the former representing the founder fathers, the latter the immigrant shopkeepers of the 1820s. The evidence is more explicit in the 1840s, when the revolt of the seat-holders associated with David Hesse was provoked by the exclusiveness of an established élite in which Abraham Franklin had become the key figure. By the time early Eastern European immigrants were in a financial position to seek the privileges of Free Membership, in the 1860s, many of the families reunited by expediency in 1851 had acquired cohesion as a new ruling class within the Old Congregation, and the stage was set for the violent clashes of 1869–72. But on this occasion, the origin of the immigrants (and perhaps their numbers) appears to have injected a new degree of bitterness into their relationships with established Anglo-Jewry. The fortunes of Henry Davis Marks were largely determined by his role as the symbol of the supposed inferiority of the one and the declared superiority of the other.[33]

The tensions generated in the Great Synagogue by the entrance and assertiveness of Eastern European seat-holders led a group of the more sophisticated and longer-established families to seek their religious fortunes elsewhere. At the very least, events within the Old Congregation converted the politically innocent and tentative idea of a southern branch into a determined move to create an independent synagogue; at most, they were the decisive factor in giving rise even to the idea of a new congregation—after all, there had been families living in south Manchester, many of them further south than Grosvenor Square, since the 1830s. At all events, the Manchester evidence suggests that the origins of a suburban synagogue lie not so much in the physical dispersal of the community, although this was a necessary prerequisite, as in the evolution by one group of a sense of collective identity as a cultural élite. The colonisation of All Saints and the foundation of the South Manchester Synagogue may be seen not so much as cause and effect but as two aspects of the Anglo-Jewish response to the extensive settlement of Eastern Europeans in Strangeways and Cheetham Hill.[34] Indirectly, too, the supposedly declining social tone of the Great Synagogue, and more clearly its political chaos, produced the Sephardi secession, for although they possessed a proud traditional identity, it was their growing sense of solidarity as a merchant class which unified the Sephardim and provided the occasion for the foundation of the Spanish and Portuguese Synagogue.

Finally, in the years before 1880, a strong immigrant middle class was already beginning to acquire a sense of its distinctive identity and collective power. The successful workshop entrepreneurs of the early 1860s, arising as they did out of the relatively small-scale immigration of the preceding decades, were few in number and for this reason they tended to seek social recognition as individuals through membership of the Old Congregation, where their presence and demands provoked the political turbulence of 1869–72. The distinguishing feature of the mid-1870s was the emergence of a far larger and more cohesive entrepreneurial class from amongst the more numerous immigrants of the 1860s. Schooled in the ethos of the *chevroth*, their search was not so much for personal acceptance through association with a reputable Anglo-Jewish congregation (although some chose this route) as for acceptance as a group on their own uncompromising terms. This was a symptom, too, of their growing confidence. By the mid-1870s they believed in the possibility of institutions which gave them prestige and embodied their own ideals rather than those of the Anglo-Jewish élite. And they were confirmed in this belief by powerful patrons—William Aronsberg, for example—who floated their ambition for influence in the English, and Anglo-Jewish, milieu upon the tide of immigrant aspirations.

The earliest evidence of these new forces was probably in the movement which began in 1875 for the creation of a Manchester *Beth Hamidrash* 'where the Holy Law can be studied and expounded and where the rising generation may obtain a thorough knowledge of Hebrew'.[35] The movement was promoted by influential, but strictly observant immigrants who viewed

with alarm and horror the ungodly way in which [young men] are allowed to grow up, deficient in religious feeling and indulging in immoral employment; and who, to remedy this awful state of things, are endeavouring to provide an antidote to the billiard rooms and the card tables on which the young men spent all their leisure moments, Sabbaths and Festivals.[36]

So attractive was the idea in Red Bank that during the winter of 1875–76 it developed into a wider scheme for the amalgamation of all the *chevroth* into a single place of worship and study which would express the full force of immigrant religious fervour.[37] Although the nominal lead was taken by immigrants of the 1850s, notably Aronsberg, but also W. S. Rothband, Joseph Mandleberg and Mark Steinart, the chief momentum was provided by entrepreneurs of a younger generation, and by their immigrant rabbis, Susman Cohen of the *Chevra Walkawischk* and Elira Tumin of the *Chevra Torah*.

The movement failed, perhaps because the immigrant middle class lacked political experience, but it was the beginning of a process of immigrant self-assertion which was to give rise in turn to the Talmud Torah (1879–80), the Shechita Board (1892), the Manchester *Beth Din* (1902), the Jewish Hospital in Elizabeth Street (1904) and the Manchester *Yeshiva* (1911),[38] each designed to raise or reinforce the community's standards of religious observance. The Manchester Burial Society of Polish Jews Limited (1877)[39] strengthened the religious life of the immigrants by freeing the people of the *chevroth* from dependence upon the burial grounds of established synagogues. In a recent thesis Mr John Shaftesley has presented a strong case for believing that the origins of Manchester's Communal Council lie in this same determination of immigrants to protect their rights.[40] Yet another feature of the whole process was the survival of many of the *chevroth* of the 1870s and their emergence as separate synagogues, rather than their incorporation into existing Anglo-Jewish institutions. This again set the stage for the religious conflicts of the 1880s and the 1890s, anticipated in the *Beth Hamidrash* controversy, in which the *chevroth*, backed by the new middle class and by rabbis of fanatical determination, sought to consolidate their distinctive identity and standards in the face of the powerful assimilatory pressures exerted by Anglo-Jewry.

Perhaps the main significance of the 1880s, apart from the substantial numerical expansion of the immigrant community, lay in the new ideological orientations—Socialism, and particularly Zionism—born in the desperation of persecution and flight. Prior to the 1870s Manchester had shown relatively little interest in the affairs of international Jewry, and when this interest first found organised expression in the establishment of a Manchester Branch of the Anglo-Jewish Association in February 1872,[41] it was in a form which laid emphasis upon assimilatory objectives. As the *Jewish Chronicle* commented, the Anglo-Jewish Association indicated 'the possibility of international Judaism' without the 'chimerical vision' of Zion.[42] The object was the elevation of Jewish life throughout the world, but not

to the detriment of that strong link of patriotism—the bond of birth—which connects in solemn union men boasting the same fatherland.[43]

This represented the outlook of the Anglo-Jewish élite, and in Manchester, as in London, the main impetus derived from the most anglicised section of the community, particularly from Reformers, who saw it as an alternative international agency to the Board of Deputies, upon which they were still not represented. It was not until the later 1880s that the political thought of the immigrants was articulated, in Manchester's earliest Zionist organisations, by the poet, printer and Hebraist (and later the close friend of Chaim Weizman) Joesph Massel.[44] Here again, once the ideological seed had been sown, the lead was taken by the immigrant entrepreneurs—Mark Steinart in particular[45]—who were at the same time building a new network of religious organisations. In each case, although it was convenient to have an Anglo-Jewish patron, with funds and influence at his disposal, the impetus came from below.[46]

II

There was something of a parallel between the tensions set up by immigrants within Anglo-Jewish society and the small beginnings of tension between Jewish immigrants and the wider community.[47] Although there was a floating population of German paupers in northern towns, from which Hermann Falk was able to recruit salt miners for his Winsford enterprise in the later 1860s,[48] other immigrant groups in Manchester, apart from the perennial Irish poor, existed on a higher social level. German residents were chiefly merchants and professional men, many of whom were members of the German Lutheran Church in Greenheys and sent their children to the school organised by its minister, Rev. H. E. Marotsky.[49] Their cultural life centred upon the *Schiller Anstalt*. Engels was at the centre of a group of radicals which included Carl Schorlemmer of the Chemistry Department at Owens College, the political exiles Louis Borchardt and Dr Wilhelm Wolff, and, occasionally, Karl Marx.[50] German nationalism found an outlet in the *Deutscher National Verein*, of which the secretary was Adolf Eller[51] (a Reform Jew, and secretary also to the Jews School) and in which Borchardt was also active.[52] Greek merchants, whatever the inroads made on their Levant trade by the Sephardim, possessed a strong and coherent communal life centring upon the new Greek Church built on the Bury New Road during 1860–61.[53] At the opening ceremony, in October 1861, their chaplain, Dr Moro, spoke indignantly of assertions that the Greek nation had 'degenerated'; their commercial activities 'proved that the spirit of enterprise was as strong and active as of old'.[54] In Manchester, the new church was seen as 'the means of preserving their nationality, their language and their religion'.[55]

The immigrant community on Red Bank was far removed from this level of aspiration and achievement. Poor, squalid, gauche, inarticulate, fearful, lacking membership of respected institutions, out of step with the major intellectual and political trends in Western Europe, Jewish immigrants were as open as the Irish to ridicule and abuse. They were 'miserable specimens of humanity' according to William Thorp,

seldom communicative or truthful. An apprenticeship under despotism in not conducive either to openness or veracity, and they never seem to comprehend that what was a crime in the country they left might be considered a credit here.[56]

Another writer saw a shop in Withy Grove (in 1865)

tenanted by a colony of Jew tailors, and a deal of information on the subject of low domestic life may be gained from an occasional glimpse through the large shop-windows which display the interior . . . the only blind consists of a fly-blown sheet of the fashions of 1817 or 1818 . . . and part of the colony is continually employed in some culinary occupation whilst the rest of it seem struggling for bare life.[57]

That 'struggle' was a source of trouble, too. In 1871 a 'numerously signed' petition was presented to the Town Clerk by the Gentile residents of Red Bank, complaining of the noise made by the sewing machines of their Jewish neighbours.[58] A correspondent to the *Jewish Chronicle* spoke of the 'constant annoyance' to Jews in the streets of Cheetham Hill, claiming to have 'actually seen lads from a neighbouring school' lie in wait for poor Jewish women coming out of shops with their purchases 'and then strike them in the face'.[59] One particularly sharp observer actually discovered a Jewish thief-trainer in the back streets of the Old Town.[60]

But although it is possible to detect in these rare incidents and minor irritations the small beginnings of the anti-alien feelings of the 1880s and 1890s, they were more than offset in the 1870s by the sobriety and social discipline of the immigrant poor, and still more by the established and growing repute of the Anglo-Jewish middle class. Moreover, Manchester men still prided themselves on their 'larger notions' and more 'catholic minded' attitudes which one local M.P. attributed to 'the blending of races' within the city.[61] Jewish immigrants were still perhaps still too few to be regarded as a serious threat to standards of living or rates of pay, and there is reason to believe that Red Bank had not yet been discovered by the community's potential critics. The noise of Jewish sewing machines on the sabbath was dismissed in the local press as a trivial matter. Jews were 'a peaceable race and give less trouble to the police . . . than any other similar class of our fellow-countrymen',[62] a view shared by the chairman of the local Poor Law Union, a J.P., who believed that he had never seen a Jew in court for 'drunkenness or anything that would reflect upon their moral character'.[63] After being called to account for an incidental reference to Jews as 'that degraded people',[64] Jacob Bright became a strong advocate of their local causes.[65] The Law Courts erred in their favour rather than the reverse. In 1862, as Manchester entered a deep commercial depression, Sampson Goodheim, an immigrant cap-making entrepreneur, was in court for continuing to trade while in a state of bankruptcy. Although the accounts he rendered to the commissioners were 'more like Egyptian hieroglyphics than anything else', he was discharged, since his failure to keep readable accounts 'did not prove any intent to defraud'.[66] In a long and notorious libel case arising out of the accusation of the *Manchester Guardian* that Louis Behrens had dealt illegally in bankrupt stock, the weight of public and commercial sympathy was with the *Guardian*, but there was no hint of anti-Semitism, in the press or elsewhere.[67]

The status and prestige of the Jewish middle classes during the 1860s and 1870s may be gauged from the level of their participation in local society. For his many spectacular gifts to local charities and visiting dignitaries—including hundreds of thousands of spectacles to the poor, and 'a beautiful aneroid barometer of solid gold' to the Sultan of Zanzibar—in 1876 William Aronsberg received a testimonial signed 'by a considerable number of noblemen, members of parliament, magistrates and local men of influence', presented by the Lord Mayor in the Town Hall.[68] Edward Salomon, already a prominent local architect by the late 1850s, was on the committee of the Manchester Art Union and amongst the promoters of a free public art gallery in 1860.[69] Although his designs for a new Liverpool Exchange in 1863 failed to win the competition, they were put on public view in the Agnew Gallery in Exchange Street.[70] Joseph Slazenger Moss was amongst the founders, and subsequently president, of the City Road Benefit Building Society.[71] In 1876 Julius Arensberg was installed as master of the De Grey and Ripon Lodge of Freemasons.[72] So prominent were Jews in local Freemasonry that in 1879 a group of eight—including Arensberg, Elias Nathan, and the ill-fated Henry Davis Marks—succeeded in establishing Zion Lodge, which, although not exclusively Jewish, was particularly intended for Jewish members.[73] In 1867 the Jewish composer Frederic Hyman Cowen was appointed to succeed Sir Charles Hallé as conductor of the Liverpool Philharmonic and Hallé Concerts.[74] In the early 1870s Charles Dreyfus, a young chemist from Alsace, arrived in Manchester, where in 1877 he founded the Clayton Aniline Dye Company, in which Chaim Weizman was subsequently to work as a research adviser.[75] David, the son of Sigismund Schloss, was Captain of Manchester Grammar School in 1869 and went on to take a First in Classics at Corpus Christi College, Oxford—'the first Jew who had obtained such a high distinction', according to the *Jewish Chronicle*.[76] Amongst the distinguished students at Owens College during the 1860s and 1870s, when Theodores was a prominent member of the professorial staff, were Max Hesse, Philip Casper and Julius Dreschfeld.[77] A practising Jew had sat on the City Council as early as 1851. In 1876 Henry Samson, partner in the cotton firm Samson & Leppoc, and then chairman of the Manchester Jewish Board of Guardians, became Manchester's first Jewish J.P.[78] Apart from the many Jewish shopkeepers and professional men, Jews were amongst 'the highest mercantile aristocracy in Manchester', considered in the later 1870s to be 'in the zenith of their prosperity'.[79]

The gradual absorption of Jews into English middle-class society affected the internal evolution of the community as much as its external image. As they improved their economic position in a class-conscious milieu, Jewish business and professional men had very rapidly assumed the social pretensions of their Gentile peers. This was expressed in the first instance as a movement into the suburbs which eroded the residential solidarity of the war years. Class distinc-

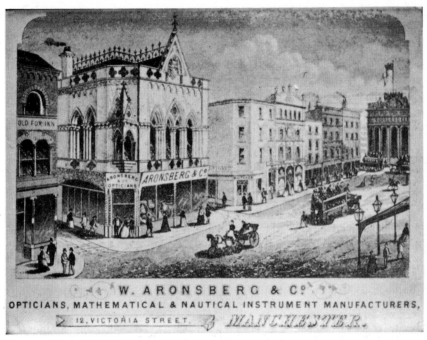

FIGURE 10   Trade card of William Aronsberg, c. 1870.

tion then made itself felt within the synagogue, particularly after an élite of immigrant merchants had superimposed their sense of social superiority upon a traditionally hierarchic structure during the 1830s. Any satisfactory explanation of the rebellions of 1844 and 1869 revolves around the premise that the Jewish businessman expected a standing within the synagogue equivalent to that which he had attained, or to which he aspired, in the town. If the economic pattern of Manchester Jewry derived very largely from communal experience and constraints, its social structure reflected the urban society in which it had evolved. Even the residential configuration of Jewish life, although centred on particular districts, had within it all the differentiations of Gentile society. The institutional development of the community was also directly affected by middle-class Gentile example. The foundation of the Jews School and the organisation of a communal Board of Guardians both suggest the degree to which the leaders of the community were prepared to seize upon Gentile models to solve communal problems. The impulses towards charity and education which were traditional in Jewish life assumed forms which were relevant to specific communal problems on the one hand and which were deeply indebted to Gentile example on the other. An open question for the urban historian is the extent to which the Jewish experience in all these respects may be taken as typical of that of other urban minorities in Victorian England.

III

By 1875 the community had determined the basic pattern of its religious life and the nature of its relationship to the Chief Rabbi. That the centralisation of ecclesiastical jurisdiction was by no means inevitable in the early nineteenth century is indicated clearly enough by the strength of Hesse's support in the early 1850s, but it was none the less the logical projection of earlier developments, in which the numerical preponderance of London Jewry had served as the basis for its religious ascendancy. In the early 1840s no provincial congregation had been confident enough to assert its independent judgement, even when, as in the case of the *cherem*, this had been at variance with the view of the Chief Rabbi and the London plutocracy. After the death of Hirschel, when the leaders of Anglo-Jewry had conferred on the arrangements to be made for a successor, the provinces were represented by only one delegate, and then only as an afterthought.[80] The London synagogues decided upon the terms of appointment for the new Chief Rabbi, and it was their influence which brought Dr Adler from Hanover. In 1847, when the new Chief Rabbi drew up regulations to govern synagogue ritual, the provincial communities were again not consulted. When called to account by the Liverpool congregation, then the largest in the provinces, he explained that he had not regarded consultation as advisable

first, because that code consisted for the most part of such laws as are beyond all question and indispensably necessary before any ulterior improvement can be effected; and secondly because it is obvious, that if it were competent for the smallest provincial congregation to throw its dissent into the opposite scale, no general measure for the benefit of all would be effectively promulgated.[81]

He went on

Relative to your statement that in the year 1843 at the time of my election it was understood that periodic meetings of the representatives of all the congregations provincial as well as metropolitan should take place to the purpose of aiding the Chief Rabbi in the consideration of general measures of ecclesiastical polity, that this is the first time I have heard of any such plan or proposal, that neither officially nor in private was it ever mentioned to me.

On my part I can assure you, that from my first arrival to this country it has been and still continues to be my anxious desire to be thoroughly acquainted with the circumstances both educational and religious of provincial congregations . . . and it has been a matter of regret to me, that the opportunity has not been afforded to me of acquiring information so interesting and desirable.[82]

The subsequent defeat of Hesse's Manchester movement and the containment of Reform were symptoms not only of Dr Adler's political skill but of the influence which could be brought to bear in the provinces through families with London connections, and of the deeply ingrained views held by the longer-established provincial settlers that the secure future of Anglo-Jewry depended upon a framework of orthodoxy determined by the Chief Rabbi. Dr Adler made no further concessions. He visited provincial congregations to settle their disputes, consecrate their synagogues and open their schools. Twenty years after his assurances to Liverpool, he made a grand tour which was said to have 'infused new life into our provincial communities'.[83] But on no occasion did he seek to consult them on important matters of ritual or religious administration. The Ashkenazi congregations of England were expected to move in orbits marked out for them in London and were encouraged to think of themselves as 'planets of the great congregational constellation' which had its centre at Duke's Place.[84]

Manchester's abortive movement towards autonomy, and partial diversion into Reform, provide only two instances of the community's contribution to the general development of Anglo-Jewry. They had tested the metal of the Chief Rabbinate and, in the process, refined it. In the early 1850s, the community took the initiative in securing State aid for Jewish education; in the 1860s, in strengthening Jewish claims to the benefits of the New Poor Law. There was some give and take between Manchester and London in dealing with such thorny questions of poor relief as the permanent integration of the Jewish poor.[85] The *Jewish Chronicle* wrote, of this particular problem: 'If Manchester . . . can learn much from London, London can also learn much from Manchester.'[86] London had already learnt a good deal from Manchester, if only indirectly. Men who had served their commercial or political apprenticeships in Manchester—Nathan Rothschild, Jacob and Ellis Franklin, Samuel Landeshut, Benjamin Hyam, Isidor Gerstenberg, Abraham Bauer, Eleazer Moses, Simon Joseph, Isaac Pariente, amongst many—conferred the future benefits of their experience on London. On one occasion during the disputes of 1869–72 M. S. Joseph wrote from London to offer the vestry room of the Borough Road Synagogue as a neutral ground for arbitration, under the mediation of former Manchester residents.[87]

Moreover, although the *Jewish Chronicle* believed that the interests of the provinces would be best served by an access of the 'genial and vivifying animation' of metropolitan leaders,[88] Manchester's experience was never a pale reflection of that of London. Manchester had a distinctive life of its own, based partly upon its central position on the route of transmigration, partly upon the unique qualities of such leaders as Hesse, Theodores and Schiller-Szinessy,[89] and partly upon the unique interaction between a community and a city, both in a dynamic state of growth during the first three-quarters of the nineteenth century. Manchester's role as an entrepôt of the cotton trade, as a major focus of the retail trades, as a centre of radical political ideas, and as the leader of a national 'school' of thought, all played their part in shaping the particular destinies of the community. The community grew *with* Manchester, and was to some extent a variation on urban themes, reflecting the social moods and prejudices, reacting to the changing economic fortunes, sharing the political *éclat* of the shock city of the age.

Appendix A Communal statistics

1 *Seat-holders of the Old Congregation, 1827–58* [a], *with seat rents*

Year	10s 6d	£1 1s	£2 2s	£3 3s	£4 4s	£5 5s	£6 6s	£7 7s
1827–28		25	14	14	7	1		
1829		20	14	19	7	1		
1830		14	11	19	5	1		
1831		16	12	19	8	1		
1832		21	11	18	8			
1833		22	12	19	9			
1834	2	21	15	22	10			
1835	5	21	18	23	9			
1836	4	22	28	28	9			
1840		34	25	33	9			
1841		39	29	33	10			
1842[b]		14	19	6	7	11	10	2
1843		12	19	10	7	11	9	4
1844		11	21	17	10	5	12	6
1845		13	21	17	9	1	16	4
1846		14	19	14	4	2	16	1
1847		16	17	13	5	5	16	—
1848		13	13	18	8	9	11	—
1849		10	12	28	10	9	11	—
1850	1	16	11	31	15	14	11	3
1851	1	34	31	29	30	32	9	5
1852	1	45	17	17	50	37	9	5
1853	1	38	13	15	48	36	8	5
1854	1	37	8	11	52	41	7	5
1855	2	35	12	16	53	33	12	5
1856	2	42	15	18	56	36	12	5
1857	3	57	21	27	52	35	11	5
1858	4	53	24	30	65	50	17	6

Notes

[a] Based on the account books of the Old Hebrew Congregation. A levelling-off of the number of seat-holders during the 1840s and the marked increase which began in 1850 reflect the discontent which culminated in the secession of 1844 and the subsequent progress towards reunion during 1850–51. It is not possible to differentiate Free Members and unprivileged seat-holders on any consistent basis.

[b] In 1842 the finances of the synagogue were rationalised. Fines for non-attendance and for non-acceptance of office, etc., were abolished in favour of a higher range of seat rents.

£8 8s	£9 9s	£10 10s	£11 11s	£12 12s	£13 13s	£19 19s	£22 1s	*Total*
								61
								61
								50
								56
		I						59
		I						63
I		I						72
I		I						78
I		I						93
								101
								111
3	8	2	9	3	I	I	I	97
5	6	I	7	3	I	I	2	98
3	3	I	5	I	I	I	2	99
3	3	I	4	I	I	—	2	96
6	4	—	4	I	I	—	2	88
6	3	I	4	I	I	—	2	90
6	3	I	4	I	I	—	2	90
7	3	I	4	I	I	—	2	99
8	3	I	4	I	I	—	2	122
7	2	—	4	I	I	—	2	188
7	2	—	4	3	2	I	I	201
7	2	—	4	3	—	2	I	183
6	I	—	4	3	—	2	I	179
5	I	—	3	3	—	—	I	181
4	—	—	3	2	—	—	I	196
5	—	—	3	2	—	—	I	222
13	—	4	—	4	—	—	I	271

2   *Finances of the Old Congregation, 1827–50*

Year	Total income (£)	Total expenditure (£)	Expenditure on poor relief (£) [a]
1827–28	337[b]	324	
1829	279	271	not differentiated
1830	407	406	
1831	280	257	37
1832	250	254	38
1833	354	271	41
1834	361	334	70
1835	437	361	88
1836	505	570	–
1840	not audited	–	113
1841	462	462	88
1842	734	729	91
1843	576	518	124
1844	630	555	168
1845	777	695	222
1846	786	757	236
1847	714	696	230
1848	698	681	215
1849	775	722	171
1850	868	828	285

Notes
[a] This does not include Passover Relief, which is separately listed in the account books, but presents problems of interpretation. Lack of clear definitions and differentiations, changing policies and idiosyncratic treasurers make it impossible to place relief payments in separate and consistent categories.
[b] All figures are given to the nearest £1.

3   *Application for Passover Relief, 1860–70* [a]

Year	Number of families	Number of people
1860	94	318
1865	100	340
1866	167	431
1867	183	531
1868	238	581
1869	283	707
1870	233	741

Note
[a] Based on the account books of the Old Hebrew
Congregation.

4   *Recipients of the Benevolent Fund, 1860–67* [a]

Year	Number of families	Number of persons	Outlay ($£$)
1860–61	58	—	101
1861–62	83	361	163
1862–63	—	—	190
1864–65	84	297	—
1865–66	94	362	239
1866–67	117	428	—

Note
[a] Based on the account books of the Old Hebrew Congregation and
reports in the *Jewish Chronicle*.

5   *Occupations of male recipients of relief*

Occupation	1864–65 [a]	1865–66	1866–67	1867	1868	1869	1870
Cap maker	8	6	8	6	7	4	5
Glazier	10	17	26	54	62	70	73
Hawker	20	19	13	10	12	8	2
Shoemaker	3	5	4	2	7	3	2
Tailor	8	15	23	30	42	40	38
Waterproofer	—	—	—	1	3	—	2
Other	1	3	4	2	5	6	9
Not given	23	13	24	45	92	126	56

Note
[a] Columns 1–3 are based on recipients of the Benevolent Fund; columns 4–7 on applications
for Passover Relief.

6 *The Jews School, 1841–75* [a]

Year	Enrolment				Total subscriptions			Pupil payments			Government grant
	Boys	Girls	Infants	Total	£	s	d	£	s	d	£
1841–42	–	–	–	24	–			–			–
1842–43	25	13	–	38	90	5	0	17	1	4	–
1843–44	24	13	–	37	107	17	0	15	15	5	–
1844–45	23	21	–	44	107	8	6	18	1	10	–
1846–47	–	–	–	60	–			–			–
1849–50	–	–	–	–	140	4	0	16	18	10	–
1850–51	–	–	–	80	165	18	0	26	9	11½	–
1851–52	60	–	–	–	262	16	6	55	7	9	–
1853–54	74	61	–	135	223	7	0	44	2	0	10
1854–55	–	–	–	–	239	5	0	36	2	8	–
1855–56	82	69	–	151	217	4	0	29	10	0	–
1856–57	93	76	–	169	249	7	6	42	6	11	–
1859–60	114	103	–	217	240	8	0	57	1	0	23
1860–61	118	109	–	227	248	11	6	54	18	7	19
1861–62	–	–	–	–	267	19	6	50	13	2½	–
1862–63	–	–	–	–	264	6	6	57	11	10	–
1863–64	128	82	50	260	317	2	6	49	1	5	81
1864–65	138	72	50	260	308	14	0	49	10	10	89
1865–66	169	104	47	320	293	2	0	54	9	4½	98
1866–67	–	–	80	–	302	13	0	60	12	5	125
1867–68	145	134	100	379	304	4	6	59	1	0	150
1868–69	188	159	106	453	282	14	6	64	5	7	160
1869–70	220	208	143	571	412	17	6	115	16	3	190
1870–71	212	–	130	–	386	3	0	103	19	3	221
1871–72	219	191	158	568	396	18	0	107	11	3	317
1872–73	232	194	183	609	507	12	6	129	5	4	314
1873–74	248	237	183	668	489	16	6	166	13	3	359
1874–75	253	243	196	692	513	19	6	165	9	8	380

Note

[a] Based on the Annual Reports of the Hebrew Association, subsequently the Manchester Jews School. These are not available for 1845–49, 1852, 1857–58. The number of pupils in 1846 is taken from a report in *JC*, 11 December 1846.

7   *Recipients of relief from the Manchester Jewish Board of Guardians, 1873–81* [a]

	1873–74	1874–75	1875–76	1876–77	1877–78	1878–79	1879–80	1880–81
Recipients	341	280	312	322	321	365	438	395
Dependent wives and children	620	481	592	682	658	870	992	846
Total persons relieved	961	761	904	1,004	979	1,235	1,430	1,241
Native-born recipients	5	11	9	8	9	11	16	21
Foreign-born recipients								
Resident under one year:								
German	26	30	28	29	30	29	43	43
Polish	128	87	88	112	100	90	118	111
Dutch	6	3	4	3	5	3	5	0
Other	11	8	11	2	6	5	5	10
Resident over one year:								
German	16	10	11	2	3	4	2	1
Polish	149	131	161	166	168	222	249	209
Dutch	0	0	0	0	0	0	0	0
Other	0	0	0	0	0	1	0	0
Marital status								
Resident under one year:								
Married	72	36	30	34	35	29	26	18
Single	82	87	95	101	104	91	147	154
Widow	7	7	8	10	3	4	2	2
Deserted [b]	10	10	4	6	5	11	10	9
Resident over one year:								
Married	115	99	118	115	118	167	177	143
Single	9	11	19	11	11	19	10	5
Widow	20	21	25	32	33	28	30	27
Deserted	20	9	13	13	12	16	36	37

Notes

[a] Extracted from the annual reports of the Board. Summaries are not available for the years 1867–73. The slight discrepancies in the totals under place of birth and marital status are in the original reports and cannot now be checked against the original returns.

[b] 'Deserted' wives: normally of husbands who had gone on ahead to America to prepare the way for their families.

8   *Expenditure of the Manchester Jewish Board of Guardians, 1867–80* [a]

Item	1868 £	s	d	1869 £	s	d	1870 £	s	d	1871 £	s	d	1872 £	s	d	1873 £	s	d
1. Relief in kind																		
4 lb loaves	97	18	0½	160	2	8	119	5	0	147	8	3	143	16	10	128	1	9
Meat	45	8	11	52	17	4	43	2	0	49	18	9	39	16	9	50	15	2
Coal	23	16	4	15	9	0		—		18	13	0	47	16	3	42	18	6
Rice	29	14	10	21	16	0	16	13	0	13	8	11	33	3	2	23	14	6
Potatoes	22	11	0		—		10	4	3	10	0	0	10	0	0	9	0	0
Groceries	22	13	1	23	2	5	17	1	10	6	15	11	5	19	6	4	11	0
2. Relief in money																		
for stock	11	16	0		—			—		19	0	⎫	1	19	9	3	13	9
equipment	6	13	0	1	9	0		17	6	13	0	⎭						
hawkers' licences [b]	2	10	0	2	8	0	2	10	0		—			—			5	0
shiva relief	4	3	6	3	6	6	3	1	6	3	17	6	3	9	6	3	0	0
clothing	1	6	6		17	0		—			2	0		—			—	
Redemption of pledges	6	1	0	2	2	4		6	1		8	3	1	0	3	1	19	7
Rent	1	16	0		—			—			—			—			—	
General relief	279	8	3	319	17	0	294	18	0	257	8	0	245	7	7	267	16	7
3. Medical relief																		
Subscriptions [c]	4	4	0	4	4	0	4	4	0	5	5	0	8	8	0	10	13	0
Medicines	9	13	9	17	16	5	8	16	3	5	5	6	5	12	3	1	19	11
Nursing	1	2	0	1	1	6		10	0		4	0		—			—	
Midwife tickets		14	0	1	2	0	1	1	0		—			—			—	
Miscellaneous		—			—		2	4	9		18	6		—			—	
4. Assisted emigration	40	15	8	65	9	11	30	10	2	24	0	11	40	17	9	21	6	4
5. Passover cakes [d]		—			—			—			—			—		96	3	4
Totals	612	5	10½	693	1	1	555	5	4	545	6	6	587	7	7	665	18	5

Notes

[a] Extracted from the annual reports. Not including the expenditure of the Board's Industrial Committee shown in the following table. Figures not available for 1867–68.

[b] Glaziers required a special licence, which cost 5s.

[c] To the Royal Infirmary, the Clinical Hospital, the Devonshire Hospital, and (from 1874–75) the Jewish Orphanage in London. Includes tickets for Southport Convalescent Hospital.

[d] By arrangement with the Old Hebrew Congregation, from 1873–74, in return for an additional congregational donation of £50.

| 1874 | | | 1875 | | | 1876 | | | 1877 | | | 1878 | | | 1879 | | | 1880 | | |
£	s	d	£	s	d	£	s	d	£	s	d	£	s	d	£	s	d	£	s	d
101	3	0	110	4	1	114	0	11	138	18	7	207	8	5	234	8	2	255	2	4
67	2	0	66	0	6	58	19	9	55	10	0	93	3	0	57	3	1	101	3	0
37	5	11	30	9	9	28	8	6	30	16	8	50	2	0	36	6	10	33	10	0
17	18	3	17	3	4	16	19	8	21	8	4	45	16	9	47	8	3	44	9	11
7	16	0	8	3	0	10	1	6	9	16	0	9	15	0	9	18	0	12	17	6
7	11	0	13	17	0	15	13	0	16	1	0	19	8	6	32	19	0	53	5	6
8	2	0	9	12	6	4	6	9	9	10	0	14	7	6	10	0	0	10	14	0
4	5	0	2	19	0		15	0		15	0	1	15	0	1	10	0	2	5	0
2	4	6	3	6	6	1	18	0	2	5	0	3	0	0	3	4	6	2	19	6
	—			—			—			—			—			—			—	
1	0	9	1	8	8	4	5	3	3	0	2	8	10	1	4	12	3	2	10	7
	—			—			—			—			—			—			—	
253	19	11	280	18	2	278	3	3	281	1	5	306	1	11	319	16	0	308	11	6
10	10	0	11	11	0	19	5	0	12	12	0	10	10	0	7	7	0	7	7	0
2	19	5	3	19	6	4	9	5	3	12	1	4	2	1	2	8	1	3	15	2
	—			—			—			—			—			—			—	
	—			—			—			—			—			—			—	
	—			—			—			—			—			—			—	
12	10	9	19	0	3	14	2	11	23	6	11	21	14	5	50	11	2	46	3	4
79	19	2	66	9	3	66	13	1	67	6	4	71	4	3	70	1	0	68	11	11
614	7	8	645	2	6	638	2	0	675	19	6	866	18	11	887	13	4	953	6	3

9   *Applications for loans to the industrial committee* [a]

Year	Number of applications	Number granted	Total loaned		
			£	s	d
1874–75	12	6	13	15	0
1875	16	9	37	0	0
1876	24	15	75	0	0
1877	37	25	115	0	0
1878	44	26	129	10	0
1879–80	42	33	121	10	0

Note

[a] Extracted from Max Hesse's paper to the Manchester Statistical Society, published in pamphlet form as *On the Effective Use of Charitable Loans to the Poor, without Interest* (Manchester, 1901), Table B.

10   *Founder members of the Manchester Congregation of British Jews, 1856–58* [a]

Name	Occupation	Area of residence	Place of birth
Amschel, Leopold	merchant	Victoria Park	Germany
Arensberg, Julius	tobacconist	Chorlton-on-Medlock	Prussia
Bauer, Philip	merchant	Chorlton-on-Medlock	Germany: Hamburg
Beaver, Dr Henry [b]	doctor	Strangeways	Prussian Poland
Beaver, Louis [c]	jeweller	Central Manchester	Prussian Poland
Behrens, Louis	merchant	Higher Broughton	Germany: Hamburg
Behrens, Rudolph	merchant	Higher Broughton	Germany: Hamburg
Benjamin Joel	rag merchant	Cheetham Hill	Prussia: Schneidemuhl
Bles, Abraham David	merchant	Higher Broughton	Holland: the Hague
Bles, David Samuel	merchant	Higher Broughton	Holland: the Hague
Da Costa, Jacob M.	merchant	Greenheys	Not known
Danziger, Isidore	importer	Old Town	Prussia: Danzig
Danziger, William	importer	Old Town	Prussia Danzig
Dreschfeld, Leopold	dentist	Chorlton-on-Medlock	Germany: Bavaria
Eller, Joseph	merchant	Chorlton-on-Medlock	Germany
Falk, David	jeweller	Cheetham Hill	Prussian Poland
Goldstein, Michael [d]	not known	not known	not known
Goodman, Joseph	cigar merchant	Strangeways	Prussia: Silesia
Goodman, Louis	cigar merchant	Strangeways	Prussia: Silesia

Name	Occupation	Area of residence	Place of birth
Haarbleicher, James Meyer	merchant	Higher Broughton	Germany: Hamburg
Hesse, David	shirt manufacturer	Cheetham Hill	Germany: Cologne
Hesse, Nathan	retired	Cheetham Hill	Germany: Leipzig
Horwitz, Max	merchant	Chorlton-on-Medlock	Germany
Isaac, John Michael	pawnbroker	Salford	Liverpool
Jacob, Eli	jeweller	Cheetham Hill	Prussia
Jacobs, Henry	tailor and draper	Old Town	Manchester
Jacoby, Ernst	calico printer	Chorlton-on-Medlock	Germany
Kaufmann, Moritz	merchant	Greenheys	Germany
Lazarus, Harry	merchant	Victoria Park	Germany: Hamburg
Lucas, Philip [e]	merchant	Cheetham Hill	Jamaica
Mayer, Nathan	jeweller	Cheetham Hill	Poland: Warsaw
Mayer, Saul	jeweller	Cheetham Hill	Poland: Sluzewo
Micholls, Henry	merchant	Chorlton-on-Medlock	Yarmouth(?)
Micholls, Horatio	merchant	Ardwick	London(?)
di Moro, Giuseppe Rabino	merchant	Bowden	Italy(?)
Rosenberg, Ferdinand	cigar merchant	Old Trafford	Germany
Rosenberg, Joseph	cigar merchant	Central Manchester	Germany
Salomon, Edward	architect	Chorlton-on-Medlock	London
Salomon, Henry Moses	merchant	Chorlton-on-Medlock	Germany
Samson, Samuel Isaac	merchant	Greenheys	Germany
Schloss, Sigismund	merchant	Greenheys	Germany: Frankfurt am Main
Simmons, William	merchant	Higher Broughton	Germany: Essen
Straus, Henry Sigismund	merchant	Ardwick	Germany: Frankfurt am Main
Straus, Ralph	merchant	Chorlton-on-Medlock	Germany: Frankfurt am Main
Theodores, Tobias	professor	Chorlton-on-Medlock	Germany: Berlin
Willing, Gabriel	merchant	Higher Broughton	Holland

Notes

[a] The records of the Reform Synagogue were destroyed during the Blitz, with the exception of one Council of Founders minute book of the late 1880s, of little value for the present purpose. The above list is compiled from many sources, including obituaries, reports in *JC*, and family reminiscences.

[b] Louis Beaver's brother, who left Manchester soon afterwards.

[c] Louis Beaver played some part in the Old Congregation's Building Fund, but appears to have left for Park Place soon after 1858.

[d] A 'Michael Goldstein' was certainly a founder member, but, on the other hand, Michael Goldstone, the jeweller and steel pen dealer of Polish origin, was on the founding committee of the Great Synagogue in 1858. On the present evidence, I cannot resolve this difficulty, particularly since there is no record of a Michael Goldstein in other sources.

[e] The evidence concerning Lucas is conflicting. He contributed heavily to the building fund of the Great Synagogue, but does not appear to have made use of it afterwards. He may be the person referred to in *JC* as belonging to both congregations; this would fit his mediating role in the *cherem* dispute.

11   *Founder Members of the South-Manchester Synagogue, 1872*

Name	Occupation	Residence
Abadi, Abraham	Merchant	Heywood St, Cheetham Hill
Aronsberg, William	Optician	Holywell House, Chorlton-on-Medlock
Barnett, H. L.	–	Heywood St, Cheetham Hill
Barnett, Lewis	Looking-glass manufacturer	Heywood St, Cheetham Hill
Bensaud, Isaac	Merchant	Oxford Rd, Chorlton-on-Medlock
Bensaud, Jacob	Merchant	Oxford Rd, Chorlton-on-Medlock
Bernstein, W. F.	Woollen merchant	Acomb St, Greenheys
Berlack, Mrs Martha	Fent dealer	Wright St, Greenheys
Bigio, S. B.	Merchant	Heywood St, Cheetham Hill
Brandt, Marcus	Cap-maker	Cannon St, central Manchester
Casper, Adam	Clothier	Trafford Terr, Old Trafford
Casper, Jacob	Clothier	Ducie St, Strangeways
Cobe, Louis	Cap maker	Moreton St, Strangeways
Cohen, Alexander	–	Brunswick St, Chorlton-on-Medlock
Cowen, David	Jeweller	Lime Grove, Chorlton-on-Medlock
Cowen, Maurice	Jeweller	Ackers St, Chorlton-on-Medlock
Davis, Alfred	Commission agent	Grosvenor St, Chorlton-on-Medlock
De Saxe, Henry	Jeweller	St Peter's Sq, central Manchester
Dreschfeld, Leopold	Dentist	Oxford Rd, Chorlton-on-Medlock
Eskell, Frederick	Dentist	St Peter's Sq, central Manchester
Fleet, Leonard	Watchmaker	Lower Mosley St, central Manchester
Golding, Henry	Merchant	Ducie St, Chorlton-on-Medlock
Goldseller, Israel	Fent dealer	Grosvenor St, Chorlton-on-Medlock
Goldstone, Sampson	Watchmaker	Elizabeth St, Cheetham Hill
Gottschalk, Isidor	Traveller	Exchange St, Cheetham Hill
Harris, Ephraim	Teacher	Broughton St, Cheetham Hill
Hope, Nathan	Cap maker	Robert St, Cheetham Hill
Hyman, Joseph	Clothier	Ackers St, Chorlton-on-Medlock
Hyman, Philip	Clothier	Stocks St, Cheetham Hill
Isaac, Samuel	Furrier	Moreton St, Strangeways
Jacksohn, Hermann	–	Oxford St, Chorlton-on-Medlock
Jacobson, Selig	Stay manufacturer	Stocks St, Cheetham Hill
Jordan, J. J.	Jeweller	Booth St East, central Manchester
Kaufman, Louis	Cigar merchant	Chapman St, Hulme
Leveson, Alexander	Perambulator manufacturer	Cheetham Hill Rd
Lewis, Albert	Jeweller	Acomb St, Greenheys
Lipman, Michael	Property owner	Elizabeth St, Cheetham Hill

Name	Occupation	Residence
Mench, J. Leo	Tobacconist	Shakespeare St, Ardwick
Michelson, Marcus	Cap maker	Brunswick St, Chorlton-on-Medlock
Mindlesohn, Myer	Merchant	Broughton St, Strangeways
Simmons, Julius	–	New Bailey St, central Salford
Simmons, Henry	–	Bloomsbury, Chorlton-on-Medlock
Simmons, Morris	Financier	Rumford St, Chorlton-on-Medlock
Simonsen, L. M.	Merchant	Richmond Grove, Longsight
Sykes, Morris	Clothier	Ducie St, Strangeways
Themans, Joel	Tobacconist	Oxford Rd, Chorlton-on-Medlock
Themans, Solomon	Cigar merchant	Exchange St, Cheetham Hill
Wahltuch, Dr Adolph	Physician	Oxford Rd, Chorlton-on-Medlock
Wahltuch, Henry	Merchant	Lime Grove, Chorlton-on-Medlock
Wilner, Henry	Bristle merchant	York Place, Cheetham Hill
Zirndorf, Dr Henry	Teacher	Oxford St, Chorlton-on-Medlock

12   *Founder Members of the Spanish and Portuguese Synagogue, 1872* [a]

Name	Occupation	Residence	Sum promised £ s d
Abadi, Abraham* [b]	merchant	Heywood St, Cheetham Hill	26 5 0
Adda, —— [c]	merchant	–	26 0 0
Ades, Habib	merchant	Petworth St, Cheetham Hill	31 0 0
Anzarut, Joseph	merchant	Heywood St, Cheetham Hill	31 10 0
Anzarut, Salomon	merchant	Cheetham Hill Rd	10 10 0
Belisha, Isaac David	merchant	York St, Cheetham Hill	52 10 0
Bensaud, Isaac*	merchant	Oxford St, Chorlton-on-Medlock	10 10 0
Benoliel, M.	merchant	Bury New Rd, Higher Broughton	10 10 0
Bensusan, Baruch	merchant	Moreton St, Strangeways	26 5 0
Bersi, L.	merchant	Albert Sq, central Manchester	5 5 0
Besso, Haim	merchant	Elizabeth St, Cheetham Hill	26 5 0
Besso, Joseph*	merchant	Oak Rd, Withington	15 15 0
Besso, Mardocheo	merchant	Mardocheo Terr, Cheetham Hill	26 5 0
Besso, Raffael	merchant	Mardocheo Terr, Cheetham Hill	52 10 0
Bianco, Moses*	merchant	Waterloo Rd, Cheetham Hill	15 15 0
Bigio, Saul*	merchant	Heywood St, Cheetham Hill	52 10 0
Cattan, B.	merchant	–	10 10 0
Cohen, Joshua	merchant	–	15 15 0
Cohen, Levy A.	merchant	Elizabeth St, Cheetham Hill	15 15 0
Dente, Marco	merchant	–	15 15 0
Esses, Moses	merchant	–	52 10 0
Farache, Moses A.	merchant	Pimblett St, Cheetham Hill	10 10 0
Guedella, Jacob	merchant	Ducie Grove, Chorlton-on-Medlock	10 10 0
Israel, Abraham S.	merchant	Elizabeth St, Cheetham Hill	5 5 0
Jeune (?), N. S.	–	–	5 5 0
Laniado, Chalom	merchant	York St, Cheetham Hill	10 10 0
Laniado, Isaac	merchant	York St, Cheetham Hill	10 10 0
Levi, Marco	merchant	Gloucester Terr, Cheetham Hill	52 10 0
Levy, Sabbato	merchant	York St, Cheetham Hill	10 10 0
Levi, Victor	merchant	Mardocheo Terr, Cheetham Hill	52 10 0
Messulam, J. B.	merchant	–	10 0 0
Messulam, Moses Ben	merchant	York St, Cheetham Hill	52 10 0
Negrin, Elias	merchant	York St, Cheetham Hill	15 15 0
Piza, Jacob	merchant	Oxford St, Chorlton-on-Medlock	10 10 0
Politi, David	merchant	York St, Cheetham Hill	26 5 0
Raphael, Moses	merchant	York St, Cheetham Hill	26 5 0
Semo, Abraham	–	–	10 10 0
Sharim, Ezra	merchant	Wilton Place, Higher Broughton	52 10 0
Sutton, Ezra	merchant	York St, Cheetham Hill	25 0 0

Notes

[a] Abstracted from a list of donations promised at the preliminary meeting of 4 February 1872.

[b] Asterisked persons were also associated with the foundation, or early development, of the South Manchester Synagogue.

[c] The name 'Adda & Co' only is given; possibly there was no one of that name living in Manchester.

Appendix B   Manchester Jewry in the Census, 1841–71

No attempt to obtain reliable demographic statistics of provincial Anglo-Jewish communities in the nineteenth century has so far proved successful. The religious allegiance of the population does not form part of the Census enquiry, and even if it did it would not necessarily provide reliable communal statistics.[1] Calculations based on places of birth given in the Census summaries are clearly of little value in the Jewish context, since when the first nominal Census was taken, in 1841, a large proportion of the community was already native-born. Only one attempt was made to take a national religious census, in 1851, and this was far from satisfactory, even in general terms;[2] Dr Lipman's interpretation of the returns to provide an analysis of Anglo-Jewry in 1851[3] is at best a rough guide, supplemented, in most instances, by speculation.[4] School attendance figures (available in Manchester Jewry from 1842) are unreliable as a guide to the general population, since only the poorer children were expected to attend a communal institution, and until 1872 they were not compelled to do so; by that time Jewish children were to be found in Board Schools and even in Christian voluntary schools. The use of synagogue membership as a guide is also risky, since the members of a synagogue represent only a fraction of the community, and that an incalculable one.[5] In Manchester, the records of the Reform Congregation (founded in 1856) were destroyed by enemy action in the Second World War, and the archives of most minor congregations (of which there were at least twenty before 1881) have been irretrievably lost, presuming that they ever existed. No form of communal statistic has been found which bears a constant relationship to the total Jewish population; contemporary estimates, by Jews and conversionists, vary wildly.

In the absence of satisfactory alternatives, I have turned to the Census Enumerators' Books for Manchester and Salford for the years 1841–71, which, whatever their defects,[6] provide the most comprehensive and accurate account of the general population, and which undoubtedly *include* the Jewish community, however difficult it might be to detect and delineate. Sampling techniques have not been used, and are perhaps inappropriate to so compact a minority grouping as the Jews; instead, an attempt has been made to extract from the enumerators' records the names of all those persons who belonged to the Jewish community between 1841 and 1871. This is not the place to discuss in any detail the methods which have been used, or to try to defend them. When the demographic research being conducted in the Jewish History Unit at Manchester Polytechnic reaches fruition, the full results will be made available.[7] Four basic processes were involved:

1. A thorough search was conducted through every Census Enumerator's Book, designed to extract the name of every person who for *any* reason (place of birth, surname, occupation, place of residence) might be thought, on basic sociological and historical premises, to be of Jewish origin. The object was not to make final judge-

ments in each case but to compile as full a list as possible, for whittling down in the light of further evidence.

2. To ensure that it *was* the fullest list, a further search was made in every available communal list of relevant date—synagogue membership lists, subscription lists, school registers, account books, marriage registers, and so on—for names which might have been omitted. In particular, this brought to light names—William Whitcover, for example, or Morris Sykes—which had no obvious Jewish connotation. Using the local Trade Directories as a guide, such persons could normally be traced back into the Census, assuming that they resided in Manchester or Salford on Census night.

3. The final, and in many ways the most difficult, task was then to eliminate from the long list those who were not, in fact, members of the community, including Jews who had broken every link with communal life. The search, after all, was for members of the *community*, and it made no sense to include Israel Napthali, missioner to the Jews, Salis Schwabe, the Unitarian calico printer, or the Anglican merchant Henry Leppoc, however Jewish their origins. The yard-stick was a proven link with the community, however tenuous. Exception was made only in the case of residents of Red Bank, whose names could not be expected to appear on subscription lists and who often avoided the major synagogues in favour of the *chevroth*, records of which have not survived. Fortunately, the internal evidence provided by name, occupation, place of birth and place of residence was less difficult to assess in cases such as these.

4. Finally, there were reservations to be made. The Census Enumerators' Books provided a *static* picture of what was, particularly in the nineteenth century, a highly mobile community. Between 1858 and 1862 alone, fifty-nine members of the Manchester Old Hebrew Congregation resigned their membership and left town, and at lower levels in the social hierarchy the state of flux was very much greater. The Jews School was constantly complaining of the 'migratory habits' of the parents of immigrant children. Every external observer agreed that the community was swollen, particularly around Passover, by large numbers of visitors, traders and travellers. On the other hand, members of the Manchester community were equally likely to be out of town on Census night, as was John Michael Isaac, the pawnbroker, in 1841, and Edward Voorsanger, a steel pen agent, ten years later. The statistical summaries below include all Jews in Manchester and Salford on the relevant Census night.

The study of historical demography is now well established, and has opened up many ways of analysing the data of enumerators' books, to reveal everything from fertility rates to social class.[8] Since my figures are at this stage provisional, I have confined myself to the presentation of basic information related to place of birth, area of residence and occupation, leaving more subtle permutations to the future. I have presented the figures in a way which may help to indicate the changing pattern of Jewish residence and economic life.

1   *Total Jewish population*

	1841	1851	1861	1871
Total of persons	625	1,092	1,755	3,444
Total of families	256	426	580	987

2   *Area of residence*

	1841		1851		1861		1871	
	Households	Persons	Households	Persons	Households	Persons	Households	Persons
Ardwick	1	6	4	16	6	20	–	–
Ancoats	–	–	1	3	4	11	2	13
Cheetham Hill	11	35	25	125	110	344	188	1,020
Chorlton-on-Medlock [a]	25	76	14 [b]	42	31	91	26	116
Crumpsall	1	6	1	4	–	–	–	–
Didsbury	–	–	–	–	–	–	4	28
Fallowfield	–	–	–	–	–	–	2	17
Higher Broughton	7	28	15	66	14	37	10	51
Lower Broughton	2	8	11	35	9	29	24	133
Manchester (central) [c]	54	146	43	196	22	64	16	65
Moss Side	1	1	3	11	–	–	–	–
Old Town [d]	67	228	69	264	90	273	55	244
Red Bank [e]	2	5	21	130	149	430	236	1,153
Rochdale Road	–	–	1	2	5	19	1	10
Salford (central)	19	64	12	50	34	112	17	108
Strangeways	9	22	31	112	92	266	79	399
Victoria Park	–	–	3	22	13	59	9	87
Elsewhere (single families)	–	–	5	14	–	–	–	–

Notes

[a] Including Greenheys.

[b] The enumerators' books of 1851 for Chorlton-on-Medlock have been defaced; an attempt has been made to reconstruct the Jewish families then living in the area, through the Trade Directories and the Censuses of 1841 and 1861. The result is almost certainly an underestimate.

[c] including all the central commercial and shopping districts outside the Old Town.

[d] The term is used here to denote the area defined on Map 3.

[e] Used to define the area between Cheetham Hill Road and the Irk, shown on Maps 4–8.

3 Occupations

	1841		1851		1861		1871	
	Male	*Female*	*Male*	*Female*	*Male*	*Female*	*Male*	*Female*
Clothing trades								
Accessories* [a] [b]	1	3	2	—	20	5	12	6
Cap maker*	4	2	36	11	56	12	49	29
Clothier and Draper [c]	12	2	19	1	15	3	23	—
Furrier	5	1	5	—	2	—	—	—
Hosier	—	—	—	—	1	—	—	—
Shirt maker	—	—	1	—	—	—	—	—
Shoe dealer [d]	—	—	—	—	—	—	—	1
Shoemaker* [e]	3	—	21	—	14	—	18	1
Tailor/dressmaker [c]	8	2	21	11	78	16	289	94
Umbrella maker	—	—	1	—	2	—	—	1
Waterproofer*	—	—	1	—	11	1	27	3
Commerce								
Broker	1	—	—	—	—	—	3	—
Commercial clerk	20	—	10	—	13	—	30	—
Commission agent	5	—	12	—	13	—	34	—
Fent dealer	1	—	2	—	7	2	11	—
Merchant	47	—	64	—	65	—	78	—
Rag merchant	—	—	1	—	—	—	—	—
Salesman	1	—	9	—	19	—	8	—
Warehouseman	6	—	9	—	10	1	9	2
Furniture trades								
Boxmaker	—	—	2	—	2	—	—	—
Cabinet maker* [f]	1	—	7	—	5	—	8	—
Glass merchant	—	—	—	—	1	—	1	—
Looking-glass maker	—	—	—	—	5	—	—	—
Upholsterer	—	—	—	—	3	1	—	1
Jewellery trades [g]								
Earthenware dealer	—	—	—	—	4	—	1	—
Hardware dealer	1	1	2	—	—	—	7	—
Musical instrument dealer	—	—	1	—	—	—	—	—
Optician	3	—	4	—	5	—	2	—
Pawnbroker	3	1	6	—	5	2	12	—
Watchmaker/jeweller	17	—	21	—	27	—	31	—
Itinerant trades								
Glazier*	—	—	14	—	18	—	107	—
Hawker/pedlar	19	1	25	2	15	7	11	1
Traveller	25	1	20	1	45	1	75	3

	1841		1851		1861		1871	
	Male	*Female*	*Male*	*Female*	*Male*	*Female*	*Male*	*Female*
The professions								
Accountant	2	—	2	—	3	—	4	—
Architect/draughtsman	—	—	—	—	1	—	2	—
Artist	1	—	—	—	1	—	1	—
Auctioneer/valuer	1	—	—	—	—	—	2	—
Chemist	1	—	1	—	—	—	—	—
Dentist	2	—	2	—	—	—	4	—
Doctor/surgeon	5	—	2	—	4	—	2	—
Engineer	—	—	—	—	—	—	2	—
Interpreter	—	—	1	—	—	—	—	—
Musician	1	—	—	—	—	2	4	—
Photographer	—	—	—	—	1	—	3	—
Religious official	4	—	6	—	6	—	5	—
Secretary	—	—	—	—	2	—	1	—
Solicitor	—	—	—	—	1	—	4	—
Teacher of Hebrew	2	—	2	—	7	—	7	—
Teacher/governess	2	2	3	5	1	6	13	9
Servants								
Cook	—	—	—	—	—	1	—	1
Domestic servant	1	2	1	5	—	13	3	21
Errand boy	—	—	—	—	—	—	4	—
Nursemaid	—	—	—	4	—	3	—	4
Porter	—	—	—	—	3	—	1	—
Waiter	—	—	—	—	—	—	1	—
Washerwoman	—	—	—	—	—	—	—	2
Service trades								
Baker	—	—	1	—	2	—	1	—
Barber	—	—	—	—	1	—	—	—
Boarding-house keeper	—	1	1	5	1	2	2	5
Butcher/poulterer	—	—	—	—	2	—	2	1
Confectioner	—	—	2	1	—	—	2	—
Fishmonger	—	—	—	—	1	—	5	1
General Dealer	9	—	7	—	—	—	7	—
Grocer/provision dealer	—	—	—	—	4	1	9	2
Marine Store dealer	—	—	1	2	2	—	2	—
Tobacconist	—	—	14	—	14	—	12	—
'Tradesman' [h]	—	—	2	—	—	—	11	4
Wine/porter dealer	—	—	2	—	—	—	1	—

	1841		1851		1861		1871	
	Male	*Female*	*Male*	*Female*	*Male*	*Female*	*Male*	*Female*
Stationery								
Artists' materials	–	–	2	–	2	–	2	–
Bookbinder	1	–	3	–	–	–	–	–
Book dealer	–	–	–	–	–	–	2	–
Ink manufacturer	–	–	2	–	4	–	–	–
Lithographer/printer*	–	–	–	–	–	–	7	–
Quill dresser	3	–	1	–	–	–	–	–
Stationer	3	1	2	1	2	–	–	–
Steel pen dealer	1	–	3	–	1	–	–	–
Textile manufacturer								
Calico printer	1	–	3	–	–	–	1	–
Fustian manufacturer	–	–	2	–	–	–	–	–
Lace weaver	1	–	2	–	2	–	–	–
Pattern designer	–	–	1	–	–	–	2	–
Silk manufacturer	–	–	1	–	–	–	1	–
Miscellaneous								
Decorator	–	–	–	–	–	–	4	–
Handbag manufacturer	–	–	–	–	–	–	4	–
Independent [i]	11	–	2	–	2	1	–	–
Leatherworker	1	–	–	–	1	1	1	–
Metal worker	–	–	3	–	–	–	4	–
Perambulator hood manufacturer	–	–	–	–	–	–	1	2
Staymaker	1	–	–	–	1	–	–	–
Other	3	–	2	–	3	1	5	–

Notes

[a] Asterisked occupations include both masters and men in the 'immigrant trades'.

[b] Includes makers of artificial flowers, tassels and fringes.

[c] The distinction between 'Clothier and Draper' and 'Tailor/dressmaker' is that between the shopkeeper and the worker or master in the tailoring industry.

[d] The same distinction divides 'shoe dealers' and 'shoemakers'.

[e] Includes slipper makers.

[f] Includes carpenter, carver, gilder, French polisher.

[g] Includes china and hardware.

[h] This is the description given in the Census: probably a general shopkeeper.

[i] Includes 'owners of property'.

4   *Place of origin 1841* [a]

Born in Lancashire [b]	258
Born elsewhere in England	127
Born in Ireland	4
Born in foreign parts	214
Not given	22

Notes

[a] In 1841 respondents were asked whether or not they were born in the country in which they were residing; if the answer was 'No' they were asked to state whether they were born elsewhere in England, in Ireland, or in foreign parts. This is regarded as an unsatisfactory census in relation to place of birth, and it can certainly be shown that a handful of Jews who said they were born outside the county, but in England, were in fact born in Germany.

[b] This figure includes persons born in Liverpool and other Lancastrian towns outside Manchester. There is no way of calculating the number born in Manchester.

5   *Place of origin, 1851–71*

Place of origin	1851	1861	1871
Overseas			
Austria–Hungary [a]	7	62	97
Belgium	2	–	–
Egypt	–	1	4
France	4	2	–
Germany [b]	195	145	220
Gibraltar	2	3	1
Greece	1	3	33
Holland	25	21	10
Morocco	1	–	8
Poland [b]	65	196	545
Prussia [b]	140	221	202
Prussian Poland [b]	28	25	30
Russia [c]	11	61	170
Russian Poland [c]	11	43	466
Sweden	1	–	1
Switzerland	–	–	4
Syria	–	2	22
Turkey	3	7	27
U.S.A.	1	6	16
West Indies	2	3	10
Elsewhere abroad	2	6	13
Great Britain			
Manchester and Salford	293	589	1,128
London	96	97	129
Provincial England [d]	198	247	297
Ireland	4	15	11

Notes

[a] includes Cracow, Bohemia and Hungary.

[b] A major problem in distinguishing place of birth arises from the uncertainty of the political terminology. The numbers given here indicate the answers given to the enumerators, but it will be clear that there were many possibilities of confusion. Some who answered 'Poland' may have lived in Russia, others in Prussia. Some who answered 'Germany' or 'Prussia' may well have been born in 'Prussian Poland'. In the text I have counted as Russian and Polish only those who described themselves to the enumerators as having been born in Russia or in Prussian or Russian Poland; those who described their place of birth as 'Prussia' are not included, even when they are known from other sources to have been born in Poland.

[c] The same possibility of confusion exists, but with less significance for the purposes of historical interpretation.

[d] The most significant numbers came from Birmingham (16, 28, 32), Hull (1, 5, 15), Liverpool (34, 58, 53) and Sheffield (5, 17, 24)

Appendix C The pattern of Jewish settlement, 1841–71[1]

The inclusion of streets, buildings and railways in the map of central Manchester is necessarily selective, and it should be remembered that they did not all exist contemporaneously. On the subsequent maps each dot indicates a household with at least one Jewish inhabitant according to the Census for the year concerned.

1. Streets, etc.

1. Ashton Road
2. Bridge Street
3. Broughton Lane
4. Bury New Road
5. Camp Street
6. Chapel Street
7. Cheetham Hill Road (York Street)
8. Chester Road
9. Collyhurst Road
10. Crescent
11. Cross Street
12. Deansgate
13. Elizabeth Street
14. Great Ancoats Street
15. Great Ducie Street
16. Greengate
17. Grosvenor Square
18. Hyde Road
19. King Street
20. Liverpool Road
21. London Road
22. Long Millgate
23. Market Street
24. Miller Street
25. Mosley Street
26. Moss Grove
27. New Bridge Street
28. North Street
29. Northumberland Street
30. Oldfield Road
31. Oldham Road
32. Oldham Street
33. Oxford Street
34. Peter Street
35. Plymouth Grove
36. Quay Street
37. Red Bank
38. St Ann's Square
39. St George's Road
40. St Peter's Square
41. St Stephen's Street
42. Shudehill
43. Stockport Road
44. Stocks Street
45. Stretford Road
46. Swan Street
47. Upper Brook Street
48. Water Street
49. Waterloo Road
50. Withy Grove

2. Synagogues

A. Halliwell Street Synagogue (1825–58)

B. Ainsworth's Court: the New Synagogue (1844–51)

C. Great Synagogue (1858)

D. Reform Synagogue (1858)

E. South Manchester Synagogue (1872)

F. Spanish and Portuguese Synagogue (1874)

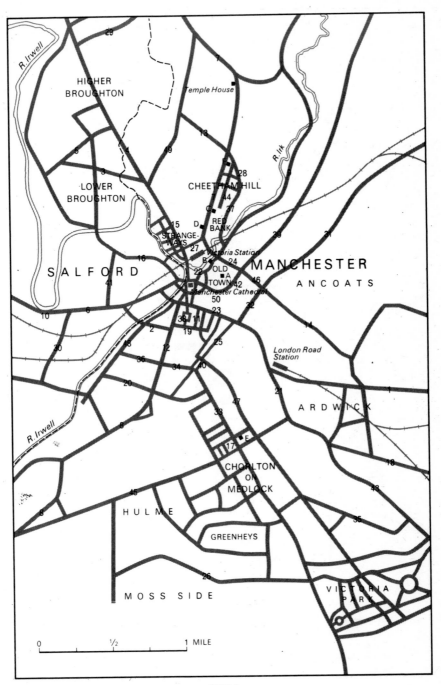

MAP 4

1841

0   ½   1 MILE

MAP 5

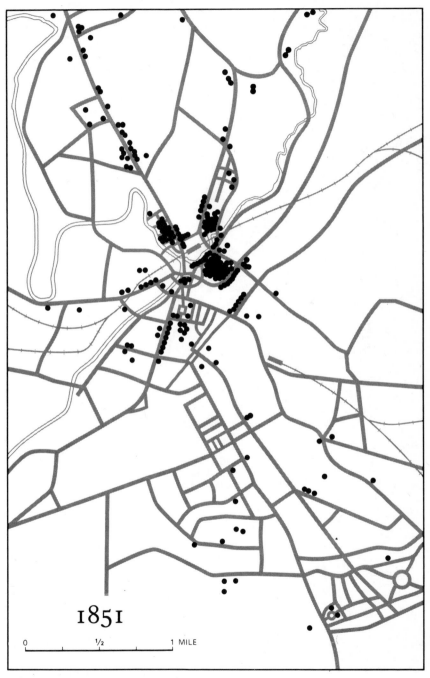

1851

0   ½   1 MILE

MAP 6

1861

0   ½   1 MILE

MAP 7

1871

0   ½   1 MILE

MAP 8

Notes

ABBREVIATIONS USED IN THE NOTES

Acc. Bk.	Account Book
BG	Manchester Jewish Board of Guardians
BD	Board of Deputies
CRO	Chief Rabbi's Office
DNB	*Dictionary of National Biography*
HA	Manchester Hebrew Association (subsequently Manchester Jews School)
JC	*Jewish Chronicle*
Lp. OHC	Archives of the Liverpool Old Hebrew Congregation
MCL	Manchester Central Library
MG	*Manchester Guardian*
Min. Bk.	Minute Book. OHC: SC Select Committee, GM General Meeting SMC: CA Council of Administrators, CF Council of Founders
OHC	Archives of the Manchester Old Hebrew Congregation
PRO	Public Record Office (H.O.: Home Office Archives)
SMC	Archives of the South Manchester Synagogue, Wilbraham Road
SPC	Archives of the Spanish and Portuguese Synagogue, Cheetham Hill Road
Tr. JHSE	*Transactions of the Jewish Historical Society of England*
VJ	*Voice of Jacob*

CHAPTER ONE

1 The widest ranging account of the origins of provincial Anglo-Jewry is in Cecil Roth, *The Rise of Provincial Jewry* (London, 1950). See also Lucien Wolf, *Essays in Jewish History* (London, 1934), pp. 137–9; Cecil Roth, *A History of the Jews in England* (Oxford, 1964), ch. x; Ernest Krausz, *Leeds Jewry* (Cambridge, 1964), ch. 1; *Provincial Jewry in Victorian Britain*, a collection of papers compiled by Dr Aubrey Newman for a conference held at University College London under the auspices of the Jewish Historical Society of England on 6 July 1975.

2 Quoted from the City of London archives by Lucien Wolf, *op. cit.*, p. 123.

3 *A Review of the Proposed Naturalisation of the Jews by A Merchant who subscribed the Petition against the Naturalisation of the Jews* (London, 1753), p. 67.

4 Israel Solomon, *Records of My Family* (New York, 1887), p. 2; cf. Lucien Wolf, *op. cit.*, pp. 137–9.

5 Israel Solomon, *op. cit.*, p. 2.

6 *Ibid.*, p. 3.

7 *London Gazette*, No. 8333, 2–5 June 1744.

8 Russel Casson and John Berry, *Plan of the Towns of Manchester and Salford* (1741). For comparable cases in Yarmouth and Liverpool, see Roth, *Provincial Jewry*, pp. 106–7, and K. L. Abrahams, 'The first Jews in Liverpool', *Greenbank Synagogue Review* (Liverpool, 1970) (not paginated).

9 *London Gazette*, No. 7995, 7–10 March 1740.

10 It is possible that the victim of the robbery may be identified with the Isaac Solomon of Darwen's Wient, Liverpool, whose failure was announced in Gore's *Liverpool General Advertiser*, 6 March 1767. Cf. K. L. Abrahams, *op. cit.*

11 S. and N. Buck, *Prospect of Manchester* (1728), quoted by W. H. Chaloner, 'Manchester in the latter half of the eighteenth century', *Bulletin of the John Rylands Library*, vol. 42, No. 1 (September 1959), p. 40.

12 Casson and Berry, *op. cit.*

13 Chaloner, *op. cit.*, p. 41.

14 Cecil Roth, 'The Portsmouth Community and its historical background', *Tr. JHSE;* vol. 13 (1932–35), pp. 158–60.

15 'John Willme and his letters to the Jews at Liverpool, 1756' in *Palatine Notebook*, vol. 1 (1881), pp. 117–20.

16 Rev. Moses Margoliouth, *The History of the Jews in Great Britain* (London, 1851), vol. 3, pp. 110–11.

17 Israel Solomon, *op. cit.*, pp. 1–2.

18 Joseph Stott, *A Sequel to the Friendly Advice to the Poor of the Town of Manchester* (Manchester, 1756), pp. 10–11.

19 Rev. John Clayton, *Friendly Advice to the Poor* (Manchester, 1755), p. 25.

20 *The New Manchester Guide; or, Useful Pocket Companion* (Manchester, 1815), p. 42.

21 Chaloner, *op. cit.*, p. 41; François Vigier, *Change and Apathy: Liverpool and Manchester during the Industrial Revolution* (London, and Cambridge, Mass., 1970), p. 41, fig. 8.

22 B. L. Benas, 'Records of the Jews in Liverpool', *Transactions of the Historic Society of Lancashire and Cheshire*, vol. 15 (1899), pp. 50–1; K. L. Abrahams, *op. cit.*

23 The name 'Synagogue Alley' does not occur in town plans of the 1750s or later.

24 *Manchester Mercury*, 1 January 1754.

25 *Ibid.*, 3 July 1753.

26 Lp. OHC, Register of Births, Deaths and Burials, 1808–19.

27 Roth, *Provincial Jewry*, p. 81.

28 *Ibid.*, p. 70.

29 *Ibid.*, pp. 87 and 35.

30 Roth, *Provincial Jewry*, pp. 17–18; 'The Portsmouth community and its historical background', p. 167.

31 Alex M. Jacob, 'The Jews of Falmouth, 1740–1860', *Tr. JHSE*, vol. 17 (1951–52), p. 67.

32 Roth, *Provincial Jewry*, p. 20.

33 *Manchester Mercury*, 30 July 1771: 'Hart Jacobs, alias Stephen Moor, alias Edward Brown, alias John Walker, removed by Habeas Corpus [from York] to Carlisle.'

34 Roth, *Provincial Jewry*, p. 18.

35 *Ibid.*, p. 18.

36 *Ibid.*, p. 20.

37 Roth, *Provincial Jewry*, p. 18.
38 Roth, *The Jews in England*, pp. 234–5. Dr Lipman has pointed out that many immigrants of the later eighteenth century were Germans from the smaller towns of the Rhineland and Franconia, where the chances of obtaining a competitive livelihood were now reduced by refugees from further east (V. D. Lipman, 'The origins of provincial Anglo-Jewry', in *Provincial Jewry in Victorian Britain*; see note 1 above).
39 *Manchester Mercury*, 12 November 1771. On the Chelsea murder, see Roth, *The Jews in England*, pp. 235–6, and bibliographical note.
40 *Manchester Mercury*, 12 November 1771.
41 *Ibid.*, 19 November 1771.
42 *Ibid.*, 12 November 1771.
43 *Ibid.*, 19 November 1771.
44 *Ibid.*
45 *Ibid.*, 26 November; Roth, *The Jews in England*, p. 236.
46 *Ibid.*
47 *Williamson's Liverpool Advertiser*, 2 June 1775.
48 *Gore's Liverpool General Advertiser*, 16 August 1776.
49 *Ibid.*, 27 December 1776.
50 *Ibid.*
51 *Ibid.*
52 *Manchester Mercury*, 24 December 1776.
53 J. Rumney, 'Anglo-Jewry as seen through foreign eyes', *Tr. JHSE*, vol. 13 (1932–35), p. 330, quoting C. P. Moritz, *Travels Chiefly on Foot through England in 1782*.
54 Rumney, *op. cit.*, p. 333, quoting G. F. A. Wendeborn, *A View of England Towards the Close of the Eighteenth Century*.
55 *VJ*, 3 February 1843, quoting a letter from Abraham Abrahams in Richard Cumberland's *Observer* of 1798.
56 Lp. OHC, Register of Births, Deaths and Burials, 1808–19, pp. 1–17.
57 Benas, *op. cit.*, pp. 50–1.
58 Chaloner, *op. cit.*, pp. 41–2.
59 *Prescott's Manchester Journal*, 31 July 1773.
60 Cf. Chaloner, *op. cit.*, p. 50; W. O. Henderson, *Britain and Industrial Europe, 1750–1870* (Manchester, 1954), pp. 46–7.
61 *Manchester Mercury*, 12 March 1774. The advertisement is repeated, with minor variations, until 16 April.
62 *Ibid.*
63 Cf. A. P. Wadsworth and J. de Lacy Mann, *The Cotton Trade and Industrial Lancashire* (Manchester, 1931), pp. 175n, 181ff; N. J. Frangopulo, 'Foreign communities in Victorian Manchester', *Manchester Review*, vol. 10 (1963–65), p. 190. Persistence of fear of foreign espionage into the 1820s is instanced in *MG*, 25 August 1821, and 1 November 1823. In November 1826 the Manchester Chamber of Commerce opposed a bill which would have legalised the export of machinery of all kinds.
64 *Manchester Mercury*, 15 January 1771.
65 *Prescott's Manchester Journal*, 13 March 1779.
66 *Ibid.*, 27 March 1773 to 9 July 1774.

67 Roth, *Provincial Jewry*, p. 81; *Manchester Mercury*, 12 February 1799. Amongst Liverpool shopkeepers with Manchester outlets was Morris Mozley, a 'silversmith, jeweller and hardware man' who moved from Portsmouth to Liverpool soon after 1785, and during 1794 began to advertise his stock in the Manchester press (*Manchester Mercury*, 20 January 1795).

68 I am indebted for this information to Mr David Bethel of Leek, Staffordshire, who is preparing material on the Solomon family of Liverpool.

69 *Manchester Mercury*, 16 October 1792; 5 February 1793.

70 'The Old Jewish Congregation of Manchester' by E. N. (Jacob Nathan's son, Elias) in the *Jewish Record*, 4 March 1887. Two masonic certificates belonging to Lemon Nathan, dated 1 November 1786 and 2 September 1787, have recently been deposited in MCL; both testify to his membership of Ancient Lodge 53. The wording of the second ('to whom it may concern') may imply that Lemon Nathan was at least considering a move from Liverpool. Much of the material in Elias Nathan's articles (*Jewish Record*, 4–18 March 1887) was based on stories told to him by his uncle, Lemon Nathan, over fifty years earlier, and must be treated with caution. One may doubt, for example, that Lemon Nathan was amongst the founders of Liverpool Jewry. Even his possession of a copy of the deed by which the Liverpool community acquired a new burial ground in 1773 (which Elias Nathan takes to suggest active participation in communal affairs) may imply no more than his need for a model for a similar transaction conducted in Manchester during 1794. Lemon Nathan was Jacob's senior partner until his retirement in 1820; he died in 1834 at the age of ninety-two. The date of Jacob Nathan's birth is based on the age he gave to the enumerators for the Census of 1851.

71 This is suggested, in particular, by the rapidity with which the earliest Jewish settlers in Manchester began to act in a corporate capacity. The relatively sudden appearance of a number of Jewish families in a compact residential district seems to imply a collective decision rather than the chance coming together of unconnected individuals. The same considerations also suggest the prior existence of some form of brotherhood.

72 *Jewish World*, 7 September 1877; Benn Franks, MS Family History, dated 25 January 1937, in the possession of Mrs Dorothy Goldstone of Cheadle.

73 Lp. OHC, Register of Births, Deaths and Burials, 1808–19, p. 17.

74 The deed is in the archives of the Great and New Synagogue, Manchester. A contemporary directory names Samuel Brierly as a silk dyer with a mill at New Richmond, Pendleton. A discussion of Brierly's motives, although with the erroneous comment that the land was a gift, appears in *Manchester City News*, 29 January 1887: 'Manchester notes and queries'.

75 The first mention of the synagogue in Withy Grove is in Joseph Aston, *Manchester Guide* (Manchester, 1804), p. 137; it was approached through a passage called Infirmary Yard (*Jewish Record*, 4 March, 1887).

76 James Butterworth, *The Antiquities of the Town . . . of Manchester* (Manchester, 1822), p. 258.

77 *Jewish World*, 7 September 1877.

78 John Aiken, *A Description of the Country from Thirty to Forty Miles around Manchester* (Manchester, 1795), pp. 192 and 194n.

79 Lp. OHC, Register of Births, Deaths and Burials, p. 20.

80 On Samuel Solomon, see Benas, *op. cit.*, pp. 57–9; Louis Hyman, *The Jews of Ireland* (London and Jerusalem, 1972), pp. 76–7; Roth, *Provincial Jewry*, p. 57; *Jewish Encyclopaedia* (1901–06) article 'Samuel Solomon'; R. C. Isaac in *Liverpool Daily Post*, 26 April 1900; R. Whittington-Egan, *Liverpool Eccentrics* (Liverpool, 1968), pp. 17–22, Alfred Rubens, *Anglo-Jewish Portraits* (London, 1935), pp. 113–14, 168.

81 Will of Isaac Solomon, a surgeon of Manchester, proved on 5 December 1796, in the Lancashire County Record Office, Preston. Israel Simon and Myer Lemon were married to the daughters who figure in the will; Myer Lemon's son later married Samuel Solomon's daughter.

82 The original document, now lost, was transcribed in *Manchester Evening Chronicle*, 20 July 1897. I have added the preposition 'by', which alone renders the agreement meaningful.

83 Aliens Licence dated 1 August 1798, in MCL.

84 The headstone is still visible in the Burial Ground at Pendleton.

85 He built a mausoleum on his own estate, in which he was subsequently buried.

86 *The British Volunteer and Manchester Weekly Express*, 30 April 1814.

87 *Ibid.*

88 Advertisement in the *Manchester Mercury*, 3 June 1806.

89 Chaloner, *op. cit.*, p. 41.

90 *Manchester Mercury*, 25 February 1800.

91 *Wheeler's Manchester Chronicle*, 3 December 1803.

92 *Ibid.*

93 Borough reeve's Muniments M1/20 in MCL.

94 *Manchester Mercury*, 18 March 1800.

95 Isaac Cohen, the hat maker, was probably the person of the same name who later 'introduced the silk hat into Scotland' and was admitted as Freeman of the City of Glasgow in 1812 (Tova Benski, 'Glasgow', in *Provincial Jewry in Victorian Britain*). Braham was known to the synagogue as Joseph Braham Danziger.

96 In the absence of access to the Rothschild family archives, little of value has been written on N. M. Rothschild's early career in Manchester. Of most value are the articles in Lucien Wolf, *op. cit.*, ch. 8(a)–(d). For general biographical detail see, in particular, Cecil Roth, *The Magnificent Rothschilds* (London, 1939), Egon Caesar Corti, *The Rise of the House of Rothschild* (London, 1928), and articles in *DNB* and *Jewish Encyclopaedia* (1901–06). My chronology of his Manchester residence is based upon local directories and the local press.

97 Roth, *Magnificent Rothschilds*, p. 19.

98 Lucien Wolf, *op. cit.*, p. 270. Wolf erroneously places Rothschild's arrival in Manchester in 1797.

99 Corti, *op. cit.*, pp. 37ff.

100 Lucien Wolf, *op. cit.*, p. 265.

101 Account said to have been given by Rothschild to Sir Thomas Foxwell Buxton at a dinner in Ham House in 1829. Quoted in *JC*, 31 October 1879.

102 *Ibid.*

103 *Ibid.*

104 Lucien Wolf, *op. cit.*, p. 265.

105 Account to Sir Thomas Foxwell Buxton, *op. cit.*
106 Michael Edwards, *The Growth of the British Cotton Trade, 1780–1815* (Manchester, 1967), pp. 13–14.
107 Estimates of the numbers of foreign merchants in Manchester, here and elsewhere, are based upon John Scholes, 'List of foreign merchants in Manchester' (MS in MCL, MS/FF/382/535).
108 Cf. Roth, *Magnificent Rothschilds*, p. 15; Frederic Morton, *The Rothschilds, a Family Portrait* (London, 1962), pp. 20–1; Corti, *op. cit.*, p. 13. A business card of Rothschild's Manchester firm has recently come to light and is now in MCL. Its presence amongst the family papers of Jacob Nathan's son, Elias, may suggest links between the families during Rothschild's Manchester period.
109 Records of the Lancashire Commercial Clerks' [Benefit] Society, MCL, M13/4/2/1.
110 Aiken, *op. cit.*, p. 205.
111 *Ibid.* The sites of other houses in Manchester occupied by Rothschild are located by T. Swindells in *Manchester City News*, 27 January 1906.
112 *Jewish World*, 7 September 1877.
113 *Ibid.*
114 Margoliouth, *op. cit.*, vol. 2, pp. 172–3.
115 Biographical material in Roth, *Provincial Jewry*, p. 83; Canon H. P. Stokes, *Studies in Anglo-Jewish History* (Edinburgh, 1913), pp. 231–2; *Jewish Encyclopaedia* (1901–06), article 'Joseph Crool'; letter from Rev. F. R. Hall, one of Crool's former students at Cambridge, in *JC*, 30 June 1848.
116 Roth, *Provincial Jewry*, p. 87.
117 Stokes, *op. cit.*, pp. 231–2.
118 [Rabbi Joseph Crool], *Service Performed in the Synagogue of the Jews, Manchester, on 19th October, 1803. Being the Day appointed for a general Fast . . . Delivered in Hebrew, by Rabbi Joseph Crool, and Translated, by him, into English* (Manchester, 1803), p. 10.
119 Document, now lost, quoted in *Manchester Evening Chronicle*, 20 July 1897.
120 Document, now lost, quoted in *Jewish Record*, 4 March 1887, by Elias Nathan, who notes that Miss Ainsworth was the aunt of the novelist, William Harrison Ainsworth. The synagogue is located in Ainsworth's Court by Joseph Aston, *Picture of Manchester* (Manchester, 1816), p. 105.
121 Edwards, *op. cit.*, pp. 15–16, 55.
122 *Manchester Mercury*, 3 June 1806. The bankruptcy of one of the three, Sylvester Mayring, was announced in the *Mercury* of 7 June 1806.
123 Edwards, *op. cit.*, pp. 17–18, 55–8.
124 *DNB*, article 'Nathan Meyer Rothschild'.
125 Margoliouth, *op. cit.*, vol. 2, pp. 162–3.
126 *Manchester Exchange Herald*, 18 November 1809 to 24 February 1810: advertisement for the sale of Rothschild's house and warehouse.
127 James Butterworth, *op. cit.*, p. 258.
128 *Manchester Exchange Herald*, 9 December 1809.
129 *Manchester Exchange Herald*, 18 November 1809 to 24 February 1810. That Rothschild spent some time in Manchester after 1805, the date usually given for his move to London, is suggested both by this advertisement and by the

subsequent statement of his wife, whom he married in 1806, that she had once been a resident of the town.

130 *Manchester Exchange Herald*, 4 July 1811. The notice is dated 'London, 25th June, 1811'.

131 Records of the Lancashire Commercial Clerks' [Benefit] Society, MCL, M13/4/7.

132 *VJ*, 12 November 1841.

133 Edwards, *op. cit.*, p. 21.

134 Biographical material in *Memoir of Sir Jacob Behrens (1806–1889)* (London, n.d., privately printed), pp. 1 and 22–3. One of the 150 copies printed is in MCL.

135 *Ibid.*, p. 22.

136 Lp. OHC, Register of Births, 31 October 1819, 12 November 1821, 13 April 1823, all described as the children of Gustavus and Sophia Gumpel of Manchester.

137 Gumpel's association with the Liverpool Synagogue and his failure to join the Manchester congregation may suggest the existence of a private *minyan* attended by a small group of mercantile families, although no evidence of such a *minyan* has survived.

138 *Manchester Exchange Herald*, 24 May 1810.

139 *MG*, 4 October 1823.

140 *Ibid.*

141 The original is in MCL, Collection of Biographical Prints.

142 Lp. OHC Building Committee Min. Bk., 25 May 1807, 7 August 1808.

143 *Ibid.*, 10 August 1808.

144 *Ibid.*, Final Accounts.

145 List of subscribers in MCL, Borough reeve's Muniments M1/20.

146 *Manchester Exchange Herald*, 3–24 January 1815.

147 List of subscribers in MCL, Borough reeve's Muniments M/1/22/6.

148 *The Admissions Register of the Manchester School* (Chetham Society Publications, 1874), vol. 3, part I, pp. 22 and 73. A third son, Elias, was sent first to the private school of a Madam Ann Broadbent and later to the academy of William Makinson in Oldham Street (*Jewish Record*, 4 March, 1887).

149 List of subscribers in MCL, MS 647.95 M7, dated 22 October 1804.

150 G. A. Marriott, *History of the Lodge of Fortitude No. 64, 1739–1939* (Manchester, 1939), List of Members. Asher Cohen was also one of the fifty members of the Manchester Lodge of Unity No. 442, held at the Trumpet Tavern (Lancashire Record Office, Freemasons' Return QDS/2/5/1).

151 Benn Franks, *op. cit.* (not paginated). In 1937 Jacob Franks' membership certificate was still extant and in the possession of Mr Edgar Franks.

152 *Manchester Mercury*, 20 January 1795.

153 Lancashire County Records Office, Freemasons' Returns QDS/2/1/43.

154 *Ibid.*, QDS/2/1/1, QDS/2/3/5, QDS/2/4/11.

155 Correspondence relating to the Manchester and Salford Volunteers in MCL, M84/1/1–3.

156 *Ibid.*

157 *Ibid.*

158 Memorial tablet in Temple Sowerby Church. The death of his first wife is noted in *Manchester Exchange Herald*, 14 June 1810.

159 *Carlisle Journal*, 23 June 1832, describes the prominent part played by Levy in the celebration in Penrith which followed the passage of the First Reform Act. He

died in 1834. Hutton Hall still stands in the town of Penrith.

160 *Manchester Exchange Herald*, 21 January 1812.

161 *Ibid.*, 5 May 1812.

162 *Ibid.*

163 *Ibid.*, 12 May 1812.

164 W. E. A. Axon, *The Annals of Manchester* (Manchester, 1886), p. 133; W. Roby, *A Sermon Preached to the Congregation assembled at St George's, Manchester, on the Death of . . . the Reverend John Johnson . . . including a Brief Memoir of his Life* (Manchester, 1804), p. 30.

165 *Manchester Exchange Herald*, 10 and 17 November 1812; *The Jewish Repository*, a conversionist journal, vol. 1 (1813), pp. 34–7, 72–6, 111–17. Surviving annual reports of the Manchester Auxiliary are in MCL.

166 *Manchester Exchange Herald*, 17 November 1812.

167 *The Jewish Repository*, vol. 1 (1813), p. 35. Cf. Roth, *The Jews in England*, pp. 244–5.

168 *Manchester Exchange Herald*, 10 November 1812.

169 *Ibid.*

170 *Ibid.*, 17 November 1812.

171 *The British Volunteer and Manchester Weekly Express*, 28 January 1815. Examples of press reporting of a mildly anti-Semitic character may be found in *The British Volunteer*, 20 August 1814, and *Manchester Exchange Herald*, 28 June 1810, 7 February 1811, and 30 March 1813.

172 S. Y. Prais, 'The development of Birmingham Jewry', *The Jewish Monthly*, vol. 2, No. 11 (February 1949), pp. 665–70.

173 Roth, *The Jews in England*, p. 241.

174 B. L. Benas, *op. cit.*, pp. 60ff; *VJ*, 16 January 1846.

175 *Manchester Exchange Herald*, 30 March 1813. Elias Nathan confirms that although there were twenty-four heads of Jewish families in Manchester by 1816, it was often difficult to raise a *minyan* for Sabbath service (*Jewish World*, 4 and 11 March 1887).

176 *Jewish World*, 7 September 1877. Subsequently 'his mental faculties . . . became impaired'. He was replaced in 1815 and survived thereafter on a small pension from the congregation; Cf. *JC*, 29 September 1854.

177 Aston, *Picture of Manchester*, p. 105. Elias Nathan provides a brief description of Ainsworth's Court in *Jewish Record* of 11 March, 1887: 'The Ark, containing only two very small scrolls of the law, was simply a deal cupboard grained as mahogany; the seats and reading desk were of the same unpretentious character. The portion allotted for the females was on the same level as the men's apartments, and was divided from it by a plain wooden partition, with wooden lattice, from about mid-distance from the floor to within a foot from the ceiling'.

178 Aston, *op. cit.*, pp. 166–7.

179 *Ibid.*, p. 31.

180 *Ibid.*, p. 220.

181 *Ibid.*, p. 219.

182 *Ibid.*, p. 84.

183 *Ibid.*, p. 31.

184 *Ibid.*, p. 25.

185 *The British Volunteer and Manchester Weekly Express*, 19 November 1814.

186 *The British Volunteer and Manchester Weekly Express*, 28 January 1815.
187 Aston, *Picture of Manchester*, pp. 30–1.
188 *Ibid.*, p. 25.

CHAPTER TWO

1 V. D. Lipman, *Social and Economic History of the Jews in England, 1850–1950* (London, 1954), p. 8.
2 *Manchester Chronicle*, 9 May 1818.
3 *Manchester Chronicle*, 9 January 1819; Lp. OHC, Register of Deaths, 1817–23; Register of Births, Deaths and Burials, 1809–19; OHC Acc. Bks., 1824–25; Roth, *Provincial Jewry*, pp. 16–22.
4 *Manchester Chronicle*, 9 January 1819.
5 *MG*, 7 June 1823.
6 *Manchester Chronicle*, 31 May and 2 August 1817.
7 *MG*, 9 March 1822.
8 *Ibid.*, 14 July 1821.
9 Dr Lamert's first advertisement is in *Cowdroy's Manchester Gazette*, 16 December 1815; Abraham Abrahams' in *Manchester Chronicle*, 15 April 1820.
10 Vigier, *op. cit.*, fig. 15.
11 The bankruptcy of Philip Hyam of Manchester, 'merchant, dealer and chapman', was announced in *Manchester Gazette*, 24 May 1806; that of Simon Jacobs, 'late of Manchester, clothes dealer, chapman, dealer', in *Manchester Gazette*, 28 September 1816.
12 *Manchester Chronicle*, 15 March and 14 June 1817.
13 Butterworth, *op. cit.*, pp. 180–1.
14 Butterworth, *op. cit.*, p. 189; Lp. OHC, Letters, D. Behrend to the President, 24 May 1832. Behrend wrote on behalf of one of Isaacs' tied pedlars.
15 *MG*, 8 January 1825.
16 *The Old Fellows Magazine*, New Series, January 1839.
17 PRO, Naturalisation papers of Phineas Henry H.O.I./20/216, 2 September 1845.
18 PRO, Naturalisation papers, H.O.I./52/1690, 8 December 1853.
19 *Ibid.*, H.O.I./20/217, 2 September 1845.
20 *MG*, 17 May 1823.
21 This paragraph is based on A. E. Franklin, *Records of the Franklin Family* (London, 1935), pp. 17–26.
22 A. E. Franklin, *op. cit.*, pp. 26–8.
23 *Admission Register of the Manchester School*, vol. 3, part 2, p. 207.
24 *MG*, 7 June 1823.
25 *Ibid.*, 26 July and 25 October 1823.
26 *Ibid.*, 27 November 1823.
27 *MG*, 8 July and 2 December 1826.
28 *Ibid.*, 20 August 1825.
29 Abraham Franklin's family pride emerges, for example, in a letter to the Liverpool Synagogue on behalf of his son Isaac: Lp. OHC, Letters, Abraham Franklin to the President, 23 May 1832. Another rare insight into Franklin's

personality is provided in the Diary of Benjamin Abraham Franklin, Franklin Papers, AJ/25/Aiii4, 22–24 October 1841, when his elder sons conspire to conceal the mild debauchery of their younger brother, Morris, whose moral conduct they take in hand.

30 *The New Manchester Guide; or, Useful Pocket Companion* (Manchester, 1815), p. 46.

31 *MG*, 25 February 1826.

32 PRO, Naturalisation Papers of George Mayer (H.O.I./35/1205) and his sons, Saul (H.O.I./20/219) and Nathan (H.O.I./8/2606).

33 Edward Baines, *History, Directory and Gazetteer of the County Palatine of Lancaster* (Liverpool, 1824–25), vol. 2, p. 141.

34 Benas (*op. cit.*, p. 65) estimated the Liverpool Jewish population to be 250 families in 1830.

35 S. Y. Prais, *op. cit.*, pp. 670–2.

36 Butterworth, *op. cit.*, pp. ii–iii.

37 *Ibid.*

38 Records of the Manchester Pitt Club in MCL, MS/ff/367/M56. The club was founded in 1812.

39 MCL, Minute Book of the Manchester Literary Society, MS/062/M3, 23 January and 6 February 1827.

40 *Wheeler's Manchester Chronicle*, 18 January 1817.

41 *Manchester Chronicle*, 18 January 1817.

42 *Ibid.*, 17 July 1819.

43 *Ibid.*, 2 August 1817.

44 *Ibid.*

45 *MG*, 7 June 1823.

46 *MG*, 27 September 1823.

47 *MG*, 23 May 1825.

48 *MG*, 27 September 1823.

49 *Ibid.*

50 *Ibid.*

51 *Ibid.*

52 *MG*, 4 October 1823.

53 *MG*, 13 September 1823.

54 *MG*, 30 May 1825.

55 The fortunes of the group of middle-class radical and professional men who served as the spearhead of new attitudes in Manchester society form the basis of Archibald Prentice's *Historical Sketches and Personal Recollections of Manchester, 1792–1832* (original edition, 1851, reprinted in London, 1970). Although at first 'a little circle of men, faithful, amongst the faithless, to liberal principles' (p. 73) and faced with considerable conservative opposition, they were responsible for the major stages of Manchester's political evolution during the nineteenth century—parliamentary representation (1832), municipal incorporation (1838) and the attack upon the Corn Laws. In religion, most were nonconformists, so that religious freedom and equality, including Jewish emancipation, ranked highly amongst their policies.

56 *MG*, 26 May 1821.

57 *MG*, 22 December 1827.

58 *MG*, 7 June 1823.

59 *MG*, 6 September 1823.

60 *MG*, 17 September 1825.

61 *MG*, 6 July 1822.

62 *MG*, 25 November 1824.

63 *MG*, 1 November 1823.

64 *MG*, 24 April 1824.

65 *MG*, 7 June 1823.

66 *MG*, 4 October 1823.

67 *MG*, 27 September 1823.

68 *MG*, 21 July 1821.

69 *MG*, 21 May 1825.

70 *MG*, 10 September 1825; 16 August 1828.

71 *MG*, 8 September 1821.

72 Cf. his funeral oration, *A Complete Memoir of the Late Rev. Canon Stowell* (Manchester, 1865); Rev. J. B. Marsden, *Memoirs of the Life and Labours of Rev. Hugh Stowell, M.A.* (London, 1868).

73 Marsden, *op. cit.*, p. 38.

74 Cf. William Gaskell, *A Letter to Canon Stowell* (Manchester, 1853).

75 Marsden, *op. cit.*, p. 123.

76 *MG*, 16 November 1833; 6 November 1847.

77 *MG*, 28 June 1837.

78 *MG*, 9 August 1837, quoting *Fraser's Magazine*.

79 *A Complete Memoir*, p. 8.

80 *MG*, 7 October 1826.

81 *MG*, 16 August 1828.

82 *MG*, 6 October 1821.

83 *MG*, 24 April 1824.

84 *MG*, 29 June 1822.

85 Letter from Trevor B. Caryll to the Manchester *Beth Din*, 21 September 1972, in the files of the Jewish History Unit, Manchester Polytechnic.

86 *MG*, 14 August 1824; for opening, *MG*, 10 September 1825.

87 Baines, *History, Directory and Gazetteer*, vol. 2, p. 141.

88 Article, 'Manchester', *The Jewish World*, 7 September 1877.

89 J. T. Slugg, *Reminiscences of Manchester Fifty Years Ago* (Manchester, 1881), pp. 191–2; *Jewish World*, 7 September 1877.

90 £287 19s was collected from the seatholders during 1823, £500 loaned by Aaron Jacob and £886 17s 11d advanced by Heywood Brothers, the Manchester bankers. Subscribers included the assimilated merchants E. B. Lomnitz and A. S. Steinthal (*Jewish Record*, 11 March 1887). The subsequent collapse of the roof is described in *MG*, 27 May 1826, and in *A Description of Manchester and Salford* (Manchester, 1826), p. 137.

91 Minute Books of the *Liverpool Hebrew Philanthropic Society*, 17 June 1818. Thanks to the efforts of Mr K. L. Abrahams, these minute books are preserved at the offices of the Liverpool Jewish Welfare Services at Rex Cohen Court.

92 *Ibid.*, 25 November 1824.

93 *MG*, 13 December 1828.

94 *VJ*, 25 December 1846.
95 *The Laws of the Congregation of the Great Synagogue, Duke's Place, London* (London, 1827), introduction, pp. vi–vii.
96 *MG*, 25 August 1832.
97 *Jewish World*, 7 September 1877; Franklin Papers in the Mocatta Library, London: file entitled 'Some family relics': Certificate signed by Solomon Hirschel, 7 August 1835.
98 OHC Acc. Bk., 1827–28, end-page.
99 Since no early law code has survived, I have used the *Revised Code of Laws for the Government of the Manchester Old Hebrew Congregation, 5607* (London, 1850) with adjustments based on information from the preceding Account and Minute Books of the Congregation.
100 S. Y. Prais, *op. cit.*, pp. 670–2. Cf. 'Synagogue organisation 100 years ago', in *JC*, 11 January 1901; V. D. Lipman, *Social History*, pp. 41–4.
101 Lp. OHC, Letters, H. Jacob to the Wardens, 8 April 1832; Isaac Franklin to the President, 12 April 1832, H. Jacob to the Wardens, 19 April 1832; Abraham Franklin to the President, 23 May 1832.
102 Diary of Benjamin Abraham Franklin, 8 March 1841. The entry includes a gesture of reconciliation.

CHAPTER THREE

1 During the period covered by this chapter, men of pedlar origin dominated the Select Committee of the synagogue and formed a majority of its Free Members.
2 *MG*, 24 October 1829.
3 *MG*, 19 February 1831.
4 *MG*, 6 June 1829.
5 *MG*, 1 August 1829.
6 *MG*, 12 July 1834.
7 *MG*, 19 February 1831.
8 *MG*, 8 December 1827. The appearance of similar reports in Archibald Prentice's radical *Manchester Times and Gazette* (e.g. 5 February 1831) suggests that the abstract defence of Jewish rights on the grounds of abstract principle (e.g. 10 April 1830) might be combined with more equivocal attitudes towards individual Jews.
9 *MG*, 1 December 1827. Cf. James Wheeler, *Manchester: its Political, Social and Commercial History* (Manchester, 1836), p. 234.
10 *MG*, 12 April 1828.
11 *MG*, 4 July 1829.
12 *MG*, 20 January 1827.
13 *MG*, 25 June 1831; Gainsborg's later success as an emancipist shopkeeper in Bathurst, New South Wales, is described in J. S. Levi and G. F. J. Bergman, *Australian Genesis: Jewish Convicts and Settlers, 1788–1850* (London and Adelaide, 1974), p. 245.
14 *MG*, 24 September 1831.
15 *MG*, 4 March 1826.

16 *MG*, 26 November 1831.
17 *MG*, 10 December 1831; 14 January 1832.
18 *MG*, 13 September 1834.
19 *MG*, 12 December 1829.
20 *MG*, 29 May 1830.
21 *MG*, 17 and 24 November 1832.
22 OHC Acc. Bk., 1835–36.
23 *MG*, 25 July 1829.
24 *Ibid.*
25 David Alexander, *Retailing in England during the Industrial Revolution* (London, 1970), pp. 243–4. Alexander concludes (p. 65) that country peddling was on the decline and urban peddling on the increase between 1830 and 1860.
26 *MG*, 1 March 1823; 22 March 1823.
27 *MG*, 1 March 1823.
28 *MG*, 29 March and 26 July 1823.
29 *MG*, 3 December 1831.
30 *MG*, 1 January 1825.
31 *MG*, 7 June 1823.
32 *Ibid.*
33 *MG*, 22 March 1823.
34 *Manchester Herald*, 9 December 1835.
35 *MG*, 9 November 1836.
36 Lp. OHC, Letters. D. Behrend to the Warden, 24 May 1832.
37 Lp. OHC, Letters, 1831–37 *passim.*
38 Lp. OHC, Letters, Henry Ephraim to the President, 19 July 1833.
39 Lp. OHC, Letters, Joseph Hyman to the Wardens, 12 August 1836.
40 Lp. OHC, Letters, Israel Barnard to the Warden, 9 May 1839.
41 *MG*, 22 November 1834.
42 *MG*, 12 January 1833.
43 *MG*, 17 January 1829.
44 *MG*, 12 November 1831.
45 *MG*, 9 June 1832.
46 Franklin Papers, MS pamphlet, 'On the use and abuse of vision: a familiar explanation of the structure and economy of the eyes with instruction for the proper adoption of optical aid' by J. A. F., 20 St Ann's Square, Manchester.
47 *MG*, 5 December 1829.
48 *MG*, 10 March 1832.
49 *MG*, 16 December 1826.
50 *MG*, 14 July 1827.
51 The early history of mass-tailoring in general, and of Jewish mass-tailoring in particular, has still to be written. Although there is useful information in Joan Thomas, *A History of the Leeds Clothing Industry* (*Yorkshire Bulletin of Economic and Social Research*, Occasional Paper 1, Leeds, 1955, pp. 1–23), Manchester evidence does not substantiate all her conclusions. If Mrs Thomas' dates for Leeds and London are accurate, then Manchester preceded both as a centre of mass-tailoring, and Hyam (with his relatives in London and other parts of England) must be counted the pioneer in the Jewish milieu. L. P. Gartner, *The Jewish Immigrant in*

England, 1870–1914 (London, revised ed. 1971), p. 85, and Lipman, *Social and Economic History of the Jews in England, 1850–1950* (London, 1954), pp. 33–4, are both in error in associating the origins of the ready-made clothing trade with the invention of the Singer Sewing Machine, shown at the Great Exhibition in Crystal Palace in 1851.

52 Information on Hyam's background and family connections is provided in Rev. Hermann Gollancz, 'A ramble in East Anglia', *Tr. JHSE*, vol. 2 (1894–95), pp. 133–40 and in a family tree of the Halford family, of which there is a copy in MCL. Hyam changed his name to Halford in 1871.

53 *MG*, 8 November 1834.

54 *MG*, 1 November 1834.

55 Circular issued by the Migration Office, Manchester, 3 November 1836; MCL Archives Misc/150. The circular speaks of Hyam's 'ready-made wearing apparel', the earliest evidence of his entry into this sector of the trade.

56 See below, Chapter 5, section 1.

57 *MG*, 13 July 1833.

58 *MG*, 2 March 1833.

59 *MG*, 13 July 1833. The Manchester strike apparently preceded the famous London stoppage, which forms part of the history of Robert Owen's Grand National Trades Union, and which began in December 1833, as a demand for a shortening of the hours of labour (Beatrice and Sydney Webb, *The History of Trade Unionism* (London, 1902), p. 134). The formation of a local Union, however, is probably related to the efforts of London's First Grand Lodge of Operative Tailors to organise the Grand National Consolidated, in February 1834 (Mary Stewart and Leslie Hunter, *The Needle is Threaded: the History of an Industry* (London, 1964), p. 34). The place of these events within the general history of trade unionism cannot obscure the changes within the industry on which the tailors' grievances were based and which relate particularly to the response of tailoring to the emergence of a mass market.

60 *MG*, 13 July 1833.

61 *MG*, 31 August 1833.

62 *MG*, 15 November 1834. An 'Address' by Edward Davies on behalf of the journeymen described the union as a 'non-political' body.

63 *MG*, 21 June 1834.

64 *MG*, 28 June and 1 November 1834.

65 *MG*, 21 June 1834.

66 Walter Tomlinson, *Bye-ways of Manchester Life* (Manchester, 1887), p. 177.

67 OHC Acc. Bk., 1833–34.

68 *MG*, 27 October 1827.

69 *MG*, 14 November 1834. Henry Leveaux's son, Moritz, was born in Preston in March 1834. (Lp. OHC, Register of Births, 30 March 1834).

70 *MG*, 5 January 1833.

71 PRO, Naturalisation Papers, H.O.I./55/1805.

72 Dr J. P. Kay, *The Moral and Physical Condition of the Working Classes in the Cotton Manufacture in Manchester* (Manchester, 1832; reprinted by the Irish University Press, Shannon, 1971), p. 10.

73 *Ibid.*, p. 7.

74 Dr J. P. Kay, *The Moral and Physical Condition of the Working Classes in the Cotton Manufacture in Manchester*, p. 10.
75 *Ibid.*, p. 6.
76 *Ibid.*, p. 20.
77 Benjamin Love, *Manchester As It Is; or, Notices of the Institutions, Manufactures, Commerce, Railways, etc, of the Metropolis of Manchester* (Manchester, 1839), pp. 136–7.
78 Aston, *Picture of Manchester*, pp. 166–7.
79 *Wheeler's Manchester Chronicle*, 29 May 1830.
80 Aston, *Picture of Manchester*, p. 223.
81 Love, *op. cit.*, p. 181.
82 J. S. Gregson, *Gimcrackiana; or, Fugitive Pieces on Manchester Men and Manners* (Manchester, 1833), pp. 88–98.
83 *MG*, 18 August 1827.
84 Cf. Asa Briggs, *Victorian Cities* (London, 1963), pp. 88–92.
85 Kay, *op. cit.*, p. 43.
86 *Ibid.*, p. 57.
87 *MG*, 26 May 1832.
88 *MG*, 2 January 1830.
89 *Ibid.*
90 *MG*, 20 March 1830.
91 Kay, *op. cit.*, p. 21.
92 *MG*, 1 June 1833.
93 *MG*, 8 June 1833.
94 *Ibid.*
95 *MG*, 21 August 1830.
96 *MG*, 11 September 1830.
97 *MG*, 13 November 1830.
98 *MG*, 25 August 1832.
99 *MG*, 21 June 1834.
100 *MG*, 12 December 1835.
101 *MG*, 21 June 1834.
102 *MG*, 6 and 13 December 1834, 14 February 1835.
103 *MG*, 5 April 1834.
104 *MG*, 14 August 1830.
105 *MG*, 6 February 1830; Minute Books of the Manchester Foreign Library in MCL, BR/MS/F./027.3/M1, 3, 17 and 22 February 1830.
106 *MG*, 31 January 1835.
107 *MG*, 1 March 1834.
108 *MG*, 22 May 1830.

CHAPTER FOUR

1 *MG*, 8 February 1834. For a general account of the struggle for Emancipation, see Roth, *The Jews in England*, pp. 247–56; 259–66.
2 *MG*, 22 May 1830.
3 e.g. *MG*, 23 May 1825; 29 November 1828.

4 *MG*, 29 November 1829, quoting the notice of a public meeting in the Manor Court Room to oppose Catholic claims; *Manchester Courier*, 22 May 1830.

5 *MG*, 8 February 1834. Reports of the meeting in London on 18 November 1833, and of a subsequent meeting in Liverpool on 28 January 1834, were inserted in all the Liverpool papers, in the *Manchester Guardian*, the *Sheffield Iris*, the *Leeds Mercury* and four London papers.

6 *MG*, 1 March 1834.

7 *MG*, 6 November 1824.

8 *MG*, 2 October 1824.

9 *MG*, 25 July 1840.

10 *MG*, 12 July 1834; 13 September 1834. After serving out his sentence at Lancaster, Sergei Tournoff returned to Manchester in the mid-1840s and secured work as a 'habit-cutter', but his connection with the synagogue was never renewed.

11 Cf. Chaim Bermant, *The Cousinhood: the Anglo-Jewish Gentry* (London, 1971), which deals chiefly with the London plutocracy.

12 *MG*, 27 August 1836.

13 Love, *op. cit.*, p. 37.

14 *Ibid.*, p. 38.

15 *Ibid.*, pp. 200–1.

16 *Ibid.*, pp. 181–2.

17 *Ibid.*

18 *The Cotton Metropolis* (first published in the *Morning Chronicle*, 1849–50, subsequently, as a tract, by W. & R. Chambers; 1972 ed. by R. Shipperbottom, Manchester), pp. 4–5.

19 *Ibid.*

20 *MG*, 7 April 1838.

21 *JC*, 19 November 1880. For Lazarus: PRO, Naturalisation Papers, H.O.I./24/50; for Hiller and Bauer: *Certificates of Naturalisation, 1844–1900, Index to Names* (Home Office, 1908); for Sington: *Jewish Record* 11 March, 1 April 1887. Sington was perhaps typical of the prospectors who lacked substantial capital backing. Born in Breslau in 1810, the son of the Reader of a small congregation, he began his working life as a clerk in a stationery business in Hamburg. The establishment of a commission agency in Manchester with Edward Nathan was his first venture in the cotton trade, although he achieved a very rapid and solid success. His religious position is described below.

22 Biographical material in *JC*, 4 September 1903; 16 October 1908; 18 November 1910.

23 *JC*, 18 November 1910: 'The family of the late Henry Lucas—an early romance'.

24 MCL Archives, M/17/4/1/1. Lucas was admitted as member No. 376 in May 1834. Subsequent members included Sigismund Stern (1837), Alexander Oppenheim (1838), Elias Mocatta of Liverpool (1848) and Julius Lipman (1848).

25 *MG*, 30 January 1836.

26 *MG*, 30 July 1836.

27 *MG*, 2 February 1839.

28 Leo Schuster, whose Jewish origin was claimed in *The Jewish World*, 7 September 1877, was the conversionist. *Commemoration of the Fifty Years of Ministry of Rev.*

William Gaskell, M.A., Sermon Preached by him . . . and Report of proceedings (Manchester, 1878?), includes Louis Schwabe, Peter Goldschmidt, H. J. Leppoc, H. M. Steinthal, E. Salomonson, and S. A. Meyer in Gaskell's flock.

29 *Jewish Record*, 1 April 1887. Later he married the daughter of Eleazer Moses.

30 Cf. *Memoir of Sir Jacob Behrens*; A. R. Rollin, 'The Jewish contribution to the British textile industry', *Tr. JHSE*, vol. 17 (1951–52), pp. 45–51; *JC*, 26 April 1889.

31 *Memoir of Sir Jacob Behrens*, pp. 29–32.

32 *Ibid.*, pp. 32–4.

33 *Ibid.*, p. 39; for Louis Behrens, cf. *JC*, 6 June 1884.

34 *Memoir of Sir Jacob Behrens*, p. 13.

35 *JC*, 11 August 1865.

36 *Memoir of Sir Jacob Behrens*, pp. 93–4.

37 *JC*, 11 August 1865; 21 October 1870; 22 November 1872; 2 October 1874 for the steps by which a Reform Synagogue emerged.

38 Franklin Papers, Esther Franklin to Jacob Prins, 22 October 1835.

39 Diary of Benjamin Abraham Franklin, 21 April 1841.

40 J. A. V. Chapple and A. Pollard, *The Letters of Mrs Gaskell* (Manchester, 1966), Letter 585, to Marianne, 6 October (1865?).

41 G. R. Catt, *Pictorial History of Manchester* (Manchester, 1843), p. 23. A small stream, the Cornbrook, which flowed through Greenheys was known locally, and not only for its smell, as 'the Oder' (*MG*, 24 June 1846).

42 Diary of Benjamin Abraham Franklin, *op. cit.*, 17 February 1842; 3 March 1842, and *passim*.

43 *VJ*, 20 January 1842.

44 *MG*, 20 July 1842.

45 *MG*, 25 January 1843.

46 *MG*, 2 March 1839; 4 March 1840.

47 *MG*, 30 April 1845.

48 *MG*, 14 June 1851.

49 Diary of Benjamin Abraham Franklin, 22 February 1841.

50 *Ibid.*

51 *MG*, 6 February 1841.

52 Alexander Behr, 'Isidor Gerstenberg, 1821–76', *Tr. JHSE*, vol. 17 (1951–52), pp. 207–13. In the Census of 1841 Gerstenberg is enumerated as a lodger in Chorlton-on-Medlock, in the same house as another of Bauer's clerks, Philip Gowa.

53 A. E. Franklin, *op. cit.*, p. 33.

54 *MG*, 8 November 1845, advertised the sale, by Behrens, of the Pyrmont Cotton Mill 'owing to family arrangements'.

55 *MG*, 26 January 1842.

56 The endorsement led Franklin into legal problems which he overcame only with the help of a loophole in the law relating to joint-stock enterprises. Reports and correspondence in *MG*, 22 November 1837 to 31 March 1838, *passim*.

57 Diary of Benjamin Abraham Franklin, 4 April 1841.

58 OHC, Min. Bk., GM, 1 November 1840: OHC Min. Bk., Burial Ground Committee, 2 April 1841. The acquisition of the new burial ground required loans of

£100 from the Philanthropic Society and £200 from Samuel Isaacs.
59 OHC, Min. Bk., GM, 25 April 1841.
60 Love, *op. cit.*, p. 20.
61 Wheeler, *op. cit.*, p. 258.
62 *Ibid.*, pp. 261–2.
63 *MG*, 14 January 1836.
64 *MG*, 28 October 1837.
65 Love, *op. cit.*, pp. 94–5.
66 The controversy is covered briefly by C. B. Dolton in *Rich Inheritance* ed. N. F. Frangopulo (Manchester, 1962), pp. 77–9, and by Arthur Redford, *The History of Local Government in Manchester*, 3 vols. (London, 1939–40), vol. 2, pp. 236–40.
67 HA, *First Annual Report* (1839), p. 6.
68 *MG*, 1 June 1839.
69 *MG*, 4 December 1850.
70 *MG*, 28 June 1837.
71 *MG*, 5 August 1837, quoting *Fraser's Magazine*.
72 *MG*, 12 June 1839.
73 *MG*, 29 October 1831. The advertisement was printed in Hebrew and framed in unmistakably Jewish terms.
74 *MG*, 24 October 1835.
75 *JC*, 13 November 1891.
76 Arthur Barnett, *The Western Synagogue through Two Centuries* (London, 1961), pp. 49–51.
77 *JC*, 2 May 1879.
78 Lucien Wolf, *op. cit.*, p. 317.
79 B. L. Benas, *op. cit.*, pp. 50–1; Margoliouth, *op. cit.*, p. 111; *JC*, 9 January 1846; 10 April 1863; Barnett, *op. cit.*, p. 51, cites an isolated English sermon in Liverpool in 1819.
80 Cf. obituary in *JC*, 2 May 1879; B. L. Benas, *op. cit.*, pp. 63–71; P. Ettinger, *Hope Place in Liverpool Jewry* (Liverpool, 1930), pp. 34–74; James Picciotto, *Sketches of Anglo-Jewish History* (London, 1956 ed.), pp. 332–3 and note; correspondence in *JC*, 9 October and 16 October 1874. His brother Samuel, who went to New York as English Lecturer to the Elm Street Synagogue in 1839, became a pillar of American orthodoxy and editor of *The Jewish Messenger* (*JC*, 31 December 1869; 7 June 1878).
81 Lp. OHC, Letters, D. M. Isaacs to the Directors of the Liverpool Synagogue, 22 October 1834.
82 *Ibid.*
83 *Ibid.*
84 Lp. OHC, Letters, B. Hyam to the President, 11 September 1838.
85 A. E. Price, MS 'History of the Jews School', based upon sources now lost, describes a meeting at the house of Abraham Franklin at which the appeal was devised.
86 HA, *First Annual Report* (1839), pp. 4–5 and Balance Sheet; Lp. OHC, Letters, Isaac Franklin to the President, 23 September and 27 September 1838.
87 Autobiographical Sketch in *The Old Fellows Magazine*, New Series, January 1839.
88 *MG*, 19 December 1835.

89 Biographical material in *MG*, 30 July and 3 August 1853; *Blackley and Crumpsall Guardian*, 17 March and 28 April 1961; *JC*, 16 November 1894, and 29 May 1896. Schwabe is said to have been 'an active member of the Glasgow Synagogue' when he first arrived in England, but he and his wife had ceased to practise Judaism before their arrival in Manchester.

90 Love, *op. cit.*, pp. 207–8. Further biographical material in *Manchester City News*, 4 April 1914, and Axon's *Annals*, 11 January 1845.

91 *MG*, 10 July 1837, announced Dr Bernstein's arrival from the University of Berlin. His Manchester referees included Dr Henry and James Heywood.

92 Margoliouth, *op. cit.*, vol. 3, p. 125. Sir Thomas Baker, *Memorials of a Dissenting Chapel* (Manchester, 1884), gives S. A. Meyer as a trustee of the Cross Street Unitarian Chapel in 1854.

93 Lucien Wolf, *op. cit.*, p. 318, quoting from Montefiore's diary.

94 HA, *First Annual Report* (1839), p. 5.

95 *Ibid.*, p. 6.

96 *Ibid.*, p. 7.

97 *MG*, 4 December 1850.

98 *JC*, 2 May 1879.

99 This is my reading of HA, *First Annual Report*, p. 5.

100 Diary of Benjamin Abraham Franklin, 8 March 16 April 18 April 1 May 1841.

101 HA, *First Annual Report*, p. 4.

102 Lp. OHC, Letters, D. M. Isaacs to the Senior Warden, 19 July 1841.

103 The dispute on this matter in correspondence in the *JC*, 9 October and 16 October 1874, in which Isaacs disputed Picciotto's claim that he had once offered himself as a candidate at Duke's Place, is decided in Picciotto's favour by Lp. OHC, Letters, D. M. Isaacs to the Senior Warden Liverpool, 19 July 1841.

104 *VJ*, 26 November 1841.

105 *VJ*, 26 November 1841; 21 January 1842.

106 HA, *First Annual Report*, pp. 7–8.

107 A. E. Price, 'History of the Jews School' (not paginated). Photocopy in MCL.

108 *Ibid.*

109 Love, *op. cit.*, pp. 95–6.

110 *VJ*, 16 September 1841.

111 A. E. Price, *op. cit.* (not paginated).

112 Liverpool Hebrew Educational Institution, *First Annual Report* (1841–42), p. 2.

113 *VJ*, 16 September 1841.

114 *VJ*, 21 January 1842.

115 *Ibid.*

116 HA, *Fifth Annual Report* (1843), p. 5; *VJ*, 25 November 1842.

117 HA, *Fifth Annual Report*, pp. 5–6.

118 *Ibid.*

119 *Ibid.*

120 *Ibid.*, p. 8.

121 *Ibid.*

122 HA, *Sixth Annual Report* (1844), p. 9.

123 HA, *Seventh Annual Report* (1845), p. 14.

124 *Ibid.*, p. 13.

125 *Ibid.*, pp. 9–10. The substance of the dispute is nowhere clarified. In spite of the Committee's attempt to retain his services, he left with a £10 gratuity and subsequently obtained a post in London.

126 *Ibid.*, p. 13.

127 *Ibid.*

128 *Ibid.*, p. 14.

129 The first public examination took place under Lucas' presidency on 1 October 1843, and was reported in *VJ*, 13 October 1843. It was conducted by Abraham Bauer and J. M. Isaac.

130 HA, *Seventh Annual Report*, p. 14.

131 HA, *Fifth Annual Report* (1843), pp. 9–10.

132 The name was changed to Manchester Hebrew Educational Society in 1850.

133 OHC, Min. Bk., 1840–46: newspaper cutting on flyleaf describing an appeal launched by the Association at the York Hotel on 30 June 1840.

134 Diary of Benjamin Abraham Franklin, 8 March 1841.

135 *VJ*, 16 September 1841; 21 January 1842.

136 *Cursory Glance at the Present Social State of the Jewish People of Great Britain* (Edinburgh, 1845), quoted in *JC*, 7 March 1845.

137 Liverpool Hebrew Educational Institution, *First Annual Report*, p. 3.

138 A brief account of the events in Damascus and the reaction in England is provided in Lucien Wolf, *op. cit.*, pp. 320–3. Cf. *The Times*, 8 April 1840, for a full immediate report.

139 *MG*, 1 July 1840.

140 HA, *Fifth Annual Report*, Balance Sheet.

141 Biographical Material in *MG*, 28 April and 1 May 1886; *JC*, 30 April 1886; *Jewish Gazette*, 10 April 1959; Rabbi P. S. Goldberg, *The Manchester Congregation of British Jews, 1857–1957* (Manchester, 1957), iv. His early alienation from Judaism is suggested (1) by his absence from the synagogal records of Manchester prior to 1842, (2) the fact that his marriage in the synagogue (1842) follows his appearance in the Census of 1841 as a married man with a young son.

142 *MG*, 16 and 24 November 1841.

143 *The Times*, 5 November 1840, summarised in P. S. Goldberg, *op. cit.*, p. 30.

144 Diary of Benjamin Abraham Franklin, 8 March 1841.

145 *VJ*, 21 June 1844.

146 *VJ*, 14 October 1842.

147 *MG*, 25 July 1840.

148 *Ibid.*

149 *Ibid.*

150 *Ibid.*

151 *Ibid.*

152 *MG*, 4 July 1840.

153 *MG*, 25 July 1840.

154 *Ibid.* There was also a perceptible softening of attitudes in the Tory Press. While still believing that Jews should be excluded from parliament on religious grounds, the *Manchester Courier* (22 December 1847) accepted that socially 'many Jews are above reproach, blameless alike in their lives and conduct'.

155 *MG*, 25 July 1840.

156 *MG*, 17 June 1840.
157 *MG*, 30 October 1844.
158 *MG*, 3 December 1845.
159 *MG*, 25 July 1840.
160 *MG*, 12 March 1845.
161 *Ibid.*
162 *MG*, 9 January 1841.
163 *MG*, 17 February 1841.
164 *MG*, 20 March 1841.
165 *MG*, 20 October 1841.
166 *MG*, 17 February 1841.
167 Dow Marmur, ed., *Reform Judaism: Essays on Reform Judaism in Britain* (London, 1973), p. 21. The article by Michael Leigh in this collection is the most recent history of Reform Judaism in England. For a more critical summary see Lucien Wolf, *op. cit.*, pp. 317ff.
168 Marmur, *op. cit.*, p. 23.
169 Lp. OHC, Letters, D. W. Marks to the Select Committee, 12 August 1840. Marks' early training and theological standpoint are treated in Marmur, *op. cit.*, pp. 25–30.
170 Lp. OHC, Letters, F. H. Goldsmid to E. S. Yates, 24 September 1840.
171 Marmur, *op. cit.*, p. 28.
172 *Ibid.*, p. 25.
173 *Ibid.*, p. 27.
174 Arthur Barnett, *op. cit.*, pp. 181–2.
175 *Ibid.*, p. 181.
176 *Ibid.*
177 *Ibid.*
178 *Ibid.*
179 OHC, Letters, Solomon Hirschel to Joseph Marks, 1 August 1836.
180 *Ibid.*
181 OHC, Min. Bk., GM, 8 January and 6 February 1842. The change was based upon the example of Liverpool (*VJ*, 16 September 1841).
182 OHC, Min. Bk., SC, 25 July 1841; GM, 3 January 1842; Special GM, 6, 20 and 27 February 1842.
183 *Ibid.*
184 *VJ*, 18 February 1842.
185 Barnett, *op. cit.*, p. 186.
186 OHC, Min. Bk., GM, 6, 20 and 27 February 1842.
187 *VJ*, 16 September 1841.
188 *JC*, 10 August 1877. The obituary was written by Abraham Benisch; a more favourable view is presented by Asher Myers in *JC*, Jubilee Supplement, 13 November 1891.
189 *The Oral Law and its Defenders. A Review by a Spiritualist* (Tobias Theodores) (London, 1842), p. 1.
190 *Ibid.*, p. 50.
191 *Ibid.*
192 *Ibid.*

193 *Ibid.*, pp. 50–1.
194 M. H. Simonson, *Holy Convocations regulated by our Rabbins, and Observed by (all) Israel in accordance with the Pentateuch and Reason* (London, 1844).
195 *Ibid.*, p. 3.
196 *Ibid.*, p. v.
197 *Ibid.*, pp. vi–viii.
198 *Ibid.*, p. iv.
199 OHC, Min. Bk., SC, 25 September 1844: GM, 1 December 1844. The number of votes allocated to Manchester (four) was based upon the congregation's contribution to the Chief Rabbi's Fund.
200 Barnett, *op. cit.*, p. 186.
201 *MG*, 28 November 1840.

CHAPTER FIVE

1 W. Cooke Taylor, *Notes on a Tour in the Manufacturing Districts of Lancashire* (London, 2nd ed., 1842), p. 8.
2 *Ibid.*
3 *Ibid.*
4 *Ibid.*, pp. 7–9, 14–19, 258–60.
5 *Ibid.*, p. 15, cf. Kay, *op. cit.*, pp. 50–7.
6 Leon Faucher, *Manchester in 1844: its Present Condition and Future Prospects* (Manchester, 1844), pp. 28–9 (translator's notes).
7 *Ibid.*, pp. 28–33n.
8 Redford, *op. cit.*, vol. 2, p. 125.
9 Faucher, *op. cit.*, p. 15.
10 Leon Faucher, *op. cit.*, p. 15; Wheeler, *Manchester: its Political, Social and Commercial History*, p. 340; Registrar General's Report on the Census of 1841: Population Summary. The Census gives 34,300 persons of Irish birth out of a population of 296,183, but this of course does not include those born in Manchester of Irish parentage.
11 Leon Faucher, *op. cit.*, p. 15.
12 *MG*, 1 March 1845.
13 *Ibid.*
14 *MG*, 25 February 1843.
15 *MG*, 8 November 1843.
16 *MG*, 4 July 1846.
17 Cooke Taylor, *op. cit.*, p. 325.
18 *MG*, 18 June 1842.
19 Cooke Taylor, *op. cit.*, p. 175.
20 *MG*, 16 May 1835.
21 Alexander, *op. cit.*, pp. 18–25; S. G. Checkland, *The Rise of Industrial Society in England 1815–1885* (London, 1964), pp. 113–15. Checkland places the beginning of a 'new age' of retail trading in the 1850s.
22 *MG*, 20 October 1841.
23 Advertisements in *MG*, 19 March 1842; 7 June 1845; 6 May 1846; 2 January 1847.

24 Advertisements in *MG*, 9 December 1843; 9 November 1844; 7 June 1845.

25 *MG*, 25 and 29 May 1839.

26 *MG*, 16 February 1850.

27 Joseph Mitchell in *MG*, 12 April 1845.

28 *MG*, 8 March 1845.

29 *MG*, 29 March 1845.

30 *MG*, 17 October 1847.

31 *MG*, 3 March 1849.

32 *Ibid.* The new copyright law was 6 and 7 Vic. cap. 45.

33 *MG*, 16 April 1836: advertisement of Edwin Taylor.

34 *MG*, 29 November 1845.

35 *MG*, 21 March 1846.

36 *MG*, 24 January 1846.

37 *MG*, 15 July 1846.

38 *MG*, 6 February 1850. See Thomas, *A History of the Leeds Clothing Industry*, pp. 10–11.

39 *MG*, 6 February 1850, under a heading 'The sweating system'.

40 *MG*, 24 March 1849.

41 Friedrich Engels, *Condition of the Working Class in England in 1844*, translated by W. O. Henderson and W. H. Chaloner (Oxford, 1958), p. 143.

42 *MG*, 17 and 24 April 1850.

43 *MG*, 25 November 1848; 24 April 1850.

44 There is an instance, in the early 1860s, of a Jewish tailor pledging a sewing machine and then selling the ticket for £2 10s and a hawker's licence. *MG*, 9 October 1861.

45 e.g. *MG*, 26 May 1832.

46 e.g. *MG*, 17 March 1832.

47 *MG*, 14 January 1843.

48 Jewish pawnbrokers appear far more frequently in the press as informants than as receivers; e.g. *MG*, 31 December 1836; 26 October 1844; 30 August 1845; 25 November 1848.

49 *MG*, 8 April 1846; cf. *MG*, 9 May 1838.

50 e.g. *MG*, 10 June 1846.

51 Scrapbook in Franklin Papers, AJ 25/Aii2.

52 *MG*, 14 March 1849.

53 *MG*, 23 March 1850.

54 MCL, M3/9/586–7.

55 *MG*, 5 October 1842.

56 *MG*, 19 February 1853.

57 *MG*, 9 June 1849.

58 *MG*, 30 October 1844. The reference to his presence in California is in A. E. Franklin, *op. cit.*, p. 30.

59 Felix Folio (John Page), *The Hawkers and Street Dealers of the North of England Manufacturing Districts* (Manchester, 1858), pp. 10, 13. For local hostility to urban pedlars, cf. *MG*, 16 September 1843. Another indication of the fate of country hawking was the declining proportion of English-born persons amongst the Jewish hawkers revealed in Manchester by the census enumerators: twenty-eight

out of fifty-two in 1841, ten out of forty-five in 1851; twelve out of fifty-seven in 1861. Hawking was becoming an immigrant trade.

60 Wheeler, *op. cit.*, p. 258.

61 *MG*, 30 August 1843.

62 *MG*, 14 January 1843, and OHC Acc. Bks., 1843–44ff.

63 *MG*, 25 January 1845.

64 The support of the Golding 'orphans' necessitated a separate clause in a treaty signed between two rival Manchester congregations in 1847; *JC*, 15 November 1847.

65 *MG*, 31 December 1831. Isaac was discharged for want of evidence.

66 *MG*, 17 May 1843. Phillips' subscriptions to the synagogue began in 1842.

67 *MG*, 18 June 1845.

68 *MG*, 26 July 1845.

69 *MG*, 27 March 1847.

70 *MG*, 6 April 1847.

71 *Mechanics Magazine*, 13 November 1841.

72 Benn Franks, MS Family History (not paginated).

73 J. G. D. Kay, typescript 'Report on optical casebook . . . written by H. Franks' (November 1970), in the possession of Mrs Dorothy Goldstone. According to this report, the casebook, now in the possession of Mr Henry Franks of Leeds, shows a knowledge of optics 'in advance of most of the general medical knowledge available at that time'. The notes on domiciliary visits include the name, address and occupation of patients, their ocular deficiencies, the approximate power of any corrective lenses required, and any observable pathological symptoms.

74 Abraham Franks, too, had begun his business life as traveller for his father (*Stamford Mercury*, 7 January and 29 April 1842, 6 January and 10 March 1843; *Lincolnshire Chronicle*, 29 April 1842, 15 and 22 December 1843; *Preston Pilot*, 13 April 1844; in a scrapbook in the possession of Mr Geoffrey Rothband, now in photocopy in MCL). The reported content of his illustrated lectures and the many recommendations from local doctors and surgeons confirm the professional knowledge and skill of Jacob Franks' sons. It is also clear that by 1844 there was a branch of the family business in Preston.

75 *MG*, 17 July 1841. Dancer went on to become an instrument maker, inventor and photographer of international repute. Cf. 'John Benjamin Dancer, F.R.S.A., 1812–1887', *Memoirs and Proceedings of the Manchester Literary and Philosophical Society*, vol. 107 (1964–65).

76 Felix Folio, *op. cit.*, p. 49. Jewish quacks, usually more literate than Sakery Moses, persisted in Manchester into the 1860s. One of the more successful was Dr David Davieson, who advertised Herb pills 'for the effectual extirpation of every species and symptom of syphilitic disease' and a Cordial Balm of Mecca, 'peculiarly efficacious in all inward wastings, loss of appetite, indigestion, depression of spirits, trembling or shaking of the hands or limbs, obstinate coughs, shortness of breath, or consumptive habits . . . all nervous disorders, fits, headaches, weakness, headiness, lowness of spirits, dimness of sight, confused thoughts, wanderings of the mind, and all kinds of hysterical complaints . . .' (advertisement in the *Manchester Examiner and Times*, 8 October 1851). Dr Davieson was a seat-holder of the

Old Hebrew Congregation; he was still in Manchester in 1861, with consulting rooms in Sidney Street, Chorlton-on-Medlock.

77 *MG*, 28 January to 23 May 1837. Solomons was one of the few surviving travelling opticians of repute, of whom others were members of the Franks family.

78 He appears in the Census of 1851 as 'Gen. Practitioner (M.R.C.S. and L.S.A. Lond.)'.

79 *MG*, 4 August 1838.

80 Franklin Papers, file entitled 'Some family relics', Certificate signed by Solomon Hirschel, 7 August 1835.

81 Lp. OHC, Letters, Isaac Franklin to the President, 21 March 1849.

82 *Ibid.*

83 *MG*, 22 December 1841.

84 A. E. Franklin, *op. cit.*, pp. 29–30.

85 *MG*, 13 August 1842.

86 *MG*, 5 October 1844.

87 *MG*, 11 August 1849.

88 *MG*, 7 November 1835; PRO, Naturalisation Papers of Louis (H.O.I./39/1248A) and Samuel (H.O.I./49/1606) Berend.

89 *MG*, 14 November 1835.

90 *MG*, 29 October 1845. Moss' business was said to have been 'slack' for the two months preceding his death.

91 *MG*, 26 January 1851: Louis Beaver had employed a boy at this wage since 1846.

92 Calculations based upon information extracted from the Census of 1841 and summarised in Appendix B.

93 I am indebted to Mr Sampson Goldstone of Ward & Goldstone, Salford, the great-grandson of Michael Goldstone, for information which extends the factual record of the Census. Michael's eldest son married Jane, the daughter of Dayan A. L. Barnett. The family firm of electrical manufacturers was founded by Michael's grandson, Meyer Hart Goldstone, in 1892.

94 Lp. OHC, Letters, Michael Goldstone to the Wardens, 1825–35 *passim*.

95 Material other than Census entries relating to Bibergeil's background and early settlement in Manchester is based upon information kindly provided by the late Leonard Stein, O.B.E., his grandson.

96 *MG*, 11 October 1843.

97 *MG*, 28 October 1843; 8 January 1861.

98 *JC*, 21 August 1846.

99 For information relating to David Hesse's background, I am indebted to his great-granddaughter, Miss Margaret Langdon, M.B.E., and to Mrs Dorothy Goldstone, into whose family (the Franks) he married.

100 *MG*, 28 March 1861.

101 CRO, Copy Bk. A2, Chief Rabbi to David Hesse, 5 February 1852. Cf. Lp. OHC, Letters, Chief Rabbi to the President, 19 October 1848, explaining the necessity of a central control of ritual.

102 OHC, SC, 24 February 1847. The committee expressed its thanks to the Chief Rabbi for his new code, and its desire to see it implemented in Manchester.

103 Briggs, *Victorian Cities*, p. 119. A movement for the incorporation of Manchester

and for the overthrow of an older urban oligarchy had reached a successful conclusion in 1838.

104 Quoted in *MG*, 4 December 1844.
105 *MG*, 7 October 1843.

CHAPTER SIX

1 B. L. Joseph, *Address to the Seatholders of the Liverpool Congregation* (Liverpool, 1838), p. 4.
2 *Ibid.*
3 Lp. OHC, Letters, Chief Rabbi to Abraham Abrahams, 13 October 1839, which includes a copy of B. L. Joseph's letter to the Chief Rabbi of 8 September 1839.
4 Lp. OHC, Minutes of a Meeting of Seat-holders, 3 April 1839.
5 *Ibid.*
6 *Ibid.*
7 B. L. Joseph, *op. cit.*, p. 4.
8 *Ibid.*, title page. Cf. K. L. Abrahams, 'Father of the congregation—a biography of Barned Lyon Joseph', *Greenbank Drive Synagogue Review* (Liverpool, 1968).
9 B. L. Joseph, *op. cit.*, p. 4.
10 Lp. OHC, Minutes of a Meeting of Seat-holders, 3 April 1839.
11 *Ibid.* The memorial called for 'remedies' to preserve harmony 'and avoid a schism'. Cf. Lp. OHC, Letters, Chief Rabbi to Abraham Abrahams, 13 October 1839, and enclosure.
12 Lp. OHC, Letters, Chief Rabbi to the President, 23 August and 13 October 1839; BD, Min. Bk., 12 September 1842.
13 BD, Min. Bk., 12 September 1842, includes a copy of a letter written by B. L. Joseph, 'President of the New Congregation', on 31 July 1842. Cf. P. Ettinger, *Hope Place in Liverpool Jewry*, p. 29.
14 BD, Min. Bk., 12 September 1842, includes a letter written by Mozeley to the Board on 7 August 1842.
15 BD, Min. Bk., 12 September 1842.
16 *Ibid.*
17 OHC, Min. Bk., GM, 27 March 1842.
18 *Ibid.*, Annual GM, 9 April 1842.
19 D. E. De Lara, *An Address Delivered at the Opening of the New Synagogue in Manchester on Friday, 5th September, 5604* (Manchester, 1844), p. 7. De Lara's pamphlet was reviewed in *JC*, 24 January 1845.
20 *Ibid.*, p. 10.
21 The tradition is reported in Rabbi P. S. Goldberg, *The Manchester Congregation of British Jews, 1857–1957* (Manchester, 1957), p. 9.
22 Margoliouth, *op. cit.*, vol. 3, p. 125. Other versions of the dispute and its origins appear in *Jewish World*, 7 September 1877; Tomlinson, *op. cit.*, p. 31, the *Jewish Encyclopaedia*, article 'Manchester'.
23 *VJ*, 18 October 1844.
24 *Ibid.*
25 OHC, Min. Bk., Annual GM, 25 April 1844; SC, 7 August 1844; De Lara, *op. cit.*, p. 8.

26 OHC, Min. Bk., Annual GM, 25 April 1844. Louis Beaver wrote 'on behalf of the Deputies of the Manchester Seatholders'.

27 De Lara, *op. cit.*, p. 8.

28 *Ibid.*, p. 8.

29 *Ibid.*, p. 8n. The only hint of compromise on the part of the authorities was the rescinding of the regulation partitioning the burial ground (OHC, Min. Bk., GM, 21 October 1844).

30 *JC*, 8 December 1848. Speech by David Hesse.

31 *Ibid.*; De Lara, *op. cit.*, p. 8.

32 De Lara, *op. cit.*, p. 9.

33 OHC, Min. Bk., SC, 25 September 1844.

34 De Lara, *op. cit.*, title-page.

35 *Ibid.*

36 *Ibid.*, pp. 8–9.

37 *Ibid.*, p. 7.

38 *Manchester Athenaeum Addresses, 1835–85* (Manchester, 1888). De Lara also offered to provide free tuition in Mathematics at the Jews School (HA, *Seventh Annual Report* (1845), p. 9).

39 Lp. OHC, Letters, circular letter from New Synagogue Chambers, Manchester, 9 February 1847. Since the records of the New Congregation have not survived, its composition and activities are reconstructed from material in the Jewish press and from some of the Congregation's letters which have survived in the Old Congregations of Manchester and Liverpool.

40 *JC*, 8 December 1848.

41 *Ibid.*

42 Lp. OHC, Letters, circular letter from New Synagogue Chambers, Manchester, 9 February 1847.

43 *JC*, 8 December 1848.

44 *MG*, 30 August 1845.

45 *MG*, 17 January 1846.

46 BD, Min. Bk., 13 August 1845. The matter was at first adjourned, but the subsequent actions of the Deputies and the Chief Rabbi confirm that the congregation was officially recognised soon afterwards.

47 CRO, Index of correspondence with British congregations, vol. 83 (1845–48), Letters 96, 98, 108, 207. The index includes brief summaries of the contents of letters now lost.

48 *Ibid.* Letter 117 and reply of 14 August 1845.

49 *JC*, 13 November 1846.

50 *Ibid.*

51 *JC*, 27 November 1846.

52 *Ibid.*, and letter from Israel Levy in *JC*, 8 January 1847.

53 Lp. OHC, Letters, circular letter from New Synagogue Chambers, Manchester, 9 February 1847, with annotations by Israel Levy.

54 *VJ*, 18 October 1844.

55 *Ibid.*

56 Margoliouth, *op. cit.*, vol. 3, p. 124.

57 OHC, Min. Bk., SC, 25 February and 23 March 1845.

58 *JC*, 18 April 1845.

59 *VJ*, 27 March 1846.

60 OHC, Min. Bk., SC, 16 March, 6 and 8 May 1846; GM, 13 May 1846.

61 *JC*, 13 November 1846; OHC, Min. Bk., SC, 22 November 1846.

62 Lp. OHC, Letters, circular letter from New Synagogue Chambers, Manchester, 9 February 1847.

63 *MG*, 22 July 1846.

64 This is to assume that the pattern of 1844–45 was similar to that of 1848–52, which is well documented. The best general account of nineteenth-century Jewish immigration into England is Lloyd P. Gartner, *The Jewish Immigrant in England* (London, rev. ed., 1971), although he may underestimate the degree of continuity between the mid-1840s and 1880. Cf. A. R. Rollin, 'Russo-Jewish immigrants in England before 1881', *Tr. JHSE*, vol. 21 (1962–67).

65 Lp. OHC, *First Annual Report of the Liverpool Mendicity Society* (1847) (not paginated).

66 *Ibid.*, and *JC*, 14 May 1847.

67 S. M. Dubnow, *History of the Jews in Russia and Poland*, translated by I. Friedlander, 2 vols. (Philadelphia, 1918). This general account of the pressures upon Russo-Polish Jewry is based upon Dubnow, pp. 47–110.

68 *MG*, 10 May 1845.

69 *MG*, 20 December 1843.

70 OHC, Min. Bk., GM, 8 July 1846; *VJ*, 14 August 1846; *JC*, 21 August 1846.

71 W. O. Henderson, *The State and the Industrial Revolution in Prussia, 1740–1870* (Liverpool, 1967), p. 161.

72 *Ibid.*, p. 161.

73 *Ibid.*, p. 167.

74 *MG*, 30 April 1845.

75 *MG*, 3 January 1844.

76 M. A. Jones, *American Immigration* (Chicago, 1960), p. 105.

77 Lp. OHC, Min. Bk. of the Liverpool Mendicity Society, Special Meeting of the Board of Managers, 7 July 1846.

78 *VJ*, 13 March 1846.

79 *Ibid.*

80 Cf. Lucien Wolf, *op. cit.*, p. 342.

81 Lp. OHC, *First Annual Report of the Liverpool Mendicity Society* (not paginated).

82 *Ibid.*

83 Lp. OHC, Min. Bk. of the Liverpool Mendicity Society, 7 July 1846.

84 Lp. OHC, *First Annual Report of the Liverpool Mendicity Society.*

85 *Ibid.*

86 *Ibid.*

87 Lp. OHC, Min. Bk. of the Liverpool Mendicity Society, 7 December 1846.

88 The Minute Book of the Society breaks off in December 1846, and does not re-open until the Institution was revived in 1853.

89 *First Annual Report of the Manchester and Salford District Provident Society* (Manchester, 1834), p. 6.

90 *Ibid.*, p. 15.

91 *MG*, 30 April 1845.

92 *First Annual Report of the Manchester and Salford District Provident Society*, p. 14.

93 *MG*, 30 April 1845.

94 OHC, Min. Bk., SC, 29 November 1846.

95 See section V below.

96 OHC, Min. Bk., GM, 28 September 1845.

97 *Ibid.*

98 *JC*, 10 December 1847.

99 OHC, Min. Bk., SC, 29 November 1846.

100 Robert Halley, *To Christians of Various Denominations in Manchester and Salford* (Manchester, 1845), pp. 2–3.

101 *Ibid.*, p. 3.

102 *The Jewish Herald*, February 1846, p. 44. The *Herald* was the official periodical of the British Society for the Propagation of the Gospel Amongst the Jews.

103 *Ibid.*, vol. I, No. I (January 1846), pp 20–23. The name of the 'confessor' is revealed in the issue of February, p. 65.

104 Rev. A. E. Pearce, *A Plea for the Jews: a Report read at a meeting of the Manchester and Salford Auxiliary of the British Society for the Propagation of the Gospel Amongst the Jews* (Manchester, 1849), p. 7.

105 *The Jewish Herald*, February 1846, pp. 63–6.

106 *Ibid.*, vol. I, No. 10 (October 1846), pp. 245–8; OHC, Min. Bk., SC, 30 August 1848.

107 *JC*, 15 September 1848.

108 Pearce, *op. cit.*, p. 6.

109 A. E. Franklin, *op. cit.*, pp. 23–6.

110 *Ibid.*

111 *Ibid.*

112 *Ibid.*, pp. 26–42.

113 *JC*, 1 May 1846.

114 OHC, Min. Bk., SC, 15 April, 30 May 1847.

115 OHC, Min. Bk., SC, 29 November 1846.

116 *Ibid.*

117 CRO, Index of Correspondence, vol. 83. Letters 1555, 1559, 1569, 1572–3, 1594, 1613–14, 1623, 1639, 1647, 1666, 1672, 1692–3, 1700, 1737, 1769, 1778, 1790–1, 1812, 1853 and 1863 all relate to the negotiations, the appointment of delegates and the terms of the final treaty. The negotiations are also summarised in OHC, Min. Bk., October 1846 to January 1847, *passim*. The terms of the treaty are given in OHC, Min. Bk., SC, 7 February 1847, and a letter from David Asher in *JC*, 15 November 1847.

118 OHC, Min. Bk., SC, 7 February 1847.

119 OHC, Letter Bk., Ansell Spier to the Chief Rabbi, 13 August 1847.

120 OHC, Min. Bk., SC, 24 February 1847.

121 OHC, Letter Bk., M. H. Simonson to Morris Harris, 2 June 1847.

122 OHC, Min. Bk., SC, 15 July 1847.

123 OHC, Letter Bk., Ansell Spier to the Chief Rabbi, 13 August 1847.

124 *Ibid.*, Ansell Spier to the Chief Rabbi, 2 September 1847.

125 *Ibid.*

126 *MG*, 10 April 1847.

127 *JC*, 21 January 1848. The society was in existence in October 1847, when its members presented a scroll to the New Congregation (*JC*, 8 October 1847). On 1 September 1847, Mrs Benjamin and Mrs Fanny Selig, widow of a Manchester tobacconist, opened a 'Cafe, Restaurant and Cigar Divan' in South Parade which became the social centre of the New Congregation (*JC*, 3 September 1847).

128 OHC, Letter Bk., Ansell Spier to the Chief Rabbi, 2 September 1847.

129 *Ibid.*, M. H. Simonson to Morris Harris (President of the New Congregation), 12 August 1847.

130 OHC, Min. Bk., SC, 27 October 1847.

131 *JC*, 26 November 1847, in an editorial comment to a Manchester correspondent.

132 OHC, Min. Bk., SC, 27 October 1847.

133 *Ibid.*, SC, 8 December 1847.

134 *Manchester Courier*, 9 December 1848.

135 *Ibid.*

136 *Ibid.*

137 *Ibid.*

138 OHC, Min. Bk., List of those relieved by the Society for the Relief of Really Distressed Foreigners, 16 December 1847.

139 OHC, Letter Bk., M. H. Simonson to the President, Society for the Relief of Really Distressed Foreigners, 9 April 1848.

140 *VJ*, 24 December 1841.

141 *JC*, 8 December 1848.

142 *JC*, 17 September 1847.

143 OHC, Min. Bk., SC, 6 June 1847.

144 BD, Min. Bk., 30 August 1847; *JC*, 3 September 1847.

145 *JC*, 22 October 1847.

146 *JC*, 29 October 1847.

147 *JC*, 21 January 1848.

148 BD, Min. Bk., 27 March 1848.

149 Quoted in full in BD, Min. Bk., 27 April 1848; summary and comments in *JC*, 22 October 1847 and 21 April 1848.

150 BD, Min. Bk., 27 April 1848.

151 *JC*, 30 June 1848.

152 *JC*, 7 January 1848.

153 *Ibid.*

154 Quoted in *JC*, 7 March 1845.

155 *JC*, 22 August 1845: letter from the Chief Rabbi to the Congregations of the British Empire.

156 Three Jews stood for election, but only Rothschild secured a majority. The object was not to enter Parliament, but to highlight the injustice of their exclusion.

157 Undated copy of a *Prospectus of the Anglo-Jewish Archives*, a monthly periodical edited by T. Theodores, is preserved in an interleaved presentation volume of Picciotto's *Sketches of Anglo-Jewish History* in the Mocatta Library, with a MS note in which Theodores suggests to Franklin an amalgamation with *The Voice of Jacob*, adding: 'Why do you not write?': vol. 2, following p. 402.

158 De Lara, *op. cit.*, p. 9.

159 Further studies of individual congregations will almost certainly reveal a series of democratic upheavals similar to those in Liverpool and Manchester. A secession synagogue which appeared in Wrottesley Street, Birmingham, in 1853, appears to be the result of such a crisis ('A portrait of Birmingham Jewry in 1851', by the Birmingham Jewish Local History Study Group, in *Provincial Jewry in Victorian Britain*, pp. 5–6).

CHAPTER SEVEN

1 *JC*, 24 November 1848.
2 *JC*, 20 August 1847; *MG*, 14 August 1847. The congregation sent a congratulatory address 'engrossed on vellum'. Rothschild's reply was printed in *MG*, 28 August 1847.
3 *MG*, 11 August 1847; 2 February 1848.
4 *MG*, 11 December 1847; 5 January 1848.
5 *MG*, 17 November 1847.
6 *MG*, 2 February 1848.
7 *MG*, 27 May 1848.
8 *MG*, 10 February 1849.
9 *MG*, 10 and 21 February, 9 May 1849.
10 *MG*, 10 February 1849.
11 *MG*, 21 February 1849.
12 *MG*, 22 January 1848.
13 *Ibid.*
14 *MG*, 6 November 1847; this was also the editorial view of the *Manchester Courier*, 12 January and 12 February 1848.
15 Pearce, *A Plea for the Jews*, p. 4.
16 *MG*, 30 November 1850.
17 *MG*, 1 November 1848.
18 *Sixth Annual Report of the Manchester and Salford Association in Aid of the British Society for the Propagation of the Gospel Amongst the Jews* (1850), pp. 9–10.
19 Pearce, *op. cit.*, p. 4.
20 *MG*, 7 November 1849.
21 *Jewish Intelligence*, June 1851, p. 217.
22 Pearce, *op. cit.*, p. 1.
23 OHC, Letter Bk., M. H. Simonson to the Chief Rabbi, 19 July 1848.
24 *Ibid.*
25 *MG*, 8 and 12 April 1848.
26 *Ibid.*
27 *MG*, 12 April 1848.
28 *Ibid.*
29 *MG*, 23 May 1849.
30 *MG*, 1 April 1848.
31 *MG*, 23 August 1848.
32 *MG*, 1 April 1848.
33 *MG*, 11 February 1846.
34 *Ibid.*

35 *MG*, 21 March 1847. While in Manchester, Mendelssohn conducted the Hargreaves Choral Society's *Elijah* and played the organ in St Luke's Church, Cheetham Hill. He died in Germany a few months later.

36 *MG*, 16 April 1845.

37 *MG*, 7 February 1846.

38 *MG*, 4 July 1849.

39 *MG*, 12 November 1851.

40 Chapple and Pollard, *The Letters of Mrs Gaskell*, Letters 70, 91B, 93–94, 116A, 118A, 582A.

41 Cf. L. P. Gartner, in Aubrey Newman (Rapporteur), *Migration and Settlement* (London, 1971), p. 123; Isaac Fein, *The Making of an American Jewish Community* (Philadelphia, 1971), pp. 70, 81, 94, 125–6. In England, immigrants divided in terms of class rather than of nationality.

42 *JC*, 25 August 1848.

43 *MG*, 1 April 1848.

44 *JC*, 24 November 1848.

45 *Ibid.*

46 *JC*, 21 January 1848.

47 L. P. Gartner, *op. cit.*, p. 17.

48 *MG*, 7 December 1850: report of annual meeting of the Society for the Relief of Really Distressed Foreigners.

49 Gartner, *op. cit.*, p. 22; Dubnow, *History of the Jews in Russia and Poland*, vol. 2, pp. 140–7.

50 This calculation, and the succeeding account of the structure and extent of relief between 1848 and 1852, is based upon OHC, Account Book of the Board of Relief, 1848–52.

51 *MG*, 24 May 1848.

52 *MG*, 28 October and 1 November 1848.

53 *MG*, 23 May 1849; Acc. Bk., of the Board of Relief, 1849–51 *passim*.

54 OHC, Min. Bk., GM, 15 December 1849.

55 *Ibid.*

56 *JC*, 24 November 1848.

57 OHC, Acc. Bk. of the Board of Relief, 27 and 30 November 1848.

58 OHC, Acc. Bk., 1848–49.

59 *Jewish Herald*, vol. 1, No. 2 (February 1846), pp. 43–4. On 21 March 1845, *JC* poured scorn on a conversionist estimate which placed Manchester's Jewish population at three thousand.

60 Pearce, *op. cit.*, p. 5.

61 Cf. V. D. Lipman, 'A survey of Anglo-Jewry in 1851', *Tr. JHSE*, vol. 17 (1951–52), pp. 184–5.

62 *MG*, 18 April 1855. The lie of the land allowed thieves to enter premises by back-bedroom windows, or by removing tiles from roofs, and to escape undetected (*MG*, 18 May 1850).

63 *MG*, 10 and 13 December 1851.

64 Manchester and Salford Sanitary Association records, MCL, M126/2/6/4–5.

65 Cf. L. P. Gartner, *The Jewish Immigrant in England*, ch. 3.

66 This arrangement resulted in a number of fires at cap-making workshops during

the 1840s and 1850s; e.g. *MG*, 14 February 1849; 22 January 1853.

67 The recipient of relief is described simply as 'the glazier'.

68 The beginnings of Mackintosh's enterprise are described by W. H. Chaloner, 'The birth of modern Manchester', in *Manchester and its Region*, ed. C. F. Carter (Manchester, 1962), p. 141.

69 *JC*, 24 November 1848.

70 OHC, Acc. Bk., 1850–51; Strangers' Offerings.

71 A. E. Franklin, *op. cit.*, p. 30.

72 *MG*, 19 January 1850.

73 HA *Thirteenth Annual Report* (1851), p. 10.

74 HA *Twelfth Annual Report* (1851), p. 8 (my italics).

75 *MG*, 24 May 1851. The speaker was Dr Schiller.

76 *MG*, 24 March 1849.

77 *MG*, 21 November 1849.

78 HA *Twelfth Annual Report* (1850), pp. 8–9.

79 Contemporaneously, Gregan was engaged on a warehouse at the corner of Portland and Parker Streets (Nicholas Taylor, in H. J. Dyos and M. Wolf, eds., *The Victorian City* (London, 1973), p. 441).

80 HA, *Thirteenth Annual Report* (1851), pp. 8–9; *MG*, 4 December 1850.

81 HA, *Thirteenth Annual Report*, p. 8. A small part of the building survives on Cheetham Hill Road.

82 HA, *Twelfth Annual Report*, pp. 11–12.

83 *JC*, 24 November 1848.

84 *Ibid.*

85 *JC*, 8 December 1848.

86 *Ibid.*

87 An excellent critical biography of Dr Schiller is provided by Raphael Loewe, 'Solomon Marcus Schiller–Szinessy, 1820–90', *Tr. JHSE*, vol. 21 (1962–67), pp. 148–52. Factual material given by Rabbi P. S. Goldberg, *op. cit.*, must be regarded with extreme caution. Except where otherwise stated the details of Dr Schiller's education and early career given below are based upon Loewe's article. See also *MG*, 14 March 1890; *The Times*, 13 March 1890.

88 Isaac Fein, *The Making of an American Jewish Community* (Philadelphia, 1971), p. 54.

89 *MG*, 9 September 1846.

90 OHC, Min. Bk., SC, 19 November 1872, when a delegate from the *Chevra Tehillim* attributed its foundation to 1854. I am inferring that this was the *chevra* described in *JC*, 9 May 1856, as meeting in Dr Schiller's house, and which may be distinguished from the nascent Reform Association meeting at the house of Horatio Micholls (*JC*, 2 May 1856).

91 *JC*, 21 and 28 June 1850.

92 *JC*, 21 June 1850.

93 *JC*, 5 July 1850.

94 A letter in *JC*, 2 August 1850, and an accompanying editorial comment make it clear that the sermon was delivered in German and not as Loewe suggests (*op. cit.*, p. 152) in English.

95 *JC*, 19 July 1850.

96 *JC*, 2 August 1850.

97 *JC*, 13 September 1850.

98 Rev. Rabbi S. M. Schiller–Szinessy, *The Olden Religion in the New Year: a Sermon Preached in the Birmingham Synagogue*, translated by Miriam Nathan (London, 1850).

99 OHC, Min. Bk., Annual GM, 3 June 1851.

100 *JC*, 27 September 1850.

101 *JC*, 4 October 1850.

102 OHC, Min. Bk., SC, 16 December 1850.

103 OHC, Min. Bk., SC, 14 October 1850.

104 *Ibid.*

105 OHC, Letter Bk., 19 March to 10 April 1850.

106 Lp. OHC, Letters, Chief Rabbi to Abraham Abrahams, 10 September 1849.

107 Lp. OHC, Letters, Chief Rabbi to the President, 19 October 1849.

108 *Ibid.*

109 *Ibid.*

110 OHC, Min. Bk., SC, 5 January 1851.

111 CRO, Copy Bk., A2, 5 February 1852, refers back to the original agreement.

112 CRO, Copy Bk., A2, 3 March 1852.

113 OHC, Letter Bk., John Michael Isaac to the Chief Rabbi, 19 December 1850; CRO, Copy Bk., A2, Chief Rabbi to David Hesse, 5 February 1852.

114 OHC, Min. Bk., SC, 5 January 1851. A summary of the negotiations is provided in OHC, Min. Bk., Annual GM, 3 June 1851, and Letters, 19 September to 23 December 1850.

115 OHC, Min. Bk., Annual GM, 3 June 1851.

116 Margoliouth, *op. cit.*, vol. 3, p. 126.

117 OHC, Min. Bk., SC, M. H. Simonson to M. Harris, 16 March and 20 March 1851.

118 *Ibid.*

119 OHC, Min. Bk., SC, 16 March 1851; GM, 20 March 1851; Meeting of the Joint Committee, 26 March 1851.

120 OHC, Letter Bk., M. H. Simonson to J. A. Franklin, 6 April 1851; Min. Bk., GM, 9 April 1851.

121 BD, Min. Bk., 14 July and 8 September 1851.

122 OHC, Min. Bk., SC, 14 April 1851.

123 OHC, Min. Bk., GM, 9 April 1851.

124 OHC, Min. Bk., Annual GM, 3 June 1851. The final details of the terms of reunion were not settled until the sub-committee revising the laws reported its findings a year later: OHC, Min. Bk., SC, 20 June to 18 September 1852.

CHAPTER EIGHT

1 OHC, Min. Bk., Annual GM, 3 June 1851.

2 OHC, Letters, David Hesse to the Chief Rabbi, 18 January 1852.

3 *JC*, 4 October 1850.

4 *Ibid.*

5 *JC*, 3 October 1851.

6 *JC*, 15 July 1853.
7 Cf. L. P. Gartner, 'Immigration and the formation of American Jewry, 1840–1925', in H. H. Ben-Sassoon and S. Ettinger, eds., *Jewish Society through the Ages* (London, 1971), pp. 299–300.
8 *JC*, 4 October 1850.
9 *MG*, 28 April 1886; *JC*, 30 April 1886.
10 *MG*, 29 October 1851.
11 *JC*, 20 March 1851.
12 *MG*, 24 May 1851.
13 *Ibid.*
14 *Ibid.*
15 *JC*, 18 December 1903: in the obituary notice of David Hesse's son, Max. In the obituary of Sarah Frances Isaac (*JC*, 9 January 1885), the wife of J. M. Isaac, it is said that she worked during the 1850s to recover the allegiance of German Jews estranged from the synagogue.
16 *JC*, 11 August 1865.
17 Cf. obituary notice in *MG*, 16 November 1883.
18 Biographical material in *JC*, 29 October 1897.
19 Quoted in *Manchester Examiner and Times*, 8 October 1851.
20 Redford, *Local Government*, vol. 2, pp. 205–7.
21 *Ibid.*, pp. 206–7.
22 *MG*, 12 November 1851.
23 V. D. Lipman, 'A survey of Anglo-Jewry in 1851', p. 183.
24 OHC, Letter Bk., M. H. Simonson to the Warden at Seel Street, 22 November 1851.
25 *Ibid.*, M. H. Simonson to Godfrey Levi, 29 November 1851.
26 *MG*, 29 October 1851.
27 *MG*, 14 June 1851.
28 *MG*, 5 November 1851.
29 *MG*, 1 January 1853.
30 Biographical material in Edward Jamilly, 'Anglo-Jewish architects and architecture in the eighteenth and nineteenth centuries', *Tr. JHSE*, vol. 18 (1953–55), p. 137. His buildings in Manchester included Princes Theatre, the Reform Club (1870), Philips Park Crematorium, and the Art Treasures Exhibition Hall of 1857.
31 *MG*, 22 June and 6 July 1850.
32 Thomas Bullock, *Bradshaw's Illustrated Guide to Manchester* (London, 1857), p. 61.
33 *MG*, 29 December 1849.
34 M. H. Simonson, *Joshua and the Sun and Moon . . . Philosophically Explained* (Manchester, 1851).
35 *Ibid.*, p. iii.
36 *Ibid.*, pp. 3, 8–9.
37 OHC, Min. Bk., SC, 15 June 1851.
38 OHC, Min. Bk., SC, 8 July 1851.
39 OHC, Min. Bk., SC, 9 July 1851.
40 Rate Book of 1861.
41 See Chapter 7, note 90 above.
42 *MG*, 25 October 1851.

43 *Ibid.*
44 *Ibid.*
45 *MG*, 24 March 1847.
46 *MG*, 28 April 1847.
47 *MG*, 18 September 1850.
48 OHC, Min. Bk., SC, 7 April 1853.
49 *Ibid.*, 25 April 1853; OHC, Miscellaneous Letters, Richard Beswick to Philip Lucas, 22 April 1853.
50 Pearce, *op. cit.*, p. 2.
51 *MG*, 23 November 1850.
52 *Sixth Annual Report of the Manchester and Salford Association in Aid of the British Society for the Propagation of the Gospel Amongst the Jews* (1850), pp. 9–10.
53 *MG*, 29 October 1845.
54 *MG*, 1 November 1848.
55 HA, *Thirteenth Annual Report* (1851), p. 8; *MG*, 24 May 1851.
56 *MG*, 24 May 1851.
57 HA, *Thirteenth Annual Report*, p. 8.
58 *Ibid.*, p. 13.
59 HA, *Twelfth Annual Report* (1851), pp. 11–12: 'Laws for the Manchester Jews School', adopted at a Special General Meeting on 12 May 1850.
60 HA, *Thirteenth Annual Report*, p. 9.
61 Rules, dated May 1853, on the flyleaf of the Minute Book of the Ladies Clothing Society, 1885–1920, in the possession of Mrs Joan Behrens of Manchester.
62 *Ibid.*
63 *Ibid.*
64 *Ibid.*
65 HA, *Sixteenth Annual Report* (1854), p. 10.
66 *MG*, 24 May 1851.
67 OHC, Miscellaneous Letters, M. Silverstein to David Hesse, 21 January 1853. Silverstein had taught for four years at the school of Rev. R. J. Cohen in Dover, and for one year had acted as a private tutor to London families, including that of Solomon Keyser of Finsbury Square.
68 A. E. Franklin, *op. cit.*, p. 30; another son, Ellis Abraham Franklin, was educated at Manchester Grammar School, where, although kindly treated by his teachers, he 'had to overcome considerable prejudice amongst his fellow pupils' (*Ulula*, the M.G.S. Magazine, vol. 19, No. 134 (May 1892)).
69 *Proceedings of the Royal Geographical Society*, vol. 21 (1876–77): obituary of Philip Lucas' son, Louis Arthur, an African explorer who died at the age of twenty-five in a ship off Jeddah.
70 *JC*, 27 May 1853.
71 *Ibid.*
72 *MG*, 15 January 1853. At its opening the school had twenty-four children of both sexes.
73 *Ibid.*
74 BD, Min. Bk., 14 July 1851, copy of letter from Philip Lucas and Isaac Franklin to Sir Moses Montefiore.
75 *MG*, 24 March 1849.

76 HA, *Thirteenth Annual Report*, p. 10.

77 HA, *Fourteenth Annual Report* (1852), p. 11.

78 HA, *Thirteenth Annual Report*, p. 10.

79 BD, 14 July 1851. J. A. Franklin was included as a member.

80 HA, *Thirteenth Annual Report*, pp. 11–12.

81 *Ibid.*

82 *Ibid.*

83 HA, *Fourteenth Annual Report* (1852), p. 7.

84 Redford, *Local Government*, vol. 2, pp. 238–9.

85 *JC*, 25 March 1853.

86 *Ibid.*

87 BD, Min. Bk., 5 January 1853; cf. *JC*, 14 January 1853. Cf. Cyril Hershon, 'Genesis of a Jewish day school' (the London Jews School) in *Provincial Jewry in Victorian Britain*, p. 14. In the light of opposition from Manchester and other centres, the deed was altered to allow each school management to nominate its own ecclesiastical controller.

88 OHC, Letter Bk., M. H. Simonson to the Chief Rabbi, 22 November 1851.

89 CRO, Copy Bk., A2, Chief Rabbi to David Hesse, 26 November 1851.

90 *Ibid.*

91 *Ibid.* From Simonson's letter of 22 November (*op. cit.*), it is clear that Dr Schiller was doing no more than enforce traditional practice in the Chief Rabbi's name.

92 OHC, Letter Bk., M. H. Simonson to the Chief Rabbi, 22 November 1851.

93 OHC, Letter Bk., M. H. Simonson to the Chief Rabbi, 3 December 1851; Min. Bk., SC, 2 December 1851.

94 CRO, Copy Bk., A2, Chief Rabbi to David Hesse, 5 December 1851.

95 OHC, Letter Bk., M. H. Simonson to the Chief Rabbi, 8 December 1851.

96 OHC, Min. Bk., SC, 16 December 1851.

97 OHC, Min. Bk., GM, 25 December 1851.

98 *Ibid.*

99 CRO, Copy Bk., A2, Chief Rabbi to David Hesse, 29 December 1851.

100 OHC, Letter Bk., David Hesse to the Chief Rabbi, 18 February 1852.

101 *JC*, 6 February 1852.

102 *JC*, 2 January 1852.

103 OHC, Letter Bk., M. H. Simonson to the Chief Rabbi, 1 January 1852.

104 CRO, Copy Bk., A2, Chief Rabbi to David Hesse, 5 January 1852.

105 OHC, Letter Bk., M. H. Simonson to the Chief Rabbi, 11 January 1852.

106 *JC*, 6 February 1852.

107 CRO, Copy Bk., A2, Chief Rabbi to David Hesse, 5 February 1852.

108 OHC, Letter Bk., David Hesse to the Chief Rabbi, 18 February 1852.

109 CRO, Copy Bk., A2, Chief Rabbi to David Hesse, 3 March 1852.

110 *JC*, 9 April 1852.

111 *JC*, 28 May 1852.

112 OHC, Min. Bk., SC, 28 April 1852.

113 *JC*, 7 May 1852.

114 *Ibid.*

115 OHC, Min. Bk., SC, 3 May 1852.

116 OHC, Min. Bk., SC, 27 May 1852.

117 *JC*, 23 May 1852.

118 *JC*, 25 June 1852.

119 OHC, Miscellaneous Letters, Dr Schiller to the President and Wardens, 15 January 1853. The letter also indicates Dr Schiller's respect for the opinions of 'our greatest authorities of Yore'.

120 OHC, Min. Bk., SC, 16 June 1852.

121 *JC*, 12 November 1852. Reference to the receipt of fourteen letters is made in *JC*, 22 October 1852.

122 *JC*, 26 November 1852.

123 CRO, Copy Bk., A2, Chief Rabbi to Simon Joseph, 8 November 1852, denying the allegation that he had prevented Dr Schiller from receiving his proper title.

124 OHC, Min. Bk., GM, 14 November 1852; SC, 18 and 22 November 1852.

125 CRO, Copy Bk., A2, Chief Rabbi to Simon Joseph, 8 November 1852.

126 *JC*, 26 November 1852. According to OHC, Min. Bk., SC, 8 November 1852, Dr Schiller had recently announced his engagement to the daughter of Michael Moses of London, but the sources make no further reference to the intended marriage, which never took place.

127 *JC*, 10 December 1852.

128 OHC, Min. Bk., GM, 6 June 1852.

129 OHC, Min. Bk., SC, 16 December 1852.

130 *Ibid.*, 19 December 1852.

131 *Ibid.*

132 *Ibid.* Isaac Franklin's official appointment is noted in OHC, Min. Bk., SC, 19 June 1855.

133 OHC, Min. Bk., SC, 9 January 1853.

134 *Ibid.*, 16 January 1853.

135 OHC, Min. Bk., GM, 27 March 1853. Rule 3: Religious Direction.

CHAPTER NINE

1 *JC*, 3 June 1853.

2 OHC, Min. Bk., GM, 5 June 1853.

3 *JC*, 10 June 1853.

4 Dr N. M. Adler, *Solomon's Judgement: a Sermon delivered at the Great Synagogue on the Sabbath of Dedication, 31st December, 5614* (1853) (London, 1854), p. 12.

5 The wider context of the *cherem* question is given in Lucien Wolf, *op. cit.*, pp. 323–7, 335–6.

6 *JC*, 15 July 1853.

7 See Lucien Wolf, *op. cit.*, p. 336 for a defence of Montefiore's position.

8 *JC*, 29 July 1853.

9 *JC*, 26 August 1853. The letter is signed 'A Manchester Deputy', but the style and the sentiment belong to Hesse.

10 Lucien Wolf, *op. cit.*, p. 335.

11 *JC*, 19 August 1853.

12 OHC, Miscellaneous Letters, J. A. Franklin to Ansell Spier, 8 May 1853.

13 OHC, Miscellaneous Letters, Isaac Lyon to David Hesse, 3 May 1853. Although

proposed by Lyon, Hyam did not appear amongst the candidates for election at the subsequent General Meeting.

14 OHC, Min. Bk., GM, 22 May 1853.
15 OHC, Miscellaneous Letters, J. S. Moss to Philip Ezekiel, 21 May 1853.
16 *JC*, 27 May 1853.
17 *Ibid.*
18 *JC*, 20 May 1853.
19 *JC*, 27 May 1853.
20 *JC*, 1 July 1853.
21 *JC*, 15 July 1853.
22 *JC*, 26 August 1853. See note 9 above.
23 *JC*, 26 August 1853: report of meeting.
24 BD, Min. Bk., 31 August 1853. Cf. *JC*, 2 September 1853; Lucien Wolf, *op. cit.*, pp. 335–6.
25 *JC*, 16 September 1853.
26 BD, Min. Bk., 8 September 1853.
27 *Ibid.*, 23 November 1853.
28 *JC*, 26 August 1853. See note 9 above.
29 *Ibid.*
30 BD, Min. Bk., 31 August 1853.
31 OHC, Min. Bk., SC, 6 September 1853.
32 *Ibid.*
33 BD, Min. Bk., 8 September 1853.
34 OHC, Min. Bk., SC, 5 December 1853; BD, Min. Bk., 7 December 1853.
35 There is no mention of the sub-committee in the minutes after its initial constitution in June 1853.
36 OHC, Min. Bk., GM, 18 December 1853. Joseph described the *cherem* as a 'Plague Spot', and avowed that if the Chief Rabbi would not remove it he would support its non-recognition in Manchester. Later he was to have second thoughts.
37 OHC, Min. Bk., GM, 18 December 1853.
38 CRO, Copy Bk., A2, undated letter to E. Moses.
39 OHC, Min. Bk., GM, 18 December 1853.
40 *JC*, 3 February 1854.
41 OHC, Min. Bk., GM, 1 January 1854.
42 OHC, Letter Bk., David Hesse to the Select Committee, 10 January 1854.
43 OHC, Min. Bk., SC, 15 June 1854.
44 Tobias Theodores, *The Rabbinical Law of Excommunication considered in its Bearing on the Case of the Margaret Street Synagogue of British Jews* (Manchester, 1854).
45 *JC*, 3 February 1854.
46 Theodores, *op. cit.*, p. 23.
47 *Ibid.*, p. 8.
48 *Ibid.*
49 *Ibid.*, pp. 24–5.
50 *Ibid.*, pp. 20–3.
51 *Ibid.*, p. 23.
52 *Ibid.*, pp. 27–28.

53 OHC, Min. Bk., SC, 25 April 1853.

54 OHC, Miscellaneous Letters, W. Goodman to the President and Committee, 27 October 1853.

55 OHC, Min. Bk., SC, 7 April, 20 June, 7 August, 18 August, 6 September 1853.

56 OHC, Min. Bk., SC, 6 September 1853.

57 e.g. OHC, Min. Bk., SC, 9 August 1854.

58 OHC, Min. Bk., SC, 18 August, 16 October and 5 December 1853; Miscellaneous Letters, Simeon Oppenheim to the Secretary, 14 October 1853; J. L. Lindenthal to the Secretary, 20 October 1853.

59 OHC, Min. Bk., SC, 5 March 1854.

60 Dr N. M. Adler, *Solomon's Judgement*, p. 14.

61 *Ibid.*, p. 13.

62 OHC, Min. Bk., GM, 18 December 1853.

63 OHC, Min. Bk., GM, 16 April 1854.

64 *Ibid.*

65 *JC*, 20 March 1857.

66 *Ibid.*

67 *JC*, 20 January 1854.

68 OHC, Min. Bk., Finance Committee, 29 June 1854; SC, 1 July 1854.

69 *JC*, 30 September 1853.

70 *JC*, 15 July and 23 December 1853; 6 January 1854.

71 *JC*, 30 December 1853.

72 *JC*, 16 December 1853.

73 OHC, Min. Bk., SC, 6 February 1854.

74 OHC, Min. Bk., GM, 27 March 1854: Rule 3.

75 OHC, Min. Bk., SC, 17 April 1854.

76 *Ibid.*

77 *Ibid.*

78 OHC, Min. Bk., GM, 30 April 1854.

79 OHC, Min. Bk., GM, 7 May 1854.

80 *Ibid.*

81 OHC, Min. Bk., GM, 25 June 1854.

82 OHC, Min. Bk., GM, 8 July 1854.

83 OHC, Min. Bk., SC, 21 December 1854.

84 *JC*, 10 November 1854.

85 OHC, Min. Bk., GM, 24 June 1855.

86 OHC, Min. Bk., Minutes of Sub-Committee, 5 August 1855. Dr Schiller met the deputation on 22 July, at the Jews School.

87 OHC, Min. Bk., GM, 8 August 1854.

88 OHC, Min. Bk., GM, 11 May 1856.

89 OHC, Min. Bk., Committee in aid of the Jerusalem Fund, 27 September 1854; cf. Rev. A. L. Green, *An Appeal on Behalf of the Famishing Jews in the Holy Land* (London, 1854).

90 OHC, Min. Bk., SC, 23 July 1855.

91 OHC, Min. Bk., GM, 12 August 1855.

92 OHC, Min. Bk., SC, 27 January 1856.

93 *JC*, 20 July 1855.

CHAPTER TEN

1 *JC*, 19 November 1858.
2 *JC*, 9 January 1885: obituary notice.
3 OHC, Miscellaneous Letters, 3 July 1853. Jacob had forfeited his membership of the synagogue, apparently because he had misapplied a congregational grant which was intended to aid his settlement in America. His attempt to recover his privileges in 1853 failed and he took no further part in the Reform controversy.
4 OHC, Min. Bk., SC, 13 January 1856.
5 OHC, Min. Bk., SC, Chief Rabbi to the Secretary, 21 January 1856.
6 *Ibid.*, Telegram to the Chief Rabbi, 22 January 1856.
7 *Ibid.*, Telegram from the Chief Rabbi, 22 January 1856; Chief Rabbi to the Secretary, 21 January 1856.
8 *Ibid.*, Chief Rabbi to the Secretary, 21 January 1856.
9 V. D. Lipman, 'A survey of Anglo-Jewry in 1851', p. 184.
10 OHC, Min. Bk., Secretary of the Hull Synagogue to the Secretary at Manchester, 11 March 1856: correspondence from Hull and London relating to the whole episode appears in the committee minute books, 10 February to 11 March 1856.
11 *Ibid.* They were reported to have purchased the scroll from a Mr Fleigeltaub of Manchester.
12 *Ibid.*
13 *Ibid.*
14 *Ibid.*
15 *Ibid.*
16 OHC, Min. Bk., Secretary of the Hull Synagogue to the Secretary at Manchester, 19 February 1856.
17 *Ibid.*, Bethel Jacobs to the Secretary at Manchester, 10 February 1856.
18 *Ibid.*, Bethel Jacobs to the Secretary at Manchester, 13 February 1856.
19 *Ibid.*, Simeon Moseley to the Secretary at Manchester, 17 February 1856.
20 *Ibid.*
21 *Ibid.*, Simeon Moseley to the Secretary at Manchester, 19 February 1856.
22 *Ibid.*
23 *Ibid.*, Bethel Jacobs to the Secretary at Manchester, 9 March 1856.
24 *Ibid.*, Chief Rabbi to the Manchester Wardens, 22 February 1856.
25 OHC, Min. Bk., SC, 20 February 1856.
26 OHC, Min. Bk., Dr Schiller to the Secretary, 21 February 1856.
27 *Ibid.*, Dr Schiller to the Secretary, 29 February 1856.
28 OHC, Min. Bk., SC, 28 February 1856.
29 *Ibid.*, SC, 4 March 1856.
30 *Ibid.*, GM, 12 March 1856.
31 *Ibid.*
32 *Ibid.*, GM, 30 March 1856.
33 *Ibid.*
34 *JC*, 18 April 1856.
35 OHC, Min. Bk., SC, transcription of letter from the Chief Rabbi to the Wardens, 18 June 1856. The ban was subsequently publicised in *JC*.
36 *JC*, 2 May 1856.

37 Correspondence between Mrs Dorothy Quas-Cohen of Bowdon and Moses Besso, 7 July to 14 December 1932 (MCL Archives) includes extracts from the minute books of the Reform Congregation which were subsequently destroyed in the Blitz. The relevant extracts are in letters dated 10 July and 5 August 1932.

38 OHC, Min. Bk., SC, 2 March 1856. The resolutions of the Reform Association are there given in full.

39 *Ibid.*

40 *Ibid.* When the Select Committee at first refused to entertain the proposals of the Association, the Reformers countered with another hint of separation (OHC, Min. Bk., SC, 16 March 1856).

41 OHC, Min. Bk., SC, 16 March 1856.

42 OHC, Min. Bk., SC, 10 April 1856, with transcription of letter sent to the Chief Rabbi on 15 April.

43 *Ibid.*

44 *Ibid.*

45 OHC, Min. Bk., Conference of Sub-Committees, 6 April 1856.

46 OHC, Min. Bk., SC, transcription of letter from the Chief Rabbi to the Wardens, 29 April 1856.

47 CRO, Index of Letters, vol. 84, No. 910, Joseph Spier to the Chief Rabbi, 16 May 1856.

48 *Ibid.*, reply of the Chief Rabbi.

49 *Ibid.*

50 Correspondence between Mrs Quas-Cohen and Moses Besso, 10 July and 7 August 1932.

51 *Ibid.*

52 OHC, Min. Bk., *SC*, S. Schloss and L. Behrens to the President, 12 and 15 June 1856.

53 CRO, Copy Bk., A4, Chief Rabbi to Joseph Spier, 3 June 1856.

54 *Ibid.*

55 OHC, Min. Bk., SC, 30 July 1856.

56 OHC, Min. Bk., SC, 3 and 4 August 1856.

57 OHC, Min. Bk., SC, Joint Meeting with the Reform Association, 17 August 1856.

58 OHC, Min. Bk., SC, 12, 15 and 22 June 1856.

59 *JC*, 22 August 1856.

60 *JC*, 5, 12 and 19 September 1856; OHC, GM, 9 November 1856.

61 *JC*, 22 August 1856.

62 The correspondence was curtailed by the editor on 10 October.

63 OHC, Min. Bk., SC, 22 October 1856.

64 OHC, Min. Bk., SC, 7 September 1857, made a final offer to the Reformers.

65 OHC, Min. Bk., SC, 15 November 1857, noted that differences with 'the other parties' had been settled.

66 OHC, Min. Bk., Building Committee, 14 January 1857.

67 Chapple and Pollard, *The Letters of Mrs Gaskell* (Manchester, 1966), Letter 422 (pp. 545–7) to Marianne Gaskell (March 1859). Worleston Grange was vacated by the family *c.* 1930 and demolished shortly after the Second World War.

68 OHC, Min. Bk., SC, 10 February 1857.

69 OHC, Acc. Bk. of the Synagogue Building Committee, 1856–60; *JC*, 20 March 1857.

70 *MG*, 26 March 1858.

71 OHC, Acc. Bk. of the Synagogue Building Committee, 1856–60.

72 OHC, Miscellaneous Letters, Dr Adler to the President, 30 June 1861.

73 OHC, Min. Bk., SC, Bethel Jacobs to the Secretary, 29 March 1856.

74 OHC, Minutes of Building Committee, Deed dated 18 May 1857; Acc. Bk. of Synagogue Building Committee, 1856–60.

75 *JC*, 20 March 1857.

76 P. S. Goldberg, *op. cit.*, pp. 17–18.

77 *The Builder*, 3 April 1858. The synagogue was destroyed by a German oil bomb on 1 June 1941 and was replaced by a new building in Jackson's Row.

78 *JC*, 20 March 1857.

79 *Ibid.*

80 *JC*, 8 May 1857. The synagogue survives, although in a poor state of preservation and repair.

81 *MG*, 24 February 1858.

82 *JC*, 22 August 1856; 8 May 1857.

83 Edward Jamilly, 'Anglo-Jewish architects and architecture in the eighteenth and nineteenth centuries', p. 137.

84 Thomas Bullock, *Bradshaw's Illustrated Guide to Manchester*.

85 *MG*, 13 February 1858.

86 OHC, *Printed Report for the Year 1857–58*, p. 6. Cf. Manchester Council Proceedings, April 1858. The motion to send a petition supporting the Bill was passed by twenty-five votes to four. The *Manchester Courier* kept up its opposition to emancipation to the bitter end, not only on 'religious grounds', but because 'being of necessity *aliens* to our religion and our nationality, the Jew millionaires may be tempted . . . to betray the cause of England at a time of national difficulty, by their votes and influence in the legislature' (editorial of 27 March 1858). The final steps towards emancipation were supported by the Cobdenite *Manchester Examiner and Times*, which regarded the subject as almost 'too threadbare for further argument' (editorial of 23 March 1858).

87 *MG*, 12 February 1858. In February 1859, however, it was decided that any Jew elected to parliament might swear the oath in an acceptable form, without further resolutions being necessary.

88 OHC, Min. Bk., SC, 5 September 1858.

89 P. S. Goldberg, *op. cit.*, pp. 25–6; *MG*, 26 March 1858.

90 Arthur Barnett, *op. cit.*, p. 178.

91 OHC, Min. Bk., SC, 2 and 16 March 1856.

92 *JC*, 20 March 1857.

93 Isaac Fein, *op. cit.*, p. 84.

94 *MG*, 7 July 1860; *Statuten und Erganzungsverordnungen der Schiller-Anstalt* (Manchester, 1860), in MCL.

95 Engels to Carl Siebel, 4 June 1862, in Helmut Hirsch, ed., *Friedrich Engels: Profile* (London, 1970), p. 250, quoted in 'Marx/Engels and Racism' by W. O. Henderson and W. H. Chaloner in *Encounter*, July 1975, p. 21. I am indebted to Dr Chaloner for providing this reference. Engels declared that he seldom visited 'the Jerusalem Club' any more because of the noisy behaviour of the Jews, whom he also believed to be unduly concerned with enlarging the premises.

96 Franklin Papers, file entitled 'Some family relics'. Letter from Elizabeth (Isaac) to her mother, sisters and brothers, 1 December 1858. Her death is recorded in *JC*, 4 March 1859.

97 *Ibid.*

98 *JC*, 4 November 1859.

99 *Ibid.*

100 Isaac Fein, *op. cit.*, p. 82.

101 *JC*, 8 April 1859.

102 *JC*, 15 April 1859.

103 *Ibid.*

104 Harry Lazarus, a founder-member at Park Place, changed his name to Langdon. One of his grandchildren was Miss Margaret Langdon, M.B.E.

105 *JC*, 20 June 1890. Laski said, 'the orthodox party had a deal to learn from Reform not only in synagogue matters, but in the part they took, locally, in the administration of charitable and educational organisations'.

106 P. S. Goldberg, *op. cit.*, p. 20.

107 Loewe, *op. cit.*, p. 165: part of a flysheet addressed to the members of the Manchester Congregation of British Jews, 16 March 1858.

108 *Ibid.*

109 *Ibid.* Loewe is incorrect, however, in accepting (p. 155) Dr Schiller's statement that the leading Reformers had taken the initiative in securing his original appointment. See Chapter 7, section IV below. Nor does Loewe correctly identify (p. 168) the founder-families of the Reform Congregation.

110 *MG*, 26 March 1858.

111 Loewe, *op. cit.*, p. 165.

112 OHC, Min. Bk., SC, 19 November 1872.

113 *JC*, 9 December 1859.

114 OHC, Min. Bk., SC, 2 September 1860.

115 *JC*, 11 and 18 May 1860.

116 *The Hebrew Review and Magazine for Jewish Literature*, vol. 1, New Series, 1 June 1860.

117 OHC, Min. Bk., SC, 30 September 1860.

118 *Ibid.*, SC, 21 October 1860.

119 *Ibid.*, SC, 10 February 1861.

120 Loewe, *op. cit.*, p. 157.

121 His subsequent career is summarised in Loewe, *op. cit.*, pp. 159–64. He died in 1890 after a distinguished academic career as Reader in Talmudic and Rabbinic Literature in Cambridge.

122 Margoliouth, *op. cit.*, vol. 3, p. 162.

123 Lp. OHC, Letters, Solomon Harris to the Warden, 22 June 1849.

124 Lp. OHC, Letters, D. M. Isaacs to the Wardens, 18 May 1849; Daniel Myers to the Wardens, 28 July 1851, Requisition to the Wardens, 23 September 1851; Memorial from nine Free Members, 2 October 1851.

125 Lp. OHC, Letters, Chief Rabbi to the Wardens, 10 October 1851, 27 November 1851; D. M. Isaacs to Daniel Myers, 10 November 1851; Ettinger, *op. cit.*, pp. 34–8; *JC*, 2 January 1852.

126 OHC, Min. Bk., SC, 4 March 1858.

127 *Ibid.*, SC, 18 April 1858.

128 *Ibid.*, SC, 24 February 1859.

129 *Ibid.*, SC, 30 May and 27 July 1859.

130 *VJ*, 29 November 1844.

131 J. Picciotto, *Sketches of Anglo-Jewish History* (London, 1875: edited by I. Finnestein, London, 1956), pp. 332–3.

132 B. L. Benas, *op. cit.*, p. 65.

133 Picciotto, *op. cit.*, p. 333.

134 *JC*, 27 June and 22 August 1862.

CHAPTER ELEVEN

1 e.g. Roth, *Provincial Jewry*, pp. 13–14, 26; Lipman, *Social and Economic History of the Jews in England*, pp. 66–7.

2 Cf. L. P. Gartner, *The Jewish Immigrant in England*, pp. 39–40.

3 *JC*, 3 April 1863.

4 *MG*, 3 July 1861.

5 *MG*, 3 July 1861; 2 May 1862; 2 January, 2 July 1863; 3 January 1865. The trends quoted apply to general emigration, of which by far the biggest proportion was from Ireland. It seems likely that the unsettled conditions in the United States had an even greater effect upon Eastern Europeans, for whom there were alternative places of refuge en route, particularly since there was a brief but virulent upsurge of anti-Semitism in America during the war years.

6 *JC*, 16 November 1866. The story of one escapee from conscription who settled in Manchester in the later 1860s is told in George Milner, ed., *Selections from 'Odds and Ends', a Manuscript Magazine issued by St Paul's Library and Educational Society* (Manchester, 1875), vol. 2, pp. 83–4.

7 *MG*, 18 April 1861; a general survey of the events in Eastern Europe which furthered emigration prior to 1881 is given in Rollin, *op. cit.*, pp. 207–8.

8 *JC*, 26 March 1869.

9 BG, *Third Annual Report* (1869–70), p. 5. The father of Israel Cohen, the Zionist, arrived in Manchester in 1870 from Lomza in Russian Poland (Israel Cohen, *A Jewish Pilgrimage* (London, 1956) p. 1).

10 *JC*, 19 February 1869: report of the Liverpool Hebrew Joint Board of Relief.

11 *JC*, 5 June 1874.

12 Roth, *Provincial Jewry*, pp. 81–2.

13 *JC*, 18 August 1865; cf. Ernest Krausz, *Leeds Jewry*, pp. 4–5.

14 *JC*, 12 October 1866. According to a conversionist estimate, there were 150 Jewish families in Hull by 1865 (*JC*, 18 August 1865); a more conservative calculation put the figure at 200 persons in 1869 (*JC*, 11 June 1869).

15 Cf. Arnold Levy, *History of the Sunderland Jewish Community* (London, 1956), p. 94; *JC*, 22 and 29 August 1873, and *passim*.

16 *JC*, 18 October and 25 October 1872; 3 January and 22 August 1873.

17 *JC*, 3 January 1873.

18 *JC*, 29 August 1873.

19 *JC*, 18 August 1880. A letter to the *Jewish Chronicle* of 29 March 1867, draws attention to the drastic decline of the Ipswich community and comments upon the 'paucity of Jews in country towns'.

20 *JC*, 17 May 1872.

21 This assumes that none of the persons who gave their place of birth as 'Prussia' were born in Prussian Poland. In fact, large numbers (probably a majority) almost certainly were, so that the Polish population was far larger than even these figures suggest. The total Jewish population was 1,755 in 1861 and 3,444 in 1871. According to a conversionist account, 'many other Jews frequently come here to purchase goods, not only from different parts of England, but also from Poland, Germany and Russia' (*JC*, 21 August 1868).

22 HA, *Twenty-first Annual Report* (1859–60), p. 10; *Thirtieth Annual Report* (1868–69), p. 35; *Thirty-sixth Annual Report* (1873–74), p. 11.

23 *JC*, 16 August 1872. The person appointed was John Crawshaw, for twenty-two years interpreter to the Society for the Relief of Distressed Foreigners.

24 In 1871 cellar-dwellings in Red Bank might be rented for between 8*d* and 1*s* 9*d*; cottages for between 1*s* 9*d* and 5*s* 6*d* (*MG*, 2 January 1861).

25 The results of their efforts are discussed in Chapter 12, section 1.

26 The phrase is taken from *JC*, 21 November 1884.

27 *Ibid.* 'The Polish Jew domiciled in England has his pet school as well as his chapel-of-ease.'

28 OHC, Min. Bk., SC, 19 November 1872. The meeting was called by Sampson Sampson, president of the Old Congregation, in a vain attempt to tap the financial resources of the *chevroth*.

29 Michael Fidler, ed., *The Holy Law Congregations One Hundred Years, 1865–1965* (Manchester, 1965), pp. 8–9, p. 30.

30 OHC, Min. Bk., SC, 19 November 1872.

31 *JC*, 18 December 1868; Asher Myers, *The Jewish Directory for 1874* (London, 1874), p. 76.

32 OHC, Min. Bk., SC, 19 November 1872; Asher Myers, *op. cit.*, p. 76.

33 Arthur Sunderland, 'The Central Synagogue story', *Jewish Gazette*, 5 March 1971.

34 OHC, Min. Bk., SC, 19 November 1872.

35 OHC, Letter Bk., Isaac Asher Isaacs to the Chief Rabbi, 16 June 1876.

36 *JC*, 18 December 1868. The *Pinkus* of the Chevra Torah also stresses the need to support the poor, particularly 'newcomers and Landsleit' (Fidler, *op. cit.*, p. 8).

37 *JC*, 12 August 1881.

38 OHC, Letter Bk., S. Landeshut to the Board of Deputies, 8 December 1868. The *Shtille Choopah* was not 'secret' in the sense commonly understood today, since it was well known within the *chevra* communities of the time, but it was 'secret' to the State authorities. Landeshut's attack may be seen as part of his general attitude towards the *chevroth*.

39 *JC*, 16 November 1866.

40 BG, *Third Annual Report* (1869–70). p. 10; *Fourth Annual Report* (1870–71), pp. 10–11.

41 In 1867 the address of one applicant for Passover Relief was given as 'No 8 in the Cellar, Back Verdon Street, off Red Bank' (OHC, Miscellaneous Letters, Hyman Nyman to the Select Committee, 19 March 1867).

42 e.g. *JC*, 3 January and 29 August 1873, when the settlement of Jews in the industrial towns of the north-east was encouraged as a means of moving immigrants away from 'a few over-stocked and unhealthy trades'.

43 *MG*, 28 March 1861.

44 HA, *Twenty-third Annual Report* (1861–62), pp. 7–8; *Twenty-seventh Annual Report* (1865–66), p. 9.

45 William Thorp, 'Poor foreigners', in George Milner, *Odds and Ends*, vol. 2, p. 85.

46 *Ibid.*, pp. 83–4.

47 BG, Min. Bk. of the Industrial Committee, 12 December 1877.

48 See Appendix A, Table 5.

49 William Thorp, 'Poor foreigners', in George Milner, *Odds and Ends*, vol. 2, p. 86.

50 *Ibid.*, p. 82.

51 *Manchester Examiner and Times*, 25 February 1871.

52 *JC*, 3 March 1871; letter from 'E.C.'

53 *JC*, 17 and 24 February, 3 March 1871. The right of Jews to work on the Christian Sabbath was safeguarded by amendments to the Factory Acts pressed home by the Manchester M.P., Hugh Birley, at the prompting of the Manchester Jewish Board of Guardians (*JC*, 5 April, 7 June 1878; BG, *Eleventh Annual Report* (1877–78), p. 7).

54 See Appendix A, Tables 3 and 4.

55 BG, *Sixth Annual Report* (1872–73), p. 6.

56 BG, *Fifth Annual Report* (1871–72), p. 7.

57 *JC*, 18 June 1880: Henry Samson attributed desertion to the 'superabundant but ill-judged affection' of an immigrant father for his wife and children; on other occasions, he was less sympathetic.

58 BG, *Fifth Annual Report* (1871–72), p. 7.

59 *Ibid.*

60 BG, *Third Annual Report* (1869–70), p. 5.

61 *MG*, 5 March 1862: report of the conversionist missionary, Israel Napthali.

62 *MG*, 21 October 1861; 8 January, 30 January, 9 July, 12 July 1862.

63 *MG*, 29 January 1862.

64 *MG*, 6 October 1862.

65 BG, *Third Annual Report* (1869–70), p. 6; *Fifth Annual Report* (1871–72), p. 6; *Eleventh Annual Report* (1877–78), p. 6.

66 BG, *Sixth Annual Report* (1872–73), p. 6.

67 Based on an analysis of the recipients of Winter Relief and Passover Relief, 1860–70.

68 BG, *Second Annual Report* (1868–69), p. 10; *Sixth Annual Report* (1872–73), p. 13. An additional factor was the lodgers 'which many occupants from sordid motives of profit have sought to cram into their houses'.

69 OHC, Min. Bk., SC, 15 December 1849.

70 OHC, Min. Bk., SC, 5 March 1854.

71 Raphael Loewe, *op. cit.*, p. 174. The *Jewish Chronicle* is in error in placing the foundation of the Fund in 1860 (*JC*, 27 May 1864), although its character may have begun to change at that time (see below, section IV).

72 OHC, Min. Bk., SC, 4 March 1858.

73 *Ibid.* Cf. *JC*, 19 March 1858.

74 OHC, Min. Bk., GM, 4 April 1858.

75 *JC*, 19 March 1858.

76 *JC*, 12 November 1858: the 'loan department' was then 'as yet in its infancy'.

77 *JC*, 26 November 1858.

78 *Ibid.*

79 *JC*, 22 November 1861.

80 *JC*, 12 November 1858.

81 *Ibid.*

82 *JC*, 25 February 1853.

83 HA, *Twenty-third Annual Report* (1861–62), p. 8.

84 The first reference to this fund is in *JC*, 4 April 1862.

85 OHC, Miscellaneous Records of the Hebrew Sick and Burial Benefit Society, 1865–68, which also mentions a Manchester Hebrew Hearse Society in 1867. Cf. *JC*, 5 January 1872; 31 December 1875; Asher Myers, *op. cit.*, p. 76.

86 *JC*, 22 February 1867. When Moss died in 1872, Cobe succeeded as president (*JC*, 10 May 1872).

87 e.g. *MG*, 3 January 1861, as part of the evidence in the case of Friedlander *v.* Sykes.

88 *JC*, 16 March 1866.

89 Max Hesse, *op. cit.*, p. 8.

90 *Manchester Courier*, 13 May 1867.

91 Michael E. Rose, *The Relief of Poverty, 1834–1914* (London, 1972), pp. 24–6; Lipman, *A Century of Social Service, 1859–1959* (London, 1959), pp. 27–31. The new approaches being developed by leading English philanthropists had in common an emphasis upon the need for a careful investigation of the circumstances of each case and the importance of avoiding indiscriminate charity in favour of curative relief.

92 *JC*, 11 March 1853. The editor commented that similar organisations 'ought to be simultaneously established in every congregation in this country, not excepting the metropolis'.

93 e.g. *JC*, 25 September and 2 October 1857. The *Chronicle's* idea was essentially for the co-ordination of existing charities, although it was understood that the co-ordinating Board would 'fill the gaps' between them.

94 On the foundation of the London Board, see Lipman, *Century of Social Service*, ch. 1.

95 *JC*, 2 March 1860.

96 *JC*, 5 February 1864.

97 *JC*, 18 November 1864. The letter is signed 'P.F.', but the sentiments are Falk's.

98 *Ibid.*

99 Obituary in *JC*, 30 November 1877.

100 *JC*, 1 July 1859. He obtained the additional post of secretary following the retirement of Godfrey Levi in January 1865.

101 *JC*, 22 May 1863. The precise structure of the Benevolent Fund is uncertain; a few Reformers appear to have contributed (HA, *Twenty-third Annual Report* (1861–62), p. 1), but on an informal, personal basis.

102 OHC, Min. Bk., GM, 1 February 1863.

103 *Ibid.*

104 *Ibid.*

105 *JC*, 18 and 25 November 1864.

106 *JC*, 25 November 1864: letter from 'S.L.'

107 OHC, Benevolent Fund Account Books, 1864–65, 1865–66.

108 OHC, Min. Bk., SC, 22 November 1865; *JC*, 8 December 1865.

109 *JC*, 16 November 1866.

110 *JC*, 8 December 1865.

111 OHC, Min. Bk., SC, 12 August 1866.

112 OHC, Letter Bk., S. Landeshut to Louis Beaver, 15 August 1866.

113 OHC, Letter Bk., Samuel Landeshut to James Craig, 16 August 1866.

114 *JC*, 25 November 1864.

115 e.g. OHC, Min. Bk., GM, 19 March, 16 April 1865, which relate to a scheme drawn up by Landeshut 'for the distribution of Charity to the poor by a Board of Guardians'.

116 The notes, headed 'Amalgamation of Delegates', occupy the final pages of the Old Congregation's Passover Relief Book for 1869–71.

117 OHC, Benevolent Fund Account Books, 1864–67.

118 *JC*, 23 November 1866.

119 *Manchester Courier*, 13 May 1867; *JC*, 17 May 1867.

120 *JC*, 28 June 1867.

121 *JC*, 5 July 1867.

122 *The Laws of the Board of Guardians for the Relief of the Jewish Poor of Manchester*, bound in with the Board's first *Annual Report*, for 1867–68.

123 *JC*, 3 July 1868; the chief difference was the allocation of delegates to corporate subscribers.

124 Following an unsuccessful attempt by Louis Cobe to set up an independent society for the distribution of *matzoth*, to which the poor might subscribe (*JC*, 26 May 1871, 12 April 1872), the Board assumed responsibility for all Passover Relief in return for an additional contribution of £50 from the Old Congregation (BG, *Sixth Annual Report* (1872–73), p. 8). The Old Congregation retained sole responsibility for the burial of paupers and the arrangements of overflow services until the formation of the Manchester Shechita Board in 1892.

125 BG, *Second* and *Third Annual Reports* (1868–70): statistical summaries.

126 BG, *Third Annual Report* (1868–70), pp. 7–8: 'Without this advantageous arrangement a great increase in resident poor would have taken place, or a still larger outlay in emigration would have been incurred.'

127 BG, *Second Annual Report* (1868–69), p. 6; *Sixth Annual Report* (1872–73), p. 7.

128 BG, Min. Bk., 6 January 1875.

129 *JC*, 16 May 1873.

130 *JC*, 29 October 1869. The architect was Edward Salomon; the new headmaster, Ephraim Harris. An infant class, commenced informally in 1858, was now an integral part of the School (*JC*, 20 January 1871).

131 HA, *Thirtieth Annual Report* (1868–69), p. 20.

132 BG, Min. Bk., 9 January 1878.

133 BG, *Fourth Annual Report* (1870–71), p. 7.

134 *Ibid.*

135 OHC, Letter Bk., S. Landeshut to Solomon Jacobs, 9 August 1865, and *passim*. In a letter to the Board of Deputies (19 September 1867) Landeshut sought a legal

means of suppressing the *chevroth*, only to be told that none existed.

136 OHC, Letter Bk., S. Landeshut to the Board of Deputies, 1 December, 8 December 1867. Landeshut drew attention to two 'secret ceremonies' and commented: 'secret marriages are a growing evil here'. Again, the Board could suggest no legal means of proceeding against them.

137 BG, *First Annual Report* (1867–68), p. 7. The phrase was used here in connection with the granting of loans.

138 BG, *Second Annual Report* (1868–69), p. 10.

139 BG, Min. Bk., 5 August, 2 September 1868. The authorities of the infirmary turned down a request for reserved beds on the grounds that it was 'inconsistent with hospital regulations'.

140 *JC*, 12 November 1869; 27 January 1871. The society raised funds by means of an annual Charity Ball in Salford Town Hall. During the first five years of its existence it provided help in four hundred cases.

141 BG, *Sixth Annual Report* (1872–73), p. 13. The Board called upon the community to support the work of the United Sisters and Hebrew Sisters Societies.

142 David Owen, *English Philanthropy, 1660–1960* (Oxford, 1965), p. 422.

143 Michael L. Rose, *op. cit.*, p. 25. Many of the methods and attitudes of the Jewish Boards of Guardians in London and Manchester had also been foreshadowed by the Liverpool Hebrew Mendicity Society in the mid-1840s (Chapter 6, Section 2).

144 *JC*, 20 November 1868.

145 BG, *Second Annual Report* (1868–69), p. 6; *Third Annual Report* (1869–70), p. 8.

146 BG, *Third Annual Report* (1869–70), p. 5.

147 *Ibid.*, p. 8.

148 This is my reading of Landeshut's letter in BG, Min. Bk., 5 August 1868.

149 BG, Min. Bk., 4 November 1869.

150 *JC*, 5 February 1869; BG, Min. Bk., following 3 February 1869.

151 *JC*, 12 February and 6 August 1869; BG, Min. Bk., following 3 February 1869.

152 On the efforts of the London Board in this direction, see Lipman, *Century of Social Service*, pp. 50–3.

153 OHC, Min. Bk., SC, 28 February 1869; *JC*, 30 November 1877.

154 OHC, Min. Bk., SC, 28 February 1869.

155 *JC*, 1 April 1864.

156 *JC*, 30 November 1877.

157 *JC*, 20 November 1857.

158 OHC, Min. Bk., SC, 19 July 1863.

159 OHC, Min. Bk., SC, 2 June 1861.

160 OHC, Letter Bk., Samuel Landeshut to the Board of Deputies, 25 November 1868, Samuel Landeshut to Jacob Franklin, 1 December 1869. Franklin declined to serve, and the community settled for representation by the London business-men, Samuel Montagu and Simeon Oppenheim.

161 BG, *Second Annual Report* (1868–69), p. 9.

162 BG, *Fifth Annual Report* (1871–72), p. 7.

163 BG, *First Annual Report* (1867–68), p. 8.

164 *Ibid.*

165 BG, *Third Annual Report* (1869–70), p. 7.

166 BG, *Sixth Annual Report* (1872–73), p. 7.

167 BG, Min. Bk., 7 May 1873.
168 BG, Min. Bk., 19 May 1873.
169 BG, Min. Bk., 5 November 1873. Except where indicated, the following account of the committee's work is based on the 'by-laws' of the Board given here in full.
170 BG, Min. Bk., 5 November 1873; *Sixth Annual Report* (1872–73), p. 7; *JC*, 11 July 1873.
171 *JC*, 27 May 1873.
172 BG, Min. Bk. of the Industrial Committee, 11 February 1874.
173 *Ibid.*, 13 January, 10 March, 12 May 1875, and *passim*.
174 BG, *Eighth Annual Report* (1874–75), p. 20; BG, Min. Bk., 2 February 1876.
175 BG, Min. Bk., of the Industrial Committee, 10 December 1873.
176 *Ibid.*, 9 July 1874.
177 Max Hesse, *op. cit.*, p. 17.
178 *Ibid.*
179 BG, *Ninth Annual Report* (1875–76), p. 7.
180 BG, Min. Bk., 11 February 1874, 8 March 1876.
181 BG, Min. Bk., 10 November 1875.
182 e.g. BG, Min. Bk., 8 May 1878.
183 e.g. BG, Min. Bk. of the Industrial Committee, 2 July 1875; 13 June 1877.
184 *Ibid.*, 13 January 1880.
185 BG, Min. Bk., 13 November 1878.
186 BG, Min. Bk., 9 December 1874.
187 Max Hesse, *op. cit.*, p. 15.
188 *Ibid.*, p. 12.
189 Lipman, *Century of Social Service*, p. 24.
190 BG, *Third Annual Report* (1869–70), p. 5.
191 BG, *Fifth Annual Report* (1871–72), p. 7.
192 Biographical material in *Manchester Faces and Places*, Old Series, vol. 2, pp. 5–7; *JC*, 21 August 1908; L. P. Gartner, *The Jewish Immigrant in England*, p. 38.
193 BG, Min. Bk., 2 March 1881. 'Secret charity' was traditionally given without the formality of an investigation and without the name of the recipient being generally revealed. Naturally, it was rejected by the Board as contrary to its objectives.
194 BG, *Ninth Annual Report* (1875–76), p. 6.
195 BG, Min. Bk., 3 November 1875.
196 BG, Min. Bk., 2 August 1876.
197 *JC*, 9 November 1877.
198 Although partly, of course, by referring a proportion of cases to the Poor Law Unions.
199 Rabbi P. S. Goldberg, *op. cit.*, pp. 32–9.
200 *JC*, 2 December 1864.
201 Rabbi P. S. Goldberg, *op. cit.*, p. 35.
202 *Ibid.*, p. 37.
203 *Ibid.* Gottheil left Manchester in 1873 to become minister of Temple Emmanuel in New York.
204 *JC*, 3 May 1872. Fragments of evidence suggest that this drift did not meet with the unanimous approval of the Congregation (*JC*, 29 August 1873), and that

Gottheil's departure was followed by a long struggle between conservatives and radicals (*JC*, 10 October and 7 November 1873), in which the former achieved final victory with the appointment of L. M. Simmons in 1877.

205 *MG*, 1 and 2 February 1861. Advertisement and counter-advertisement noted that Richard Brown, butcher, had transferred his services from the Old Congregation to Park Place.

206 *JC*, 4 March 1870: Gottheil is reported to have delivered a sermon in the Great Synagogue and to have read a prayer for the Royal Family; soon afterwards, D. M. Isaacs attended a confirmation service at Park Place (*JC*, 3 June 1870).

207 *JC*, 29 April 1870.

208 OHC, Min. Bk., SC, 17 January 1872.

209 OHC, Letter Bk., H. D. Marks to the President of the Manchester Reform Synagogue, 1 January 1872.

210 OHC, Min. Bk., SC, 21 March 1872.

211 BG, Min. Bk., inserted letter: Samuel Landeshut to Philip Falk, 7 March 1869.

CHAPTER TWELVE

1 OHC, Min. Bk., GM, 18 and 22 February 1858.

2 OHC, Min. Bk., GM, 23 December 1860.

3 OHC, Min. Bk., GM, 21 May 1865.

4 OHC, Min. Bk., GM, 23 February 1868.

5 e.g. OHC, Min. Bk., SC, 6 April, 11 June 1865, when new safeguards discussed included a black-balling system.

6 *JC*, 20 October 1865.

7 *JC*, 2 June 1865.

8 *JC*, 9 June 1865.

9 *Ibid.*

10 *Ibid.*

11 OHC, Min. Bk., GM, 4 July 1869. Biographical material on H. D. Marks in *JC*, 9 July 1869, 13 and 27 February 1885.

12 OHC, Min. Bk., SC, 1 July 1869; Letter Bk., H. D. Marks to the Chief Rabbi, 19 August 1869.

13 OHC, Min. Bk., SC, 1 July 1869.

14 OHC, Min. Bk., GM, 4 July 1869.

15 OHC, Min. Bk., SC, 19 August, 29 September 1869; *JC*, 27 August, 3 September 1869; 28 October 1870.

16 OHC, Min. Bk., GM, 5 February 1871: ballot for the admission of members of the New Congregation.

17 Based on OHC, Min. Bk., July 1869 to March 1871.

18 *JC*, 27 January 1865.

19 *Ibid.*

20 OHC, Min. Bk., SC, 17 September 1865; GM, 15 April 1866.

21 OHC, Min. Bk., GM, 8 July 1866.

22 *Ibid.*

23 *Ibid.*

24 *JC*, 15 and 22 January 1869. The object of the society was apparently to arrange cultural events suited to the tastes of young, anglicised middle-class Jews. It disappeared in June 1869 after organising a number of 'entertainments' and lectures, and a conversazione in Cheetham Town Hall (*JC*, 19 March, 4 June 1869). The president of the society was David Meyer Isaacs.

25 OHC, Letter Bk., H. D. Marks to the Chief Rabbi, 19 August 1869.

26 OHC, Min. Bk., GM, 12 September 1869.

27 OHC, Letter Bk., H. D. Marks to the Chief Rabbi, 30 September 1869.

28 OHC, Min. Bk., GM, 12 September 1869.

29 *Ibid.*

30 OHC, Letter Bk., H. D. Marks to the Chief Rabbi, 11 February 1870.

31 OHC, Letter Bk., H. D. Marks to the Chief Rabbi, 30 September 1869.

32 OHC, Min. Bk., SC, 4 November 1869.

33 OHC, Letter Bk., H. D. Marks to the Chief Rabbi, 19 August 1869.

34 OHC, Letter Bk., H. D. Marks to the Chief Rabbi, 30 August 1869.

35 OHC, Min. Bk., SC, 10 February 1870.

36 *JC*, 4 March 1870.

37 *JC*, 5 August 1870.

38 *Ibid.*

39 *JC*, 10 and 17 September 1869.

40 *JC*, 28 October 1870.

41 OHC, Min. Bk., GM, 1 January 1871.

42 OHC, Min. Bk., GM, 15 January 1871.

43 *Ibid.* A proposal to impose an additional entrance fee of one guinea was defeated.

44 OHC, Min. Bk., SC, 5 February 1871.

45 OHC, Min. Bk., GM, 5 February 1871.

46 OHC, Min. Bk., GM, 12 February 1871.

47 OHC, Min. Bk., GM, 9 April 1871.

48 *Ibid.*; *JC*, 10 March 1871.

49 OHC, Min. Bk., GM, 23 April 1871.

50 OHC, Letter Bk., H. D. Marks to the Secretary of the Board of Deputies, 23 April 1871.

51 OHC, Min. Bk., GM, 26 January 1873.

52 OHC, Min. Bk., GM, 8 June 1873.

53 OHC, Min. Bk., GM, 16 June 1873.

54 *JC*, 17 September 1869.

55 *JC*, 28 April 1871.

56 *Ibid.*

57 OHC, Min. Bk., SC, 30 October 1871.

58 OHC, Min. Bk., SC, 5 November 1871.

59 OHC, Min. Bk., GM, 5 November 1871.

60 OHC, Min. Bk., SC, 10 March, GM, 17 March 1872.

61 OHC, Min. Bk., SC, 6 August 1872.

62 OHC, Min. Bk., GM, 4 August 1872.

63 OHC, Min. Bk., GM, 11 August 1872.

64 OHC, Min. Bk., SC, 20 August, GM, 8 September 1872.

65 OHC, Min. Bk., SC, 9 and 17 September 1872.

66 OHC, Min. Bk., SC, 10 March 1872.

67 OHC, Min. Bk., SC, 20 August 1872.

68 A lucid narrative of the events leading to the foundation of the South Manchester Synagogue is given in I. W. Goldberg, *The South Manchester Hebrew Congregation: Eighty Years of Progress* (Manchester, 1952), pp. 5–13.

69 *JC*, 6 September 1872: letter from 'Albatross'.

70 Biographical information in *Jewish Encyclopaedia*, article 'Henry Zirndorf', which wrongly attributes Zirndorf's period of residence in England (1860–73) to London.

71 HA, *Twenty-fifth Annual Report* (1863–64), p. 7; *Twenty-sixth Annual Report* (1864–65), p. 8; *Twenty-seventh Annual Report* (1865–66), p. 8.

72 *JC*, 29 November 1895.

73 *JC*, 6 July 1861, 10 July 1863.

74 On Julius Dreschfeld, see William Brockbank, *The Honorary Medical Staff of the Manchester Royal Infirmary, 1830–1948* (Manchester, 1965), pp. 73–6.

75 *JC*, 29 October 1897.

76 *JC*, 25 October 1872: letter from 'Veritas'.

77 *JC*, 27 September 1872.

78 *JC*, 6 September 1872.

79 *JC*, 11 October 1872; this account was the subject of correspondence in the issue of 25 October.

80 SMC, Min. Bk., Preliminary Meeting, 1 September 1872.

81 *JC*, 11 October 1872.

82 SMC, Min. Bk., Preface, September 1872.

83 OHC, Letter Bk., Isaac Asher Isaacs to the Chief Rabbi, 16 June 1876; cf. SMC, Min. Bk., CA, 16 September 1873.

84 Resignations from the Old Congregation, 1872–74; SMC, Membership Book.

85 SMC, Min. Bk., Meeting of the Provisional Committee, 12 September 1872.

86 SMC, Min. Bk., CA, 20 October 1872.

87 OHC, Min. Bk., SC, 30 September 1872, *passim*.

88 OHC, Min. Bk., SC, 21 January 1873.

89 SMC, Min. Bk., CA, 15 December 1872; I. W. Goldberg, *op. cit.*, pp. 14–15.

90 OHC, Min. Bk., SC, 17 November 1872; SMC, Min. Bk., CA, 15 December 1872.

91 SMC, Min. Bk., CA, 9 August 1874.

92 OHC, Min. Bk., SC, 1 July 1873; Letter Bk., I. A. Isaacs to the Chief Rabbi, 2 July 1873.

93 OHC, Letter Bk., I. A. Isaacs to the Chief Rabbi, 11 September 1873.

94 OHC, Min. Bk., SC, 15 September 1873.

95 *JC*, 25 October 1872.

96 *Jewish World*, 19 September 1873; *JC*, Special Supplement, 19 September 1873.

97 SMC, Min. Bk., CA, 16 September 1873.

98 *JC*, 19 September 1873: since the representative of the paper was not allowed into the meeting, his report was based on hearsay.

99 *JC*, 19 September 1873.

100 OHC, Letter Bk., I. A. Isaacs to the Chief Rabbi, 5 October 1873.

101 OHC, Min. Bk., SC, 19 October 1873.

102 *Ibid.*

103 e.g. OHC, Min. Bk., SC, 18 May 1874; 5 January, 15 April 1879.

104 OHC, Letter Bk., I. A. Isaacs to the Chief Rabbi, 16 June 1876.

105 OHC, Min. Bk., SC, 7 March 1878.

106 The general effect of mass immigration was to move the South Manchester Congregation from a position of comparative isolation towards increasing co-operation with other Anglo-Jewish congregations: SMC, Min. Bk., CA, 11 December 1882; 18 September 1883.

107 OHC, Letter Bk., I. A. Isaacs to the Chief Rabbi, 16 June 1876.

108 *Ibid.*

109 SMC, Min. Bk., CF, 2 February, 4 May 1873.

110 The result was to put an end to the possibility of a merger with the Sephardim, who were preparing the way for a new synagogue at the same period. The only Reformer to associate himself with the South Manchester Synagogue was Leopold Dreschfeld.

111 SMC, Min. Bk., Preliminary General Meeting, 8 September 1872; CF, 2 February 1873.

112 *JC*, 13 September 1872.

113 SMC, Min. Bk., CA, 24 June 1873.

114 *JC*, 18 December 1896.

115 *JC*, 29 May 1874.

116 The subsequent growth of Ashkenazi settlement in south Manchester, and the movement of Jewish families farther south along Oxford Road, led to the transfer of the congregation from the converted house in Sidney Street to a new building in Wilbraham Road, Fallowfield, in 1913.

117 On the participation of Moroccans, Greeks and Jews in the Mediterranean trade, there is useful information in Louis M. Hayes, *Reminiscences of Manchester* (Manchester, 1905), pp. 205–12, 291–3, 299–307.

118 MS notes on Mardocheo and Haim Besso by Haim Besso's daughter (1948) in the possession of the Jewish History Unit, Manchester Polytechnic, kindly donated by Mr Vivian Besso.

119 Biographical material in *JC*, 30 July 1897; reference to Spanish antecedents in R. J. Minney, ed., *Leslie Hore Belisha, First Baron Hore Belisha: the Private Papers of Hore-Belisha* (London, 1960), p. 21; Leslie Hore Belisha was Isaac Belisha's grandson.

120 *MG*, 29 January, 11 February 1861.

121 OHC, Min. Bk., SC, 11 September 1865: reference to 'the house rented by the Gentlemen of the Portuguese minhag'.

122 OHC, Min. Bk., SC, 13 December 1864; 21 March 1865. An attempt was made to induce the Sephardim to make a corporate payment for the right to the Old Congregation's facilities for *shechita* and burial.

123 Rev. B. Rodrigues-Pereira and Rev. J. Pereira-Mendoza, *History of the Manchester Congregation of Spanish and Portuguese Jews, 1873–1923* (Manchester, 1923), pp. 18–19.

124 *JC*, 21 August 1868.

125 *JC*, 30 August 1872.

126 *JC*, 30 January 1874: letter of 'S Levy' of 49 York Street, Cheetham Hill.

127 Short MS account of family history by Miss Eileen Bianco, Moses Bianco's

granddaughter, in the possession of the Jewish History Unit, Manchester Polytechnic. Subsequently the coffee house became the Cafe Royal, under Bianco's management.

128 *Ibid.*

129 *JC*, 13 June, 17 October 1873.

130 The phrase was used in 1890 by Isaac Pariente, then in London (*JC*, 12 September 1890).

131 SPC, Min. Bk., Preliminary Meeting, 4 February 1872.

132 *Ibid.*

133 SPC, Min. Bk., GM, 25 February 1872.

134 SPC, Min. Bk., GM, 31 March 1872.

135 SPC, Min. Bk., GM, 7 July 1872; GM, 18 September 1872; Report of laying of corner-stone, 11 June 1873.

136 SPC, Min. Bk., GM, 22 February 1874; GM, 24 May 1874.

137 *JC*, 8 May 1874.

138 A. M. Hyamson, *The Sephardim in England* (London, 1951), pp. 358–60. During the 1880s Haim Besso broke away from the main congregation to found a private congregation—the 'Besso Synagogue' in Bent Street—which survived until 1932 (*MG*, 18 January 1932).

139 OHC, Letter Bk., I. A. Isaacs to the Chief Rabbi, 16 June 1876.

140 SMC, Min. Bk., CA, 19 September 1872; SPC, Min. Bk., GM, 3 November 1872.

141 SMC, Min. Bk., CA, 17 June 1873. The Sephardim also broke off negotiations for the purchase of a common burial ground (CA, 8 June 1875).

142 OHC, Min. Bk., GM, 8 March 1874.

143 At the time of its foundation the synagogue had a handful of Sephardi members, particularly the merchants Abraham Abadi and Isaac and Jacob Bensaud; subsequently it attracted a few disaffected members of the Spanish and Portuguese Synagogue, notably Moses Bianco.

144 The growth of a colony of rich Sephardi families in south Manchester in the last decade of the nineteenth century led to the foundation of a Sephardi synagogue in Withington in 1904 (Rodrigues-Pereira and Pereira-Mendoza, *op. cit.*, p. 38; Minute Book of the Withington Congregation of Spanish and Portuguese Jews, Preliminary Meeting, 25 October 1903).

145 *JC*, 3 May 1872. Cf. *Jewish World*, 7 September 1877: Manchester 'possesses synagogues adapted to every locality and party among us'.

146 The northern equivalent, in social terms, was the Higher Broughton Congregation, founded in similar circumstances, in 1905. Cf. Samuel Davies, ed., *The Higher Broughton Hebrew Congregation: the First Fifty Years, 1907–1957* (Manchester, 1957).

147 OHC, Letter Bk., I. A. Isaacs to the Chief Rabbi, 16 June 1876.

148 *Ibid.*

149 BG, Min. Bk., 6 December 1882.

150 OHC, Min. Bk., SC, 31 January 1881.

CONCLUSION

1 L. P. Gartner, while noting an early influx in *The Jewish Immigrant in England*,

confines his analysis to the phenomena of the 1880s and later.

2 Gartner, *op. cit.*, p. 38; Lipman, *Social and Economic History*, p. 66; J. A. Garrard, *The English and Immigration* (Oxford, 1971), p. 23.

3 Preliminary work on the Birmingham Census of 1851, conducted under the supervision of Mrs Zoe Josephs, appears to indicate that there too a substantial body of Eastern European immigrants had settled in the later 1840s.

4 *JC*, 3 August 1877; another estimate of the same year put the figure at nine to ten thousand (BG, Min. Bk., 4 July 1877).

5 *JC*, 29 August 1873.

6 *JC*, 3 January 1873.

7 *Ibid.*

8 *JC*, 29 August 1873.

9 Joan Thomas, *op. cit.*, p. 10.

10 *Ibid.*, p. 20.

11 e.g. *JC*, 25 February 1881, in Sheffield; the *Jewish Chronicle* was constantly urging strong central control as a means of promoting harmony.

12 *JC*, 5 January 1855, where correspondence suggests the priority of London in the substantial development of Jewish waterproofing; Lipman, *Social and Economic History*, pp. 106–7, which indicates the important part played by immigrants in London as operatives in the tobacco trade; Joan Thomas, *op. cit.*, p. 22, which notes that in tailoring the workshops of Leeds were larger than those of Manchester, and their subdivisional structure more advanced.

13 It is arguable that, in so doing, immigration promoted the development of a Local Rabbinate, and, more indirectly of a Reform movement.

14 A Joint Board of Relief was operating in Liverpool by 1869 (*JC*, 19 February 1869), and subsequently, Manchester assisted in the formation of a Liverpool Board of Guardians (BG, *Ninth Annual Report* (1875–76), p. 9). By 1887 there were also Boards in Birmingham, Sheffield and Hull (BG, Min. Bk., 7 December 1887: notes on a conference of Jewish Boards of the United Kingdom, called by E. M. Henriques).

15 *JC*, 28 November 1873.

16 Cf. Stephen Sharot, 'Native Jewry and the religious anglicisation of immigrants in London, 1870–1905', *The Jewish Journal of Sociology*, vol. 16, No. 1 (June 1974), pp. 39–56.

17 *JC*, 26 December 1873.

18 HA, *Twenty-third Annual Report* (1860–61), pp. 10–11.

19 HA, *Nineteenth Annual Report* (1857–58), p. 8.

20 HA, *Twenty-ninth Annual Report* (1867–68), p. 7.

21 HA, *Twenty-third Annual Report* (1861–62), p. 8. This orientation may explain the increasing number of Jewish domestic servants during the 1860s (see Appendix B: Occupations).

22 HA, *Twenty-third Annual Report* (1861–62), p. 8.

23 *Ibid.*

24 HA, *Thirty-third Annual Report* (1871–72), p. 9.

25 HA, *Twenty-sixth Annual Report* (1864–65), pp. 3–4, 8; *Twenty-seventh Annual Report* (1865–66), p. 8; *passim.*

26 BG, Min. Bk. of the Industrial Committee, 14 January 1874.

27 HA, *Twenty-fifth Annual Report* (1863–64), pp. 8–9.

28 *JC*, 6 January 1865. Isaacs died in 1879 while convalescing in Southport, and was succeeded as minister by Dr Berendt Salomon.

29 *Ibid.*

30 *JC*, 8 February 1867.

31 *Ibid.*

32 *JC*, 19 September 1873.

33 H. D. Marks left his post in Manchester in 1882 and died in Cape Town in 1885 (*JC*, 13 February 1885).

34 This again underlines the danger of regarding new suburban synagogues as a precise guide to the spread of Jewish suburban settlement, a theme pursued by Lipman in 'The rise of Jewish suburbia', *Tr. JHSE*, vol. 21 (1962–67), pp. 78–103. In this article (p. 79) Lipman is also wrong in describing Jewish settlement in Manchester and Salford as 'compressed geographically into a stretch of road four miles along the road to Bury'.

35 *JC*, 27 August 1885.

36 *JC*, 28 April 1876.

37 *JC*, 19 May 1876.

38 Cf. I. W. Slotki, *Seventy Years of Hebrew Education, 1880–1950* (Manchester, 1950); I. W. Slotki, *The History of the Manchester Shechita Board, 1892–1952* (Manchester, 1954); *Manchester Talmudical College: Fortieth Anniversary Souvenir Report* (Manchester, 1950).

39 This Society (a registered limited company) offered burial rights to shareholders, whatever their synagogal allegiance. It was founded and controlled by immigrants and, in effect, served *chevroth* without burial grounds of their own. MCL has the minute books of the society from 1901 (M 129).

40 Unpublished paper read to the Manchester Branch of the Jewish Historical Society of England, 11 September 1974. Mr Shaftesley challenged the view that the Communal Council owed its origin to an Anglo-Jewish élite. He based his thesis on MS minute books of preliminary committees from 1913, now on micro-film in MCL by courtesy of Mr Shaftesley.

41 *JC*, 23 February 1872; the founder was the Reform merchant, Arthur Q. Henriques.

42 *Ibid.*

43 *JC*, 20 January 1871.

44 On Massel see J. M. Shaftesley, 'Nineteenth-century Jewish colonies in Cyprus', *Tr. JHSE*, vol. 22 (1968–69), p. 97.

45 *JC*, 28 November 1890.

46 A case in point is the participation of Dr Charles Dreyfus in the foundation of the Manchester Jewish Hospital, which was built substantially on the efforts and pennies of the poor (Annual Reports available in the Hospital in Elizabeth Street). Cf. on the *Beth Hamidrash*, *JC*, 21 April 1876.

47 The parallel was drawn by Lionel Kochan in a talk, 'Jews on the move', reported in *The Listener*, 27 May 1971.

48 W. H. Chaloner, 'William Furnival, H. E. Falk and the Salt Chamber of Commerce: some chapters in the economic history of Cheshire', *Transactions of the Historic Society of Lancashire and Cheshire*, vol. 112 (1960), pp. 141–3.

49 *MG*, 17 January 1860.

50 Cf. W. O. Henderson and W. H. Chaloner, 'Friedrich Engels in Manchester', *Memoirs and Proceedings of the Manchester Literary and Philosophical Society*, vol. 98 (1956–57), No. 2. In the Burial Register of Ardwick Cemetery (in MCL) the burial of Wilhelm Wolff, on 13 May 1864, was witnessed by Louis Borchardt and Charles (*sic*) Marx.

51 *MG*, 30 January 1864.

52 *MG*, 7 December 1863: meeting of 150 Germans in Manchester to discuss the Schleswig–Holstein Question.

53 *MG*, 9 May 1860; 7 October 1861. The first Greek church was in a house in Parker Street (1843), the second in Waterloo Road (1848), in a building later occupied by a Jewish *chevra*.

54 *MG*, 7 October 1861.

55 *Ibid.*

56 Milner, *Odds and Ends*, vol. 2, pp. 80–1, 86.

57 *Ibid.*, vol. 1, p. 124.

58 *JC*, 1 December 1871.

59 *JC*, 2 May 1873, and correspondence in *JC*, 9 and 23 May 1873.

60 Milner, *Odds and Ends*, vol. 1, pp. 127–8.

61 HA, *Thirtieth Annual Report* (1868–69), p. 25.

62 *Manchester Examiner and Times*, 25 February 1871.

63 *Ibid.*

64 *JC*, 6 December 1867; 10 January, 21 August 1868.

65 HA, *Thirtieth Annual Report* (1868–69), pp. 24–7.

66 *MG*, 7 March 1862.

67 *MG*, 10 May 1862 to 30 August 1862, *passim*; David Ayerst, *The Guardian: Biography of a Newspaper* (London, 1971), pp. 140–1. When the *Guardian* was found guilty of libel, 1,100 merchants, manufacturers and bankers presented the proprietor, Edward Taylor, with a cheque for £1,457, together with a written expression of their gratitude for his exposure of fraud.

68 *JC*, 3 November 1876. For examples of Aronsberg's eccentric and conspicuous generosity, see *JC*, 1 May, 8 May, 26 June, 30 October, 27 November, 1874; 1 January, 5 February, 30 April, 4 June, 16 July, 19 November 1875. He claimed to be a friend of Disraeli, and in January 1876 received a signed edition of Disraeli's works. During the 1880s he played a prominent role as founder and patron of new institutions, particularly the New Synagogue and *Beth Hamidrash*, founded in 1889, specifically to meet the needs of the immigrant bourgeoisie.

69 *MG*, 5 and 6 March 1860.

70 *MG*, 17 July 1863.

71 *MG*, 4 and 18 February 1860.

72 *JC*, 30 June 1876.

73 *JC*, 16 May 1879.

74 *JC*, 14 February 1896. Cowen was born in Jamaica in 1852; his family settled in England in 1856.

75 *JC*, 2 November 1900.

76 *JC*, 2 January 1874. David Schloss became a prominent lawyer and communal leader in London; he married the daughter of Jacob Waley at the London

Reform Synagogue (*JC*, 23 April 1886).

77 *JC*, 6 July 1861; 10 July 1863; 28 January 1876. In 1869 Philip Falk founded a scholarship to Owens College in honour of his uncle, David Falk, tenable by competition by a pupil of the Jews School (*JC*, 29 October 1869). Theodores was Professor of Oriental and Modern Languages until 1879 and Professor of Oriental Languages until his retirement in 1884; he died in 1886. Gottheil lectured in German until his departure for the United States in 1873.

78 *JC*, 8 December 1876. Aronsberg became a J.P. in the following year (*JC*, 29 June 1877).

79 *JC*, 17 August 1877.

80 Printed circular letter from Elias Mozley to provincial congregations, 22 November 1844: copy in the Mocatta Library in an interleaved presentation copy of Picciotto's *Sketches of Anglo-Jewish History*.

81 Lp. OHC, Miscellaneous Letters, Dr Adler to the President, 19 October 1849.

82 *Ibid.*

83 *JC*, 12 May 1871: an important leader article on 'Provincial congregations', which pays some respect to 'local associations, local traditions and local individuality'.

84 *JC*, 28 November 1873.

85 *JC*, 16 and 23 May 1873.

86 *JC*, 16 May 1873.

87 *JC*, 25 October 1872.

88 *JC*, 28 November 1873.

89 Cf. Moses Margoliouth, *op. cit.*, vol. 3, p. 126.

APPENDIX B

1 The difficulty here is one of definition. Assuming the object is to be a statistical description of the *community*, the use of religious ascription alone would rule out those whose allegiance took some other form, e.g. membership of Jewish secular societies, or of a Zionist organisation.

2 E. A. Wrigley, ed., *Nineteenth Century Society* (Cambridge, 1972), pp. 15–19.

3 V. D. Lipman, 'A survey of Anglo-Jewry in 1851', *Tr. JHSE*, vol. 17 (1951–52).

4 In modifying his general hypothesis (p. 173) to interpret the Manchester returns, Lipman appears to apply no recognisable yardstick, and arrives at a figure over 40 per cent in error (p. 183).

5 I cannot accept Lipman's formulae (pp. 172–3) as valid, even in general terms, particularly since membership lists, even assuming that they embraced seat-holders, included an unknown number of brothers, and of women who were full members in their own right. In Manchester the lists provided to the Board of Deputies included non-resident members, living as far away as Bradford, Leeds, Hanley, Preston, Whitchurch and Bangor.

6 Cf. P. M. Tillot, 'Sources of inaccuracy in the 1851 and 1861 censuses', in Wrigley, *Nineteenth Century Society*, pp. 82–133.

7 The work of the group in Birmingham working on the Census Enumerators' Books for 1851 will also soon become available for comparative purposes. This

kind of census work lies well within the powers of an interested local history society.

8 The most recent summary of the methodology of historical demography is Wrigley, *Nineteenth Century Society*, which also includes a full bibliography of the subject.

APPENDIX C

1 Maps 4 to 8 are designed to provide a general impression of the changing *pattern* of Jewish settlement. They are in no way a guide to *density* of Jewish settlement in each district. There were, in fact, no exclusively Jewish districts in Manchester, and only six streets (all in Red Bank) in which Jews outnumbered Gentiles by 1871; a fact which no doubt contributed to the acceptance of Jews by the host society in the first three quarters of the nineteenth century. There was no large area characterised by an 'alien culture' or by physical and social conditions which could be put down to Jewish residence, as those in Angel Meadow were attributed to the Irish. Again, the Irish attracted much of the odium which in different circumstances might have attached itself to working-class Jews. It was not until the 1880s and 1890s, as first Red Bank and then Strangeways and Cheetham Hill became dominated by poorer immigrant families, that working-class Jewry could be seen as 'alien menace' and became subject (although on a much smaller scale than in London) to caricature and abuse. The only households outside the area shown were those which in 1871 comprised six Reform Jewish families, three in Prestwich and three in Bowdon. These households, totalling not more than thirty persons in all, and headed in each case by an overseas merchant of German origin, are not included in Appendix B.

Glossary

Aliyah (pl. Aliyoth)   A calling-up to the Reading of the Law during Divine Service.

Ashkenazi (pl. Ashkenazim)   Jew of Central or Eastern European origin, whose vernacular language is Yiddish.

barmitzvah   Traditional ceremony of acceptance when a boy attains his religious majority at the age of thirteen.

Beth Din   Ecclesiastical court of at least three members which administers Jewish Law.

Beth Hamidrash   Literally House of Study. Centre for the study of Hebrew and religion, occasionally associated with a small place of worship.

Chazan   *see* Hazan

cheder (pl. chedarim)   Private class held for the study of Hebrew and religion.

cherem   Ecclesiastical ban, equivalent to excommunication.

chevra (pl. chevroth)   Voluntary association for religious purposes, often constituting a small, independent congregation, with associated social and charitable functions.

Chevra Tehillim   Literally Psalm Society. The name given to the *chevroth* in Manchester and Hull with which Dr Schiller-Szinessy was associated during the period 1854–56.

Chief Rabbi   Spiritual leader of the Ashkenazim of Great Britain and the British Empire.

Cohanim   Members of the priestly caste; descendants of the priests of the Temple.

Dayan (pl. Dayyanim)   Ecclesiastical judge; member of the *Beth Din*.

haftorah   Reading of a portion of the Prophets following the Reading of the Law.

Haham   Spiritual head of the English Sephardi community.

halakhah (adj. halakhic)   Jewish law, especially the accepted traditional interpretation of the Written Law.

Hanukkah   Literally Dedication. Post-biblical festival commemorating the victory of Judah the Maccabee over the Syrians in 167 B.C. and the subsequent rededication of the Temple.

Hoshana Rabbah   The Seventh Day of the Feast of Tabernacles.

Hazan (pl. Hazanim)   Cantor, Reader; alternatively Chazan (pl. Chazanim).

herem   *see* cherem.

kaddish   Literally Sanctification. Prayer recited by persons in mourning for their parents and certain close relatives.

kahal   Community, used particularly of the semi-autonomous communities of the Russian Pale of Settlement.

Karaites   One of the earliest and best known dissident sects in Judaism, which accepted the written, but not the Oral Law. Used colloquially to describe other forms of dissidence.

Kashruth   Jewish dietary laws.

kehillah   Jewish community.

kethuba (pl. kethuboth)   Marriage contract.

kosher (pl. kashruth)   Food fit according to Jewish dietary law.

landsman (pl. landsleit)   Literal Yiddish for a fellow-countryman. Used to describe a person from the same district of Central or Eastern Europe.

maftir   Last portion of the reading of the Law.

mahamad   Executive committee of the Spanish and Portuguese Synagogue.

'makadesh'   Literally To consecrate. Used colloquially in correspondence of the Old Congregation to mean enforced cohabitation.

matzo (pl. matzoth)   Cake or biscuit of unleavened bread eaten at Passover.

melamed (pl. melamdim)   Private teacher of Hebrew and religion.

mikvah   Ritual bath.

minhag   Religious rite or custom.

minyan (pl. minyanim)   Quorum of ten adult males for divine worship; colloquially used to describe a small group meeting unofficially for divine service, occasionally in the past as a synonym for *chevra*.

misheberach   The initial words of a prayer formula invoking God's blessing, recited for every person called to the Reading of the Law and sometimes specifying the donation being made to the congregation. The word has no plural form in Hebrew, and it has become customary in Anglo-Jewry to use the English form *misheberachs*, a style adopted in the present work.

Mishna   Oral tradition as expounded by the *Tannaim* (rabbinical teachers), finalised in about 200 C.E. and forming the basis of the Talmud.

mitzva (pl. mitzvaoth)   literally a favour. Used to describe an honour bestowed upon a member of the synagogue, such as a call to the reading of the Law.

mohel (pl. mohalim)   Person qualified to perform circumcision in accordance with Jewish religious ordinances.

Morenu   The title given in honour of a distinguished rabbi.

parnass   President of a community, or synagogue warden.

Pinkus   A document formalising the foundation of a *chevra*, usually incorporating a code of rules and a list of founder-members.

piyyutim   Liturgical hymns or poems, often additional to the main body of the order of service.

Purim   Festival commemorating the rescue of Persian Jewry by Esther when Haman threatened to annihilate them.

Rabbi   Person possessed of full rabbinical qualifications, properly atttested by eminent, established rabbis.

Rosh Hashana   Festival of the Jewish New Year.

Sabbath Nahamu   The Sabbath of Comfort.

Second Days (of festivals)   Obligation on the orthodox in the Diaspora to observe two days of any festival, derived from the difficulty of ascertaining its precise calendrical day.

seder   Family ritual and banquet held on the eve of Passover.

semikhah   Rabbinical diploma.

Sephardi (pl. Sephardim)   Jew originating in Spain or Portugal. They possess their own ritual, vernacular language (Ladino) and distinctive pronunciation of Hebrew.

Sepher Torah   Scroll of the Law.

shamash   Beadle or caretaker of a synagogue.

shechita The slaughter of cattle and poultry for food in a manner prescribed by Jewish law by a properly qualified *shochet*.

shechita board Communal organisation for the control of matters relating to *shechita*.

Shemona Asra (alternatively Shemone Esrei) The prayer of the Eighteen Blessings.

shiva Seven days of mourning for the dead.

shochet (pl. shochetim) One properly qualified to slaughter animals according to Jewish law.

shomer One who supervises the sale, manufacture or cooking of kosher food.

shtille choopah 'Secret' Marriage, valid in Jewish law but not registered by the State.

succah Tabernacle or booth erected against the synagogue or in private homes during the Festival of the Tabernacles.

Succoth Festival of Tabernacles, when Jews gave thanks for their delivery from the wilderness.

Talmud The classic collection of Rabbinic law and commentary.

Talmud Torah School for the study of Hebrew and religion, usually for children who obtain their secular education elsewhere.

trefa Food forbidden by Jewish law.

Yamin Noraim Literally Days of Awe. Referring to the ten days commencing with the New Year festival and culminating in the Day of Atonement.

Yeshiva (pl. Yeshivot) Academy for higher Jewish learning.

yiddishkeit Yiddish description of the sum of Jewish orthodox religious and social observance and culture.

Yom Kippur Day of Atonement.

Bibliography

A. *Archival sources* in (*a*) Manchester, (*b*) Liverpool, (*c*) Preston, and (*d*) London
B. *Contemporary newspapers and periodicals*
C. *Printed reports*
D. *Contemporary pamphlets, guides, autobiography, and printed correspondence*
E. *Secondary sources: general national and local background*
F. *Secondary sources: general Jewish background,* including only the major works consulted and cited. Full bibliographic material on Anglo-Jewry may be found in Cecil Roth, *Magna Bibliotheca Anglo-Judaica: a Bibliographical Guide to Anglo-Jewish History* (London, JHSE, 1937) and Ruth Lehmann, *Nova Bibliotheca Anglo-Judaica: a Bibliographical Guide to Anglo-Jewish History* (London, JHSE, 1961) and *Anglo-Jewish Bibliography, 1937–70* (London, JHSE, 1973).
G. *Secondary sources: Manchester Jewry, 1740–1875*

A. *Archival sources*

(*a*) in *Manchester*

Account Books (from 1824), Minute Books (from 1840), Letter Books (from 1847), Codes of Law, Letters and Miscellaneous Records of the Manchester Old Hebrew Congregation, 1794–1945, in MCL (M/139).

Minute Books and Account Books of the South Manchester Synagogue, 1872–, in the offices of the synagogue in Wilbraham Road.

Minute Books, Account Books and miscellaneous records of the Spanish and Portuguese Synagogue, 1872–, in the offices of the synagogue in Cheetham Hill Road.

Minute Books of the Manchester Jewish Board of Guardians, from 1867, including the Minute Book of the Industrial Committee, from 1873, in MCL (not yet calendared).

Minute Book of the Manchester Jewish Ladies Clothing Society, 1885–1920, in the possession of Mrs Joan Behrens of Manchester. The flyleaf includes the original rules of the society, drawn up in 1853.

Miscellaneous records relating to Jacob Nathan and his son, Elias, recently deposited in MCL by Mr Geoffrey Kershaw of Didsbury. The collection includes letters, Masonic documents, trade cards and photographs.

Minute Books of the Manchester Foreign Library, in MCL (BR/MS/F/027.3/Ml).

Correspondence relating to the Manchester and Salford Volunteers, in MCL (M84/1/1–3).

Records of the Lancashire Commercial Clerks Society in MCL (M13/4/7).

John Scholes, List of Foreign Merchants in Manchester, 1784–1870, in MCL (MS/FF/382/535).

Records of the Franks family, in the possession of Mrs Dorothy Goldstone of Cheadle, including letters, agreements, scrapbooks, photographs, and other materials from c. 1840. These include a brief MS history of the family, by Benn Franks and a report by J. G. D. Kay on the casebook of Henry Franks.

(b) in *Liverpool*

Correspondence of the Liverpool Old Hebrew Congregation, in the Princes Road Synagogue, Liverpool, c. 1820–1945. The archives of the congregation have not yet been systematically surveyed or calendared.

Minute Books and Account Books of the Liverpool Hebrew Mendicity Society, 1840–47, in the archives of the Princes Road Synagogue, Liverpool.

Minute Books of the Liverpool Hebrew Philanthropic Society, from 1811, in the archives of the Liverpool Jewish Welfare Services, Rex Cohen Court. These archives which owe their preservation to Mr Karl Abrahams of Liverpool, have not yet been calendared.

(c) in *Preston*

Freemasons' Returns, 1799–1803 in the Lancashire County Record Office (QDS/2/5/1).

(d) in *London*

The Franklin Papers in Anglo-Jewish Archives (AJ/25) in the Mocatta Library, University College, London.

Copy Books and Indexes of Correspondence in the Chief Rabbi's Office, London, particularly Copy Book A2 and Index of Correspondence with British Congregations, vol. 83 (1845–48).

Minute Books of the Board of Deputies of British Jews, in the archives of the Board.

Home Office Naturalisation Papers in the PRO (H.O.1).

B. *Contemporary newspapers and periodicals*: the dates given indicate the life-span of each periodical.

Aston's Manchester Exchange Herald, 1809–26
British Volunteer and Manchester Weekly Express, 1804–1825
Cowdroy's Manchester Gazette, 1795–1829
Jewish Chronicle, 1841–
Jewish World, 1873–1934
Manchester Courier, 1825–1916
Manchester Guardian, 1821–
Manchester Mercury, 1752–1830
Prescott's Manchester Journal, 1771–81
Voice of Jacob, 1841–46
Wheeler's Manchester Chronicle or Weekly Advertiser, 1781–1843

C. *Printed reports*

Annual Reports of the Manchester Hebrew Association (subsequently the Manchester Jews School) from 1838, in MCL.

Annual Reports of the Manchester Jewish Board of Guardians, from 1867, in MCL.

Annual Reports of the Society for the Relief of Really Deserving Distressed Foreigners, 1853–97, in MCL (incomplete).

Annual Reports of the Society for the Propagation of the Gospel Amongst the Jews, from 1845, in the Mocatta Library, University College, London (incomplete).

Annual Reports of the Manchester and Salford Auxiliary of the Society for Promoting Christianity Amongst the Jews, from 1817, in MCL (incomplete).

D. *Contemporary pamphlets, guides, autobiography and printed correspondence*

Aiken, John, *A Description of the Country from thirty to forty miles around Manchester* (Manchester, 1795).
Anon., *A Description of Manchester and Salford* (Manchester, 1826).
Anon., *The New Manchester Guide; or, Useful Pocket Companion* (Manchester, 1815).
Anon., *A Complete Memoir of the Late Reverend Canon Stowell* (Manchester, 1865).
Aston, Joseph, *Manchester Guide* (Manchester, 1804).
— *Picture of Manchester* (Manchester, 1816).
Baines, Edward, *History, Directory and Gazetteer of the County Palatine of Lancaster*, 2 vols. (Liverpool, 1824–25).
[Behrens, Sir Jacob], *Memoir of Sir Jacob Behrens, 1806–1889* (London, privately printed, n.d.).
Bullock, Thomas, *Bradshaw's Illustrated Guide to Manchester* (London, 1857).
Butterworth, James, *Antiquities of the Town of Manchester* (Manchester, 1822).
Catt, G. R. *Pictorial History of Manchester* (Manchester, 1843).
Chapple, J. A. V. and Pollard, A. *The Letters of Mrs Gaskell* (Manchester, 1966).
Clayton, Rev. John. *Friendly Advice to the Poor* (Manchester, 1755).
Crool, Rabbi Joseph, *Service Performed in the Synagogue of the Jews, Manchester, on 19th October, 1803* (Manchester, 1803).
De Lara, D. E., *An Address Delivered at the Opening of the New Synagogue in Manchester on Friday, 5th September, 5604* (Manchester, 1844).
Engels, Friedrich, *Conditions of the Working Class in England in 1844*, translated by W. O. Henderson and W. H. Chaloner (Oxford, 1958).
Faucher, Leon, *Manchester in 1844: its Present Condition and Future Prospects* (Manchester, 1844).
Folio, Felix [John Page], *The Hawkers and Street Dealers of the North of England Manufacturing Districts* (Manchester, 1858).
Gaskell, Rev. William, *A Letter to Canon Stowell* (Manchester, 1853).
Gregson, J. S., *Gimcrackiana; or, Fugitive Pieces on Manchester Men and Manners* (Manchester, 1833).
Halley, Robert, *To Christians of Various Denominations in Manchester and Salford* (Manchester, 1845).

Harris, Joseph, *Random Notes and Reflections* (Liverpool, 1912).

Hayes, Louis, *Reminiscences of Manchester* (Manchester, 1905).

Joseph, B. L., *Address to the Seatholders of the Liverpool Congregation* (Liverpool, 1838).

Kay, Dr J. P., *The Moral and Physical Condition of the Working Classes in the Cotton Manu-facture in Manchester* (Manchester, 1832; reprinted by the Irish University Press, Shannon, 1971).

Love, Benjamin, *Manchester As It Is* (Manchester, 1839).

Myers, Asher, *Jewish Directory for 1874* (London, 1874).

Pearce, Rev. A. E., *A Plea for the Jews: a Report Read at a Meeting of the Manchester and Salford Auxiliary of the British Society for the Propagation of the Gospel Amongst the Jews* (Manchester, 1849).

Playfair, Dr Lyon, *Health of Towns Commission: Report of the State of Large Towns in Lancashire* (London, 1845).

Roby, W., *A Sermon Preached . . . on the Death of the Reverend John Johnson* (Manchester, 1804).

Schiller-Szinessy, Rev. Rabbi S. M., *The Olden Religion in the New Year* (London, 1850).

Simonson, M. H., *Holy Convocations regulated by our Rabbins, and Observed by (all) Israel in accordance with the Pentateuch and Reason* (London, 1844).

— *Joshua and the Sun and Moon . . . Philosophically Explained* (Manchester, 1851).

Slugg, J. T., *Reminiscences of Manchester Fifty Years Ago* (Manchester, 1881).

Solomon, Israel, *Records of my Family* (New York, privately printed, 1887).

Stott, Joseph, *A Sequel to the Friendly Advice to the Poor of the Town Manchester* (Manchester, 1756).

Taylor, Dr William Cooke, *Notes on a Tour in the Manufacturing Districts of Lancashire* (London, 2nd ed., 1842).

[Theodores, Tobias], *The Oral Law and its Defenders. A Review by a Spiritualist* (London, 1842).

— *The Rabbinical Law of Excommunication considered in its Bearing on the Case of the Margaret Street Synagogue of British Jews* (Manchester, 1854).

— *Prospectus of Anglo-Jewish Archives* (London, 1844?).

Tomlinson, Walter, *Bye-Ways of Manchester Life* (Manchester, 1887).

Wheeler, James, *Manchester: its Political, Social and Commercial History* (Manchester, 1836).

Willme, John, 'Letters to the Jews at Liverpool, 1756', Palatine Notebook, vol. 1 (1881), pp. 117–19.

E. *Secondary sources: general, national and local background*

Alexander, David, *Retailing in England during the Industrial Revolution* (London, 1970).

Ashton, T. S., *Economic and Social Investigation in Manchester, 1833–1933* (Manchester, 1933).

Axton, W. E. A., *The Annals of Manchester* (Manchester, 1886).

Baker, Sir Thomas, *Memorials of a Dissenting Chapel* (London and Manchester, 1884).

Briggs, Asa, *Victorian Cities* (London, 1963).

Carter, C. F., ed., *Manchester and its Region* (Manchester, 1962).

Chaloner, W. H., 'Manchester in the latter half of the eighteenth century', *Bulletin of the John Rylands Library*, vol. 42, No. 1 (September, 1959).

Edwards, Michael, *The Growth of the British Cotton Trade, 1780–1815* (Manchester, 1967).

Frangopulo, N. J., ed., *Rich Inheritance* (Manchester, 1962).

— 'Foreign communities in Victorian Manchester', *Manchester Review*, vol. 10 (1963–1965).

Harte, N. B. and Ponting, K. G., eds., *Textile History and Economic History: Essays in Honour of Miss Julia de Lacy Mann* (Manchester, 1973).

Henderson, W. O., *The Lancashire Cotton Famine, 1861–5* (Manchester, 1934).

Marshall, L. S., *The Development of Public Opinion in Manchester, 1780–1820* (London, 1946).

Marsden, Rev. J. B., *Memoir of the Life and Labours of Reverend Hugh Stowell, M.A.* (London, 1868).

Nicholls, W., *History and Traditions of Prestwich* (Manchester, 1905).

Owen, David, *English Philanthropy, 1660–1960* (Oxford, 1965).

Perkin, Harold, *The Origins of Modern English Society, 1780–1880* (London, 1971 ed.).

Prentice, Archibald, *Historical Sketches and Personal Recollections of Manchester, 1792–1832* (new ed., London, 1970).

Read, Donald, *Press and People, 1790–1850* (London, 1961).

Redford, A., *The History of Local Government in Manchester*, 3 vols. (London, 1940).

— *Manchester Merchants and Foreign Trade*, 2 vols. (Manchester, 1956).

Thomas, Joan, *A History of the Leeds Clothing Industry, Yorkshire Bulletin of Economic and Social Research*, Occasional Paper I (Leeds, 1955).

Valimigli, A., *La colonia Italiana di Manchester* (Florence, 1932).

Vigier, François, *Change and Apathy: Liverpool and Manchester during the Industrial Revolution* (London and Cambridge, Mass., 1970).

Wadsworth, A. P., and Mann, J. de Lacy, *The Cotton Trade and Industrial Lancashire* (Manchester, 1931).

F. *Secondary sources: general Jewish background*

Abrahams, K. L., 'The first Jews in Liverpool', *Greenbank Drive Synagogue Review* (Liverpool, 1970).

— 'Father of the Congregation—a biography of Barned Lyon Joseph', *Greenbank Drive Synagogue Review* (Liverpool, 1968).

Anon., 'John Willme and his letters to the Jews at Liverpool', *Palatine Notebook*, vol. 1 (1881).

Barnett, Arthur, *The Western Synagogue through Two Centuries* (London, 1961).

Behr, Alexander, 'Isidor Gerstenberg, 1821–76', Tr. *JHSE.*, vol. 17 (1951–52).

Benas, B. L., 'Records of the Jews in Liverpool', *Translations of the Historic Society of Lancashire and Cheshire*, vol. 15 (1899).

Ben-Sassoon, H. H. and Ettinger, S., eds., *Jewish Society through the Ages* (London, 1971).

Bermant, Chaim, *The Cousinhood: the Anglo-Jewish Gentry* (London, 1971).

Corti, Egon Caesar, *The Rise of the House of Rothschild* (London, 1928).

D'Arcy Hart, R. J., *The Samuel Family of Liverpool and London* (London, 1958).

Duschinsky, C., *The Rabbinate of the Great Synagogue* (Oxford, 1921).

Ettinger, P., *Hope Place in Liverpool Jewry* (Liverpool, 1930).

Fein, Issac, *The Making of an American Jewish Community* (Philadelphia, 1971).

Franklin, A. E., *Records of the Franklin Family* (London, 1935).

Freedman, Maurice, ed., *A Minority in Britain* (London, 1955).

Gainer, B., *The Alien Invasion* (London, 1972).

Garrard, J. A., *The English and Immigration* (Oxford, 1971).

Gartner, Lloyd P., *The Jewish Immigrant in England, 1870–1914* (London, revised ed., 1971).

— 'Notes on the statistics of Jewish immigration to England', *Jewish Social Studies*, vol. 22 (1960).

Gollancz, Rev. Hermann. 'A ramble in East Anglia', *Tr. JHSE*, vol. 2. (1894–95).

Hyamson, A. M., *The Sephardim in England* (London, 1951).

Hyman, Louis, *The Jews of Ireland* (London and Jerusalem, 1972).

Jacob, Alex M., 'The Jews of Falmouth, 1740–1860', *Tr. JHSE*, vol. 17 (1951–52).

Jamilly, Edward, 'Anglo-Jewish architects and architecture in the eighteenth and nineteenth centuries', *Tr. JHSE*, vol. 18 (1953–55).

Jewish Encyclopaedia (New York, 1901–06).

Krausz, Ernest, *Leeds Jewry* (Cambridge, 1964).

Levy, Arnold, *History of the Sunderland Jewish Community* (London, 1966).

Lipman, V. D., ed., *Three Centuries of Anglo-Jewish History* (London, 1961).

— *Social and Economic History of the Jews in England, 1850–1950* (London, 1954).

— *A Century of Social Service, 1859–1959* (London, 1959).

— 'The rise of Jewish suburbia', *Tr. JHSE*, vol. 21 (1962–67).

— 'A survey of Anglo-Jewry in 1851', *Tr. JHSE*, vol. 17 (1951–52).

Loewe, Raphael, 'Solomon Marcus Schiller-Szinessy, 1820–90', *Tr. JHSE*, vol. 21 (1962–67).

Magnus, Laurie, *The Jewish Board of Guardians and the Men Who Made It* (London, 1909).

Margoliouth, Rev. Moses, *The History of the Jews of Great Britain*, 3 vols. (London, 1851).

Marmur, Dow, ed., *Reform Judaism: Essays on Reform Judaism in Britain* (London, 1973).

Newman, Aubrey (Rapporteur), *Migration and Settlement* (London, 1971).

Newman, Aubrey, ed., *Provincial Jewry in Victorian Britain*. Papers for a conference at University College, London, convened by the Jewish Historical Society of England, 6 July 1975.

Picciotto, James, *Sketches of Anglo-Jewish History*, ed. I. Finestein (London, 1956).

Prais, S. Y., 'The development of Birmingham Jewry', *The Jewish Monthly*, vol. 2, no. 11 (February 1949).

Rollin, A. R., 'The Jewish contribution to the British textile industry', *Tr. JHSE*, vol. 17 (1951–52).

— 'Russo-Jewish immigrants in England before 1881', *Tr. JHSE*, vol. 21 (1962–67).

Roth, Cecil, *The Rise of Provincial Jewry* (London, 1950).

— *A History of the Jews in England* (Oxford, 1964).

— *The Magnificent Rothschilds* (London, 1939).

— 'The Portsmouth Community and its historical background', *Tr. JHSE*, vol. 13 (1932–35).

Rumney, J., 'Anglo-Jewry as seen through foreign eyes', *Tr. JHSE*, vol. 13 (1932–35).

Shaftesley, John M., ed., *Remember the Days: Essays in Honour of Cecil Roth* (London, 1966).
Stokes, Canon H. P., *Studies in Anglo-Jewish History* (Edinburgh, 1913).
Wolf, Lucien, *Essays in Jewish History*, ed. Cecil Roth (London, 1934).

G. *Secondary sources: Manchester Jewry, 1740–1875*

Anon., 'Jewish life in Manchester', *Manchester Evening Chronicle*, 16 July to 17 August 1897.
Anon., 'Manchester', in *The Jewish World*, 7 September 1877.
Davies, Samuel, *The Higher Broughton Hebrew Congregation: the First Fifty Years, 1907–1957* (Manchester, 1957).
Fidler, Michael, ed., *The Holy Law Congregation: One Hundred Years, 1865–1965* (Manchester, 1965).
Goldberg, I. W., *The South Manchester Hebrew Congregation: Eighty years of Progress* (Manchester, 1952).
Goldberg, Rabbi P. S., *The Manchester Congregation of British Jews, 1857–1957* (Manchester, 1957).
Gottheil, Richard, *The Life of Gustav Gottheil, Memoir of a Priest of Israel* (New York, n.d.).
Gouldman, Hyman, *The Manchester Great Synagogue, 1858–1958* (Manchester, 1958).
Gouldman, Hyman, and Morgan, J. B., *The Mancester Jewish Board of Guardians: the Story of One Hundred Years* (Manchester, 1967).
Harris, Frank, 'The story of Manchester Jewry', in *The Jewish Telegraph*, January–March 1956.
Hesse, Max, *On the Effective Use of Charitable Loans to the Poor, without Interest* (Manchester Statistical Society, 1901).
Jewish Encyclopedia (New York, 1901–06), article 'Manchester'.
Laski, Neville J., 'The history of Manchester Jewry', *Manchester Review*, vol. 7 (1956), pp. 366–78.
—— 'The Manchester and Salford Jewish Community, 1912–1962', *Manchester Review*, vol. 10 (1965), pp. 97–108.
[Nathan, Elias], 'The Old Jewish Congregation of Manchester', in the *Jewish Record*, 4–18 March, 1887.
Rodrigues-Pereira, Rev. B. and Pereira-Mendoza, Rev. J., *History of the Manchester Congregation of Spanish and Portuguese Jews, 1873–1923* (Manchester, 1923: subsequently published with a supplement covering the years 1924–49).
Salomon, Sidney, 'The Manchester Great Synagogue', *Common Ground*, vol. 12, No. 1 (1958), pp. 17–22.
Slotki, Rev. I. W., *The History of the Manchester Shechita Board, 1892–1952* (Manchester, 1954).
—— *Seventy Years of Hebrew Education, 1880–1950* (Manchester, 1950).
Steiner, Mrs Miriam, 'Philanthropic activity and organisation in the Manchester Jewish Community, 1867–1914' (unpublished M.A. dissertation, University of Manchester, June 1974).
Swindells, Thomas, 'The Jews in Manchester: a review of the past one hundred years', *Manchester City News*, 27 January 1906.

Index